Fodor's

FIRST 1st EDITION

The Netherlands, Belgium, Luxembourg

Linda Burnham
Eric Sjogren
Nancy Coons

D1166929

Fodor's Travel Publications, Inc.
New York • Toronto • London • Sydney • Auckland

Fodor's The Netherlands, Belgium, Luxembourg

Editor: Nancy van Itallie
Editorial Contributors: Robert Blake, Ellen Browne, Caroline Liou, Denise Nolty, Alexander Parsons, Melanie Roth
Creative Director: Fabrizio La Rocca
Cartographer: David Lindroth
Illustrator: Karl Tanner
Cover Photograph: Peter Guttman

Design: Vignelli Associates

About the Authors

The Netherlands: Linda Burnham, author of a guidebook to Amsterdam and a contributor to *Fodor's Europe*, has also written for *Travel & Leisure*. She lives in Connecticut.

Belgium: Eric Sjogren, a Swedish travel writer based in Brussels, is a contributor to *Fodor's Europe* and to *The New York Times* and other publications.

Luxembourg: Nancy Coons, author of *Fodor's Switzerland '92* and a contributor to *Fodor's Europe*, has written for *The Wall Street Journal* and *European Travel and Life*.

Special Sales

Contents

Foreword

We would like to express our gratitude to Barbara Veldkamp and Eline van Bon of the Netherlands Board of Tourism, Frédérique Raeymaekers and Marleen Bervoets of the Belgian Tourist Office, and Anne Bastian of the Luxembourg National Tourist Office for their generous cooperation during the preparation of *Fodor's The Netherlands, Belgium, Luxembourg*.

While every care has been taken to ensure the accuracy of the information in this guide, the passage of time will always bring change, and consequently, the publisher cannot accept responsibility for errors that may occur.

All prices and opening times quoted here are based on information supplied to us at press time. Hours and admission fees may change, however, and the prudent traveler will avoid inconvenience by calling ahead.

Fodor's wants to hear about your travel experiences, both pleasant and unpleasant. When a hotel or restaurant fails to live up to its billing, let us know and we will investigate the complaint and revise our entries where the facts warrant it.

Send your letters to the editors of Fodor's Travel Publications, 201 E. 50th Street, New York, NY 10022.

Highlights and Fodor's Choice

Highlights

The Netherlands Relatively speaking, 1993 is a quiet year in the Netherlands. No major commemorative events are planned until the celebration of **Mondrian Year 1994,** and no major festivals are scheduled until the next meeting of the tall ships in Amsterdam harbor for **Sail Amsterdam 1995.** This breathing time in the calendar puts new and deserved emphasis on several major events held annually in the Netherlands (*see* The Netherlands, Festivals and Seasonal Events, *below*).

Also in 1994, the National Museum H. W. Mesdag in The Hague reopens after an extensive two-year renovation. Formerly a private collection, it displays principally 19th-century landscape paintings of The Hague and Barbizon schools.

In May 1993, **Amsterdam Schiphol Airport,** the national airport of the Netherlands, opens Terminal West and further expands its passenger capacity from 18 million to 27 million passengers per year. The new terminal, reserved for non-European arrivals and departures, is connected to the existing facility, which handles only flights from European Community member nations. Terminal West incorporates state-of-the-art technical systems, an expanded laser-managed baggage handling operation, and a full-service business travelers' meeting and communications center. Within a few years, both a 3,500-car parking garage and an expanded rail station are also scheduled to open.

Belgium One of the more pleasing features of the European Community is the opportunity provided to the smaller member states to occupy center stage in world politics. For the second half of 1993 it will be Belgium's turn to chair the European Council, and given the country's commitment to the European ideal it is certain that Belgium will seek to use its turn at the helm to accelerate the pace of European integration.

Antwerp has been designated the European Community's **Cultural Capital** for 1993. Festivities kick off March 26–28, when the entire city becomes a stage for theatrical and musical happenings. The fourth centenary of the birth of the painter Jacob Jordaens occurs in 1993, celebrated with an extensive exhibition of his work at the Museum of Fine Arts (March 27–June 27). The remarkable Rubens's Studio exhibition from Copenhagen, with drawings by Rubens, Van Dyck, and others illustrating a 16th-century artist's workshop, is on show at the Rubens House in May and June. The great medieval Flemish masters of polyphonic choral music are honored by a series of concerts in the Church of St. Augustine, and chamber music returns to the milieu for which it was created as 25 Antwerp families open their homes for concerts in July and August. In defiance of the xenophobic tendencies of some political parties, *Antwerpen 93* plans to demonstrate how the culture of recent immigrants can enrich the host city through bringing the music of Morocco, Turkey, Indonesia, and other countries to Antwerp. The 150-year-old Bourla Theater, restored to mint condition, is staging works by young dramatic talents. The Frankfurt Ballet comes to the City Theater April 19 through May 2, and the cultural center De Singel hosts a Contemporary Opera Festival in May. From May through September, The Ark, a new kind of showboat on the River Scheldt, offers performances by young artists from 15 European cities.

The Middelheim Open-Air Museum is showing its new sculpture acquisitions. The Museum of Fine Arts puts on an exhibition of International Contemporary Art July 25 to October 10, while the Museum of Contemporary Art displays works by the youngest generation.

Other dates to remember are August 14 to 18, when some 70 Tall Ships from all over the world are moored in the heart of Antwerp, and the last week of December for the closure festivities.

The restorations undertaken for Antwerp's year as Cultural Capital of Europe include the Bourla Theater, the Central Railway Station, and the Cathedral, which after years of work again becomes the largest Gothic church in the Low Countries. The Carolus Borromeus Church, St. Paul's Church, St. Augustine's Church, and several of the city's museums have all undergone important refurbishing and renovation. It's a rejuvenated historic city that welcomes its visitors in 1993.

The biennial **Europalia Festival** features Mexico this year. The principal exhibition is at the Palais des Beaux-Arts in Brussels, supplemented by numerous exhibitions and events in both the capital and other Belgian cities, celebrating the art, music, drama, and culture of Mexico. Europalia begins in September, with most exhibitions remaining open until mid-December.

The American painter Edward Hopper is honored with a retrospective at the Beaux-Arts in Brussels from February to May, and in May choreographer Maurice Bejart and his company arrive for a limited engagement at the Cirque Royal. The year's major musical event is the Queen Elisabeth Music Competition in Brussels in May and June, attracting young violin virtuosos from around the world. The second round of concerts at the Conservatoire Royale is open to the public, as of course are the finals at the Palais des Beaux-Arts during the week leading up to the proclamation of the laureates on June 5.

The borderline between some modern sports and the arts is frequently blurred. Rhythmic gymnastics is a case in point.

The world championships take place at Brussels's Parc des Expositions November 13 to 15.

Travel The hotel expansion in Brussels continues unabated. Two major new hotels are scheduled to open in 1993, the 283-room Conrad Hilton in fashionable Avenue Louise and the 226-room Meridien (an Air France hotel) near the Grand'Place.

A much-needed modernization and expansion program for Brussels National Airport at Zaventem nears completion in 1993. Preparations to link major Belgian cities with the TGV (Train Grande Vitesse) rail network have slowed to a crawl due to the usual Belgian conundrum of equal work and benefits for each linguistic community, but the super-fast trains should be rolling by 1994.

Luxembourg As Luxembourg prepares for two big events—the 1994 anniversary of the Battle of the Bulge, and its role in 1995 as the Cultural Capital of Europe—museums, monuments, memorials, and landmarks are being upgraded and buffed to a high sheen. That means that the Ducal Palace in Luxembourg City, its Renaissance treasure, will remain behind scaffolding this year, but that castles (especially the newly reconstructed one at Bourscheid) and museum collections have never been in better shape. The Museum of the Battle of the Bulge in Diekirch, devoted to neutral fact-finding on the battle, continues to solicit firsthand accounts from veterans who fought on either side and to welcome their often emotional visits to territory weighted with painful memories.

Fodor's Choice

Hotels

Netherlands The Grand, Amsterdam (*Very Expensive*)

Hotel Derlon, Maastricht (*Very Expensive*)

Hotel de l'Europe, Amsterdam (*Expensive*)

Kasteel Elsloo, Elsloo (*Moderate*)

City Hotel, Scheviningen (*Inexpensive–Moderate*)

Canal House, Amsterdam (*Inexpensive*)

Auberge Corps de Garde, Groningen (*Inexpensive*)

Belgium De Rosier, Antwerp (*Very Expensive*)

De Tuilerieen, Brugge (*Very Expensive*)

SAS Royal Hotel, Brussels (*Very Expensive*)

Amigo, Brussels (*Expensive*)

Firean, Antwerp (*Expensive*)

Oud Huis Amsterdam, Brugge (*Expensive*)

Egmond, Brugge (*Moderate*)

Erasmus, Ghent (*Moderate*)

Manos Stephanie, Brussels (*Moderate*)

La Truite d'Argent, Brussels (*Inexpensive*)

Le Mosan, Dinant (*Inexpensive*)

Le Vieux Logis, Rochefort (*Inexpensive*)

Luxembourg Hostellerie du Grunewald, Luxembourg City (*Expensive*)

Auberge du Coin, Luxembourg City (*Moderate*)

Hiertz, Vianden, Luxembourg (*Moderate*)

Restaurants

Netherlands Prinses Juliana, Valkenburg aan de Geul (*Very Expensive*)

Excelsior, Amsterdam (*Very Expensive*)

American Cafe, Amsterdam (*Expensive*)

Kastel Doorwerth, Arnhem (*Expensive*)

Bistro at Nolet Het Reymerswale (*Moderate*)

Polman's Huis, Utrecht (*Moderate*)

Brasserie Lido, Amsterdam (*Moderate*)

Bodega Keyzer, Amsterdam (*Moderate*)

Haesje Claes, Amsterdam (*Inexpensive*)

Belgium Comme Chez Soi, Brussels (*Very Expensive*)

Den Gouden Harynk, Brugge (*Very Expensive*)

Sir Anthony Van Dijck, Antwerp (*Very Expensive*)

Les Capucines, Brussels (*Expensive*)

Du Midi, La Roche (*Moderate/Expensive*)

De Grotte Ganz, Antwerp (*Moderate*)

De Zinc, Brugge (*Moderate*)

La Quincaillerie, Brussels (*Moderate*)

Siphon, Damme (*Inexpensive/Moderate*)

Chez Leon, Brussels (*Inexpensive*)

Luxembourg Le Bergerie, Echternach, (*Very Expensive*)

Saint-Michel, Luxembourg City (*Very Expensive*)

Bamberg, Ehnen, (*Moderate–Expensive*)

Mousel's Cantine, Luxembourg City (*Moderate*)

Lëtzebuerger Kaschthaus, Frisange,
(*Inexpensive–Moderate*)

Aal Vienen, Vianden, (*Inexpensive*)

Ancre d'Or, Luxembourg City (*Inexpensive*)

Landmarks and Monuments

Netherlands Begijnhof, Amsterdam

Caves of St. Pieter, Maastricht

Dom Toren, Utrecht

Lang Jan Tower, Middelburg

Nieuwe Kerk, Delft

Portuguese Synagogue, Amsterdam

Prinsenhof, Delft

Sint Servaas Basilik, Maastricht

St. Jan Kathedraal, 's Hertogenbosch

Belgium Bouillon Castle, Bouillon

Burg and canals, Brugge

Butte de Lion, Waterloo

Cathedrale Notre-Dame, Tournai

Cloister, Onze Lieve Vrouw-basiliek, Tongeren

Eglise St-Jacques, Liège

Graslei and Spires, Ghent

Grand'Place, Brussels

Onze-Lieve-Vrouwekathedraal, Antwerp

Orval Abbey, Orval

Luxembourg Eglise St-Laurent, Diekirch

Vianden Castle, Vianden

Museums

Netherlands Anne Frank House, Amsterdam

Kröller-Müller Museum, Otterloo

Paleis Het Loo, Apeldoorn

Rijksmuseum, Amsterdam

Vincent Van Gogh Museum, Amsterdam

Belgium Centre Belge de la Bande Dessinée (Comic Strip Museum), Brussels

David and Alice Van Buuren Museum, Brussels

Groeninge Museum, Brugge

Horta Museum, Brussels

Mayer van den Bergh Museum, Antwerp

Modern Art Museum, Brussels

Museum of Contemporary Art, Ghent

Plantin-Moretus Museum, Antwerp

Royal Museum of Fine Arts, Antwerp

Luxembourg Battle of the Bulge Museum, Diekirch

Art Treasures

Netherlands *Destroyed City* by Zadkine, Rotterdam

The Night Watch by Rembrandt, Rijksmuseum, Amsterdam

Rietveld-Schroeder House by Rietveld, Utrecht

Sunflowers by Van Gogh, Vincent Van Gogh Museum, Amsterdam

Belgium *Adoration of the Mystic Lamb* by van Eyck, Sint Baafskathedraal, Ghent

Dulle Griet (Mad Meg) by Bruegel, Mayer van den Bergh Museum, Antwerp

Descent from the Cross by Rubens, Onze-Lieve-Vrouwekathedraal, Antwerp

Works of Magritte, Ensor, and Delvaux, Modern Art
Museum, Brussels

Madonna with Canon van der Paele by van Eyck,
Groeninge, Brugge

Altarpiece of St. John the Baptist and St. John the
Evangelist by Memling, Memling Museum, Brugge

Baptismal font by Renier de Huy, St-Barthelemy, Liège

Perfect Moments

Netherlands Eating oysters fresh from the Oosterschelde in Zeeland.

Joining the merriment of Carnival in Maastricht.

Riding a bike along a dike road anywhere in the country.

Walking along the canals of Amsterdam after dark.

Watching fireworks over the beach in Scheveningen.

Belgium Antiquing around Grand Sablon, Brussels

Wandering at dusk through the churchyard of l'Eglise de
Notre Dame, Damme

Retreating from a steady drizzle to a dark-wood pub for an
abbey beer and cheese bits

Spotting wild boar in the forests of the Ardennes

Walking the windmill-lined canal between Damme and
Brugge

Following a winter walk along a North Sea beach with a
plate of steaming mussels in a café with a view of the sea

Horseback riding in the beech woods of the Forêt de
Soignes near Brussels

Listening to the Last Post being blown for the soldiers of
World War I at the Menin Gate in Ieper

Riding a kayak down the River Lesse in the Ardennes

Sunday morning Marché du Midi in Brussels

Finding a quiet side street where time has stood still in
Brugge

Munching french fries out of a twist of paper at a roadside
stand

Walking the misty moorland of the Hautes Fagnes near
Malmedy

Singing along with amateur performers in a *café chantant*
in Liège

Luxembourg Looking out over the Alzette Valley from Sigefroid's Bock.

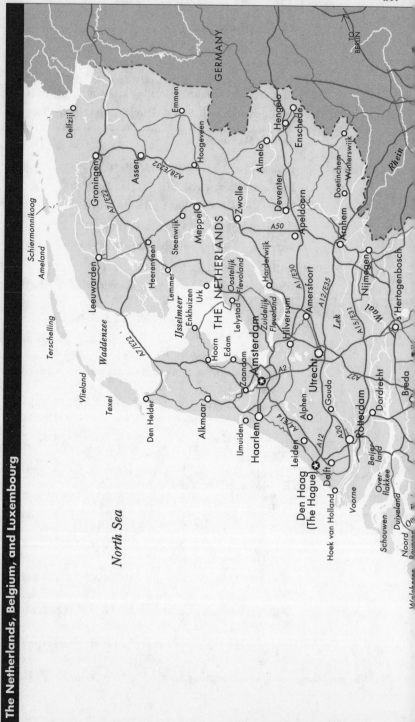

The Netherlands, Belgium, and Luxembourg

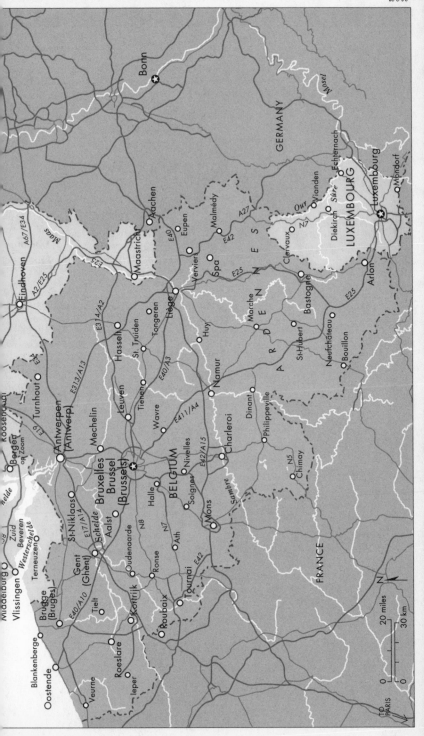

Europe

World Time Zones

MONDAY
SUNDAY

+12 +13

International Date Line

+11

+12

-9

-10

-11

-10

-10

+11

+12

-4

-3

-5 -4

-3:30

-7

-8

-6

-5

-4

-4

-5

-4 -3

-3

3

7

4

14 **15**

13

5 **8** **9**

16

6 **17**

10

11

18

2

12

19 **22**

20

23

1

21 **24**

+11   +12 -   -11   -10   -9   -8   -7   -6   -5   -4   -3   -2

Numbers below vertical bands relate each zone to Greenwich Mean Time (0 hrs.).
Local times frequently differ from these general indications,
as indicated by light-face numbers on map.

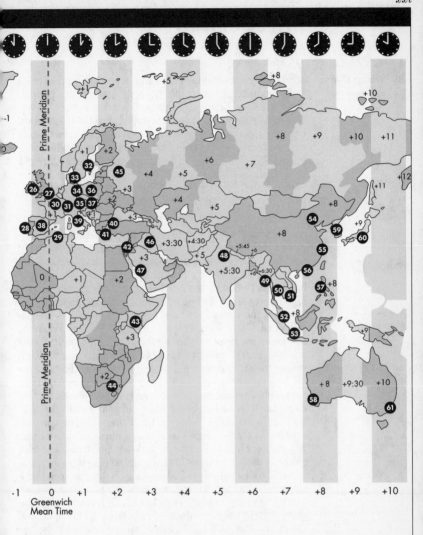

-1
0

Prime Meridian

Prime Meridian

+1 +2
+5
+8
+10
+5
+8 +9 +10 +11
+6 +7
33 32 45 +4 +5
26 27 34 36 +3 +11 +12
30 31 35 37 +2 +4 +8 +9
28 38 39 40 +4 +5 +8 54 59 60
29 41 +8 55
42 46 +3:30 +4:30 +5:45 +6
47 +3 +5 48 56
+5:30 +6:30 57 +8
0 +1 +2 49
50 51
43 52 +8
+3 53
+2 +8 +9:30 +10
44 58 61

-1 0 +1 +2 +3 +4 +5 +6 +7 +8 +9 +10
Greenwich
Mean Time

Introduction

By Nancy Coons

Slate-colored skies curve like a pewter bowl over an undulating landscape, the long, low horizon punctuated by blunt steeples and a scattering of deep-roofed farmhouses that seem to enfold the land like a mother goose spreading wings over her brood. Inky crows wheel over spindle-fingered pollards, jackdaws pepper the ocher grainfields, and a magpie, flashing black and white, drags a long, iridescent tail through the damp air. These are the 16th-century landscapes of Bruegel the Elder—stained-glass planes in sepia tones, leaded by black branches, crooked spires, dark-frozen streams.

And these, too, are the 20th-century landscapes of Belgium, the Netherlands, and Luxembourg—a wedge of northern Europe squeezed between the massive and ancient kingdoms of France and Germany, bounded by the harsh North Sea to the northwest, defined by the rough, high forests of the Ardennes to the southeast. No wonder so much of their appeal, past and present, is interior—bountiful, sensual still lifes, the glowing chambers of Vermeer, the inner radiance in the portraits of Rembrandt: Their weather-beaten cultures have turned inward over the centuries, toward the hearth. Indoors, Bruegel's otherwise sepia scenes warm subtly with color—earthy browns, berry reds, loden greens, muted indigos, coral cheeks. So it is today: The Netherlanders gather in gold-lit, smoke-burnished "brown cafés," old bentwood chairs scraping across weathered stone floors; the Flemish nurse goblets of mahogany beer by candlelight in dark-beamed halls, a scarlet splash of paisley runner thrown over the pine tabletop; red-vested Walloons—French-speaking Belgians—read the newspaper in high-backed oak banquettes polished blue-black by generations of rough tweed. In Luxembourg, the glass of light beer and *drüp* of eau-de-vie go down behind the candy-colored leaded glass of spare, bright-lit *stuff* or pubs, where village life finds its social focus, day in, day out. In each of these small northern lands, so often lashed by rain, soaked by drizzle, wrapped in fog, with winter dark closing in at 4 PM and winter daylight dawdling until 9 AM, the people live out the rich-hued interior scenes of the Old Masters.

Yet the skies do clear, come spring, and at last the light lingers until well after 10 at night. Then the real pleasure begins—an intense appreciation that residents of moderate climates would be hard-put to understand. As if the people's gratitude took physical form, it manifests itself in flowers, a frenzy of color spilling from every windowsill, spreading like ocean waves across tulip fields, over rose trellises, through wisteria-woven archways. Fruit trees explode like fireworks, and whole orchards shimmer pink. Chestnut branches sag under the weight of their leaves and the heavy, grapelike clusters of blossom that thrust upward, defying gravity. In the midst of this orgy of scent and color, Dutch university students bicycle along canals in loose batik-print cotton; blue-overalled Flemish farmers open their half-doors and bask; the international bankers of Luxembourg swing their Versace suitcoats over their shoulders and head for the benches in the green Petrusse Valley.

Then café society, and home life with it, moves lock, stock, and barrel outdoors, to bask lizardlike in the rare warmth. Terrace cafés on the Grote Markts and Grand' Places rival any piazza in Italy. And when there's no café around, the family simply sets out a cluster of folding chairs, perhaps a checkered-cloth card table, whether smack on the sidewalk or behind the barn door, to make the most of fine weather. A suntan remains (as it does in sun-starved North Germany) the most sought-after of status symbols—doubly prestigious if flaunted in midwinter, as northerners, once pale and prune-skinned, return from the ski slopes of the Alps or the beaches of the Canary Islands.

The extremes of their climate, from inexorable gray to luxurious sun, may form a common bond, but the three countries of the Netherlands, Belgium, and Luxembourg sustain sharply different cultures, languages, and terrain. The Netherlands itself is a tangle of inner conflicts—Catholic versus Protestant (they lean 60–40 toward the latter, that 60 percent still functioning as one of Europe's Reformation strongholds); puritanical versus prurient (though you can't buy liquor on Sunday in some areas, in others prostitutes sit, gartered and whalebone-stayed, in display windows like so much grade-A beef). In fact, in narrow, low rowhouses up and down town streets, whole blocks-full of ordinary people live without curtains, their evening lives and possessions open to viewing by passersby; yet they are the soberest, most courteous and conservative drivers in Europe. Open to the North Sea for hundreds of miles, each summer the Netherlanders turn their back on the beach, load up their trailers, and migrate south; though they're leaving behind the most heavily populated land on the Continent, they flock together in crowded trailer parks wherever they go, rank on cozy rank decked with lace curtains and black-and-yellow Dutch license plates.

The Belgian situation goes beyond mere contradiction: It is a country torn in two, split by two tongues and two distinct cultures. The division between Wallonie and Flanders traces back to Merovingian times, and the Walloon patois and Belgian French represent the last northward wave of the Roman empire and its lingual residue. Twice in this century Flemish citizens (and possibly a king) were known to collaborate with German invaders, allying themselves against what they saw as French-speaking domination.

And today the bickering over bilingual rights leaves Brussels a no-man's-land, with extra-wide enamel signs naming every street and alley in two tongues. The cultures are as different as their languages: The Flemish are proud and tidy, their homes filled with the exterior light that pours in tall, multipaned windows; a spare, avant-garde current in fashion, film, and literature shows their Dutch leanings. The Walloons, on the other hand, remain more laissez-faire, their homes often dark, cozy, and cluttered with knick-knacks and lace. A women's clothing shop in Ghent is likely to include progressive, trendy, severe clothing, while the equivalent in Liège will show cardigans, A-line skirts, and fussy florals. Of the two separate worlds, only Catholicism runs between them, as mutual as their government, uniting them in conservatism on divorce and abortion laws.

If Belgium and the Netherlands show inner conflict, the natives of little Luxembourg present a solid front to the outside, interacting in French, German, or English, but maintaining their private world in their own native *Lëtzebuergesch* (Luxembourgish). Thus, having survived centuries of conquest and occupation, they can open their country to European Community "Eurocrats" and more than a hundred international banks, and still keep to themselves. Luxembourg sustains two, parallel cultures, with some cafés catering to trendy, international, or tourist crowds and others reserved for the loden-coated locals, who may greet an aberrant visitor with stunned silence as thick as the cigarette smoke that fills the air.

The Netherlands, Belgium, and Luxembourg—as diverse within themselves as they are to each other. And yet all this diversity has been thrown together by the dominant cultures pressing in at the borders—France and Germany. Having been conquered, wartorn, and economically dwarfed for generations, the three little countries felt compelled, in 1958, to form an alliance, an early and seminal economic union that served as a foundation for the European Community. Since then, "Benelux" has become a convenient abbreviation for a small, independent wedge of northern Europe where fruit juice is packaged bisymmetrically, one side labeled in French and the other in Dutch; only a few, local products have yet been labeled in Luxembourgish.

But, of course, Benelux is considerably more than an arbitrary economic unit. It is a rich and varied region, laced with canals, sprinkled with orchards, its cities burnished with age, where museum visitors can browse through the landscapes of Bruegel and Van Ruisdael and the interiors of Van Eyck, Vermeer, and Rembrandt—then experience their inspiration firsthand, in the magnificent, brooding countryside and time-polished interiors that remain much unchanged since they first inspired the Old Masters.

1 Essential Information

Before You Go

Government Tourist Offices

In the United States Belgian Tourist Office, 745 5th Ave., New York, NY 10151, tel. 212/758–8130. **Luxembourg National Tourist Office**, 801 2nd Ave., New York, NY 10017, tel. 212/370–9850. **Netherlands Board of Tourism**, 355 Lexington Ave., New York, NY 10017, tel. 212/370–7360; 90 New Montgomery St., Suite 305, San Francisco, CA 90410, tel. 415/543–6772; 225 N. Michigan Ave., Suite 326, Chicago, IL 60601, tel. 312/819–0300.

In Canada Netherlands Board of Tourism, 25 Adelaide St. E, Suite 710, Toronto, Ont. M5C 1Y2, tel. 416/363–1577.

In the United Kingdom Belgian Tourist Office, Premier House, 2 Gayton Rd., Harrow, Middlesex HA1 2XU, tel. 081/861–3300. **Luxembourg National Tourist Office**, 36–37 Piccadilly, London W1V 9PA, tel. 071/434–2800. **Netherlands Board of Tourism**, 25–28 Buckingham Gate, London SW1E 6LD, tel. 071/630–0451.

Tour Groups

With their wealth of artistic treasures, medieval castles, story-book villages, and picturesque landscapes, Belgium, Luxembourg, and the Netherlands (Holland) offer nearly limitless options to the visitor. How to enjoy them is up to you. If you're heading to the region for the first time, consider an escorted tour. Just sit back and enjoy yourself; all the details will have been taken care of. Group tours also tend to save you money on airfare and hotels. If you prefer more independence, there are still plenty of creative alternatives available. You can enjoy a fly/drive package, follow a prearranged itinerary independently, or plan a visit from an à la carte menu of package options.

Before selecting a tour, be sure to find out exactly what expenses are included (particularly tips, taxes, service charges, side trips, additional meals, and entertainment) and expect only what is specified. In addition, check the ratings of all hotels on the itinerary and their facilities, cancellation policies for you and the tour operator, and, if you are traveling alone, the cost of a single supplement.

Listed below is a sample of the tours and packages available. Most tour operators request that bookings be made through a travel agent—there is no additional charge for doing so. For additional resources, contact your travel agent or the tourist offices of the Netherlands, Belgium, and Luxembourg.

General-Interest Tours *From the U.S.* **Abercrombie & Kent** (1520 Kensington Rd., Oak Brook, IL 60521, tel. 708/954–2944 or 800/323–7308) takes a six-night cruise through the waterways of Holland and Belgium, including stops in Amsterdam, Rotterdam, Ghent, and Brugge. **American Express Vacations** (300 Pinnacle Way, Norcross, GA 30093, tel. 800/241–1700 or 800/421–5785 in GA) spends 10 days touring Amsterdam, Brussels, Ghent, Brugge, Luxembourg, and Paris. A variety of other tours of the Continent include visits to the Netherlands. **Caravan Tours** (401 N. Michigan Ave., Chicago, IL 60611, tel. 312/321–9800 or 800/227–2826) offers a "Four-Country Highlight" of Holland, Belgium, Luxembourg, and Germany in 12 days. **Globus-Gateway** (95–25 Queens Blvd.,

Rego Park, NY 11374, tel. 718/268–7000 or 800/221–0090) also includes Holland and Belgium in many of its tours of continental Europe. **Maupintour** (Box 807, Lawrence, KS 66044, tel. 913/843–1211 or 800/255–4266) offers the highlights of Belgium and Germany in 10 days, including Brussels, Ghent, and a Rhine cruise. A 10-day tour of Luxembourg and Paris includes side trips to Belgium and Germany. Another tour offers Holland and Brussels for 10 days. **Olson Travelworld** (Box 10066, Manhattan Beach, CA 90226, tel. 310/546–8400 or 800/421–2255) begins its two-week excursion with highlights of Holland, heads into Belgium and Luxembourg, then winds up in Paris. **Trafalgar Tours** (11 E. 26th St., Suite 1300, New York, NY 10010, tel. 212/689–8977 or 800/854–0103) includes Holland and Belgium on a number of its trips through continental Europe. **Travcoa** (Box 2630, Newport Beach, CA 92658, tel. 714/476–2800 or 800/992–2004) offers "Medieval Holland and Flanders," an 18-day tour including Antwerp, Ghent, Brugge, Brussels, The Hague, Amsterdam, and the cities of Northern Holland.

From the U.K. **Amsterdam Travel Services Ltd.** (Bridge House, Ware, Herts SG12 9DF, tel. 0920/467444) has short breaks and package holidays to Amsterdam. Cycling holidays, excursions, and packages to Delft, The Hague, and Scheveningen are available. **Cresta Holidays** (Cresta House, 32 Victoria St., Altringham, Cheshire WA14 1ET, tel. 0345/056511) offers package holidays to Amsterdam with optional bulb-field excursions, day trips, and canal cruises. Three-center holidays, which include Brussels and Paris, are also available. **Holland Travel Service** (Holland House, 24–28 The Broadway, Old Amersham, Buckinghamshire HP7 0HP, tel. 0494/729333) offers weekend breaks to Amsterdam and packages based in seven Dutch cities; Valkenburg is ideally placed for visiting Belgium, Luxembourg, and Germany. Castle and country house holidays are also available. **Shearing Holidays** (Miry Lane, Wigan, Lancashire WN3 4AG, tel. 0942/824824) features five-day city breaks centered in Brugge or Amsterdam, with excursions to Brussels and other places of interest; seven-day tours covering Belgium, Luxembourg, and Holland; a "Belgian House Party" tour; and holidays based in various Dutch cities. **Time Off Ltd.** (Chester Close, Chester St., London SW1X 7BQ, tel. 071/235–8070) has two- to seven-night packages to Brussels, Brugge, and Luxembourg. A Rhine cruise and excursions to Ghent, Antwerp, and Waterloo are available. Holidays to Amsterdam and The Hague feature optional tours to see the windmills, tulip fields, a cheese market, and a Delft pottery factory. **Travelscene Ltd.** (Travelscene House, 11–15 St. Ann's Road, Harrow, Middlesex HA1 1AS, tel. 081/427–4445) offers short breaks to Amsterdam in all price ranges, with optional sightseeing excursions and canal cruises. **Wallace Arnold Tours Ltd.** (8 Park La., Croyden CR0 1JA, tel. 081/686–2378) has several coach tours featuring sights in Belgium and Holland.

Special-Interest Tours Among the operators of special-interest tours that include two or more countries of the Benelux area: for art and culture, **Unitours** (8 S. Michigan Ave., Chicago IL 60603, tel. 312/782–1590 or 800/621–0557) and **Art Horizon International** (14 E. 63rd St., New York, NY 10021, tel. 212/888–2299); for art and flowers, **Travel Time** (203 N. Wabash Ave., Chicago, IL 60601, tel. 312/726–7197 or 800/621–4725); for flowers and castles, **Tauck Tours** (11 Wilton Rd., Westport, CT 06880, tel. 203/226–6911 or 800/468–2825); for jazz, **Ciao! Travel** (810 Emerald St.,

Suite 107, San Diego, CA 92109, tel. 619/272–1543 or 800/942–2426). For people age 18–30, bicycling tours including all three countries are available from **College Bicycle Tours** (Sept.–Apr.: 415 W. Fullerton Pkwy., Chicago, IL 60614, tel. 312/404–1710; May–Aug.: 21188 Harvard, Southfield, MI 48076, tel. 800/736–2453).

Package Deals for Independent Travelers

American Airlines Fly Away Vacations (tel. 800/832–8383) offers independent packages for as long as you like for visits to Brussels, Brugge, and Antwerp. **Extra Value Travel** (683 S. Collier Blvd., Marco Island, FL 33937, tel. 813/398–4848 or 800/255–2847) offers self-drive tours of Belgium, Luxembourg, and Holland, including hotel choices and car rental. **Jet Vacations** (1775 Broadway, New York, NY 10019, tel. 212/474–8700 or 800/538–0999) offers Flexiplan Europe, a choice of hotels, car rentals, airport transfers, and sightseeing options for Brussels, Antwerp, Brugge, Liège, Luxembourg, and a number of cities in Holland. **Northwest WorldVacations** (tel. 800/692–8687) provides visitors to Amsterdam or Brussels with preferred hotel and car-rental rates and tour options for a minimum of two nights. **Travel Bound** (599 Broadway, Penthouse, New York, NY 10012, tel. 212/334–1350 or 800/456–8656) offers a week-long "Brussels Grand" package for independent travelers, as well as packages to Holland, Belgium, and/or Luxembourg for a minimum of three to six nights. **United Vacations** (United is getting a new phone number for European vacations in about mid-April; to get that number, call 708/952–6252) will customize your itinerary to this region.

When to Go

Late spring, when the northern European days are long, but the summer crowds have not yet filled the beaches, the highways, or the museums, and fall are the best times to visit these three countries.

Climate *See* individual country chapters, below, for temperature charts. Current weather information for foreign and domestic cities may be obtained by calling **The Weather Channel Connection** (tel. 900/932–8437) from a touch-tone phone. In addition to the weather report, The Weather Channel Connection offers the local time and helpful travel tips as well as hurricane, foliage, and ski reports. Calls cost 95¢ per minute.

What to Pack

Clothing In the Netherlands, Belgium, and Luxembourg a sweater and a raincoat are indispensable. More expensive restaurants tend toward formality, making a jacket and tie useful items for men.

Miscellaneous Bring converters and adapter plugs for electrical appliances; outlets take plugs with two round prongs.

Carry-on Luggage Airlines generally allow each passenger one piece of carry-on luggage on international flights from the United States. The bag cannot exceed 45 inches/114 centimeters (length + width + height) and must fit under the seat or in the overhead luggage compartment.

Checked Luggage Passengers are generally allowed to check two pieces of luggage, neither of which can exceed 62 inches/157 centimeters (length + width + height) or weigh more than 70 pounds/31.5 kilograms. Baggage allowances vary among airlines, so check with the carrier or your travel agent before departure.

Taking Money Abroad

Before going, you may want to chart the U.S. dollar for a couple of weeks against the currencies of the Benelux countries. If the dollar is weakening, consider buying traveler's checks in foreign currency and paying in advance for such costly items as hotel rooms and train or plane tickets. If the dollar is improving, buy traveler's checks in U.S. dollars and use a credit card to pay for costly items after you've arrived at your destination. (Overseas credit charges often don't appear on your bill for two or three months, and you pay the exchange rate of the day the vendor posted the charge.) Always carry some cash with you, however, especially in smaller cities and rural areas where credit cards and traveler's checks may not be widely accepted. Regardless of how the dollar is faring abroad, it's wise to change a small amount of money before you go; lines at airport currency-exchange booths can be very long. If your local bank can't change your currency, you can exchange money through a local office of **Thomas Cook Currency Services** (630 5th Ave., New York, NY 10111, tel. 212/757–6915).

The most widely recognized traveler's checks are those of American Express, Barclay's, and Thomas Cook, plus those issued through major commercial banks such as Citibank and Bank of America. American Express now issues **Travelers Cheques for Two**—a system that allows both you and your traveling companion to sign and use the same checks. Some banks will issue the checks free to established customers, but most charge a 1% commission fee. Buy part of the traveler's checks in small denominations to cash toward the end of your trip. This will save you from having to cash a large check and ending up with more foreign money than you need. (Hold on to your receipts after exchanging your traveler's checks; it's easier to convert foreign currency back into dollars if you have the receipts.) Remember to take the addresses of offices where you can get refunds for lost or stolen traveler's checks. The American Express Traveler's Companion, a directory of offices to contact worldwide in case of loss or theft of American Express Traveler's Checks, is available at most travel service locations.

Getting Money from Home

Cash Machines It's easy to use automated-teller machines (ATMs) to withdraw
Withdrawals money from your checking account with a bank card. Just get the names of affiliated cash-machine networks before your departure. Note that you may be charged a fee for withdrawals away from your home turf. Of course, you will need to get a personal identification number (PIN) if you don't have one already.

Cash Advances You can also use ATMs to get cash advances on your credit card, providing you have a PIN number for your card. As with cash advances from tellers, you pay interest from the day of posting, and some banks tack on an additional service charge. The amounts of both withdrawals and cash advances are usually limited within given time periods. Know before you go.

Bank Transfers Just call your local bank and have money sent to a bank in the area you're visiting. It's faster and cheaper to transfer money between like branches.

American Express Cardholder Services The company's **Express Cash** system links your U.S. checking account to your Amex card. You can withdraw up to $1,000 in a seven-day period (more if your card is Gold or Platinum). For each transaction there's a 2% fee (minimum $2, maximum $6). Call 800/227–4669 for information.

Cardholders can also cash personal or counter checks at any American Express office for up to $1,000, of which $500 may be claimed in cash and the balance in traveler's checks carrying a 1% commission.

Wiring Money To send or receive up to $10,000, you can use an American Express MoneyGram, and you don't need an American Express card. The sender goes to an American Express MoneyGram agent, specifies an amount, pays up to $1,000 with a credit card (anything over that in cash), and telephones the receiver with the reference number he is given. The receiver goes to the nearest MoneyGram agent, presents identification and the reference number, and picks up cash. Fees are 5% to 10%, depending on the amount and method of payment (AE, D, MC, V are accepted). For agent locations, call 800/543–4080.

If there are no American Express offices nearby, you can use Western Union (tel. 800/325–6000). A friend at home can bring cash or a check to the nearest Western Union office or pay over the phone with a credit card. Delivery usually takes two business days, and fees are roughly 5% to 10%.

Currencies

The monetary unit in Belgium is the Belgian franc (BF); in Luxembourg, the Luxembourg franc (Flux); and in the Netherlands, the guilder (Fl). The currency exchange rates quoted in the following chapters fluctuate daily, so check them at the time of your departure.

Passports and Visas

Americans All U.S. citizens must have valid passports to enter the Netherlands or Belgium for stays of up to 90 days. U.S. citizens must have valid passports to enter Luxembourg, but their length of stay is not restricted.

To obtain a new passport, apply in person; renewals can be obtained in person or by mail. First-time applicants should apply to one of the 13 U.S. Passport Agency offices at least five weeks in advance of their departure date. In addition, local county courthouses, many state and probate courts, and some post offices accept passport applications. Necessary documents include (1) a completed passport application (Form DSP-11); (2) proof of citizenship (certified birth certificate issued by the hall of records of your state of birth, or naturalization papers); (3) proof of identity (valid driver's license or state, military, or student ID card with your photograph and signature); (4) two recent, identical, two-inch-square photographs (black-and-white or color head shot with white or off-white background); and (5) a $65 application fee for a 10-year passport (those under 18 pay $40 for a five-year passport). You may pay with a check, a money order, or an exact amount of cash; no change is given. Passports are mailed to you in 10 to 15 working days. To renew your passport by mail, you'll need to send a completed Form DSP-82; two recent, identical passport photographs; your current passport (if less than 12 years old and issued after your 16th birthday); and a check or money order for $55.

Britons You need a valid 10-year passport or a British Visitor's Passport to enter the Netherlands, Belgium, or Luxembourg. Application forms are available from most travel agents and major post offices and from the Passport Office (Clive House, 70 Petty France, London SW1H 9BR, tel. 071/279–3434 for recorded information or 071/279–4000). A standard 32-page passport costs £15, a 94-page passport £30. A British Visitor's Passport is valid for one year only and costs £7.50. You'll need two passport photographs and identification.

Canadians All Canadian citizens must have a valid passport to enter the Netherlands, Belgium, or Luxembourg for stays of up to 90 days. To obtain a passport, send a completed application (available at any post office or passport office) to the Bureau of Passports (Suite 215, West Tower, Guy Favreau Complex, 200 René Lévesque Blvd. W, Montreal, Quebec H2Z 1X4). Include $25, two photographs, a guarantor, and proof of Canadian citizenship. Applications can be made in person at regional passport offices in many locations, including Edmonton, Halifax, Montreal, Toronto, Vancouver, and Winnipeg. Passports are valid for five years and are nonrenewable.

Customs and Duties

On Arrival *See* the chapters below for regulations applying to visitors entering individual countries.

On Departure
Americans You may bring home duty-free up to $400 worth of foreign goods, as long as you have been out of the country for at least 48 hours and haven't made an international trip in the past 30 days. Each member of the family is entitled to the same exemption, regardless of age, and exemptions may be pooled. For the next $1,000 worth of goods, a flat 10% rate is assessed; above $1,400, duties vary with the merchandise. Included in the allowances for travelers 21 or older are one liter of alcohol, 100 cigars (non-Cuban), and 200 cigarettes. Only one bottle of perfume trademarked in the United States may be imported. There is no duty on antiques or works of art more than 100 years old. Anything exceeding these limits will be taxed at the port of entry and may be taxed additionally in the traveler's home state. Gifts valued at under $50 may be mailed duty-free to friends or relatives at home, but you may not send more than one package per day to a single addressee, and packages may not include perfumes costing more than $5, tobacco, or liquor.

The U.S. Customs Service (1301 Constitution Ave., Washington, D.C. 20029) publishes a free brochure, "Know Before You Go," that outlines what returning residents may and may not bring back to this country, and at what cost.

Canadians Exemptions for returning Canadians range from $20 to $300, depending on length of stay out of the country. For the $300 exemption, you must have been gone for one week. In any given year, you are allowed only one $300 exemption. You may bring in duty-free up to 50 cigars, 200 cigarettes, 2.2 pounds of tobacco, and 40 ounces of liquor, provided these are declared in writing to customs on arrival and accompany you in hand or checked-through baggage. Personal gifts should be mailed labeled "Unsolicited Gift—Value under $40." Obtain a copy of the Canadian Customs brochure "I Declare" for details.

Britons As all the countries are members of the EC, the following customs allowances apply upon entering the Netherlands, Belgium, or Luxembourg and returning to the United Kingdom. Travelers age 17 and over have two different allowances: one for goods bought in a duty-free shop, and the other for goods obtained elsewhere (i.e., tax paid) within the EC.

In the first category you may bring in (1) 200 cigarettes or 100 cigarillos or 50 cigars or 250 grams of tobacco; (2) two liters of still table wine and (3) one liter of spirits over 22% volume or two liters of spirits under 22% volume (fortified or sparkling wine) or two more liters of table wine; (4) 60 milliliters of perfume and 250 milliliters of eau de toilette; and (5) other goods to a value of £32, but not more than 50 liters of beer or 25 mechanical lighters.

In the second category you may bring in (1) 300 cigarettes or 150 cigarillos or 75 cigars or 400 grams of tobacco; (2) five liters of table wine and (3) 1.5 liters of alcoholic drink over 22% volume or three liters of alcohol under 22% volume (fortified or sparkling wine) or three more liters of table wine; (4) 90 milliliters of perfume and 375 milliliters of toilet water; and (5) other goods to a value of £425, but not more than 50 liters of beer or 25 lighters.

Traveling with Film

If your camera is new, shoot and develop a few rolls before leaving home. Pack some lens tissue and an extra battery for your built-in light meter. Film doesn't like hot weather, so if you're driving in summer, don't store film in the glove compartment or on the shelf under the rear window. Put it behind the front seat on the floor, on the side opposite the exhaust pipe.

On a plane trip, never pack unprocessed film in check-in luggage; if your bags are X-rayed, your film may be ruined. Always carry undeveloped film with you through security and ask to have it inspected by hand. Inspectors at American airports are required by law to honor requests for hand inspection; abroad, you'll have to depend on the kindness of strangers. The newer airport scanning machines used in all U.S. airports are safe for anything from five to 500 scans, depending on the speed of your film.

Languages

Belgium has three official languages: Flemish, French, and German. In Flemish-speaking parts of the country you are likely to get a better reaction if you speak English rather than French. Luxembourg's languages are mixed throughout the population rather than divided geographically; they include Luxembourgish (a language descended from an ancient dialect of the Franks), French, and German—as well as a fair amount of English. In the Netherlands, Dutch is the official language, but most people know some English as well.

Staying Healthy

If you have a health problem that may require the purchase of prescription drugs, have your doctor write a prescription using the drug's generic name, as brand names vary from country to country.

The **International Association for Medical Assistance to Travelers** (IAMAT) is a worldwide organization that offers listings of approved physicians and clinics whose training meets British and American standards. For lists of Dutch, Belgian, or Luxembourgian physicians and clinics that are part of this network, contact IAMAT (417 Center St., Lewiston, NY 14092, tel. 716/754–4883; in Canada, 40 Regal Rd., Guelph, Ont. N1K 1B5; in Europe, 57 Voirets, 1212 Grand-Lancy, Geneva, Switzerland). Membership is free.

In Washington, the U.S. Department of State **Citizens Emergency Center** (tel. 202/647–5225) provides information about health conditions in other nations; on what U.S. citizens can do in the event of an emergency overseas; on whether any notices, cautions, or warnings exist in the area to which you're traveling; and on how to obtain passports and visas.

Insurance

Travelers may seek insurance coverage in four areas: health and accident, lost luggage, trip cancellation, and flight. Your first step is to review your existing health and home-owner policies; some health insurance plans cover health expenses incurred while traveling, some major medical plans cover emergency transportation, and some home-owner policies cover the theft of luggage.

In the U.S.
Health and Accident

Several companies offer coverage designed to supplement existing health insurance for travelers:

Carefree Travel Insurance (Box 310, 120 Mineola Blvd., Mineola, NY 11501, tel. 516/294–0220 or 800/323–3149) provides coverage for emergency medical evacuation and accidental death and dismemberment. It also offers 24-hour medical phone advice. **International SOS Assistance** (Box 11568, Philadelphia, PA 19116, tel. 215/244–1500 or 800/523–8930), a medical assistance company, provides emergency evacuation services, worldwide medical referrals, and optional medical insurance. **Travel Assistance International** (1133 15th St., NW, Suite 400, Washington, DC 20005, tel. 202/331–1609 or 800/821–2828) provides emergency evacuation services, 24-hour medical referrals, and medical insurance. **Travel Guard International,** underwritten by Transamerica Occidental Life Companies (1145 Clark St., Stevens Point, WI 54481, tel. 715/345–0505 or 800/782–5151), offers emergency evacuation services and reimbursement for medical expenses with no deductibles or daily limits. **Wallach and Company, Inc.** (Box 480, Middleburg, VA 22117–0480, tel. 703/687–3166 or 800/237–6615) offers comprehensive medical coverage, including emergency evacuation services worldwide.

Lost Luggage

On international flights, airlines are responsible for lost or damaged property of up to $9.07 per pound ($20 per kilogram) for checked baggage, and up to $400 per passenger for unchecked baggage. If you're carrying valuables, either take them with you on the plane or purchase additional insurance for lost luggage. Some airlines will issue extra luggage insurance when you check in, but many do not. Insurance for lost, damaged, or stolen luggage is available through travel agents or directly through various insurance companies. Lost-luggage coverage is usually part of a comprehensive travel insurance package that includes personal accident, trip cancellation, and sometimes default and bankruptcy. Two companies that issue luggage insurance are **Tele-Trip** (Box 31685, 3201 Farnam St., Omaha, NE 68131–0618, tel. 800/228–9792), a subsidiary of Mutual of Omaha, and **The Traveler** (Ticket and Travel Dept., 1 Tower Square, Hartford, CT 06183–5040, tel. 203/277–0111 or 800/243–3174). Tele-Trip operates sales booths at airports and also issues insurance through travel agents. Rates vary according to the length of the trip. The Traveler will insure checked or hand luggage at $500–$2,000 valuation per person, for a maximum of 180 days. The rate up to five days for a $500 valuation is $10; for 180 days, $85. Other companies with comprehensive policies include **Access America, Inc.,** a subsidiary of Blue Cross–Blue Shield (Box 11188, Richmond, VA 23230, tel. 800/334–7525 or 800/284–8300); **Near Services** (450 Prairie Ave., Suite 101, Calumet City, IL 60409, tel. 708/868–6700 or 800/654–6700); and **Travel Guard International** and **Carefree Travel Insurance** (*see* Health and Accident Insurance, *above*).

Before you go, itemize the contents of each bag in case you need to file an insurance claim. Be certain to put your home or business address on each piece of luggage, including carry-on bags. If your luggage is lost or stolen and later recovered, the airline will deliver the luggage to your home free of charge.

Trip-Cancellation and Flight Insurance
Consider purchasing trip-cancellation insurance if you are traveling on a promotional or discounted ticket that does not allow changes or cancellations. You are then covered if an emergency causes you to cancel or postpone your trip. Trip-cancellation insurance is usually included in combination travel-insurance packages available from most tour operators, travel agents, and insurance agents. Flight insurance, which covers passengers in the case of death or dismemberment, is often included in the price of a ticket when paid for with American Express, MasterCard, or other major credit cards.

In the United Kingdom
For general advice on all aspects of holiday insurance, contact **The Association of British Insurers** (51 Gresham St., London BC2V 7HQ, tel. 071/600–3333) or **Europ Assistance** (252 High St., Croyden Surrey CRO 1NF, tel. 081/680–1234).

Car Rentals

All major car-rental companies are represented in the Netherlands, Belgium, and Luxembourg, and visitors are advised to make a reservation in advance. Usually, you must be over 21 to rent a car (some rental companies require a driver to be 25) and some restrictions may apply to drivers over 60 years of age. Most companies will accept your current driver's license from home, but some may require an International Driver's Permit, available through your automobile club (AAA or CAA) office.

In metropolitan areas, rates can range from $69 plus tax per day for an economy car to as high as $219 plus tax for a large car, with unlimited free mileage. Costs may be higher if you rent outside major cities. One-way rentals can be arranged, although they usually involve a drop-off charge. Special packages, such as fly/drive combinations in conjunction with your international airline ticket, offer discount rental rates. Campers, motor homes or four-wheel-drive vehicles may also be available. Call well in advance.

For car rental reservations call **Avis** (tel. 800/331–1084 in the U.S., 800/879–2847 in Canada), **Budget** (tel. 800/472–3325 in the U.S. and Canada), **Dollar** (tel. 800/800–4000 in the U.S. and Canada), and **Hertz** (tel. 800/654–3001 in the U.S., 800/654–3131 in AK and HI, 800/263–0600 in Canada).

Rail Passes

The **EurailPass,** valid for unlimited first-class train travel through 20 countries, including the Netherlands, Belgium, and Luxembourg, is an excellent value if you plan to travel around the Continent.

The ticket is available for periods of 15 days ($430), 21 days ($550), one month ($680), two months ($920), and three months ($1,150). For two or more people traveling together, a 15-day rail pass costs $340 each. Between April 1 and September 30, you need a minimum of three in your group to get this discount. For those 25 and under (on the first day of travel), there is the Eurail Youthpass, for one or two months of unlimited second-class train travel at $470 and $640, respectively.

For travelers who like to spread out their train journeys, there is the **Eurail Flexipass.** With the 15-day Flexipass ($280), travelers get five days of unlimited first-class train travel but can spread that travel out over 15 days; a 21-day pass gives you nine days of travel ($450), and a one-month pass gives you 14 days ($610). The Eurail Youth Flexipass allows for 15 days of unlimited second-class travel within a two-month period ($420).

The EurailPass is available only if you live outside Europe or North Africa. You can apply through an authorized travel agent or through **Rail Europe, Inc.** (230 Westchester Ave., White Plains, NY 10604, tel. 914/682–5172 or 800/345–1990).

Rail Europe also offers the **Benelux Tourrail Pass,** a special unlimited mileage ticket for travel in the Netherlands, Belgium, and Luxembourg, good for any five days in a 17-day period, for $154 (C$180) first class and $103 (C$125) second class. The **Benelux Junior Pass** costs $109 (C$129) first class and $74 (C$89) second class for travelers under 26 years old and $54 (C$65) and $36 (C$45) for children 4–11.

Student and Youth Travel

The **International Student Identity Card** (ISIC) entitles students to special fares on local transportation, rail passes, intra-European student charter flights, and discounts at museums, theaters, sports events, and many other attractions. If the ISIC card is purchased in the United States, the $14 cost also includes $3,000 in emergency medical coverage, plus hospital coverage of $100 a day for up to 60 days. Apply to the **Council on International Educational Exchange** (CIEE), 205 E. 42nd St., New York, NY 10017, tel. 212/661–1414). In Canada, the ISIC is available for C$13 from **Travel Cuts** (187 College St., Toronto, Ont. M5T 1P7, tel. 416/979–2406). In the United Kingdom, students enrolled in university programs can purchase the ISIC at any student union or student travel company upon presentation of a valid university ID.

Travelers (students and nonstudents) under age 26 can apply for a **Youth International Educational Exchange Card** (YIEE) issued by the **Federation of International Youth Travel Organizations** (Islands Brygge 81, DK-2300 Copenhagen S, Denmark). It provides benefits similar to those of the ISIC card and is available in the United States from CIEE (*see above*).

An **International Youth Hostel Federation** (IYHF) membership card is the key to inexpensive dormitory-style accommodations at more than 6,000 hostel locations in 70 countries around the world. Hostels provide separate sleeping quarters for men and women at rates ranging from $7 to $20 a night per person, and many have family accommodations. Youth Hostel memberships, valid for 12 months from the time of purchase, are available in the United States through **American Youth Hostels** (AYH, Box 37613, Washington, DC 20013, tel. 202/783–6161), in Canada through the **Canadian Hostelling Association** (CHA, 1600 James Naismith Dr., Suite 608, Gloucester, Ont. K1B 5N4, tel. 613/748–5638), and in the United Kingdom through the **Youth Hostel Association of England and Wales** (Trevelyan House, 8 St. Stephen's Hill, St. Albans, Herts AL1 2DY, tel. 0727/55215). By joining one of the national (American, Canadian, or British) youth hostel associations, members automatically become part of the International Youth Hostel Federation, and are entitled to reductions on rail and bus travel worldwide. Handbooks listing these special concessions are available from the associations. The cost for a first-year membership is $25 for adults 18–54. Renewal thereafter is $20. For youths (17 and under) the rate is $10, and for seniors (55 and older) the rate is $15. Family memberships cost $35.

Economical bicycle tours for small groups of adventurous, energetic students are a popular AYH student travel service. For information on these and other AYH activities and publications, contact the AYH.

Council Travel, a CIEE subsidiary, is the foremost U.S. student travel agency, specializing in low-cost charters and serving as the exclusive U.S. agent for many student airfare bargains and tours. CIEE's 72-page "Student Travel Catalog" and "Council Charter" brochures are available free from any Council Travel office in the United States (enclose $1 postage if ordering by mail). In addition to CIEE headquarters (205 E. 42nd St., tel. 212/661–1450) and a branch office (W. 8th St.) in New York City, there are Council Travel offices in Arizona (Tempe), California (Berkeley, La Jolla, Long Beach, Los Angeles, San Diego, San Francisco, and Sherman Oaks), Connecticut (New Haven), Washington, DC, Florida (Miami), Georgia (Atlanta), Illinois (Chicago, Evanston), Louisiana (New Orleans), Massachusetts (Amherst, Boston, Cambridge), Michigan (Ann Arbor), Minnesota (Minneapolis), North Carolina (Durham), Ohio (Columbus), Oregon (Portland), Rhode Island (Providence), Texas (Austin, Dallas), Washington (Seattle), and Wisconsin (Milwaukee).

Students who would like to work abroad should contact **CIEE's Work Abroad Department** (206 E. 42nd St., New York, NY 10017, tel. 212/661–1414, ext. 1130). The council arranges paid and voluntary work experiences overseas for up to six months. CIEE also sponsors study programs in Europe and produces several books of interest to the student traveler. These include *Work, Study, Travel Abroad: The Whole World Handbook* ($12.95 plus $1.50 book-rate postage or $3 first-class postage), *Volunteer! The Comprehensive Guide to Voluntary Service in the U.S. and Abroad* ($8.95 plus $1.50 book-rate postage or $3 first-class postage), and *The Teenager's Guide to Travel, Study, and Adventure Abroad* ($11.95 plus $1.50 book-rate postage or $3 first-class postage.)

The Information Center at the **Institute of International Education** (IIE, 809 UN Plaza, New York, NY 10017, tel. 212/984–5413) has reference books, foreign-university catalogues, study-abroad brochures, and other materials that may be consulted free. The Information Center is open weekdays 10–4 and is closed on holidays.

Traveling with Children

Publications   *Family Travel Times* is a newsletter published 10 times a year by **TWYCH** (Travel With Your Children, 45 W. 18th St., 7th Floor Tower, New York, NY 10011, tel. 212/206–0688). A one-year subscription costs $35 and includes access to back issues. The organization also offers a free phone-in service with advice and information on specific destinations.

Great Vacations with Your Kids, by Dorothy Jordan and Marjorie Cohen, offers complete advice on planning your trip with children, from toddlers to teens ($12.95, E.P. Dutton, 375 Hudson St., New York, NY 10014, tel. 212/366–2000).

Kids and Teens in Flight, a useful brochure about children flying alone, is available from the U.S. Department of Transportation. To order a free copy, call 202/366–2220.

Innocents Abroad: Traveling with Kids in Europe, by Valerie Wolf Deutsch and Laura Sutherland, is a new guide to child- and teen-friendly activities, food, and transportation in Britain and on the Continent, with individual sections on each country ($15.95 paperback, New American Library, Penguin USA, 375 Hudson St., New York, NY 10014, tel. 212/366–2000).

Traveling With Children—And Enjoying It, by Arlene K. Butler, offers tips on how to cut costs, keep kids busy, eat out, reduce jet lag, and pack properly ($11.95 paperback, Globe Pequot Press, Box Q, Chester, CT 06412).

Tours   **Grandtravel** (600 Wisconsin Ave., Suite 706, Chevy Chase, MD 20815, tel. 301/986–0790 or 800/247–7651) offers dozens of international and domestic tours tailored for grandparents and grandchildren traveling together.

Getting There   All children, including infants, must have valid individual passports for foreign travel. On international flights, children under 2 not occupying a seat pay 10% of the adult fare. Various discounts apply to children 2–12, so check with your airline when making reservations.

Regulations about infant travel on airplanes are changing. If you want to be sure your infant is secure, you must bring your own infant car seat and buy a separate ticket. Check with the airline in advance to be sure your seat meets the required standard. If possible, reserve a seat behind one of the plane's bulkheads, where there's usually more legroom and enough space to fit a bassinet (which is available from the airlines). The booklet "Child/Infant Safety Seats Acceptable for Use in Aircraft" is available from the Federal Aviation Administration (APA-200, Independence Ave., SW, Washington, DC 20591, tel. 202/267–3479). If you opt to hold your baby on your lap, do so with the infant outside the seat belt rather than inside it so he or she isn't crushed in case of a sudden stop.

When reserving tickets, also ask about special children's meals or snacks. The February 1990 and 1992 issues of *Family Travel Times* include TWYCH's *Airline Guide*, which contains a rundown of the children's services offered by 46 different airlines.

Home Exchange Exchanging homes is a surprisingly inexpensive way to enjoy a vacation abroad, especially if you plan a lengthy visit. The largest home-exchange company, **Intervac U.S./International Home Exchange** (Box 590504, San Francisco, CA 94159, tel. 800/756–4663), publishes three directories a year. The $45 membership entitles you to one listing and all three directories (there is an additional charge for postage). Photos of your property cost an additional $11, and listing a second home costs $10.

Loan-a-Home (2 Park La., Apt. 6E, Mount Vernon, NY 10552, tel. 914/664–7640), which publishes two worldwide directories (in December and June) and two supplements (in March and September) each year, is popular with professors on sabbatical, business persons on temporary assignment, and retired people on extended vacations. There is no annual membership fee or charge for listing your home, but one directory and a supplement cost $35. All four books cost $45.

Vacation Exchange Club (Box 820, Halweiwa, HI 96712, tel. 800/638–3841) specializes in both international and domestic home exchanges. The club publishes four directories a year, in January, March, July, and September, and updated late listings throughout the year. Annual membership, which includes your listing in one book, a newsletter, and copies of all publications (mailed first class), is $50.

Apartment/Villa Rentals **Interhome, Inc.** (124 Little Falls Rd., Fairfield, NJ 07004, tel. 201/882–6864), Europe's largest vacation rental company, has some 22,000 homes and apartments to rent throughout Europe. Properties are available in major resort areas and quiet, rustic settings.

Villas International (605 Market St., Suite 510, San Francisco, CA 94105, tel. 415/281–0910 or 800/221–2260) has houses, apartments, villas, and cottages to rent in a variety of towns, cities, and resort areas.

Hotels At the **Best Western** hotels (reservations tel. 800/528–1234) in Brussels, Ostend, and Brugge in Belgium; the city of Luxembourg; and more than 40 cities in the Netherlands, children under 12 may stay free when sharing a room with two paying adults. A maximum of five persons is allowed per room. The **Intercontinental** hotels (reservations tel. 800/327–0200) in Brussels, Amsterdam, The Hague, and Luxembourg allow one child of any age to stay free in his or her parents' room. Many hotels throughout the region have family rooms.

Baby-sitting Services Check with your hotel concierge or the tourist office for information about local child-care services.

Hints for Disabled Travelers

Hotels The **Ramada Inns** (reservations tel. 800/228–2828) in Brussels, Liège, and Amsterdam have rooms for handicapped guests. The **Intercontinental** Hotel (reservations tel. 800/327–0200) in Luxembourg has two handicapped-accessible rooms. Wheelchair-accessible rooms are also available at the **Hilton** hotels (reservations tel. 800/531–5900) in Brussels, Amsterdam, and Rotterdam.

Associations The **Information Center for Individuals with Disabilities** (Fort Point Pl., 1st floor, 27–43 Wormwood St., Boston, MA 02210; voice and TDD, tel. 617/727–5540) offers useful problem-solving assistance, including lists of travel agents who specialize in tours for the disabled. The center also publishes two fact sheets, "Tips on Planning a Vacation" and "Tour Operators and Travel Agencies." Enclose $5 (to cover postage) for each sheet.

Mobility International USA (Box 3551, Eugene, OR 97403; voice and TDD, tel. 503/343–1284) coordinates exchange programs for disabled people around the world and offers information on accommodations and organized study programs for a $20 annual fee. It also publishes *A World of Options for the 90s*, a guide to international exchange and travel for people with disabilities ($16 including postage, from the address above).

Moss Rehabilitation Hospital Travel Information Service (1200 W. Tabor Rd., Philadelphia, PA 19141, tel. 215/456–9600 or TDD 215/456–9602) for a small fee provides information on tourist sights, transportation, and accommodations in destinations around the world. They also provide toll-free telephone numbers for airlines with special lines for the hard of hearing.

The **Society for the Advancement of Travel for the Handicapped** (SATH, 347 5th Ave., Suite 610, New York, NY 10016, tel. 212/447–7288) offers access information and lists of tour operators specializing in travel for the disabled. Annual membership costs $45, or $25 for students and seniors. Send $2 and a self-addressed, stamped envelope for information on a destination.

Travel Industry and Disabled Exchange (TIDE, 5435 Donna Ave., Tarzana, CA 91356, tel. 818/368–5648) publishes a quarterly newsletter and a directory of travel agencies and tours catering to the disabled. The annual membership fee is $15.

In the U.K. The main British sources of advice on travel for the handicapped are the **Royal Association for Disability and Rehabilitation** (RADAR, 25 Mortimer St., London W1N 8AB, tel. 071/637–5400), the **Holiday Care Service** (2 Old Bank Chambers, Horley, Surrey RH6 9HW, tel. 029/377–4535), and **Mobility International** (228 Borough High St., London SE1 1JX, tel. 071/403–5688).

Publications *The Itinerary* (Box 2012, Bayonne, NJ 07002, tel. 201/858–3400) is a bimonthly travel magazine for the disabled. Call for a subscription ($10 for one year, $20 for two); it's not available in bookstores.

Twin Peaks Press (Box 129, Vancouver, WA 98666, tel. 206/694–2462 or 800/637–2256 for orders only) specializes in books for the disabled: *Travel for the Disabled* offers helpful hints as well as a comprehensive list of guidebooks and facilities geared to the disabled. *The Directory of Travel Agencies for the Disabled* lists more than 350 agencies throughout the world. *Wheelchair Vagabound* and *The Directory of Accessible Van Rentals* provide information for the RV/camping traveler. Twin Peaks also offers a "Traveling Nurse's Network," which provides registered nurses to accompany and assist disabled travelers.

Hints for Older Travelers

When renting a car, be sure to ask about special promotional rates, which might offer greater savings than the available discount. Senior discounts may also be applicable on train travel; check when you buy tickets.

The American Association of Retired Persons (AARP, 601 E St., NW, Washington, DC 20049, tel. 202/662–4850) arranges group tours, cruises, and apartment living in Europe through "AARP Travel Experience from American Express" (400 Pinnacle Way, Suite 450, Norcross, GA 30091, tel. 800/927–0111). AARP members must be 50 years or older; annual dues are $8 per person or couple. Members can purchase land tours through their local travel agent or any American Express office and pay for them with a credit card.

Elderhostel (75 Federal St., 3rd floor, Boston, MA 02110, tel. 617/426–7788) is an innovative educational program for people 60 and older. Participants live in dorms on 1,600 campuses around the world. Mornings are devoted to lectures and seminars; afternoons, to sightseeing and field trips. Fees for two- to three-week international trips—including room, board, tuition, and transportation—range from $1,800 to $4,500.

Saga International Holidays (120 Boylston St., Boston, MA 02116, tel. 800/343–0273) specializes in group travel for people over 60. A selection of variously priced tours allows you to choose the package that meets your needs.

Publications *The International Health Guide for Senior Citizen Travelers*, by W. Robert Lange, M.D., is available for $4.95, plus $1.50 for shipping, from **Pilot Books** (103 Cooper St., Babylon, NY 11702, tel. 515/422–2225).

Hotels SAS Royal hotels in Brussels and Amsterdam offer weekend reductions for senior citizens and traveling companions based on age. If you're 65 years old, you qualify for a 65% reduction, those aged 75 are eligible for a 75% reduction, and so on. Travelers aged 100 stay for free.

Arriving and Departing

From the U.S. by Plane

There are three types of flights: nonstop—no changes, no stops; direct—no changes, but one or more stops; and connecting—two or more planes, one or more stops.

Airlines Major airlines that fly nonstop or direct from the United States or Canada to the Benelux countries include **KLM Royal Dutch** (tel. 800/777–5553), **Sabena** (tel. 800/955–2000), **Icelandair** (tel. 800/223–5500), **American** (tel. 800/433–7300), **Delta** (tel. 800/221–1212), **TWA** (800/892–4141), and **United** (tel. 800/241–6522).

Flying Time Flights from New York to Amsterdam take just over seven hours; to Brussels, just under seven; to Luxembourg, eight. Flights from Los Angeles to Amsterdam take 10½ hours.

Enjoying the Flight Because the air on a plane is dry, it helps, while flying, to drink plenty of nonalcoholic beverages; drinking alcohol contributes to jet lag, as does eating heavy meals on board. Feet swell at high altitudes, so it's a good idea to remove your shoes at the beginning of your flight. Sleepers usually prefer window seats to curl up against; those who like to move about the cabin should ask for aisle seats. Bulkhead seats (located in the front row of each cabin) have more legroom, but seat trays are attached to the arms of the seat rather than to the back of the seat ahead. Generally, bulkhead seats are reserved for the disabled, the elderly, or parents traveling with babies.

Discount Flights The major airlines offer a range of tickets that can increase the price of any given seat by more than 300%, depending on the day of purchase. As a rule, the further in advance you buy the ticket, the less expensive it is and the greater the penalty (up to 100%) for canceling. Check with airlines for details.

The best buy is not necessarily an APEX (**advance purchase**) ticket on one of the major airlines, because these tickets carry certain restrictions: They must be bought in advance (usually 21 days); they restrict your travel, usually with a minimum stay of seven days and a maximum of 90; and they also penalize you for changes—voluntary or not—in your travel plans. But if you can work around these drawbacks (and most travelers can), they are among the best-value fares available.

Travelers willing to put up with some restrictions and inconveniences, in exchange for a substantially reduced airfare, may be interested in flying as an **air courier.** A person who agrees to be a courier must accompany shipments between designated points. There are several sources of information on courier deals: 1) A telephone directory lists courier companies by the cities to which they fly. Send $5 and a self-addressed, stamped, business-size envelope to **Pacific Data Sales Publishing** (2554 Lincoln Blvd., Suite 275-F, Marina Del Rey, CA 90291). 2) **"A Simple Guide to Courier Travel"**; send $15.95 (includes postage and handling) to Box 2394, Lake Oswego, OR 97035. For more information, call 800/344–9375. 3) **Now Voyager** (74 Varick St., Suite 307, New York, NY 10013, tel. 212/431–1616). 4) **Courier Travel Service** (530 Central Ave., Cedarhurst, NY 11516, tel. 516/374–2299 or 800/922–2359).

Charter flights offer the lowest fares but often depart only on certain days. Though you may be able to arrive at one city and return from another, you may lose all or most of your money if you cancel your trip. Don't sign up for a charter flight unless you've checked with a travel agency, the Better Business Bureau, or your local consumer protection agency about the reputation of the packager. It's particularly important to know the packager's policy concerning refunds should a flight be canceled; some travel agents recommend that travelers purchase trip-cancellation insurance if they plan to book charter flights. One of the most popular charter operators to Europe is **Council Charter** (205 E. 42nd St., New York, NY 10017, tel. 212/661–0311 or 800/800–8222), a division of the Council on International Educational Exchange (CIEE). Other companies advertise in Sunday travel sections of newspapers.

Somewhat more expensive—but up to 50% below the cost of APEX fares—are tickets purchased through **consolidators**, companies that buy blocks of tickets on scheduled airlines and sell them at wholesale prices. Tickets are subject to availability, so passengers must generally have flexible travel schedules. Here again, you may lose all or most of your money if you change plans, but at least you will be on a regularly scheduled flight with less risk of cancellation than on a charter. As an added precaution, you may want to purchase trip-cancellation insurance. Once you've made your reservation, call the airline to confirm it. Among the best-known consolidators are **UniTravel** (Box 12485, St. Louis, MO 63132, tel. 314/569–2501 or 800/325–2222) and **Access International** (101 W. 31st St., Suite 1104, New York, NY 10001, tel. 212/465–0707 or 800/825–3633). Others advertise in Sunday newspaper travel sections.

Another option is to join a **travel club** that offers special discounts to its members. Several such organizations are **Discount Travel International** (114 Forrest Ave., Narberth, PA 19072, tel. 215/668–7184), **Moment's Notice** (425 Madison Ave., New York, NY 10017, tel. 212/486–0503), **Travelers Advantage** (CUC Travel Service, 49 Music Square W, Nashville, TN 37203, tel. 800/548–1116), and **Worldwide Discount Travel Club** (1674 Meridian Ave., Miami Beach, FL 33139, tel. 305/534–2082). Compare cut-rate tickets with APEX tickets on the major airlines.

Smoking It is best to request a nonsmoking seat at the time you book your ticket. If a U.S. airline representative tells you there are no seats available in the nonsmoking section, insist on one: Department of Transportation regulations require U.S. flag carriers to find seats for all nonsmokers on the day of the flight, provided they meet check-in time restrictions. On foreign carriers, ask for a seat far from the smoking section.

Lost Luggage *See* Insurance—Lost Luggage, *above.*

From the U.S. by Ship

Only one firm now offers transatlantic crossings: **Cunard** (tel. 800/221–4770; in the U.K., through British Airways, tel. 081/897–4000), sailing the *Queen Elizabeth 2* between New York and Southampton, England. The trip takes five days, and passengers fly home. Ferries connect with Belgium and the Netherlands from ports on the English Channel.

From the U.K. by Plane, Train, Bus, and Car

See individual country chapters, *below.*

Staying in the Benelux Countries

Getting Around

Travel in the Netherlands, Belgium, and Luxembourg is convenient by almost any mode of transportation.

By Plane Both KLM and Sabena airlines have flights between Amsterdam and Brussels, and KLM has flights from Amsterdam to Luxembourg.

By Car A network of well-maintained superhighways and other roads covers the three countries, making car travel convenient. Traffic can be heavy around the major cities, on the roads to southern Europe on June 30, and on those approaching the North Sea beaches on summer weekends.

By Train Several express trains daily, including Eurocities and Intercities international rail service, connect the main cities of the Benelux region; regularly scheduled frequent service links smaller cities as well. *See* individual country chapters, *below*, for specific information.

By Bus Bus service between the Benelux countries is minimal.

By Boat Canal boats and ferries link many parts of Belgium and the Netherlands (*see* individual country chapters, *below*).

Shopping

These three countries, in the center of the EC and participating in the sophisticated, modern, high-tech culture of 1990s Europe, offer a full spectrum of goods, but they are especially known for diamonds, lace, porcelain, antiques, tulip bulbs, chocolate, and cheese.

Sports and Outdoor Activities

Bicycling, boating, camping, and hiking rate high among the outdoor activities available in the Benelux countries. *See* individual country chapters, *below*, for specific information.

Beaches

The long North Sea coast of Belgium and southern Holland attracts droves of sun lovers during the long northern days of summer, despite the bracing temperature of the water.

Dining

In these cosmopolitan countries food from around the world is readily available. Currently the single strongest influence, even on Dutch cooking, seems to be the cuisine of France—at least in restaurants. All three countries revel in the bounty of the sea: mussels and shrimp, as well as fish, are major delicacies. Vegetables and fruit are freshest here where they are grown. Paralleling these are the local, old-fashioned specialties of each country: *waterzooi* (a rich chicken or fish stew) or *carbonnade* (beef stew with beer) in Belgium; *judd mat gardebohn'en* (smoked pork shoulder with fava beans) or *gromperekichelcher* (fried potato patties) in Luxembourg; and soup, sausage, and potatoes in the Netherlands.

Belgium supports a significant number of the foremost restaurants in Europe; the Netherlands offers Indonesian *rijstafel* (rice served with many small meat, poultry, and vegetable dishes and sauces) rivaling the original halfway around the world; and tiny Luxembourg has more *gastronomique* restaurants per capita than any other country in Europe.

Lodging

All three countries offer a range of choices, from the major international hotel chains to small, modern local hotels to family-run restored inns and historic houses to elegant country châteaus and resorts. Prices in metropolitan areas are significantly higher than those in outlying towns and the countryside.

Credit Cards

The following credit card abbreviations have been used: AE, American Express; D, Discover; DC, Diners Club; MC, MasterCard; and V, Visa. It's a good idea to call ahead to check current credit card policies.

Great Itineraries

Haute Cuisine and Country Air

The peripatetic gourmet first chooses overnight stops to ensure that each evening meal is a feast. It is an added bonus that many of the finest small hotels with outstanding restaurants are located in out-of-the-way places that you might not otherwise visit. This kind of travel obviously does not come cheap.

Length 15 days

Getting Around In the Netherlands the drive from Amsterdam to Kerkrade by
By Car way of Oisterwijk is 380 kilometers (228 miles). In Belgium, highways link Antwerp and Noirefontaine by way of the coast for an arc of some 600 kilometers (370 miles). To travel from meal to meal in Luxembourg, you'll cover a lot of ground, much of it inaccessible except by car.

By Train In the Netherlands there are good train and taxi connections from Amsterdam by way of Middelburg and Den Bos. Trains in Belgium connect through Brussels with the main towns on the route; a car is necessary in the Ardennes. In Luxembourg, only Luxembourg City is easily reached by direct rail lines.

The Main Route **Three Nights: Netherlands.** From Amsterdam, travel south toward Middelburg; take the Yerseke-Kruiningen exit on the highway toward **Kruiningen.** Restaurant Inter Scaldes sits alone in the countryside, offering fine French cuisine and luxury accommodations. The following day can be a leisurely drive to **Oisterwijk** between Tilburg and s'Hertogenbosch, for an overnight stay at Hotel-Restaurant De Swaen, located on the town square. The following day travel south through Limburg province to **Kerkrade** for dinner in the castle at Hotel Kasteel Erenstein and overnight in the luxury accommodations of the half-timbered former Limburg farmstead. A word of advice: book your overnight stays well in advance.

Nine nights: Belgium. Start the Belgian portion of your trip in **Antwerp,** where Sir Anthony van Dijck is the top restaurant. The ten exquisite rooms of De Rosier are only minutes away. Make your next stop **Brugge,** to eat and sleep at the revered De Karmeliet or the young, imaginative Den Gouden Harynk, both within easy walking distance of the aristocratic rooms of De Tuilerieen. As an eating alternative, Waterput in nearby **Oostkerke** is highly recommended. From Brugge, head for the coast and the elite resorts of **Knokke-Heist,** where you can dine in the lavish Aquilon and stay in the charming old Katelijne. At the west end of the coast, dine and stay in **De Panne** at the sumptuous Le Fox.

As you head inland, pride of place among restaurants in **Ghent** goes to Het Cooremetershuys. The most delightful small hotel is Erasmus. Near Brussels you can enjoy lake views and superb game at Chateau du Lac in **Genval.** An embarrassment of choices in rustic country inns with world-class food lie throughout the Ardennes, from Le Vivier d'Oies in **Dorinne** and Auberge de Bouvignes in **Bouvignes** to Au Gastronome in **Paliseul.** At **Noirefontaine,** near Bouillon, you can stay and dine at the Auberge du Moulin Hideux. To get from here to the Grand Duchy of Luxembourg, turn eastward to Arlon. To continue in Belgium, go north in the province of Luxembourg to **Nadrin,** home of Le Cabri, a great inn with a great view. In the province of Limburg, head for Clos Saint-Denis outside ancient **Tongeren.**

Three nights: Luxembourg. In **Luxembourg City,** settle for the night in either the traditional Hotel Cravat or the modern luxury of Le Royal. You'll dine in the medieval intimacy of St-Michel, in the oldest quarter of town. The next day, head south toward the French border for **Frisange,** where Lea Linster will serve a world-class lunch. Drive through the vineyards of the Moselle Valley, and spend the night in atmospheric little **Ehnen,** where you can dine and sleep at either waterfront landmark: Bamberg's or Simmer. The next day, visit **Echternach,** and book for the night in La Bergerie. You can drive or be shuttled from there into the country for an extraordinary meal at the restaurant of the same name.

The North Sea Coast

From De Panne to Knokke on the Dutch border the pattern does not change: beach, largely covered by the sea at high tide, then a sea wall that is often lined with shops, restaurants, and motels, and dunes partially covered by marram grass. While sea dikes block your view of the water from the road throughout much of the Netherlands, you can approach the water and, in places where you see boardwalks and staircases, walk over the dikes to the beaches and the dunes. As if to make up for blocking your view while you are on land, there are roads over the two major enclosing dikes, one in the south and one in the north, that more than compensate with sweeping water views.

Length 6 days (or more)

Getting Around The trip from De Panne to Breskens in Holland is about 90 ki-
By Car lometers (56 miles), so theoretically driving time should not be much more than an hour. In fact it is likely to take two, three, or even more during the holiday season. From Vlissingen to Harlingen by way of the Benelux tunnel is 370 kilometers (222 miles).

By Train There is train service from Brussels to several points on the coast. Along the coast you have to rely on the tram service, which operates all the way from De Panne to Knokke-Heist. Train service in the Netherlands runs between major cities and coastal towns but not along the coast.

The Main Route **Three nights: Belgium. De Panne,** where the beach is at its widest, and neighboring resorts are your best choice for a stay if you are traveling with children. Sportslovers tend to make the yacht harbor of **Nieuwpoort** their base, while **Oostende,** the largest city on the coast, offers more sophisticated pleasures in the form of a casino, a race track, and museums. The most fashionable resort is **Knokke-Heist,** where the stylish shops are open on Sunday and the casino attracts not only gamblers but also world-class entertainers. Right on the border you'll find the peaceful and fascinating bird sanctuary of **Het Zwin.**

Two nights: The Netherlands. On the Dutch side of the border, the beach continues, and Cadzand Bad is one of the attractive resorts. Farther on, in **Breskens,** you can take the car ferry to **Vlissingen** on the island of Walcheren. Follow the Zeeland coastal route across the Oosterscheldekering sea dike, with its massive storm surge barriers towering over the road and the Delta Expo museum. Stay overnight in **Scheveningen** to enjoy the busy beach and the nightlife. You can get to the beach next at towns such as **Katwijk** or **Egmond aan Zee.** Beyond there, the drive across the 22-mile Afsluitdijk enclosing dike offers you mile after mile of sweeping views over the water on two sides. **Harlingen** is the port for ferries to the Wadden Islands, where you can enjoy the natural beauty of the seaside.

Information *See* Chapters 3 and 4.

Ancient Crafts of the Low Countries

The extraordinary flourishing of decorative crafts in the Low Countries in the Middle Ages was the result of the insatiable appetite for ornamentation of their rulers and shared by local gentry and wealthy burghers. The clothing and jewelry lovingly depicted in 15th-century Flemish paintings indicate the very high standards of the artisans of the era, and those artisanal traditions have been continued to the present.

Length 11 days

Getting Around Luxembourg City is easy to reach by car, though difficult to ne-
By Car gotiate once you're inside. The Villeroy & Boch complex lies just outside the center, on the northwest edge, toward Wiltz. The Belgian section of the itinerary (Luxembourg City to Rotterdam) is about 780 kilometers (485 miles), driving time some 10 hours. The Dutch section (Antwerp to Delft to Amsterdam to Hindeloopen) is about 290 km (175 mi).

By Train If you're visiting Luxembourg by train, city buses pass the Villeroy & Boch outlet. All Belgain cities on this itinerary are accessible by train, but you'll have to double back from Brugge to Brussels to get to Antwerp. Train travel in the Netherlands is efficient.

The Main Route **One night: Luxembourg.** A weekday stop in **Luxembourg** will give you a chance to visit the on-site factory outlet store of Villeroy & Boch, whose popular vitro-porcelain sells here at discount prices. Watch for specials on patterns being phased out, and be sure to dig through the bargain bin. The factory does not ship, so be prepared to schlep. If you can round up a group of 20, you can take a guided tour of the factory.

Two nights: Liège and Sint-Truiden. Arriving from Luxembourg, start your Belgian crafts tour in **Liège.** The Val Saint-

Lambert glassworks in Seraing, on the outskirts of the city, is one of the finest in the world; you can visit the showroom and watch glassblowers in action. Lace-making is an age-old Belgian specialty. You'll have an opportunity to see traditional lace-making elsewhere, but in **Sint-Truiden** one can inspect the results of a modern revival of this craft at the Kanttentoonstelling (Lace Exhibition) in the school of the Ursuline Sisters.

Three nights: Brussels. Mechelen, halfway between Brussels and Antwerp, boasts the only workshops in Belgium where traditional tapestry weaving is still practiced; Gaspard De Wit's Royal Tapestry Manufacture is located at the Refuge van Tongerlo. In **Brussels,** some of the finest examples of Belgian tapestry from the 14th to 16th century are on view in the Musées Royaux d'Art et d'Histoire (Royal Museums of Art and History), and lace and needlework are on view in the Musée du Costume et de la Dentelle (Costume and Lace Museum). Tapestry weaving has been revived in **Tournai** (southwest of Brussels), one of the old centers of this craft, where the new Museum of Tapestry shows how it is done.

One night: Brugge. Brugge is intimately associated with lace-making, and there are a large number of shops selling everything from lace souvenirs to works of art. The best place to get a real understanding of the craft is the Kantcentrum (Lace Center), incorporating a museum and a lace-making school.

One night: Antwerp. Diamonds are big business in **Antwerp,** where the origins and history of diamond cutting are shown at the Provincial Diamond Museum, while Diamondland, where you can also see diamond cutting demonstrations, is probably the most spectacular diamond showroom in the world.

Three nights: Netherlands. Begin in **Delft** with a visit to the factory De Porcelyn Fles to see painting of the famous blue and white ceramic ware known as Delft. Continue to **Amsterdam** for a visit to a diamond factory. Continue north to the village of **Makkum** in Friesland, where the prized Dutch polychrome, or multicolor, ceramic ware is produced at the factory of Tichelaars Koninklijk Makkumer Aardewerk en Tegelfabriek (Tichelaars Royal Makkum Pottery and Tile Factory). In nearby **Hindeloopen** you can see the traditional painted furniture of Friesland in Museum Hidde Nieland Stichting.

Information *See* Chapters 3, 4, and 5.

The Ardennes

To experience the Ardennes fully, you owe it to yourself to take your time. Explore the hamlets and river valleys off the highway. Stop in the small towns along the way for a meal of hearty Ardennaise fare—smoked ham, cheese and farm bread, crayfish and trout from the rushing streams—enjoy the inns, visit the churches and castles. You will be amply rewarded!

Length 8 days

Getting Around The Belgain portions of the trip add up to about 430 kilometers
By Car (270 miles). Much of this is on secondary routes, so reckon on a driving time of some 8 hours. To see the best of the Luxembourg Ardennes, you'll need a car for the *routes nationales* and secondary roads that snake through the forests.

By Train   The cities on the itinerary are accessible by train, but they are
not necessarily interconnected in the same sequence. Rail connections in Luxembourg are minimal, though a train does run
from Luxembourg City to Clervaux, in the north.

The Main Route   **Two nights: Belgium.** From Liège, go by way of Eupen toward
Malmédy, stopping to explore the high moorland known as the
Hautes Fagnes.

One night: La-Roche-en-Ardenne. Passing Stavelot, continue to
La-Roche-en-Ardenne in the heart of the Belgian mountain
range. Here in the valley of the River Ourthe, you will see the
finest scenery the Ardennes has to offer.

Two nights: Luxembourg. Enter the Grand Duchy of Luxembourg from the north, stopping to visit **Clervaux's** castle museums before winding through rolling countryside toward
Vianden, where the spectacular castle dominates the hill village. Head south to **Diekirch** to visit the Romanesque church
with its Merovingian sarcophagi and the evocative Battle of the
Bulge museum. Then, though it falls just below the Ardennes
plateau, drive on into **Luxembourg City,** for the Vauban fortifications, cathedral, and old-town streets.

Three nights: Belgium. Driving west from Luxembourg City
you follow the Semois River, with a stop to see the romantic
ruins of Orval Abbey, to **Bouillon** with its mountain-top fort.
Through dense woods you reach **Saint-Hubert,** going on to **Hansur-Lesse** with its remarkable caves and nature reserve. Follow
the Lesse to **Dinant**—part of the way by kayak, if you wish—
spectacularly situated on the River Meuse. As you drive along
the Meuse, sheer cliffs line the river bank on the opposite side.
Continuing along the river, with stops in **Huy** and **Modave,** you
arrive back in Liège.

2 Portraits of the Netherlands, Belgium, and Luxembourg

The Netherlands, Belgium, and Luxembourg at a Glance: A Chronology

By Anita Guerrini

55 BC Julius Caesar's legions extend Roman control to the Meuse and Waal rivers.

ca AD 300 Inundation of the Frisian plain causes Rome to abandon it.

ca 400 Roman rule retreats before invading Frisians in the north and Franks in the south.

481–511 Under their king, Clovis, the Frankish Merovingians extend their rule north.

ca 700 Christianity is extended to the Netherlands by Saints Willibrord and Boniface.

800 Charlemagne, king of the Franks, is crowned emperor of the Romans by the pope. His domains extend from the marches of Denmark to Spain.

843 The Treaty of Verdun divides Charlemagne's empire into three. Luxembourg and the Netherlands are included in the middle kingdom of Lotharingia; Belgium is divided at the Scheldt River between France and Lotharingia. Viking attacks begin along the coast.

862 Baldwin Iron-Arm establishes himself as first count of Flanders, but rule of the Lotharingian lands is constantly disputed.

963 Siegfried, count of Ardennes, purchases an old Roman castle named Lucilinburhuc along the Alzette river. His descendants are named counts of Luxembourg.

1196–1247 Reign of Countess Ermesinde of Luxembourg, who enlarges and unifies the county, grants privileges to its cities, and founds the ruling house of Luxembourg-Limburg.

ca 1200 With the rise of towns, the collection of duchies and counties that constitutes the Low Countries gains economic power.

1302 The men of Flanders revolt against French attempts at annexation and defeat Philip the Fair's army at the Battle of the Golden Spurs, near Kortrijk. Flanders remains a desirable prize.

1308 Henry VII of Luxembourg is elected Holy Roman emperor; he grants the rule of the county of Luxembourg to his son, John the Blind (d. 1346).

1354 John's son, Charles, also Holy Roman emperor, raises the status of Luxembourg to a duchy.

1361 Philip the Bold, son of John II of France, establishes the great duchy of Burgundy, which, by Philip's marriage in 1369 to Marguerite, heiress of the count of Flanders, grows to include Flanders, Artois, Limburg, and Brabant.

1419–1467 Philip's grandson Philip the Good extends Burgundian rule over Holland, Zeeland, and Hainaut and presides over the golden age of the Flemish Renaissance. Painters include the van Eycks, Hans Memling, and Rogier van der Weyden.

1443   Philip gains Luxembourg.

1464   Philip calls the deputies of the states—nobles, merchants, and churchmen—to meet together, thus beginning the States-General, the Dutch representative assembly.

1477   The death of Philip's son Charles leaves his granddaughter Mary of Burgundy as heiress. Mary marries the Hapsburg heir, Maximilian of Austria; their son Philip marries Juana, heiress to the throne of Spain.

1500   Birth in Ghent of Charles, son of Philip and Juana, who inherits the collective titles and holdings of Burgundy, Spain, and Austria as Charles V, Holy Roman emperor.

ca 1520–1540   Protestantism spreads through the Netherlands.

1549   By the Pragmatic Sanction, Charles declares that the 17 provinces constituting the Netherlands will be inherited intact by his son Philip.

1555   Charles V abdicates, dividing his empire between his brother Ferdinand and his son Philip, who inherits Spain and the Netherlands. A devout Catholic, Philip moves to suppress Protestantism in the Netherlands.

1566   Revolt in Antwerp against Spanish rule provokes ruthless suppression by the Spanish governor, the duke of Alva.

1568   Beginning of eighty years of warfare between the 17 provinces and Spain.

1572   The "Sea Beggars" under William of Orange take to the natural Dutch element, water, and harass the Spanish.

1579   The Spanish succeed in dividing the Catholic south from the Protestant north with the Treaty of Arras. The seven Protestant provinces in the north—Holland, Friesland, Gelderland, Groningen, Overijssel, Utrecht, and Zeeland—declare themselves the United Provinces, under the hereditary *stadtholder* (city elder), William the Silent of Orange.

1585   Antwerp falls to the Spanish, and the division of the Netherlands between north and south is effectively completed; the Dutch close the Scheldt to navigation, depriving Antwerp of its egress to the sea and leading to its rapid decline.

1602   With the founding of the Dutch East India Company, the United Provinces emerges as a major trading nation and a cultural force. Rembrandt, Vermeer, and Hals chronicle an era of wealth, while in Belgium, Rubens and Van Dyck epitomize Flemish Baroque.

1609   The Twelve-Years' Truce temporarily ends fighting between the United Provinces and Spain.

1624   The Dutch land on Manhattan and found New Amsterdam.

1648   By the Treaty of Westphalia, the Spanish finally recognize the independence of the United Provinces. What will become Belgium remains under Spanish control, but is a battleground between the ambitions of France and a declining Spain.

1652–1654   First Anglo-Dutch War, over trading rivalries.

1653–1672   The Dutch fail to elect a new stadtholder and are ruled as a republic under the grand pensionary Johan de Witt.

1667 By the terms of the Peace of Breda, which ends the second Anglo-Dutch War, the Netherlands exchanges New Netherland, renamed New York, for England's Suriname.

1672 William III of Orange, great-grandson of William the Silent, is named stadtholder; de Witt is murdered.

1678 By the Treaty of Nijmegen William ends yet another war with France.

1689 William III is named joint ruler of England with his wife, Mary Stuart.

1697 The Treaty of Ryswick ends the War of the League of Augsburg against France, instigated by William.

1701–1713 The War of the Spanish Succession ends with the Treaty of Utrecht, which transfers the Spanish Netherlands (including Luxembourg) to Austria. Depleted of men and money, the Netherlands declines in the eighteenth century.

1785–1787 Revolt of the Patriot Party in the Netherlands, which temporarily drives out the stadtholder William V; he is restored with the help of his brother-in-law, Frederick William of Prussia.

1789–1790 Inspired by events in France, the Brabançonne revolution succeeds in overthrowing Austrian rule in Belgium, but divisions between conservatives and liberals allow the Austrians to regain their territory.

1795 In the Netherlands, the Patriots eject the stadtholder and establish the Batavian Republic; the French defeat the Austrians and annex the Belgian provinces and Luxembourg.

1806–1810 Napoleon establishes the Kingdom of Holland, ruled by his brother Louis Bonaparte, but finally annexes the Netherlands to France.

1813 Upon Napoleon's defeat at Leipzig, the prince of Orange is called back to the Netherlands, not as stadtholder but as King William I.

1815 Napoleon defeated at Waterloo, near Brussels. By the terms of the congress of Vienna, the Netherlands and Belgium are reunited under William I, but the union proves an unhappy one. Luxembourg is divided between William and Prussia.

1830 Again inspired by a revolution in France, the Belgians rise against William I and declare their independence.

1831 With the guarantees of the great powers, the Belgians draw up a constitution and elect as king Leopold of Saxe-Coburg (an uncle to soon-to-be-Queen Victoria of England).

1839 The Netherlands finally recognizes Belgium as an independent, neutral state. Luxembourg is again divided, with 60% going to Belgium while the rest remains a duchy, with William I of the Netherlands as grand duke.

1840 Faced by mounting popular opposition, William I abdicates in favor of his more liberal son, William II, who enacts reforms.

1865 Leopold II succeeds his father as king of the Belgians; begins reign as empire builder in Africa and rebuilder of Brussels at home. By the terms of an international agreement, the Prussian garrisons withdraw and Luxembourg's independence and neutrality are guaranteed.

1885 The establishment of the Congo Free State brings Belgium into the ranks of colonial powers.

1890 King William III of the Netherlands is succeeded by his daughter Wilhelmina; because Luxembourg bars female succession, the grand duchy passes to the house of Nassau-Weilburg.

1903 Birth of Georges Simenon (d. 1989), creator of Inspector Maigret and Belgium's most widely read author.

1908 Congo Free State annexed to Belgium.

1909 Albert succeeds Leopold II of Belgium; leads Belgian resistance from exile during World War I.

1914 In violation of the terms of the 1839 treaty, Germany invades and conquers Belgium at the outset of World War I. Luxembourg is also occupied; the Netherlands remains neutral.

1919 The Franco-Belgian alliance ends Belgian neutrality and signals the dominance of the French-speaking Walloons. Universal male suffrage is granted; in the Netherlands, where this had been enacted in 1917, women are now given the right to vote. In Luxembourg, a plebiscite confirms the continuation of the grand duchy under Grand Duchess Charlotte.

1934 Leopold III succeeds Albert on Belgian throne.

1940 May 10: Nazi Germany launches blitzkrieg attacks on Belgium, the Netherlands, and Luxembourg. The Dutch army surrenders May 14, the Belgians May 28. Grand Duchess Charlotte and Queen Wilhelmina flee; King Leopold III remains in Belgium, where he is eventually imprisoned. The Nazi occupation leaves lasting imprints on all three countries.

1942 Dutch Indonesia falls to the Japanese.

1944 Luxembourg City is liberated.

1947 The Marshall Plan helps rebuild devastated areas. Belgium, Netherlands, and Luxembourg form customs union.

1948 Queen Wilhelmina abdicates in favor of her daughter Juliana; the first of a series of Socialist governments initiates a Dutch welfare state. Women gain the vote in Belgium.

1949 The Netherlands and Luxembourg join NATO; the Dutch recognize Indonesian independence after much fighting.

1951 Amid controversy over his wartime role and continued ethnic dissension, King Leopold III of Belgium abdicates in favor of his son, Baudouin.

1957 Belgium, Netherlands, Luxembourg are charter members of the European Economic Community (EEC).

1960 A 50-year treaty establishes the Benelux Economic Union. The Belgian Congo gains independence.

1964 Grand Duchess Charlotte of Luxembourg abdicates in favor of her son, Jean.

1967 Already the center of the EC, Brussels becomes host to NATO.

1975 Suriname wins its independence from the Netherlands.

1981 Queen Juliana of the Netherlands abdicates in favor of her daughter, Beatrix.

1989 The latest of many Belgian attempts to establish greater linguistic and regional autonomy is enacted.

Les Moules Sont Arrivées!

By Nancy Coons

Damp and cold mist the leaded-glass windows, but inside the café glows a scene worthy of a Flemish Master. The burnished wooden banquettes are Rembrandt's; the lace curtain, Vermeer's. Hals would have painted the diner, a lone bearded man in rumpled black leather and heavy, worn wool, his thick fingers clasping a broad-stemmed bowl of mahogany-brown beer. Before him lies a spread of crockery and mollusks, a still-life in themselves: The two-quart pot is heaped high with blue-black mussels, their shells flecked with bits of onion and celery, the broth beneath them steaming; beside them a bowl piled high with yellow *frites* (french fries), crisp and glistening; in the corner, a saucer of slabs of floury-gold cracked-wheat bread. The man works studiously, absorbed in a timeless ritual: Fish out the shell from the broth with fingers inured to the heat by years of practice. Pluck out the plump flesh with a fork and, while chewing the morsel, chuck the shell aside on a crockery plate. Sometimes he sets down the fork and uses the empty shell as pincers to draw out the meat of the next shell. As the meal progresses, the pile in the pot shrinks and the heap of empty shells grows. As the beer follows the mussels, its strong tonic paints the man's cheeks until two ruby patches radiate above his beard. The painting's caption: "Man eating moules."

It is the central image of the Flemish lowlands—the Netherlands, Flanders, even leaking into landlocked Wallonie and Luxembourg—and from the middle of September, when the first signs appear on brasserie doors to announce *Les moules sont arrivées!*, through the end of April, when the signs (now withered with steam and smoke) come down, the ritual repeats itself.

But this warmly lit interior scene wouldn't be as striking without its harsh exterior foil: Mussels, like the Dutch and the Flemish, are creatures of the sea; they flourish in cold, inky waters along rock-crusted shores, clustered and stacked like blue-black crystals in muddy tidal pools. They're a product of caustic sea winds and briny, chilly damp, and their bite tastes like salt air itself.

Most of the mussels consumed in the Benelux region come from the North Sea, above all in the Waddenzee, off the northern coast of the Netherlands. Captured by the billions in great nets along the bottom of specially protected, fenced-off nursery beds, they are sorted by weight and auctioned to wholesalers in Zeeland, who return them to shallow tidal waters to recover from the trip, to mature, and to purge themselves of sandy mud. From there, they are harvested en masse and shipped live across Europe.

The cultivation of mussels dates from Roman times, though legend credits an Irish shipwreck victim who settled in La Rochelle, on the west coast of France; he is said to have noticed great colonies of the mollusks clinging to posts he planted to hold fishing nets. By placing posts closer together and arranging branches between them, he was able to create an ideal breeding ground and, in essence, mass-produce the delicacy. (The French, predictably enough, prefer their own, smaller mussels from the coasts of Brittany and Normandy, insisting that North Sea mussels are fleshy, dull, and vulgarly oversized.)

Scrubbed with stiff brushes under running water, soaked with salt to draw out the sand, and often fed flour to plump and purge them, mussels are served throughout the region in dozens of ways. The building block for French or Walloon recipes: simmering them *à la marinière*, in a savory stock of white wine, shallots, parsley, and butter. It's difficult to improve on this classic method, which brings out the best in mussels' musky sea essence—but chefs have been trying for centuries. Another common version is *à la crème*, the marinière stock thickened with flour-based white sauce and a generous portion of heavy cream. Flemish mussels, on the other hand, are nearly always served in a simple, savory vegetable stock, with bits of celery, leek, and onions creeping into the shells. The Dutch have been known to pickle them, or even to fry them in batter. Those who don't want to get their fingers messy may order their mussels *meunière*, removed from the shells in the kitchen and baked in a pool of garlicky butter.

Regardless of the preparation, the Belgians and the Dutch wash their mussels down with beer, the Luxembourgers with an icy bottle of one of the coarser Moselle wines—an Elbling or a Rivaner. Mussels are only available in autumn, winter, and spring (months that have the letter "r" in them); this is their breeding period, when they are relatively thin and small. Hence one of the great tragedies of gastronomic tourism in the region: Summer visitors miss out on this quintessential experience altogether.

Those who come in season, be warned: Mussels rations are anything but stingy here, and on your first venture you may be appalled by the size of the lidded pot put before you. It's the shells that create the volume, and once you've plucked out the tender flesh, thrown away the shells, and sipped the broth and succulent strays from a colossal soup spoon, you'll soon find yourself at the bottom of the pot. Don't worry: Many restaurants will whisk it away and come back with Round Two—another mountain of the steamy blue creatures, another pool of savory broth. It's called *moules à volonté* (all you can eat), so gird yourself for a feast: The locals have been doing it for 2,000 years.

Battle Scars from the Bulge

By Nancy Coons

The first thing the sleepy American soldiers noticed was light—pinpoints of light blinking to the east, distinct in the pitch-black of an early midwinter morning. A second, or seconds, later (depending on their distance from the German frontier), there followed the roar of a thousand exploding shells, the pounding percussion of heavy artillery. Rockets and mortars screamed overhead while at five well-spaced points German foot soldiers poured through gaps in the sparsely protected front line, their way lit by searchlights that bounced off the clouds, flooding the land with eerie, artifical "moonlight."

It was 5:30 AM on December 16, 1944, along the eastern border of Belgium and Luxembourg. The Allied armed forces—having landed at Normandy in June and southern France in August and pressed steadily inland; having pushed the German armies back to the old Siegfried line and liberated France, Belgium, and Luxembourg by September; and having fought viciously, died in droves, and been hungry, filthy, and sleepless for weeks at a time—were reveling in the role of heroes in the relatively calm days before Christmas. That morning they were caught with their pants down in one of the most massive and successful surprise attacks in World War II. It was Hitler's last, desperate effort to regain western Europe, and it was one of the greatest failures of Allied intelligence in the war.

In September 1944, when Hitler first announced secret plans for an all-out attack on the western front, his army could scarcely have been in more desperate straits. More than 3½ million German men had died over the preceding five years, and massive Allied bombing raids were leveling German cities day by day. Not only had the enemy driven the Wehrmacht out of France, Belgium, and Luxembourg, but Italy was being lost in bitter fighting as well, and Russia had penetrated west to Warsaw and Bucharest. The Third Reich was in danger of being choked off from all sides, and Hitler—though not his more prudent commanders—saw no option but to strike out offensively. His goal: To take the all-important port at Antwerp, from where the River Schelde flowed from Belgium through the Netherlands and into the North Sea. By closing in on Antwerp, they would not only cut off the most likely source of new supplies, but also surround and capture some 1 million remaining Allied forces. His strategy: To surprise the Allies by attacking through the improbably rough, virtually impassable forest terrain of the Ardennes in southeastern Belgium and northern Luxembourg. He intended to overwhelm them with massive artillery fire, press on to take the strategic bridges of the River Meuse, reinforce with a second wave, and close out defenders with strong flanks at the north and south. Antwerp could be reached in a week, he insisted, and the Allies would be crippled by winter fog, snow, and mud.

For the task of inspiring a bitter, war-weary army to what seemed even then to be a suicidal mission, Hitler named the aristocratic Gerd von Rundstedt commander in chief in the West. And, in a decision that was to set the tone for one of the most vicious and bloody conflicts in the war, in charge of the Sixth Panzer Army he placed Joseph "Sepp" Dietrich, an early Nazi loyalist and SS commander, chief executioner in the 1934 Nazi Party purge (the Night of the Long Knives), notorious for ordering the execution of more than 4,000 prisoners taken over three days at the Russian front. His kindred spirit: SS Lt. Col. Joachim Peiper, in charge of the SS Panzer Division called Leibstandarte Adolf Hitler and also notorious for brutal executions in Russia. It was Dietrich who passed on Hitler's inspirational message that this was "the decisive hour of the German people," that the attacking army was to create a "wave of terror and fright" without "humane inhibitions."

While the Germans were building up staggering quantities of materiel along the Siegfried line—tanks, artillery, rafts, and pontoons—and moving in men from all corners of the shrinking Reich, the Allied command remained remarkably unperceptive. Reconnaissance pilots flew over unwonted activity near Bitburg, Trier, and Koblenz—trains, truck convoys, heaps of equipment along the roads. Messages were intercepted and deciphered, some asking for increased forces, some for more detailed information on Ardennes and Meuse terrain. Yet Generals Bradley, Eisenhower, Middleton, and Patton continued to misinterpret, anticipating instead a predictable counterattack around Aachen and Cologne, well north of the Ardennes. (Hitler, in fact, counted on this interpretation, strutting a visible buildup of forces in the north while secretly preparing to attack elsewhere.) On December 12, an optimistic Allied intelligence summary described the vulnerability and "deathly weakness" of German forces in the area.

On the evening of December 15, the German soldiers—until then as unaware of the plan as the Allies—were finally told what morning would bring. The message from von Rundstedt: "We gamble everything . . . to achieve things beyond human possibilities for our Fatherland and our Führer!" Some, convinced the cause was lost, faced the news of further carnage with dismay; others saw a final opportunity to avenge the civilian death toll in German cities. Members of the SS, the greatest believers in the Nazi effort and thus the least restrained by the niceties of the Geneva Convention, welcomed the "holy task" with a blood lust that was to be more than sated in the weeks to come.

That night, across the border in Luxembourg, German-born film star Marlene Dietrich performed for American soldiers and went to bed early.

They attacked at 5:30 AM with a thoroughness and a ruthlessness that impressed soldiers even through their bewilderment. The assault crippled communications, and word moved as slowly as in the era before telegraph. Twenty miles from one prong of the attack, Gen. Omar Bradley had breakfast at the Hotel Alfa in Luxembourg City and, blithely unaware of the change in situation, headed toward Paris for a meeting with Eisenhower, who had just that day been promoted to five-star General of the Army. Neither heard of the conflict until late afternoon; neither believed, at first sketchy report, that it was anything more than a flash in the pan.

It was. From the first wave of "artillery-prepared" assaults—meaning systems stunned by a barrage of shells, followed by a surge of infantry attacks—to the sharp, startled, and for the most part instinctive defense of the Allies, the offensive was to escalate quickly into a battle of staggering scale, the Americans surprising the Germans in their tenacity, the Germans surprising the Americans with their almost maniacal dedication.

Over a month and a half, the two sides bludgeoned each other, struggling through harsh terrain and winter muck, reducing medieval castles to smoking rubble, and razing villages that had been liberated only months before. The ferocious tone of the fight was set early on: On December 17, SS officers of Lieutenant Colonel Peiper ordered the execution of 130 American prisoners outside Malmédy. The victims were left where they fell, periodically kicked for signs of life, and shot again. A few who survived, hiding the steam of their breath, crawled away when night fell and told their story, and the massacre at Malmédy became a rallying point for the bitter Allies. Prisoners of war were murdered on both sides, and at times the gunfights took on a guerrilla aspect, with those in danger of capture, fearing execution, dissolving into the dense forest to go it alone.

And not only soldiers were killed. On December 18, in and near Stavelot, Peiper's SS troops ordered whole families of civilians from their cellars—women, children, elderly men—and shot them methodically; the toll reached 138. On December 24, SS security men assembled all the men of Bande, screened out those over 32, stripped them of watches and rosaries, and executed them one by one. The sole survivor, before he slugged his way free and dashed for the forest, noticed that his would-be executioner was weeping.

And on December 23, Americans wrought their own kind of horror in Malmédy when Army Air Corps Marauders, headed for the German railroad center of Zulpich, mistak-

enly emptied 86 bombs on the village center, killing as
many of its own troops as innocent citizens. As the people
dug out from the rubble on December 24, another mis-
guided swarm of American bombers dropped an even more
lethal load, leveling what was left of the center. On December 25, four more planes mistook Malmédy for St. Vith and
dropped 64 more bombs. Civilian victims—refugees and
residents alike—were laid in rows in the school playground.

It wasn't a very merry Christmas anywhere in the Ardennes that year. Sleepless, shell-shocked, often out of
touch, soldiers from both sides huddled in icy pillboxes and
snowy foxholes. Propaganda flyers fluttered down, carefully phrased in the recipients' mother tongue. For the Americans, the not-so-inspirational message admonished them:
"Why are you here? What are you doing, fighting somebody
else's war? You will die and your wife, your mother, your
daughters will be left alone. Merry Christmas!" For the
Germans, the American pamphlets simply assured them
they were losing the war, and that they'd long since lost the
battle.

That wasn't altogether clear until well into January. By the
time the carnage slowed and the tide turned, the Germans
had pressed deep into Belgium, the central thrust "bulg-
ing" west to within miles of the Meuse and Dinant. Though
Hitler grudgingly ordered retreat from the farthest point
of the Bulge on January 8, the Germans fought through
January 28, as they were driven all the way back to the
Siegfried line.

Some 19,000 American soldiers died, and at least as
many Germans. Hundreds of Belgian and Luxembourg citizens died as well, and survivors came back
to find their villages flattened, their churches gaping
shells, their castles—having survived assault for centuries—reduced to heaps of ancient stone. In Luxembourg,
the towns of Diekirch, Clervaux, Vianden, and Echternach
were prime battle zones, charred and crumbled. In Belgium, St. Vith, Houffalize, and myriad Ardennes resort
towns like La Roche were wasted by artillery "preparation" and the gun-and-grenade battles that ensued. And
Bastogne, surrounded, besieged, and pounded by artillery
for days, lost what was left of its town center in the concentrated bombing Hitler ordered for Christmas Eve.

Today, throughout the Ardennes region, the faces of monuments and main streets are incongruously new and shiny,
their resourceful owners having taken charred, roofless,
windowless shells and made the best of the worst by install-
ing new plumbing, modern wiring, efficient windows, central heat. Yet there are scars, visible and invisible. Behind
the caulked shrapnel holes, which pock foundations and
farmhouse walls here and there, lurk bitter memories that
weren't altogether appeased at Nuremburg. And the ugli-

ness of the conflict, distorted by a new generation, occasionally rears its head: On the stone memorial at the crossroads outside Malmédy, where the names of the victims of the massacre have been carved, someone has spray-painted a swastika.

The cultural chasm between the two sides of the battle seems embodied in the two military cemeteries outside Luxembourg City. The American plot at Hamm is a blaze of white-marble glory, its 5,000 graves radiating in graceful arcs under open sun, its well-tended grass worn by the shoes of visitors. The German plot, just down the road at Sandweiler, lies apart, heavily shaded and concealed from view, with a few hundred low, dark-stone crosses marking the graves of some 5,000 men. Yet another 5,000, gathered in battle by the U.S. Army Burial Service and dumped unceremoniously in mass graves, were transferred here and buried under one heavy cross, as many as possible identified in fine print crowded on a broad bronze plaque. Those graves are tended today by busloads of German schoolchildren, who visit in the name of a concept long overdue: *Versöhnung über den Gräbern—Arbeit für den Frieden* (Reconciliation over the graves—work for peace).

Through the Dutch Waterways

By William
Golding

The Nobel prizewinning English novelist here describes a boat trip in the Netherlands that he took with his family. The piece first appeared in Holiday *magazine in January 1962.*

My old boat, the *Wild Rose*, is technically a converted Whitstable oyster smack. She has a sort of eccentric inelegance and ought to be in a maritime museum, for she was built in 1896. My wife and I, with our children David and Judith, planned a trip in her through the canals of Holland and across the old Zuider Zee. We took my friend Viv with us, partly because we like him, partly because he knew a little about Holland and partly because he is the only man I know who can keep the *Wild Rose*'s ancient auxiliary engine running.

We started at Flushing—an ancient port, clinging to, rambling along, and at one point piercing the ancient sea-wall, the dike that surrounds the island of Walcheren. We moved in through two locks, and then into a yacht basin, and at once some Dutch characteristics commended themselves to our notice. Except in show places like Cowes, a yachtsman expects the smell of decaying wood, slime, weed, mud, rusted and insecure ladders, and stanchions which once had a use but now are nothing but paint-threatening hazards. But the basin at Flushing was an oblong of still water with a neat, cemented edge, and a wooden gangway leading round it. At each berth there were piles driven into the bottom, enamelled white, their iron caps picked out in vivid orange. There was no notice forbidding the dumping of rubbish in the water; and there was no rubbish either. There was no rubbish anywhere, unless you count my ancient boat; for the basin was crowded with Dutch craft, eccentric in build, but charming—and all more glossily enamelled than the piles.

We were to find that this is a Dutch habit, and sometimes a mania. When you cannot think what else to do with something in Holland, you give it a coat of paint. Out of any ten Dutchmen you see, as they go about their business, at least one will be covering an object with bright paint—a fence, or a post, or a gate, or a stone, or a hole in the road—anything that has a paint-holding surface.

We had barely realized our status as a slumship in these spotless surroundings when we saw a number of tradesmen waiting for us on the gangway. They took our orders politely, with neither truculence nor subservience. Then they rode off on bicycles. Out of our ten typical Dutchmen, at least three will be riding bicycles. They came back quickly, with goods of moderate price and high standard; and I have always found this to be the case in Holland, whether it be car rental at the Hook, boat rental at Rotterdam, theatre tickets in Amsterdam, a haircut in Groningen, lunch in Enkhuizen or a bunch of flowers in Utrecht. A Dutchman trades fairly, asking a fair price and giving a fair service, and the same cannot be said of Europe as a whole. In Holland a sucker is safe, though frowned on with a sort of tut-tutting compassion.

We stocked up, spent a quiet night and then moved out into the canal that divides Walcheren in two. In the centre of Flushing we came to a bridge and had to wait while it was opened for us. Perhaps because we were in the mood to enjoy anything, the bridge, flooded with traffic and neat and powerful in construction, seemed to us wholly charming. As we approached, the red-and-white bars descended to cut off the traffic, and the middle span lifted. It was a stripped mechanism, functional, with long arms that seemed to need no effort to raise a weight of many tons. Yet the whole was so exactly balanced that there was a dream quality of ease in the movement. Nothing of the whole mechanism but had a use and was confined to it; and yet the occasion, the smooth water, the silent bridge, the calmly controlled traffic, combined to make what I can only call the poetry of order. As we moved through, we exclaimed and nodded to one another. The bridge was so modern, we said, it had the delicate elegance you see in a high-speed plane or racing car. It was the Dutch equivalent of achievements in that engineering world which produced jet aircraft and atomic submarines, the world of streamlining and calculations to the nth. This is not mere tourist country, we said—even their bridges are the newest in the world!

Viv put his head out of the hatch.

'This dam' engine won't run much longer.'

'Never mind,' said Ann. 'Enjoy yourself. Look at that bridge. Whatever will they think of next?'

Viv wiped his forehead with a wad of waste, and peered aft.

'*That* bridge?'

He gave a short, cynical engineer's laugh and disappeared again.

The bridge sank into place behind us and we turned to look forward at the most typical sight in Holland. The canal that would take us across the island lay like a sword-blade, shining and drawn to a point. There were trees looking at us over the bank, clouds and blue sky mirrored, a towpath, and miles away, a huddle of buildings that looked quaint even at that distance.

There was something shining in the air over the houses. At first we thought it might be an airliner catching the sun. But since when have airliners been made of gold and hung motionless? My wife said it was a captive balloon, and the children decided it was a flying saucer. Yet this single gleaming point of light in the soft, blue sky seemed to be causing no distraction. Dutchmen passed along the towpath on their inevitable bicycles, and they were as phlegmatic as ever. Whatever was gleaming there, in a local suspension of the law of gravity, was causing no panic. But could anything in Holland cause a panic? Would not the day of judgement find them doing no more than insuring that the dikes were holding and all accounts in order? With one of those flashes of common sense which come late in such situations, I got out the binoculars and focused them on the gleam.

The huddle of quaint houses was a town—Middelburg, in the centre of the island. The gleam suspended over it was a golden crown; and with the binoculars I could see that this topped a fantastic, not to say frivolous, tower. This, then, is the scene which repeats itself all over Holland—a canal leading to a huddle of houses, with a golden crown hanging over them. Sometimes you see the gleam first, then gradually make out the tower or spire hardening into sight below it. All spires in Holland, apart from the crowns, have an air of modest fantasy. This one at Middelburg rose up first as a tower with tall, lancet windows. The tower supported a bulbous structure, topped at last by the golden crown. The whole thing looked like a graceful piece from some antique chess set.

Viv appeared once more in the hatch.

'You'd better cut the motor.'

'Can't we even go slow ahead?'

'Not unless you want to blow up. What d'you think these blue fumes are?'

There was indeed a faint haze of gasoline round the afterend of the boat. David dropped his book, ran for'ard and hoisted our tattered brown staysail as I switched off. There was the faintest breath of wind to give us way, but so little that the ripples from our bow were moving up and down against the bank before our stern had passed them. Viv sat down on the deck. Ann turned over on the catwalk in the sun, said 'Mmmm!' and went to sleep again.

Holland is a huge country. I say this in the full knowledge that I am stating an apparent paradox. I have flown across Holland in a few minutes. I have driven a car from one end to the other in a single day. But for all that, I declare Holland to be a huge, ample country, full of silences and vast airs. Moving stealthily towards the gold crown over Middelburg, we knew that the right speed for a visitor to Holland is the speed of a slow boat. That way you get the feel of the country into your blood. How else to appreciate the most remarkable quality of geographical Holland, its wide, wide light? The sky seems always not moist, but soft, as though water were hung in it like scent in a girl's hair. The softness conditions the light. We saw no hard shadows, only defined luminosities.

How strange that the Dutch, these foursquare, practical people, these sailors, farmers and engineers, should live in a pastel country that seems woven of light itself! The water-heart of Holland is a scatter of islands—mudpats, if you like—lying at the mouths of the great rivers of northern Europe. They are part of a plain that stretches from the Pennines of England to the Urals in Russia. To be out-of-doors in the water-heart of Holland is like being at sea. Uninterrupted sky comes right down to a horizon that is close at hand at every point of the compass. Whenever we went below, dazzled by this abundance of light, we descended into a darkness that drove us on deck again, into the bland, enormous air, where the fluffy white clouds rode high, and the gold crown sparked nearer. This happened wherever we went. The pastel earth seems to swing like a basket from a balloon of sky.

Halfway to Middleburg we met what must have been almost our only example of Dutch rubbish. We drew alongside a pair of wooden objects floating in the water and found they were castoff clogs. What unusual Dutchman had been so carefree as to fling them into the sparkling water? We felt this was so unlikely that there must have been an accident; and indeed the clogs, floating soles upward, looked for all the world as though a drowned Dutchman were hanging from them, his feet on the surface and his head brushing the bottom. But there was no Dutchman, of course. If there had been, he would have been rescued, neatly and methodically, and fined for causing a disturbance. So the ownerless clogs drifted astern, turning their toes apart slowly.

The Dutch call these wooden boots *klompen,* which is exactly what they are. For presently we passed another Dutchman busy being typical. He was repairing an inch or two of canal bank that had got out of place. He wore bright yellow *klompen* and whenever he moved they went 'Klomp! klomp!' over the stones.

Out of our ten Dutchmen we have not many left. One, we said, would be painting something, three riding bicycles—and now we found that another two would be repairing an earthwork. All over Holland all the time, armies are at work repairing earthworks to keep the sea out, or to keep a canal in. In Friesland I have seen them busy in a field in high summer, cutting back the long grass to insure that a mere runnel of water went where is was wanted, and more important still, did not go where it was not wanted.

We docked with surprising neatness in Middleburg, under sail only. David and Judith got the dinghy into the water and sailed it. Viv emerged from the engine room.

'I think she may last a few hours longer now. Next time may I bring my own engine? Ah—Middleburg! Come with me.'

He led us away through the cobbled streets with an expression of deep purpose and stopped at last in front of an antique shop.

'Yes. It's still there. See?'

There was the usual display in the window—every sort of disused article from copper warming-pans, through nineteenth-century jewellery, to some not very inspiring prints.

'See what?'

'Your bridge.'

It was our lovely bridge at Flushing, accurate in every detail, even to the red and white bars that regulated traffic. But *this* bridge was made of wood, and the picture had been made in the seventeenth century.

'They were building that sort of bridge when Newton was writing his *Principia*. It's a design even older than your engine.'

I can hardly describe the revolutionary effect of this discovery on our ideas about Holland. What we had taken, in our innocence, as a triumph of technology, we now saw to be an old Dutch custom. In this country, men have always worked sensibly with things, always made a bank as wide as it need be, and no more, given the span of a bridge the exact thickness it required. That print saved us from making the common tourist's mistake. We were not to be deceived by the fairy-tale charm of the houses, their quaint gables and profuse ornamentation, into thinking that this was a doll's country. The houses were the homes of commercial giants of the seventeenth century, and those imposing buildings backing on to the inner canal, decorated as if for some eternal party, were warehouses that had held the riches of the world.

Yet this love of decoration is a strange quirk in the Dutchman's character. Wherever you go you find even the cottages are not thought properly dressed until they have been set with patterns of different-coloured brick, or plaster moulding. More important buildings—town halls, guildhalls and churches—sometimes break out into sheer fantasy. The result is usually pleasant to see; and perhaps this is reason enough for a practical people. . . .

We sailed across to Staveren in Friesland and entered canals again. Friesland, famous for cattle, impressed us most by its barns. These are vast structures with the farmhouses built into one end. They ride in the lush countryside like ships and the foliage of trees breaks against their tall sides like spray. We dawdled in winding canals not much wider than our boat, through an Arcadian country, a land of woods and shallow lakes, and sunshine and flowers. Each little town is a knot of canals filled with small boats of every description. It is a place in which to waste time, to refuse to move, to be indifferent to everything but the birds perched in the rigging, the waterlilies in the side canals, the sun sleeping in a green glade.

And then it was time to think about home.

We returned to the Ijsselmeer and came to our last, perhaps most impressive, vision of Holland. We stood north from Staveren and presently there appeared a stain on the horizon, a stain that hardened, lifted. It looked like a cliff but it was man-made: the Afsluitdyk, the Enclosing Dam. It cuts off the whole of the Ijsselmeer from the open sea, a bank in the sea that is eighteen miles long. There are small harbours of refuge inside it, probably built for the ships that worked on the original construction, but now very convenient for small boats. So we were able to moor, and climb on the bank.

It is stupendous. There is a motorway across it and sheep crop the short turf where so many Germans died in the retreating army. There is an observation tower too, built at the point where the breach was finally closed. There are sluices at either end a hundred yards wide. As the tide falls, the captive waters of the Ijsselmeer run through them and as the tide rises, the sluices close. The rivers of Holland bring in new water all the time. Nature is harnessed to defeat herself. Hoorn was once a salt-water port; but now the waters of the Ijsselmeer are fresh.

There is a lock at the west end of the Afsluitdyk, but the day was a Sunday; and by a mixture of business and piety only too familiar to an Englishman, the lock was closed on Sundays. So we waited there for the morrow, the Texel and the long haul home.

There was an old Dutchman beside us in his small yacht, who taught us more about the truth of the country than anyone else. He was a very distinguished old man, the equivalent of a judge of the supreme court. When he discovered how much we liked Holland, he expanded. He told us of the awful fix the Dutch were in, with the Ijsselmeer and the project for Port Europe. Both schemes were running out of money.

'But,' said he thoughtfully, 'it is more sensible than making H-bombs, don't you think?'

I looked at the fresh waters of the Ijsselmeer.

'Haven't you done enough,' I said, 'Can't you stop for a moment?'

'While there is still land to be reclaimed? My dear sir! We have a proverb. "God made the world, but the Dutch made Holland."'

And you feel that this is true. You feel it in the opening of a bridge or a lock, in the rich, cultivated earth of a polder, in the sight of a factory, looming like a ship over the level land. Is not this how men should live, making their country and keeping it? On the map of the world Holland is a very small country: but in every way save mere extent of miles it is a very great country indeed.

3 The Netherlands

By Linda
Burnham

If you come to the Netherlands expecting to find its residents shod in wooden shoes, you're years too late; if you're looking for windmills at every turn, you're looking in the wrong place. The bucolic images that brought tourism here in the decades after World War II have little to do with the Netherlands of the '90s. Sure, tulips grow in abundance in the bulb district of Noord and Zuid Holland provinces, but today's Netherlands is no backwater operation: This tiny nation has an economic strength and cultural wealth that far surpass its size and population. Sophisticated, modern Netherlands has more art treasures per square mile than any other country on earth, as well as a large number of ingenious, energetic people with a remarkable commitment to quality, style, and innovation.

The 41,040 square kilometers (15,785 square miles) of the Netherlands are just about half the number in the state of Maine, and its population of 15 million is slightly less than that of the state of Texas. Size is no measure of international clout, however. The Netherlands owns more property in the United States than Japan does, and is second only to Great Britain as an investor in the American economy. The Netherlands encourages internal accomplishments as well, particularly of a cultural nature. Within a 120-kilometer (75-mile) radius are ten major museums of art and several smaller ones that together contain the world's richest and most comprehensive collection of art masterpieces from the 15th to the 20th centuries, including the majority of paintings by Rembrandt and nearly every painting produced by Vincent van Gogh. In the same small area are a half dozen performance halls offering music, dance, and internationally known performing arts festivals.

The marriage of economic power and cultural wealth is nothing new to the Dutch; in the 17th century, for example, money raised through their colonial outposts overseas was used to buy or commission portraits and paintings by young artists such as Rembrandt, Hals, Vermeer, and van Ruisdael. But it was not only the arts that were encouraged: the Netherlands was home to the philosophers Descartes, Spinoza, and Comenius; the jurist Grotius; the naturalist van Leeuwenhoek, inventor of the microscope; and others like them who flourished in the country's enlightened tolerance. The Netherlands continues to subsidize its artists and performers, and it supports an educational system in which creativity in every field is respected, revered, and given room to express itself.

The Netherlands is the delta of Europe, located where the great Rhine and Maas rivers and their tributaries empty into the North Sea. Near the coast, it is a land of flat fields and interconnecting canals; in the center of the country it is surprisingly wooded, and in the far south are rolling hills. The country is too small for there to be vast natural areas, and it's too precariously close to sea level, even at its highest points, for there to be dramatic landscapes. Instead, the Netherlands is what the Dutch jokingly call a big green city. Amsterdam is the focal point of the nation; it also is the beginning and end point of a 50-kilometer (31-mile) circle of cities that includes The Hague (the Dutch seat of government and the world center of international justice), Rotterdam (the industrial center of the Netherlands and the world's largest port), and the historic cites of Haarlem, Leiden, Delft, and Utrecht. The northern and eastern provinces are rural and quiet; the southern provinces that

hug the Belgian border are lightly industrialized and sophisti- cated. The great rivers that cut through the heart of the coun- try provide both geographical and sociological borders. The area "above the great rivers," as the Dutch phrase it, is peopled by tough-minded and practical Calvinists; to the south are more ebullient Catholics. A tradition of tolerance pervades this densely populated land; aware that they cannot survive alone, the Dutch are bound by common traits of ingenuity, personal honesty, and a bold sense of humor.

Before You Go

Government Tourist Offices

In the U.S. **Netherlands Board of Tourism** (355 Lexington Ave., 21st floor, New York, NY 10017, tel. 212/370–7367, fax 212/370–9507; 90 New Montgomery St., Suite 305, San Francisco, CA 90410, tel. 415/543–6772, fax 415/495–4925; 225 North Michigan Ave., Suite 326, Chicago, IL 60601, tel. 312/819–0300, fax 312/819–1740).

In Canada **Netherlands Board of Tourism** (25 Adelaide St., Suite 710, Toronto, Ont. M5C 1Y2, tel. 416/363–1577, fax 416/363–1470).

In the U.K. **Netherlands Board of Tourism** (25–28 Buckingham Gate, London SW 1E 6LD, tel. 071/630–0451).

Tour Groups

General-Interest Tours **Abercrombie & Kent** (1520 Kensington Rd., Oak Brook, IL 60521, tel. 708/954–2944 or 800/323–7308) runs six-night barge cruises through the waterways of Holland in the early spring. **Holland Approach, Inc.** (550 Mountain Ave., Gillette, NJ 07933, tel. 908/580–9200 or 800/225–1699 outside NJ) offers nine-day tours, and **Maupintour** (Box 807, Lawrence, KS 66044, tel. 913/843–1211 or 800/255–4266) offers eight-day tulip-time excursions through Holland while the flowers are blooming. **Olson Travelworld** (Box 10066, Manhattan Beach, CA 90226, tel. 310/546–8400 or 800/421–2255) tailors tours for individuals and groups.

Special-Interest Tours The **Netherlands Board of Tourism** offices in North America maintain a data bank for special-interest travel that includes specialized tours for senior citizens, gays, and handicapped travelers; information is continually updated, and printouts of requested material are available.

Architecture **Art Express** (4500 Campus Dr., Suite 410, Newport Beach, CA 92660, tel. 800/325–7103, fax 714/852–1234; **Art Horizon International** (14 E. 63rd St., New York, NY 10021, tel. 212/888–2299, fax 212/888–2148); and **Horizon Holidays** (160 John St., Toronto, Ont. M5V2X8, tel. 416/585–9911 or 800/387–2977, fax 416/585–9614) all offer tours.

Arts, Culture, and Music **Unitours** (8 S. Michigan Ave., Chicago IL 60603, tel. 800/621–0557 or 312/782–1590, fax 312/726–0339); **International Education** (301 Alhambra Pl., Madison WI 53713, tel. 608/274–8574 or 800/558–0215, fax 608/274–8421); **Travel Time** (203 N. Wabash Ave., Chicago IL 60601, tel. 312/726–7197 or 800/621–4725, fax 312/726–0718); **Witte Travel** (3250 28th St. SE, Grand Rapids, MI 49512-1640, tel. 616/957–8113 or 800/253–0210, fax

616/957–9716); and **Ciao! Travel** (810 Emerald St., Suite 107, San Diego, CA 92109, tel. 619/272–5116 or 800/942–2426, fax 619/272–1543) offer a variety of arts and music tours.

Bicycling **Country Cycling Tours** (140 W. 83rd St., New York, NY 10024, tel. 212/874–5151 or 800/284–8954, fax 212/874–5286); **International Bicycle Tours** (Box 754, 7 Champling Sq., Essex, CT 06426, tel. 203/767–7005, fax 203/767–3090); **Four Seasons Cycling** (Box 203, Williamsburg, VA 23187–0203, tel. 804/253–2985); and **Revatours** (1256 Philips Sq., Suite 906, Montreal, Que. H3B3G1, tel. 514/392–9016 or 800/363–6339, fax 514/392–9015) arrange cycling vacations.

Barge Cruising **The Barge Lady** (230 E. Ohio St., Suite 210, Chicago IL 60611, tel. 312/944–2779); **European Waterways** (230 S. Beverly Dr., Suite 203, Beverly Hills, CA 90212, tel. 310/247–8612 or 800/438–4748, fax 310/247–9460); **Waterways & Byways** (1027 S. Palm Canyon Dr., Palm Springs, CA 92264, tel. 619/320–5754, 800/925–0444); **SeaAir Holidays Ltd.** (733 Summer St., Stamford, CT 06901, tel. 203/356–9033, 800/732–6247); and **Inclusive Tours** (2 Carleton St., Suite 910, Toronto, Ont. M5B1J3, tel. 416/977–5074, fax 416/977–7759) offer cruising on Holland's waterways.

Horticulture **Quinn's International Holidays** (333 Vaughn St., Suite 2, Winnipeg, Man. R3B3J9, tel. 204/942–5380 or 800/665–2626, fax 204/957–0322) and **Silverline Tours** (112 Athol St. 204, Whitby, Ont. H3B3G1, tel. 416/666–1404 or 416/436–2253, fax 416/430–2911) specialize in Holland's flora.

Package Deals for Independent Travelers

Jet Vacations (1775 Broadway, New York, NY 10019, tel. 212/474–8700 or 800/538–0999) offers a Flexiplan Europe package, which includes a choice of hotels, car rentals, airport transfers, and sightseeing options for a number of cities in Holland. **Northwest WorldVacations** (call your travel agent or 800/692–8687) provides visitors to Amsterdam with hotel, car rental, and tour options for a minimum of two nights. **Travel Bound** (599 Broadway, New York, NY 10012, tel. 212/334–1350 or 800/456–8656) offers packages for a minimum of three to six nights. **United Vacations** (106 Calvert St., Harrison, NY 10528, tel. 800/678–0949) will plan customized itineraries.

When to Go

The Netherlands' high season begins late-March to late-April, when the tulips come up, and runs through October, when the Dutch celebrate their Autumn Holiday. June, July, and August are the most popular traveling months with both international visitors and the Dutch themselves—it can be difficult to obtain reservations, particularly in beach towns on the North Sea coast and at campgrounds, during midsummer. The cultural season lasts from September to June, but there are special cultural festivals and events scheduled in summer months.

Climate The Netherlands has a mild maritime climate, with bright, clear summers and damp, overcast winters. The driest months are from February through May; the sunniest, May through August. In the eastern and southeastern provinces, winters are colder and summers warmer than along the North Sea coast. The following are average daily maximum and minimum temperatures for Amsterdam.

Amsterdam	Jan.	40F	4C	May	61F	16C	Sept.	65F	18C
		34	1		50	10		56	13
	Feb.	41F	5C	June	65F	18C	Oct.	56	13C
		34	1		56	13		49	9
	Mar.	47F	8C	July	70F	21C	Nov.	47F	8C
		38	3		59	15		41	5
	Apr.	52F	11C	Aug.	68F	20C	Dec.	41F	5C
		43	6		59	15		36	2

Festivals and Events

Jan.–Feb.: The international **Filmfestival Rotterdam** celebrates avant-garde cinema.

Mar./Apr. (end of Lent): **Carnival** dances through the cities of Brabant and Limburg provinces.

Mar.: **European Fine Arts Fair** gathers artists and works in Maastricht, and international crews compete in Amsterdam's **Head of the River Race.**

Apr.: **Rotterdam Marathon** draws runners from around the globe, and the **Flower Parade** passes through Lisse to open the **National Floral Exhibition** at Keukenhof gardens.

May: **National Bicycle Day** races through the Netherlands; an international modern dance festival, **Spring Dance,** bounces into Utrecht; and the **International Traditional Jazz Festival** makes Breda jump.

May/June: The **Eleven Cities by Bicycle Race** and the five-day **Eleven Cities Walking Tour** circle Friesland.

June: **Holland Festival of the Performing Arts** captures Amsterdam, spilling over to The Hague, Rotterdam, and Utrecht; **Parkpop,** a pop music festival, livens up The Hague; and **Pinkpop** bursts into Landgraf.

July: The Hague hosts the **North Sea Jazz Festival;** the **International Organ Competition** brings musicians to Haarlem in even-numbered years; and the **International Four Days Walking Event** strides through Nijmegen.

July/Aug.: *Skutsjesilen* **Sailing Regattas** skim the lakes in Friesland.

Aug.: Utrecht enjoys the **Festival of Ancient Music.**

Sept.: The **Floral Parade** makes a day-long procession of floats from Aalsmeer to Amsterdam; **Gaudeamus Muziekweek** honors music in Amsterdam; and the **Opening of Parliament** takes place in The Hague on the third Tuesday—the queen arrives in her golden coach.

Oct.: **Delft Art and Antiques Fair** fills the Prinsenhof with treasure.

Nov.: With the **St. Nicolas Parade** in Amsterdam and in cities throughout the country, the arrival of Sinterklaas launches the Christmas season.

What to Pack

The best advice for a trip to the Netherlands in any season is to pack light, be flexible, bring an umbrella (and trench coat with a liner in winter), and always have a sweater or jacket available. For daytime wear and casual evenings, turtlenecks and flannel shirts are ideal for winter, alone or under a sweater, and cotton shirts with sleeves are perfect in summer. For women, high heels are nothing but trouble on the cobblestone streets of Amsterdam and other old cities, and sneakers or running shoes are a dead giveaway that you are an American tourist; a better choice is a pair of dark-colored walking shoes and for women, with skirts, low-heeled pumps. Pants are not commonly worn by Dutch women, by the way, except on weekends or in the country, and then only by some; blue jeans are becoming a fashion item in Amsterdam, but elsewhere they are generally worn only by students, and not all the time; sweats suits, by the way, are never seen outside of fitness centers.

Dutch Currency

The official monetary unit of the Netherlands is the **guilder,** which may be abbreviated as Dfl, Fl, F, Hfl, and occasionally as NLG. There are 100 cents in a guilder; coins are minted in denominations of 5, 10, and 25 cents, and 1, 2½, and 5 guilders. Bank notes are printed in amounts of 10, 25, 50, 100, 250, and 1,000 guilders, with the denominations embossed in Braille in the corner of each bill. In spring 1992 the exchange rate was 1.55 guilders to the dollar, 2.78 to the pound sterling, and 1.30 to the Canadian dollar.

What It Will Cost

Prices in the Netherlands include an 18.5% **BTW/VAT** (value added tax). Residents of countries outside the European Community are entitled to a refund of 15.6% of the BTW, minus commission, on purchases over Fl 300 that are personally carried out of the country within 30 days of purchase. To get your refund, ask the store clerk to complete the Shopping Cheque export certificate (Form OB90). Turn in this form at customs when you leave the Netherlands—it will be returned to the store for processing, and you will be issued a refund.

Sample Costs Cup of coffee, Fl 2–2.50; glass of beer, Fl 2.50–3; glass of wine, Fl 4; soda or juice, Fl 2.50–4; a sandwich Fl 4–10; a pastry or dessert, Fl 4–8.

Passports and Visas

A valid passport or a national identity card within five years of its expiration date is all the documentation needed to enter the Netherlands for up to three months for citizens of the United States, Canada, or the United Kingdom. A rabies certificate no less than 10 days old is required to bring a dog or cat into the country.

Customs and Duties

On Arrival Residents of the United States, Canada, and the United Kingdom arriving in the Netherlands from a European Community (EC) country are entitled to import free of duty either 300 cigarettes, 75 cigars, 150 small cigars, or 400 grams of tobacco; either 1.5 liters of alcohol (over 22% alcohol), three liters under 22% alcohol, three liters of sparkling wine or three liters of fortified wine and five liters nonsparkling wine and eight liters non-sparkling Luxembourgian wine; 75 grams perfume and .375 liter cologne or lotions; one kilogram coffee or 400 grams coffee extracts and essences; 200 grams tea or 80 grams tea extracts and essences; and other goods valued at a maximum of Fl. 1400. Entering from a non-EC country, you may bring in duty-free 200 cigarettes or 50 cigars or 100 small cigars or 250 grams of tobacco; one liter of alcohol (more than 22%) or two liters (less than 22%), 50 grams of perfume and .25 liter cologne, 500 grams of coffee, 100 grams of tea, and other goods valued up to Fl. 125.

There are no restrictions regarding the import or export of currency.

On Departure To export Dutch flower bulbs, a health certificate issued by the **Nederlandse Planteziektenkundige Dienst** (Dutch Phytopathological Service) is required; these are provided with packages you buy from specialized flower bulb companies.

Language

Dutch is the official language of the Netherlands, though local dialects are used in Friesland and Limburg provinces. Almost everyone speaks good English, but in rural areas you may need a phrase book, at least until the residents overcome their shyness about using the English they know.

Staying Healthy

Travelers covered by medical insurance are entitled, by law, to medical care in Holland. All inquiries about medical care should be addressed to **Afdeling Buitenland van het Ziekenfond** (ANOZ, Health Service Foreign Affairs Department) Postbus 9069, 3506 GB Utrecht, tel. 030/618881.

Car Rentals

Major international car rental companies, including **Avis, Hertz, Europcar/National,** and **Eurodollar/Dollar** operate desks at Amsterdam Schiphol Airport and have rental offices in Amsterdam and other key cities throughout the Netherlands. In addition, there are two Dutch firms operating at the airport and other locations: **ai/Ansa International Rent A Car** (Amsterdam Schiphol Airport, tel. 020/601–5518) and **Van Wijk Amsterdam** (Amsterdam Schiphol Airport, tel. 020/601–5277).

Rail Passes

The **Holland Leisure Card,** offered by the Netherlands Board of Tourism (NBT), provides discounts of 10% to 50% on transportation as well as on admissions to tourist attractions and excursions in major cities. Valid for one year, it costs $15. The NBT also can sell you one of three special rail passes available for first- or second-class travel; these are the **Holland Rail Pass,** offering unlimited rail travel for any three days in a 10-day period; the **7-Day Rail Rover,** for unlimited travel during seven consecutive days; and the **Benelux Tourrail Pass,** for unlimited rail travel in the Netherlands, Belgium, and Luxembourg for any five days within a 17-day period. NS Nederlands Spoorwagen (Netherlands Railways, tel. 06/899–1121) offers special passes, including **One Day Rail Rover,** and **Day Excursions, Multi-Rovers** for off-peak travel, and **Summer Tour** passes for three days of travel in a 10-day period in July or August. There is also a **Teenage Rover** discounted ticket for travelers under age 18, allowing four days of travel in a 10-day period.

Student and Youth Travel

In addition to the YHA hostels, young visitors to Holland may want to consider staying at a **youth hotel**, or "Sleep-in," which provides basic, inexpensive accommodations for young people. A list of these is available from the NBT (tel. 212/370–7367 in New York). During the summer months (and in some cases all year round), the IVN, Institute for Nature Protection Education (Postbus 201123, 1000 HC Amsterdam, tel. 0020/228115) organizes **work camps** popular among English-speaking visitors aged 15–30 in scenic locations. Another organization to consider for **voluntary work experiences** in Holland is S/W, International Volunteer Projects (Willemstraat 7, 3511 RJ Utrecht, tel. 030/317721).

Hints for Disabled Travelers

The Netherlands leads the world in providing facilities for handicapped people. Train and bus stations are equipped with special telephones, elevators, and toilets. Visitors can obtain special identity cards to ensure free escort service on all public transportation. Modern intercity train carriages have wheelchair-accessible compartments. Train timetables are available in braille, and some restaurants have menus in braille. There are also special gardens for the blind at some tourist sites. For information on accessibility in the Netherlands, contact the national organization, **De Gehandicaptenraad** (Postbus 169, 3500 AD Utrecht, tel. 03/667–78–86).

Each year the **Netherlands Board of Tourism** publishes a booklet listing hotels, restaurants, hostels and campsites, museums and tourist attractions, as well as gas/petrol stations with 24-hour srvices and boat firms with adapted facilities. **The Netherlands Railways (Nederlanse Spoorwagen NS)** offers special assistance at railway stations by reservations before noon at least one day in advance or by 2 PM Friday for travel Saturday, Sunday, Monday, or on public holidays (Mon.–Fri., 8–4, tel. 030/355–5555); many Intercity carriages are designed to accommodate wheelchairs in the compartments; special elevators, phone booths, refreshment facilities, and toilets are accessible at nearly all railway stations, and many have a free Red Cross wheelchair available. For the blind, railway timetables area available in braille; also, all Dutch paper currency is embossed in braille with the applicable denomination. For information on tours and exchanges for the disabled, contact **Mobility International Nederland** (Postbus 165, 6560 AD Grosebeek, tel. 08891–71744, Wed. 9–4).

Hints for Older Travelers

There are special discount museum admissions available to senior citizens in the Netherlands. **Saga International Holidays** (120 Boylston St., Boston, MA 02116, tel. 617/434–0273 or 617/451–6808 or 800/343–0273, fax 617/451–6474) operates special-interest tours and cruises for travelers age 60 and up.

Further Reading

A visit to the Netherlands is greatly enhanced by a knowledge of the nation's history and a familiarity with its rich art heritage. Books of particular value and interest include *Amsterdam: The Life of a City*, by Geoffrey Cotterell (Little Brown, 1972), a comprehensive history of the city; *Diary of Anne Frank*, by Anne Frank, the diary of young Jewish girl that details the experience of living in hiding in Amsterdam during World War II; and *Images of a Golden Past*, by Christopher Brown (Abbeville, 1984), a guide to Dutch genre painting of the 17th century.

Some worthwhile histories include *The Dutch Revolt*, by Geoffrey Parker (Peregrine/Penguin, 1977), a history of the development of the Dutch nation; *The Dutch Seaborne Empire 1600–1800*, by C.R. Boxer (Penguin, 1965), which traces the development of the great Dutch trading companies in the 17th and 18th centuries; and *The Embarrassment of Riches*, by Simon Schama (Alfred A. Knopf, 1987/University of California Press, 1988), which interprets the Dutch culture in its Golden Age. *Evolution of the Dutch Nation*, by Bernard H.M. Vlekke (Roy, 1945), is a comprehensive history of the Netherlands.

In addition, Janwillem Van de Wetering's mystery novels (Ballantine), set in Amsterdam, can make for good light reading on the plane.

Arriving and Departing

From North America by Plane

Airports and Airlines **Amsterdam Schiphol Airport** (tel. 020/601–0966) is located 25 kilometers (15 miles) southeast of Amsterdam and is linked by rail to every part of the country.

KLM Royal Dutch Airlines (tel. 800/777–5553) is the national carrier of the Netherlands. Other airlines serving the country include **Delta** (tel. 800/221–1212), **Northwest** (tel. 800/225–2525), **TWA** (tel. 800/221–2000), and **United** (tel. 800/241–6522).

Flying Time Flying time to Amsterdam from New York is just over seven hours; from Chicago, closer to eight hours; and from Los Angeles, 10½ hours.

Discount Flights **Martinair** (tel. 800/366–4655) offers reduced-fare flights to Amsterdam from Detroit, Fort Lauderdale, Los Angeles, Miami, New York, Oakland, San Francisco, Seattle, Tampa, and Toronto.

From the United Kingdom by Plane, Train, Bus, and Ferry

By Plane *Airlines* Airlines that serve the Netherlands from the United Kingdom include **KLM City Hopper** (tel. 081/750–9000), **British Airways** (tel. 081/897–4000), and **Aer Lingus** (tel. 081/569–5555).

Flying Time Flying time to Amsterdam from London is one hour; from Belfast, 1½ hours.

By Train **EuroCity** (tel. 071/8288361) and **InterCity** expresses include seven trains a day from London to Amsterdam.

By Bus Bus/ferry combination service between the United Kingdom and the Netherlands is operated from London to Amsterdam by **Eurocity** (tel. 071/8288361).

By Ferry Ferries are run between Harwich and Hook of Holland twice daily by **Sealink/Stena** (tel. 0255/243333), overnight between Hull and Rotterdam by **North Sea Ferries** (tel. 0482/77177), and between Sheerness and Vlissingen twice daily by **Olau Line** (tel. 0795/666666). The trip can last between six and 14 hours, depending on the route taken.

Staying in the Netherlands

Getting Around the Netherlands

By Plane **KLM City Hopper** (tel. 020/674–7747) provides regular service between Amsterdam Schiphol Airport and Rotterdam, Eindhoven, and Maastricht, though air travel in a country this small is really unnecessary.

By Train **NS/Nederlands Spoorwagen** (Netherlands Railways) (tel. 06/899–1121) operates a minimum of one train per hour throughout its system, and major cities are connected by three or more trains each hour. Nearly every corner of the country is covered, supplemented by local and regional bus services. The modern, clean trains have first- and second-class coaches and nonsmoking and smoking cars. Rail fares are based upon distance; there are one-way fares and day-return fares for same-day round-trip travel; and bicycles may be carried aboard for a nominal fee. Children under 3 travel free and children under 11 are charged just Fl 1 if they are accompanied by an adult. (*See* Chapter 1, *above*, for details on special multiday train fares.)

By Ferry An extensive ferry system serves the Netherlands. Ferries in **Zeeland** province operate from Breskens (tel. 01172/1663 or 01172/3350), Vlissingen (tel. 01184/65905 or 01184/78899), Perkpolder (tel. 01148/1234 or 01148/2692), and Kruiningen (tel. 01130/1466 or 01130/2828). In **Friesland** province they run from Lauwersoog (tel. 05193/9050 or 05193/9079), Harlingen (tel. 05620/2969 or 05620/2770), and Holwerd (tel. 05191/6111) to the Frisian Islands, and from Den Helder (tel. 02220/19393) in **Noord Holland** province. Ferries across the IJsselmeer run from Enkhuisen to Stavoren (tel. 02290/17341; no cars) or Urk (tel. 05277/3407).

By Car The Dutch superhighway system is extensive and very well maintained; there are European, national, provincial, and local roads designated as E, A, N, and S, respectively. The **ANWB (Royal Dutch Touring Club)** operates telephone road information services (tel. 070/3313131) and has a 24-hour-a-day fleet of bright yellow cars and trucks equipped to handle routine repairs free of charge for members of AAA, CAA, or any affiliate of Alliance International du Tourisme. A temporary membership is available for a monthly fee of Fl 125. The speed limit in the Netherlands is 120 kilometers (75 miles) per hour, and driving is on the right. A valid driver's license from your home country is all that is required to operate a vehicle in the Netherlands.

Telephones

The country code for the Netherlands is 31.

The area code for Amsterdam is 020 (or simply 20 if you are calling from outside the Netherlands), and it is used only when you call from other parts of the Netherlands to Amsterdam. Within the immediate environs of any municipality you do not need to use an area code.

Local Calls Coin-operated telephones are becoming a rarity in the Netherlands; most public phones take PTT (Dutch telephone company) credit cards. The public telephones take Fl .25 coins: Short local calls may only require one *kwartje* (25-cent coin), but for longer calls or calls to other parts of the country insert several coins before dialing, and they will drop automatically as needed during your conversation. Calls will be cut off abruptly when all the coins are used, so keep an eye on how many are left and add more accordingly.

International Calls To call outside the Netherlands, dial 09 followed by the country code (1 for the United States and Canada, 44 for the United Kingdom), area code, and number. In Amsterdam, **Tele Talk Center** (Leidsestraat 101, tel. 020/620–8599) is open daily 10 AM–midnight; it also has a fax service.

Operators and Information Dial 008 for **directory assistance** within the Netherlands, 0018 for numbers elsewhere. Operators speak English. To place collect, person-to-person, or credit-card calls, dial 06/022–9111 to reach an **AT&T USA Direct** operator in the United States, or 06/022–9122 to reach an **MCI Call USA** operator.

Mail

Postal Rates Airmail letters up to 10 grams (⅓ ounce) cost Fl 1.40 to the United States and Canada, postcards cost Fl 0.80; to the United Kingdom, letters up to 20 grams (⅔ ounce) cost Fl 0.80, postcards, Fl 0.60.

Tipping

Service is included in the prices you pay in the Netherlands, though it is customary to round up to the nearest guilder or two on small bills, and up to the nearest five, 10, or even 25 guilders for good service on large bills.

Opening and Closing Times

Banks are open weekdays, 8 or 9 AM to 4 or 5 PM; post offices are open weekdays from 8:30 to 5 and often on Saturday from 8:30 to noon. Shopping hours, regulated by the government, are Monday 1–6, Tuesday–Friday 9–6, and Saturday 9–5; each city may designate one night a week as a late shopping night, when stores are open until 9 PM. Drugstores are open weekdays from 8 or 9 AM to 5:30 PM, with a rotating schedule in each city to cover nights and weekends. All national museums are closed on Mondays.

Shopping

The Netherlands is a good place to shop for diamonds, Delft and Makkumware, art, antiques, tulip bulbs, and cheese. Amsterdam has numerous department stores, shops, and boutiques that range in character from conservative to funky; Utrecht is the site of the largest enclosed shopping malls in the Netherlands for general shopping; and Maastricht is known for its elegant shops and boutiques. Diamonds are found exclusively in Amsterdam, as is the best selection of antiques. Amsterdam, The Hague, 's-Hertogenbosch, and Eindhoven are art centers. Delft and Makkumware are available throughout the country. And though tulip bulbs are available in the bulb district and cheese can be bought directly from farmers in Noord Holland province, it is easier to buy these items at the airport where bulbs are packaged with the required health certificates attached.

Sports and Outdoor Activities

Biking To the Dutch, biking is not a sport, it's a primary means of transportation. Wherever you go in the Netherlands, even in a city as bustling as Amsterdam, there are separate bike lanes on major thoroughfares and special road signs and traffic signals for cyclists on smaller streets. In Amsterdam and other major cities, be sure to lock your bike, or it may not be there when you return.

Boating and Sailing Pleasure sailing was invented by the Dutch, who are among the world's best designers of small sailing craft, and in the Netherlands you'll find a variety of boating opportunities ranging from the rough North Sea to the wide river deltas of Zeeland province and the gentler Frisian lakes. **ANWB** (Royal Dutch Touring Club) stores in Amsterdam (Museumplein 5, tel. 020/ 673–0844) sell very good nautical maps.

Camping Prices at the country's numerous camping locations range from Fl 25 to Fl 35 per site per night. Reservations can be made through the **Netherlands Reservation Centre** (Postbus 404, 2260 AK Leidschendam, tel. 070/320–3611, fax 070/320–2611).

Canoeing Canoeing and kayaking are popular on the small rivers and canals in the eastern regions of the country. The **Netherlands Board of Tourism** booklet "Canoeing in Holland" provides a good overview of canoeing sites throughout the country and annual canoeing events. For more detailed information on canoeing in the Netherlands, contact the **Dutch Canoe Union** (Postbus 1160, 3800 BD Amersfoort, tel. 033/622341).

Fishing Visitors need a national fishing document, or *sportvisakte*, which is valid for one year and is available at any post office. Additional licenses to fish certain areas are also necessary and are available from local fishing clubs. No license is required for saltwater fishing on the North Sea or the Wadden Sea. Ports throughout the Netherlands offer deep-sea trips; tackle and bait can be rented or bought.

Golf There are a number of public courses throughout the Netherlands that are open to players of all levels; most are open year-round, except during tournaments. **De Nederlandse Golf Federatie** (Postbus 221, 3454 ZX De Meern, tel. 03406/21888) can provide information on golfing around the country.

Beaches

The North Sea is visited by the Dutch and their landlocked German neighbors in droves during the summer months. The principal beach areas of the Netherlands are in Zeeland at **Zoutelande, Westkapelle,** and **Domburg;** along the coast of Zuid Holland province at **Oostvoorne, Brielle, Hook of Holland, Kijkduin, Scheveningen, Katwijk,** and **Nordwijk;** and in Noord Holland at **Zandvoort, Ijmuiden, Egmond aan Zee, Bergen,** and **Den Helder.** There also are beaches on the Frisian islands of **Texel, Vlieland, Terschelling, Ameland,** and **Schiermonnikoog.**

Dining

The Dutch have a dining advantage over other Europeans in the quantity and quality of the fresh ingredients available to them. Their national green thumb produces the Continent's best and greatest variety of vegetables and fruits, and their dairy farms supply a rich store of creams, cheeses, and butter for sauces; the forests yield a wide range of game meats in the winter wild season, and the sea dikes are covered with rare herbs and other vegetation that offer a rich diet to their lambs and calves to produce exceptionally tasty, tender meats year-round; plus, the waters of the Netherlands, both salt and fresh, are well known for the extraordinary quality and variety of the fish and shellfish they yield. Remarkably, for centuries Dutch cuisine failed to take advantage of this national bounty. But the days of home-style, stick-to-the-ribs cooking are nearly gone in the Netherlands, even in many smaller cities and rural areas. In its place are imaginative dishes designed and prepared to take advantage of the high-quality fresh ingredients so readily available. Many Dutch chefs also have spent time in the kitchens of France and Belgium to learn the techniques of both traditional and nouvelle cuisine. The rest of the population travels as well, and that fact has influenced dining in the Netherlands. You find Chinese, Italian, Mexican, and Indian restaurants even in small cities, and Indonesian restaurants are found everywhere because the Dutch, having colonized the country, developed a taste for the multi-dish Indonesian meal *rijstafel.* Potatoes, cabbage, sausage and other ingredients of traditional cooking remain important to the cuisine; soup continues to be the appropriate, and delicious, beginning of a meal on a daily basis. Also unchanging in the Netherlands is fresh flowers on the tables.

The Dutch prefer small, formal restaurants that emphasize service and leisurely dining; quick, casual meals can be had in French-style *grandes cafés* and café-pubs, also called *eetcafes* (eat cafés).

In Amsterdam and major cities dinner is served until 10 or later in most restaurants, though most diners eat between 7 and 9; elsewhere, dining hours vary by local custom. In the northern and eastern provinces, people dine from as early as 6 PM, while in the southern provinces, dinner is later, 8 to 9 PM.

Prix fixe and pretheater menus are found at restaurants throughout the country; vegetarian menus also are available, particularly in university cities.

The price ranges below are for an average three- or four-course meal and include taxes and tip, but not wine or drinks. The most highly recommended restaurants in each price category are indicated with a star.

Category	Amsterdam, The Hague, & Rotterdam	Metro Cities & Maastricht	Other Cities
Very Expensive	over Fl 80	over Fl 70	over Fl 60
Expensive	Fl 60–Fl 80	Fl 50–Fl 70	Fl 40–Fl 60
Moderate	Fl 40–Fl 60	Fl 35–Fl 50	Fl 30–Fl 40
Inexpensive	under Fl 40	under Fl 35	under Fl 30

Lodging

Accommodations in the Netherlands of the 1990s have changed from Old Dutch "cozy" to European cosmopolitan: Even small hotels and family-owned inns have redecorated in trendy colors and added televisions to guest rooms. International chains have opened hotels throughout the country, and golf and fitness resorts are being widely developed. In the southern province of Limburg, castles and manor houses have been converted to luxury hotels, and in many ancient city centers, a new generation of hoteliers has created attractive family-run hotels in canal houses and historic buildings. All rooms in the hotels reviewed below have baths and/or showers unless otherwise specified.

The **Netherlands Reservation Center** (NRC, Postbus 404, 2260 AK Leidschendam, tel. 070/3203611, fax 070/320–2611) handles bookings for most lodgings in the Netherlands.

Rates are for two people sharing a double room, including taxes and service; breakfast is generally included in the lower price categories only. Highly recommended hotels are indicated with a star.

Category	Amsterdam, The Hague, & Rotterdam	Metro Cities & Maastricht	Other Cities
Very Expensive	over Fl 500	over Fl 400	over Fl 300
Expensive	Fl 400–Fl 500	Fl 300–Fl 400	Fl 200–Fl 300
Moderate	Fl 300–Fl 400	Fl 200–Fl 300	Fl 150–Fl 200
Inexpensive	under Fl 300	under Fl 200	under Fl 150

Amsterdam

Amsterdam is a city with a split personality: This gracious, formal cultural center built on canals is also the most off-beat metropolis in the world. There is an incomparable romance about the canals at night, and a depth of cultural heritage in its great art museums; but there is also a houseboat crawling with stray cats permanently parked in front of an elegant gabled canal house, and prostitutes display their wares in the windows facing the city's oldest church. Only in Amsterdam can you marvel at the acoustics of the Concertgebouw concert hall one evening and be greeted by a hurdy-gurdy barrel organ pumping out happy tunes on the shopping street the next morning. When you know what to expect, Amsterdam is a delight to visit; when you don't, it can be a disconcerting experience.

The city is laid out in concentric rings of canals around the old center, crosscut by a network of access roads and alleylike connecting streets; visitors easily can see the city on foot, though there are also trams and water taxis for the weary. Most of the art museums are clustered conveniently at the edge of the canal district.

Important Addresses and Numbers

Tourist Information The **VVV Amsterdam Tourist Office** is in front of Amsterdam's neo-baroque Centraal Station. *Stationsplein 10, tel. 06/340–34066 (costs 50¢ per minute), fax 020/625–2869. Open Easter–Sept. daily 9–5; Oct.–Easter, Mon.–Sat. 9–5. A second information office at Leidsestraat 106 keeps the same hours.*

Consulates The **U.S. Consulate** (Museumplein 19, Amsterdam, tel. 020/664–5661), **British Consulate** (Koningslaan 44, Amsterdam, tel. 020/676–4343).

Emergencies The **National Emergency Alarm Number** is 06–11 for police, ambulance, and fire.

Police Call 555–5555 to report **accidents.** The **police** can be reached at 622–2222. City police stations are located at Elandsgracht 117, Lijnbaansgracht 219, Warmoesstraat 44–46, and at the entrance to IJtunnel.

Hospital Emergency Rooms **Academisch Medisch Centrum** (Meibergdreef 9, tel. 020/566–9111), **Boven 't IJ Ziekenhuis** (Statenjachtstraat 1, tel. 020/634–6346), **VU Ziekenhuis** (de Boelelaan 1117, tel. 020/548–9111), **Lucas Ziekenhuis** (Jan Tooropstraat 164, tel. 020/510–8911), **Onze Lieve Vrouwe Gasthuis** (le Oosterparkstraat 197, tel. 020/599–9111), and **Slotervaartziekenhuis** (Louwesweg 6, tel. 020/512–9333).

Doctors/Dentists/Pharmacy Call 020/664–2111 for a 24-hour referral service for all medical services. For dental emergencies, contact **Dentist Surgery AOC** (W.G. Plein 167, tel. 020/616–1234).

Where to Change Money **GWK/Grenswisselkantoren** (Centraal Station, tel. 020/32–06–0566, Mon.–Sat. 8–8, Sun. 10–4) is a nationwide financial organization, specializing in foreign currencies, where travelers can exchange cash and traveler's checks, receive cash against major credit cards, and receive Western Union money transfers. Many of the same services are available at banks, and cash can be exchanged at any post office.

English-language Bookstores The Dutch read English as well as they read their own language, so you will find English-language book sections in most bookstores in Amsterdam. The city's best selection of English-language reading material, including magazines, is found at the **American Discount Book Center** (185 Kalverstraat, tel. 020/625–5537).

Travel Agencies Major travel agencies in Amsterdam include **American Express International** (66 Damrak, 020/520–7777); **Thomas Cook** at four locations (Damrak 1–5, tel. 020/620–3236; Dam 23–25, tel. 020/625–0922/626–2194; Muntplein 12A, tel. 020/620–4016; and Leidseplein 31A, tel. 020/626–7000), **Holland International Travel Group** (Rokin 54, tel. 020/551–2812), **Key Tours** (Dam 19, tel. 020/624–7310 or 623–5051), **Lindbergh Excursions** (26 Damrak, tel. 020/622–2766), and, for student travel, **NBBS** (Rokin 38, tel. 020/624–0989).

Arriving and Departing by Plane

Airports and Airlines **Amsterdam Schiphol Airport** (tel. 020/601–0966) is located 25 kilometers (15 miles) southeast of the city; it is directly linked by rail to Amsterdam.

Between the Airport and Center City
By Bus **KLM Road Transport** (tel. 020/649–5651 or 020/649–5631) operates a regular morning shuttle bus service between Amsterdam Schiphol Airport and major city hotels. The trip takes about half an hour and costs Fl 15.

By Train The **Schiphol Rail Line** (tel. 06/899–1121) operates between the airport and the city 24 hours a day, with service to the central railway station or to stations in the south part of the city. The trip takes about 15 minutes and costs Fl 4.25.

By Taxi There is a taxi stand directly in front of the arrival hall at Amsterdam Schiphol Airport. All taxis are metered, and the fare is approximately Fl 48 to various points within central Amsterdam. Service is included, but small additional tips are not unwelcome.

Arriving and Departing by Car or Train

By Car Major European highways leading into the city from the borders are E22 from western Belgium, E25 from eastern Belgium, and E 22, E 30, and E35 from Germany. Follow the signs for *Centrum* to reach center city. Traffic is heavy but not stationary at rush hour.

By Train The city has several substations, but all major Dutch national as well as European international trains arrive at and depart from **Centraal Station** (tel. 06/899–1121 for national services information, tel. 020/620–2266 for international service), which also houses the travel information office of **NS/Nederlandse Spoorwagen** (Dutch National Railways).

Getting Around Amsterdam

Amsterdam is a small city, and most major sites are located within its central district. The canal-laced central core is surrounded by concentric rings of 15th- to 17th-century canals, built following the pattern of earlier city walls and drainage ditches. Six roads link the city center with the more modern outer neighborhoods. Once you understand the fanlike pattern of Amsterdam's geography, you will have an easier time getting around. All trams and most buses begin and end their journeys at Centraal Station, sightseeing and shopping are focused at Dam Square, and the arts and nightlife are centered in the areas of Leidseplein, Rembrandtsplein, and Waterlooplein.

By Tram/Bus/Metro The transit map published by **GVB** (main information office: Prins Hendrikkade 108–114, tel. 020/551–4911) and available at their ticket office across from the central railway station is very useful; you also can get a copy at the VVV tourist information offices next door, or you will find it reprinted as the center spread in *What's On in Amsterdam*, the weekly guide to activities and shopping published by the tourist office. The map shows the locations of all major museums, monuments, theaters, and markets, and it tells which trams to take to reach each of them. Single-ride tickets valid for one hour can be purchased from the tram and bus drivers for Fl 2.85, but it is far more practical to buy a *strippenkaart* (strip ticket) that includes from two to 45 "strips," or ticket units. The best buy for most visitors is the 15-strip ticket for Fl 9.35. By tradition, Dutch trams and buses work on the honor system: Upon boarding the vehicle, punch your ticket at one of the machines situated in the rear or center section of the tram or bus. The city is divided into zones, which are indicated on the transit map, and it is important to punch the correct number of zones on your ticket. (one for the basic tariff; one for each additional zone traveled). Occasional ticket inspections can be expected: A fine of Fl 100 is the price for "forgetting" to stamp your ticket.

By Taxi Taxi stands are located at the major squares and in front of the large hotels, or call **Taxicentrale** (tel. 020/677–7777), which is the central taxi dispatching office. Fares are Fl 4.60, plus Fl 2.28 per kilometer.

By Water Taxi A **Water Taxi** (tel. 020/622–2181) can be hailed anytime you see one cruising the canals of the city. The boats are miniature versions of the large sightseeing canal boats, and each carries up to seven passengers. You pay by time elapsed, at a rate of approximately Fl 27 per 15 minutes. The rate is per ride, no matter how many passengers are traveling.

By Bicycle There are bike lanes on all major streets and bike racks in key locations in the city, including special bike parking indentations in the pavement. For information on renting a bicycle, *see* Sports and Fitness, *below*.

Opening and Closing Times

Opening and closing times are uniform throughout the Netherlands (*see* Staying in the Netherlands, *above*). It's important to remember that state museums are closed on Mondays, including, in Amsterdam, both the Rijksmuseum and the Rijksmuseum Vincent van Gogh.

Guided Tours

Orientation The quickest, easiest way to get your bearings in Amsterdam is to take a canal-boat cruise. Trips last from an hour to an hour and a half and cover the harbor as well as the main canal district; a commentary is available on tape in four languages. Excursion boats leave from piers in various locations in the city every 15 minutes from March to October, and every half-hour in winter months. Most launches are moored in the inner harbor in front of Centraal Station. Fares range from Fl 8.50 to Fl 12.50. Operators of canal cruises include **Rederij D'Amstel**, (Nicolaas Witsenkade, opposite Heineken Brewery, tel. 020/626–5636), **Holland International** (Prins Hendrikkade, opposite Centraal Station, tel. 020/622–7788), **Rederij P. Kooy B.V.** (Rokin, near Spui, tel. 020/623–3810 or 020/623–4186), **Rederij Lovers B.V.** (Prins Hendrikkade 76, opposite Centraal Station, tel. 020/622–2181), **Meyers Rondvaarten** (Damrak, quays 4–5, tel. 020/623–4208), **Rederij Noord/Zuid** (Stadhouderskade 25, opposite Parkhotel, tel. 020/679–1370), and **Rederij Plas C.V.** (Damrak, quays 1–3, tel. 020/624–5406 or 020/622–6096).

Bus Tours Afternoon bus tours of the city operate daily. Itineraries vary, and prices range from Fl 25 to Fl 35. A three-hour city tour, including a drive through the suburbs, is offered by **Key Tours** (Dam 19, tel. 020/624–7304 or 020/624–7508, fax 020/623–5107). A three-hour tour focusing on the central city and including a canal-boat cruise is offered by **Lindbergh Excursions** (Damrak 26, tel. 020/622–2766, fax 020/622–2769).

Special-Interest There are several boat trips to museums available: **Canalbus**
Tours (Nieuwe Keizersgracht 8, tel. 020/623–9886), which makes
By Boat three stops along a route between the Centraal Station and the Rijksmuseum, costs Fl 12.50. Following a longer route is **Museumboot Rederij Lovers** (Stationsplein 8, tel. 0020/622–2181), which makes seven stops near 20 different museums. The cost is Fl 15 for a day ticket that entitles you to a 50% discount on admission to the museums, or Fl 25 for a combination ticket that includes admission to three museums of your choice.

By Bike During the extended summer season, March–October, guided 3½-hour bike trips through the central area of the city are available through the **VVV Amsterdam Tourist Office** (Stationsplein 10, tel. 020/626–6444, fax 020/625–2869).

On Foot Walking tours focusing on art and architecture are run by **Stichting Arttra** (Staalstraat 28, 1011 JM, tel. 020/625–9303) and **Archivisie** (Postbus 14603, 1001 LC, tel. 020/625–8908). For walking tours of the Jewish Quarter, contact **Joods Historisch Museum** (Jonas Daniel Meyerplein 2–4, Postbus 16737, 1001 RE, tel. 020/626–9945, fax 020/624–1721), and for a guided walk through the red-light district, contact **Stichting FIS** (Postbus 1566, 1001 ND, tel. 020/627–3978).

Personal Guides The **VVV Amsterdam Tourist Office** (Stationsplein 10, tel. 020/626–6444, fax 020/625–2869) maintains lists of guides and can advise you on making arrangements. The costs range from Fl 80 to Fl 350 for a half day; from Fl 120 to Fl 450 for a full day.

Walking Tours The **VVV Amsterdam Tourist Office** (Stationsplein 10, tel. 020/626–6444, fax 020/625–2869) sells brochures outlining easy-to-follow theme tours through the central part of the city. Among them are "A Journey of Discovery Through Maritime Amsterdam," "A Walk Through the Jordaan," "Jewish Amsterdam," and "Rembrandt and Amsterdam." An interesting selection of walking-tour brochures focusing on the city's development is available at the **Amsterdam Physical Planning Department** exhibition at Zuiderkerk (Zandstraat 5, tel. 020/625–8908).

Highlights for First-Time Visitors

Amsterdam Historisch Museum (*see* Tour 1: City of the Arts)
Anne Frank huis (*see* Tour 3: The Canals)
Museum het Rembrandt huis (*see* Tour 2: The Jewish Quarter and the Old Town)
Museum van Loon (*see* Tour 1: City of the Arts)
Rijksmuseum (*see* Tour 1: City of the Arts)
Rijksmuseum Vincent Van Gogh (*see* Tour 1: City of the Arts)

Exploring Amsterdam
Tour 1: City of the Arts

Numbers in the margin correspond with points of interest on the Amsterdam map.

❶ Your tour begins where Amsterdam began. In the 12th century **Dam (Dam Square)** was the site of a dam across the Amstel River and the location of the local weigh house. The monument in the center was erected in 1956 to commemorate the liberation of the Netherlands at the end of World War II.

❷ Follow the shopping street Kalverstraat south to the entrance to the **Amsterdam Historisch Museum** (Amsterdam Historical Museum). In the halls of this former orphanage you will learn all you need to know about the history of Amsterdam, from its beginnings in the 13th century as a marketplace for farmers and fishermen through the glorious period in the 17th century when Amsterdam was the richest, most powerful trading city in the world. A towering, skylit gallery is filled with the guild paintings that document that period of power. *Kalverstraat 92, tel. 020/523–1822. Admission: Fl 5 adults, Fl. 2.50 children. Open daily 11–5.*

❸ Passing through the painting gallery of the historical museum brings you to the entrance of the **Begijnhof** (Beguine Court). Walk inside and you are in the courtyard of a peaceful residential hideaway. Built in the 14th century as a conventlike residence for unmarried lay women, it is typical of many found throughout the Netherlands. No. 34 is the oldest house in Amsterdam. The small church is the Church of Scotland. *Begijnhof 29, tel. 020/623–3565. Admission free. Open June–Aug., daily 2–4 pm.*

Time Out At the end of the alley that passes the Beguine Court you come to Spui, an open square that is the focal point of the University of Amsterdam and the site of its library. Several nice choices for a break can be found in the pubs and eateries here, including **Caffe Esprit** (Spui 10, tel. 020/627–8281), attached to the store of the same name. For a quick sandwich, **Broodje van Kootje** (Spui 20, tel. 020/623–7451) sells the classic Amsterdam *broodje* (sandwich).

❹ Cut through the canals by way of the Heisteg and its continuation the Wijde Heisteg. The corner of Herengracht (Gentleman's Canal) and Leidsegracht, the **Gouden Bocht** (Golden Bend), was the most prestigious section of the city in the 17th century, and it still is. You'll notice that houses are wide, doors are centrally placed, and there is an imposing look to the architecture. Follow Herengracht to the left to Vijzelstraat and turn right. Cross the Keizersgracht and turn left to find the **Museum van Loon.** This is the city's best look at life in those magnificent canal houses. Still a private residence for a descendant of one of Amsterdam's powerful families, the house is filled with portraits, many of them traditional paired marriage portraits and paintings of children. *Keizersgracht 672, tel. 020/624–5255. Admission: Fl5 adults, Fl4 children. Open Mon. 10–5, Sun. 1–5.*

❺ Directly across the canal is **Museum Fodor,** a small museum of modern art that showcases the work of rising Dutch painters, sculptors and photographers. *Keizersgracht 609, tel. 020/624–9919. Admission: Fl1. Open daily 11–5.*

Turn right and follow Keizersgracht to Nieuwe Spiegelstraat, where you turn left and walk toward Museumplein. The wealth of art Amsterdam offers its visitors is largely concentrated around this grassy plain, which also serves as a transition point between the central canal area and the modern residential sections of the city.

⑥ The **Rijksmuseum** (State Museum), a turreted, turn-of-the-century building designed by Petrus J. Cuypers, has more than 150 rooms displaying paintings, sculpture, and objects from both Western and Asian art traditions, dating from the 9th through the 19th centuries. The primary collection is 15th- to 17th-century paintings, mostly Dutch (the Rijksmuseum has the largest concentration of these masters in the world); there are also extensive collections of Dutch drawings and prints from the 15th to 20th centuries. The main attraction of the Rijksmuseum are the works of Rembrandt, such as *The Night Watch. Stadhouderskade 42, tel. 020/673–2121. Admission: Fl 6.50 adults, Fl 3.50 children. Open Tues.–Sat. 10–5, Sun. and holidays 1–5.*

When you leave the Rijksmuseum, walk through the covered gallery that divides the building. Directly ahead is Museumplein; to your right is Paulus Potterstraat (look for the diamond factory on the far corner), where you'll find the
⑦ **Rijksmuseum Vincent Van Gogh** (Vincent van Gogh Museum). As the Rijksmuseum honors Rembrandt with the major concentration of his work, so the Van Gogh Museum honors the short, but prolific, career of the 19th-century Dutch painter with a collection that includes *nearly all* of his paintings, drawings, and letters. In a light-filled building designed by Gerrit Rietveld and opened in 1973, the galleries present van Gogh's development as an artist, step by step, from the early dark and roughhewn drawings of potato farmers he did in the Dutch province of Drenthe to his brooding final painting of crows circling above a wheat field. *Paulus Potterstraat 7, tel. 020/570–5200. Admission: Fl 10 adults, Fl 5 children. Open Tues.–Sat. 10–5, Sun. and holidays 1–5.*

Continuing along Paulus Potterstraat, at the corner of Van
⑧ Baerlestraat, you reach the **Stedelijk Museum** (Municipal Museum), where you'll find a collection of paintings and sculptures by Cézanne, Picasso, Monet, and other artists dating from 1850 to the present. Major movements that are well documented here are COBRA (Appel, Corneille), American pop art (Johns, Oldenburg, Liechtenstein), American action painting (de Kooning, Pollock), and neorealism (de Saint-Phalle, Tinguely). *Paulus Potterstraat 13, tel. 020/573–2911. Admission: Fl 7 adults, Fl 3.50 children. Open daily 11–5.*

Time Out On the corner of Van Baerlestraat and Brouwersstraat, facing the side of the Concertgebouw concert hall, is **Restaurant Bodega Keyzer** (Van Baerlestraat 96, tel. 020/671–1441), something of an institution in the neighborhood as the spot for a preconcert dinner or postconcert supper.

Facing the back of the Rijksmuseum across Museumplein is the
⑨ **Concertgebouw** (Concert Building), filled since the turn of the century with the music of the Concertgebouw Orchestra as well as visiting international artists. There are two concert halls in the building, Grote (large), and Kleine (small): It is the larger hall that is well known to music lovers and musicians around the world as one of the most acoustically perfect anywhere. You will recognize the building at once (it is topped with a lyre); enter through the glass extension along the side. There

Amsterdam

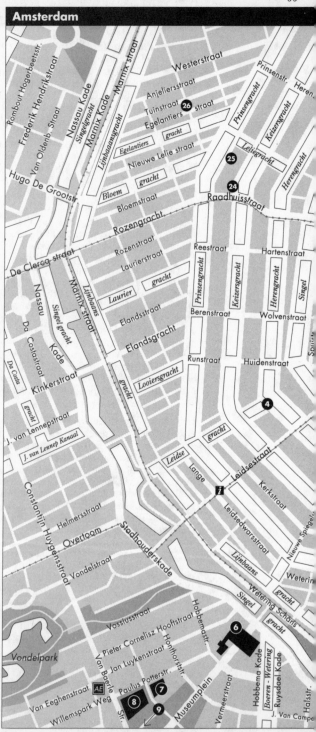

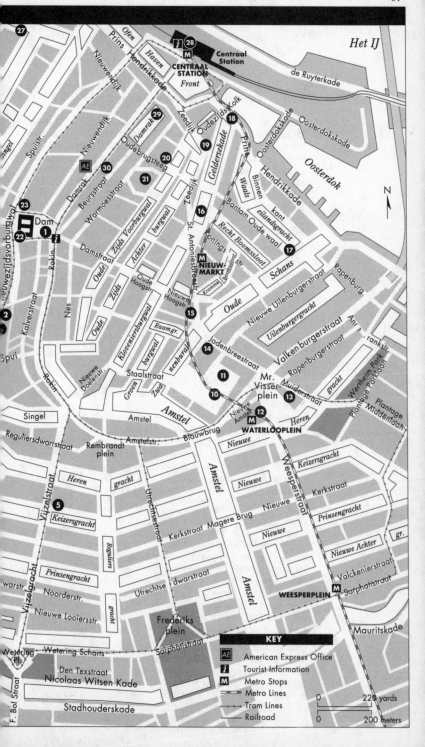

are no tours of the building, so you will need to buy a ticket to a concert to see beyond the broad lobby, or, if you visit on a Wednesday before 12:30, you can attend a free lunchtime concert. *Concertgebouwplein 2–6, tel. 020/675–4411 (information and concert schedules 24 hours) or 020/671–8345. AE, DC, MC, V.*

Tour 2: The Jewish Quarter and the Old Town

Start on Waterlooplein, where the large and modern **Muziektheater/Stadhuis** (Music Theater/Town Hall) complex is the cornerstone of a revival of this part of the city. Built as a home for everything from opera performances to welfare applications, it is a multifunctional complex that includes theaters, offices, shops, and even the city's wedding chamber (Dutch marriages all must be performed in the Town Hall, with church weddings optional). Feel free to wander through the lobbies; there is interesting sculpture as well as a display that dramatically illustrates Amsterdam's position below sea level.

Wrapped around two sides of the Music Theater/Town Hall complex is the **Waterlooplein** flea market. The pushcarts are gone, but a stroll past the stalls provides a colorful glimpse of Amsterdam entrepreneurship in action, day in and day out, in every sort of weather. *Waterlooplein. Admission free. Open weekdays 9–5, Sat. 8:30–5:30.*

From the time in the 15th century when the diamond cutters of Antwerp first arrived to find refuge from the Spanish Inquisition, this area east of the Zwanenburgwal has been the traditional Jewish Quarter of Amsterdam.

East of Waterlooplein, across Mr. Visserplein, is a statue erected after World War II to honor a solidarity strike by Amsterdam's dockworkers in protest of the deportation of Amsterdam's Jews during the war. Facing it is the entrance to the **Joods Historisch Museum** (Jewish Historical Museum), which incorporates four synagogues within its complex and contains documents, paintings and objects related to the history of the Jewish people in Amsterdam and the Netherlands. *Jonas Daniel Meyerplein 2–4, tel. 020/626–9945. Admission: Fl 7 adults, Fl 3.50 children. Open daily 11–5.*

Just to the east, on the corner of Mr. Visserplein and Jonas Daniel Meyerplein, is a square brick building behind brick courtyard walls. This is the **Portugees Israelitische Synagogue** (Portuguese Israeli Synagogue), built between 1671 and 1675 by the Sephardic Jewish community that had emigrated from Portugal during the preceding two centuries. Its spare, elegantly proportioned, wood interior has remained virtually unchanged since it was built and still is lighted by candles in two immense candelabras during services. *Mr. Visserplein 3, tel. 020/625–3509. Admission: Fl 2.50. Open May–Oct., Sun.–Fri. 10–4; Nov.–Apr., Mon.–Thurs. 10–4, Fri. 10–2.*

Up Jodenbreestraat (once the main street of the Jewish Quarter) from Mr. Visserplein, the second house from the corner by the Zwanenburgwal is **Museum het Rembrandthuis** (Rembrandt's House). This was the house that Rembrandt, flush with success, bought for his family. He later lost it to bankruptcy when he fell from popularity following his wife's death. He came under attack by the Amsterdam burghers, who refused to accept his liaison with his housekeeper. The house today is a museum of Rembrandt prints and etchings and includes one of his presses. *Jodenbreestraat 4–6, tel. 020/624–9486. Admission: Fl 4 adults, Fl 2.50 children. Open Mon.–Sat. 10–5, Sun. and holidays 1–5.*

Time Out   Grab a bite in the Waterlooplein flea market or in the café of the Muziektheater.

Cross the bridge into St. Antonies Brestraat and follow it to the **⑮ Zuiderkerk** (South Church), built between 1603 and 1611. The city planning office maintains a display here that offers a look at the future of Amsterdam. *Zandstraat. Admission free. Tower open June–Oct., Wed. 2–5, Thurs.–Fri. 11–2, Sat. 11–4.*

Cut through on Zandstraat to Kloveniersburgwal and follow it **⑯** north to **Nieuwe Markt** (New Market) square. The **Waag** (Weigh House) in the center of the square was built between 1488 and 1614 as a town gate, and it was part of the city walls in 1500. After 1617 this was the weighing house; one of its towers became a teaching hospital for the academy of surgeons of the Surgeons' Guild. It was here that Rembrandt came to watch Professor Tulp in action prior to painting *The Anatomy Lesson.*

Take Koningsstraat to the Kroomboomsloot canal and turn left; turn right at Rechtboomsloot canal and follow it through its homey neighborhood to Montelbaans Straat, turn left, and cut **⑰** through to Oudewaal canal. Follow it right to **Montelbaanstoren** (Montelbaans Tower), which dates from 1512 and now houses the City Water Office. Since 1878, this department has maintained the water levels in the canals and engineered the nightly flushings of the entire city waterway system, closing and opening the sluices to change the direction of the flow and cleanse the waters. (The canals remain murky green despite the process, due to algae.) The elegant clock tower was added early in the 17th century. Up Kalk Markt from the tower, at Prins Hendrikkade, is the **Oosterdok** (Eastern Dock) of Amsterdam Harbor. Continue west along Prins Hendrikkade to **⑱** Gelderskade and **Schrierstoren** (Weeper's Tower). There's a shop for nautical instruments, maps, and books in the building now, but in the 16th century it was a lookout tower for the women whose men were fishing at sea. A plaque on the side of the building tells you that it was from this location that Henry Hudson set sail on behalf of the Dutch East India Company to find a shorter route to the East Indies, discovering instead Hudson's Bay in Canada and, later, New York harbor and the Hudson River.

⑲ Follow Oudezijds Kolk south to the small alley of **Zeedijk**, once known throughout the country as the black hole of Amsterdam for its concentration of drug traffic and usage. In one night in the late 1980s, however, the city fathers cleared the area with an onslaught of horse patrols and fire hoses. The planned attack was immediately followed by a brigade of carpenters, who reclaimed the area's dilapidated buildings. No. 1 Zeedijk is one of only two timbered houses left in the city.

⑳ From Zeedijk, take Oudezijds Voorburgwal south to **Museum Amstelkring** ("Our Lord in the Attic" Museum). It looks to be just another canal house, and on the lower floors, it is. The attic of the building is unique, however; it is a small chapel that dates from the Reformation in Amsterdam, when open worship by Catholics was outlawed. *Oudezijds Voorburgwal 40, tel. 020/ 624–6604. Admission: Fl 3.50 adults, Fl. 2 children. Open Mon.–Sat. 10–5, Sun. and holidays 1–5.*

Continue south on Oudezijds Voorburgwal through part of the red-light district (where semi-nude women display their wares in canal-side windows) to the **Oude Kerk** (Old Church), built between 1366 and 1566 and restored from 1955 to 1979. Rembrandt's wife, Saskia, is buried here. *Oudekerksplein 23, tel. 020/624–9183. Admission: Fl. 3. Open Apr.–Oct., Mon.–Sat. 11–5, Sun. 1:30–5; Nov.–Mar., Mon.–Sat. 1–3, Sun. 1:30–3. Tower accessible June–Sept., Mon. and Thurs. 2–5, Tues.– Wed. 11–2.*

From here you can continue south on Oudezijds Voorburgwal through more of the red-light district to Damstraat and the Dam.

Tour 3: The Canals

This tour, too, begins at Dam Square. On its western side are two of Amsterdam's most imposing structures. **Het Koninklijk Paleis te Amsterdam** (Royal Palace at Amsterdam), built in the mid-17th century as the city's town hall, is Dutch classical in design and stands solidly on 13,659 pilings sunk deep into the marshy soil of the former riverbed. Restored as a royal residence during the Napoleonic period and filled with furnishings of that time, it has been the official residence of the House of Orange since 1808. Queen Beatrix, like her mother and grandmother before her, uses it only on the highest of state occasions, however. If you are in Amsterdam while it is open, be sure to visit; this is the Dutch equivalent of touring the White House. *Dam, tel. 020/624–8698. Admission: Fl 5 adults, Fl 1.50 children. Open Easter, summer, and autumn holidays, Mon.–Sun. 12:30–4; most Wed. afternoons during the rest of the year.*

To the right of the palace is the **Nieuwe Kerk** (New Church). Built in the 16th and early 17th centuries, this is the royal church of the Netherlands, in which every monarch has been crowned since 1815. It is often the site of special exhibitions. *Dam, tel. 020/626–8168. Admission free. Open daily 11–5.*

Circle around behind the Royal Palace, follow the tram tracks into the wide and busy Raadhuisstraat, and continue along it to the Westermarkt. The **Westerkerk** (Western Church) is on the right, facing the next canal. Built between 1602 and 1631, it has a tower topped by a copy of the crown of the Habsburg emperor Maximilian I, and its carillon is the comforting "clock" of the canal area of Amsterdam whose chiming was mentioned often by Anne Frank in her famous diary. Rembrandt and his son Titus are buried here; the philosopher René Descartes lived on the square facing the church. *Prinsengracht (corner of Westermarkt), tel. 020/624–7766. Tower open June–Sept., Tues.– Wed. and Fri.–Sat. 2–5.*

Make a right past the church and follow the Prinsengracht canal to the **Anne Frankhuis** (Anne Frank House), one of the most frequently visited places in the world. It was in this unimposing canal house that two Jewish families hid from the Nazis for more than two years during World War II. They were eventually discovered and sent to concentration camps, but young Anne's diary survived as a detailed record of their life in hiding. If you have time to see nothing else in Amsterdam, don't miss a visit to this house. *Prinsengracht 263, tel. 020/626–4533. Admission: Fl 6 adults, Fl 3 children. Open Sept.–Apr., Mon.–Sat. 9–5, Sun. and public holidays 10–5; May–Aug., Mon.–Sat. 9–7, Sun. and public holidays 10–7.*

Time Out Sugared or fruit-filled crepe-style pancakes are a Dutch specialty, and the **Pancake Bakery** (Prinsengracht 191, tel. 020/625–1333) is one of the best places in Amsterdam to try them; the menu offers a choice of more than 30 different flavor combinations.

Continue north along the Prinsengracht canal. The neighbor-
㉖ hood to your left, across the canal, is known as the **Jordaan**, the traditional working-class area of the city. Developed during the Napoleonic era and filled with streets and former canals named for flowers and trees, it was originally referred to as the *jardin*, French for "garden."

At the intersection of the Prinsengracht and Brouwersgracht
㉗ canals, turn left. A leisurely stroll along the **Brouwersgracht** (Brewers Canal) is one of the prettiest in the city; the canal is lined with homes and former warehouses of the brewers who traded here in earlier centuries and is blessed with long views down the canals and plenty of sunlight. Cross the canal at Willemsstraat and follow it back to the Singel canal. On the other side, follow the tram tracks to the left toward the harbor.
㉘ Ahead is **Centraal Station** (Central Station), an imposing example of Dutch Renaissance style. It opened in 1885 and has been the hub of transportation for the Netherlands ever since.

The inner harbor along the broad avenue leading to the station
㉙ is the **Damrak** (Dam Port), once completely filled with piers bringing fish and other cargo to the weigh house at the Dam and now lined with a curious assortment of shops, attractions,
㉚ hotels, and eating places. On the far side, the **Beurs** (Stock Exchange), built at the turn of the century, overlooks the Dam.

Amsterdam for Free

Free demonstrations are given at a number of Amsterdam's diamond-cutting factories and showrooms, including the **Amsterdam Diamond Centre** (Rokin 1–5, at Dam Square, tel. 0201/624–5787), **Coster Diamonds** (Paulus Potterstraat 2–4, behind the Rijksmuseum, tel. 0201/676–2222), and **Van Moppes Diamonds** (Albert Cuypstraat 2–6, in the middle of the daily green market street, tel. 0201/676–1242). Free lunchtime concerts are given on Wednesdays at 12:30 during the winter concert season (Sept.–June) at the Concert Building.

What to See and Do with Children

Keep young travelers entertained with a visit to the **Plantage quarter,** east of the city center beyond the expressway leading to the IJ Tunnel. Built in the mid-19th century as a garden city, this area includes a 14-hectare (37-acre) park called **Artis** that is home to Amsterdam's collection of natural-history museums, a zoo with an aviary and an aquarium, and a planetarium. A special Artis Express canal boat from the central railway station provides an amusing means of transportation. *Plantage Kerklaan 40, tel. 020/523–3400. Admission: Fl 17.50 adults, Fl 10 children. Open daily 9–5. Zoological Museum closed Mon., planetarium opens Mon. at 1.*

The Netherlands' link to Indonesia and the West Indies is honored at the Tropen Museum (*see* Off the Beaten Track, *below*) located beyond the Artis complex. The **Kindermuseum** (Children's Museum), was recently added here. Adults may visit, but only under the supervision of a child aged 6–12. *Linnaeusstraat 2, tel. 020/568–8295. Admission: Fl 6 adults, Fl. 4 children. Open weekdays 10–5, weekends and holidays noon–5.*

The nearby **Museumwerf 't Kromhout** (Museum Wharf The Kromhout), a small 19th-century shipyard in which old ships are being restored, is sure to hold the attention of nautically minded youngsters. *Hoogte Kadijk 147, tel. 020/627–6777. Admission: Fl 3.50 adults, Fl 1.50 children. Open weekdays 9–4.*

Stick with this theme by visiting a replica of the VOC (Dutch East India Company) ship *Amsterdam* (*see* Off the Beaten Track, *below*), permanently moored at the end of the harbor.

A branch of the world-famous wax museum, **Madame Tussaud's,** is located at Dam Square above the P&C department store. *P&C Building, Dam 20, tel. 020/622–9949. Admission: Fl 16 adults, Fl 11 children. Open daily 10–5:30.*

Off the Beaten Track

The early development of Western civilization, from the Egyptians to the Romans, and of the Near Eastern cultures (Anatolia, Persia, Palestine) are documented in the displays of the **Allard Pierson Museum,** the archaeological collection of the University of Amsterdam. *Oude Turkmarkt 127, tel. 020/525–2556. Admission: Fl 5. Open Tues.–Fri. 10–5, weekends and holidays 1–5.*

Well beyond the bustle of the city center, housed in a magnificent tiered, galleried, and skylighted building decorated in gilt and marble, is the **Tropen Museum** (Tropical Museum), where displays and dioramas portray everyday life in the world's tropical environments. *Linnaeusstraat 2, tel. 020/568–8295. Admission: Fl 6 adults, Fl 4 children. Open weekdays 10–5, weekends and holidays noon–5.*

If you have always wanted to sort out your knowledge of the Dutch role in the development of world trade, the **Rijksmuseum Nederlands Scheepvaart/VOC Schip *Amsterdam*** (State Museum of Netherlands Shipping/East India Ship *Amsterdam*) is the place to do it. Once the warehouse from which trading vessels were outfitted for their journeys with everything from cannons to hardtack, the building now incorporates room after room of displays related to the development and power of the Dutch East and West Indies companies as well as the Dutch fishing industry. Moored alongside the building at the east end of Amsterdam Harbor is the trading ship *Amsterdam.* *Kattenburgerplein 1, tel. 020/523–2222. Admission: Fl 10 adults, Fl 7.50 children. Open Tues.–Sat. 10–5, Sun. and holidays 1–5.*

In the Plantage section of the city is the remarkable **Hortus Botanicus,** a botanical garden that was first laid out as an herb garden for doctors and pharmacists in 1638. It has since been expanded to incorporate an ornamental garden, where 6,000 species are represented. *Plantage Middenlaan 2, tel. 020/625–8411. Admission: Fl 5 adults, Fl 3 children. Open Apr.–Sept., weekdays 9–5, weekends and holidays 11–5; Oct.–Mar., weekdays 9–4, weekends and holidays 11–4.*

Shopping

The variety of goods available here, plus the convenience of a shopping district that snakes through the city in a continuous parade of boutiques and department stores, are the major joys of shopping in Amsterdam. Be sure to visit the year-round outdoor flea market at Waterlooplein, a holdover from the pushcart days in the Jewish Quarter. Shopping hours in the Netherlands are regulated by law: One night a week is reserved for late shopping. In Amsterdam, department stores and many other shops are closed on Monday morning but open on Thursday evening.

Shopping Districts/Streets **Dam Square** is home to two of Amsterdam's main department stores, and several popular shopping streets lead away from the square in different directions: **Nieuwendijk** is good for bargain buys, **Rokin** for high-priced fashion and jewelry items. **Kalverstraat** is the city's main pedestrian-only shopping street. **Leidsestraat** offers a range and variety of shopping similar to Kalverstraat's. **Max Euweplein** is a small plaza-style shopping mall surrounding a summer café and adjacent to the Amsterdam Casino. The posh and prestigious **P. C. Hooftstraat,** generally known as the P. C. (pronounced "pay-say"), and its companion shopping avenue, **Van Baerlestraat,** leading to the Concertgebouw, are both good choices. For a variety of trendy shopping opportunities, try **Utrechtsestraat.**

Department Stores The city's best-known department store is **De Bijenkorf,** located on one of the main corners of Dam Square, which offers a full range of goods and services. Directly across the square is **P&C,** specializing in clothing. In the middle of the Kalverstraat are the gracious and conservative **Maison de Bonneterie en Pander,** for clothing and household items, and the Amsterdam branch of England's **Marks & Spencer,** for low-priced clothing. Other lower-priced department stores include **C&A,** spanning the block between Nieuwendijk and Damrak, and **Vroom & Dreesman,** at the end of the Kalverstraat near Muntplein. One other department store to mention is **Metz & Company,** at the corner of Leidsestraat and Keizersgracht.

Street Markets Few markets compare with Amsterdam's **Waterlooplein** flea market, which partially surrounds the city's Music Theater/Town Hall complex at the convergence of the Oude Schans canal and the Amstel River. It is a descendant of the haphazard pushcart trade that gave this part of the city its distinct and lively character in the early part of the century. You're unlikely to find anything of value here, but it's a good spot to look for the secondhand clothing young Amsterdammers favor, and it is a gadget lover's paradise. The **Bloemenmarkt** on the Singel between Koningsplein and Muntplein is another of Amsterdam's must-see markets, where flowers and plants are sold from permanently moored barges. Sunday art markets are held in good weather from April to October on **Thorbeckeplein** and from April through November at **Spui.** The **Postzegelmarkt** stamp market is held twice a week (Wed. and Sat. 1–4) on Nieuwezijds Voorburgwal.

Specialty Stores Antiques always have been a staple item of shopping in Am-
Antiques sterdam, and the array of goods available at any time is broad
enough to meet the demands and suit the budget of most visitors. There are more than 150 antiques shops scattered
throughout the central canal area of the city. The greatest concentration of shops offering fine antiques and specialty items is
in the **Spiegel Quarter.** Nieuwe Spiegelstraat and its continuation, **Spiegelgracht,** constitute the main thoroughfare of the
quarter, with shops on both sides of the street and canal for five
blocks, from the Golden Bend of the Herengracht nearly to the
Rijksmuseum, including several dealers under one roof in the
Amsterdams Antiques Gallery (Nieuwe Spiegelstraat 34, tel.
020/625–3371). **Rokin,** which runs between Dam and
Muntplein, is the location of the Amsterdam branch of **Soth-
eby's** (Rokin, tel. 020/627–5656). Shops on **Rozengracht** and
along **Prinsengracht** near the Westerkerk tend to offer country
Dutch furniture and household items; you'll also find antiques
and curio shops along the side streets in that part of the city.
For a broad range of vintage and antique furniture, curios, jew-
elry, clothing, and household items, **Antique Market de Looier**
(Elandsgracht 109, tel. 020/624–9038; open Sat.–Wed. 11–5,
Thurs. 11–9) houses more than 50 dealers. Nearby **De
Rommelmarkt** (Looiersgracht 38, tel. 020/627–47–62; open
Sat.–Thurs. 11–5) is an indoor flea market.

There are sure to be old maps and prints (including botanicals)
in antiques shops all over Amsterdam, but for a broad selection
of high quality, **A. van der Meer** (P.C. Hooftstraat 112, tel. 020/
662–1936) is a gallery that has specialized in 17th-, 18th-, and
19th-century works for more than 30 years. Daumier etchings,
hunt prints, and cityscape engravings can be found here.

There is considerable interest in Art Deco and Jugendstil items
in the Netherlands, particularly in Amsterdam. **Tangram**
(Herenstraat, tel. 020/624–4286), **De Haas** (Kerkstraat 155,
tel. 020/626–5952) and **Galerie Frans Leidelmeyer** (Nieuwe
Spiegelstraat 58, tel. 020/625–4627) all specialize in Art Deco
and/or Jugendstil.

Art *What's On in Amsterdam*, published by the tourist office, is a
good source of information on current exhibitions; another is
the Dutch-language publication *Uit Krant/Going Out News*,
which has the most comprehensive listings available. Among
the dealers specializing in 20th-century art in Keizersgracht
are **Collection D'Art 1970** (Keizersgracht 516, tel. 020/622–
1511), **Kunsthandel M.L. De Boer** (Keizersgracht 542, tel. 020/
623–4060), **Galerie Espace** (Keizersgracht 548, tel. 020/624–
0802); and in the Spiegel Quarter, **E. Den Biemen de Haas**
(Nieuwe Spiegelstraat 34, tel. 020/620–0520), **Marie-Louise
Woltering** (Nieuwe Spiegelstraat 53, tel. 020/622–2240), **C.M.
Kooring Verwindt** (Spiegelgracht 14–16, tel. 020/623–6538),
Galerie Asselijn (Lange Leidsedwarsstraat 200, tel. 020/624–
9030), **Galerie Oppo** (Spiegelgracht 30, tel. 020/624–1192),
Wetering Galerie (Lijnbaansgracht 288, tel. 020/623–6189), and
Galerie Guido de Spa (2e Weteringdwarsstraat 34, tel. 020/622–
1528). Also dealing in art, including old paintings, engravings,
and Asian art, are **Waterman** (Rokin 116, tel. 020/623–2958), **J.
Denijs 1912** (Nieuwe Spiegelstraat 29, tel. 020/624–3258), **E.H.
Ariens Kappers** (Nieuwe Spiegelstraat 32, tel. 020/623–5356),

Eurasia Antiques (Nieuwe Spiegelstraat 40, tel. 020/626–1594), **Cserno Antiek** (Spiegelgracht 28, tel. 020/626–3697), **Art Galerie Bruns** (Lijnbaansgracht 290, tel. 020/626–6777), **N. Veeman** (Weteringstraat 20, tel. 020/623–5358), **Couzijn Simon** (Prinsengracht 578, tel. 020/624–7691), **Kunsthandel J. Polak** (Spiegelgracht 3, tel. 020/627–9009), **Aalderink** (Spiegelgracht 15, tel. 020/623–0211). In the Spiegel Quarter, **Galerie Animation Art** (Berenstraat 19, tel. 020/627–7600) offers original Disney and other cartoon sketches.

Books   The Dutch love books, and most read in at least two or three languages. You'll have no trouble finding reading material in English. **Albert de Lange** (Damrak 60–62, tel. 020/624–6744) has a good selection of travel books, history, and fiction, as does **W.H. Smith** (Kalverstraat 152, tel. 020/638–3821). Near the art museums and the Concertgebouw, **Premsela** (Van Baerlestraat 78, tel. 672–4266) specializes in art books. The very best, and best located, place to shop for English-language books in Amsterdam is **American Discount Book Centers** (Kalverstraat 185, tel. 020/625–5537). True in character to every word in its name, American Discount Book Centers' selection is strongly oriented to American tastes and expectations.

Cigars and   Dutch cigars are famous for their unique taste and character; a
Smokers' Materials   cigar is also a customary after-dinner offering among men in the Netherlands. One of the best places in the world to buy cigars and other smoking materials is **Hajenius** (Rokin 92, tel. 020/623–7494), in business since 1826. Another option near the Concert Building is **Davidoff** (Van Baerlestraat 84, tel. 020/671–1042).

Coffee/Tea/Spices   While other nations sent ships to plunder the world's stores of gold and jewels, the Dutch of the 17th century got rich carrying shiploads of coffee, tea, and cinnamon. **Jacob Hooy & Co.** (Kloveniersburgwal 12, tel. 020/624–3041), in the same canalside location since 1743, sells spices and herbs from gold-lettered wooden drawers, barrels, and bins, and it offers a daunting array of *dropjes* (hard candies and medicinal drops) as well as teas. Directly across town near the Anne Frank House is **H. Keijzer's Koffie- en Theehandel N.V.** (Prinsengracht 180, tel. 020/624–0823), which offers nearly 100 different kinds of tea and more than two dozen coffees.

Crystal/Porcelain/   **Focke & Meltzer** (P.C. Hooftstraat 65–67, tel. 020/664–2311;
Ceramics   Hotel Okura Shopping Arcade, tel. 020/678–7111; Rokin 124, tel. 020/231944) is the primary source in Amsterdam of authenticated Delft and Makkumware as well as fine crystal.

Diamonds/Jewelry   The **Amsterdam Diamond Center** (Rokin 1, tel. 020/624–5787) houses several diamond sellers, and across the street, **Bonebakker** (Rokin 88/90, tel. 020/623–2294) is one of the city's oldest and finest jewelers. At the head of the Kalverstraat, **Schaap and Citroen** (Kalverstraat 1, tel. 020/626–6691) is a century-old jeweler and watch dealer.

On Rokin, **Premsula & Hamburger** (Rokin, tel. 020/624–9688; closed weekends) has sold fine antique silver and jewelry since 1823. On Nieuwe Spiegelstraat, two other dealers are **Schilling** (Nieuwe Spiegelstraat 23, tel. 020/623–93–66) and **A.S.M. Hemke Kuilboer** (Nieuwe Spiegelstraat 52, tel. 020/624–62–85).

Duty-Free If you find you have no time to shop in Amsterdam, save your guilders for the airport. **Amsterdam Airport Shopping Centre** (Box 7501, 1118 ZG Schiphol Airport Holland, tel. 020/601–2497) is bigger, better, and cheaper than almost any other airport duty-free shopping area in the world. The departure hall at Amsterdam Schiphol Airport looks more like a shopping mall than a transportation facility, and auxiliary shops for the most popular items (liquor, perfume, chocolates) are found in every wing of the terminal.

Men's Clothes In addition to the main department stores, which have good men's departments, the best places to shop for menswear in Amsterdam are on the Kalverstraat or in the P.C. Hoofstraat/Van Baerlestraat shopping district. Two of the best shops are **Meddens** (Heiligeweg 11–17, tel. 020/624–0461) and **The English Hatter** (Heiligeweg 40, tel. 020/623–4781). There are nearly a dozen shops on the P.C. (pronounced "pay-say"). For conservative clothes, try **Richfield** (P.C. Hoofstraat 58, tel. 020/675–6203), **McGregor** (P.C. Hoofstraat 113, tel. 020/662–7425), **Mulberry Company** from England (P.C. Hoofstraat 46, tel. 020/673–8080), and **Society Shop** (Van Baerlestraat 20, tel. 020/664–9281). For more highly styled apparel, head to **Players** (Singel 540, tel. 020/626–8005), **Dik** (P.C. Hoofstraat 35, tel. 020/662–4328), **Inpetto** (P.C. Hoofstraat 53, tel. 020/675–1676), **Ogger** (P.C. Hoofstraat 81, tel. 020/676–8695) and **Gaudi** (P.C. Hoofstraat 116, tel. 020/679–9319).

Women's Clothes Dutch women are conscious of their clothes, although they tend to be conservative in both style and colors. The department stores carry mainstream styles, while boutiques along the side streets between the canals and in the Jordaan neighborhood are where generation after generation of experimental designers have set up shop to show their imaginative creations. Antique- and used-clothing shops also can be found in these parts of town. Two Dutch minichains stand out among the crowd for the quality of both design and craftsmanship; they are **Claudia Strater** (Beethovenstraat 9, tel. 020/673–6605) and **Boetiek Pauw** (van Baerlestrasse 66 and 72, tel. 020/662–6253), which also operates men's and children's shops. At Spui, you will find **Esprit** (tel. 020/626–3624), but some of the best shopping for women's clothes in a variety of styles is in the P.C. Hoofstraat/Van Baerlestraat shopping area, including **Reflections** (P.C. Hoofstraat 77, tel. 020/664–6772), **Champs Élysées** (Strawinskylaan 63, tel. 020/671–6499), **Benetton** (P.C. Hoofstraat 72, tel. 020/679–5706), **Alain Manoukian** (P.C. Hoofstraat 95, tel. 020/673–3822), **Max Mara** (P.C. Hoofstraat 110, tel. 020/671–7742), **Leeser** (P.C. Hoofstraat 117, tel. 020/679–5020), **Azzurro** (Van Baerlestraat 17, tel. 020/671–6804), and designer **Edgar Vos** (P.C. Hoofstraat 134, tel. 020/662–6336).

Shoes and Hats For men, **Bally Shoes** is on the Leidsestraat (8–10, tel. 020/622–2888). For women's shoes, three of the best shops are **Smit Bally** (Leidsestraat 41, tel. 020/624–8862), **Charles Adams** (P.C. Hoofstraat 90, tel. 020/662–3835), and **Shoe Ba Loo** (Koningsplein 7, tel. 020/626–7993). **Houden M/V** (422 Herengracht, tel. 020/626–3038) is a well-stocked hat shop in a canal house with Borsalino hats for men and women as well as Dutch and international designer hats.

Sports and Fitness

Biking The most convenient place to rent a bicycle is **Centraal Station** (Stationsplein 15, 1012 AB, tel. 020/620–2266) or **Koenders Take-a-Bike** (Stationsplein 33, 1012 AB, tel. 020/624–8391). Expect to pay from Fl 7 per day, plus a deposit from Fl 50 to Fl 200 per bicycle.

Golf The new and luxurious **Golf Resort Purmerend** (NHM Hotels, Westerweg 60, 1445 AD Purmerend, tel. 03438/15304, fax 03438/12336) is now open outside Amsterdam in Noord Holland province.

Health Clubs Several hotels in Amsterdam have fitness facilities for guests; these facilities generally include exercise machines, weights, sauna, and whirlpool. The **Holiday Inn Crowne Plaza** (N.Z. Voorburgwal 5, 1012 RC, tel. 020/620–0500) has a large indoor swimming pool. Two of the more comprehensive hotel-based fitness facilities are **Splash Sonesta** (Kattengat 1, tel. 020/271044) and **Splash Palace Executive Fitness Club** (Prins Hendrikkade 59–72, tel. 020/556–4899), both of which offer personal training, aerobics, weight training, massage, solarium, Turkish bath, sauna, and whirlpool. **Sporting Club Leidseplein** (18 Korte Leidsedwarsstraat, tel. 020/620–6631) offers fitness facilities, sauna and super-fast tanners. Day rates at all of the above are Fl 25, with extra charges for special services.

Jogging Sunday morning is about the only time in Amsterdam when it is possible to jog in the city center. **Vondelpark** (Vondel Park), near the art museums, and **Oosterpark** (Eastern Park), behind the Tropenmuseum, are the only parks within the city proper. Beyond the city near the suburb of Amstelveen, **Amsterdamse Bos** (Amsterdam Woods) is a large and spacious place to run.

Squash The **Sporting Club Leidseplein** (18 Korte Leidsedwarsstraat, tel. 020/620–6631) is a squash and fitness club. There are eight courts (sauna use is included); you can rent equipment as well, and instruction is available. Day cards for all facilities are Fl 25, weekdays until 4 PM; services are priced separately in the evening and on the weekend.

Spectator Sports

Rowing There are monthly rowing events at Stedelijk Beheer Sport en Recreatie (tel. 020/643–1414) in **Amsterdamse Bos** (Amsterdam Woods), a large park located south of the city. There are also canoeing events four times a year in the Bos. In the city, the **Dutch Marine Academy** stages a rowing event (tel. 020/624–7699) on the canals in September.

Soccer Soccer is a near obsession with the Dutch, and if you want to impress an Amsterdam host, you would best be advised to know the current standing of the local team, Ajax (pronounced "eye-axe"), relative to that of its archrivals, Rotterdam's Feyenoord (pronounced "fie-nord") and PSV (Philips Sports Vereninging). The Dutch soccer season runs from August to June, with a short break in midwinter; matches are played at the **Ajaxstadion** (Ajax Stadium; Middenweg 401, tel. 020/665–4440).

Beaches

After their long, dreary winter, Amsterdammers count the days until they can hit the beaches at **Zandvoort,** a beach community directly west of the city, beyond Haarlem, where clean beachfront stretches for miles and many of the dunes are open for walking. The train station is close by, and there are lifeguards on duty. Separate areas of the beach are reserved for nudists, though topless bathing is common practice everywhere in the Netherlands.

Dining

Like everyone, Amsterdammers enjoy good food, particularly when shared with good company. In couples or small groups, they seek out the quieter, cozier places or go in search of the new culinary stars of the city; to celebrate or entertain, they return to the institutions that never disappoint them with the quality of their cuisine or service; and in large groups, you invariably find the Dutch trooping into their favorite Indonesian restaurant to share a *rijstafel* (rice served with many small meat, poultry, and vegetable dishes). There are more than 700 restaurants in Amsterdam spanning a wide variety of ethnic cuisines. Styles range from international fast-food joints to chandeliered waterfront dining rooms frequented by the royal family. In between you'll find small, chef-owned establishments on the canals and their side streets, restaurants that have stood the test of time on the basis of service, ambience, and consistency.

Very Expensive **Dikker en Thijs.** This gracious restaurant overlooks the busy corner of the Leidestraat and the Prinsengracht from the second floor of a French-style, late-19th-century building. It is a quiet place, with large well-spaced tables and patient service that encourages diners to linger over their coffee. Chefs Wim Bastiaanse and Jan Borst have brought an imaginative touch to the traditional cuisine that has been produced at this restaurant since it first opened in 1915. Among the selections you might find on the menu are turbot salad on artichoke hearts with olive paste, lamb cutlet with salami, and *zeeduivel* (fish) with sauerkraut. *Prinsengracht 444, tel. 020/626–7721. Reservations advised. Jacket and tie required. AE, DC, MC, V. Closed Sun. and Aug. 3–16.*

★ **Excelsior.** The Excelsior's view over the Amstel River, to the Muntplein on one side and to the Music Theater on the other, is the best there is in Amsterdam. The dining room is a gracious, chandeliered hall with plenty of room for diners, waiters, dessert trolleys, preparation carts, towering palms, tall candelabras, and a grand piano. The approach is traditional French with a twist: You might choose from smoked eel with dill, potato soup with caviar, lobster salad with smoked goose liver, fillet of halibut with caper sauce, and breast of dove with mushrooms and truffles. For dessert, try the orange pie with frozen yogurt. There are five prix fixe menus. *Hotel de L'Europe, Nieuwe Doelenstraat 2–8, tel. 020/623–4836. Reservations advised. Jacket and tie required. AE, DC, MC, V.*

De Kersuntuin. De Kersuntuin means "cherry orchard," and cherry red is the overwhelming color of the decor and dinnerware at this cheerful restaurant. The ceilings are high, and the large windows overlook a residential street. It is a good place for a leisurely meal, although some complaints about service may be justified; see for yourself. Chef Jon Sistermans is the star here: The kitchen is open behind glass panels, and you are welcome to watch the chef and his staff prepare such specialties as fried eel with parsley sauce, ravioli of truffles, and goose liver with carpaccio of goose breast and rosemary. *Dijsselhofplantsoen 7, tel. 020/664–2121. Reservations required. Jacket and tie required. AE, DC, MC, V. Closed Sun.*

Lido. Located on the site of the original 1930s Lido theater restaurant, the new Lido is part of the complex that incorporates the Holland Casino Amsterdam. The Lido is actually several restaurants in one: The quiet dinner restaurant, Gauguin, mixes French and Asian cuisines with menu choices such as pork with sesame pasta, grilled tuna with adzuki beans, or rice parfait with kiwi sauce. The pièce de résistance is the Lido Dinner Show, where for Fl 200, diners enjoy a four-course dinner served by waiters and waitresses who then perform a lively musical revue. *Leidsekade 105, tel. 020/626–2106. Reservations required. Jacket and tie required. AE, DC, MC, V. Closed Sun.–Wed.*

Les Quatre Canetons. The Four Ducklings is a very personal, chef-owned Amsterdam institution. Chef/owner Wynand Vogel shows some flair in his traditional offerings: Try stuffed roast suckling pig, a combination of three goose livers, envelope of tongue with salmon and salmon roe, or goose steak with marinated red-pepper kernels. The wine cellar here is well stocked. There is also a vegetarian menu. *Prinsengracht 1111, tel. 020/624–6307. Reservations advised. Jacket and tie required. AE, DC, MC, V. Closed Sun.*

De Trechteur. Located beside a canal in the residential part of the city, this very small restaurant has a very big reputation, so reservations, if you can get them, are absolutely necessary. Chef Jan de Wit offers such specialties as carpaccio of Angus beef and Scotch salmon, fillet of lamb in potato crust with ratatouille and rosemary sauce, or smoked oxtails with cubes of goose liver, garlic mayonnaise, and croutons. *Hobbemakade 62–63, tel. 020/671–1263, fax 020/685–2571. Reservations necessary. Jacket and tie required. AE, DC, MC, V. Closed Sun.–Mon.*

Expensive **Beddington's.** The decor is eye-catching, and the location is good: Near the Concertgebouw and the art museums, Beddington's sits at the junction between the business district and the city's most prestigious modern residential neighborhoods. The chef is an Englishwoman with a multicultural approach in the kitchen, mixing Japanese and other East Asian influences with English, Spanish, and even West Indian concepts. A sample of the sort of imaginative meal you might put together for yourself here would be *zeeduvil* (fish) tandoori followed by—why not?—trifle. *Roelof Hartstraat 6–8, tel. 020/676–5201. Reservations advised. Jacket required. AE, DC, MC, V. Closed Sun.*

★ **Café Americain.** Though thousands of buildings in Amsterdam are designated as historic monuments, this is the only one where the interior, an Art Deco treasure, is also protected. Opened in 1882 and said to have been the site of Mata Hari's wedding reception, the Americain is a hybird restaurant-café serving everything from light snacks to full dinners. To one side are formal tables topped with white linens, where traditional entrées such as medallions of beef with béarnaise sauce are served; to the other side are tiny bare-topped tables, per-

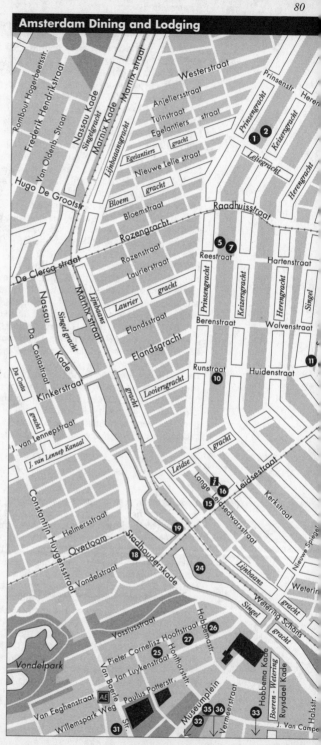

Amsterdam Dining and Lodging

Dining
Beddington's, **35**
Brasserie Lido, **24**
Brasserie
van Baerle, **32**
Cafe Americain, **19**
Caffe Esprit, **13**
Christophe, **1**
De Kersuntuin, **36**
De Kooning
van Siam, **9**
De Oesterbar, **15**
De Prinsenkelder, **16**
De Trechteur, **33**
Dikker en Thijs, **16**
D'Vijff Vlieghen, **11**
Dynasty, **20**
Excelsior, **23**
Haesje Claes, **12**
Het Tuynhuis, **21**
Keyzer, **31**
Les Quatre
Canetons, **30**
Lido, **24**
Manchurian, **15**
Meghna, **28**
Padi Mas, **25**
Sama Sebo, **26**
Sancerre, **7**
Sluizer, **29**
Tony's Pasta and Pizza
Company, **22**
Tout Court, **10**
Treasure, **6**

Lodging
American, **19**
Amstel Hotel, **34**
Avenue Hotel, **3**
Canal House, **2**
De l'Europe, **23**
Golden Tulip Barbizon
Centre, **18**
Golden Tulip Barbizon
Palace, **4**
Grand Amsterdam, **14**
Jan Luyken, **27**
Pulitzer, **5**
SAS Royal Hotel, **17**
Swissôtel Amsterdam
Ascot, **8**

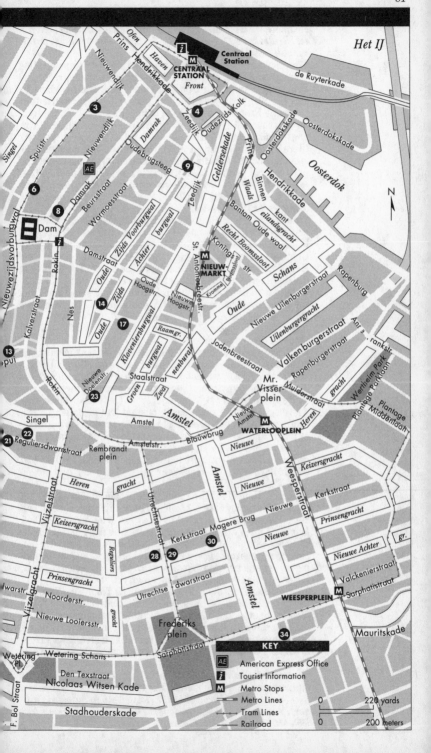

Het IJ

Centraal Station

i

M CENTRAAL STATION
Front

de Ruyterkade

Ofen

Prins Hendrikkade

Haven

Oosterdokskade

3

Nieuwendijk

Zeedijk

Oudezijds Kolk

Prins

Oosterdok

4

Singel

Spuistr.

Damrak

Oudebrugsteeg

Gelderschekade

Hendrikkade

AE

9

Binnen

Waals

kant

eilandsgracht

6

Beursstraat

Warmoesstraat

Oude Zijds Voorburgwal

Zeedijk

Bantam Oude waal

Recht Boomssloot

8

Damrak

Dijk

St. Antoniesbreestr.

Konings str.

Oude

Schans

Rapenburg

Nieuwezijdsvoorburgwal

Dam

i

Damstraat

Achter burgwal

Oude Hoogstr.

Nieuwe Hoogstr.

M NIEUW-MARKT

Kromme Waal (Oo...straat)

Oude

Nieuwe Uilenburgerstraat

Uilenburgergracht

Rokin

Kalverstraat

Nes

14

Oude Zijds

17

Kloveniersburgwal

Raamgr.

Jodenbreestraat

Valkenburgerstraat

Rapenburgerstraat

Anne Frankstr.

13
pui

Nieuwe Doelenstr.

Staalstraat

Groen burgwal

Zuid enburg...

Mr. Visser-plein

Muiderstraat

Wertheim Park
plantae Parklaan

Plantage Middenlaan

23

Amstel

Amstel

Nieuwe Amstel

Blauwbrug

Nieuwe Amstel

M WATERLOOPLEIN

Heren

Plantage

21 **22** Reguliersdwarsstraat

Singel

Rembrandt plein

Amstelstr.

Nieuwe

Keizersgracht

Heren gracht

Amstel

Nieuwe

Weesperstraat

Kerkstraat

Vizelstraat

Keizersgracht

Nieuwe

Magere Brug

Prinsengracht

Reguliers

Kerkstraat

Magere Brug

30

Nieuwe

Nieuwe Achter

gr.

Prinsengracht

28 **29**

Utrechtse dwarstraat

Nieuwe

Valckenierstraat

dwarstraat

Amstel

Sarphatistraat

Noorderstr.

gracht

Nieuwe Looiersstr.

M WEESPERPLEIN

Frederiks plein

Wetering Pl.

Wetering Schans

Sarphatistraat

Mauritskade

34

KEY

Den Texstraat

Nicolaas Witsen Kade

AE American Express Office

i Tourist Information

M Metro Stops

F. Bol Straat

Stadhouderskade

Metro Lines

Tram Lines

Railroad

0 — 220 yards

0 — 200 meters

fect for a quick coffee and pastry. There is a well-stocked buffet complete with hot dishes, salads, and desserts. *American Hotel, Leidsekade 97, tel. 020/624–5322. No reservations. Dress: casual/jacket. AE, DC, MC, V.*

Christophe. Christophe Royer opened his *eet tempel* (eating temple) on a small cross canal between the Keizersgracht and Prinsengracht, not far from the Anne Frank House, where he and his all-French kitchen staff were quickly recognized for their fine French cuisine. Some of Royer's specialties are Indian corn soup with oysters, *crevettes à l'orange* (shrimp with orange sauce), and *pigeon à la marocaine* (Moroccan pigeon); there is also a selection of vegetarian dishes. The menu may be special, but at Christophe's, the welcoming atmosphere and personalized service are worth noting as well. *Leliegracht 46, tel. 020/625–0807. Reservations required. Jacket and tie required. AE, DC, MC, V. Closed Sun.–Mon., New Year's week and 2 weeks in July–Aug.*

Dynasty. At this trendy, interesting spot, the decor is a fanciful mating of Oriental and Art Deco. A mural in red, white, and black encircles the room, and dozens of amber and dove-gray Chinese paper umbrellas hang upended from the ceiling. Chef K.Y. Lee's menu is as fascinating as the decor: The medley of Asian cuisines includes authentically prepared, classic Chinese dishes, such as Three Meats in Harmony, and selections from the cuisines of Thailand, Malaysia, and Vietnam. There are two prix fixe menus. *Reguliersdwarsstraat 30, tel. 020/626–8400. Reservations advised. Jacket required. AE, DC, MC, V. Closed Tues.*

De Prinsenkelder. Though it's especially pleasant in summer, when the doors are thrown open and tables overflow outside, a visit to this former warehouse cellar is a trip into the history of Amsterdam at any time. The ceiling is beamed, the walls are whitewashed, and the floor is tiled in traditional black-and-white squares; one could easily mistake the place for a 17th-century guild meeting room. The kitchen produces a traditional menu and specializes in house pâtés and straightforward dishes such as leek soup, steamed halibut with butter sauce, and medallions of veal with mustard sauce. *Prinsengracht 438, tel. 020/626–7721. Reservations advised. Jacket and tie required. AE, DC, MC, V. Closed Mon.*

Sancerre. Named for the region that produced the wines that fill its cellar, Sancerre is the home of imaginative French cuisine. The kitchen is directed by an award-winning young chef, Martin Hoppers, who offers choices such as fried mussels with sesame seeds and curried beurre blanc, or guinea hen with fennel and gorgonzola. There are several prix fixe menus, including a vegetarian one. *Reestraat 28–34, tel. 020/627–8794. Reservations advised. Jacket required. AE, DC, MC, V.*

★ **Tout Court.** Chef John Fagel, who hails from a well-known Dutch family of chefs, has stuck by his intention to serve "good food without a fuss." This comfortable, casual restaurant is tucked away on a side street between the canals: You'll know it by the napkins that hang in the window, as if strung on a laundry line. The menu is direct and uncomplicated, with selections such as roasted rib of lamb with basil, guinea fowl stuffed with mushrooms, roast brill with leeks, and watercress soup. At dinner there are three menus, including a seven-course feast. *Runstraat 13, tel. 020/625–8637. Reservations advised (dinner), required (cooking lessons). Dress: casual/jacket. AE, DC, MC, V. Closed Sun.–Mon.*

Het Tuynhuis. This stylish newcomer to the Reguliersdwars-straat's restaurant row is drawing crowds of Amsterdammers in search of the latest and best. The cream-white and black tile, art deco–inspired borders and panels, and frothy palms that separate the tables create a feeling of the Riviera. The menu is French, with selections such as crisp fried sweetbreads with mustard sauce, roasted lamb kidneys, grilled quail, and, after dinner, gratinéed goat cheese. Beyond the French doors is a spacious summer garden. There are three menus, including a theater menu. *Reguliersdwarsstraat 28, tel. 020/627–6603. Reservations advised. Jacket required. AE, DC, MC, V.*

D'Vijff Vlieghen. Dining in a traditional canal-house environment is part of the Amsterdam experience, though you are more likely to find yourself seated among closely packed tables of Swedes and Japanese than with Dutch diners. But don't let that stop you. "The Five Flies" is one of the city's best-known restaurants, and its menu has recently undergone a major face-lift. Long a follower of the meat-and-potatoes approach to traditional Dutch fare, it now makes greater use of fresh native ingredients. The menu offers choices such as smoked calves' tongue on spinach, baby turbot with bay, and pheasant with endive. Housed in five adjoining houses that date from 1627, the restaurant incorporates a series of small timbered dining rooms, each well adorned with mementoes and bric-a-brac ranging from music boxes, liqueur kegs, and violin cases to two etchings by Rembrandt. *Spuistraat 294–302, tel. 020/624–8369. Reservations advised. Jacket and tie required. AE, DC, MC, V.*

Moderate **Brasserie van Baerle.** Begun as a neighborhood lunch and Sunday brunch restaurant, it now even draws late diners who come following performances at the Concertgebouw nearby. The restaurant is bright and appealing, with an uncomplicated European modern decor, but Chef Esther Hageman's creativity is the main attraction. Imaginative dishes from the kitchen include fried brill prepared with fresh ginger, leek, and shiitake mushrooms served in a rice paper wrap. There is outdoor dining in good weather. *Van Baerlestraat 158, tel. 020/679–1532. Reservations accepted. Dress: casual/jacket. AE, DC, MC, V. Closed Sat., Dec. 25–Jan. 2.*

Brasserie Lido. The Brasserie is the heart of the new Lido dining and casino complex at Leidseplein; it is a relaxing place, with tall windows overlooking the boardwalk and terrace to the canal. It's open all day and into the night for everything from breakfast and light snacks to complete suppers. Choices include French, Dutch, or Morning After (including Alka-Seltzer) breakfasts; quiches and Chinese dim sum, and for dinner, leg of rabbit with leeks and prunes. *Leidsekade 105, tel. 020/626–2106. No reservations. Dress: casual. AE, DC, MC, V.*

★ **Keyzer.** After 85 years spent serving musicians, concert goers, and residents of the neighborhoods surrounding the art museums and Concertgebouw, the Keyzer has evolved into something as familiar and comfortable as an old shoe. Come to this half restaurant, half café-bodega in almost any attire, at almost any hour, for a simple drink or a full meal. Everything about this place is traditional: The interior is paneled with dark woods, the lights are dim, and oriental carpets cover the tables. The menu is largely traditional as well—among the meat and fish selections are tournedos, schnitzel, and sole meunière—though you may also come across a more adventurous *ris de* *veau* (veal sweetbreads) with orange and green pepper sauce or fricassee of veal with nut-basil sauce. *Van Baerlestraat 96, tel. 020/671-1441. Reservations advised. Dress: casual/jacket. AE, DC, MC, V. Closed Sun.*

De Kooning van Siam. This restaurant sits smack in the middle of the red-light district, but don't let that deter you from enjoying a meal in the Thai restaurant that is favored by Amsterdam's Thai population. While the beams and wall panels are still visible in this old canal house, there is nothing Old Dutch about the furniture or wall decorations. Choices are somewhat limited: Selections might include very hot stir-fried beef with onion and chili peppers, or a milder chicken and Chinese vegetables with coconut, curry, and basil. *Oude Zijds Voorburgwal 42, tel. 020/623-7293. Reservations accepted. Jacket required. AE, DC, MC, V. Closed Dec. 25, Dec. 31, Feb.*

Manchurian. Vivid touches of Chinese red and black, standing urns, and Oriental statuary set the tone here. The menu is richly varied, with selections representing a number of Southeast Asian cuisines; Manchurian also offers rijstafel. There is a prix fixe menu that might include Szechuan beef, Hong Kong crisp duck, or a simple steamed fish in season. The wine list is extensive. *Leidseplein 10A, tel. 020/623-1330. Reservations advised. Jacket required. AE, DC, MC, V. Closed Jan.*

Meghna. This comfortable, friendly Indian restaurant is part of a small restaurant row among the neighborhood shops of the Utrechtsestraat. Small and darkly decorated, it is the pride and joy of owner/chef Roy Sankar. Prices are quite reasonable, and there are two prix fixe menus that are good values: choices might include *rogan josh*, a mild and creamy East Indian fish curry, or chicken tandoori badami with cashew nuts. *Utrechtesstraat 28, tel. 020/625-1392. Reservations not necessary. Dress: casual/jacket. AE, DC, MC, V.*

De Oesterbar. "The Oyster Bar," like its namesake in New York, is an Amsterdam institution and the first place to think of when you hanker for a half dozen oysters fresh from the Oosterschelde or the simply prepared catch of the day. There is no prix fixe, but the choices are straightforward: grilled, baked, or fried fish served with tartar sauce, potatoes, and salad. Live lobster is also available in season. The no-nonsense main-floor room, which has a small bar at the back, has white tile walls incorporating nautical murals and a long row of eerily lighted fish tanks along one side of the restaurant. In the upstairs dining room, the mood is oddly bordellolike, with elaborately patterned wallpaper and an assortment of innocuous paintings dotted around the walls. *Leidseplein 10, tel. 020/623-2988. Reservations advised. Dress: casual/jacket. AE, DC, MC.*

Padi Mas. The new owners have high hopes that theirs will be the next star in the firmament of top Dutch restaurants, with their interpretations of traditional Indonesian dishes. Found among the shops on the fashionable P.C. Hooftstraat shopping street, this small dining room is also convenient to the Concertgebouw and the art museums. The decor is straightforward to the point of being boring, but that, too, may change. Two rijstafels are served (with 15 and 17 dishes), and a children's menu is available. *P.C. Hooftstraat 87, 020/664-6421. Reservations suggested. Dress: casual/jacket. AE, DC, MC, V.*

Sluizer. Sluizer is really two side-by-side restaurants—one serves only fish, the other serves only meats. Both are simply decorated and unpretentious; both are known for good food that is honestly prepared without a lot of fanfare or creativity; both are known to be reasonably priced; and, not surprisingly, both are crowded every night. *Utrechtsestraat 43, tel. 020/622–6376. Reservations advised. Dress: casual. AE, DC, MC, V.*

Treasure. This traditional Chinese restaurant has its own very loyal following in this neighborhood near Dam Square. Peking duck is a specialty of the house; the menu also offers samples from the Szechwan, Peking, Shanghai, and Mongolian cuisines. Owner Ho Min Kin contributed his own figurative paintings to the decor. *N.Z. Voorburgwal 115, tel. 020/626–0915. Reservations suggested. Jacket required. AE, DC, MC, V.*

Inexpensive **Caffe Esprit.** Clean-cut and trendy, it has tall windows that
★ overlook the busy Spui square; the decor is simple black, white, and gray. There is just a handful of small tables, with a small counter to take care of overflow. The menu is California American in character, with choices such as a Surf Burger garnished with avocado and bacon, or an Archie Bunker burger covered with melted swiss cheese. Salads include Chinese almond chicken and spinach salad with hot tarragon mustard dressing. There also are pastas, pizzas, sandwiches; at breakfast (served until noon) fresh-squeezed orange juice is available, as well as yogurt with muesli and scones with butter and jam. There is a children's menu. *Spui 10, tel. 020/627–8281. No reservations. Dress: casual. No credit cards. Closed Sun.*

Haesje Claes. This is as Old Dutch cozy as you can get. The beams are dark and heavy, the walls are chockablock with copper pots and farmstead curios, and the lampshades that hang low over the tabletops are draped with kerchiefs in the traditional way to shadow the light. The food, too, is Old Dutch, and the prices are as basic as the food. Come here for calves' liver with bacon and onions, or tournedos with pepper sauce. A nightly tourist menu is served; there also is a children's menu. *Spuistraat 273–275, tel. 020/624–9998. No reservations. Dress: casual. AE, DC, MC, V. Closed Sun.*

Sama Sebo. Come to this relaxed neighborhood Indonesian restaurant near the State Museum for rijstafel, a simple *bami goreng* (spicy fried rice with vegetables), or a *nasi goreng* (spicy fried noodles with vegetables) lunch. The colors are muted tans and browns with rush mats covering the walls. This is a small restaurant, and when it's busy it can be somewhat cramped. *P.C. Hoofstraat 27, tel. 020/662–8146. Reservations accepted. Dress: casual. AE, DC, MC, V. Closed Sun.*

Tony's Pasta and Pizza Company. Although trendy decor seems to be the criterion for success on the Reguliersdwarsstraat, not all the restaurants in the row are expensive. Tony's is a bright and cheerful place decorated in Italian red, white, and green, with small white tables and stiff black chairs that don't encourage anyone to linger over any long, relaxing meals. Pizzas, pastas, and simple grilled meats are offered. *Reguliersdwarsstraat 55, tel. 020/627–3833. Reservations not necessary. Dress: casual. AE, DC, MC, V.*

Lodging

There are some 270 hotels to choose among in Amsterdam, though most are small mom-and-pop operations, best described as pensions, found along and among the canals or in residential neighborhoods beyond the center. The larger hotels, including the expensive international chains, are clustered in the area around Central Station, at Dam Square, and near Leidseplein. Amsterdam is a busy city; reservations are advised at any time of the year and absolutely necessary in tulip season (late Mar.–June). Should you arrive without a room, the **VVV Logiesservice** (VVV Accommodation Service, Stationsplein 10 or Leidsestraat 106, open Easter–Sept., daily 9–5; Oct.–Easter, Mon.–Sat. 9–5) is a same-day hotel booking service that helps you find a room for a modest service charge of Fl 3.50.

Very Expensive
★
Amstel Hotel. After months of renovation, this grand old 125-year-old hotel reopened in 1992 with a completely new interior designed by Pierre Yves Rochon of Paris, who has created a Dutch atmosphere with a European touch. The Amstel's rooms always have been the most spacious in the city; they still are, and the new decor is like that of a gracious home, with Oriental rugs, brocade upholstery, Delft lamps, and a color scheme that borrows from the warm tones of Makkum pottery. Everything about this hotel has been reconsidered and redesigned, including the format of its well-known restaurant, La Rive. *Professor Tulpplein 1, tel. 020/622–6060, fax 020/622–5808. 79 rooms with bath. Facilities: 2 restaurants, sauna, fitness center, swimming pool. AE, DC, MC, V.*

The Grand Amsterdam. This hotel is located on a historically important site—it was built into a group of buildings dating from the 14th century that served for more than 185 years as the Town Hall of Amsterdam. Maria de Medici once stayed here, as did William of Orange, and it was the site of Queen Beatrix's wedding. The hotel that has been incorporated into these buildings is a deluxe property. Special touches include Gobelin tapestries, Jugendstil stained-glass windows, and, in the café, a wall mural by Karl Appel created early in his career to repay a debt to the city of Amsterdam. The rooms vary in size and are attractively done in deep tones of burgundy damask and bold floral prints; the best of them overlook the garden courtyard. *Oude Zijds Voorburgwal 197, tel. 020/555–3111. 170 rooms with bath. Facilities: 2 restaurants, sauna, solarium, heated swimming pool. AE, DC, MC, V.*

Expensive
★
De l'Europe. Quiet, gracious, and understated in both decor and service, the hotel lives by its motto, "Where stylishness is a tradition." Overlooking the Amstel River, the Muntplein, and the flower market, its location near the Music Theater is one of Amsterdam's most convenient. Rooms are not as large as you might wish, but the lack of elbow room is generally compensated for by the views through the tall French windows that let in generous amounts of light. The marble baths are large and luxurious. A junior suite might be a worthwhile choice here. *Nieuwe Doelenstraat 2–8, tel. 020/623–4836, fax 020/524–2962. 101 rooms. Facilities: restaurant, sauna, solarium, fitness room, small swimming pool. AE, DC, MC, V.*

Golden Tulip Barbizon Centre. The intimate lobby and minimal public spaces belie the size and popularity of this elegant but unpretentious hotel overlooking the busy Leidseplein. Personal and congenial service is an outstanding characteristic of this hotel, and its location is one of the best in Amsterdam: The historic city center is a short walk or tram ride in one direction, and the art museums, shops, and Concertgebouw are a short walk in the other. Rooms are somewhat small, but are brightly decorated and thoughtfully equipped with two phones.

Stadhouderskade 7, tel. 020/685–1351. 239 rooms. Facilities: restaurant, bar, fitness center, sauna. AE, DC, MC, V.

Golden Tulip Barbizon Palace. One of the newest hotels in Amsterdam also has one of the most convenient locations, directly across from Central Station. The exterior was designed to blend with the neighboring row of old houses overlooking the inner harbor. Inside, however, the historic Amsterdam mood is replaced by a towering, skylighted, Roman-atrium-style lobby that stretches across the full length of the hotel, with cafés, shops, restaurants, and club rooms opening to the sides. Guest rooms are small, but they are decorated nicely and support the Old Dutch theme with dark beams across the ceilings. *Prins Hendrikkade 59–72, tel. 020/556–4564. 268 rooms with bath. Facilities: 2 restaurants, fitness center. AE, DC, MC, V.*

Moderate **American.** The American is one of the oldest hotels in Amster-
★ dam, housed in one of the city's most fancifully designed buildings. Its location directly on the Leidseplein is ideal for anyone who likes to be in the middle of everything—nightlife, dining, sightseeing, and shopping are all near at hand. A complete renovation in the late 1980s did wonders for the place: Rooms are comfortably sized and furnished in an art deco style. *Leidsekade 97, tel. 020/624–5322. 188 rooms with bath. Facilities: restaurant, fitness room. AE, DC, MC, V.*

Pulitzer. Twenty-four 17th-century houses were combined to create this hotel, which faces both the Prinsengracht and the Keizersgracht canals and is just a short walk from Dam Square. The beamed ceilings in most guest rooms help to maintain the historic atmosphere fitting for these old buildings, and, thankfully, the central gardens in the middle of the block were left open. From here you may hear the hourly chiming of the Westerkerk clock, located nearby. Renovations are in the works, but even in its current worn state, the Pulitzer is one of the best places to stay to experience some of Amsterdam's historic ambience. *Prinsengracht 315–331, tel. 020/523–5235. 236 rooms with bath. Facilities: restaurant. AE, DC, MC, V.*

SAS Royal Hotel. Located on a side street in the oldest part of the city, not far from the Muziektheater, is one of the newest hotels in Amsterdam. The lobby features a towering, skylighted atrium with a Japanese garden—in contrast, the adjoining bar is housed in the vicarage of an old church that previously stood on the site. A second building filled with guest rooms is located across the street and is connected to the main hotel by underground passage. Rooms are comfortable in size and are furnished in Dutch, Scandinavian, or Oriental decor. *Rusland 17, tel. 020/623–1231. 245 rooms with bath. Facilities: 2 restaurants, sauna, solarium, fitness room. AE, DC, MC, V.*

Inexpensive **Avenue Hotel.** Fully renovated in 1990, the Avenue is a stylish,
★ miniature version of its large, chain-hotel neighbors on the Nieuwe Zijds Voorburgwal. The staff is uniformed, the rooms and baths are larger than one would expect in this level of hotel, and the decor, done in restful moss green and khaki, is fashionably contemporary. Located not far from Central Station, this is one of the best values in Amsterdam. *Nieuwe Zijds Voorburgwal 27, tel. 020/623–8307. 51 rooms with bath. Facilities: elevator. AE, DC, MC, V.*

★ **Canal House.** This is what you imagine a canal-house hotel to be like: a beautiful old home with high plastered ceilings, antique furniture, and old paintings, and a backyard garden bursting with plants and flowers. Rooms are unique in both size and decor, and antiques are found throughout. The elegant chandeliered breakfast room overlooks the garden, and there is a small bar in the front parlor. The American owners have put a lot of love and style into the Canal House: The end result is an intimate hotel that seems more like the private home of a well-to-do family. *Keizersgracht 148, tel. 020/622–5182. 26 rooms. Facilities: breakfast room, elevator. AE, DC, MC, V.*

★ **Jan Luyken.** This small, out-of-the-way place is barely noticeable among the homes and offices of a residential Amsterdam neighborhood. The personal approach is a relaxing alternative to the large hotels, yet it also is well equipped to handle the needs of the many business travelers who stay here regularly, with office services and small meeting rooms available. *Jan Luykenstraat 58, tel. 020/573–0730. 63 rooms with bath. Facilities: elevators. AE, DC, MC, V.*

Swissotel Amsterdam Ascot. Located just off Dam Square, this attractive Swiss-run hotel has spacious rooms decorated in subtle shades of gray and purple, and marble baths that one would expect to find in a much more expensive hotel. There is a true French-style bistro on the premises, and a no-smoking floor. *Damrak 95–98, tel. 020/626–0066. 109 rooms with bath. Facilities: restaurant. AE, DC, MC, V.*

The Arts and Nightlife

The Arts More than 18,000 performances are staged each year in Amsterdam's theaters, churches, museums, and assorted other locations throughout the city. The arts overflow into the streets as well: There are barrel organs playing on the shopping streets, carillon concerts from the church towers, and impromptu street performers at locations such as Dam Square and Leidseplein.

The grand and elegant new **Muziektheater** (Music Theater, Waterlooplein) is Amsterdam's equivalent of Lincoln Center in New York. It seats 1,600 people and is home to both the Netherlands Opera and the Netherlands National Ballet; it also hosts international opera, ballet, and chamber orchestra performances throughout the year.

Amsterdam's theater and music season begins in September and runs through June, when the Holland Festival of Performing Arts is held. *What's On in Amsterdam* is a comprehensive, English-language publication distributed by the tourist office that lists art and performing-arts events around the city. Look, too, for a magazine called *City Life Amsterdam;* it is a monthly English-language publication sold on newsstands that includes advertisements and listings for movies and clubs. Reserve tickets to performances at the major theaters before your arrival through the **National Reservation Center** (Postbus 404, 2260 AK Leidschendam, tel. 3170/320–2500, telex 33755, fax 3170/320–2611). Tickets can also be purchased in person at the tourist information offices through the **VVV Theater Booking Office** (Stationsplein 10; open Mon.–Sat. 10–4), at the **AUB Ticketshop** (Leidseplein/corner Marnixstraat; open Mon.–Sat. 10–6), or at theater box offices.

Multicultural Performances Three stages known for their eclectic mix of offerings are **Akhnaton** (Nieuwezijdskolk 25, tel. 020/624–3396), which is a multicultural stage that offers, for example, South American or African music at Friday and Saturday night performances;

Paradiso (Weteringschans 6, tel. 020/626–4521 or 020/624–8492), a former church with a calendar of various national and international offerings; and **De Melkweg** (Lijnbaansgracht 234A, tel. 020/624–1777 or 020/624–8492), internationally known as a multicultural center for music, theater, film, and dance, with live music performances every Wednesday and Sunday.

Music   Amsterdam's critically acclaimed **Koninklijk Concertgebouworkest** (Royal Concert Orchestra) is often joined by other internationally known performers. There are two concert halls, large and small, under one roof at the **Concertgebouw** (Concertgebouwplein 2–6, tel. 020/671–8345). Contemporary music is on the program at **IJsbreker** (Weesperzijde 23, tel. 020/668–1805).

Opera and Ballet   **De Nederlandse Opera** (The Netherlands National Opera) and **Het Nationale Ballet** (The Netherlands National Ballet) are the resident companies at Amsterdam's **Muziektheater** (Amstel 3, tel. 020/625–5455). Both offer largely classical repertoires, but the dance company has, in recent years, gained a large measure of fame throughout Europe for its performances of 20th-century ballets as well.

Theater/Cabaret   Performances of American and British plays as well as English-language revues and cabaret are common in multilingual Amsterdam, and touring companies from Broadway and West End musical hits come to town on a regular basis. For traditional theater, check the program of **Stadsschouwburg** (Leidseplein 26, 020/523–7700); for large-scale productions, **Koninklijk Theater Carre** (Amstel 115–125, tel. 020/622–55225); and for cabaret, **Kleine Komedie** (Halvemaansteeg 56, tel. 020/624–0534). Amsterdam's off-Broadway-type theaters, **Frascati** (Nes 63, tel. 020/623–5723 or 020/623–5724) and **Brakke Grond** (Nes 45, tel. 020/624–0394), are found on a small street off Dam Square.

Film   First-run American feature films are common and are usually shown undubbed: It's like you never left home. Cinemas are concentrated near the Leidseplein; the largest is the seven-screen **City 1–7** (Kleine Garmanplantsoen 13–25, tel. 020/623–4579); directly across the street is the four-screen **Alfa 1–4** (Kleine Gartmanplantsoen 4A, tel. 020/627–8806). Also near Leidseplein are **Alhambra 1–2** (Weterinschans 134, near Fredericksplein, tel. 020/623–3192), **Bellevue Cinerama** (Marnixstraat 400, tel. 020/623–4876), and **Calypso** (Marnixstraat 402, tel. 020/626–6227). Worth visiting if only to have the pleasure of sitting in its Art Deco auditorium is the **Tuschinski** (Reguliersbreestraat 26, tel. 020/626–2633).

Puppets/Marionettes   The young and the young at heart will enjoy puppet and marionette shows at **Amsterdam Marionette Theater** (Nieuwe Jonkerstraat 8, tel. 020/620–8027) and **Mirakel Poppentheater** (Miracle Puppet Theater, Stromarkt 4a, tel. 020/625–5675).

Nightlife   Most of Amsterdam's nightlife is concentrated at Leidseplein and Rembrandtsplein, which bustle until late at night on weekends, and even until a relatively late hour during the week. The city has something for everyone, be it disco or jazz club, piano bar, or rowdy revue, gay or straight; and if all else fails, you can always fall back on the quieter pleasure of downing a few Dutch beers in a brown café (*see* Brown Cafés *below*). Amsterdam also has a full-scale casino right in the heart of the city.

Nightclub/Casino One of the best additions to the nightlife scene of Amsterdam in recent years is the **Lido Dinner Show** (Leidsestraat 105, tel. 020/626–2106) and, under the same roof, the **Holland Casino Amsterdam** (Max Euweplein 62, tel. 020/620–1006), which is one of the largest in Europe (more than 9,500 square meters/90,000 square feet) and offers everything from your choice of French or American roulette to computerized bingo, with the obligatory slot machines to eat up your supply of loose guilders.

Brown Cafés *Broene cafes* (brown cafés), loosely equivalent to an English pub, are an indispensable part of the city's lifestyle, and they can be found on many corners throughout Amsterdam. A few of the brown cafés you may come across in your travels are **De Admiraal** (Herengracht 319, tel. 020/625–4334), **De Drie Fleschjes** (Gravenstraat 18, tel. 020/624–8443), and **In de Wildeman** (Kolksteeg 3, tel. 020/638–2348). In the Jordaan neighborhood are **Nol** (Westerstraat 109, tel. 020/6245380), **Rooie Nelis** (Laurierstraat 101, tel. 020/624–4167), and **'t Smalle** (Eglantiersgracht 12, tel. 020/623–9617). **De Reiger** (Nieuwe Leliestraat 34, tel. 020/624–7426) has a distinctive Jugendstil bar and serves food. When you want to hear the locals sing folk music on Sunday afternoons, stop by **De Twee Zwaantjes** (Prinsengracht 114, tel. 020/625–2729).

Jazz Clubs The Dutch love jazz, and a number of establishments in Amsterdam have been meccas for music lovers for years. At **Bimhuis** (Oude Schans 73–77, tel. 020/623–3373), the best-known jazz place in town, you'll find top musicians, including avant-gardists, performing on Friday and Saturday nights, and weeknight jam sessions. Other jazz clubs include **Alto** (Korte Leidsedwarsstraat 115, tel. 020/626–3249), **Bamboo Bar** (Lange Leidsedwarsstraat 64, tel. 020/624–3993), **Bourbon Street Jazz & Blues Club** (Leidsekruisstraat 6–8, tel. 020/623–3440); **Grand Jazzcafe de Heeren van Amstel** (Thorbeckeplein 5, tel. 020/620–2173), and **Joseph Lam** (Van Diemenstraat 242, tel. 020/622–8086).

Piano Bars Hotel piano bars include **Le Bar** (Hotel de l'Europe, Nieuwe Doelenstraat 2–8, tel. 020/623–4836) and **Golden Palm Bar** (Grand Hotel Krasnapolsky, Dam 9, tel. 020/554–9111). Others found near Leidseplein and Rembrandtsplein are **Pianobar Maxim** (Leidsekruisstraat 35, tel. 020/624–1920) and **Pianobar the Melody** (Reguliersdwarsstraat 74, tel. 020/626–3962).

Discos and Rock Clubs Among the hotel discos are **Boston Club** (Kattengat 1, tel. 020/624–5561) and **Juliana's** (Apollolaan 138–140, tel. 020/673–7313). Near Leidseplein are **Cash** (Leidseplein 12, tel. 020/627–6544), open Thurs.–Sun. 10 PM–4 AM, and **Hard Rock Cafe** (Korte Leidsedwarsstraat 28–32, tel. 020/625–3180 or 020/626–6422). At Rembrandtsplein there is the huge, popular **Escape** (Rembrandtsplein 11–15, tel. 020/622–3542; open Thurs. and Sun. to 4AM, Fri.–Sat. to 5AM), which can handle 2,500 people dancing to a DJ or live bands. There are also laser light shows and videos here. Not far away is the theatrical **Roxy** (Singel 465, tel. 020/620–0354; open Sun., Wed., and Thurs. to 4 AM, Fri.–Sat. 11 PM–5 AM), which is considered to be the trendiest discotheque in the Netherlands at the moment. **Bunnies** (Korte Leidsedwarsstraat 26, tel. 020/622–6622; open weeknights to 4 AM, Fri.–Sat. to 5 AM) features a mix of house music, Motown, and reggae. **It** (Amstelstraat 24, tel. 020/625–0111; open Thurs.–Sun. to 4 AM) has four bars, special acts and bands, and celebrities in the crowd. This place tends toward a gay crowd on

Friday and Saturday nights, straight on Thursday and Sunday nights. Also attracting an artsy crowd, both gay and straight, is **Mazzo** (Rozengracht 114, tel. 626–7500; open weeknights to 4 AM, Fri.–Sat. to 5 AM), which features trendy dance music and specialty acts and bands. To find a smoke- and alcohol-free dance call **Dance Jam** (tel. 020/644–3571) for the schedule.

Gay Bars   Gay visitors to Amsterdam should check the major newsstands for one of the specialized publications that include ads and listings for entertainment possibilities oriented to the interests of gays and lesbians. The gay scene in Amsterdam is concentrated mostly on Warmoestraat, Reguliersdwarsstraat, Amstelstraat and along the Amstel, and Kerkstraat near Leidseplein. The **Gay & Lesbian Switchboard** can provide information (tel. 020/623–6565, 10–10), as can **COC** action group (Rozenstraat 14, tel. 020/626–3087), which also operates a coffee shop, youth café, pub, and weekly dance.

Gay cafés include **Amstel Taveerne** (Amstel 54, tel. 020/623–4254), **Chez Manfred** (Halvemaansteeg 10, tel. 020/626–4510), **Downtown** (Reguliersdwarsstraat 31, tel. 020/622–9958), and, for lesbians, **Saarein** (Elandsstraat 119, tel. 020/623–4901). **Exit** (Reguliersdwarsstraat 42, tel. 020/625–8788) is a gay discotheque with a large bar.

Excursions from Amsterdam

Numbers in the margin correspond with places of interest in the Excursions from Amsterdam map.

The Bulb Fields and Flower Auction   Though the bulb fields are in full bloom in April and May, flowers are a year-round business in the Netherlands: Visitors in the dead of winter can still gain a sense of the magnitude and magnificence of Dutch tulips and countless other varieties of flowers.

The **Bollenstreek Route** (Bulb District Route) is a special itinerary through the heart of the flower-growing region that was designed by the Dutch auto club, ANWB. The route begins in Oegstgeest, near Leiden, and circles through Rijnsburg (site of one of Holland's three major flower auction houses), the beach communities of Katwijk and Noordwijk, Hillegom, **Lisse** (site of Keukenhof Gardens, *see below*), and Sassenheim. The route is marked with small blue and white signs that read "Bollenstreek."

Keukenhof is a 28-hectare (70-acre) park and greenhouse complex that is especially planted each year to be a special spring exhibition of bulb flowers. It also serves to introduce the newest hybrids developed by Dutch botanists. Keukenhof is open only in April and May. *Lisse, tel. 02521/19034. Admission: Fl. 14 adults, Fl. 6.50 children. Open late Mar.–late May, daily 8 AM–8 PM.*

At any time during the year, it is an easy trip from Amsterdam to the small village of **Aalsmeer.** This is the site of the **Bloemenveiling Aalsmeer** (Aalsmeer Flower Auction) that is held five days a week from the predawn hours until mid-morning. It is the largest flower auction in the world, with three auction halls operating continuously in a building the size of several football fields. You walk on a catwalk above the rolling four-tier carts that wait to move on tracks past the auctioneers. The buying system is what is called a Dutch auction; the price

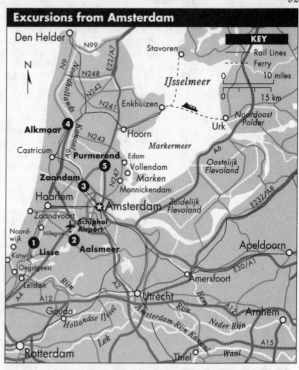

Excursions from Amsterdam

goes down, not up, on a large "clock" on the wall. The buyers sit lecture-style with buzzers on their desks; the first to register a bid gets the bunch. *Legmeerdijk 313, tel. 02977/34567. Admission: Fl. 4 adults, children free. Open weekdays 7:30–11.*

Folkloric Holland ❸ Over the Noordzee Kanaal from Amsterdam and just beyond the city of **Zaandam** is the restored village of **Zaanse Schans,** gateway to the windmill-studded countryside of Noord Holland province. Many of the buildings here have been restored as private homes, but a small cluster along the river edge includes a clock museum, the shops of a clog maker and a cheese maker, a bakery museum, and a restaurant. *Kraaienest 2, tel. 075/ 152221. Admission: Fl. 3.50 adults, Fl. 1.50 children. Open daily 10–5.*

❹ ❺ Open-air **cheese markets** are held in **Alkmaar** (tel. 072/114284; Apr.–Sept., Fri. mornings) and **Purmerend** (tel. 02990/52525 Feb.–Aug., Thurs. mornings). To see how cheese is made, visit one of more than a dozen *kaasboerderij* (cheese farms) in the area: **Kaasboerderij De Witte Saander** (Braakdijk 37, Zaandam, daily 9–6); **Kaasboerderij De Domme Dirk** (Roomeinde 17, Broek in Waterland, daily 10–5), and **Kaasboerderij Zeilzicht** (Westdijk 15, Alkmaar, Tues. and Thurs. 10–4) are three of them.

Metropolitan Holland and The Hague

Like filings around the end of a magnet, the population of the Netherlands clusters in the arc of Amsterdam's attraction. More than 25% of the country's 15 million residents live in and around ten small to medium-size cities that are within 80 kilometers (50 miles) of the capital. And that doesn't count the tulip growers, vegetable farmers, dairy farmers, and villagers that fill in what little open land remains in this area. The Dutch refer to the circle formed by the four cities of Amsterdam, Den Haag (The Hague in English), Rotterdam, and Utrecht as the Randstad (Round City); the megalopolis also is called "The West" by young Randstad wannabes waiting for their opportunity to hit the big time in the same way young Americans and Britons dream of making it in New York, Los Angeles, or London. In addition to harboring the capital of international justice (The Hague) and the world's largest port (Rotterdam), Metropolitan Holland is the political and historic heart of the Dutch nation.

Important Addresses and Numbers

Tourist Information
VVV Delft (Markt 85, tel. 015/126100; open Apr.–Sept., weekdays 9–6, Sat. 9–5, Sun. 11–3; Oct.–Mar., Sat. 9–5). VVV Haarlem (Stationsplein 1, 2011 LR, tel. 023/319059, fax 023/340537; open Apr.–Sept., Mon.–Sat. 9–5:30; Oct.–Mar., Sat. 10–4). **The Hague Information Office** (Koningin Julianaplein 30, Babylon shopping center, tel. 070/354–6200; open mid-Apr.–mid-Sept., Mon.–Sat. 9–9, Sun. 10–5; mid-Sept.–mid-Apr., Mon.–Sat. 9–6, Sun. 10–5). **Scheveningen Information Office** (Gevers Deynootweg 1134, Palace shopping center Promenade, tel. 070/354–6200). VVV Leiden (Stationsplein 210, tel. 071/146846) open Apr.–Aug., Mon.–Sat. 9–6; Sept.–Mar., weekdays 9–5:30, Sat. 10–4). VVV Rotterdam (Coolsingel 67, tel. 06/34034065, fax 010–4130124; Open Mon.–Thurs. 9–5:30, Fri. 9–9, Sat. 9–5, and Sun. 10–4; Oct.–Mar., Mon.–Thurs. 9–5:30, Fri. 9–9, and Sat. 9–5). VVV Utrecht (Vredenburg 90, tel. 030/331544, fax 030/331417; open weekdays 9–6, Sat. 9–4.

Emergencies
The **national emergency number** for police, fire, and ambulance is 06/11.

Hospital Emergency Rooms
Emergency care is available in **Delft** (R. De Graafweg 3–11, tel. 015/603060), **Haarlem** (Velserstraat 19, tel. 023/14 15 16), **The Hague** (Bronovolaan 5, tel. 070/312 4141), **Leiden** (Rijnsburgerweg 10, tel. 071/269111), **Rotterdam** (Dr. Molewaterplein 40, tel. 010/463–9222), and **Utrecht** (Heidelberglaan 100, tel. 030/509111).

Late-night Pharmacies
In **Delft** (tel. 015/121568), in **Haarlem** (tel. 023/319148), in **The Hague** (tel. 070/345–1000), in **Rotterdam** (tel. 010/411–0370), and in **Utrecht** (tel. 030/441228).

Arriving and Departing

By Car
N5/A5 goes to **Haarlem** from Amsterdam (from there N208 leads through the bulb district to Leiden); to reach **Leiden, The**

Hague, Delft, and **Rotterdam** directly from Amsterdam, take E19 via Schiphol Airport; to continue to **Utrecht** from Rotterdam, take E25, or to reach **Utrecht** directly from Amsterdam, take E35. Take E30/A12 from The Hague to Utrecht to bypass the congestion of Rotterdam.

By Train **Intercity express trains** (tel. 06/899–1121) run twice an hour between Amsterdam and Leiden, The Hague, and Rotterdam, and four times an hour between Amsterdam and Haarlem and Utrecht. To get to Delft from Amsterdam, change trains in The Hague. Four trains an hour also run between The Hague and Rotterdam, and three per hour between The Hague and Utrecht, and Rotterdam and Utrecht. There are two railway stations in The Hague (one in the central business district and another in the residential area); for reasons that have more to do with politics than practicality, trains from Amsterdam do *not* stop at the central station, which means you either must change trains in Leiden to disembark directly at the central station, or take a bus from the high station into the center.

Getting Around

By Bus or Tram Bus service is available in all cities in this region, and trams run in The Hague, between Delft and The Hague, in Rotterdam, and in Utrecht; Rotterdam also has an excellent underground metro system with two major lines (red/east–west and blue/north–south) that extend into the suburbs and cross in the city center for easy transfers from one to the other. For **information** on public transportation in all major Dutch cities, call 06/899–1221. For further local information on public transportation: Haarlem, tel. 06/899–1177; Rotterdam, tel. 010/454–6890; and Utrecht, tel. 030/317031.

By Taxi Taxis are available at railway stations; at major hotels; and, in larger cities, at taxi stands in key locations. Call to order a taxi in Delft (tel. 015/620621), Haarlem (tel. 023/151515), The Hague (tel. 070/390–7722 or 070/364–2828), Leiden (tel. 071/212121), Rotterdam (tel. 010/462–6060 or 010/425–7000), or Utrecht (tel. 030/515151 or 030/331122).

By Bike Bicycles can be rented at railway stations or by contacting local rental facilities (*see* Sports and Fitness, *below*, for names of firms in each town).

Guided Tours

In Leiden, **Jaap Slingerland** (tel. 071/134938 or 071/413183; fare: Fl. 15 per person) runs 3½-hour boat trips every summer afternoon except Saturdays from the *haven* (harbor) across the Braassemer Lake and the Kager Lakes, including a windmill-cruise. In July and August there are also day trips across the Braassemer Lake to visit the bird and recreation center **Avifauna** in Alphen aan den Rijn (tel. 01720/87575; fare: Fl 6, includes admission to Avifauna park). In The Hague, a **Royal Tour** (tel. 070/354–6200) is run during the summer that takes in the palaces and administrative buildings associated with Queen Beatrix. The cost is Fl 19 adults, Fl 15 children. The **Rotterdam City Tour** (Coolsingel, tel. 06/34034065) is available daily from April through September for Fl 16. The best way to see Rotterdam's waterfront is by boat. **Spido Harbor Tours** (Willemsplein, tel. 010/413–5400), offer excursions lasting from just over an hour to a full day. In Utrecht, carriages drawn by Gelderland horses tour the city on weekends from April through October. Another option in Utrecht is the **Walkman Tour,** available from the tourist office (Vredenburg 90, tel. 06/3403–4805) for Fl. 5.

Exploring Metropolitan Holland

Numbers in the margin correspond with places of interest on the Metropolitan Holland map.

Haarlem Often eclipsed by Amsterdam, **Haarlem** is an important small
① city in its own right. It is home to one of the finest church organs in the world, and its museums contain artworks that fill gaps in, or expand upon, the collections of Amsterdam's major museums.

The heart of any Dutch town is its market square. Surrounding Haarlem's Grote Markt are the medieval town hall, the old fish- and meat-market halls dating from the 17th century and often used by the Frans Hals Museum for special exhibitions, and the imposing late-Gothic **Grote Kerk** (St. Bavo's Church) built on the square in the 15th century and the burial place of Frans Hals. The church is the home of the world-famous Müller Organ, on which both Handel and Mozart played (Mozart at age 10). Installed in 1738 and long considered to be the finest in the world, this gilded and gleaming instrument has been meticulously maintained and restored through the years to protect the sound planned by its creators, the master organ builder Christian Müller and the sculptor Jan van Logteren. Between May and October the official town organists of Haarlem give free weekly or twice-weekly concerts. *Grote Markt. Admission: Fl 2 adults, Fl 1 children. Open Apr.–Aug., Mon.–Sat. 10–4; Sept.–Mar., Mon.–Sat. 10–3:30.*

Just off the Grote Markt in a small gabled town building is the **Corrie ten Boom House,** which honors a family of World War II resistance fighters who successfully hid a number of Jewish families before being captured themselves by the Germans in 1944. Most of the ten Boom family lost their lives in the concentration camps, but Corrie survived and returned to Haarlem to tell the story in her book, *The Hiding Place.* The family clock shop is preserved on the street floor, and their living quarters now contain displays, documents, photographs, and memorabilia. Visitors can also see the hiding closet, which the Gestapo never found, although they lived six days in the house hoping to starve out anyone who might be hiding there. *Barteljorisstraat 19, tel. 023/310823. Admission free (donations appreciated). Open Apr.–Oct., Mon.–Sat. 10–4:30; Nov.–Mar., Mon.–Sat. 11–5:30.*

Time Out Not far from the Grote Markt is **Het Stadscafe** (Zeijlstraat 56–58, tel. 023/325202), a good place to stop for a reasonably priced snack or a quick meal.

Crossing back through the Grote Markt, take Warmoesstraat and its continuations, Schagchelstraat and Groot Heilig Land, to the entrance to the **Frans Hals Museum.** What once was a series of small houses is now galleries for paintings, period furniture, silver, and ceramics. The 17th-century collection of paintings that is the focal point of this museum includes the

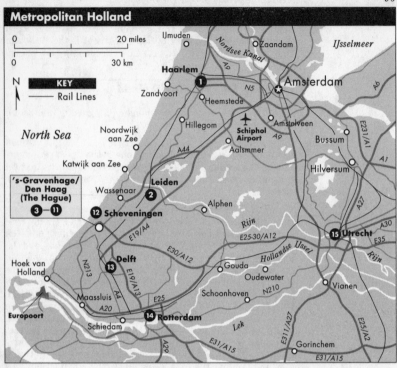

Metropolitan Holland

KEY
— Rail Lines

North Sea

IJmuden · Zaandam · IJsselmeer

Haarlem ①

Zandvoort · Heemstede · Amsterdam

Hillegom · Schiphol Airport · Amstelveen · Bussum

Noordwijk aan Zee · Aalsmeer · Hilversum

Katwijk aan Zee

's-Gravenhage/ Den Haag (The Hague) ③–⑪

Wassenaar · **Leiden** ② · Alphen · Rijn

⑫ Scheveningen

Hoek van Holland

Delft ⑬ · Gouda · Oudewater · Vianen · ⑮ Utrecht

Maassluis · Schoonhoven

Europoort · Schiedam · ⑭ **Rotterdam** · Lek · Gorinchem

works of Frans Hals and other masters of the Haarlem School, including Hendrick Goltzius, Judith Leyster, Johannes Verspronck, Pieter Claesz, Willem Heda, Adriaen van Ostade, and Jacob van Ruisdael. The museum has a modern art collection as well, with the works of Dutch impressionists and expressionists, including sculpture, textiles, and ceramics, as well as paintings and graphics; there are also an 18th-century dollhouse and a recreated 18th-century pharmacy. *Groot Heilig Land 62, tel. 023/319180. Admission: Fl 4.50 adults, Fl 2 children. Open Mon.–Sat. 11–5, Sun. and public holidays 1–5.*

From the Hals Museum, follow the canals around to the left, past the Turfmarkt to Spaarne to reach the **Teylers Museum.** This is the oldest museum in the Netherlands and possibly the most curious in the world. The major artistic attraction is the collection of master drawings and prints by Michelangelo, Rembrandt, and others that once belonged to Queen Christina of Sweden. Among the scientific curiosities are collections of fossils and crystals and examples of early machines and scientific tools. There is also a collection of coins and medals and even a rare 31-pipe Fokker organ. *Spaarne 16, tel. 023/319010. Admission: Fl 6.50 adults, Fl 3 children. Open Tues.–Sat. 10–5, Sun. and public holidays 1–5.*

Leiden ② Birthplace of Rembrandt and site of the nation's oldest and most prestigious university, **Leiden** is also noted for its significant historic role. In 1574, Leiden was the object of a major siege at the hands of the Spanish; the story of that siege, and the city's deliverance by the uniquely Dutch tactic of breaching the dikes to flood out an invader, is an important part of national lore. A place where windmills still rise over the cityscape, Leiden derives its charm today from its relaxed and spirited university-town atmosphere.

Founded in 1575, **Leiden University** was a mecca for the great thinkers and scientists of the 16th and 17th centuries, including the philosopher René Descartes. Follow the wide Rapenburg canal from the center of town to the university's **Hortus Botanicus.** This botanical garden is the oldest in Europe and includes extensive beds filled with flowers, rare plants, and towering trees; there is an orangery, a Japanese garden, and several greenhouses. *Rapenburg 73, tel. 071/275188. Admission: Fl 2. Garden open Mon.–Sat. 9–5, Sun. 10–5. Greenhouses open Apr.–Sept., weekdays 9–12:30 and 1:30–4:30, weekends 10:30–12:30, 1:30–4; Oct.–Mar., weekdays 9–12:30 and 1:30–4:30, Sun. 10:30–12:30 and 1:30–4.*

After visiting the gardens, continue into Kaiserstraat to the next canal, where you will find the **Pilgrim Collection.** In a small house behind the city archives, this collection includes documents, models, and books related to the period when a group of English Puritans later known as the Pilgrims lived in Leiden before sailing to found the Plymouth Colony in what is now Massachusetts. *Vliet 45, tel. 071/120191. Admission free. Open weekdays 9:30–4:30.*

Return to the gardens and cross the canal; take Kloksteeg to the square in front of the **Pieterskerk** (St. Peter's Church), which is the oldest church in the city, dating from 1428. Also on the church square is the Gravensteen, which once was the home of the Counts of Holland. *Pieterskerkhof, tel. 071/124319. Admission: Fl 1.50 adults, Fl 0.75 children. Open daily 1:30–4.*

Behind the church on Pieterskerkchoorsteeg is the former home of William Brewster, spiritual leader of the Pilgrims. At the entrance is a small plaque placed by the Society of Mayflower Descendants. Return to the Rapenburg canal and stroll past the city's most gracious houses to reach the **Rijksmuseum van Oudheden** (National Museum of Antiquities), which has a particularly fine Egyptian and classical collection, as well as Dutch archaeological artifacts. Pass through a soaring gallery in which the Egyptian temple of Taffah has been reconstructed, and continue through two floors of Greek and Roman sculpture, Egyptian tombs, funerary urns, and collections of everyday items from the pre-Christian eras, including glassware, ceramics, jewelry, and weapons. *Rapenburg 28, tel. 071/146246. Admission: Fl. 3.50 adults, Fl. 2 children. Open Tues.–Sat. 10–5, Sun. 1–5.*

Time Out   In summer the place for a break is on the nearly water-level café **Annie's Verjaardag** (Oude Rijn 1A, tel. 071/125737) at the confluence of the New and Old Rhine rivers. In winter, a better choice is the pancake house **Pannekoekkenhuysje** (Steenstraat 51, tel. 071/133144).

At the end of the Rapenburg canal, continue straight ahead through the Turfmarkt to the second canal, the Oude Singel. On the far side is the **De Lakenhal** museum, which contains an impressive collection of paintings as well as furniture and silver and pewter pieces. The galleries are hung with paintings by Rembrandt, Gerrit Dou, Jan Steen, and Salomon van Ruysdael, as well as an impressive collection of the works of Lucas van Leyden, including his triptych, *Last Judgment*. Also of interest here are the reconstructed guild rooms. *Oude Singel 28–32, tel. 071/25420. Admission: Fl 2.50 adults, Fl 1.25 children. Open Tues.–Sat. 10–5, Sun. and public holidays 1–5.*

The Hague and Scheveningen

While Amsterdam is the official capital of the Netherlands, 's-Gravenhage/Den Haag (The Hague) is the seat of government and home of the reigning monarch, Queen Beatrix. An elegant city dotted with parks and open squares, it exudes a graciousness that Amsterdam lacks, and has a formal and traditional lifestyle that befits its role as a diplomatic capital and world center of international peace and justice. Almost seamlessly connected to The Hague is the fishing port and stylish beach resort community of Scheveningen, where a small and dwindling community of women still dresses in traditional costumes on a daily basis.

Numbers in the margin correspond with places of interest on the The Hague map.

The governmental heart of the Netherlands is the Parliament Complex, which is situated in the center of The Hague beside ❸ the **Hofvijver** (Court Lake), a small rectangular reflecting pool. ❹ The late-13th-century **Ridderzaal** (Knight's Hall) is where the queen comes each fall to address her government at the annual Opening of Parliament (the third Tuesday in September). Built ❺ around this is the **Binnenhof** (Inner Court) complex; it incorporates the buildings used by the First and Second Chambers of the Staten Generaal (States General, equivalent to the U.S. Senate and House of Representatives). There is a special exhibition on the origin and methods of the Dutch governmental system, and there are guided tours into the legislative chambers (when they are not in session) and the Knight's Hall, with its provincial flags and stained-glass windows displaying the coats of arms of the major Dutch cities. *Binnenhof, tel. 070/364–6144. Reservations required. Admission: tour Fl 4, Parliament exhibition free. Open Mon.–Sat. 10–4; last guided tour at 3:55 PM.*

Tucked into a corner behind the Parliament Complex and overlooking the waters of the Court Lake is a small 17th-century ❻ palace, the **Mauritshuis,** known as the Royal Gallery of Paintings, which contains an outstanding collection of Dutch masterpieces, including three Rembrandt self-portraits and his breakthrough painting, *The Anatomy Lesson*. Also here are three highly prized paintings by Vermeer *(Girl with the Pearl, View of Delft, Diana with the Nymphs);* more than a dozen works by Jan Steen, who portrayed daily life and ordinary people in the Netherlands in the 17th century; and paintings by other Dutch and Flemish masters, including Hals, Ruysdael, Potter, Rubens, and Van Dyck. *Korte Vijverberg 8, tel. 070/365–4779. Admission: Fl 6.50 adults, Fl 3.50 children. Open Tues.–Sat. 10–5, Sun. 11–5.*

Included in the admission to the Mauritshuis is the opportunity to visit the **Painting Gallery of Prince Willem V,** which is located on the far side of the Parliament Complex on the open Buitenhof (Outer Court). This small gallery in a Louis XIV-style town house contains additional works by 17th-century masters that illustrate life in the Netherlands in that time. *Buitenhof 35, tel. 070/318–2487. Admission: Fl 2.50 adults, Fl 1 children. Open Tues.–Sun. 11–4.*

Binnenhof, **5**
Haags
Gemeentemuseum, **9**
Hofvijver, **3**
Mauritshuis, **6**
Museon, **10**
Museum Bredius, **7**
Omniversum, **11**
Ridderzaal, **4**
Vredespaleis, **8**

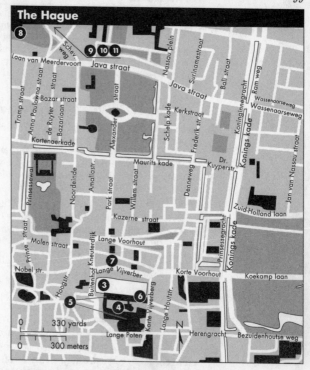

The Hague

7 Facing the Parliament Complex across the Court Lake is **Museum Bredius.** Housed in an 18th-century mansion, it displays a former private collection that includes additional works by the masters as well as lesser-known works of the period. *Lange Vijverberg 14, tel. 070/362–0729. Admission: Fl 2.50 adults, Fl 2 children. Open Tues.–Sun. noon–5.*

Time Out Follow Gravenstraat toward the center to a small square facing the old Town Hall. Opening onto the square is '**T Goude Hooft** (De Groenmarkt 13, tel. 070/346–9713), the oldest restaurant in The Hague, with both a street café and a traditional Dutch dining room.

8 Beyond the city center and facing the world across a broad lawn is the **Vredespaleis** (Peace Palace), which houses the International Court of Justice. The court was initiated in 1899 by Czar Nicolas II of Russia, who invited 26 nations to meet in The Hague to set up a permanent world court of arbitration. The present building was constructed in 1903 with a $1.5 million gift from the Scots-American industrialist Andrew Carnegie. Gifts from each of the participating nations embellish the architecture with examples of their national craftsmanship in the form of statuary, stained-glass windows, gates, doors, clocks, and such. *Carnegieplein 2, tel. 070/346–9680. Admission: Fl 5 adults, Fl 3 children. Open May–Oct., weekdays 10–4; Nov.–Apr. weekdays 10–3; guided tours 10 AM, 11 AM, 2 PM, and 3 PM; May–Oct., additional guided tour 4 PM.*

Continuing by way of Groot Hertoginnelaan to Stadhouder-
⑨ slaan, you find the **Haags Gemeentemuseum** (Hague Municipal
Museum), which is best known for housing the world's largest
collection of works by Piet Mondrian, as well as 50 drawings by
Karl Appel. In addition there are paintings from the Hague
school and an arts-and-crafts section that displays magnificent
local silverware, old glass, earthenware, ceramics, and Dutch
and Chinese porcelain. *Stadhouderslaan 41, tel. 070/338–1111.
Admission: Fl 7 adults, Fl 6 children. Open Tues.–Sun. 11–5.*

⑩ Also at the Hague Municipal Museum is the **Museon,** which incorporates science exhibits on the origins of the universe and
evolution with three themes: Earth, Our Home; Between Man
and the Stars; and Ecos, an environmental show. *Stadhouderslaan 41, tel. 070/338–1338 and 070/338–1305. Admission: Fl 5
adults, Fl 3 children. Open Tues.–Fri. 10–5, weekends and
public holidays noon–5.*

⑪ Next door to Museon is the Imax theater **Omniversum,** which
shows a rotating program of spectacular presentations, including several with natural and futuristic themes, on a film screen
that is six stories high. *Pres. Kennedylaan 5, tel. 070/354–
5454. Reservations suggested. Admission: Fl 14 adults, Fl 11
children. Shows Tues.–Thurs. hourly 11–4, Fri.–Sun. and
holidays hourly 11–9.*

*Numbers in the margin correspond with places of interest on
the Metropolitan Holland map.*

Leaving Omniversum, follow Johan De Wittlaan to Scheven-
⑫ ingseweg, which leads to the beach resort community of **Scheveningen.** Here you can enjoy a variety of relaxing pleasures,
including a walk on the beach promenade or a swim in a wave
pool. The famous and grand old hotel, the **Kurhaus,** (*see* The
Arts and Nightlife, *below*) houses a casino as well as several restaurants. There is also shopping seven days a week (it is the
only Sunday shopping in the Netherlands). Scheveningen is the
departure point for deep-sea fishing trips.

Delft Delft is a special little city: Perhaps more than any other in the
⑬ Netherlands it preserves a historic look that is best appreciated by simply wandering along its small canals with their
graceful, humpback bridges. Delft rivals Leiden in its importance to the history of the Netherlands; it was here that William of Orange (known as William the Silent), founder of the
nation, was assassinated in 1584. The Dutch monarchs that followed him are all buried here in the Nieuwe Kerk (New
Church), in the shadow of which the painter Jan Vermeer was
born and lived. And, of course, Delft also is the crafts center
known around the world for its famous blue-and-white porcelain.

Begin your tour of Delft at the market square, flanked at one
end by the **Stadhuis** (Town Hall). Facing it across the square is
the 14th-century **Nieuwe Kerk** (New Church), which is the royal
burial church of the House of Orange; it entombs all but a few of
the Dutch monarchs. The mausoleum of William the Silent, a
massive and ornate structure of black marble and alabaster,
dominates the chancel. Nearby in the floor is the stone that covers the entry to the royal crypt, and throughout the church are
paintings, stained-glass windows, and memorabilia associated
with the Dutch royal family. In summer it is possible to climb
the church tower for the view that stretches as far as The

Hague and Scheveningen. *Markt, tel. 015/123025. Admission: Fl 2 adults, Fl 0.75 children, Fl 1.50 groups. Combination card (Old and New churches): Fl 3 adults, Fl 1 children. Open May–Oct., Mon.–Sat. 9–5; Nov.–Apr., Mon.–Sat. 11–4. Tower Admission: Fl 3.25 adults, Fl 2.40 children. Open May–Aug., Tues.–Sat. 10–4:30; July 15–Aug. 19, daily 10–4:30.*

Time Out   On a corner at the center of the market square is a small pastry shop and tearoom, **Bankerbakkerij van Leeuwen** (Markt 57, tel. 015/12 37 20), in a building also identified as *In Den Beslagen Bijbel*, honoring the fact that it was in this building that the first Dutch printed Bible was produced.

Behind the Town Hall is a row of buildings that formerly served as the butter market, the town weigh house, and the guild halls of gold- and silversmiths and pharmacists. Cut through and cross the second canal, which is the **Oude Delft.** This was the first canal dug in the city and is said to be the first city canal dug in the Netherlands. If you turn right, you walk toward the now-leaning tower of the **Oude Kerk** (Old Church). Founded in 1200, this is the oldest church in Delft and the final resting place of several important Dutch military and naval heroes and of Antonie van Leeuwenhoek, the Delft resident who invented the microscope. The tower, which now leans too precariously to be ascended, holds the largest carillon bell in the Netherlands; weighing nearly 20,000 pounds, it now is used only on state occasions. *Heilige Geestkerkhof, tel. 015/123015. Admission: Fl 2 adults, Fl 0.75 children. Combination card (Old and New churches): Fl 3 adults, Fl 1 children. Open Apr.–Nov., Mon.–Sat. 10–5.*

Directly across the canal from the Oude Kerk is **Het Prinsenhof** (Prince's Court), the most famous sight in Delft. Built as a convent in the early 15th century, the complex of buildings was taken over by the government of the new Dutch Republic in 1572 and given to William of Orange for his use as a residence. It was here that William was assassinated. The complex of buildings now houses a museum devoted to the history of the Dutch Republic; there is also a museum of ethnology and a church. *St. Agathaplein 1, tel. 015/602358. Admission: Fl 3.50 adults, Fl 1.75 children. Open Sept.–May, Tues.–Sat. 10–5, Sun. 1–5; Jun. to Aug., Tues.–Sat. 10–5, Sun.–Mon. 1–5.*

Rotterdam ⑭   Were it not for the devastation of World War II, when the city and its port were leveled in the crossfire between Hitler's forces and the Allies, **Rotterdam** might never have become the dynamic and influential world port it is today. A busy harbor since the 17th century, it built bigger facilities in the 19th and early 20th centuries, playing a key role in European trade. The massive 48-kilometer (30-mile) -long **Europoort** complex of piers, warehouses, and refineries is best seen by boat (*see* Guided Tours, *above*).

Walk along the Leuvehaven inner harbor past several old ships moored along the quay to the nautical museum at the head of the harbor. This is the **Prins Hendrik Maritime Museum,** devoted to the history of Rotterdam harbor and its historic role in world trade. The museum building contains both changing exhibitions and a permanent collection of models and memorabilia; the warship *De Buffel*, moored alongside the museum, is part of the collection. *Leuvehaven 1, tel. 010/413–2680. Admis-*

sion: Fl 3.50, children free; free Wed. Open Tues.–Sat. 10–5, Sun. and holidays 11–5.

Take the red line from the Metro station outside the museum to the next stop at Eendrachtsplein; walk along Westersingel toward the park and turn right on Mathenesserlaan. The **Boymans-van Beuningen Museum** is another of the Netherlands' exceptional fine-arts museums. Its collection spans the 15th to 20th centuries and includes a number of extraordinary early primitives by painters such as Hieronymus Bosch, Sint Jans, and the van Eycks, as well as Bruegel the Elder and van Scorel. Later painters, including Rubens and Van Dyck, are also represented. Rembrandt's portrait of his son Titus is part of the collection, as are prints and drawings by Dürer, da Vinci, and later artists such as Cezanne and Picasso. Add to this a remarkable collection of impressionist, surrealist and contemporary art, and as the final fillip, a fine collection of objects, including glassware, silverware, and earthenware. *Mathenesserlaan 18–20, tel. 010/441–9400. Admission: Fl 3.50 adults, children free; free Wed. Open Tues.–Sat. 10–5, Sun. and holidays 11–5.*

Utrecht Birthplace of the 16th-century Adrian VI, the only Dutch
15 pope, Utrecht has been a powerful bishopric since the 7th century and is still is a major religious center. It was in Utrecht that the Dutch Republic was established in 1579 with the signing of the Union of Utrecht.

While the surrounding city is among the busiest and most modern in the Netherlands, the central core of Utrecht retains a historic character, particularly along its two main canals. The best place to begin a tour is from the bridge that connects Lange Viestraat to Potterstraat just beyond Vredenburg square. There's a pleasant view over the **Oude Gracht** (Old Canal), which winds through the central shopping district. The unique feature of this lively water esplanade is that there are both upper and lower levels, with shops opening onto the street level, restaurants and cafés opening onto the walkway that is just above water level.

Follow the canal along to the Steenweg and jog left to visit one of the most delightful museums in the Netherlands. Housed in an old church, the **Rijksmuseum van Speelklok tot Pierement** (National Museum from Musical Clock to Street Organ) is a happy place filled with ticking clocks, music boxes, player pianos, and traditional Dutch barrel organs. *Buurkerkhof 10, tel. 030/312789. Admission: Fl 6 adults, Fl 3 children. Open Tues.–Sat. 10–5, Sun. and public holidays 1–5; guided tours every hour.*

Time Out Before or after you tackle the steps of the Dom Tower, a pleasant spot for a quick bite of lunch is the **Brasserie Domplein** (Domplein 20, tel. 030/322895), on the corner as you enter the square. The decor is no-nonsense French (bare tables and art on the walls), and the menu is typical of a brasserie, with a choice of quiches, salads, and croissant sandwiches.

Return to the Old Canal and cross at the Zadelstraat bridge. The **Domtoren** (Dom Tower) in front of you is the highest tower in the Netherlands (112 meters/367 feet), and it is well worth the effort to climb its 465 steps for the panoramic view it offers over the city and surrounding countryside of Utrecht province.

Built in the late 14th century, the stone tower was originally the bell tower of a cathedral that was destroyed in a hurricane late in the 17th century (the outline of its nave can still be seen in the paving squares of the Domplein). Soaring lancet windows add to the impression of majestic height. *Domplein, tel. 030/919540. Admission: Fl 3.50 adults, Fl 1 children. Open Apr.–Nov., weekdays 10–5, Sat. 11–5, Sun. and public holidays noon–5; Dec.–Mar., Sat. 11–5, Sun. and public holidays noon–5, last tour at 4.*

Across the square is the Gothic-style **Domkerk** (Dom Church), built in the 13th and 14th centuries and designed after the pattern of the Tournai Cathedral in Belgium. It has five chapels radiating around the ambulatory of the chancel, as well as a number of funerary monuments, including that of a 14th-century bishop. *Domplein, tel. 030/310403. Admission free; guided tours Fl 2. Open May–Sept., daily 10–5; Oct.–Apr., Mon.–Sat. 11–4, Sun. 2–4.*

The 15th-century cloister garden adjacent to the Dom Church, the **Pandhof** (House Garden) of the Dom, is planted with herbs and offers a peaceful respite. *Between Domplein and Achter den Dom. Admission free. Open Dec.–Mar., Sat. 11–5, Sun. noon–5; Apr. and June–Nov., weekdays 10–5, Sat. 11–5, Sun. noon–5; May, Mon., Wed., and Fri 10–5, Tues. and Thurs. 10–8:30, Sat. 11–5, Sun. noon–5.*

Turn right on Achter den Dom and walk toward the **Nieuwe Gracht** (New Canal). **Het Catharijneconvent,** a vast and comprehensive museum of religious history and sacred art housed in a former convent is just past the second bridge. There are magnificent altarpieces, ecclesiastical garments, manuscripts, sculptures, paintings, and the country's primary collection of medieval art. *Nieuwegracht 63, tel. 030/317296 or 030/313835. Admission: Fl 3.50 adults, Fl 2 children. Open Tues.–Fri. 10–5, weekends and public holidays 11–5.*

Continue to the end of the Nieuwegracht and turn right at Agnietenstraat, where you will find the **Centraal Museum,** also housed in a former convent. Primarily dedicated to painting and the decorative arts, it contains collections of costumes, coins, and medals and an archaeological section as well. The paintings here include excellent works from the 16th-century Utrecht school, reflecting the strong Italian influence on painters such as van Scorel, van Heemskerk, and Terbrugghen. There are also examples of the 20th-century Dutch de Stijl movement, though this school is best represented at the Rietveld-Schroder House (*see* Off the Beaten Track, *below*). *Agnietenstraat 1, tel. 030/362362 or 030/362359. Admission: Varies per exhibition; guided tours Fl. 2.50. Open Tues.–Sat. 10–5, Sun. and public holidays 1–5.*

What to See and Do with Children

Leiden's **Molenmuseum de Valk** (Windmill Museum de Valk) may be the best place and the best way to learn more about the windmill heritage of the Netherlands. *2e Binnenvestgracht 1, tel. 071/254639. Admission: Fl 3 adults, Fl 1.50 children. Open Tues.–Sat. 10–5, Sun. and official holidays 1–5.*

Near Leiden, in the beach community of Noordwijk, is Europe's first permanent space exhibition, **Noordwijk Space**

Expo, which includes real satellites, engines, and space stations, as well as models and pieces of moon rock. *Keplerlaan 3, Noordwijk, tel. 01719/46446 or 01719/46448. Admission: Fl 10 adults, Fl 7.50 children. Open Tues.–Sat. 10–6.*

Madurodam, in The Hague, is a collection of small reproductions of typically Dutch buildings set into a sprawling "village" with pathways, tram tracks, and railway stations. All of the most important buildings of the Netherlands have been reproduced; if you are there at sunset you will see the lights come on in the houses. During July and August, there also is an after-dark sound-and-light presentation, free to park visitors. *Haringkade 175, tel. 070/355–3900. Admission: Fl 11 adults, Fl 9 senior citizens, Fl 6 children. Open Mar.–May, daily 9 AM–10:30 PM; June–Aug., daily 9 AM–11 PM; Sept., 9 AM–9:30 PM; Oct.–Mar., 9–6.*

Off the Beaten Track

June is the time to visit **Westbroek Park** in The Hague, when its 20,000 rosebushes are in magnificent bloom. *Kapelweg. Admission free. Open daily 9–1 hour before sunset.*

The **Euromast** tower affords a panorama of Rotterdam Harbor. You reach it on the **Spacetower** revolving elevator. *Parkhaven 20, tel. 010/436–4811. Admission: Fl 13 adults, Fl 8 children. Open mid-Mar.–mid-Oct., 10–7. Spacetower open Mar.–Dec., daily 10–6; Jan.–Feb., weekends only 11–4.*

An adjunct exhibit of Utrecht's Centraal Museum, located several blocks away, the **Rietveld-Schroder House** exemplifies several key principles of the de Stijl movement—its open plan, the direct communion with nature from every room, and the use of neutral white or gray on large surfaces with primary colors to identify linear details. *Prins Hendriklaan 50A, tel. 030/517926. Reservations required. Admission (includes guided tour): Fl 9 adults, Fl 6 children. Open Tues.–Sun. 12:30–5.*

The charming old city of **Dordrecht,** at the busiest river junction in Europe, rewards a visit with medieval town gates, a 15th-century church with a leaning tower, and an 18th-century period house museum. It is the oldest town in Holland, given its charter in 1220.

Shopping

The late shopping nights (*see* Essential Information, *above*) in this region: in **Leiden,** Thursdays; in **The Hague,** Thursdays; in **Scheveningen,** Fridays and, during the summer at the Palace Promenade, Mondays through Saturdays; in **Rotterdam,** Fridays; and in **Utrecht,** Thursdays.

Shopping Districts The best shopping in this region of the Netherlands is in the larger cities of The Hague, Rotterdam, and particularly Utrecht, which has two American-style enclosed shopping malls.

Street Markets Street markets are an integral part of Dutch city life. **Leiden's** street market is held in the city center on the Nieuwe Rijn on Wednesday and Saturday 9–6 and at Vijf Mei plein on Tuesday 9–2. In **The Hague,** the Farmers' Market is Wednesday 10–6, and there is an antiques market on Lange Voorhout on summer Thursdays. In **Delft,** market day is Thursday 9–5, and there is a flea market on the canals in the town center on summer Saturdays. In **Rotterdam** an antiques, curiosities, and general market is held on Mariniersweg on Tuesday and Saturday 9–5, and the stamp, coin, and book market on Grotekerkplein is on Tuesday and Saturday 9:30–4; there is also a Sunday market at Schiedamsedijk April–September 11–5. In **Utrecht** the general market at Vredenburg is Wednesday 9–5 and Saturday 8–5; the antiques market at the Ossekop (Voorstraat 19) is Saturday 9–5; flowers and plants are sold at Janskerkhof on Saturday 7–4, and by the Old Canal on Saturday 8–5; there is a health-food market at Vredenburg on Friday noon–6; and a flea market at Waterstraat is held Saturday 8–2.

Specialty Stores
Delft
De Porceleyne Fles (The Royal Delftware Factory, Rotterdamseweg 196, tel. 015/569214) is home to that famous blue-and-white Delft pottery. The galleries here exhibit famous pieces from throughout Delft's history, and regular demonstrations of molding and painting pottery are given by the artisans. Other Delftware pottery factories are **De Delftse Pauw** (Delftweg 133, tel. 015/124920 or 015/124743), and **Atelier de Candelaer** (Kerkstraat 13, tel. 015/131848).

Sports and Fitness

Biking
Bicycling is popular in this flat land, and rentals are available in virtually every city. Delft: the **railway station** (tel. 015/143033). Leiden: **Van der Laan** (Merelstraat 13, tel. 071/155915) and **Bicycle Depot** (next to the railway station, tel. 071/131304). Haarlem: **Van Bentum** (Stationsplein, tel. 023/317066) and **De Volkenfietser** (Koningstraat 36, tel. 023/325577). The Hague: **Cycle Garage** (Hollands Spoor, tel. 070/389–0830; or at Central Station, tel. 070/385–3235) and **Garage due Nord** (Keizerstraat 27, Scheveningen, tel. 070/355–4060). Rotterdam: **Stationsrijwielstalling Centraal Station** (Stationsplein 1, tel. 010/412–6220). Utrecht: **Ottevanger and Co.** (Loeff Berchmakerstraat 20, tel. 030/314705), **Bicycle Parking** (Central Station Utrecht, tel. 030/311159), and **Verleun and Co.** (Van Bijnkershoeklaan 413, tel. 030/936368).

Canoeing
A canoe may be the very best way to get a close view of the bulb fields that fill the countryside between Haarlem and Leiden. The **VVV Leiden tourist office** (tel. 071/146846) has mapped out four different routes of varying lengths through the Dune and Bulb Area. Ask, too, about the Singel sightseeing route through Leiden's canals and moats. For information on canoe rentals contact **Jac. Veringa** (tel. 071/149790).

Sea Fishing
Sea fishing is one of the main reasons many people visit Scheveningen. For information and reservations, contact **Sportviscentrum Trip** (Dr. Lelykade 3, Scheveningen, tel. 070/354–1122 or 070/354–0887).

Sports Complex
In Utrecht, the sports center **De Vechtsebanen** (Mississippidreef 151, tel. 030/627878) is a multisport complex offering bowling, badminton, volleyball, squash, curling, and a number of other sports possibilities; there is a small running track as well as both indoor and outdoor tennis courts and ice-skating rinks.

Tennis/Squash
In Leiden, you can play squash and tennis at the **Holiday Inn Racket Center** (Haagse Schouwweg 10, tel. 071/355100). In Delft, squash courts are available at **Squash Delft** (Sportring 3,

tel. 015/146983). In Utrecht, both squash and tennis are available at the sports center **De Vechtsebanen** (Mississippidreef 151, tel. 030/627878).

Spectator Sports

Auto Racing One of Europe's best-known auto racing tracks is **Circuit Park Zandvoort** (Burgemeester van Alphenstraat, tel. 02507/16004 or 02507/18284); the racing season runs from April to October.

Horse Racing Near The Hague, **Duindigt Racecourse** (Waalsdorperlaan 29, Wassenaar, tel. 070/324–4427) is one of two racetracks in the Netherlands (the other is in Hilversum, between Utrecht and Amsterdam). The racing season runs from mid-March to mid-November and includes both flat and trotting races with betting. Race days are Wednesday and Sunday.

Marathon Run in late April each year (in close time proximity to both the Boston and London marathons) the City of Rotterdam Marathon is the major European running event of the year, where the last two world bests were set, in 1985 and 1988.

Soccer Rotterdam's Feyenoord team (pronounced "fie-nord") plays at **Feyenoord Stadion** (Olympiaweg 50, tel. 010/492–9499 or 010/492–9444).

Beaches

The beach community of **Scheveningen** has a boardwalk and amusement pier. Beaches near Leiden are at **Katwijk** and **Noordwijk**. Near Haarlem, **Zandvoort** is also the principal beach for Amsterdam (busy, but very large); the beaches at **Bloemdaal** are also open to the public.

Dining and Lodging

Delft **L'Orage.** A bright and gracious small French restaurant facing
Dining the Old Canal, it has an owner/chef who is partial to fish dishes. *Oude Delft 111b, tel. 015/123629. Reservations advised. Jacket and tie required. AE, DC, MC, V. Closed Sun.–Mon. Expensive.*

De Prinsenkelder. Located in the old storerooms of the former convent that now is the Prinsenhof Museum, this restaurant has a French menu. Entry is by way of a small alley opening onto the Oude Delft canal. *Schoolstraat 11, tel. 015/121860. Reservations advised. Jacket and tie advised. AE, DC, MC, V. Closed Sun. Expensive.*

Dining and Lodging **Les Compagnons.** This is a one-family hospitality package in the heart of Delft. The younger generation operates a small and comfortable hotel on the market square that offers a variety of brightly decorated rooms with a range of amenities that you wouldn't expect in so small a hotel. Dad hosts a restaurant on the next canal, and Mom operates a deli and tearoom in the adjoining store. *Markt 61, 2611 GS, tel. 015/140102. 11 rooms with bath. Facilities: restaurant nearby. AE, DC, MC, V. Inexpensive/Moderate.*

Lodging **Delft Museumhotel & Residence.** This elegant small hotel has been created within a complex of 11 historic buildings in the prime neighborhood of Delft. Among the choices are small apartments in the adjacent Residence building that opens onto the side alley. *Oude Delft 189, 2611 HD, tel. 015/140930. 51 rooms with bath. Facilities: bar. AE, DC, MC, V. Moderate/ Expensive.*

Hotel Leeuwenbrug. Facing one of Delft's canals, it is a traditional hotel with an Old Dutch–style canalside lounge. The rooms are large, airy, and contemporary in decor; those in the annex are particularly appealing. *Koornmarkt 16, 2611 EE, tel. 015/147741. 37 rooms with bath. Facilities: bar. AE, DC, MC, V. Inexpensive/Moderate.*

Haarlem
Dining

Peter Cuyper. This gracious restaurant is convenient to both the Frans Hals and the Teyler museums. Its small, traditional beamed dining rooms are brightened with flowers, crisp linens, and light from an enclosed garden (open in summer) filtering through the windows. *Kleine Houtstraat 70, 2011 DR, tel. 023/ 320885. Reservations advised. Jacket and tie advised. AE, DC, MC, V. Closed Mon. dinner and Sun. Expensive.*

Lodging

Carlton Square Hotel. This modern high-rise hotel in a residential district beyond the center has rooms that are bright and spacious with white art deco–inspired furniture. *Baan 7, 2012 DB, tel. 023/319091, fax 023/329853. 106 rooms with bath. Facilities: 2 restaurants, bar. AE, DC, MC, V. Expensive.*

Golden Tulip Lion d'Or. This traditional hotel near the railway station has been here since the early 18th century. Thoroughly modernized, it has spacious rooms. A jogging path runs behind the hotel. *Kruisweg 34–36, 2011 LC, tel. 023/321750, fax 023/ 329543. 36 rooms with bath. Facilities: restaurants, garage, business center. AE, DC, MC, V. Moderate/Expensive.*

Hotel Faber. Located within walking distance of the beaches of Zandvoort, this is a small, family-style hotel with bright, tidy rooms and a summer terrace. *Kostverlorenstraat 15, 2042 PA Zandvoort, tel. 02507/12825, fax 02507/16886. 35 rooms, 5 without bath. Facilities: lounge. No credit cards. Inexpensive.*

The Hague
Dining and Lodging

Corona Hotel. Elegant lodging seems appropriate to an elegant city of diplomacy, and this hotel fits the requirement perfectly. It is conveniently located across from the Parliament Complex, near the Mauritshuis and Museum Bredius at the edge of the shopping district. The rooms are restfully decorated in a muted scheme of white, cream, and dove gray. *Buitenhof 39–42, 2513 AH, tel. 070/363–7930, fax 070/361–5785. 26 rooms with bath. Facilities: restaurant, bar. AE, DC, MC, V. Very Expensive.*

Hotel Des Indes. With a grace and graciousness that make it one of the world's very special hotels, it is located on one of The Hague's most prestigious squares. Once a private town residence, the mansion was built principally for grand balls and entertainments. The former inner courtyard is now a towering reception area leading to the restaurant. The spacious rooms, already pleasant, are slated for major renovation in 1993. One suite, which enjoys a magnificent view over the city toward the beach, is fought over by rock stars who come to perform in nearby Rotterdam. *Lange Voorhout 54–56, 2514 EG, tel. 070/363– 2932, fax 070/345–1721. 76 rooms with bath. Facilities: restaurant, bar. AE, DC, MC, V. Very Expensive.*

Kurhaus Hotel. Holding the prime position at the center of the beach at Scheveningen, this grand hotel of the old school is nevertheless fully modern and bustling. Now engulfed by shops and apartments on the street side, it still has its famous turn-of-the-century profile from the amusement pier, and you still can dine in the magnificent Kurzaal with its fancifully painted, coffered ceiling high overhead. Rooms here are grand and grandly decorated in a variety of modern and traditional styles. *Gevers Deynootplein 30, 2586 CK, Scheveningen, tel. 070/352–0052, fax 070/350–0911. 241 rooms with bath. Facilities: 2 restaurants, sauna, swimming pool, casino. AE, DC, MC, V. Very Expensive.*

Lodging **Novotel Hotel.** Well located for both the sights and the shopping of The Hague, Novotel is a new and well-appointed full-service hotel with modestly sized rooms; the decor is a bland but restful beige and white. *Hofweg 5–7, 2511 AA, tel. 070/364–8846, fax 070/356–2889. 106 rooms with bath. Facilities: restaurant, bar, sauna. AE, DC, MC, V. Expensive.*

Hotel Petit. On a residential boulevard between the Peace Palace and the Hague Municipal Museum, this quiet, family-style mid-20th-century brick hotel is operated by a young couple. Bright and graciously furnished, it has a pleasant guests-only bar-lounge for relaxing after a day of sightseeing. *Groot Hertoginnelaan 42, 2517 EH, tel. 070/346–5500, fax 070/346–3257. 20 rooms with bath. Facilities: bar. AE, DC, MC, V. Inexpensive/Moderate.*

Hotel Sebel. The friendly owners of this hotel have expanded into two buildings located between the city center and the Peace Palace. Tidy and comfortable, the rooms are large and have high ceilings and tall windows for lots of light and air. *Zoutmanstraat 38, 2518 GR, tel. 070/360–8010. 14 rooms with bath. Facilities: bar-lounge. AE, DC, MC, V. Inexpensive/Moderate.*

City Hotel. Just off the beach in Scheveningen, this spanking clean, brightly decorated, and very friendly small family hotel spreads through several houses on a main street leading to the waterfront. It has its own restaurant, rare in a hotel of this size. *Renbaanstraat 1–3 and 17–23, 2586 EW, Scheveningen, tel. 070/355–7966, fax 070/354–0503. 20 rooms with bath. Facilities: restaurant, bar. AE, DC, MC, V. Inexpensive.*

Leiden **De Bisschop.** On a small street off the fashionable Rapenburg
Dining canal, this restaurant offers a traditional French-Dutch menu in a cheery pink-and-white environment; there's a small bar and a quieter upstairs dining room. Choices might include tuna with lime sauce, or veal cutlets with port sauce. *Kloksteeg 7, tel. 071/12 50 24. Reservations advised. Jacket and tie advised. AE, DC, MC, V. Expensive.*

Bistro La Cloche. Another chic and attractive French-Dutch restaurant just off the Rapenburg canal on the small street leading to St. Peter's Church, this one is done up in soft pastels, with flowers everywhere. It has a pleasant, but small, streetside café area. *Kloksteeg 3, tel. 071/12 30 53. Reservations advised. Jacket and tie advised. AE, DC, MC, V. Expensive.*

Oudt Leyden/'t Pannekoekenhuysje. These side-by-side restaurants with a shared kitchen have totally different menus and environments. Oudt Leyden is a formal, Old Dutch–style restaurant with a traditional menu of simple grilled and sautéed meats and fishes; 't Pannekoekenhuysje is a traditional Dutch pancake house with red-check tablecloths, a relaxed mood, and easy-on-the-budget prices. *Steenstraat 51–53, tel. 071/13 31 44. Reservations advised. O.L.: jacket and tie advised; 't P.: casual. AE, DC, MC, V. Closed Sun. O.L.: Expensive; 't P: Inexpensive.*

De Trommelaar. A delightful part of the New Age/Whole Earth

university scene, this easy-going enterprise features vegetarian and fish dishes imaginatively prepared with natural ingredients (sea salt, soy, brown sugar) and served in generous
portion. There are three all-vegetable plates, heaping with a
variety of earthy combinations—lasagne with sunflower
seeds, cauliflower with nutmeg sauce, sesame potatoes—and
three simple fish options as well, expansively garnished. Even
the wine is organic, and there's no smoking allowed, whether in
the airy dining room, with its mix of polished antique tables, or
in the lush courtyard garden behind. Moosewood lives on!
Apothekersdijk 22, tel. 071/13 00 55. Reservations suggested.
Casual. No credit cards. Inexpensive.

Schildknegt. In a lively canal-side shopping area full of san-
daled students, this pleasant new restaurant takes the step up
from hippie to yuppie, offering imaginative food in a chic but
casual cafe-like setting. Spare post-modern plank pine and halogen set the tone for cress salad with crushed strawberries and
onion, wild mushroom broth, carpaccio with capers and frisée,
and calf brains in browned butter, all served with a minimum of
pretense and a maximum of style. *Oude Rijn 1a, tel. 071/14 11*
00. Reservations suggested. Casual. No credit cards. Inexpen-
sive.

Lodging **Holiday Inn Leiden.** Located just off the secondary highway between Leiden and The Hague and not far from the beaches at
Katwijk, this is more a resort than a hotel. There is a vast interior garden lobby, and the decor of the guest rooms carries out
the garden theme with bold floral-patterned bedspreads.
Haagse Schouwweg 10, 2332 KG, tel. 071/35 55 55, fax 071/35 55
53. 200 rooms with bath/shower. Facilities: 2 restaurants, bar,
swimming pool, tennis and squash, bowling, sauna/solarium,
casino. AE, DC, MC, V. Expensive/Very Expensive.

De Ceder. This is a small, friendly, and very tidy family-style
hotel in a converted home out near the teaching hospital of Leiden University. The garden rooms are particularly desirable,
but the breakfast room overlooks the garden, too. *Rijnsbur-*
gerweg 80, 2333 AD, tel. 071/17 59 03, fax 071/15 70 98. 13
rooms, 9 with bath/shower. Facilities: bar-lounge for guests,
garden. AE, DC, MC, V. Inexpensive.

Rotterdam **Raden Mas of Rotterdam.** At this elegant and exotically deco-
Dining rated Indonesian restaurant, rijstafel is served both traditional style (from a number of small dishes) and Oriental style (all
on your plate from the kitchen). Among the traditional elements of a rijstafel you will find are *sate* (a kebob of chicken or
pork in peanut sauce), *gado-gado* (Oriental vegetables), and
sambal (a red-pepper condiment that is very, very hot).
Kruiskade 72, tel. 010/411-7244. Reservations advised. Jacket
and tie advised. AE, DC, MC, V. Very Expensive.

La Gondola. In this Italian restaurant there is a picture wall
that reads like a history of modern pop music. Located directly
across from the Rotterdam Hilton, where pop stars tend to
stay, it is a relaxing, friendly place with a good selection of traditional Italian specialties. *Kruiskade 6, tel. 010/411-4284.*
Reservations advised. Jacket required. AE, DC, MC, V. Ex-
pensive.

Pasta Pasta. On the second floor of an office building, this elaborately decorated Italian restaurant offers music nightly during
dinner. The wine list includes the best Italian vintages, and
there is a raw bar. *Kruiskade 78, tel. 010/413-6211. Reserva-*

tions advised. Jacket and tie advised. AE, DC, MC, V. Expensive.

De Wagon. This pleasant little restaurant is an old railway dining car now situated at Leuvehaven harbor. It is a casual sort of place with a friendly bar and a traditional menu of grilled meats and fish. *Geldersekade 10, tel. 010/433–1728. No reservations. Dress: casual. AE, DC, MC, V. Moderate.*

Dining and Lodging **Hotel Inntel Rotterdam.** This modern high rise, built in 1990 at the opening to the Leuvehaven inner harbor, has a water view over the port from all its rooms, as well as from the dinner restaurant and the rooftop health club. *Leuvehaven 80, 3011 EA, tel. 010/413–4139, fax 010/413–3222. 150 rooms. Facilities: restaurant, café, sauna, indoor swimming pool. Credit cards. AE, DC, MC, V. Expensive.*

Rijnhotel. This 10-story, business-oriented hotel is located next to the major theater of Rotterdam and across from the congress center. It has attractive, art deco–style rooms, recently renovated, and an appealing small restaurant overlooking the street that offers a prix fixe dinner arrangement with private limousine transportation for nonhotel guests. *Schouwburgplein 1, 3012 CK, tel. 010/433–3800, fax 010/414–5482. 100 rooms. Facilities: restaurant, café. AE, DC, MC, V. Expensive.*

Lodging **Rotterdam Hilton.** Don't be surprised if you run into Mick Jagger or Diana Ross if you choose to stay here. This is the hotel of choice for many of the pop and rock performers who bring their tours to Holland; it provides top facilities, a number of suites, and luxury appointments and amenities. It also has one of the best downtown locations in Rotterdam. *Weena 10, 3012 CM, tel. 010/414–4044, fax 010/411–8884. 254 rooms. Facilities: restaurant, café, bar, discotheque, garage, casino, barber/beauty shop. AE, DC, MC, V. Very Expensive.*

Hotel Van Walsum. On a residential boulevard within walking distance of the Boymans–van Beuningen Museum, Hotel van Walsum is not far from the Euromast. The gregarious owner proudly restores and reequips his rooms, floor by floor, on a continuously rotating basis, with the always-modern decor of each floor determined by that year's best buys in furniture, carpeting, and bathroom tiles. There is a bar-lounge and a small restaurant that has a summer garden extension. *Mathenesserlaan 199–201, 3014 HC, tel. 010/436–3275, fax 010/436–4410. 25 rooms. Facilities: restaurant, café. AE, DC, MC, V. Inexpensive.*

Utrecht **Het Grachtenhuys.** There is the feeling of a gracious home at
Dining this restaurant in a canal house that overlooks the fashionable New Canal. The young owners offer a choice of four- or five-course menus of traditionally French-influenced Dutch cuisine. Tempting selections might include rabbit fillet with a puree of various nuts, or truffle and potato soup with smoked eel. *Nieuwegracht 33, tel. 030/31 74 94. Reservations advised. Jacket and tie advised. AE, DC, MC, V. Closed Mon. and weekend lunch. Expensive–Very Expensive.*

Le Piano. One of the restaurants on the lower quay of Utrecht's main canal, it has waterside tables in the summer. The dining room is hung with amusing art; the menu offers traditional grilled dishes, including choices such as salmon with chervil, and a salad of smoked duck with almond dressing. *Oudegracht* a/d Werf 101–103, tel. 030/334939. Reservations advised. Dress: casual/jacket and tie. AE, DC, MC, V. Moderate.

Polman's Huis. This grand café of the old school is a Utrecht institution. Its Jugendstijl/Art Deco interior is authentic. Other reasons to find your way to Polman's are its relaxing atmosphere and range of meal choices, from a simple quiche to a steamed fish dinner. Keistraat 2, tel. 030/31 33 68. No reservations. Dress: casual. No credit cards. Closed Dec. 25. Moderate.

Lodging **Holiday Inn.** Primarily a business hotel (it looks like an office building), it serves the convention and exhibition hall next door and makes a convenient choice for other travelers as well. It has the only hotel swimming pool in town. Jaarbeursplein 24, 3521 AR, tel. 030/910555, fax 030/94 39 99. 280 rooms with bath/shower. Facilities: restaurant, bar, sauna, indoor swimming pool. AE, DC, MC, V. Expensive.

Hotel Smits. On the main square between the station and the old city center, this medium-size hotel has all the comforts of the larger, business-oriented establishments. The rooms are bright, comfortable, and decorated in mauve and black, in an art deco–influenced manner; nonsmoking rooms are available. Vredenburg 14, 3511 BA, tel. 030/33 12 32, fax 030/32 84 51. 85 rooms with bath/shower. Facilities: restaurant, bar. AE, DC, MC, V. Moderate/Expensive.

Malie Hotel. Located on a quiet residential street in a 19th-century row house, this is a modern and attractive family hotel. Rooms are brightly decorated though simply furnished. The bar-lounge doubles as a small art gallery. Maliestraat 2–4, 3581 SL, tel. 030/31 64 24, fax 030/34 06 61. 29 rooms with bath/shower. Facilities: bar. AE, DC, MC, V. Moderate.

Hotel Ouwi. A convivial family hotel, it is just off one of the main transit routes to the city center. The rooms are tight and simple in furnishings and decor, but they're very clean and tidy. F.C. Dondersstraat 12, 3572 JH, tel. 030/71 63 03. 21 rooms, 18 with bath/shower. No credit cards. Inexpensive.

The Arts and Nightlife

The Arts The cities of the Randstand are a cultural mecca, harboring world-class music and dance programs, master classes, major festivals, and pop/rock extravaganzas.

For information on cultural events, call the *Uit (Going Out)* information telephone numbers in The Hague (Uitpost Den Haag, tel. 070/363–3833) and Rotterdam (Uit Promotie Rotterdam, tel. 010/413–6540; or VVV Rotterdam, tel. 06/340–40655), or contact the VVV tourist information office in Utrecht (Vredenburg 90, tel. 06/340–34085) for both schedules and ticket information. In addition, in The Hague you can pick up the monthly *Info: Den Haag, Scheveningen en Kijkduin, Day to Day Tourist Information,* which lists (in Dutch) what's going on in major theaters in that area, with English copy describing major events. Similar publications are *Punt Uit Agenda* in Rotterdam, and *Uit in Utrecht* in Utrecht.

Music Haarlem hosts the **International Organ Competition** in even-numbered years during the first week of July. In The Hague, the **Residentie Orkest** is the city's excellent orchestra, which performs at **Dr. Anton Philipszaal** (Houtmarkt 17, tel. 070/360–9810) and **Nederlands Congresgebouw** (Churchillplein 10, tel.

070/354–8000). In Rotterdam, the concert orchestra is the fine **Rotterdam Philharmonic Orchestra,** which performs at the large concert hall **Concert- en Congresgebouw de Doelen** (Kruisstraat 2/Schouwburgplein 50, tel. 010/413–2490 or 010/413–2400). Utrecht is the site of the **Festival of Early Music** (tel. 030/34 09 21) late in each summer. It also offers a full program of concerts in its fine churches, including the Dom Church (tel. 030/31 04 03), St. Peter's Church (tel. 030/31 14 85), and St. Catharine's Church (tel. 030/31 40 30), and there are programs including both concerts and master classes in the **Conservatory** of the **K&W-gebouw/Arts and Sciences Building** (Mariaplaats 27, tel. 030/31 40 44).

Dance **Nederlands Danstheater** is the national modern dance company of the Netherlands, which makes its home in The Hague and performs at the **AT&T Danstheater** (Schedeldoekshaven 60, tel. 070/360–4930). **Scapino Ballet** is Rotterdam's resident dance company; performances are at **Rotterdamse Schouwburg** (Schouwburgplein 25, tel. 010/411–8110), which was designed by Dutch architect Wim Quist. In Utrecht you will find dance on the programs of **Stadsschouwburg** (Lucas Bolwerk 24, tel. 030/33 13 43), which has a major performance hall as well as the Blauwe Zaal (Blue Room) for small productions.

Theater/Opera In The Hague, the national theater company **Het Nationale Toneel** performs at **Royal Schouwburg** (Korte Voorhout 3, tel. 070/346–9450); the **De Appel** company performs at its own **Appeltheater** (Duinstraat 6–8, tel. 070/350–2200). **Musicals,** including occasional world tours from Broadway, can be seen at **Nederlands Congresgebouw** (Churchillplein 10, tel. 070/355–8000) or in the adjoining beach resort community of Scheveningen at **Circustheater** (G. Deijnootplein 50, tel. 070/355–8800). The theater company of Rotterdam is **RO-theatergroup,** which performs at the new **Rotterdamse Schouwburg** (Schouwburgplein 25, tel. 010/411–8110); **cabaret and musicals** in Rotterdam are performed at **Luxor Theater** (Kruiskade 10, tel. 010/413–8326). Theater (and opera) in Utrecht is performed in the *zaals* (auditoriums—large and small) at **Stadsschouwburg** (Lucas Bolwerk 24; tel. 030/33 13 43).

Film Films are shown in the original language, except Disney movies and other films for the very young. In addition to the annual avant-garde **Film Festival Rotterdam** (tel. 010/413–6540), Rotterdam offers mixed media and film performances at **Lantaren/Venster** (Gouvernestraat 129–133, tel. 010/436–1311) and has a special publication for film listings titled *Cargo,* available in bars, cafés, and some shops.

Pop/Rock When the big stars come to Rotterdam, they perform either at the **Sportpaleis Ahoy** (Zuiderparkweg 20–30, tel. 010/481–2144) or at the major soccer stadium, **Feyenoord Stadion** (Olympiaweg 50, tel. 010/492–9499 or 010/492–9444).

Jazz One of the festivals for which the Netherlands is well known is the annual **North Sea Jazz Festival** (tel. 070/350–2034), which is the largest of its kind in the world. It is held in The Hague and Scheveningen for four days in July and regularly attracts the greats of jazz as well as thousands of jazz lovers from around the world. In addition, the **Heineken Jazz Festival** (tel. 010/413–3972) is held in Rotterdam's streets and cafés in October.

Nightlife You'll find brown cafés (the traditional pub-bars of the Netherlands, which still have their locals who come in for a quick drink

or a nightcap) in every town in the Netherlands and discos in
any of the student towns, such as Leiden, but for real nightlife,
with plenty of variety, look to the large cities. In The Hague,
you will find discos in the streets around Central Station, especially on Herengracht, and in the beach resort of Scheveningen;
in Rotterdam, nightlife is concentrated in Oude and Nieuwe
Binnenweg, on 's Gravendijkswal, Oude Haven, Katshoek,
Witte de Wittsstraat, and at Stadhuisplein; and in Utrecht,
cafés are found on Oude Gracht and at 't Wed (near the canals,
in the center). Among the favorite newer places to go are the
Paris-style grand cafés and brasseries, which have terraces
(open or covered) on busy streets and squares of the major cities.

Cafés In the beach community of Scheveningen, **Plaza Bar** (Gevers
Deynootplein 118, tel. 070/355–5056) is a chic and exclusive
place, open until 4 AM, that offers all sorts of music, live and recorded. In Rotterdam, **De Consul** (Westersingel 28B, tel. 010/
436–3323) offers movies, New Age and pop music; **De Pul**
(Weena 115), not far from the Casino, is open until 6 AM (closed
Mon.) and has 30 brands of whiskey and Indonesian (and Dutch)
food. In Utrecht, **Het Oude Pothuis** (Oude Gracht 279, tel. 030/
31 89 70) has both music and meals six nights a week, plus a
stage with instruments available for jam sessions; another
place in Utrecht is **Polman's Huis** (*see* Dining and Lodging,
above), which stays open until 2 AM on weekdays, 3 AM on weekends.

Discotheques In The Hague, the huge **Marathon** (Wijndaelerweg 3, tel. 070/
368–0324) offers a wide variety of music, as does **The Corniche
Club** (Gevers Deynootplein 155–156, tel. 070/354–4510) in
Scheveningen. **Rebel Rebel** (Herengracht 7, tel. 070/345–7616)
and, in Scheveningen, **Thahiti** (Strandweg 43, tel. 070/350–
2068) have some live performances. In Rotterdam, **Beat Corner**
(Nieuwe Binnenweg 182, tel. 010/436–6070) is open all night (to
6 or 7 AM) with swing, house music, and, on Wednesday, quiet
music; **Carrera** (Karel Doormanstraat 10–12, tel. 010/213–
1180, open Thurs.–Sun. to 5 AM) has a variety of music and an
all-night French terrace serving snacks; **Full Moon** ('s
Gravendijkswal 130, tel. 010/436–7172) has dance music until 4
AM nightly except Monday (no house music). In Utrecht, the top
place is **Fellini** (Stadshuisbrug 3, tel. 030/31 72 71), in the cellars
of the old town hall.

Dancing In Rotterdam, **Tudor** (Nieuwe Binnenweg 210–212) has dance
music Thursday through Sunday until 6 AM. **Le Toucan** (L.
Berchmakerstraat 4, tel. 030/31 71 07) in Utrecht is a "swingcafé" with a dance floor that's open Wednesday to Saturday until 3 AM.

Jazz/Blues After Amsterdam, Rotterdam is the place for jazz. **Dizzy** ('s
Gravendijkswal 127A, tel. 010/477–3014) is a jazz café with a
big terrace out back that has performances by Dutch and inter-
national musicians every Tuesday and Sunday. **Thelonious**
(Lijnbaan 120, tel. 010/411–2231) has concerts on Friday and
Saturday nights, with jam sessions on Thursdays. **De
Twijtelaar** (Mauritsstraat 173, tel. 010/413–2671, open Tues.–
Sat.) has jazz sessions on Wednesdays. In Utrecht, **Zeezicht**
(Nobelstraat 2, tel. 030/31 99 57) offers jazz and blues on Tues-
days.

For Gays In Rotterdam, **Gay Palace** (Schiedamnsesingel 139, tel. 010/
414–1486) is a discotheque that's open Thursday–Monday until
4 AM; and in Utrecht, **De Roze Wolk** (Oude Gracht 45, tel. 030/32
20 66) is a canalside gay and lesbian disco with two bars that's
open Thursday–Saturday until 4:30 AM.

The Border Provinces and Maastricht

The long, shared border between the Netherlands and Belgium
runs like a drunkard's test path from the North Sea coast to the
German frontier. The long, shared heritage of religion, architecture, food, and lifestyle makes Brussels as alluring as Amsterdam to the residents of the southern provinces of the
Netherlands: These southern Dutch are more gregarious and
outspoken than those of the north; they also pursue the good
life of food, drink and conviviality with more gusto, and less
guilt, than their Calvinist-influenced countrymen who live
"above the Great Rivers."

Three provinces hug the Belgian border: Zeeland (Sea Land) is
a collection of flat, open, and windswept islands and peninsular
extensions of the mainland, known for its agriculture and shellfish; Noord Brabant, also known simply as Brabant, is a
wooded and water-laced industrial area bordered on both east
and north by the River Maas; Limburg is a region of hills and
half-timbered farmhouses that extends along the River Maas
deep into the south, a peninsula of land surrounded on one side
by Belgium and the other by Germany.

Important Addresses and Numbers

Tourist Information The tourist information offices of the major cities of the border
provinces are **VVV Breda** (Willemstraat 17–19, 4811AJ, tel.
076/22 24 44), **VVV Eindhoven** (Stationsplein 17, 5611 AC, tel.
040/44 92 31), **VVV 's-Hertogenbosch** (Markt 77, Box 1039, 5200
BA, tel. 073/12 30 71), **VVV Maastricht** (Het Dinghuis, Kleine
Staat 1, 6211 ED, tel. 043/25 21 21, fax 043/21 37 46), and **VVV
Middelburg** (Markt 65a, Postbus 730, 4330 AS, tel. 01180/
16851).

Emergencies The **national emergency number** for police, fire, or ambulance is
06–11.

Medical There are **hospitals** in Breda (tel. 076/23 30 00 or 076/25 80 00),
Eindhoven (tel. 040/33 59 33), 's-Hertogenbosch (tel. 073/41 45
45 or 073/86 91 11), Maastricht (tel. 043/87 65 43), and
Middelburg (tel. 01180/37000).

Arriving and Departing

By Plane There are airports in Eindhoven and Maastricht. In addition to
regular flights to both cities from Amsterdam, **KLM City Hopper** (tel. 081/750–9000) also operates service direct from London Gatwick to Maastricht and from London Heathrow to
Eindhoven. Additional services to Eindhoven from the United
Kingdom are scheduled by **Base Business Airlines** (tel. 061/489-
2808) from Birmingham and Manchester.

By Car To reach **Zeeland** take E19 from Amsterdam to Rotterdam and pick up A29 south; connect with N59 west to Zierikzee and N256 across the Zeelandbrug toll bridge to Goes, where you can pick up E312/A58 west to Middelburg, capital of Zeeland province.

To reach the provinces of Brabant and Limburg take E25/A2 from Amsterdam south through Utrecht. Pick up A27 south to Breda, or stay on E25 through Den Bosch to reach Eindhoven and other points south.

By Train There are **Intercity express trains** (tel. 06/899–1121) twice each hour from Amsterdam direct to 's-Hertogenbosch and Eindhoven, once each hour direct to Middelburg or Maastricht. To reach Breda by train, it is necessary to connect either in Roosendaal or 's-Hertogenbosch.

Getting Around

By Bus The **national bus information** number is 06/9292. Local and regional buses leave and return from the Dutch railway stations. For local information call in **Breda** (tel. 06/821–2115 or 076/22 38 50), **Eindhoven** (tel. 06/821–2115), **Maastricht** (tel. 045/73 51 00), and **Middelburg** (tel. 01110/19111).

By Train There is an Intercity train line (tel. 06/899–1121) that crosses the country, west to east **within the Border Provinces,** twice each hour. From Breda there also is twice-hourly service direct to Eindhoven, for connections to Maastricht.

By Taxi To summon a taxi, call in **Breda** (tel. 076–22 21 11), **Eindhoven** (tel. 040/52 52 52), **'s-Hertogenbosch** (tel. 073/12 85 85), **Maastricht** (tel. 043/47 77 77), and **Middelburg** (tel. 01180/12600).

Guided Tours

The **Maastricht Tourist Office** (Kleine Staat 1, tel. 043/25 21 21) offers a guided tour of the city for Fl 4–Fl 7.50 for adults, Fl 2.50–Fl 4 for children. Tours last from 1 to 1½ hours. For cruises on the River Maas, contact **Stiphout Cruises** (Maaspromenade 27, 6211 HS Maastricht, tel. 043/25 41 51); the fare is Fl 10–Fl 47.50 adults, Fl 6–Fl 18 children.

The **Middelburg Tourist Office** (Markt 65a, tel. 01180/16851) occasionally offers guided walking tours during the summer for Fl 2 (1 hour) to Fl 4 (2 hours) per person. Tours of the province also are available through **Holland International Reisbureau Van Fraassen** (Londensekaai 19, tel. 01180/27758), **Carlier Tours** (Elektraweg 9, tel. 01180/15015), and **Holland International Reisbureau** (Langeviele 7, tel. 01180/27855).

Exploring the Border Provinces and Maastricht

Numbers in the margin correspond with places of interest on the Border Provinces map.

Zeeland On the fingerlike peninsulas and islands of the province of Zeeland (the name means Sea Land), you are never more than a few kilometers from a major body of water. You also are never more than a meter or two above sea level, if you are above it at all: Floods have put this province almost completely under water on several occasions, most recently in 1953. Today, major dikes, dams, and bridges connect the four chief islands and penin-

116

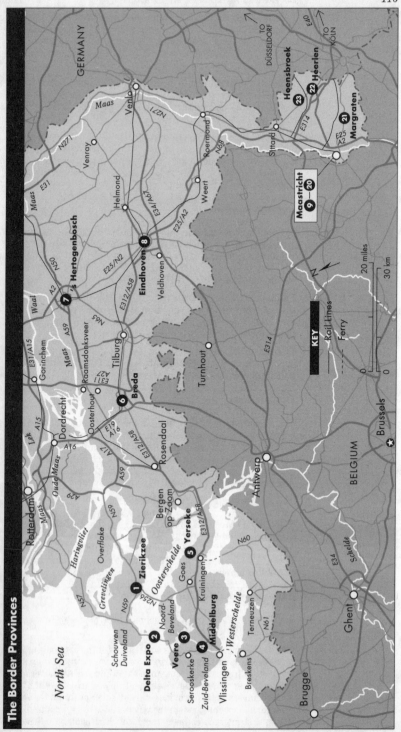

The Border Provinces

North Sea

GERMANY

BELGIUM

KEY

Rail Lines

Ferry

0   20 miles

0   30 km

N

1 Zierikzee
2 Delta Expo
3 Veere
4 Middelburg
5 Yerseke
6 Breda
7 's Hertogenbosch
8 Eindhoven
9 — 20 Maastricht
21 Margraten
22 Heerlen
23 Heensbroek

Rotterdam
Dordrecht
Gorinchem
Raamsdonksveer
Oosterhout
Rosendaal
Bergen op Zoom
Goes
Kruiningen
Vlissingen
Breskens
Terneuzen
Serooskerke
Zuid-Beveland
Noord-Beveland
Schouwen Duiveland
Turnhout
Antwerp
Ghent
Brugge
Brussels
Tilburg
Veldhoven
Helmond
Venray
Venlo
Weert
Roermond
Sittard
Maastricht
Heerlen
Margraten

Maas
Waal
Lek
Oude Maas
Haringvliet
Grevelingen
Overflake
Oosterschelde
Westerschelde
Schelde

N57
N59
N256
N59
N61
N60
N68
N65
N50
N271
N271
A2
A15
A16
A17
A27
A29
A59
A58
E31
E31/A15
E19/A16
E311/A27
E312/A58
E312/N2
E34/A67
E25/N2
E25/A2
E314
E40
A2/E25
E34

TO DÜSSELDORF
TO KÖLN

sulas of Zeeland, guarding against the possibility of the sea's reclaiming the land already reclaimed by the Dutch.

From the north, follow A29 to N59, which leads to the small old

❶ city of **Zierikzee,** a yachting port with a canal connecting it to the open waters of the Oosterschelde. Continue on N59 to Serooskerke, where you can turn onto N57 to cross the Oosterscheldekering dam. This dramatic ride may be restricted in times of high winds; you have the North Sea to one side, the Oosterschelde bay to the other, and the looming storm surge barriers beside the road remind you that it requires massive constructions of steel and concrete to resist the forces of the sea. Your destination is Neeltje Jans Island, approximately halfway across the dam. Used as a work island during the two decades this massive enclosure was under construction, it now

❷ is the site of **Delta Expo,** which documents the 2,000-year history of Dutch hydraulic engineering. There are films and slide shows, working scale models, and displays of the materials used to construct dikes, dams, and underwater supports. The visit includes a boat trip in good weather, and there is an opportunity to walk inside a sample of one of the multistory pilings that make up the support system of the storm surge barriers. *Eiland Neeltje Jans, Burgh-Haamstede, tel. 01115/2702. Admission: Apr.–Oct., Fl 12 adults, Fl 8 children; Nov.–Mar., Fl 9 adults, Fl 6 children. Open Apr.–Oct., daily 10–5; Jan.–Feb., Thurs.–Mon. 10–5; Mar. and Nov.–Dec., Fri.–Tues. 10–5.*

Beyond the dam you briefly cross a corner of Noord Beveland Island and travel over another small dam, the Veersegatdam.

❸ Take the dike road to **Veere,** which is one of the prettiest small towns in the Netherlands. Now the principal sailing port of the Veerse Meer (Veerse Lake), it was an important seaport in the 16th century, with a busy trade in items such as wool, linen, and salt. **Museum De Schotse Huizen** (The Scots' Houses) is found in side-by-side 16th-century buildings facing the town's small inner harbor that once were the offices and warehouses of Scots wool merchants. Highly decorated, the buildings are named Het Lammetje (The Little Lamb) and De Struys (The Ostrich); you'll know which is which by the facade stones. Inside is a collection of local costumes, porcelain, household items, and paintings. *Kaai 25–27, Veere, tel. 01181/1744. Admission: Fl 2 adults, Fl 1.25 children. Open Apr.–Oct., Mon. 1–5, Tues.–Sat. 10–5.*

❹ From Veere take the local road to **Middelburg,** the capital of the province of Zeeland. It was an important trading post of the Dutch East and West India companies in the 17th century. The **Stadhuis** (Town Hall) on the market square is an elaborately decorated structure begun in the mid-15th century. The heart of this small city, however, is the 12th-century **Abdij** (Abbey Complex), which incorporates three churches, countless provincial government offices, a major research library, the provincial cultural and historical museum, and a tall tower that overlooks the city and surrounding countryside. Although it was badly damaged in World War II, the entire complex has been faithfully reconstructed. **Onze Lieve Vrouwe Abdij** (Our Beloved Lady Abbey) was founded in 1150 as a Premonstrant abbey and served as a monastery until 1574. The tours offered here include the three churches of the Abbey Complex, the Council Hall of the government, and the tapestry hall of the

Zeeland Museum. *Abdij 9, tel. 01180/16851. Admission (including visit to Zeeland Museum): Fl 5 adults, Fl 3.50 children. Tours May–Nov., Mon.–Sat. 1:30 and 3; July–Aug., Tues–Fri. 11, 1:30, and 3.*

Zeeuwse Museum (Zeeland Museum) is best known for its series of tapestries illustrating the major Dutch sea battles with Spain during the 16th century. The varied collection also includes an Egyptian mummy, votive stelae dating from the Roman period, a rare seashell collection of the Royal Zeeland Science Association, and a costume hall that is one of the best in the Netherlands. *Abdij, tel. 01180/26655. Admission: Fl 3.50 adults, Fl 2 children, Fl 9 family. Open Tues.–Fri. 10–5, Sat.–Mon. 1:30–5.*

Time Out **Restaurant De Abdij** (Abdijplein 5, tel. 01180/35022 or 01180/36196) is a convenient place to stop for a bite of lunch. Located within the Abbey Complex next to the Zeeuwse Museum, it offers a menu of sandwiches, salads, and light meals.

Also part of the Abbey complex, and of particular interest to American visitors to Zeeland, is the **Roosevelt Studiecentrum** (Roosevelt Study Center), a library, research center, and exhibition hall. Theodore Roosevelt and Franklin Delano Roosevelt were descendants of a Zeeland family; the purpose of this center is to make known the historical links between the United States and the Netherlands and particularly to publicize the role of the United States in Europe during the 20th century. *Abdij 9, tel. 01180/31590. Admission free. Open Wed.–Thurs. 9:30–12:30 and 1:30–4:30.*

You can climb the 207 steps to the top of the octagonal **"Lange Jan" Abdijtoren** ("Long John" Abbey Tower), which is attached to the Choral Church of the Abbey Complex. The 85-meter (280-foot) stone tower was constructed in the 14th century and is topped with an onion-shaped dome from the 18th century. *Abdij, tel. 01180/82255. Admission: Fl 1.95 adults, Fl 1.30 children. Open Apr.–Sept., Mon.–Sat. 10–5.*

5 Leave Middelburg on E312/A58 toward Bergen Op Zoom. At the Kruiningen/Yerseke exit, follow signs to **Yerseke,** a small fishing port that is the oyster nursery of Europe. Along the waterfront here, you'll see lobster boats docked at the piers; below the seawalls in pits are the beds in which are nurtured what some say are the finest, sweetest, and most flavorful oysters and mussels in the world. Peek into the small buildings on the docks and you will see shellfish being sorted and packed for shipment.

Brabant **6** Follow A58 all the way to **Breda.** Dotted with parks, this small city maintains a quiet medieval charm that is unexpected in a city also known as a major manufacturing center.

From the railway station, walk toward the center through **Stadspark Valkenburg** (Valkenburg Park), which dates from 1350 and was originally the castle garden of the counts of Breda. The former castle, **Kasteel van Breda** (Breda Castle), sits imposingly beyond the moat; it now houses the KMA (Royal Military Academy) and can be visited only on a group tour, which the VVV organizes on an occasional basis.

Follow Kasteelplein to Kerkplein and the imposing 15th- and 16th-century **Grote Kerk** (Great Church). Built in the French-influenced Brabant Gothic style in brick and sandstone, it was the family church of the House of Orange-Nassau: William of Orange's first wife and child are buried here, as are several of his ancestors. The church was looted of its brass ornamentation when Napoleon's soldiers used it as a barracks. The splendor of the architecture remains, as does the magnificence of the blue-and-gold-painted 18th-century organ. *Kerkplein, tel. 076/ 218267. Admission: Fl 2. Open weekdays 10–5, Sat. 10–5, Sun. 1–5.*

Facing the Grote Markt just beyond the church is the **Stadhuis** (Town Hall), which counts among its treasures a copy of the Velázquez painting of the surrender of Breda in 1625. Also on this elongated square is the municipal museum, **Het Stadelijk en Bisschoppelijk Museum** (The Municipal and Episcopal Museum), worth a quick visit to learn something of the city's eventful history. *Grote Markt 19, tel. 076/223110. Admission: Fl 1.50 adults, Fl 0.75 children. Open Wed.–Sat. 10:30–5, Tues., Sun., and holidays 1–5.*

Time Out When it's time to take a break, you'll find a good selection of restaurants and cafés circling the Grote Markt. **In The Mood** (Grote Markt 46, tel. 076/21 79 75 or 076/21 99 01) has a dramatic coffered ceiling and serves a simple grill menu.

From the head of the Grote Markt behind the church, follow Catharinastraat to the **Waalse Kerk** (Walloon Church, Catherinastraat 83a, tel. information 076/21 82 67), which marks the entrance to the **Begijnhof** (Beguine Court). A home for unmarried or widowed lay women who dedicate their lives to prayer and charitable works, this is one of only two remaining cloisters of this type in the Netherlands (the other is in Amsterdam).

➐ From Breda, take E311/A27 north to Raamsdonksveer and connect with A59 to **'s-Hertogenbosch.** 'S-Hertogenbosch means The Duke's Woods in Dutch, and while that is the official name of this stylish medieval city, the name you will hear more commonly is simply Den Bosch (pronounced "den-boss"), The Woods. Not much remains of the woods for which it was named, however: The forests have been replaced by marshes and residential and industrial development. The principal attraction of Den Bosch is the magnificent **St. Janskathedraal** (St. John's Cathedral), the only cathedral in the Netherlands. Built between 1380 and 1520 in the Brabant Gothic style, it is a cruciform, five-aisle basilica with numerous side chapels and a Romanesque tower. Abundantly decorated with statuary, sculptural details, and grotesques, its nave is supported by double flying buttresses that are unique in the Netherlands. *Parade, tel. 073/ 13 97 40. Admission free. Open weekdays 10–5.*

Time Out There is a very special sweet treat in store for you in 's-Hertogenbosch. Called a *Bossche bol*, it is a whipped-cream-filled, ball-shaped *choux* (cream puff) pastry that is completely dipped in dark chocolate and served cool. **Patisserie Jan de Groot** (Stationsweg 24, tel. 073/13 38 30), on the road leading to the railway station, is the only producer in town.

From the Parade, follow Lange Putstraat to Verwersstraat and turn left for the **Noordbrabants Museum** (North Brabant Museum), the foremost provincial museum in the country. Housed in the imposing former residence of the provincial governor, the museum contains historical, archaeological, and cultural exhibits related to the history of Brabant, as well as an outstanding art collection that includes many 17th- and 18th-century Dutch floral paintings as well by Brabant artists of various periods. *Verwersstraat 41, tel. 073/13 96 64. Admission: Fl 5 adults, Fl 2.50 children. Open Tues.–Fri. 10–5, weekends noon–5.*

❽ From 's-Hertogenbosch, take E25/N2 to **Eindhoven.** This bustling, modern city has no traditional, historic center to explore, thanks to heavy bombing in World War II, but there are remarkable examples of contemporary architecture throughout the city (even the bus shelters are designed by well-known architects), and there is an exceptional museum of modern art. The **Stadelijk Van Abbemuseum** (Municipal van Abbe Museum) began in 1936 as the simple wish of a local cigar maker, Henri van Abbe, to visit a museum in his own town; today it has one of the world's finest collections of contemporary art and owns more works than can be displayed at one time. The galleries and exhibitions are rotated and rearranged continually. The collection includes major works by artists such as Picasso and Christo. There are examples to be seen here of every major trend of the last 100 years, including cubism, constructivism, de Stijl, German expressionism, minimalism, and American pop. *Bilderdijklaan 10, tel. 040/38 97 30. Admission: Fl 2.50. Open Tues.–Sun. 11–5.*

Leaving the Van Abbe Museum, you can take an interesting walk past shops and art galleries. Turn right on Wal and left at Grote Berg, right again at Bergstraat and take another right at Kleine Berg.

Continue left onto Keizersgracht and its continuation, Willemstraat, or return from Keizersgracht to the tourist office and railway station.

Time Out **Grand Cafe Berlage** (Kleine Berg 16, tel. 040/45 74 81) is a spacious, Art Deco brasserie with a streetside terrace that serves French-influenced dishes such as grilled fish and meats with simple butters and sauces.

Continue left onto Keizersgracht and its continuation, Willemstraat, or return from Keizersgracht to the tourist office and railway station.

Numbers in the margin correspond with places of interst on the Maastrict map.

Maastricht From Eindhoven, take E25/A2 south through Limburg province to reach the city of Maastricht. The oldest city in the Netherlands, established by the Romans more than 2,500 years ago, Maastricht has enjoyed a long history as a crossroads between Germanic and Latin cultures. The lighthearted lifestyle, meticulous attention to service, and the exceptionally fine French cuisine further reflect the blending of these influences. Maastricht straddles the River Maas: The old city is on the river's western bank, its newer neighborhoods and the railway station **❾** are on the eastern side. Connecting the two is **St. Servaasbrug** (St. Servatius Bridge), one of the oldest and busiest bridges in the Netherlands. Built solidly of gray Namur stone in the late 13th century, it replaced an earlier wooden bridge. It offers the

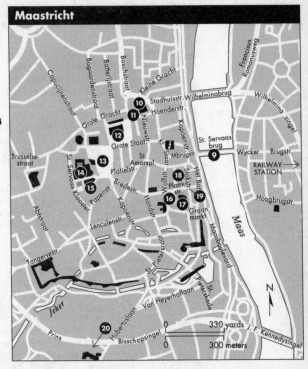

best views of the old city—an expanse of jumbled rooflines and whitewashed houses facing the river. The St. Servatius Bridge leads directly into both the old city and the heart of the shopping district. Follow Maastrichter Brugstraat to its end and bear right on Kleine Staat to find the tourist office, housed in a building that dates from 1470. Take Muntstraat directly ahead to Markt, the market square, dominated by the 1662 **Stadhuis** (Town Hall). Every Wednesday and Friday are market days in Maastricht, when this square is chockablock with stalls and stands offering fruits, vegetables, meats, and household items. You'll notice that business here is conducted in three currencies (Dutch, Belgian, and German) and four languages (Dutch, French, German, and English). *Markt 78, tel. 043/29 22 22. Admission free. Open weekdays 8:30–12:30 and 2–5:30.*

Leave the market square by way of Spilstraat, near the jolly statue of a roly-poly woman carrying a basket of vegetables, known affectionately as **Moosewief** (Greengrocer's Wife). Take Spilstraat to Grote Staat and turn right into Dominikerkstraat; directly ahead is the **Bonnefantenmuseum** (Bonnefanten Museum), the provincial museum of Limburg. Among the displays are one on the archaeological history of the province, a model of the city of Maastricht, and an art collection that focuses on 13th- to 15th-century Romanesque and Gothic Mosan sculpture of the Meuse region, 14th- to 16th-century Italian painting, and 16th- to 18th-century paintings of the South Netherlands, including works by Jan Bruegel and Pieter Bruegel the Younger. There also is a collection of contemporary art by important Dutch painters of the 20th century, several of whom are from

Limburg. *Dominikanerplein 5, tel. 043/25 16 55. Admission:
Fl 5 adults, Fl 3 children. Open Tues.–Fri. 10–5, weekends
11–5.*

13 Leaving the museum, turn toward the large open **Vrijthof**
square. Ringed with restaurants, grand cafés, discotheques
and traditional pubs, this is the major public gathering place of
Maastricht and the focal point of the annual Carnival.

Time Out A cheerful place to stop at any time of the day is the plant-filled,
Jugendstil-decorated **Cafe Britannique** (Vrijthof 6, tel. 043/21
86 91). They serve breakfast (with champagne if you like) as
well as simple, light meals throughout the day and drinks, including a house beer, until midnight.

Tucked into a corner of Vrijthof are two churches. The larger of
14 these is the magnificent and historic 7th-century **St.
Servaasbasiliek** (St. Servatius Basilica) named for and built
above the site of the burial place of a 4th-century saint whose
choice of Maastricht for his see stimulated the development of
the city following the departure of the Romans in 402. The basilica has a dark but warmly carved interior, the focal point of
which is its **Schatkamer van Sint Servaas** (Treasure Chamber of
St. Servatius) in the 12th-century chapel. The extraordinary
collection dates from 827 and contains religious relics (some of
them donated by Charlemagne) and exquisitely wrought liturgical objects. The most important item in the collection is the
12th-century **Noodkist**, an elaborately decorated oak chest
that is adorned with gold and silver figures and contains bones
and relics of St. Servatius and other local bishops. *Vrijthof, tel.
043/25 21 21. Admission: Fl 3.50 adults, Fl 1 children. Open
Dec.–Mar., daily 10–4, Apr.–June and Sept.–Nov. 10–5;
July–Aug., daily 10–6.*

15 Next to St. Servatius is the 14th-century Gothic **St. Janskerk**
(St. John's Church), the white interior of which is a notable con-
trast to the darkness of St. Servatius Basilica. *Vrijthof (enter
Henric van Veldekeplein), tel. 043/25 21 21. Admission free.
Open mid-June–mid-Sept., Tues.–Fri. 11–4; Jul.–Aug.
Tues.–Sat. 11–4.*

Cross the Vrijthof in front of the Spanish Government House
and continue on the Bredestraat to reach the intimate residen-
16 tial square **Onze Lieve Vrouweplein** (Our Beloved Lady
17 Square). Dominating the tree-shaded, quiet square is the **Onze
Lieve Vrouwebasiliek** (Our Beloved Lady Basilica). Recent ex-
cavations on the square indicate that the basilica may have replaced a Roman temple. The Westwork, a massive flat facade in
Romanesque style that is topped with two round turrets, is the
oldest part of the structure, dating from the 11th and 12th centuries. Inside is a two-story apse with a double row of columns
and a half-domed roof. *Onze Lieve Vrouweplein, tel. 043/25 18
51. Admission: Fl 2 adults, Fl 0.50 children. Open Easter–
Oct., Mon.–Sat. 11–5, Sun. 1–5.*

From Onze Lieve Vrouweplein, take Plankstraat to the small
18 entry to **Op de Thermen**. This small interior square was discovered in 1840 to be the site of the Roman baths; recently laid paving stones indicate the outline of the chambers of the ancient
complex. Beyond the entry to the square, the next street is
19 **Stokstraat**, a fashionable residential street that extends on either side of Plankstraat and was the heart of the original Ro-

man settlement of Maastricht. Follow Stokstraat left to the small square at the end; a few steps up a small stairway will bring you back to the St. Servatius Bridge.

㉙ South beyond Maastricht's city walls and the busy Prins Bisshopsingel (N278) encircling highway are the **Grotten St. Pieter** (Caves of St. Peter), man-made corridors carved deep into the limestone hills since Roman times to produce building stone. There are approximately 200 kilometers (124 miles) of chambers and passageways here; in some areas the mining has been so extensive that the ceiling height now is nearly 12 meters (40 feet); this means that graffiti left by the Romans are now far above your head, while the signatures of such visitors as Napoleon can still be seen. The caves are complex and can be visited only with a guide; they are also chilly and damp, so bring a sweater. *Grotten Noord (Northern System) Luikerweg 71; Zonneberg Caves, Slavante 1 (near Enci Cement Works); tel. 043/25 21 21 for times of tours. Admission: Fl 4 adults, Fl 2.25 children. Open hours vary, call ahead.*

Numbers in the margin correspond with places of interest on the Border Provinces map.

South Limburg Take the encircling highway N278 east from the caves toward Vaals and Aachen. Approximately 10 kilometers (6 miles) beyond the city, near the town of **Margraten,** you will find the entrance to the 26-hectare (65-acre) **Netherlands American Cemetery and Memorial.** This is the only American military cemetery in the Netherlands and is the final resting place of more than 8,000 Americans killed in World War II. *Rijksweg 2, tel. 04458/1208. Admission free. Open summer, daily 8–6; winter, daily 8–5.*

㉒ From here, take N281 toward **Heerlen,** the second of the Roman cities in this part of the Netherlands. The discovery in 1940 of the foundations of a large and elaborate Roman bathhouse was proof of the importance of Heerlen as a meeting place for the Roman troops stationed in this northern outpost. Now enclosed in a large, open, glass-encircled building, the **Thermenmuseum** (Thermae Museum) has catwalks over the perfectly preserved complex. The *thermae* (baths) incorporated open-air sports fields, a large swimming pool, shops, restaurants, and the enclosed bathhouse complex, which included a large dressing room, the hot-air sweating room, and a series of baths (warm, lukewarm, cold, and immersion). *Coriovallumstraat 9, Heerlen, tel. 0445/76 45 81. Admission: Fl 2.50 adults, Fl 1.50 children. Open Tues.–Fri. 10–5, weekends and holidays 2–5.*

㉓ Follow N281 northwest to **Hoensbroek** and the largest and best preserved of the castles in South Limburg, the **Kastel Hoensbroek** (Hoensbroek Castle), which incorporates sections dating from the 13th century and represents various architectural styles, including Baroque and Maasland-Renaissance. You can visit several sparsely but appropriately furnished rooms and an unexpected small museum of Afro-Asian art. There is an art gallery in the attic and a photography gallery in the gatehouse. *Klinkertstraat 118, tel. 045/21 11 82. Admission: Fl 4 adults, Fl 3 children. Open May–Sept., 10–5:30; Oct.–Apr., 10–noon and 1–5:30.*

What to See and Do with Children

Miniatuur Walcheren (Miniature Walcheren) is a miniature city in a garden not far from the Abbey Complex in Middelburg. Typical buildings and landmarks of the area have been duplicated at 1:20 scale, including houses, churches, and windmills. Even the trees and plants are miniature, and there is a reconstruction of Veerse Lake, with motorized boats. *Molenwater, Middelburg, Zeeland, tel. 01180/12525. Admission: Fl 5 adults, Fl 3 children. Open Apr. 12–Oct. 21, daily 9:30–5, July–Aug., daily 9:30–6.*

The **Remschip de Schorpioen** (Ramship *Scorpion*) is one of only three iron ramming ships of its kind in the world and the oldest surviving Dutch naval vessel. It is docked across from the railway station in Middelburg and can be visited in summer. *Loskade, Middelburg, Zeeland, tel. 01180/39649. Admission: Fl 3.50 adults, Fl 2.50 children. Open Apr.–Oct., daily 10–5.*

De Efteling is a children's fairy-tale park in Brabant, approximately halfway between Breda and 's-Hertogenbosch. Rides and amusements are enhanced by the fanciful and witty depiction of classic fairy tales by the Dutch artist Anton Pieck. *Box 18, 5170 AA Kaatsheuvel, Brabant, tel. 04167/88111, fax 4167/81095. Admission: Fl 25 adults, Fl 22 children. Open mid-Apr.–late Oct., daily 10–6.*

Hundreds of animals live in an open, natural environment at **Safaripark Beekse Bergen** in Brabant, near Tilburg. There is a safari bus to take you through the park, or you can rent your own safari jeep. There is also a children's farm. *Beekse Bergen 1, Hilvarenbeek, Brabant, tel. 013/36 00 35. Admission: Fl 14.50 adults, Fl 11.50 children. Open Apr.–Oct.*

Off the Beaten Track

Just east of Tilburg is **Oisterwijk,** a wooded community and resort town that's perfect for a weekend getaway or a quiet day in the country. The charming central square is planted with lime trees, and there is a bird sanctuary with a number of exotic species.

As you travel south toward Maastricht, the small town of **Thorn,** known as the "white village" because of its abundance of white-painted 18th-century houses and buildings, is also well worth a detour. Visit the 10th-century abbey church, which has an outstanding Baroque altar and three choirs (for canons, princesses, and noblewomen); there also is a small museum.

Shopping

While there is shopping in every city mentioned in this section, you are well advised to save your guilders for Maastricht. This sophisticated small city is a mecca for goods from all over Europe, drawing merchants and shoppers from as far as Amsterdam, Brussels, and Cologne.

In Maastricht, as well as Breda, 's-Hertogenbosch, and Middelburg, stores are open late (until 9 PM) on Thursday; in Eindhoven, on Friday.

Shopping Districts The concentration of shopping in **Maastricht** is in the pedestrian cross streets that connect and surround the three main squares of the old city. Maastrichter Brugstraat takes you into the network of shopping streets from the St. Servaasbrug. Maastrichter Smedenstraat and Plankstraat are lined with exclusive shops, with Wolfstraat and the exceptionally fashionable Stokstraat intersecting both of them. In the other direction, Kleine Staat and Grote Staat lead to Vrijthof, with a mixed bag of shopping opportunities. Off Grote Staat is a trio of small shopping streets—Spilstraat, Nieuwestraat, and Muntstraat—that end at the Markt. Off Helmstraat is a shopping square, W.C. Entre Deux.

Street Markets **Breda** has a secondhand market at Grote Markt Tuesday through Friday, **'s-Hertogenbosch** holds a large general market every Wednesday and Saturday; **Maastricht** has its tri-country general market in front of the Town Hall on Wednesday and Friday mornings, and a flea market opposite the railway station on Saturday; **Middelburg's** market day is Thursday, and the fruit market is held there on Saturday. The summer antiques and curiosities market is held at the Vismarkt from mid-June through August on Thursdays from 9 to 4.

Art and Antiques Fair Each year Maastricht's MECC Congress and Exhibition Hall is the site of the **European Fine Art Fair** (European Fine Art Foundation, Box 1035, 5200BA, 's-Hertogenbosch, tel. 073/14 51 65), for a week beginning in mid-March. Major dealers in antiques and fine art from all over Europe participate, showing paintings, drawings, and prints (traditional and contemporary), furniture and objects, textiles, tapestries, and rugs; there also are music programs and lectures.

Specialty Stores *Antiques/Art Galleries* Eindhoven is an art and antiques mecca. Among the dealers in modern art is **Kunsthandel Beckers B.V.** (Kleine Berg 14, tel. 040/441381). Antiques dealers include **De Verleeden Tijd** (Kleine Berg 19, tel. 040/454041, especially for rocking horses; **Mimore** (Keizersgracht 22, tel. 040/435358) for 20th-century articles, including Art Deco; and **'t Harlekijntje** (Bergstraat 38, no tel.) for small antique items.

Art Books The shop of the **North Brabant Museum** (Verwersstraat 41, tel. 073/13 96 64) in 's-Hertogenbosch offers an exceptional collection of art books covering many periods and styles of Dutch and international art.

Sports and Fitness

Biking To rent a bicycle, contact, in Breda, **Rijwielstalling NS** (Stationsplein 16–20, tel. 076/210501); in 's-Hertogenbosch, **Stationsfietsstalling** (Stationsplein 22, 5211 AP, tel. 073/134737 or 073/134033) or **Cyclepoint** (Hoek Zuid-Willems-vaart-Hinthamereinde, tel. 073/139020); in Middelburg, **Stationsrijwielstalling** (Kanaalweg 22, tel. 01180/12178) or **Rijwiel- en bromfietsenhandel De Pree** (Zusterstraat 10–12, tel. 01180/2344); in Maastricht, the Railway Station (Stationsplein, Maastricht, tel. 043/211100).

Canoeing/Kayaking There are two areas of interest to canoeists in Noord Brabant province. One is the **Biesbosch** area near Breda, which combines small creeks with stretches of open water (busy with power boats in the summer season); the other is the tiny **Dommel River,** which meanders through the countryside between s'Hertogenbosch and Eindhoven and beyond. To rent a canoe in the Biesbosch area, contact **Nion Watersport**

(Oosterhoutseweg 20, Raamsdonksveer, tel. 01621/12997); along the Dommel, contact **Adventure Trips** (Sint Oedenrode, tel. 04138/77267), **De Kanovriend** (Geenhovensedreef 10, Valkenswaard, tel. 04902/14632), or **Kanobouw/knoverhurr Rofra** (Luikerweg 74, Valkenswaard, tel. 04902/42593). To kayak on the River Maas in Maastricht, contact **Kayak Tours Limburg** (Chambertinlaan 19, 6213 EV Maastricht, tel. 043/474899; cost Fl 23–Fl 45; day trips May–Sept.).

Tennis/Squash   To play in Maastricht, visit **Squash Centre Erik van der Pluijm** (Brusselsestraat 74a, tel. 043/216387), **Tennis Centre De Dousberg** (Dousbergweg, tel. 043/434404), or **Sportpark Mulder** (Mockstraat 36–38, tel. 043/637295). Rates are around Fl 12.50 per 30 minutes court time during the day; Fl 18, after 5 PM.

Sailing   To arrange a day on the water in Zeeland, contact **Jachtwerf Oostwatering** (Polredijk 13 B, Veere, tel. 01181/665), **WSVW en RYCB,** (Wolphaartsdijk, tel. 01198/1565), **Keur Marina B.V.** (Kanaalweg wz 5, Veere, tel. 01181/223), or **Jachtwerf Wolphaartsdijk** (Zandkreekweg 5, Wolphaartsdijk, tel. 01198/1562).

Spa   One of the special treats of South Limburg is a luxurious hill spa that offers a complete range of services, including indoor and outdoor spring-fed pools, sauna, steam bath, yoga/meditation and hydrogymnastics, aerobics, sports massage, herbal and mud baths, and more. **Thermae 2000** (Cauberg 27, 6301 BT Valkenburg aan de Geul, Valkenburg, tel. 04406/16060) is open daily 9 AM–11 PM.

Spectator Sports

Racing/Trotting Races   There is Friday-night racing at the **Limburg Race** in Landgraff (Hofstraat 13–15, tel. 045/319191) starting at 7.

Soccer   Eindhoven's team, **PSV** (Philips Sport Vereniging), plays from September through May at **PSV-stadion Eindhoven** (Frederiklaan 101A, tel. 040/501505.

Beaches

In the vicinity of Middelburg, you will find the best beaches at the towns of **Domburg, Kouderkerke, Oostkapelle, Vrouwenpolder/Serooskerke, Westkapelle,** and **Zoutelande;** all have beach houses to rent, and all but Vrouwenpolder/Serooskerke have beach pavilions.

Dining and Lodging

When Amsterdammers want to spend a weekend eating well and staying in luxurious small hotels, they think first of the southern provinces of their own country. The freshness of Zeeland shellfish, and the Burgundian lifestyle and French kitchens of the border provinces make for restaurants of exceptional quality, and Limburg's castles are often the site of luxurious hotels.

Breda   **Auberge De Arent.** The ceiling murals in this elegant white,
Dining   step-gabled 15th-century house, thought to be among the oldest in western Brabant, are of pheasants, rabbits, and snails, all of which are found on the menu in wild season (the fall and winter months). The Arent has a French kitchen; there is a sep-

arate bistro and also a wine cellar with tasting room. *Schoolstraat 2, tel. 076/14 46 01. Reservations advised. Jacket and tie required. AE, CB, DC, MC, V. Closed Sat. lunch and Sun. Expensive (restaurant)/Moderate (bistro).*

Dining and Lodging **De Klok.** This small hotel is a busy and friendly part of the lively market square of Breda. There is a café on the street in summer, and a bar and restaurant take up the lobby. Double rooms are generously sized, and beds have *dekbedden* (comforters) to keep you warm. Baths may have shower or tub; some quads are available. *Grote Markt 26–28, 4811 XR, tel. 076/21 40 82, fax 076/14343. 28 rooms with shower/bath. Facilities: restaurant/café, bar. AE, DC, MC, V. Moderate.*

Lodging **Pullman Hotel Breda.** Located next to the railway station in a building that formerly housed the offices of the telephone company, the Pullman is a straightforward business hotel with a no-nonsense approach to decorating. Still, rooms are spacious, and there are welcoming touches such as flowers in the bathroom window. *Stationsplein 14, 4811 BB, Breda, tel. 076/22 02 00, fax 076/21 40 67. 40 rooms with bath/shower. Facilities: restaurant, bar. AE, DC, MC, V.*

Eindhoven **Ravensdonck.** The Ravensdonck is located in a large and elegant house with tall windows. The dining room is on the second floor and, with windows all around, affords the feeling of a gracious home. There is an amusing touch here, in that you can buy boxes of chocolates in the shape of light bulbs. Why not? It was a light-bulb factory that transformed Eindhoven from a sleepy village at the turn of the century to an international business mecca. *10 Hagestraat 2, tel. 040/44 31 42. Reservations advised. Jacket and tie required. AE, DC, MC, V. Closed weekend lunch. Expensive.*

Dining and Lodging **The Mandarin Hotel.** Prepare yourself for a pleasant surprise: The Mandarin is unique in that it was designed to meet East Asian standards of service. Its Asian decor includes small bridges spanning water gardens as part of the traffic pattern through the lobby. The restaurants are all Asian in theme and cuisine: One serves fine Chinese specialties, another offers a range of Indonesian and Oriental dishes, and the third is a Japanese steak house; there also is a Parisian coffee shop. Nonsmoking rooms are available. *Geldropseweg 17, 5615 EB, tel. 040/12 50 55. 105 rooms and suites with bath. Facilities: 3 restaurants, café, indoor swimming pool, saunas, parking. AE, DC, MC, V. Expensive.*

Elsloo **Kasteel Elsloo.** This manor-house castle with its own park and **Dining and Lodging** botanical garden sits at the edge of the village, which owns and operates the hotel restaurant. Thoroughly renovated in the late 1980s, rooms are spacious and restfully decorated. The restaurant, too, has a manor house ambience and restful decor; the kitchen is traditional French. *Maasberg 1, 6181 GV, tel. 046/37 76 66, fax 046/37 75 70. 27 rooms. Facilities: restaurant, bar, botanical garden. AE, DC, MC, V. Moderate (hotel)/Expensive (restaurant).*

's-Hertogenbosch **Auberge de Koets.** *Koets* means "carriage" in Dutch, and that is **Dining** the theme of the decor of this moderately formal restaurant on the Parade, near the cathedral. Bridles, old saddles, and brass carriage lamps decorate the walls on all five dining levels. The interior is light and bright, with touches of brass. The menu is

French influenced. *Korte Putstraat 23, tel. 073/13 27 79. Reservations advised. Jacket advised. AE, DC, MC, V. Expensive.*

Dining and Lodging **Hotel Central.** This is more than just your typical full-service business hotel: The Hotel Central is a family-run place that has grown along with the city, and the warmth of the service here reflects this. The rooms have a modern, tailored look. The restaurant, De Leeuwenborgh, with a separate entrance on the square, is graciously appointed and intimate; mirrors are etched with views of the city's important buildings; the menu is traditional and French. *Burg. Loeffplein 98, 5211 RX, tel. 073/ 12 51 51. 125 rooms with bath. Facilities: restaurant, bar. AE, DC, MC, V. Expensive.*

Kerkrade **Hotel Kasteel Erenstein.** A 14th-century moated château
Dining and Lodging houses the restaurant; a traditional whitewashed Limburg farmstead across the road is the luxury hotel. Many of the rooms have beamed ceilings, and some are bi-level and skylighted; others have rooftop balconies. The menu and the wine cellar are French. *Oud Erensteinerweg 6, 6468 PC, tel. 045/46 13 33, fax 045/46 07 48. 45 rooms. Facilities: restaurant, bar, fitness center, sauna, massage, sun lounge. AE, DC, MC, V. Very Expensive.*

Kruiningen **Restaurant Inter Scaldes.** In the past ten years the owner/chef
Dining and Lodging of this small, gracious country restaurant has earned acclaim in the European culinary world for her imaginative use of the products of her region. To accommodate the diners who were traveling from all over the Netherlands and Belgium to sample her French cooking, a luxuriously appointed 12-room *manoir* was added on the far side of the small formal garden beyond the windows of the restaurant. *Zandweg 2, 4416 HA, tel. 01130/ 1753. Reservations required. Jacket and tie required. AE, DC, MC, V. Closed Mon.–Tues. Very Expensive.*

Maastricht **Chateau Neercanne.** This gracious château has a wide summer
Dining terrace and a wine cellar carved into the hillside overlooking the Belgian border. Dining in the elegant and quietly decorated dining rooms is like attending a dinner party in a private home. The cuisine, regularly honored in European culinary circles, is French, with an emphasis on seasonal and country specialties. In a former chapel there is a second, less formal, lunch restaurant, L'Auberge. *Cannerweg 800, tel. 043/25 13 59, fax 043/21 34 06. Reservations required. Jacket and tie required. AE, DC, MC, V. Closed Mon. Very Expensive.*

't Klaöske. This pleasant, somewhat formal restaurant facing Onze Lieve Vrouweplein is owned by an established Limburg restaurant family. Oyster-shell globe lamps hang from the beamed ceiling to light the tables of the spacious open dining room. French and Belgian country cuisine are the inspiration for the original dishes served here. *Plankstraat 20, tel. 043/21 81 18. Reservations advised. Jacket and tie advised. AE, DC, MC, V. Closed Sun. Expensive.*

't Hegske. This romantic spot is near St. Amorsplein off Vrijthof. Window boxes full of flowering plants decorate the street side, and there is a bubbling fountain in the year-round covered interior courtyard. The warmth of half-timbered walls, hanging baskets, and antique collectibles here and there add to the intimacy. The kitchen is open, the cuisine Dutch with strong French influences. *Heggenstraat 3a, tel. 043/25 17 62. Reservations advised. Dress: jacket and tie advised. AE, DC, MC, V. Closed Tues. Moderate/Expensive.*

De Blindgender. Not far from Onze Lieve Vrouweplein, De Blindgender is a particularly warm and cheerful eating pub with large windows looking onto the street. The tables are plain and unadorned, the service is relaxed, and the menu offers straightforward Dutch pub food. *Koestraat. 3, tel. 043/25 06 19. No reservations. Dress: casual. No credit cards. Inexpensive.*

Dining and Lodging **Old Hickory.** The location seems at first to be an odd one (behind the railway station), but it is in fact quite convenient to both the city of Maastricht and the surrounding Limburg countryside. The spacious restaurant, focused around a large central fireplace, emphasizes traditional French gastronomy. Fish and shellfish are the basis for many dishes, and game is served in season. Most rooms are spacious and bright, decorated in a country-house manner, but the standards of decor may vary, so be warned. The owner/chef often invites overnight guests to visit his extensive, naturally climate-controlled wine cellar. *Meerssenerweg 372/6224 AL, tel. 043/62 05 48. 8 rooms with bath. Facilities: restaurant, AE, DC, MC, V. Moderate (hotel)/ Expensive (restaurant).*

Lodging **Hotel Derion.** The relaxed and quiet elegance of Onze Lieve Vrouweplein is perfectly reflected in this small luxury hotel. There is a personal quality to the service, and its intimacy and warmth is reflected throughout. Guest rooms are graciously sized and decorated in relaxing, muted, sand-and-seashell tones; they face either the medieval side street or, if you are particularly fortunate, the tree-filled square. *Onze Lieve Vrouweplein 6, 6211 HD, tel. 043/21 67 70, fax 043/25 19 33. 42 rooms with bath. Facilities: restaurant, shops. AE, DC, MC, V. Very Expensive.*

L'Empereur. A variety of rooms, done in either European modern or traditional decor, is available in this busy hotel's two buildings. Conveniently located directly across from the railway station, it attracts business travelers. The large restaurant serves seasonal specialties. *Stationsstraat 2, 6221 BF, tel. 043/21 38 38, fax 043/21 68 19. 80 rooms with bath. Facilities: restaurant, bar, sauna, solarium, indoor swimming pool. AE, DC, MC, V. Moderate.*

Hotel Bergere. The Bergere, located in an elegant 19th-century building not far from the railway station, was completely redone in 1990 by the new generation of family owners. A *grand café* was added with a separate entrance, an elevator was added, and comfortable and well-appointed rooms were created upstairs (most new rooms have showers rather than tubs). The color scheme is light and fresh in pinks, grays, and beiges. *Stationsstraat 40, 6221 BR, tel. 043/25 16 51, fax 043/25 54 98. 40 rooms with bath. Facilities: restaurant, parking. AE, MC, V. Inexpensive.*

Middelburg **Het Groot Paradys.** Facing the market square in a house that
Dining dates from the mid-16th century, this intimate restaurant retains a traditional town-house decor. Dishes feature ingredients from the region, and fresh-baked breads are the pride of the kitchen. *Damplein 13, tel. 01180/26764. Reservations advised. Jacket advised. AE, DC, MC, V. Closed Sun.–Mon. Very Expensive.*

Lodging **Hotel Arneville.** Beyond the city center near the railway station, this bright and comfortable small hotel was built in 1987. Guest rooms have fluffy comforters on the beds. *Buitenrust-*

straat. 22, 4337 EH, tel. 01180/38456. 43 rooms with bath. Facilities: restaurant, bar, sauna/solarium. AE, DC, MC, V. Inexpensive/Moderate.

Oisterwijk
Dining and Lodging

Hotel Restaurant De Swaen. This French-Victorian streetside town hotel faces a tree-shaded square and is more the sort of place you expect to see in the American Southwest, not the middle of the Netherlands. The shallow front porch is equipped with rocking chairs and a café terrace in the summer; there is also a patio terrace. The crystal-chandeliered restaurant, overlooking the elegant formal garden in back of the hotel, serves excellent French cuisine. There is also a small *auberge* (inn) restaurant, De Jonge Swaen (The Young Swan), that serves simpler, less expensive, traditional Dutch choices. The Swan's hotel rooms are gracious and homey; baths are marble. *De Lind 47, 5061 HT, tel. 04242/19006, telex 52617, fax 04242/85860. 18 rooms with bath. Facilities: restaurant, bar, lounge, garden. AE, DC, MC, V. Expensive.*

Valkenburg
Dining and Lodging

Prinses Juliana. Food is everything here; the French cuisine served here was recognized internationally more than ten years ago and continues to be honored by the harshest French food critics. The decor is elegant in an unadorned way so you can pay attention to the food. The suite-style rooms are bright and spacious. *Broekhem 11, Postbus 812, 6300 AV Valkenburg a/d Geul, tel. 044406/12244, fax 04406/14405. 15 rooms with bath. Facilities: lounge, restaurant. AE, DC, MC, V. Expensive (hotel)/Very Expensive (restaurant).*

Wittem
Dining and Lodging

Kasteel Wittem. This fairy-tale castle hotel, with its duck-filled moat, spindle-roofed tower, and series of peek-a-boo dormers dotting the roof is human in scale. The family who has owned it for more than 20 years welcomes you to a comfortable environment of vintage Dutch furnishings. The intimate dining room, where the cuisine is French, has towering windows open to the view of gardens and fields. There is even a summer terrace beside the moat. *Wittemer Allee 3, 6286 AA, tel. 04450/1208. 12 rooms with bath. Facilities: restaurant, lounge. AE, DC, MC, V. Expensive.*

Yerseke
Dining

Nolet's Restaurant Het Reymerswale. After a stroll along the harbor, stop in at the Nolet family's restaurant for a bite. The traditional, beamed second-floor dining room overlooking the water is spacious and graciously decorated with a comfortable lounge area with a fireplace and a summer porch to the back. The menu's focus is on fish and seafood, traditionally and simply prepared to finest French standards. In a separate building, with shared kitchen, is an informal bistro. *Jachthaven 6, tel. 01131/1642. Reservations advised. Dress: casual. AE, DC, MC, V. Closed Feb. and Tues.–Wed. Moderate/Expensive.*

The Arts and Nightlife

The Arts Maastricht is the arts capital of the border provinces. It has a resident orchestra, a well-known men's choir, and several small theater companies. For information on what is going on during your visit, check *Maandagenda*, a monthly calendar you will find around town, or *Uit in Maastricht*, published biweekly by the VVV tourist office.

Music In Maastricht, the **Limburgse Symfonie Orkest** (Limburg Symphony Orchestra), the leading regional orchestra, performs at the newly renovated Theater aan Het Vrijthof (Vrijthof 47, tel. 043/29 38 28; box office open Mon. 1–4, Tues.–Fri. 11–4, Sat. 11–2). In addition, there are regular student performances at both the Conservatoire Concert Hall (Bonnefanten 15, tel. 043/29 98 30) and the College of Music Concert Hall (St. Maartenspoort 2, tel. 043/29 31 41). Also of interest are the free twice-weekly open rehearsals of Maastreechter Staar, the male choir of Maastricht, which are held Monday and Thursday at 8 PM (except July–Aug.).

Carillon Concerts   Once a week, **'s-Hertogenbosch** offers back-to-back carillon recitals from two sets of bells. The town hall bells play every Wednesday morning from 10 to 11, followed by another carillon concert from the cathedral from 11:30 to 12:30. In **Maastricht,** there is a summer series of evening concerts played by carilloneurs on various church bells of the city; and throughout the year there are midday concerts every Friday from 11:30 to 12:30 from the cheerful carillon on the town hall in the market square.

Theater   The main theater of Maastricht is the **Theater aan Het Vrijthof** (Theater at Vrijthof, Vrijthof 47, tel. 043/29 38 28); in addition, there is a small theater hall, Podium (Het Generaalshuis, Vrijthof 47, tel. 043/29 38 28), and next door, Het Verlog Theater (Vrijthof 47a, tel. 043/25 53 33). The student theater is Studio Toneelacademie (Drama Academy, Lenculenstraat 31–33, tel. 043/46 66 90).

Nightlife   Among the bars and cafés in the heart of the old city of **Maas-**
Bars   **tricht** on or near Onze Lieve Vrouweplein are **De Boonte Kooi** (Koestraat 14–16, tel. 043/21 48 12); **De Lanteern** (O.L. Vrouweplein 26, tel. 043/21 43 26); and **Charlemagne** (O.L. Vrouweplein 24, tel. 043/21 93 73). A very special pub to visit is the very old **In den Ouden Vogelstruys** (Vrijthof 15, tel. 043/21 48 88); first mentioned in town records in the 13th century, it has remained virtually unchanged since 1730 (except, of course, for the modern conveniences of electricity and beer on tap).

In **'s-Hertogenbosch,** try **Castell** (Markt 79–81, tel. 073/13 84 71), **Galaxy** (Karrenstraat 29, tel. 073/14 36 58), or the late-night **King's Cross** (Vughterstraat 99a, tel. 073/13 44 79).

Discos   The disco life of Maastricht is centered in, on, or near the main nightlife squares. On Vrijthof, **Momus** (Vrijthof 8, tel. 043/21 19 37) is a Top 40 discotheque with a neoclassical decor of marble and statues; **Satyricon** (St. Bernardusstraat 16, tel. 043/21 03 21) is a mellow, jazz-oriented place.

Casinos   There are two casinos in this part of the Netherlands: **Holland Casino Breda** (Bijster 30, tel. 076/22 76 00) and **Holland Casino Valkenburg** (Odapark, tel. 04406/15 55 0), not far from Maastricht.

Gay Bars   Three gay bar/dancing cafés in the old city of Maastricht are **Cafe Rembrandt** (Markt 32, tel. 043/21 42 18), on the market square; **Esquire** (Kommel 11–13) not far from Vritjhof; and on the "new" side of the city, **La Ferme** (Rechtstraat 29). All are open until 2 AM.

Carnival   The Catholic heritage of the southern provinces of the Netherlands is most dramatically felt during the days preceding Ash Wednesday each year. The public celebration of Carnival survives in its full bloom of conviviality and relative recklessness in both **Breda** and **Maastricht,** with celebrations also in 's-Hertogenbosch and Eindhoven.

The Green Heart

Like a mystery package that opens in a series of ever smaller, ever more intriguing boxes, the wooded heart of the Netherlands is an unfolding treasure. The national park is the wrappings; its ultimate and most precious gift is a museum of art that is buried deep in the forest; another of its surprises is a small palace.

Important Addresses and Numbers

Tourist Information
The tourist offices in the region are: **Apeldoorn** (Stationsplein 6, tel. 055/78 84 21), **Arnhem Region** (Stationsplein 45, tel. 085/42 03 30), **Deventer** (De Drie Haringen aan de Brink 55, tel. 05700/16200), **Zutphen** (Groenmarkt 40, tel. 05750/19355), and **Zwolle** (Grote-Kerkplein 14, tel. 038/21 39 00).

Emergencies
The national emergency number for police, fire, and ambulance is 06/11.

Hospital Emergency Rooms
Hospital numbers are: **Apeldoorn** (tel. 055/77 44 11 or 055/77 31 31), **Arnhem** (tel. 085/52 91 11), **Deventer** (tel. 05700/46666; or ambulance, tel. 05700/33222), **Zutphen** (tel. 05750/92911; or ambulance, tel. 05750/15555), and **Zwolle** (tel. 038/29 99 11 or 038/26 22 22).

Arriving and Departing

By Car
From Amsterdam, take A1 to Apeldoorn and Deventer or Zutphen; A2 and A12 to Arnhem; or A1 and A28 to Zwolle. Nijmegen is easily reached from Arnhem by A52.

By Train
There are **express Intercity trains** (tel. 06/899–1121) twice each hour from Amsterdam to Apeldoorn and Deventer, Zwolle, and Arnhem; there is hourly service to Nijmegen, with an additional train each hour connecting in Arnhem. To reach Zutphen by train, change in either Arnhem or Zwolle.

Getting Around

By Bus
For local and regional bus service, contact tourist offices (*see* Tourist Information, *above*).

By Taxi
Taxis wait at city railway stations; additional stands may be available in central shopping and hotel districts. To call a taxi: **Apeldoorn** (tel. 055/41 34 13 or 055/22 32 23), **Arnhem** (tel. 085/45 00 00), **Deventer** (tel. 05700/26200 or 05700/22537); **Nijmegen** (tel. 080/22 60 00 or 080/23 30 00); **Zutphen** (tel. 05750/25345, 05750/12935, 05750/19217, or 05750/13717); **Zwolle** (tel. 038/55 11 33, 038/21 30 00, or 038/66 00 77).

By Bike
Free bicycles are provided in the national park De Hoge Veluwe for visitors. In the cities of this region, you can also rent a bicycle at railway stations or from **Blakborn** (Soerenseweg 3, tel. 055/215679), **Harleman** (Arnhemseweg 28, tel. 055/334346), **M. Janssen** (Koninginnelaan 54, tel. 055/21 25 82), and **Van 't Slot** (Groeneweg 4, tel. 03417/5916) in Apeldoorn; **Mantel** (95 Lawick van Pabststraat, tel. 085/420624), **H. Matser** (784 Kemperbergweg, tel. 085/423172), or **R. W. Roelofs** (1 G.A. van

Nispenstraat, tel. 085/426014) in Arnhem; and **Scholten** (Luttekestraat 7, tel. 038/217378) in Zwolle.

Guided Tours

The tourist offices in most cities in the region organize walking tours in the summer months. Inquire for times, minimum group size, and whether or not English translation is offered or can be arranged.

In summer (late June–late Aug.) the VVV Apeldoorn offers a nature tour of the royal forests on weekday evenings, called **Game Quest** (tel. 055/788421). The 2½-hour drive brings visitors into sections of the woods normally closed to the public to observe the wildlife and the indigenous trees and plants. The tours are by reservation only; the cost is Fl 14.

Exploring The Green Heart

Numbers in the margin correspond with places of interest on the Green Heart map.

The Royal Forest The small and gracious city of **Apeldoorn** is the gateway to the
❶ royal forest. On its outskirts you will find **Palace Het Loo.** Built in 1685 on the site of a 14th- and 15th-century castle and hunting lodge as a country residence for William III and his wife Mary Stuart (daughter of James II of England), it was further expanded into a full-blown royal palace when the couple became king and queen of England, with Mary's quarters in the east wing and William's to the west. Built of brick and outfitted with what are said to be the world's first sash windows, the palace is Dutch Baroque in style and has formal French gardens. An avenue of tall beeches leads to the central courtyard, where you enter through a high, grilled fence. Exhibits fill some of the rooms, and there is a video show that documents the building's history and restoration prior to its opening to the public in 1984. Many other rooms are furnished as they had been for William and Mary, but rooms are also maintained in the manner in which they were used by later Dutch monarchs, including Queen Wilhelmina, who was the grandmother of the current queen. Wilhelmina was the last regent to make this her home and died here in 1962. Queen Mary's kitchen, where she made jam, is particularly appealing for the sense of hominess it gives to the palace. The four gardens, meticulously and formally planted, are decorated with statues and fountains, and lined with tall trees. There are separate King's and Queen's Gardens; the King's is dominated by plantings in blue and orange, the colors of the Dutch royal family. Don't miss the stable; it is full of old royal carriages, including the toy car that was used by the current crown prince of the Netherlands when he was a child. *Koninklijk Park 1, tel. 055/21 22 44. Admission: Fl 7.50 adults, Fl 5.50 children. Open Tues.–Sun. 10–5.*

❷ **De Hoge Veluwe** (tel. 5768/1627) is a public nature reserve that covers more than 5,200 hectares (13,000 acres). The traditional hunting land of the Dutch royal family is populated with deer, boar, and many birds; it is also filled with towering pines and hardwood trees (oak, beech, and birch), dotted with small villages (Hoge Soeren, near Apeldoorn, is particularly charming), and riddled with paths for cars, bicycles, and walkers. There is a landlocked, always shifting sand dune to marvel at,

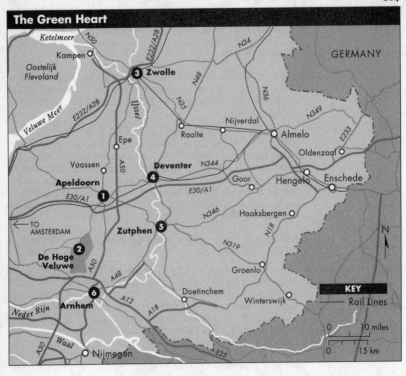

The Green Heart

Ketelmeer · N50 · Kampen · E232/A28 · Zwolle ③ · N34 · GERMANY · Oostelijk Flevoland · N48 · Veluwe Meer · E232/A28 · IJssel · N35 · Nijverdal · N349 · Raalte · Almelo · E233 · Epe · A50 · Oldenzaal · Vaassen · Deventer ④ · N344 · Enschede · Apeldoorn ① · Goor · Hengelo · E30/A1 · E30/A1 · N346 · Haaksbergen · TO AMSTERDAM · Zutphen ⑤ · N18 · De Hoge Veluwe ② · A50 · N319 · A48 · Groenlo · Arnhem ⑥ · A12 · Doetinchem · Winterswijk · KEY · Neder Rijn · A18 · Rail Lines · A50 · Waal · Nijmegen · E35 · N

0 — 10 miles
0 — 15 km

plus an old hunting lodge beside a dam that provides a nice stopping place. You'll find racks of bikes here and there in the park, available free of charge; just be sure to return the bike to any bike rack when you are finished using it. If you need an idea for a destination, there is a visitors' center that contains exhibits on the park and also an observation point for animal watching.

In the heart of the national park is the **Kröller-Müller Museum**, the third most important museum of art in the Netherlands, after the Rijksmuseum and the Vincent van Gogh Museum in Amsterdam. Opened in 1938, it is the repository of a remarkable private collection of late-19th-century and early 20th-century paintings, including 278 works by van Gogh that, when combined with the collection in the Amsterdam museum, constitute nearly his entire *oeuvre*. Helene Kröller, née Müller, the wife of a prosperous industrialist, had a remarkable eye for talent and a sixth sense about which painters and paintings would be important. Her first purchase was van Gogh's *Sunflowers*. Among his other well-known paintings in her collection are *Potato Eaters*, *The Bridge at Arles*, and *L'Arlesienne*, copied from a drawing by Gauguin. But Helene Kröller-Müller was not myopic in her appreciation and perception. She added to her collection of van Goghs works by Seurat, Picasso, Redon, Braque, and Mondrian. The collection also contains 16th- and 17th-century Dutch paintings, ceramics, Chinese and Japanese porcelain, and contemporary sculpture. The museum building itself, which was designed by Henry van de Velde, artfully brings nature into the galleries through its broad windows, glass walkways, and patios. The gardens and woods around the museum form another gallery in the open air, with a collection of 20th-century sculptures by Aristide Maillol, Jean Dubuffet, Richard Serra, and Claes Oldenburg; works by Barbara Hepworth and Alberto Giacometti are under a special pavilion added in 1953. *National Park De Hoge Veluwe, tel. 8382/1041. Admission (to park and museum): adults Fl 6.50, children Fl 3.25, cars Fl 6 Open Dec.–Mar., Tues.–Sat. 10–5, Sun. and public holidays 11–5; Apr.–Nov., Tues.–Sat. 10–5, Sun. and public holidays 1–5. Sculpture Garden open Apr.–Nov., Tues.–Sat. 10–4:30, Sun. and public holidays 11–4:30.*

Hanseatic Towns Seven hundred years before the European Common Market or the European Community, there was an association of northern European trading cities called the Hanseatic League. It began as a pact among itinerant merchants to travel together for mutual safety, but in time it became an alliance of more than 80 cities scattered over the Continent, including major ports such as London, Lübeck, Bremen, Hamburg, Cologne, Danzig, Stockholm, Novgorod, and Bergen, as well as 17 cities located on the rivers and coastline of what is now the Netherlands. Their purpose was to consult with one another on matters of trading routes, tolls, and uniformity of regulations governing trade. Three of the cities that were important Dutch members of that league are scattered along the River IJssel, which connects the Rhine with the body of water known today as IJsselmeer, an open sea (the Zuider Zee) in the 13th century.

❸ The small city of **Zwolle** was an important depot for trade between the Netherlands and Germany during the time of the Hanseatic League, located as it is between the IJssel and another important Dutch river, the Vecht. Founded in 800, it officially became a town in the 12th century. An important Latin school was located in Zwolle, and the religious philosopher Thomas à Kempis lived here in the early 1400s, when he wrote his influential work, *Imitation of Christ.* Zwolle continued in this century as an important center of cattle trading, grain processing, coffee roasting, and linen manufacture.

A pleasant short walk through the town begins at the brick-and stone-embellished **Sassenpoort,** which is the only one of the original town gates of 1406 left standing on the eastern edge of the city center. From there you can weave your way on and off Sassenstraat to the **Grote Kerkplein,** the main square of Zwolle. It is the site of the Town Hall as well as the local tourist office and a charming shop, **Zwolse Balletjes Huis** (Grote Kerkplein 13, tel. 038/21 88 15), that sells the local sweet specialty, *Zwollse balletjes* (fruit-and-spice-flavored hard candies).

Time Out A pleasant place to stop for a simple lunch in the middle of your wandering might be the mustard factory **De Wijndragers** (Broerenkerkplein 63, tel. 038/22 67 25), where you also can buy the mustard that is processed in the tower room upstairs.

The Romanesque **St. Michaelskerk,** which dates from 1040, dominates the square; within are a fine organ and the final resting place of the 17th-century painter of interiors Gerard Terborch, who was born in Zwolle. Farther along on the Voorstraat is the provincial **Overijssel Museum,** housed in a building that dates from the mid-16th century. Its principal display is the wainscoted living-dining Blokzil Room, which came from a house in the north part of the province and exemplifies the lifestyle of a well-to-do 17th-century family. *Melkmarkt 41 or Voorstraat 41, tel. 038/21 46 50. Admission: Fl 2.50 adults, Fl 1 children. Open Tues.–Sat. 10–5, Sun. 2–5.*

Leaving Zwolle, follow signs for Wijhe-Olst for a scenic drive along the IJssel River, passing rich marshes filled with wildlife and lush plants. This region between the river and the German border, known as the Salland, is the Provence of Holland, a quiet farming area that has a local dialect and produces asparagus, and food specialties such as *kruitmoes* (hot porridge with raisins).

❹ As you near **Deventer,** follow signs to *Centrum.* Founded late in the 8th century by an English cleric named Lubuinus, whose mission in life was to convert the Saxons to Christianity, by the 9th century Deventer was already a prosperous port and a powerful bishopric; the town center still reflects this medieval heritage. A center of learning as well, it had a printing industry to disseminate the thoughts of its scholars. It was home at various times to Thomas à Kempis, Pope Adrian VI, Erasmus, and, in the 17th century, French philosopher René Descartes. Still under restoration, Deventer has won prizes for the renovation of its historic houses and public buildings. In Brink, the main square, the late-Gothic **Waag** (Weigh House), begun in 1528, holds periodic exhibits on town history. Uphill is the 13th-century Romanesque-Gothic **Bergkerk;** though the church is not open to visitors, it sits high on a square with pleasing views down medieval side streets (Bergstraat and Roggestraat are particularly appealing).

Time Out Just below the Bergkerk is **Chez Antoinette** (Roggestraat 10–12, tel. 05700/16630), a restaurant-pub that honors the owners' fascination with everything Portuguese in both its menu and the fado entertainment in the pub (open for lunch or snacks). The building dates from 1303, and the pub is the oldest in the city (from 1881).

The principal sight in Deventer is **Lubuinuskerk,** a huge stone cross basilica that was built in the 10th century on the site of Lubuinus's small wooden church. It is known for its mural paintings, its massive size, and its 15th-century tower, which can be climbed in the summer months for a wide view over the town; the carillon is played at least twice a week. *Grote Kerkhof. Admission free. Open weekdays 10–5, Sat. 1:30–5.*

❺ Known as the Tower City for the many spires that rise above the city center, **Zutphen** is located on a small hill at the juncture of the Rivers IJssel and Berkel. It was one of the region's wealthiest towns in the 14th and 15th centuries. The tourist office offers town tours twice a week from mid-June to mid-September (Tues. and Thurs. 1:30). The charming, once-walled town has medieval houses and courtyards, churches and monasteries, and towers and water gates. The small **Henriette Polak Museum** contains a portrait of the former Dutch queen, Wilhelmina, at age 10, by Mari Andriessen. *Zaadmarkt 88, tel. 05750/16878. Admission: Fl 2.50 adults, Fl 2 children. Open Tues.–Fri. 11–5, weekends 1:30–5.*

Time Out Not far from the Henriette Polak Museum is **De Pelikaan** (Pelikaanstraat 6, tel. 05750/17035), a century-old coffee and tea emporium; the adjacent tearoom is a good place to stop for refreshment.

St. Walburgskerk (St. Walburgis Church) was begun in the 12th century in Romanesque style and enlarged in the 16th century in Gothic style. It is busy with roofs and a wide variety of building materials. Within, the side walls and vaults are ornamented with 14th- and 15th-century frescoes; the richly decorated organ loft contains a Baeder organ. In the **Librije** side chapel are found the true treasures of Zutphen: This library dates from 1561, and under its white vaulted ceilings are rare and beautiful early manuscripts and incunabula, chained to rows of reading stands. *Kerkhof. Admission: Fl 2.50 adults, Fl 1.50 children; in combination with the walking tour, Fl 5 adults, Fl 3 children. Open May–Sept., tours Mon. at 2 and 3, Tues.–Sat. at 11, 2, and 3.*

Arnhem
6

Arnhem is best known as the "bridge too far." Near the end of World War II the Allies followed up the invasion of Normandy by seeking to cut off the German army entrenched in the eastern Netherlands. The battle involved the largest airborne operation of the war, and 3,000 British, American, and Canadian lives were lost in three weeks of fighting that left the Allies still short of their goal, which was finally achieved seven months later. **Museum Hartenstein** includes a large scale model of the region and incorporates memorabilia, weapons, and equipment to depict the battle. Tanks and guns sit on the lawn, and an audiovisual presentation describes the progress of the battle. *Utrechtseweg 232, Oosterbeek, tel. 085/33 77 10. Admission: Fl 3 adults, Fl 2 children. Open weekdays 11–5, Sun. and public holidays noon–5.*

Among the other attractions of Arnhem are its parks (including the 75-hectare/185-acre **Sonsbeek Park**), its trolley buses, its weekly market held in the shadows of the **Grote Kerk** (Great Church), and its cozy entertainment area, the **Korenmarkt**, where old warehouses have become pubs, cafés, restaurants, and discotheques. Situated on the River Rhine, Arnhem also is the southern gateway to the national park De Hoge Veluwe (*see above*). North of the city in an 18-hectare (44-acre) park is the **Nederlands Openlucht Museum** (Open Air Museum), which recreates Dutch country life through farm buildings typical of their regions, transported to the site from every province of the Netherlands. Here you can see furnished farmhouses, outbuildings, windmills, and craft shops in a setting that reflects the variety of the Dutch landscape. *Schelmseweg 89, tel. 085/57 61 11. Admission: Fl 10 adults, Fl 6 children. Open Apr.–Oct., weekdays 9–5, weekends 10–5.*

What to See and Do with Children

More than 2,000 animals inhabit **Burgers' Zoo** in Arnhem. Established in 1913 on the principle that there should be as few barriers as possible between humans and animals, this zoo includes a large safari park with roaming lions, zebras, giraffes, and rhinos, plus a tropical rain forest. *Schelmseweg 85, 6816 SH Arnhem, tel. 085/42 45 34 or 085/45 03 73. Admission: Fl 16 adults, Fl 12 children. Open summer 9–7, last safari 5 PM; winter 9–sunset, last safari 4 PM.*

In Apeldoorn's **Alpenheul** park, more than 300 monkeys, apes, chimpanzees and gorillas wander free in the woods. *J.C. Wilslaan 21, tel. 055/55 25 56. Admission: Fl 9.50 adults, Fl 6.50 children. Open Apr.–June, daily 9:30–5; July–Aug., daily 9:30–6, Sept.–Oct., daily 10–5.*

The **Speelgoed- en Blikmuseum** (Toys and Tin Museum) is an enchanting collection of toys (including mechanical toys), dolls, puppets, and electric trains in a town house just off the main square and only a few doors down from the tourist office in Deventer. *Brink 47, tel. 05700/93786. Admission: Fl 3 adults, Fl 1.50 children. Open Mon.–Sat. 10–5, Sun. 2–5.*

Off the Beaten Track

From Zwolle it is a short drive to another Hanseatic town, **Kampen.** Once a herring port, it lies near the point where the IJssel River empties into IJsselmeer. To see the oft-painted skyline at its best, approach the city from across the river by way of the old bridge rather than on the highway: Take N50 and follow signs for IJsselmuiden. The **Schepenzaal** (Magistrates' Hall) in the 14th-century Oude Raadhuis (Old Town Hall) is an excellent example of a medieval courtroom.

Near Zutphen on the road to Doetinchem is **Bronkhorst,** the tiniest town in the Netherlands; its population is 160, and the entire town is protected by the national historic preservation program. There are curious little museums and shops here, as well as a choice of gracious restaurants. The 14th-century chapel is particularly attractive and peaceful.

From Arnhem it is an easy 30-minute drive to the pre-Roman city of **Nijmegen,** situated strategically near the junction of the Maas–Waalkanal and the River Waal. The river is the main branch of the Rhine and the second of the "great rivers" of the Netherlands that lead to the North Sea. Nijmegen is a lively university town and shopping center for the region, as well as the gateway to the southern provinces. The city's **Belvedere Park** offers a splendid view over the river below and a restaurant in a tower. The nearby Waalkade riverfront esplanade, lined with restaurants, shops, and a casino, is also a pleasant place to stroll.

Shopping

The late shopping nights in the cities in this region are: in Apeldoorn, Thursday in the city center, Friday in the suburbs; in Arnhem, Thursday; in Nijmegen, Thursday; in Zutphen, Friday; and in Zwolle, Thursday.

Street Markets The market days in the region are: in Apeldoorn, Monday and Wednesday mornings and on Saturday at Marktplein in the city center; in Arnhem, Friday morning and Saturday at Kerkplein; in Deventer, Tuesday–Friday morning and Saturday (also antiques); in Nijmegen, Monday and Saturday at Agustijnenstraat, Grote Markt, and Burchstraat; in Zutphen, Thursday mornings; in Zwolle, Friday morning and Saturday.

Sports and Fitness

Biking There is a program of *free* bicycles (a total of 400 vehicles) for use on the 42 kilometers (26 miles) of bicycle paths in **De Hoge**

Veluwe National Park (*see above*); special cycles for the handicapped are also available.

Canoeing In summer it's possible to canoe on the canals of Zwolle. **Vadesto Kanocentrum** (Veenrand 5, 8051 DW Hattem, tel. 05206/45428) at the Potgietersingel rents canoes. The VVV Zwolle tourist information office (*see* Tourist Information, *above*) sells canoeing maps.

Fishing Fishing in the streams of Overijssel province near Zwolle is easy and pleasurable. The VVV Zwolle tourist information office (*see* Tourist Information, *above*) sells one-day fishing licenses for Fl 5. The license includes a list of the fishing places, and the tourist office also has a helpful map of the area.

Golf Among the best golf facilities in the area are **Publi Golf De Berendonck** (Panhuysweg 39, Wijchen, tel. 08894/20039) and **Golfbaan Het Rijk van Nijmegen** (Postweg 17, 6561 KJ Groesbeek, tel. 08891/76644), near Nijmegen, and **Golfclub Zwolle** (Heinoseweg 26, Zwolle, tel. 05290/1930).

Jogging There is a training circuit in Zwolle at the **Haersterveerweg.** Near the center of town are two places suitable for jogging, **Park De Weezenlanden** and **Park 't Engelse Werk.**

Tennis/Squash Facilities in the region include **Squash Matenpark** (Heemradenlaan 130, tel. 055/296222) and **De Maten Sports** (Ambachtsveld 2, tel. 055/425044) in Apeldoorn; **Tennis en Squashcentrum** (Bremenweg 29, tel. 05700/22107) in Deventer; **Gofferthal** (Nieuwe Dukenburgseweg, tel. 080/564260) in Nijmegen; and in Zwolle, **Squash Zwolle** (near Winkelcentrum Aalanden, tel. 038/548485), **Sportpark Wilhelmina** (Wilhelminastraat), **Sportpark de Marslanden** (Marsweg), **Sportpark De Pelikaan** (Haersterveerweg), **Tenniscentrum Zwolle** (Palestrinalaan), and **Tenniscomplex Zwolle** (Peterskampweg).

Spectator Sports

Walking/Cycling Each summer during the third week of July the **Nijmegen Annual Four-Day Walking Event** is held; it draws as many as 30,000 participants from all over the world. A similar event is held for cyclists.

Dining and Lodging

The Royal Game Reserve in the north and the fruit- and vegetable-growing region to the east provide the restaurants of the Green Heart with abundant, high-quality ingredients. The area is well supplied with hotels of all sizes and types, small resorts, and country inns in the woods.

Apeldoorn **Echoput.** Located not far from Palace Het Loo, Echoput is a
Dining much-honored and gracious country restaurant. The large fireplace in the lounge welcomes in winter; the terrace invites in summer. In the fall wild season, the menu specializes in game from the royal hunting lands. *Amersfoortseweg 86, tel. 05769/248. Reservations advised. Jacket and tie advised. AE, DC, MC, V. Closed Monday. Expensive.*

Lodging **De Keizerskroon.** A nice cross between a business hotel and a country inn, it is located within easy walking distance of Palace Het Loo. Renovations over the past 20 years have obliterated all traces of traditional architecture; in its place is a stylish hotel, with rooms decorated in tones of cream and Wedgwood blue, with furniture that, like the hotel, is a cross between business practical and weekend comfortable. *Koningstraat 7, 7315 HR, tel. 055/21 77 44, fax 055/21 47 37. 101 rooms. Facilities: sauna, solarium, swimming pool. AE, DC, MC, V. Expensive.*

Astra. Located on a quiet residential side street, Astra is a small pension-style family hotel that is comfortably furnished in the manner of a Dutch home. Rooms are large for this type of accommodation. *Bas Backerlaan 12–14, 7316 DZ, tel. 055/22 30 22, fax 055/22 30 21. 27 rooms. Facilities: recreation room. AE, DC, MC, V. Inexpensive.*

Arnhem
Dining

Kasteel Doorwerth. This restaurant offers a rare experience: to dine in a small castle set along the banks of the Rhine 8 kilometers (5 miles) from Arnhem. The timbered dining room is furnished with antiques, and the cuisine is in the new, French-inspired Dutch mode; vegetables and herbs come from the castle gardens. *Fonteinalle 4, Doorwerth, tel. 085/33 34 20. Reservations advised. Jacket and tie advised. AE, DC, MC, V. Closed Tuesday. Expensive.*

Lodging

Hotel de Bilderberg. In the suburb of Oosterbeek, it is located in a wooded setting. The rooms are spacious and bright, with comfortable modern furnishings. De Bilderberg caters to business travelers as well as weekenders. *Utrechtseweg 261, 6862AK, Oosterbeek, tel. 085/34 08 43. 144 rooms. Facilities: indoor swimming pool, sauna/solarium, fitness room, tennis courts. AE, DC, MC, V. Expensive.*

Hotel Blanc. This small hotel is not far from the railway station in central Arnhem. In a turn-of-the-century town house, the Blanc offers bright and comfortable rooms and a friendly café for guests. *Coehoornstraat 4, 6811 LA, tel. 085/42 80 72. 10 rooms. Facilities: café, lounge. AE, DC, MC, V. Inexpensive.*

Hotel Molendal. In an Art Deco–era house in a residential neighborhood near Sonsbeek Park, the hotel has spacious and high-ceilinged rooms; decorative elements carry out the Art Deco heritage of the building. *Cronjestraat 15, 6814 AG, tel. 085/42 48 58. 32 rooms. Facilities: lounge. AE, DC, MC, V. Inexpensive.*

Bronkhorst
Dining and Lodging

Herberg de Gouden Leeuw. This peaceful country restaurant is in the smallest town in the Netherlands. There are formal and informal dining areas and a fireplace in the lounge, and on Saturday nights diners are entertained with piano music. The cuisine is traditional Continental, with such choices as beef bourguignonne and veal cordon bleu. The guest room is simple. *Bovenstraat 2, 7226LM, tel. 05755/1231. 1 room with bath. Facilities: restaurant. AE, DC, MC, V. Expensive (restaurant)/ Inexpensive (room).*

Hoog Soeren
Dining and Lodging

Hotel Oranjeoord. In a small woodland village that seems to be right out of a Grimms' fairy tale, the Oranjeoord is a relaxed country hotel with garden rooms, terraces, and a sunny dining room. It is a pleasant choice for a country weekend. *Hoog Soeren 134, 7346AH, tel. 05769/1227. 27 rooms. Facilities: Restaurant. MC. Inexpensive.*

Nijmegen
Dining

Belvedere. Housed in a tall tower set high on a hill in the middle of a park overlooking a wide bend in the River Waal, it has possibly the best river view in the Netherlands. In the beamed dining room are only a handful of tables; the menu is new Dutch cooking, including choices such as peppered fillet of beef with goat cheese. *Kelfkensbos 60, tel. 080/22 68 61. Reservations required. Jacket and tie advised. AE, DC, MC, V. Moderate/Expensive.*

Zutphen
Lodging

Hotel Inntel. If you like to mix sports and fitness with sightseeing, this is a good choice. The emphasis here is on activities rather than decor. *De Stoven 37, 7206 AZ, tel. 05750/25555, fax 05750/29676. 150 rooms with bath. Facilities: 2 restaurants, outdoor/indoor heated pool, indoor and outdoor tennis courts, bowling, sauna/solarium. AE, DC, MC, V. Moderate.*

Zwolle
Lodging

Grand Hotel Wientjes. Convenient to both the railway station and the city center, this hotel occupies a stately old building. Most rooms are in the modern wings and are both spacious and brightly decorated. It also has theme rooms, including one styled in Old Dutch and a Chinese-style bridal suite with a two-person tub. *Stationsweg 7, tel. 038/25 42 54. 57 rooms. Facilities: restaurant. AE, DC, MC, V. Expensive.*

The Arts and Nightlife

The Arts

In Apeldoorn, there are concerts the last Friday of every month at **Paleis Het Loo** (Koninklijk Park 1, tel. 055/21 22 44); in Nijmegen, performances take place at **Stadsschouwburg Nijmegen Concertgebouw De Vereeniging** (tel. 080/22 11 00 or 080/22 83 44).

Nightlife

In Deventer, there is a concentration of brown cafés at the main square, including **Het Wapen van Overijssel** (also known as **Floors;** Brink 37, tel. 05700/13811), **La Balance** (Brink 72, tel. 05700/19277), and **De Waagschaal** (Brink 77, tel. 05700/17190); in Zutphen, there is **Oma** (Beukerstraat 52a, tel. 05750/18003); and in Zwolle, **Petit Restaurant de Casteleijn** (Kamperstraat 33, tel. 038/218099) and **La Galleria** (Oude Vismarkt 9a, tel. 038/212153).

The North

In the northern provinces of the Netherlands, life is more peaceful; there are quiet streams and a chain of sparkling lakes 64 kilometers (40 miles) long to tempt you to sample the outdoor life. For the most part, museums are small and quiet but have surprisingly rich displays, and there are luxury resorts hidden in small wooded villages that rival the attractions of the more cosmopolitan parts of the country. Particularly in Friesland, there are opportunities to watch an unusual array of sporting activities, including sailing regattas, bike races, long-distance walks, a local version of pole-vaulting, and—*if* the canals freeze in the winter—one of the world's most famous ice-skating races, which flashes through 11 cities before it is done.

Important Addresses and Numbers

Tourist
Information

The tourist office in **Groningen** (Naberpassage 3, 9712 JV, tel. 050/13 97 00) provides information on the capital city and also the province of the same name. The tourist office in **Leeuwarden** (Stationsplein 1, 8911 AC, tel. 058/13 22 24, fax 058/13 65 55) is the central source for information for both the city and the province of Friesland.

Emergencies	The **national emergency number** for police, fire, and ambulance is 06/11.
Police	**Groningen:** tel. 050/16 22 22; for breakdown and towing service, tel. 050/56 52 74. **Leeuwarden:** tel. 058/13 24 23.
Hospital Emergency Rooms	**Groningen:** tel. 050/61 91 11, 050/25 88 88, or 050/25 86 54. **Leeuwarden:** tel. 058/93 33 33 or 058/96 66 66.

Arriving and Departing by Car, Train or Ferry

By Car To reach the northern provinces from Amsterdam, you can take A6 across the province of Flevoland to Emmeloord, then A50 to Joure, and from there E22 to Groningen. Turn north on N32 for Leeuwarden. You can also follow E22 through Noord Holland province and across the 35-kilometer (22-mile) Afsluitdijk (Enclosing Dike) that divides the IJselmeer from the North Sea; from the end of the Enclosing Dike, take A31 to Leeuwarden or continue on E22 to Groningen. A third option is to drive to Enkhuizen and take the car ferry to Urk (*see* By Ferry, *below*). From Urk, take N351 to A50 and continue as above.

By Train **Intercity** express trains (tel. 06/899–1121) operate once an hour direct from Amsterdam to both Leeuwarden and Groningen; there is an additional once-hourly Intercity service to both cities that requires a connection in Amersfoort. Whatever train you take, however, be sure you are in the right car; trains split en route, so there are separate cars for each destination in both classes of service.

By Ferry Two ferry lines cross the Ijsselmeer from May to September to connect the town of **Enkhuizen** with the northern province of Friesland. One service, **Rederij Naco B. V.** (Stationsplein, Hoorn, tel. 02290/17341; adult fare: Fl 9.50 one way, Fl 15 round-trip; children: Fl 4.75 one way, Fl 7.75 round-trip), is for passengers only (or passengers with bicycles) and takes travelers to **Stavoren,** from where there is a direct train connection to Leeuwarden; the ferry operates three times a day and there is no need for a reservation. The other service, **Friese Recreatie Onderneming B. V.** (Slenk 5A, Urk, tel. 05277/3407; fare: Fl 15 per person, Fl 25 per car, Fl 8 per bicycle) is a car ferry to the port of **Urk** in Flevoland province that operates two or three times a day; reservations are required.

Getting Around

By Car Roads are excellent throughout the northern provinces of Friesland and Groningen. In Friesland signs are in two languages, however, with the town names shown in Frisian as well as in Dutch. For example, the provincial capital Leeuwarden also is seen on signs by its Frisian name, Ljouwert.

By Train In addition to the national rail lines connecting Leeuwarden with the south, local trains link the Enkhuizen–Stavoren ferry service to Leeuwarden; another connects Leeuwarden with Harlingen (departure point for ferry and hydrofoil services to the Wadden Islands); and another links Leeuwarden with Groningen and continues to the German border. A small local train in Groningen province connects Groningen with Winsum (a canoeing center), Uithuizen (departure for guided walks to the Wadden Islands at low tide), and the port of Eemshaven. For

train information in Leeuwarden, call 058/12 22 41; in Groningen, call 050/12 27 55 (closed weekends).

By Taxi   Taxis wait at the railway stations in both Leeuwarden and Groningen. For a taxi in Leeuwarden, call 058/12 22 22 or 058/12 33 33; in Groningen, call 050/12 80 44.

Guided Tours   **Canal cruise trips** are available in summer; in Leeuwarden, contact **H. Geertsma** (Tijnjedijk 31, tel. 058/88 75 88); in Groningen, **Verbindingskanaal Groningen** (tel. 050/12 83 79 or 050/12 27 13). Another guided option, as much sport as sightseeing, is to join a **wadlopen** excursion to the Wadden Islands. Permissible *only* with a guide who knows well the timing of the tidal waters on the Wadden Sea, these are walks across the sand at low tide from the mainland to the islands from May to September. Don't even think about attempting this on your own; the tides are very, very tricky. If you are interested, the tourist offices can give you information and recommend qualified guides, or you can contact **De Stichting Wadloopcentrum Pieterburen** (Postbus 1, Pieterburen, tel. 05952/300).

Exploring the North

Numbers in the margin correspond with places of interst on the North map.

Leeuwarden
❶   An odd mixture of distinctions identifies the small provincial capital of **Leeuwarden**. On one hand, it was the official residence of the first hereditary *stadtholder* (king) of the Netherlands; on the other, it is presumed to have been the birthplace of the notorious dancer/spy, Mata Hari. It is well known as the focal point of the Dutch dairy industry and site of one of the largest cattle markets in Europe, yet it also is home to the one of the world's finest collections of Oriental ceramics. The world-famous 200-kilometer (124-mile) Elfstadentocht (Eleven Cities Tour) ice-skating race departs from Leeuwarden when—or if—there is ice on the canals connecting the capital with 10 other cities of the province (including Harlingen, Franeker, Workum, Hindeloopen, Stavoren, and Sloten).

From the railway station, follow the wide street just ahead, across the Nieuwestade canal, where you jog left to the next bridge before continuing along Kleine Kerkstraat. At Grote Kerkstraat is the **Museum Het Princessehof** (Netherlands Ceramic Museum), housed in the former residence of Marie-Louise of Hesse-Kassell, who was the widow of the first prince of Orange and whose gracious dining room has been preserved. The museum documents the history of fine ceramics, Oriental as well as European, and modern as well as ancient. The remarkable collection of Chinese stoneware and porcelain dates from the third millennium BC through the 20th century. Look closely at the plates and tiles commissioned in China by the Dutch East India Company; you'll notice decidedly Oriental features on Dutch-costumed merchants and their ladies. *Grote Kerkstraat 9–15, tel. 058/12 74 38. Admission: Fl 3 adults, Fl 2 children. Open Mon.–Sat. 10–5, Sun. 2–5.*

The 13th-century **Grotekerk** (Great Church), a Jacobin church, has been reconstructed and restored over the centuries, most recently in 1976; it is the traditional burial place of the Nassau line, ancestors of the royal family. *Jacobinerkerkhof, tel. 058/ 15 12 03. Admission free. Open June–Aug., daily 2–4.*

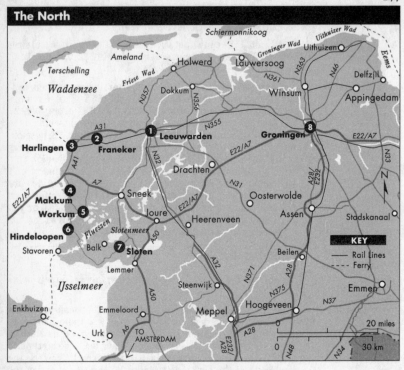

From the church, follow Bij de Put and its continuation, Sacramentsstraat, across the Voorstreek canal; follow Tuinen canal and turn right at Turfmarkt. There, facing one another across the small street, are the highly decorated Renaissance buildings known as the **Kanselarij** (Chancellery), which was the residence of George of Saxony when he governed the region in the 16th century, and the provincial **Fries Museum** (Frisian Museum), which houses a varied collection documenting the history and culture of Friesland. Among its treasures is a portrait by Rembrandt of his wife, Saskia; she was the daughter of the mayor of Leeuwarden. The couple married in 1634 in the nearby village of St. Annaparochie. *Turfmarkt 24, tel. 058/12 30 01. Admission: Fl 3 adults, Fl 2 children. Open Tues.–Sat. 10–5, Sun. 1–5.*

From the Frisian Museum, continue along Turfmarkt to Korfmakersstraat and turn right. At the canal you will see a tiny statuette of a dancer. You guessed it; this is **Mata Hari,** a statue erected in the late 1970s to honor the town's most colorful citizen.

Time Out If you follow the canal into the center, you will come to the Waagplein, which is dominated by the red brick **Waag** (Weigh House), decorated with heraldic lions. Built at the end of the 16th century, it was used as a weigh house for butter and cheese until the late-19th century; it now houses a cozy restaurant called **De Waag** (Nieuwestad 148B, tel. 058/13 72 50).

Beyond the Weigh House, take Weerd to the Raadhuisplein and its extension, the Hofplein. Facing one another here are the **Stadhuis** (Town Hall) and the **Hof,** which was the former residence of the Frisian stadtholders. In the center of the square is a statue of Willem Louis, the first stadholder, locally known as *Us Heit* (Our Father).

Follow St. Jacobobstraat and its continuation, Wirdumerdijk, back to the railway station where you began. Across the bridge, the **Verzetsmuseum Friesland** (Resistance Museum) is an intriguing collection of memorabilia and exhibits honoring the strong Frisian resistance movement under the German occupation during World War II. *Zuiderplein 9–13, tel. 058/13 33 35. Admission: Fl 2 adults, Fl 1.50 children. Open Tues.–Sat. 10–5, Sun. 2–5.*

Friesland The province of Friesland offers a number of fascinating small museums, particularly in the craft towns that dot the coast of the IJsselmeer. To explore the province, take N355 from Leeuwarden toward Harlingen. In the late 18th century a clergyman in the town of **Franeker** convinced the inhabitants that the end of the world was imminent due to a collision of the planets. When his dire prediction failed to materialize, a local scoffer set out to help his neighbors understand why. The **Eise Eisinga Planetarium** is one man's attempt to demonstrate why the planets do not collide. One wonders what his wife must have thought, but Eise spent years turning his living-room ceiling into a continuously moving display of interplanetary action, and his home's closets and attic into the storage place for the workings needed to carry out his unusual experiment in education and home decoration. *Eise Eisingastraat 3, Franeker, tel. 05170/3070. Admission: Fl 3.50 adults, Fl 3 children. Open Oct.–Apr., Tues.–Sat. 10–12:30, and 1:30–5; May–Sept., Mon.–Sat. 10–12:30 and 1:30–5, Sun. 1–5.*

Just a short drive farther on is the small port city of **Harlingen.** A walk along its main canal will remind you of Amsterdam in that several homes are copies of canal houses in the capital.

Time Out Facing the main canal is the pleasant, small hotel-restaurant **Anna Caspari** (Noorderhaven 69, tel. 05178/12065), where you can have a bite of lunch or dinner while overlooking the canal.

Take the scenic coastal road south along the dike toward Zurich and from there toward **Makkum.** If you are a lover of fine pottery, you will know that multicolored Makkumware is as important and treasured in Dutch homes as the better-known blue-and-white Delftware. The small, family-owned factory, **Tichelaars Koninklijke Makkumer Aardewerk en Tegelfabriek** (Tichelaar's Royal Makkumer Potteries), which has made Makkumware under license from the royal family for 10 generations, invites you to watch the craftsmen at work; they also operate a shop where you can buy the products of the sole supplier of Makkumware to the world. *Turfmarkt 61, Makkum, tel. 05158/1341. Admission: Fl 3. Open weekdays 10–4; factory showrooms open weekdays 9–5:30, Sat. 9–4.*

Nearby, in a former weigh house, is the **Fries Aardewerkmuseum DeWaag** (Frisian Pottery Museum), a small collection of ceramic tiles and other pottery that includes many contributions by the Tichelaar family. *Waaggebouw, Pruikmakershoek*

2, Makkum, tel. 05158/1422. Admission: Fl 1.50. Open May–Sept. 15, Mon.–Sat. 10–5, Sun. 1:30–5.

Continuing along the dike road through the villages of Piamm and Gaast, you come to **Workum,** where, in a house on the main ⑤ street near the church, you will find the **Jopie Huisman Museum.** This is an art museum devoted to one man, who was born in Workum and lives there still in a house by an eel stream where he fishes every night. What is unusual about the man, and his art, is that he was a junk man all his life; sketching and painting every chance he had, without benefit of formal instruction, he produced an abundance of fine canvases and drawings, many reminiscent of the careful duplication of fabric and texture in the work of the early Dutch masters. Jopie Huisman, however, has made haunting compositions of the rags, worn shoes, and discarded dolls he collected in his travels. *Noard 5, Workum, tel. 05151/3131. Admission: Fl 4 adults, Fl 2.50 children. Open Mar.–Nov., Mon.–Sat. 10–5, Sun. 2–5.*

⑥ Just beyond Workum is the coastal town of **Hindeloopen,** which is known for its traditional painted furniture. The **Museum Hidde Nijland Stichting** is an exhibition of the local craft that is worth a quick detour. *Dijkweg, tel. 05142/1420. Admission: Fl 3.50 adults, Fl 1.75 children. Open Mar.–Nov., Mon.–Sat. 10–5, Sun. 1:30–5.*

From Hindeloopen you are within easy driving distance of the **Frisian Lakes,** which lure Dutch and international sailors and boating enthusiasts every summer. N359 just outside Hindeloopen or Workum takes you across the countryside and across the connecting land between one of the largest lakes and ⑦ its outlet. The small fortified towns of **Sloten** and **Balk** are focal points in this area of southwestern Friesland known as **Gaasterland.**

Groningen and Groningen is a university town; it also is a major commercial
Environs center of the northern provinces of the Netherlands. A member
⑧ of the Hanseatic League in medieval times, it enjoyed six centuries of prosperity as a grain market. The province still leads Western Europe in the production of sugar beets; another of its riches is a large supply of natural gas. Street life is busy in the city, and the region offers pleasant drives in the countryside.

To tour the town on foot, start at the Grote Markt, the market square in front of the **Stadhuis** (Town Hall). Walking by way of Sint Jansstraat, you come to the **Martinikerk,** which dates from 1230 and was begun as a Romanesque-Gothic cruciform basilica. Finished in the 15th century, it has an organ that was installed in 1470, as well as splendid murals from that period; the stained-glass windows date from the late 18th century. *Martinikerkhof, tel. 050/12 07 98. Admission: Fl 1. Open May–Aug., Tues.–Sat. noon–5.*

Behind the church is the **Prinsenhoftuin** herb and rose garden, which has an 18th-century sundial in its gate and hedges cut in the shapes of *A* and *W,* after the first names of former governors of Friesland and Groningen provinces. *St. Walburgstraat Kattenh, no tel. Admission free. Open mid-Mar.–mid-Oct.*

Leaving the garden, follow the canal around to the left. Turn back into the city at Oude Boteringestraat, where you will pass a number of fashionable homes built by prominent 18th-century citizens and, on the corner of the Broerstraat, a medieval stone house that is one of the oldest in town.

Turn there and you will pass the main building of the **university.** Founded in 1614 and today one of the largest in the Netherlands, it was chosen by Descartes in 1645 to arbitrate his conflicts with Dutch theologians. The university building you see is neo-Renaissance in style, built in 1909. Allegorical figures of Science, History, Prudence, and Mathematics adorn the gable; across the street is the University Library opened in 1985.

Time Out   As might be expected in a university town, there are plenty of terrace cafés and inexpensive eating places (*eetcafes* in Dutch) clustered around the Grote Markt. When you are hungry or want to take a break, head for **Time Out** (Poelestraat 34, tel. 050/13 15 35) or **Cafe Oblomov** (Poelestraat 11, tel. 050/18 19 97).

Ten sculptures on major city access roads are part of the **City Identification Project,** conceived by the Municipal Physical Planning Department to restore to the city the identity once derived from its medieval city gates. Two architects, three artists, a historian, a philosopher, a choreographer, a playwright, and an economist were each commissioned to design an "identification feature," each of which was given an identifying letter spelling out *Cruoninga,* an ancient name for the city; the resulting sculptures and structures circle the city clockwise from the south and carry such mystifying titles as *Earth, water and gas flames; A steel book on posts; The missing factor X.*

What to See and Do with Children

From April through October you can follow the **Aldfaers Erf** (Our Forefathers' Heritage) route, which weaves through the Frisian countryside in a small area bounded by the towns of Makkum, Bolsward, and Workum, stopping at 12 restored buildings and workshops. In Exmorra you can visit the agricultural museum, a village grocery, and a schoolroom; in Allingawier, a farm, a church, a painter's workshop, a forge, a bakery, and two residences; in Piaam, an ornithological museum; and in Ferwoude, a carpenter's workshop. *Postbus 176, 8700 AD Bolsward, tel. 05157/5681. Open Apr.–Nov. Mon.–Sat. 9–5:30, Sun. 10–5.*

Near Groningen, children will enjoy a stop at **Abraham's Mostermakerij,** a museum-restaurant in the village of Eenrum/Pieterburen. The convivial manager invites diners and visitors into the mustard factory to see how mustard and vinegar are made. *Molenstraat 5, 9967SL Eenrum/Pieterburen, tel. 05959/1600. Open daily 10 to 10.*

Off the Beaten Track

If you happen to be in Leeuwarden on Friday morning, find your way to the Frieslandhal on the perimeter of town for the **weekly cow market.** It is one of the largest in Europe and offers a look into what this part of the Netherlands is really all about.

Of all the unexpected places in the Netherlands, perhaps the most intriguing are the offshore **Wadden Islands,** which shelter the northern coastline from the North Sea. They offer varying degrees of seclusion or socialization and plenty of opportunity for water sports, beach walking, and bird-watching. Ferries leave from Harlingen to Terschelling (tel. 05620/6111) and Vlieland (tel. 05620/4141; no cars); ferries to Ameland leave from Holwerd (tel. 05191/6111), and to Schiermonnikoog from Lauwersoog (tel. 05193/9050 or 05193/9079; no cars.) For information on accommodations on the islands, contact the VVV Friesland (Stationsplein 1, 8911 AC Leeuwarden, tel. 003158/ 13 22 24, fax 003158/13 65 55).

Shopping

Shopping is not the lure of the northern provinces, though standard merchandise is available. The late shopping night in both Leeuwarden and Groningen is Thursday, until 9 PM.

Street Markets Market days in **Leeuwarden** are Friday (to 3:30) and Monday afternoon at Wilhelminaplein and Wednesday morning at Akkerstraat. In **Groningen** the market is held on the Grote Markt on Tuesday, Wednesday, and Friday; there also is a Sunday flea market between June and mid-October in Groningen on the Grote Markt.

Antiques/Antique Books There are a number of antique book dealers in the city center of Groningen, including **De Groninger Boekverkoper** (Oude Kijk-in-'t-Jatstraat 60, tel. 050/135858), **Isis Antiquarian Bookshop** (Folkingestraat 20, tel. 050/184233), **Odysee** (Oude Ebbinge-straat 79, tel. 050/133139), and **Succes Bookshop** (Oude Kijk-in-'t-Jatstraat 62, tel. 050/189725). A number of general antiques shops are clustered on the broad shopping street **Gedempte Zuiderdiep.**

Ceramics There is a particular pleasure in buying from a factory store, even if no special savings are involved. The factory shop at the **Tichelaars Koninklijke Makkumer Aardewerk en Tegelfabriek** sells a good selection of Makkumware (*see* Friesland, *above*).

Sports and Fitness

Camping With more than 100 campgrounds in the province of Friesland alone, the North offers plenty of opportunity for camping. The national reservations service, **NRC/National Reservations Centre** (Box 404, 2260 AK Leidschendam, tel. 070/320–2500, telex 33755), takes campsite reservations. For camping in Leeuwarden, **De Kleine Wielen** (De Groene Ster 14, 8926 XE, tel. 05118-1660; may be closed mid-Oct.–mid-Mar.) has sites for 350 tents and touring caravans and has places for hikers. **Camping Stadspark** (Campinglaan 6, 9727 KH, tel. 050/25 16 24; may be closed Nov.–Mar.) in Groningen has 50 sites; it also has accommodation for hikers.

Canoeing In both Friesland and Groningen, canoeing routes have been laid out and special maps have been printed. Check with the respective tourist offices. Three of the largest canoe renting facilities in Friesland are **Watersportbedrijf De Drijfveer** (U. Twijnstrawei 31, 8491 CJ Akkrum, tel. 05665/2789), **Pean** (Pean 1, 8490 AB Akkrum, tel. 05663/1392), and **De Ulepanne/ Balk** (Tsjamkedijkje 1, 8571 MS Balk, tel. 05140/2982). In the province of Groningen, **Horizon** (Hoffdstraat W.4, 9951 AB Winsum, tel. 05958/1980 or 05958/1792), **De Zijlsterhoeve/HR** (Zijlsterweg 5, 9892 TE Aduarderzijl, tel. 05941/1423), **Hinrichs Watersport** (Damsterweg 32, 9629 PD Steendam, tel. 05960/29137) rent canoes.

Sailing/Boating Friesland is bordered by the large and windswept Ijsselmeer (Lake Ijssel). The province is also cut with a swath of lakes, canals, and small rivers that offer sailing or boating opportunities. The more than 150 boat- and sailboat-rental firms throughout Friesland include **Watersportbedrijf Anja** (Meersweg 9a, 9001 BG Grouw, tel. 05662/1373), **Botenverhuurbedrijf Grouw** (Yn 'e Lijte 18a, 9001 ZR Grouw, tel. 05662/3810), **A.E. Wester en Zn., 'De Blieken'** (Garde Jagersweg 4–5, Postbus 51, 9000 AB Grouw, tel. 05662/1335, fax 05662/3840), **Watersportcamping Heeg** (De Burd 25a, 8621 JX Heeg, tel. 05154/2328), **L. Van Der Pol** (Oude Oppenhuizerweg 93, Priorstraat 2, 8603 VR Sneek, tel. 05150/11771), **Jachtwerf Frisia** (Oude Oppenhuizerw 79, 8606 JC Sneek, tel. 05150/12814, fax 05150/18182), **Top En Twel Zeilcentrum** (It Ges 6, 8606 JT Sneek, tel. 05150/19192), and **Scheepers Schepen** (Postbus 21, 8715 ZH Stavoren, tel. 05149/1555, fax 02975/40514).

Although less blessed with open water, the province of Groningen offers opportunities for sailing and boating as well, particularly on the Schildmeer from the boating center at Steendam; contact **Hinrichs Watersport** (Damsterweg 32, 9629 PD Steendam, tel. 05960/29137) for information on boat rentals.

Windsurfing Where the sailboats go, so go the Windsurfers. In Friesland the following firms rent both equipment and wet suits: **De Ulepanne/Balk** (Tsjamkedykje 1, 8571 MS Balk, tel. 05140/2982), **Jeugdherberg Oer 'T Hout** (Raadhuisstraat 18, 9001 AG Grouw, tel. 05662/1528), and **Top En Twel Zeilcentrum** (It Ges 6, 8606 JT Sneek, tel. 05150/19192).

Spectator Sports

Kaatsen **(a Frisian ball game)** During the summer months, you will find local matches of the Frisian ball game *kaatsen* (similar to baseball) played in the villages throughout Friesland; major tournaments are held in August.

Polsstokspringen **(pole-vaulting over canals)** Another uniquely Frisian sport is *polsstokspringen*, which involves pole-vaulting over canals. The main competition is held in Winsum in August.

Sailing Throughout the summer you will find weekend racing on the Frisian lakes. The summer's main event, however, is the two-week series of **Skûtjesilen Races** (late July) using the uniquely Dutch vessels, *skûtjes*, which are wide-bottom sailing barges.

Beaches

The need for dikes to hold back the sea makes broad beaches impossible along the long northern coastline of the Netherlands, but there are plenty of wide sandy beaches on the offshore Wadden Islands (*see* Off the Beaten Track, *above*).

Dining and Lodging

Beetsterzwaag *Dining and Lodging* **Hotel Lauswolt.** This golf and spa resort is set in a sprawling manor-house hotel at the back of a sweeping lawn in a quiet wooded village. The fine restaurant is a member of the Alliance Gourmandise Néerlandaise. The rooms are large, and suites have separate living rooms. Special golf, spa and gastronomic packages are available. *Van Harinzmaweg 10, 9244 ZN, tel.*

05126/1245. 54 rooms with bath. Facilities: restaurant, sauna, swimming pool, tennis/squash courts. AE, DC, MC, V. Expensive.

Groningen
Dining

Ni Hao. Located across the canal from the city center, not far from the railway station, this antique-filled and elaborately decorated Chinese-Indonesian restaurant is large, but thanks to an imaginative layout of open dining areas alternating with semiprivate rooms for groups, there is no feeling of the crowd that regularly fills the tables. Groups (4–6 people) can order from the extravagant 10-course menus, but if it's just two of you, the Surprise Menu mixes a variety of Chinese regional specialties; another possibility is an all-duck dinner, including whole roast Peking duck. *Hereweg 1, tel. 050/18 14 00. Reservations advised. Jacket and tie advised. AE, DC, MC, V. Expensive.*

De Pauw. This chic, highly styled restaurant done in cream and black has a sophisticated and imaginative French-influenced menu that includes choices such as a cream soup of carrots, tomatoes, and gorgonzola cheese, and mussels with chopped fennel and anise butter. Art decorates the walls, and the bouquets are peacock feathers. *Gelkingestraat 52, tel. 050/18 13 32. Reservations advised. Jacket and tie advised. AE, DC, MC, V. Expensive.*

Salle a Manger. Not far from Grote Markt, it has three dining rooms, traditional Dutch decor, and a Dutch-traditional menu as well, with an emphasis on meat dishes, although it does offer low-calorie and vegetarian selections as well. *Poelestraat 41, tel. 050/18 11 14. Reservations advised. Dress: casual. AE, DC, MC, V. Moderate.*

Dining and Lodging

Golden Tulip Familiehotel. Located in a comfortable suburb of Groningen on the edge of the area's largest lake, this small family hotel has grown over the years into a semiresort. There is a spaciousness and an elegantly modern but homey feeling about the rooms and suites. The lakeside café is particularly busy and entertaining in summer; boats can be rented nearby. *Groningerweg 19, Paterswolde, tel. 05907/5400. 78 rooms with bath. Facilities: 3 restaurants, bikes, whirlpool, sauna, tennis, indoor swimming pool, pier, bus to city center. AE, DC, MC, V. Expensive.*

Lodging

Auberge Corps de Garde. This small hotel is located in a gracious 18th-century house. It is partially furnished with antiques and faces the city center's encircling canal. Family-owned, it is a congenial place with pleasant, spacious rooms that are brightly decorated in tones of green and rose. *Oude Boteringestraat 74, 9712 GN, tel. 050/14 54 37. 8 rooms, 6 with bath. Facilities: lounge. AE, DC, MC, V. Inexpensive.*

Altea Hotel. Essentially a business traveler's hotel that serves the local exhibition hall across the street, the Altea is well located on one of the major roadways to the city center. The rooms have a bland but restful cream-and-white or gray-and-white decor. *Expositielaan 7, 9727 KA, tel. 050/25 84 00. 157 rooms with bath. Facilities: restaurant, bar, sauna, indoor swimming pool. AE, DC, MC, V. Moderate.*

Leeuwarden
Dining

Mata Hari. Located just off the main shopping street of Leeuwarden is a bright and cheerful small restaurant that serves French specialties in an atmosphere of crisp white linens accented with pinks and blues. *Weerd 7, tel. 058/12 01 21. Reser-*

vations advised. Jacket and tie advised. AE, DC, MC, V. Closed Sun. Moderate/Expensive.

Dining and Lodging   **Oranjehotel.** Primarily a business hotel, Oranjehotel is located directly across from the railway station. The rooms are comfortable and newly renovated; the hotel is a local gathering place with a busy pub and a fine restaurant serving traditional Continental cuisine. *Stationsweg 4, 8901 BL, tel. 058/12 62 41, fax 058/12 14 41. 78 rooms with bath. Facilities: restaurant, bar. AE, DC, MC, V. Closed Dec. 25–26. Moderate.*

Oudkerk
Dining and Lodging   **De Klinze.** In a wooded town not far from Leeuwarden, De Klinze is a semiresort created from a 17th-century country estate. The handful of roomy suites in the manor house are decorated with vintage furniture and antiques; the bright and spacious guest rooms, decorated in a cheerful lemon-yellow and white, are in a separate, modern wing that also includes the spa. Dinner here is in the former parlors, with views to the woods. The cuisine is French. *Van Sminiaweg 32–36, 9064 KC Oudkerk; tel. 05103/1050; fax, 05103/1060. 22 rooms and 5 suites all with bath. Facilities: indoor swimming pool, sauna, whirlpool, solarium, beauty salon. AE, DC, MC, V. Very Expensive.*

Nightlife

Casino   **Holland Casino** (Gedempte Kattendiep 150, tel. 050/12 34 00), the only casino in the northern half of the Netherlands, is in Groningen.

Discos   The influence of 20,000 university students in **Groningen** insures the easy availability of dancing to the latest music. In the Grote Markt neighborhood are **Night Spot Monrow** (Herestraat 75, tel. 050/13 22 22), **Gdansk** (Poelestraat 53, tel. 050/18 82 00), **The Palace** (Gelkingestraat 1, tel. 050/13 91 00), **Troubadour** (Peperstraat 19, tel. 050/13 26 90), and **Warhol** (Peperstraat 7, tel. 050/12 13 50).

Jazz/Rock Clubs   In **Leeuwarden** the generally tame nightlife scene is enlivened by two music cafés. **De Brouwershoeck** (Poststraat 21) offers jazz, and **Kings Inn** (Nieuwesteeg 1) has a novel combination of gospel and rock.

Gay Bars   In Groningen there are two gay discotheques: **Duke** (Hoogstraatje 9, tel. 050/13 46 09) and **MacDonald** (Hoge der A–3, tel. 050/12 71 88).

4 Belgium

By Eric Sjogren

Belgium packs just over 5 million Dutch-speaking Flemings and almost as many French-speaking Walloons into a country only slightly larger than the state of Vermont. The presence of two language cultures inevitably creates tension, but it also enriches the cultural heritage. Diversity of geography, too, enhances the country's attractions. The Belgian landscape ranges from the beaches and dunes of the coast and the tree-lined, placid canals of the "platte land" (flat land) to the sheer cliffs of Ardennes River valleys and the dense forests of the south.

In many ways, Belgium is a country for connoisseurs: This is the land of van Eyck, Bruegel, and Rubens, and this is where their best work can be seen. The spirit of the Middle Ages and its great humanists—Erasmus, his friend Thomas More, and others—lives on in cities of great renown like Brugge and Ghent, and in others that are waiting to be discovered, like Mechelen and Lier. The art of living well has been cultivated in Belgium since the days of the great Burgundian feasts. Today, the country boasts an astonishing number of gourmet restaurants, including some of the world's finest.

In Belgium flourishes an unapologetically bourgeois culture. Dukes, counts, and lesser lords have built many a feudal castle on Belgian land, and abbots and cardinals have constructed towering religious edifices, but it was the merchants who built the cities and commissioned the works of art we admire today. The endless variations of Art Nouveau in the town houses of the Belle Époque are another manifestation of bourgeois individualism. So are the comfortable proportions of today's private homes and public spaces.

Until quite recently the Belgians had no common history. Rather, their fate was determined by the dynastic marriages whereby princely families sought to extend their influence and perpetuate their power. It was through marriage that the possessions of the dukes of Flanders passed into the hands of the dukes of Burgundy in the 14th century, and then to the Habsburg family in 1477. A scion of that family, born in Ghent, became Emperor Charles V in 1519 when he inherited the Holy Roman Empire from his father and Spain from his mother. This was the beginning of 200 years of Spanish rule, and when eventually the Austrian branch of the Habsburg family gained the upper hand, the only real difference for Belgium was that it came to be ruled from Vienna instead of Madrid.

After the fall of Napoleon in 1815, the victorious powers aimed to settle matters by awarding the Belgian provinces to the Netherlands. But a cultural divide had opened up between the Low Countries to the north and those to the south, and it was a foregone conclusion that the staunchly Catholic southerners would not get along with the adamantly Protestant northerners. In military terms Belgium's 1830 war of independence did not amount to more than a few skirmishes, but the purpose was served. The new nation included the former principality of Liège, which under elected prince-bishops had maintained its independence for 800 years.

Colonialism, too, was thrust upon the Belgians. The Congo was the personal fiefdom of King Leopold II (son of Leopold I, first king of independent Belgium), who bequeathed it to the nation in 1908 only shortly before his death. The Belgians may have reaped the reward, but they also had to pay the consequences

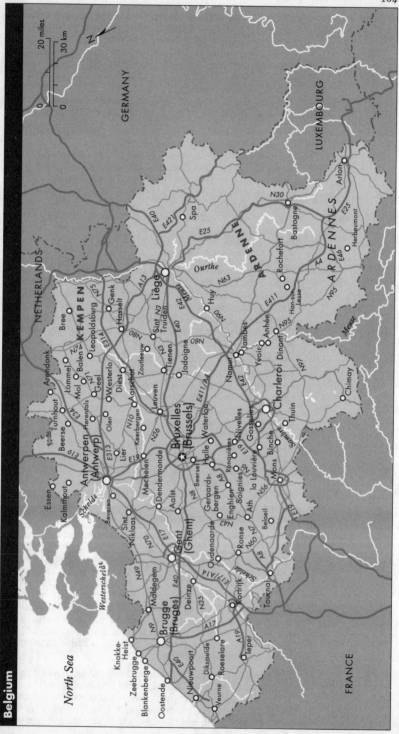

Belgium

when colonialism came to its painful end and the independent Congo (now known as Zaire) was born 52 years later.

When Belgian forces put up unexpected resistance against the Germans in 1914, the country became known, a little patronizingly, as "brave little Belgium." In 1940 another war that Belgium basically had nothing to do with ravaged the country.

This is perhaps why Belgium is one of the staunchest supporters of the European Community (EC). Brussels is the home of the European Commission, where most decisions affecting the EC are made. Writers and politicians tend to refer to "Brussels" as a synonym for the commission, and this can be a bit of a mixed blessing. It is a heady sensation, but of secondary importance, to be the capital of Europe. What matters is the commonality of interests. The EC will survive only if it is successful in fashioning unity out of diversity. Exactly the same thing applies to the kingdom of Belgium.

Before You Go

Government Tourist Offices

In North America Belgian Tourist Office (745 5th Ave., New York, NY 10151, tel. 212/758–8130, fax 212/355–7675).

In the U.K. Belgian Tourist Office (Premier House, 2 Gayton Rd., Harrow, Middlesex, HA1 2XU, tel. 081/861–3300, fax 081/427–6760).

Tour Groups

General-Interest Tours Listed below is a sample of the tours and packages that concentrate on Belgium. *See* Tour Groups in Chapter 1, *above*, for tours that cover more than one country in the region.

From the U.K. **Shearing Holidays** (Miry La., Wigan, Lancashire WN3 4AG, tel. 0942/824824) features a five-day city break centered in Brugge with excursions to Brussels and other places of interest, and a Belgian House Party tour. **Time Off Ltd.** (Chester Close, Chester St., London SW1X 7BQ, tel. 071/235–8070) has packages from two to seven nights to Brussels and Brugge. Excursions to Ghent, Antwerp, and Waterloo are also available.

Special-Interest Tours
From the U.K. **Travel Art** (54 Vanderbilt Rd., London SW18 3BQ, tel. 081/870–6094), specializes in Art Nouveau. Their three-day guided tours to Brussels include buildings not normally open to the public and Art Nouveau restaurants and hotels. **Prospect Music and Art Tours** (454–458 Chiswick High Rd., London W4 5TT, tel. 081/995–2151) operates an "Art Treasures" tour of Flanders, with an accompanying guest lecturer, that takes in the sights of Brugge, Ghent, Antwerp, and Brussels. **The Belgium Travel Service** (Bridge House, Ware, Herts. SG12 9DG, tel. 0920/467–345) specializes in inclusive holidays on the Belgian coast and in the Ardennes, and it also operates tours covering all Belgium. Some include noteworthy festivals such as the Oostende Carnival.

Package Deals for Independent Travelers

American Airlines Fly Away Vacations (tel. 800/832–8383) offers independent packages for as long as you like for visits to

Brussels, Brugge, and Antwerp. **Extra Value Travel** (683 S. Collier Blvd., Marco Island, FL 33937, tel. 813/398–4848 or 800/255–2847) offers self-drive tours of Belgium, including hotel choices and car rental. **Jet Vacations** (1775 Broadway, New York, NY 10019, tel. 212/474–8700 or 800/538–0999) offers Flexiplan Europe, a choice of hotels, car rentals, airport transfers, and sightseeing options for Brussels, Antwerp, Brugge, and Liège. **Northwest WorldVacations** (tel. 800/692–8687) provides visitors to Brussels with preferred hotel and car-rental rates and tour options for a minimum of two nights. **Travel Bound** (599 Broadway, Penthouse, New York, NY 10012, tel. 212/334–1350 or 800/456–8656) offers a week-long "Brussels Grand" package for independent travelers, as well as packages to Belgium for three to six nights. **United Vacations** (tel. 800/678–0949) will customize your itinerary in Belgium.

When to Go

Because the Belgians take vacations in July and August, these months are not ideal for visiting the coast or the Ardennes, but summer is a very good time to be in Brussels, Antwerp or Liège. In the summer you may also be able to get a break on hotel prices. On the other hand, this is also vacation time for many restaurants. For touring the country and visiting much-frequented tourist attractions like Brugge, the best times are April–June and September–October.

The following are average daily maximum and minimum temperatures for Brussels.

Brussels								
Jan.	40F	4C	**May**	65F	18C	**Sept.**	70F	21C
	31	–1		47	8		52	11
Feb.	45F	7C	**June**	72F	22C	**Oct.**	59	15C
	32	0		52	11		45	7
Mar.	50F	10C	**July**	74F	23C	**Nov.**	49F	9C
	36	2		54	12		38	3
Apr.	58F	14C	**Aug.**	72F	22C	**Dec.**	43F	6C
	41	5		54	12		34	1

Festivals and Seasonal Events

Feb. 23–25: Carnival is celebrated with great gusto, especially at Binche with its extravagantly costumed Gilles, at Malmédy, and at Eupen.
Mar. 21–23: In Stavelot, the hilarious Blancs Moussis with their long red noses swoop through town during the **mid-Lent carnival.**
Mar. 27–Dec. 31: Antwerp's year as **Cultural Capital of Europe** (tel. 03/234–1188) is celebrated with exhibitions, concerts, drama, and other special events, including the reopening of newly restored historical monuments.
April 1: The **Bal Rat Mort** (tel. 059/50–05–12) in Oostende is one of Europe's most extravagant fancy-dress balls. Advance bookings are essential.
Late Apr.–early May: The **Royal Greenhouses** (tel. 02/513–0770), at Laeken Palace near Brussels, with superb flower and plant arrangements, are open to the public for a limited period.
May 3–June 5: The **Queen Elisabeth International Music Com-**

petition (tel. 02/513–0099) is one of the most demanding events of its kind. In 1993, the focus is on young violinists.

May every 5th year (next in 1995): The **Floralies of Ghent,** in the Flanders Expo halls, are considered the world's most prestigious international flower shows.

Late May: The **Brussels Jazz Rally** (tel. 02/735–8629) encompasses gigs and informal sessions in over 60 cafés and pubs, plus outdoor concerts in the Grand'Place.

May 20: The **Ascension Day** Procession of the Holy Blood (tel. 050/44–86–86) in Brugge is one of the oldest and most elaborate religious and historical processions in Europe. Early seat reservations are recommended.

June 6: The **Trinity Sunday** procession of the Golden Carriage and St. George's battle with Lumeçon the dragon are enacted in Mons (tel. 065/33–55–80).

June 20: The **Folklore and Shrimp Festival** (tel. 058/51–11–89) in Oostduinkerke features shrimp fishermen on horseback, brass bands, floats, and folklore ensembles.

July–Oct.: The **Festival of Wallonie** (Rue du Jardin Botanique 29, 4000 Liège, tel. 041/22–32–48) is a four-month series of concerts throughout Wallonie.

June 29 and July 1: The **Ommegang** (tel. 02/512–1961) takes over Brussels's Grand'Place. It's a sumptuous and stately pageant reenacting a procession honoring Emperor Charles V in 1549.

July 17: The **Ghent Festivities** (tel. 091/24–15–55) start, a 10-day sequence of music-making, entertainment, and assorted happenings in the streets of the city.

Aug.: The **Francorchamps Formula I Grand Prix** (tel. 02/287–0911) is one of the key events in the annual cycle of international motor racing.

Aug. 15: The **Outremeuse Festival** in Liège combines religious and folkloric elements in a joyous tide that sweeps through this section of the *cité ardente*.

Sept.–mid-Oct.: The **Festival of Flanders** (Eugeen Flageyplein 18, 1050 Brussels, tel. 02/640–1525) brings concerts to all the old Flemish cities, including a Czech music week in Brussels and Baroque music in Ghent.

Sept.–Dec.: Every other year, the **Europalia Festival** honors a different country with exhibitions, concerts, and other events amounting to a thorough inventory of its cultural heritage. In 1993, the country thus honored in Brussels and other cities is Mexico (tel. 02/507–8550).

Sept. 12: On **National Heritage Day** (tel. 02/511–1840) buildings of architectural or historical interest throughout Belgium that are not normally accessible to the public open their doors to all comers.

Nov. 30–Dec. 6: The **European Community Championship** (tel. 03/326–1010) in Antwerp is a major event on the international tennis circuit.

Dec. 10–12: The **European Christmas Market** in the Grand Sablon in Brussels features the traditions and products of the 12 countries of the European Community.

What to Pack

Clothing No season is totally immune to rainfall in Belgium, even though the rain is usually rather light. For visits from April/May to October, you would be well advised to bring a raincoat, and you will need an overcoat at other times. Bring a sweater at all times. The more expensive restaurants expect patrons to wear jacket and tie.

Miscellaneous If you're bringing electrical appliances from the U.S., you'll need a converter and adapter plug. More expensive hotels often feature hair dryers and 100V shaver outlets.

Taking Money Abroad

Cash Machines The two major ATM networks in Belgium are Mister Cash and Bancontact. Provided you have a PIN code and have arranged direct debit to your bank at home, you can withdraw cash from these machines using major credit cards. There's a minimum charge of BF125 per transaction and interest is charged.

There is an American Express cash machine in the arrival hall at the National Airport in Brussels, and Diners Club, Visa, and MasterCard cash advances can be obtained at SCS Weckers, also in the arrival hall.

Belgian Currency

The monetary unit in Belgium is the Belgian franc. There are bills of 100, 500, 1,000 and 5,000 francs, and coins of 1, 5, 20, and 50 francs. At press time (fall 1992), one dollar was worth about BF29; one pound sterling, BF50; and one Canadian dollar, BF23.

What It Will Cost

The Belgian economy is stable and inflation is low to moderate, currently standing at 2.77%. Brussels, with its vast influx of business travelers and officials on EC business, can be very expensive. This applies especially to hotels, which can be twice as expensive as elsewhere in the country, but perfectly acceptable accommodations are available at more reasonable prices as well.

Taxes Sales tax (TVA) is always included in the price quoted for accommodations and meals. It ranges from 6% on basic items to 33% on luxury goods. *See also* Shopping in Staying in Belgium, *below*.

Sample Costs A cup of coffee in a café will cost you BF45–60; a glass of beer, BF35–85; a glass of wine, about BF100. Train travel averages BF6 per mile, the average bus/metro/tram ride costs BF40, theater tickets are about BF500, and movie tickets cost about BF200.

Languages

Belgium is bisected by a linguistic border, with Flemish spoken to the north and French to the south of it. Written Flemish is indistinguishable from Dutch, but spoken Flemish may include dialect variations. Some French speakers have Wallon, a separate German-influenced tongue, as a second language. German, spoken by a couple of hundred thousand people at the eastern end of the country, is Belgium's third official language. Brussels is officially bilingual (Flemish/French).

Language is a sensitive subject in Belgium, loaded with political implications. A foreigner is well advised to use English rather than French in Flanders, even though both are widely understood. You will have no problem finding English-speakers in Brussels. In Wallonie you may have to muster whatever French you possess, but in tourist centers you will always be able to find people who speak at least basic English.

Staying Healthy

Medical services are highly developed in Belgium, and should the need for hospitalization arise, it's almost always possible to be admitted immediately. English is more widely spoken by doctors and paramedics of Flemish mother tongue than among French-language colleagues. This is worth bearing in mind when, as in Brussels, you have a choice among hospitals where Flemish or French predominates.

It used to be the rule that seafood should not be consumed during months without an "r" in the name. Nowadays you can safely eat mussels and the like the year round in restaurants with good hygienic standards, but avoid those where the produce is displayed all day long (as in some places in Brussels's Ilôt Sacré area).

Car Rentals

There are 20 pages of ads for car-rental firms in the Brussels Yellow Pages, so a wide choice is available. Half a dozen firms have desks in the baggage claim area at the Brussels airport, in addition to several locations around town. Some also have offices at hotels—Avis at the Hilton, Hertz at the SAS Royal. The major firms also have offices in the larger provincial cities, supplemented by local enterprises.

Rail Passes

Belgian **rail passes** can be bought in the U.K. from Belgian National Railways (10 Premier House, Greycoat Place, London SW1P 1SB, tel. 071/223–0360). They are not available in the U.S. or Canada.

Student and Youth Travel

The youth information service in Brussels is **Infor-Jeunes** (Boulevard de Smet de Nayer 145, tel. 02/426–3333), and there's also an English-language **Help Line** (tel. 02/648–4014), which provides both practical information and crisis intervention. **Acotra** (Rue de la Madeleine 53, tel. 02/512–8607) will help in finding inexpensive accommodations.

Youth hostels are inexpensive and numerous. For information on facilities in Wallonie, write to **Fédération Belge des Auberges de la Jeunesse** (Belgian Youth Hostel Federation, Rue Van Oost 52, 1030 Brussels, tel. 02/215–3100); for Flanders, contact **Vlaamse Jeugdherbergcentrale** (Flemish Youth Hostel Center, Van Stalenstraat 40, Antwerp, tel. 03/232–7218).

Traveling with Children

Hotels The Brussels Best Western is the Bedford Hotel (Rue du Midi 135); there are also Best Westerns in Brugge, Knokke,

Blankenberg, and Oostende. Children under 19 stay free at
Holiday Inn. Children of whatever age stay free at the Hilton.

Apartment/Villa Rentals A large choice of properties in Wallonie is available through
Belsud Reservation (Rue Marché-aux-Herbes 61, 1000 Brus-
sels, tel. 02/504–0280, fax 02/514–5335). This organization is
part of the government tourist authority. They publish a cata-
logue with illustrations of all accommodations.

Hints for Disabled Travelers

For information on facilities for disabled travelers in Belgium,
contact **Fonds National de Reclassement Social des Handicapés**
(Rue du Meiboom 14, 1000 Brussels, tel. 02/218–3080) or
Vlaamse Federatie voor Gehandicapten (VFG) (Rue St. Jean
32–38, 1000 Brussels, tel. 02/515–0260).

Two holiday centers have facilities built especially for the disabled: **De Ceder** (Parijsestraat 34, 9800 Astene-Deinze, tel. 091/
86–30–28) in Flanders, and **Les Riezes et les Sarts** (Rue Grande
84, 6404 Cul-des-Sarts, Couvin, tel. 060/37–76–64) in the Ardennes.

Hotels The following hotels in Brussels have rooms for physically disa-
bled guests: Hilton, SAS Royal, Carrefour de l'Europe and
Sodehotel Brussels (Sabena), Copthorne Stephanie, Sheraton
Brussels Airport, Cadettt Mövenpick, Le Dome, Euro-Flat,
Jolly Atlanta, Mercure, Jolly Grand Sablon, Novotel Brussels
off Grand'Place, Palace, Albert Premier, Arcade Sainte Cath-
erine, Atlas, Colonies, Fimotel Brussels Airport, Fimotel
Expo, Ibis Brussels Center and Ibis Brussels Airport, Orion,
Auberge du Souverain, Campanile, Gerfaut, de France.

The same applies for Best Western, Holiday Inn, Novotel,
Mercure, Sofitel and Ibis hotels throughout Belgium, for
Ramada Hotel in Liège, the Switel in Antwerp, Hotel Pullman
in Brugge, and Hotel Ardennes in Spa-Balmoral.

Further Reading

Barbara Tuchman's *A Distant Mirror*, describing 14th-century
European affairs, gives valuable insights, illuminated by memorable vignettes, into the conflicts between Flemish towns and
the crown of France. *The Guns of August* applies Tuchman's
narrative technique to the events, largely in Belgium, of the
first month of World War I. Leon Wolff's *In Flanders Fields* is a
classic account of the catastrophic campaign of 1917, while John
Toland's *No Man's Land* covers the events on the Western
Front in 1918.

Toland has also written *Battle: The Story of the Bulge*. William
Wharton's *A Midnight Clear* is a fictional account of the Ardennes battle, as seen by American GIs. *Outrageous Fortune*
by Roger Keyes is a sympathetic account of the role played by
Leopold III up to 1940. Hugo Claus's *The Sorrow of Belgium*,
an outstanding novel of life during the occupation, has been
translated into many languages from the original Dutch.

Two 19th-century novels well worth dipping into are Georges
Rodenbach's *Bruges-la-Morte*, which was contemporaneous
with the rediscovery of Brugge, and Charles de Coster's pica-
resque *La legende d'Ulenspiegel*, which captures the spirit of

Belgian defiance of outside authority. Both have been translated into English.

Maurice Maeterlinck, Marguerite Yourcenar, and Georges Simenon were all Belgian writers working in French. So was Jacques Brel, many of whose songs also contain outstanding poetry. Hergé, finally, set many of the *Tintin* cartoon adventures in foreign lands, but Tintin himself remained always the quintessential "bon petit Belge."

Arriving and Departing

From North America by Plane

Airports and Airlines All intercontinental and the vast majority of other international flights arrive at the Brussels National Airport at Zaventem. The airport is linked with Antwerp by coach service and with all other Belgian cities by rail.

Sabena (tel. 02/511–9030), the Belgian national carrier, flies to Brussels from New York, Boston, Chicago, Toronto, and Montreal; **American Airlines** (tel. 02/508–7700), from New York and Chicago; **United** (tel. 078/11–43–76), from Washington; and **Delta** (tel. 02/751–8195), **TWA** (tel. 02/513–7916), and **Tower Air** (tel. 02/218–5320), all from New York.

Sample eastbound flying times are: 6 hours, 50 minutes from New York to Brussels; 6 hours, 25 minutes from Montreal to Brussels; and seven hours from Boston to Brussels. Westbound flights are about an hour longer.

From the U.K. by Plane, Car, Ferry/Ship, Train, and Bus

By Plane **Sabena** (tel. 02/511–9030), **British Airways** (tel. 02/725–3000), and **British Midland** (tel. 02/772–9400) fly to Brussels from London (Heathrow); **Dan-Air** (tel. 02/722–4608), from London (Gatwick); and **Air UK** (tel. 02/507–7052), from London (Stansted). Other U.K. cities with direct or nonstop flights to Brussels include Birmingham, Manchester, Newcastle, Leeds, Bristol, Edinburgh, and Glasgow. Flying time from London to Brussels is one hour; Brussels to London is 1 hour, 10 minutes.

By Car The ferry routes to Belgium are from Dover to Oostend or Zeebrugge. Unless you're traveling in the dead of winter, and sometimes even then, it's essential to book well in advance (*see* By Ferry/Ship, *below*, for addresses). Rates vary according to the length of your vehicle, the time of your crossing, and whether you travel in peak, shoulder, or low season.

Both the **Automobile Association** (Fanum House, Basingstoke, Hants. RG21 2EA, tel. 0345/500600) and the **Royal Automobile Club** (RAC House, Box 100, South Croydon CR2 6XW, tel. 081/686–2525) operate on-the-spot breakdown and repair services across Belgium. Both companies will also transport cars and passengers back to Britain in case of serious breakdowns. AA has 5-day, 12-day, and 31-day coverage; RAC offers 10-day and 31-day coverage.

By Ferry/Ship The principal routes across the English Channel to Belgium are Dover–Oostende (operated by **P&O European Ferries**, Channel View Rd., Dover, Kent CT17 9TJ, tel. 0304/203–388) and

Felixstowe–Oostende (operated by P&O European Ferries).
The Dover–Oostende crossing takes four hours, depending on
sea states. The passengers-only Dover–Oostende Jetfoil (book
through P&O European Ferries) is a good bet if you're traveling by train. It makes the crossing in only 100 minutes, but it is
more expensive than the regular ferries and much more liable
to cancellation in bad weather.

By Train   Boat trains timed to meet ferries at Dover leave London and
connect with onward trains at Oostende. The Dover–Oostende
Jetfoil service is the fastest rail connection to Brussels (about
5½ hours, station to station). Contact InterCity Europe, the international wing of BritRail, at London/Victoria station (tel.
071/834–2345, information; tel. 071/828–0892, bookings).

By Bus   **Euroways/Eurolines**—an international consortium of bus operators—offers a range of day and night services linking London
with Antwerp, Brussels, and Brugge. Citysprint offers one-
day round-trips to Antwerp and Brussels. Trips on both bus
lines can be booked at **National Express** offices at Victoria
Coach Station (52 Grosvenor Gardens, London SW1W OAU,
opposite Victoria Rail Station; or through agents throughout
Britain) and at the **Coach Travel Centre** (13 Regent St., London
SW1, for credit card reservations, tel. 071/730–3499; for inquiries, tel. 071/730–0202).

Staying in Belgium

Getting Around

By Plane   There are no domestic air services.

By Train   The Société Nationale des Chemins de Fer Belge (SNCB/Bel-
gian National Railways, Rue de France 89, B-1070 Brussels,
tel. 02/219–2640) provides frequent train service—first and
second class—from Brussels to all major cities in the country.
Very few are more than an hour away. This means that you can,
if you wish, see most of the country on day trips while remaining based in Brussels and traveling on reduced-price same-day
return tickets. Tickets are sold only at railway stations.

Rail Passes   **Tourrail Tickets** allow unlimited travel on the Belgian network
for any five days during a 17-day period. For those over 26 the
price is BF2,550 first class and BF1,700 second class. For those
under 26, the pass costs BF1,950 first class and BF1,300 second
class. A **Go-Pass,** available at BF990 for those between 12 and
26, is good for nine one-way trips in a six-month period; it is not
individual and can thus be used by a group traveling together.

By Bus   Intercity bus travel is not well developed in Belgium. You can,
however, reach a number of localities surrounding each city by
the local bus company. Generally speaking, this would correspond to getting to those places that are mentioned under Off
the Beaten Track in each chapter.

By Car   Belgium has a magnificent network of well-marked motorways, and in contrast with the railroads, they are not all spokes
from the Brussels hub. Thus you can, for instance, drive along
fast, four-lane highways from Antwerp to Ghent, or Liège to
Tournai or Brugge to Kortrijk without passing through the
capital. There are no tolls, and most highways are illuminated
at night.

You must carry a warning triangle, to be placed well behind the car in case of a breakdown. There are emergency telephones at intervals along the motorways. The speed limit is 120 kph (74 mph) on motorways, 90 kph (56 mph) on secondary roads and 50 kph (31 mph) in built-up areas. Driving with the flow may mean higher speeds than most U.S. drivers are accustomed to. At intersections, always check traffic from the right even if you're on a thoroughfare; Belgian drivers can be reckless in insisting on "priority on the right." Gas costs about the same as in other European countries, which means quite a bit more than in the U.S. (about a dollar a liter).

Telephones

Local Calls   Pay phones work with 5- and 20-franc coins or (increasingly) with Telecards, available in a number of denominations starting at BF200. These cards can be purchased at any post office and at many newsstands. Most phone booths that accept Telecards have a list indicating where cards can be bought. A local call costs BF10 or BF20.

International Calls   The least expensive way is to buy a high-denomination Telecard and make a direct call from a phone booth. A five-minute call to the United States at peak time will cost about BF750 by this method. Most hotel rooms are equipped with direct-call telephones, but nearly all add a service charge that can be quite substantial. It's better to ask beforehand what service charges are applied.

To call collect, or by credit card, dial 078/11–00–10 (AT&T), 078/11–00–12 (MCI), or 078/11–00–14 (US Sprint) for the United States; 078/11–00–44 for the United Kingdom.

Mail

Postal Rates   A 5-gram airmail letter to the United States costs BF32; add BF4 for each additional 5 grams. Postcards cost BF32. Letters (up to 20 grams) and postcards to the United Kingdom cost BF15.

Receiving Mail   If you do not know where you will be staying, you can have mail sent care of American Express (Place Louise 1, 1000 Brussels). The service is free for cardholders, otherwise $2 per letter.

Tipping

A service charge is included in restaurant and hotel bills, and tips are also included in the amount shown on the meter in taxis. Additional tipping is unnecessary unless you wish to say thank you for really superior service. Hotel porters generally get a gratuity of BF100 for carrying bags to your room. Tip doormen BF50 for getting you a cab. Porters in railway stations ask a fixed per-suitcase price of BF30–35. In movie theaters, ushers expect a BF20 tip when you present the ticket. Washroom attendants get a BF10 tip. Hairdressers usually receive 10% to 20%.

Shopping

Good quality **lace** is available in several shops in Brussels (but not in cheap souvenir shops); even so, you may wish to wait until you've seen what is available in Brugge before making your choice. Similarly, if you're interested in **fashion,** wait until you've checked out the avant-garde boutiques in Antwerp. If your visit includes Liège, go first to the Val St.-Lambert factory shop before buying **crystal** elsewhere.

Chocolate is best bought as close to departure as possible. In fact, some of the best brands (Godiva, Neuhaus, Daskalides) are available in the tax-free shop at the airport. The Godiva shop in Place Stephanie will mail boxes anywhere in the world.

Many shops, especially perfumeries and electronic equipment stores, advertise that goods are available tax-free. It's worthwhile, but not as simple as it sounds. You have to request a special form or itemized invoice showing the amount of TVA (value added tax) that you have paid. When leaving the country, declare the goods and have the customs officer stamp the documents. Back home, send the stamped forms to the shop, and your sales tax will be refunded.

Sports and Outdoor Activities

Cycling   From Eddy Merckx on, Belgium has produced champion cyclists. The flat land of Flanders is made for this sport, but it can get windy at times. The steep hills of the Ardennes separate the men from the boys. You can rent bikes cheaply at many railway stations, but they aren't your state-of-the-art models. Specialized rental shops exist in most tourist centers. The **Fédération Belge de Cyclotourisme** (Belgian Cycling Federation) is at Avenue H. Limbourg 34, Brussels (tel. 02/521–8640).

Golf   Until recently strictly a rich man's sport in Belgium, golfing is becoming more and more popular, and there are now courses near all major cities. The **Fédération Royale Belge de Golf** (Royal Belgian Golf Federation) is at Chemin de Baudemont 23, Nivelles (tel. 067/22–04–40).

Mountaineering   The Ardennes may not be the Alps, but the many cliffs, especially along the Meuse River valley, provide excellent opportunities for rockface climbing. The **Club Alpin Belge** (Belgian Alpine Club) is at Rue de l'Aurore 19, Brussels (tel. 02/648–8611).

Tennis   There are tennis courts aplenty, but so popular is this sport that you are well advised to book one as early as you can. Your hotel concierge will generally help. For more information, contact the **Fédération Royale Belge de Tennis** (Royal Belgian Tennis Federation), Centre International Rogier, Brussels (tel. 02/217–2200).

Water Sports   All along the coast, but also on lakes and man-made bodies of water, you'll see large numbers of people windsurfing. In summer it seems every second car has a surfboard strapped to its roof rack. For information on this and other sports, contact the **Vlaamse Watersportvereiningen** (Flemish Water Sport Association), Beatrijslaan 25, Antwerp (tel. 03/219–6967).

Beaches

Belgium's entire North Sea Coast is one long beach, and some resorts are so close to each other that you can wander from one to the next without really noticing. Generally speaking, Knokke-Heist draws a youngish, well-heeled clientele, De

Haan is more middle-aged, Oostende caters to a mixed crowd, and De Panne attracts families with young children. If you crave a secluded beach, cross the border into the Dutch province of Zeeuwsch-Vlaanderen.

Dining

The Belgians, by and large, take dining seriously and are discerning about fresh produce and innovative recipes. Because they put a high value on the pleasures of the table, they are also prepared to pay a price that in the best restaurants can be quite steep. You will almost always find families or groups of friends sharing a celebratory meal even in the most expensive restaurants.

As in France, nouvelle cuisine has meant a liberation of creative spirits, and the standards have improved greatly over the past few decades. More recently, the trend has been back to regional and traditional dishes, and now you can enjoy old-fashioned recipes with a modern twist in many restaurants. These may include such hearty dishes as *waterzooi* (a rich chicken or fish hot pot), *faisan à la brabançonne* (pheasant with braised chicory), *lapin à la bière* (rabbit cooked in beer), or *carbonnade* (chunky beef stew with beer).

The quintessential Belgian vegetable is not the brussels sprout but the *witloof* (*chicon* to French-speakers, and endive or chicory to the rest of the world). We owe it to an act of pure serendipity. During one of the many wars in Belgium, a farmer near Mechelen had to abandon the chicory roots (used to produce a coffee substitute) that he had just harvested. When he returned, he found they had sprouted leaves; he tried them and found them good. The witloof was born, and you'll find it in many guises—braised, au gratin, or in salads, always with a slightly bitter edge. Many other good things come from Belgium: superb asparagus, smoked ham and sausages from the Ardennes, crayfish, and trout. But the mussels the Belgians eat with such gusto and proclaim as their own actually come from Holland.

Belgians also swear by the humble *frite*—chips or french fries. They are served in every restaurant and home. You can also get them on street corners and at roadside stands known as *fritures* (Dutchified *frituur*), served with mayonnaise, catsup, or, catering to more advanced tastes, béarnaise or curry sauce. You're not likely to encounter a cheaper or more Belgian dish.

Mealtimes Most hotels serve breakfast until 10. Belgians usually eat lunch between 1 and 3, but restaurants are open from noon. The two-hour lunch is generally expense-account related. The main meal of the day is dinner, generally eaten between 7 and 10. Peak dining time used to be about 8 but seems to be getting later, and reservations are readily accepted for 9 or 9:30.

Dress Belgians are getting less and less formal, and conservative dress is now de rigueur only in the most expensive restaurants. The younger generation in particular favors stylish but casual dress when dining out.

Ratings Prices are per person and include appetizer, entrée and dessert, but no beverages. *See* also separate ratings for Brussels, *below*. Highly recommended restaurants are indicated by a star ★.

Category	Cost: Belgium except Brussels
Very Expensive	BF2000 and up
Expensive	BF1200–BF2000
Moderate	BF600–BF1200
Inexpensive	under BF600

Lodging

You can trust Belgian hotels, almost without exception, to be clean and of a high standard. Modern hotels catering to business travelers, especially in Brussels, can be very expensive, but there is also a wide choice of perfectly acceptable and reasonably priced hotels, where the only difference is the size of the room and number of amenities. Hotel prices in the rest of the country are considerably lower than in the capital. Taxes and service charges are always included in the quoted price. Hotel lists are available from local tourist offices.

Apartment Hotels If you are staying for a week or longer, this may be an interesting option. There are 20-odd such hotels in Brussels, with prices ranging from BF12,000 to BF30,000 per week for a furnished flat with kitchenette.

Pensions Pensions offer a double room with bath or shower and full board from BF2,500 to BF3,500 in Brussels, about BF500 less elsewhere. There's often a minimum stay requirement of two to three days. For information, check the local tourist office.

Youth Hostels *See* Student and Youth Travel in Before You Go, *above.*

Camping Belgium is well supplied with camping and caravaning sites. For details, contact the **Royal Camping and Caravaning Club of Belgium** (Rue Madeleine 31, Brussels, tel. 02/513–1287).

Ratings Hotel prices are exclusive and are posted in each room. All prices in this book are for two people sharing a double room. *See also* separate ratings for Brussels, *below.* Highly recommended hotels are indicated by a star ★.

Category	Cost: Belgium except Brussels
Very Expensive	BF6,000 and up
Expensive	BF3,500–BF6,000
Moderate	BF2,500–BF3,500
Inexpensive	under BF2,500

Brussels

Brussels (Bruxelles in French, Brussel in Flemish) is a provincial city at heart, even though it has assumed a new identity as capital of the European Community. Within the Belgian framework, Brussels has equal status with Flanders and Wallonie as an autonomous region. It is a bilingual enclave just north of the border that divides the country into Flemish- and French-speaking parts.

The battle for dominance of the city began long ago. A village on the site of present-day Brussels had begun to emerge during the latter half of the 10th century. A population of craftsmen and traders settled gradually around the castle of the counts of Leuven, who were later succeeded by the dukes of Brabant.

Philip the Good, duke of Burgundy, took possession of Brabant in 1430, and Brussels became a center for the production of tapestry, lace, and other luxury goods. When Charles V abdicated in 1555, his son, Philip II of Spain, dealt ruthlessly with advocates of the Reformation, which had taken hold in the Low Countries. His governor, the duke of Alva, had the leaders of the revolt, the counts of Egmont and Hoorn, executed in the Grand'Place. A monument to them stands in the square of the Petit Sablon.

In 1695, the French Marshal Villeroy had the city bombarded with red-hot cannonballs. Four thousand houses and 16 churches were destroyed by the ensuing fires, including all of the Grand'Place with the exception of the Town Hall. The Austrian Habsburgs, nominal masters of the Low Countries from 1713 on, recovered the lands in 1744. A new era of prosperity began, and the Upper Town around Place Royale, the Sablon, and the Parc de Bruxelles was restyled in something like its present form.

The next large-scale rebuilding of Brussels was initiated by Leopold II in the second half of the 19th century. He applied the profits from what was the Congo Free State to grand urban projects. Present-day Brussels is indebted to him for the generous proportions of the city's avenues and thoroughfares.

At the end of the 19th century, Brussels was one of the liveliest cities in Europe, known for its splendid cafés and graceful Art Nouveau architecture. The Germans stamped out that gaiety when they occupied the city during World War I, and again from 1940 to 1945. The comeback of Brussels on the international scene was heralded by the World's Fair and Universal Exposition of 1958.

International business has invaded the city in a big way, but a few steps from the steel-and-glass office blocks there are cobbled streets and forgotten spots where the city's eventful past is plainly visible, and all over the city fanciful Art Nouveau town houses testify to the individualistic tastes of their builders.

Over the centuries, Brussels has been shaped by the different cultures of the foreign powers that have been its rulers. It has learned the art of accommodating them and in the process prepared itself for the role of capital of Europe.

Important Addresses and Numbers

Tourist Information The **Tourist Information Brussels** (TIB) office is in the Hotel de Ville (Town Hall) on the Grand'Place (tel. 02/513–8940), open Monday–Saturday 9–6; Sunday same hours in summer, 10–2 in winter, closed December–February. There's a separate tourist office in Waterloo at Chaussée de Bruxelles 149 (tel. 02/354–

9910), open April–November 15, daily 9:30–6:30; November 16–March, daily 10:30–5.

Embassies **U.S.:** Bd du Regent 27, tel. 02/513–3830. **Canadian:** Av de Tervuren 2, tel. 02/735–6040. **U.K.:** Rue d'Arlon 85, tel. 02/287–6211.

Emergencies **Police,** tel. 101. **Ambulance,** tel. 100. **Hospital emergency rooms:** Hôpital St. Pierre (Rue Haute 322, tel. 02/535–3111) and Institut Edith Cavell (Rue Edith Cavell 32, tel. 02/348–4111). **Doctors,** tel. 02/648–8000. **Dentists,** tel. 02/426–1026.

Where to Change Major banks have offices at the airport and all over the city.
Money Many *bureaux de change* stay open outside banking hours but may charge a higher rate. Your safest bet is to go to **American Express** (Place Louise 2, tel. 02/512–1740) or **Thomas Cook** (Grand'Place 4, tel. 02/513–2844).

English-language **W. H. Smith** (Boulevard Adolphe Max 71, tel. 02/219–2708) car-
Bookstores ries a large selection of paperbacks, specialized hardbacks, and periodicals. The **Librairie de Rome** (Av Louise 50, tel. 02/511–7937) sells paperbacks, guidebooks, and newspapers from all over Europe.

Late-night One pharmacy in each district stays open 24 hours; the roster is
Pharmacies posted in all pharmacy windows. In an emergency, call 02/479–1818.

Travel Agencies **American Express** is at Place Louise 2 (tel. 02/512–1740), **Wagons-Lits** at Rue Ravenstein 22 (tel. 02/512–9878) and other locations. For travel to the United Kingdom, most requirements can be handled by the **British Reservation Centre** (Av Louise 306, tel. 02/646–4210). For others, ask at your hotel.

Arriving and Departing by Plane

Airport and All flights arrive at and depart from Brussels's national air-
Airlines port, **Zaventem** (tel. 02/732–3111). **Sabena, American, Delta, TWA, United,** and **Tower Air** fly into Brussels from the United States. **Sabena, British Midland,** and **British Airways** fly to Brussels from London's Heathrow Airport; **Air UK,** from Stansted; and **Dan-Air,** from Gatwick.

Between the Express trains leave the airport for the Gare du Nord and Gare
Airport and Centrale every 20 minutes (one train an hour continues to the
Downtown Gare du Midi). The trip takes 20 minutes and costs BF110 one
By Train way in first class, BF70 second class. You can buy tickets at a booth in the baggage area or on the train (BF30 surcharge). The trains operate 6 AM to midnight.

By Taxi Airport taxis are plentiful. A taxi to the city center takes about half an hour and costs about BF1,000. You can save 25% on the fare by buying a voucher for the return trip if you use the Autolux taxi company.

By Bus Free courtesy buses serve airport hotels and a few downtown hotels. Inquire when making reservations.

Arriving and Departing by Car, Train, and Bus

By Car Belgium is covered by an extensive network of four-lane motorways. Brussels is 204 kilometers (127 miles) from Amsterdam on E19, 222 kilometers (138 miles) from Düsseldorf on E40, 219 kilometers (136 miles) from Luxembourg City on

E411, 308 kilometers (191 miles) from Paris, and 115 kilometers (71 miles) from Oostende.

Brussels is surrounded by a beltway, marked "Ring." Exits to the city are marked "Center." Among several large underground parking facilities, the one close to the Grand'Place is particularly convenient for users of downtown hotels.

By Train Train services from London connect with the Dover–Oostende ferry or Jetfoil, and from Oostende the train takes you to Brussels. The whole journey by Jetfoil takes some five hours, but by ferry it's quite a bit longer. For reservations and times, contact **P&O Ferries** in London (tel. 081/575–8555).

Brussels is linked with Paris, Amsterdam, and the German rail network by fast intercity trains, and there are direct services to Switzerland, Italy, and Austria. **Belgian State Railways** (SNCB, tel. 02/219–2640) is the national rail line.

The main station is the **Gare du Midi** (South Station, off Boulevard du Midi). Trains also stop at the **Gare du Nord** (Rue du Progrès); this is the one to use if your hotel is in the Place Rogier area. In between is the **Gare Centrale** (Boulevard de l'Impératrice), the most convenient for the downtown area, but served (apart from the Airport Express) mostly by commuter trains. For train information, tel. 02/219–2640.

By Bus From London, the **Hoverspeed City Sprint** bus connects with the Dover–Calais Hovercraft, and the bus then takes you to Brussels, where it stops at Rue Antoine Dansaert 101, near the Bourse. The journey takes 6½ hours. For reservations and times, call **Hoverspeed** in London (tel. 081/554–7061. Overnight services by **National Express-Eurolines** in London (tel. 071/730–0202) take the ferry.

Getting Around Brussels

By Metro, Tram, and Bus The **Metro** system consists of one line running east–west and another north–south. Tram and bus routes are less predictable and subject to change. Maps of the total system are available in many Metro stations and from the TIB in the Grand'Place.

Multifare cards can be purchased in Metro stations and at newsstands. Single tickets, good for one transfer, cost BF45 and can be bought on buses and trams. The best buy is a 10-trip ticket at BF275, or a 24-hour card at BF180. You need to stamp your card in the appropriate machine on buses and trams; in the Metro your card is stamped as you pass through the turnstiles.

By Taxi Taxis are expensive, but tips are included in the fare. Even a short trip will cost you about BF250, and longer in-town trips are up to BF500. To call a cab, phone (or have the restaurant or hotel call) **Taxis Verts** (tel. 02/511–2244) or **Taxis Oranges** (tel. 02/513–6200), or catch one at a cabstand.

Opening and Closing Times

Businesses are open weekdays 9–5 or 9–5:30. Banks are open weekdays 9–4, with some open Saturday 9–noon. Administrative offices are a law unto themselves; call ahead. Shops are generally open Monday–Saturday 10–7; smaller shops often close for lunch. Nearly all museums are closed on Monday. Restaurants usually stay open until the last guest leaves; last food orders are about 10 PM. Theaters and concerts normally start at 8:30. In discos and nightclubs, the action begins around midnight.

Guided Tours

De Boeck Sightseeing (tel. 02/513–7744) operates city tours (BF600) with multilingual cassette commentary and guides. Passengers are picked up at major hotels and at the TIB in the Town Hall. De Boeck also operates tours of Waterloo. **Chatterbus** (tel. 02/673–1835 evenings only) organizes walking tours from June to September (BF275).

Special Interest **ARAU** (Rue Henri Maus 37, tel. 02/513–4761) organizes a variety of city architectural tours (BF500 for a half-day tour, Saturday only) in English.

Personal Guides Qualified guides, collectively speaking a total of 14 languages, are available for individual tours from TIB in the Town Hall (tel. 02/513–8940). The cost for three hours is BF2,600, and up to 20 persons can share the same guide.

Highlights for First-Time Visitors

Cathédrale St-Michel (Tour 1: The Grand'Place and Surroundings)
Grand'Place (Tour 1: The Grand'Place and Surroundings)
Grand Sablon (Tour 2: The Upper Town and the Marolles)
Manneken Pis (Tour 1: The Grand'Place and Surroundings)
Musée d'Art Ancien (Tour 2: The Upper Town and the Marolles)
Musée d'Art Moderne (Tour 2: The Upper Town and the Marolles)
Petit Sablon (Tour 2: The Upper Town and the Marolles)
Place Royale (Tour 2: The Upper Town and the Marolles)

Exploring Brussels

Start in the historic heart of Brussels, the Lower Town, centered on the Grand'Place with its 17th-century guild houses. You can devote a second day to the Upper Town of the 18th and 19th centuries.

Tour 1: The Grand'Place and Surroundings

Numbers in the margin correspond with places of interest on the Brussels map.

❶ The most famous citizen of Brussels is the insouciant **Manneken Pis.** The small bronze statue of a chubby boy peeing into a fountain stands at the corner of the Rue de l'Etuve and the Rue du Chêne, southwest of the Grand'Place. A similar stone figure, of unknown origin, is first mentioned in a document from 1377. To replace it, the city ordered the present bronze statue in 1619 from the sculptor Jerome Duquesnoy. It was hidden during the 1695 bombardment but was later briefly kidnapped by British soldiers in 1745 and French soldiers in 1747. King Louis XV of France presented Manneken Pis with a gold-embroidered suit in 1747, and the statue has many other costumes for ceremonial occasions.

❷ Rue de l'Etuve leads to the **Grand'Place,** one of Europe's most ornate market squares and a true jewel box, close to the hearts of all the people of the city. At night, you experience the full theatrical effect of the burnished facades of the guild houses and their gilded statuary. From April to September, the square is floodlighted after sundown with changing colored lights. There is a daily flower market in the Grand'Place, and a bird market on Sunday mornings.

The **Hôtel de Ville** (Town Hall), in Brabant Gothic style, is some 300 years older than the guild houses. The left wing was begun in 1402 but was soon found to be too small. Charles the Bold laid the first stone for the extension in 1444, and it was completed in just four years. The change in plans left the slender belfry, designed by Jan van Ruysbroeck, off center. It is topped by a bronze statue of St. Michael crushing a figure of the devil beneath his feet. Over the gateway are statues of the prophets, female figures representing lofty virtues, and effigies of long-gone dukes and duchesses. The Town Hall contains some excellent Brussels and Mechelen tapestries, some of them in the Gothic Hall, where there are frequent recitals and chamber-music concerts. *Grand'Place. Admission: BF75. Open Tues.–Fri. 9:30–12:15 and 1:45–4 (Apr.–Sept. until 5). Guided visits only; suspended when City Council is in session.*

The guild houses of the Grand'Place were built soon after the 1695 bombardment in ornate Italo-Flemish Baroque style. Among the buildings on the north side of the square, No. 1–2, **La Maison du Roi d'Espagne,** belonged to the bakers' guild. It is decorated with a relief honoring Charles II of Spain, and is surmounted by a cupola on which the figure of Fame is perched. **La Maison du Sac,** No. 4, commissioned by the guild of joiners and coopers, and No. 6, **La Maison du Cornet,** built for the boatmen, were both designed by Antoon Pastorana, a gifted furniture maker. **La Maison du Renard,** No. 7, was designed for the guild of haberdashers and peddlers. A sculpture of St. Christopher, their patron, stands on top of the gable.

Time Out   On the ground floor of No. 1 there's a vast and popular cafe, **Au Roy d'Espagne,** with an open fire and solid wooden furniture.

On the same side as the Town Hall, **La Maison des Brasseurs** (No. 10), the brewers's guild, appropriately houses a Brewery Museum, making it the only guild hall in the world still serving its original purpose. *Grand'Place 10, tel. 02/511–4987. Admission: BF50. Open weekdays 10–noon and 2–5, Apr.–Sept. also Sat. 10–noon.*

Next to it stands No. 9, **La Maison du Cygne,** formerly owned by the guild of butchers, now one of the city's most elegant restaurants. Before going posh, it housed a tavern much frequented by Karl Marx, who lived in Brussels for three years before being expelled.

On the side opposite the Hotel de Ville stands the **Maison du Roi,** in which no king ever lived, although legend has it that it was the scene of Emperor Charles V's abdication in 1555 in favor of his son, Philip II. Now it houses the **Musée Communal,** with some fine tapestries, altarpieces, and paintings, notably Pieter Bruegel the Elder's *Marriage Procession.* On the top floor you can see the extensive wardrobe of costumes donated to Manneken Pis. *Grand'Place, tel. 02/511–2742. Admission:*

172

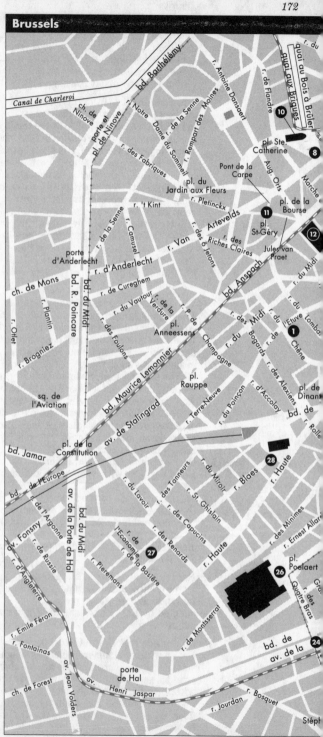

Brussels

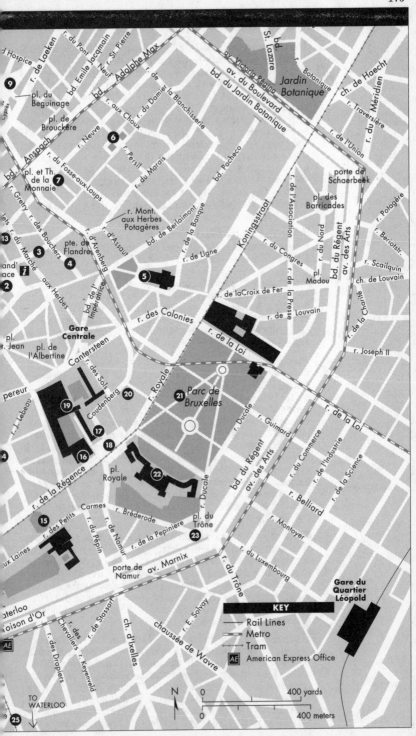

r. d'Hospice
r. de Laeken
r. du Pont
bd. Emile Jacqmain
r. St. Pierre
r. Neuf
Adolphe Max
av. Victoria Régina
av. du Boulevard
St. Lazare
bd.
bd. du Jardin Botanique
Botanique
ch. de Haecht

Jardin
Botanique

9 pl. du
Béguinage
r. Cyprès
pl. de
Brouckère
bd. Anspach
r. du Fossé-aux-Loups
r. Neuve
r. aux Choux
r. du Damier
r. de la Blanchisserie
6
r. aux Choux
r. du Damier
r. Traversière
r. du Méridien
r. de l'Union

7 pl. et Th.
de la
Monnaie
r. Grétry
r. des Bouchers
r. du Persil
r. du Marais
bd. Pacheco
porte de
Schaerbeek
r. Potagère
r. Berlolstr.

13
3 r. du Marché
r. Mont.
aux Herbes
Potagères
pte. de
Flandre
r. d'Arenberg
r. d'Assaut
bd. de Berlaimont
r. de la Banque
r. de Ligne
Koningsstraat
r. de l'Association
r. du Congrès
r. du Nord
pl. des
Barricades
bd. du Régent
av. des Arts
r. Scailquin
ch. de Louvain

2 grand'
place
i
r. aux Herbes
4
5
r. des Colonies
r. de la Croix de Fer
r. de la Presse
pl.
Madou
r. de Louvain
r. de la Charité

bd. de l'Impératrice

Gare
Centrale
Cantersteen
r. des Colonies
r. de la Loi
r. Joseph II

pl.
r. Jean
pl. de
l'Albertine
empereur
r. J. Lebeau
19
r. des Sols
Coudenberg
20
17
Royale
21
Parc de
Bruxelles
r. Ducale
r. Guimard
bd. du Régent
av. des Arts
r. de la Loi
r. de la Loi

4
16
18
r. de la Régence
pl.
Royale
22
r. du Commerce
r. de l'Industrie
r. de la Science
r. Belliard

15
Carmes
r. Bréderode
r. de Namur
r. de la Pepinière
r. du Pépin
pl. du
Trône
r. Ducale
23
r. Montoyer

aux Laines
r. des Petits
porte de
Namur
av. Marnix
r. du Trône
r. du Luxembourg

Gare du
Quartier
Léopold

aterloo
Toison d'Or
r. de Stassart
r. des
Chevaliers
r. des Drapiers
r. Keyenveld
ch. d'Ixelles
chaussée de Wavre
r. E. Solvay
r. du Trône

AE

KEY
—— Rail Lines
==== Metro
++++ Tram
AE American Express Office

TO
WATERLOO
25
N

0   400 yards
0   400 meters

BF80. Open weekdays 10–12:30 and 1:30–4 (Apr.–Sept. 10–12:30 and 1:30–5), weekends 10–1.

The alley next to the Maison du Roi leads out of the Grand'Place to Rue du Marché-aux-Herbes and, across the way, the narrow Petite Rue des Bouchers. We're now in the **Quartier de l'Ilôt Sacré**, the liveliest area in Brussels, where restaurants and cafés are cheek by jowl, with tables spilling out on the sidewalk. In the evening it grows very crowded; be careful not to provide temptation for pickpockets. The restaurants make strenuous efforts to pull you in with huge displays of seafood and game. As a general rule, the more extravagant the display, the more dubious the quality (*see* Dining, *below*). Down an even narrower alley off Petite Rue des Bouchers, called Schuddeveld, lies the **Théâtre Toone** (Impasse Schuddeveld, tel. 02/511–7137), a famous old puppet theater where satirical plays are performed in broad Bruxellois dialect. You won't understand a word, but it's fun anyway.

To the right at the top of Petite Rue des Bouchers, past several more restaurants, the **Galeries St-Hubert** (also known as the Galeries Royales) branch off right and left. They were built in 1847 as the world's first covered shopping galleries, using the new engineering techniques that allowed architects to design soaring constructions of glass with iron girders. Neoclassical gods and heroes in their sculpted niches look down on the crowded scene below, and even the buskers play classical music, while from high above, diffused daylight penetrates the gallery from the glassed arches.

At the northern exit of the galleries, to the right on Rue d'Arenberg and up the slight incline, is the **Cathédrale St-Michel** (Parvis Ste-Gudule 20, tel. 02/217–3845), begun in 1226, whose twin Gothic towers gleam white after the removal of centuries of grime. Stay to the right side of the street in front of the church before crossing to the side entrance, for there are no marked crossings, and pedestrians are fair game. The restoration of the interior is underway, but the remains of an 11th-century Romanesque church can be glimpsed through glass apertures set into the floor. Among the windows, designed by various artists, those by Bernard van Orley, a 16th-century court painter, are outstanding. The window of the Last Judgment, at the bottom of the nave, is illuminated from within in the evening.

Cross the boulevard into the Rue d'Assaut. Making a right on Rue Montagne aux Herbes Potagères, turn into Rue du Fossé-aux-Loups or proceed straight ahead and turn left through the narrow Rue du Persil into the **Place des Martyrs**. This nobly proportioned square, in the cool style favored by the Austrian Habsburgs of the 18th century, contains an underground shrine to the 445 patriots who died in the brief war of independence against the Dutch.

If you return to Rue du Fossé-aux-Loups on Rue Neuve (a busy pedestrian shopping street) you arrive in Place de la Monnaie, where the revolt began. It was here, during a performance of Auber's *La Muette de Portici* in the **Théâtre de la Monnaie** (Place de la Monnaie, tel. 02/218–1202) on August 25, 1830, that some members of the audience became so inflamed by the duet "Amour sacré de la patrie" that they stormed out and started a riot that led to independence. The opera house is very pleasing, and among Europe's leading opera stages. Concerts and recitals are also given here, as are lunchtime chamber music performances.

Past the modern Centre Monnaie and across the broad and busy Boulevard Anspach, is the Place de Brouckère on the right, which is recovering from a past as a sort of Times Square of Brussels. Straight ahead toward the Place Ste-Catherine are **(8)** the rather forlorn remnants of the **Tour Noire,** which dates from the 12th century and was part of the city's oldest fortifications.

The short Rue des Cyprès is one of several streets that converge on the Place du Beguinage and the **Eglise de St-Jean (9) Baptiste.** *Beguinages* are enclosures once inhabited by an order of lay sisters. The one in Brussels exists no more, except for the beautiful church in Flemish Baroque. The facade is divided into three bays, each with a curlicued scroll gable.

Down the block-long Rue du Peuplier is the **Quai aux Bois à Bruler,** formerly a quay along the harbor of the River Senne. The other side of the street is called the Quai aux Briques. The river, long since gone underground, is represented only by a symbolic pool, but the legacy of the harbor is present in a collection of good fish restaurants.

(10) To the left past the **Eglise Ste-Catherine,** which looks centuries old but is in fact barely 150, is the square of the same name, which was the old fish market. There is still generally a stall where you can taste some oysters or mussels and wash them down with a glass of chilled muscadet.

The second left on the square, **Rue Antoine Dansaert,** has in recent years become a center for chic boutiques featuring young Belgian designers, home furnishings shops, galleries, and bars.

Time Out | **Le Pain Quotidien** (Rue Antoine Dansaert 16) is a bakery that produces superior bread, and you can enjoy it, in sandwiches or with salad, seated at a big old refectory table.

(11) Rue du Pont de la Carpe affords a brief detour to the **Place St-Géry,** the oldest part of Brussels. A 6th-century church once stood here; now it is the site of a covered market. Some of its old brick houses have been restored, and a short stretch of the river has been uncovered.

Rue Jules Van Praet leads to Boulevard Anspach opposite the **(12)** rather magnificent **Bourse** (Palais de la Bourse, tel. 02/512–5110), built in 1871 on a scale that Brussels's modest stock-exchange trading has never quite justified.

Tucked away behind the Bourse and hemmed in by tiny houses **(13)** is the small **Eglise de St-Nicolas** (Bourse—Grand'Place, tel. 02/511–8178). Once the parish church of Brussels's merchants, it is also the traditional church of aspiring dancers. Here Mass is said in English on Sundays at 10. One short block on Rue au Beurre leads back to the Maison du Roi and the Grand'Place.

Tour 2: The Upper Town and the Marolles

(14) There are few more pleasant places in Brussels than the **Grand Sablon,** once, as the name implies, nothing more than a sandy hill. Today it is an elegant square, surrounded by numerous restaurants, cafés, and exclusive antiques shops, some in intriguing alleys and arcades, as well as Wittamer, a pastry shop of such renown that its products are flown to Belgian embassies around the world. On Saturdays and Sunday mornings there's a lively antiques market at the upper end of the square.

At the eastern end stands the **Eglise Notre-Dame du Sablon,** a Flamboyant Gothic church founded in 1304 by the guild of crossbowmen and rebuilt in the 15th century. Its chief glory is the stained-glass windows. After nightfall they are illuminated from within, suffusing the Grand Sablon with kindly light.

⑮ Across Rue de la Régence lies the **Place du Petit-Sablon.** The square is surrounded by columns topped by small bronze statues representing the city's 48 guilds. Inside the garden are statues of the Flemish patriots, Counts Egmont and Hoorn, on their way to the scaffold in 1568. On the square, the **Musée Instrumental** (Musical Instruments Museum) contains over 4,000 instruments. The collection is scheduled to be transferred to a house on the Place Royale that is now undergoing restoration. *Place du Petit Sablon 17. Admission free. Open Tues., Thurs., Sat. 2:30–4:30, Wed. 4–6, Sun. 10:30–12:30.*

Immediately beyond the square is the **Palais d'Egmont,** where Queen Christina of Sweden, France's Louis XV, and Voltaire resided at various times. The garden is open to the public and can be entered from a gate on Rue du Grand Cerf.

To the left from Petit Sablon at Rue de la Régence 30 is the Conservatoire Royale (the Royal Conservatory, tel. 02/511–0427), site of numerous concerts, and Synagogue de Bruxelles (No. 32, tel. 02/512–4334), the city's main synagogue. Down Rue de **⑯** la Régence to the right lies the **Musée d'Art Ancien** (Museum of Classical Art), which holds paintings by Flemish primitives of the 15th century such as Memling, Petrus Christus, and Gerard David. The collection of works by Pieter Bruegel the Elder is outstanding; it includes *The Fall of Icarus,* in which the figure of the mythological hero disappearing in the sea is but one detail while people continue going about their business. An excellent Rubens collection is on the floor above. The 19th-century collection on the ground floor includes the *Assassination of Marat* by Jacques-Louis David, who like many other French artists and writers spent years of exile in Belgium. *Rue de la Régence 3. Admission free. Open Tues.–Sun. 10–12 and 1–5.*

⑰ The new **Musée d'Art Moderne** can be reached by an underground passage, or you can enter it from the house on Place Royale where Alexandre Dumas (père) once lived and wrote. This original subterranean gallery circles downward eight floors, rather like the Guggenheim Museum in reverse. Here you can see how the art movements of the past hundred years have been interpreted in works by Belgian painters. The handful of Belgians who have acquired international prominence— the expressionist James Ensor and the surrealists Paul Delvaux and René Magritte—are well represented. *Place Royale 1. Admission free. Open Tues.–Sun. 10–12 and 1–5.*

⑱ The white, elegantly proportioned **Place Royale** is the centerpiece of the Upper Town as conceived in Louis XVI style in the 18th century. Its buildings are being restored one by one, leaving the facades intact. From the center you have a splendid view of the Lower Town and its spires. In the other direction is the attractive church of St-Jacques-sur-Coudenberg, and down the Rue Montagne de la Cour and the flight of steps on the left you reach the neoclassical **Ancien Cour** on the right, all that remains of the palace built for Charles of Lorraine in 1760.

Back on Rue Montagne de la Cour, the blackened walls of the **Hotel Ravenstein** loom across the street. Built in the 15th century, it is the only aristocratic house from that period to have survived and is now a restaurant. A bit farther on is the main entrance of the **Palais des Beaux-Arts,** designed in the 1920s in Art Deco style by Victor Horta, known for the Art Nouveau architecture of his earlier years. Here stood the pension where the Brontë sisters, Charlotte and Emily, stayed in 1842.

From Rue Baron Horta a flight of curving steps leads up to **Rue Royale.** The white and quietly elegant buildings lining this street contain the headquarters of the Société Générale, which formerly had enormous holdings in Africa and remains powerful in Belgian banking and industry. In front of you is the **Parc de Bruxelles,** once a wild and woodsy hunting ground but tamed into rigid symmetry in the late 18th century.

The huge **Palais Royal** occupies the entire south side of the park. It was built by Leopold II at the beginning of this century on a scale corresponding to his own megalomaniacal ambitions. The present monarch, King Baudouin, lives at the Laeken Palace on the outskirts of Brussels but comes here for state occasions. As a constitutional monarch he wields no direct power but exercises discreet influence behind the scenes, especially on the not infrequent occasions when a new government is being formed. *Place des Palais. Admission free. Open July 22– early Sept., Tues.–Sun. 10–4.*

Up Rue Ducale in the **Place du Trône** stands Leopold II himself in the form of an equestrian statue. Here, too, is the Luxembourg Metro station; two stops on the subway take you to Place Louise. Here, Boulevard du Régent forms part of *la ceinture* (the belt) that surrounds the heart of the city. It changes names every few blocks and, to make the confusion complete, the two sides of the street also have different names. To the south past the intersection Porte de Namur lies the real shopping section. On the **Boulevard de Waterloo** side you'll encounter the same luxury brand names as on Rodeo Drive or Fifth Avenue. The other side is appropriately named the **Avenue de la Toison d'Or** (Golden Fleece Avenue). Two shopping arcades branch off from here, the warrenlike Galerie de la Toison d'Or and the more prestigious **Galerie Louise** with its recent upmarket addition, Espace Louise. Fashion boutiques predominate in the arcades, interspersed with cafés and perfumeries. At the other end Galerie Louise has its exit on **Place Stephanie.** To the right is **Avenue Louise,** the city's top shopping street, built in the mid-19th century to link the city with the Bois de la Cambre to the south.

Time Out   **Nemrod** (Boulevard de Waterloo 61, near Place Louise) is a popular place for a shopping break or a drink after a movie.

Past Place Louise to the northwest stands the gigantic **Palais de Justice,** another of Leopold II's brainchildren, on the site of the old Gallows Hill. The terrace in front of it offers great views of the Lower Town and, to the northwest, another huge and eccentric building, the Basilique, begun in 1905 but not completed until 1970. On its right, straight north, you can see the Atomium, a 122-meter (400-foot) -high structure representing the nine atoms of an iron crystal, designed for the World's Fair in 1958.

The contrast of the grand scale of the works of Leopold II with the past is immediately apparent as you descend the ramps and proceed down Rue de l'Epée into **Les Marolles,** an area once deemed dangerous and still with a slightly raffish reputation. If the Grand'Place has an ambience of old money, Les Marolles has one of old poverty. Settled by weavers in the Middle Ages, it has survived many occupations and welcomed many waves of immigrants. Here you might still hear the Brussels dialect, mixing Flemish with French and bits of Spanish.

On your right at Rue Haute is the **Maison de Bruegel** (No. 132), a step-gabled building where the painter probably lived; we know for certain that it was owned by his descendants. To
㉗ the left on Rue Haute and right on Rue des Renards is **Place du Jeu de Balle,** scene of a huge daily flea market. Early morning is the best time for spotting value. Leave your handbag at the hotel. Rue Blaes, lined with curio shops, parallels Rue Haute.

㉘ At the end of Rue Blaes stands the unusual **Eglise Notre-Dame de la Chapelle,** where Pieter Bruegel the Elder was married in 1563 and, just six years later, buried. The transept is Romanesque, while the nave and aisles are in Brabant Gothic style, and the church tower is Baroque. Across the Place de la Chapelle is Rue de Rollebeek, lined with a multitude of restaurants; it leads back to the Place du Grand-Sablon.

Excursion to Waterloo

The decisive Battle of Waterloo, where Napoleon was finally stopped by the British and Prussian armies under Wellington and Blücher, was fought on June 18, 1815. Once every five years (next in 1995) the Battle of Waterloo is reenacted by thousands of volunteers in period uniforms. The town of **Waterloo** is 19 kilometers (12 miles) south of Brussels on N5. The **Waterloo Tourist Office** (Chaussée de Bruxelles 149, tel. 02/354–9910) is in the center of town. Next door is the well-laid-out **Wellington Museum,** in the building where Wellington had his headquarters. It presents maps and models of the battle along with military memorabilia. *Chaussée de Bruxelles 147, tel. 02/345–7806. Admission: BF60. Open Apr.-mid Nov., daily 9:30–6:30; mid-Nov.–Mar., daily 10:30–5.*

South of the city is the actual **battlefield,** where the **Visitors' Centre** (Route du Lion 252, tel. 02/385–0625) has an audiovisual presentation that shows scenes of the battle and a model of the battlefield that lights up to indicate the battle's progress.

Expert guides, **Les Guides 1815,** can be booked through the Visitors' Centre to take you around the battlefield (cost: BF1,400 for a one-hour tour and BF2,200 for a three-hour visit; group visits in English, BF100 per person, weekends 4 PM July–Aug). A red tourist train also runs from Waterloo station (tel. 02/354–7806) to all the main sights (July–Aug.).

The victorious combatants were quick to erect battle monuments. The most famous, the **Butte du Lion,** a pyramid 226 steps high and crowned by a 28-ton lion, was erected by the Dutch on a spot of no military significance, but it provides a great view of the battlefield. The adjacent **Battle Panorama Museum** illustrates the crucial mistake that cost Napoleon the battle. *Chemin des Vertes Bornes 90, tel. 02/384–3139. Admission: BF70. Open daily 9:30–6.*

Napoleon's headquarters were at what is now the small **Musée du Caillou** in **Genappe,** south of the battlefield. It contains the room where he spent the night before the battle and some personal effects. *Chaussée de Bruxelles 66, tel. 02/384–2424. Admission: BF60. Open Apr.–Sept., Tues.–Sun. 10–6:30; Nov.–Mar., Tues.–Sun. 1:30–5.*

Dining **La Mère Pierre.** In the tiny suburban town of Limal, just south
★ of Brussels between Waterloo and Wavre, this gem of a restaurant offers the rare opportunity to dine as a guest in a Belgian household. The owner of this comfy old redbrick house is an easygoing woman who cooks, chats, and serves you a well-priced four-course menu (sole in a delicate curry, guinea fowl in orange sauce) of such generous proportion and unaffected style, you feel you're at a family dinner party. There are toys for the grandchildren, hydrangea-print linens, and a garden for summer dining. *Rue Charles Jaumotte 3, Ottignies-Louvain-la-Neuve, tel. 010/41–16–42. Reservations suggested. Dress: Casual, but jacket suggested. AE, DC, MC, V. Moderate.*

What to See and Do with Children

There are few kids who don't fall in love with the **Musée des Enfants** (Children's Museum) even though its purpose is educational for 2- to 12-year-olds: learning to handle both objects and emotions. Kids get to plunge their arms into sticky goo, dress up in eccentric costumes, crawl through tunnels, or take photographs with an oversize camera. *Rue du Bourgmestre 15, tel. 02/640–0107. Admission: BF150. Open Sept.–July, Wed. and weekends 2:30–5.*

Under the high glass roof of the south hall in the Parc du Cinquantenaire, you'll find **Autoworld,** one of the handsomest collections of vintage cars—over 450 of them—in the world. *Palais Mondial/Cinquantenaire, tel. 02/736–4165. Admission: BF150. Open daily 10–5, Apr.–Sept. until 6.*

Mini-Europe consists of a collection of 1:25 scale models of 300 famous European buildings and high-tech achievements in a five-acre park near the Atomium. *Boulevard du Centenaire 20, tel. 02/478–0550. Admission: adults BF350, children BF290, under 6 free. Open Apr.–Dec. weekdays 9–6 (July–Aug. until 8), weekends 9–9.*

The adjoining **Oceade** offers water slides, an ocean wave pool, and other watery attractions. *Tel. 02/478–4320. Admission: adults BF389, children BF240. Open Tues.–Thurs. 2–10, Fri. 2–midnight, Sat. 11 AM–midnight, Sun. 10–8.*

Out of town, **Walibi** draws Brussels kids and teenagers with its advanced rides and shows, while attractions at the adjoining **Aqualibi** include a tropical river adventure. *Exit 6 (N238) at Wavre from E411, tel. 010/41–44–46. Walibi admission:*

BF530. Open Apr.–Sept., daily 10–6. Aqualibi admission: BF360. Open Apr.–Sept., Tues–Sun. 10–10; Oct.–March, Tues.–Sun. 2–10.

From mid-July until the end of August, all of Belgium's carnival barkers and showmen and their carousels, ghost trains, Ferris wheels, shooting galleries, rides, swings, and roundabouts congregate along the Boulevard du Midi for the giant and hugely popular **Foire du Midi.**

Off the Beaten Track

West of the city center, in Anderlecht, the **Maison d'Erasme/Erasmushuis** (House of Erasmus) has been restored to its condition in 1521. In addition to Erasmus's study, the house contains works by Hieronymous Bosch and Albrecht Dürer and first editions of Erasmus's books. *Rue du Chapitre 31, tel. 02/ 521–1383. Metro to St–Guidon; tram 103; buses 47 and 49. Admission: BF20. Open Wed–Thurs., Sat.–Mon. 10–12 and 2–5.*

In the boroughs just south of the center St.-Gilles and Ixelles, are Brussels's best examples of the pre–World War I Art Nouveau architecture of Victor Horta and his colleagues and followers. The **Horta Museum,** the house where the architect lived and worked until 1919, is the best place to see his joyful interiors and furniture. *Rue Americaine 25, tel. 02/537–1692. Trams 81 and 92; buses 81 and 92. Admission: BF100. Open Tues.– Sun. 2–5:30.*

The **David and Alice Van Buuren Museum,** in the borough of Uccle, preserves a perfect Art Deco interior. The made-to-order carpets and furnishings are of an exceptional standard, and the art treasures include paintings by the Van Buurens' contemporaries as well as old masters. *Avenue Leo Errera 41, tel. 02/343–4851 or 02/733–7152. Trams 23 and 90. Admission: BF100. Open Mon. 2–4 and by appointment (groups only).*

The late Hergé, creator of Tintin, elevated the comic strip to an art form. The new **Centre Belge de la Bande Dessinée** (Belgian Comic Strip Center) contains over 400 original plates by Hergé and his many successors and 25,000 cartoon works. *Rue des Sables 20, tel. 02/219–1980. Metro Rogier/Botanique: trams 90, 92, and 93; bus 38. Admission: BF120. Open Tues.–Sun. 10–6.*

Toward the southern end of Avenue Louise is the **Bois de la Cambre,** a natural park that is a favorite among joggers and families with children. The park merges on the south into the beech woods of the 4,455-hectare (11,000-acre) **Forêt de Soignes,** extending as far south as Genval with its lake and restaurants.

From Square Montgomery, Tram 44 passes the rolling Parc de Woluwe and through the forest all the way to **Tervuren.** Nearby is the **Musée Royal d'Afrique Centrale,** the final vestige of Belgium's colonial adventure. It contains a fine collection of masks, sculpture, and memorabilia of the journeys of the explorers of Africa. *Leuvensesteenweg 13, tel. 02/767–5401. Admission free. Open mid-Mar.–mid-Oct. daily 9–5:30; mid-Oct.–mid-Mar. daily 10–4:30.*

North of the center of Brussels stands the **Atomium,** a model of a molecule enlarged 165 billion times, constructed for the 1958 World's Fair. There's an express elevator to the highest point, where you have a panoramic view of Brussels. *Boulevard du Centenaire, tel. 02/477–0977. Metro Heysel. Admission: BF150. Open mid-Mar.–mid-Oct. daily 9:45–6:30 mid-Oct.–mid-Mar., daily 9:30–5.*

Shopping

The Belgians started producing high-quality luxury goods in the Middle Ages, and this is what they are skilled at. This is not a country where you pick up amazing bargains. Value added tax (TVA) further inflates prices, but visitors from outside the European Community can obtain refunds.

Shopping Districts The chic shopping area comprises the upper end of **Avenue Louise** plus the avenue branching off at a right angle from it at Place Louise, **Avenue de la Toison d'Or** and **Boulevard de Waterloo** (the other side of the street), plus **Galerie Louise,** which links the two avenues and, a couple of blocks away, another arcade, the **Galerie de la Toison d'Or.** The **Place du Grand Sablon** is equally expensive but more attractive. Here and in the adjoining streets and alleys you will find exclusive antiques dealers and smart art galleries. The **Galeries St-Hubert** is a rather stately shopping arcade lined with high-class shops selling men's and women's clothing, books, and interior design products. The **City 2** mall on Place Rogier and the pedestrian **Rue Neuve** are fun and inexpensive shopping areas (but not recommended for women alone after dark). **Rue Antoine Dansaert** and **Place du Nouveau Marché aux Grains,** near the Bourse, form the newest chic shopping area, specializing in clothes by young designers, interior design, and art.

Department Stores The best department stores in town are **Inno** (rue Neuve 111, tel. 02/211–2111; Chaussée d'Ixelles 41, tel. 02/512–7800; and Chaussée de Waterloo 699, tel. 02/345–3890) and **Sarmalux** (rue Neuve 15, tel. 02/212–8714; and av Louise 12, tel. 02/513–8494).

Street Markets Bruxellois with an eye for fresh farm produce and low prices do most of their food shopping at the animated open-air markets in almost every borough. Among the best are those in **Boitsfort** in front of the Maison Communal (Sun. AM), on **Place du Chatelain** (Wed. afternoons), and on **Place Ste-Catherine** (all day Mon.–Sat.). In addition to fruits, vegetables, meat, and fish, most markets include traders with specialized products, such as wide selections of cheese and wild mushrooms. The most exotic market is the **Marché du Midi** (Sun. AM), which transforms the area next to the railway station into a vast bazaar as the city's large North African community gathers to buy and sell foods, spices, and plants.

In the Grand'Place there's a **Flower Market** (every day but Mon.) and a **Bird Market** (Sun. AM). You need to get to the flea market, **Vieux Marché** (Place du Jeu de Balle; open daily 7–2) early. The **Antiques and Book Market** (Place du Grand Sablon; Sat. 9–5 and Sun. 9–1) is considerably more upscale and is frequented by established dealers. The TIB (tel. 02/513–8940) has the details on other specialized markets.

Specialty Stores *Antiques*	**Costermans** (place du Grand Sablon 5, tel. 02/512–2133) and **Jean Tollemans** (place du Grand Sablon 15, tel. 02/511–3405) are among the leading dealers in the Sablon area. **Afrique Congo** (av Louise 138, tel. 02/640–6948) specializes in African art; **L'Ecuyer** (av Louise 187, tel. 02/648–0684), in Art Nouveau.
Books	**Tropismes** (Galerie des Princes 11, tel. 02/512–8852) carries more than 40,000 titles and will help you find out-of-print books. **Libris** (av de la Toison d'Or 29, tel. 02/511–6400) is very well stocked with current French-language titles. **Candide** (place Brugmann 1–2, tel. 02/344–8194) is where you'll find your Sunday *New York Times*, but not before Wednesday. Shops specializing in comic strip albums include those at Chaussée de Wavre Nos. 167, 179, and 198, and the **Tintin Shop** (rue de la Colline 13).
Children's Clothing	**Dujardin** (av Louise 8–10, tel. 02/513–0748) is still one of the world's greatest (and priciest) children's outfitters, from infants to preteens—though not what it once was.
Chocolates	**Godiva** (Grand'Place 22 and other locations) is the best known. **Neuhaus** (Galerie de la Reine 25–27 and other locations) is the runner-up and is preferred by many. **Leonidas** (Chaussée d'Ixelles 5 and other locations) is the budget alternative, still high quality. The best handmade pralines, which are the crème de la crème of Belgian chocolates, are made and sold at **Nihoul** (av Louise 298–302, tel. 02/648–3796), **Mary** (rue Royale 180, tel. 02/217–4500), and **Wittamer** (Place du Grand Sablon 6, tel. 02/512–3742).
Crystal	**Art et Sélection** (rue du Marché-aux-Herbes 83, tel. 02/511–8448) and **Buss** (across the street at No. 84, tel. 02/511–6652) both carry Val St-Lambert hand-blown crystal tableware.
Home Furnishings	**Ligne** (Galerie de la Reine 12–16, tel. 02/511–6030), **Projection** (bd Anspach 85, tel. 02/511–5452), and **Théorèmes** (place du Nouveau Marché-aux-Grains 22–23, tel. 02/511–6574) carry avant-garde furniture.
Lace	**Manufacture Belge de Dentelle** (Galerie de la Reine 6–8, tel. 02/511–4477) and **Maison F. Rubbrecht** (Grand'Place 23, tel. 02/512–0218) sell local handmade lace. At the many souvenir shops in the area it is likely to come from the Far East. An introductory visit to the **Musée du Costume et de la Dentelle** (rue de la Violette 6, tel. 02/512–7709; admission: BF80; open weekdays 10–12:30 and 1:30–5, weekends 2–4:30) is a good idea.
Leather Goods	**Delvaux** (av de la Galerie 31, tel. 02/512–7198 and bd de Waterloo 27, tel. 02/513–0502) makes outstanding, classic, and long-lasting handbags, wallets, belts, and attaché cases. Be prepared to part with a hefty sum.
Men's Clothing	**Dean** (av Louise 50A, tel. 02/511–2718), **Deman** (bd de Waterloo 45, tel. 02/512–2367), and **De Vlaminck** (bd de Waterloo 32, tel. 02/512–4203) carry classic Italian and English ready-to-wear and accessories. **Stijl Men** (rue Antoine Dansaert 20, tel. 02/512–0313) caters to younger tastes.
Women's Clothing	**Bouvy** (av de la Toison d'Or 52, tel. 02/513–0748) carries a good selection of upscale ready-to-wear. **Olivier Strelli** (av Louise 72, tel. 02/511–2134) is the best-known Belgian fashion designer. Other designers are represented by boutiques in the Avenue Louise and Boulevard de Waterloo district.

Sports and Fitness

Golf The top clubs in the area are **Royal Golf Club de Belgique** (Château de Ravenstein, Tervuren, tel. 02/767–5801), **Royal Waterloo Golf Club** (Vieux Chemin de Wavre 50, Ohain, tel. 02/633–1850) and **Keerbergen Golf Club** (Vlieghavenlaan 50, Keerbergen, tel. 015/23–49–61). For more information, call the Belgian Golf Federation (tel. 067/22–04–40).

Health and Fitness Several hotels have well-equipped fitness centers open to the public. The best are at the **Europa Brussels** (rue de la Loi 107, tel. 02/230–1333), **Holiday Inn** (Holidaystraat 7, Diegem, tel. 02/720–5865), **SAS Royal** (rue du Fosse-aux-Loups 47, tel. 02/219–2828), and **Sheraton** (place Rogier 3, tel. 02/219–3400). Fees are about BF750 a session. Prices are considerably lower at independent health clubs such as **European Athletic City** (av Winston Churchill 25A, tel. 02/345–3077), **Golden Club** (aerobics; place du Chatelain 33, tel. 02/538–1906) and **Feminigym** (women only; rue de Namur 86, tel. 02/512–0780).

Horseback Riding Stables/schools near the Forêt de Soignes include **Centre Equestre de la Cambre** (Chaussée de Waterloo 872, tel. 02/375–3408), **L'Etrier** (Champ du Vert Chasseur 19, tel. 02/374–2860), and **Le Relais Equestre de Groenendael** (Groenendalsesteenweg 139, Hoeilaart, tel. 02/657–2177). For more information, call the Fédération Royale Belge des Sports Equestres (Belgian Riding Federation) (tel. 02/478–5056).

Jogging For in-town jogging, use the **Parc de Bruxelles** (rue de la Loi to the Palace); for more extensive workouts, head for the **Bois de la Cambre** (southern end of av Louise).

Tennis Popular clubs include the **Racing Club** (av des Chênes 125, tel. 02/374–4181), **Royal Leopold** (av Dupuich 42, tel. 02/344–3666), and **Wimbledon** (Chaussée de Waterloo 220, Rhode-St-Genèse, tel. 358–3523). For more information contact the Fédération Royale Belge de Tennis (Belgian Tennis Federation) (tel. 02/217–2200).

Swimming Hotel swimming pools are few and far between (Copthorne Stephanie, Holiday Inn, Sheraton). Among covered public pools, the best are **Calypso** (av Wiener 60, tel. 02/673–3929), **Longchamp** (Square de Fré 1, tel. 02/374–4396), and **Poseidon** (av des Vaillants 2, tel. 02/771–6655).

Spectator Sports

Horse Racing Going to the races comes second in popularity only to soccer, and there are three major racecourses: **Boitsfort** (Chaussée de la Hulpe 51, tel. 02/660–2839), which has an all-weather flat track; **Groenendael** (Sint-Jansberglaan 4, Hoeilaart, tel. 02/673–6792), for steeplechasing; and **Sterrebeek** (Du Roy de Blicquylaan 43, Sterrebeek, tel. 02/767–5475), for trotting and flat racing. For information, contact the **Jockey Club de Belgique** (tel. 02/771–4286).

Soccer Soccer is the most popular spectator sport, and the leading club, **Anderlecht**, has many fiercely loyal fans. Their home pitch is Parc Astrid (av Theo Verbeeck 2, tel. 02/522–9400). Major international games are played at Heysel Stadium (av du Marathon 135, tel. 02/479–3654). For information and tickets, contact the **Maison du Football** (av Houba de Strooper 145, tel. 02/477–1211), which is open weekdays, 9–4:15.

Dining

When the history of the European Commission is written, the real reason for the choice of Brussels as capital of Europe will be revealed: the excellence of its restaurants. There are more than 1,600 of them, and 25 are internationally acclaimed. They are not cheap; a meal with wine in a medium-class restaurant with some gastronomic distinction is likely to cost about BF2,000 per person. In this country, cooking has the status of a fine art. The Belgians take the pleasures of the table seriously and are happy to save up to give themselves, their families, and friends a treat. Formal wear is de rigueur only in Very Expensive restaurants.

You can reduce the check almost by half by choosing a set menu. Menus and prices are always posted outside restaurants. You should never feel that you're under an obligation to eat a three-course meal; many people order just a salad and a main course.

If you don't want two full restaurant meals a day, there are plenty of snack bars for a light midday meal, and most cafés serve sandwiches and light hot meals both noon and night. Vegetarian restaurants are another inexpensive alternative. The city is also richly endowed with good Oriental restaurants.

The TIB booklet "Gourmet Restaurants," food journalists' evaluations of some 250 restaurants, is available for BF30 at the Tourist Office in Grand'Place. Listings include the cost of set menus and of *plats du jour* (daily specials).

Ratings Prices are per person and include a first course, main course, and dessert, but no beverages. The check always includes 6% value added tax (TVA) and 16% service charge. There is no need for any additional tipping. Highly recommended restaurants are indicated by a star ★.

Very Expensive	over BF3,000
Expensive	BF2,000–BF3,000
Moderate	BF1,000–BF2,000
Inexpensive	under BF1,000

Very Expensive
★

Comme Chez Soi. Pierre Wynants, the third-generation owner/chef, has redecorated the tiny restaurant in Art Nouveau style. Every detail at this temple of gastronomy is authentic, from the stained-glass panels to the stylish menus. The kitchen is larger than the dining room, and the wine cellar bigger than the kitchen. Wynants cooked with only minimal amounts of butter and cream before nouvelle cuisine was heard of, and among his recent creations are *emincé* (slices) of crayfish with green asparagus and basil in a vinaigrette with ground nuts, and sautéed duck's liver with blackberry vinaigrette and angelica leaves. *Place Rouppe 23, tel. 02/512–2921. Reservations required. Jacket and tie required. AE, DC. Closed Sun.–Mon., July, and Christmas week.*

Les Délices de la Mer. Master chef Michel Buyls presides at this splendid villa in Uccle. His trademark is poached egg on a mousse of wild mushrooms. As the name implies, seafood has pride of place on the menu, but there's also a selection of excellent meat dishes. The sautéed scallops in light curry sauce are superb, as is the back of turbot with breadcrumbs and basil, and the salmon and duck's liver baked in a vine leaf. *Chaussée de Waterloo 1020, tel. 02/375-5467. Reservations required. Jacket and tie required. AE, DC, MC, V. Closed Sat. lunch and Sun.*

L'Ecailler du Palais Royal. At this dark and clubby place just off the Grand Sablon, many of the patrons seem to have known each other and the staff for years. The menu is uncompromisingly fishy: soufflé of sea urchins, ragout of monkfish and prawns, and roast turbot. *Rue Bodenbroek 18, tel. 02/511-9950. Reservations essential. Jacket and tie required. AE, DC, MC, V. Closed Sun., first week of Mar., Aug.*

La Maison du Cygne. Dining at the Cygne is a sensuous experience. The setting, in one of the old guild houses on the Grand'Place, is incomparable. The paneled dining room upstairs is hung with old masters, while the ground floor is less formal. Tailcoated waiters glide rather than rush to attend your every wish. The cuisine is classic French: saddle of lamb, braised turbot, duckling with onions. *Rue Charles Buls 2, tel. 02/511-8244. Reservations advised. Jacket and tie required. AE, DC, MC, V. Closed Sat. lunch, Sun., first 3 weeks of Aug., Christmas week.*

La Truffe Noire. Luigi Ciciriello's "Black Truffle" attracts a sophisticated clientele with its discreet modern design, well-spaced tables, and a cuisine that draws on classic Italian and modern French cooking. Carpaccio is prepared at the table and served with long strips of truffle and Parmesan. Entrées include ravioli filled with minced truffles and wild mushrooms, and leg of Pauillac lamb in pie crust. *Boulevard de la Cambre 12, tel. 02/640-4422. Reservations required. Jacket and tie required. AE, DC, MC, V. Closed Sat. lunch, Sun., Easter week, second half of Aug., Christmas week.*

Villa Lorraine. Generations of American business travelers have been introduced to the three-hour Belgian lunch at the opulent Villa, on the edge of the Bois de la Cambre. The green terrace room is light and airy, and there's alfresco eating under the spreading chestnut tree. You can dine supremely well on such standbys as red mullet in artichoke vinaigrette, crayfish cooked in chicken stock with white wine and a dash of Armagnac, and duckling with peaches and green pepper. *Avenue du Vivier-d'Oie 75, tel. 02/374-3163. Reservations advised. Jacket and tie required. AE, DC, MC, V. Closed Sun. and July.*

Expensive **Castello Banfi.** On the Grand Sablon in beige-and-brown
★ postmodern surroundings, you can enjoy classic dishes with little added refinements such as toasted pine kernels with the pesto. There's excellent carpaccio with Parmesan and celery, red mullet with ratatouille, and unbelievable mascarpone. The quality of the ingredients (sublime olive oil, milk-fed veal imported from France) is very high. The wine list is strong on fine Chiantis aged in wood. *Rue Bodenbroek 12, tel. 02/512-8794. Reservations advised. Jacket and tie required. AE, DC, MC, V. Closed Sun. dinner, Mon., and second half of Aug.*

La Charlotte aux Pommes. This is a light and airy ground-floor restaurant that has friendly service and a clientele composed largely of thirtysomething executives. It is situated on a pleasant square with a lively market every Wednesday afternoon. Chefs come and go, but the standard remains high. House specialties include oysters poached in a cream of watercress, sea bass coated with coconut, and sweetbreads in lentil cream. Ask

Central Brussels Dining and Lodging

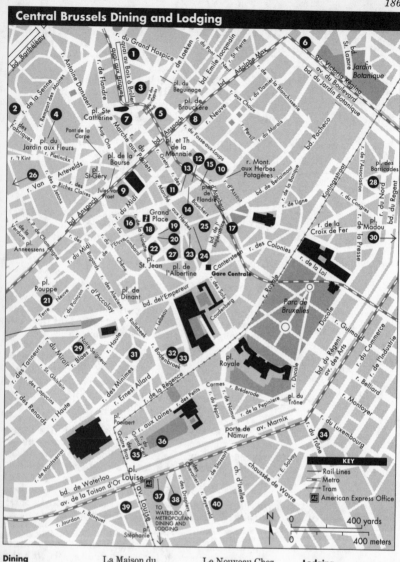

Dining

Adrienne, **38**

Aux Armes de
Bruxelles, **13**

Boccaccio, **20**

Castello Banfi, **32**

Chez Jean, **19**

Chez Leon, **14**

Comme Chez Soi, **21**

Falstaff, **9**

In 't Spinnekopke, **4**

La Charlotte aux
Pommes, **46**

La Maison du
Cygne, **18**

La Manufacture, **2**

La Porte des Indes, **49**

La Quincaillerie, **45**

La Roue d'Or, **22**

La Truffe Noire, **50**

L'Ecailler du Palais
Royal, **33**

Le Cambodge, **48**

Le Faste Fou, **35**

L'Elephant Bleu, **53**

Le Nouveau Chez
Nous, **54**

Le Paradoxe, **43**

Le Wine Bar, **31**

Les Capucines, **39**

Les Delices de la
Mer, **51**

Les Petits Oignons, **29**

Michel Meyers, **5**

Ogenblik, **15**

Villa Lorraine, **52**

Vincent, **12**

Lodging

Albert Premier, **6**

Amigo, **16**

Arcade St.-
Catherine, **7**

Arenberg, **17**

Arlequin, **11**

Cadettt, **44**

Carrefour de
l'Europe, **23**

Château du Lac, **55**

Clubhouse, **42**

Metropolitan Brussels Dining and Lodging

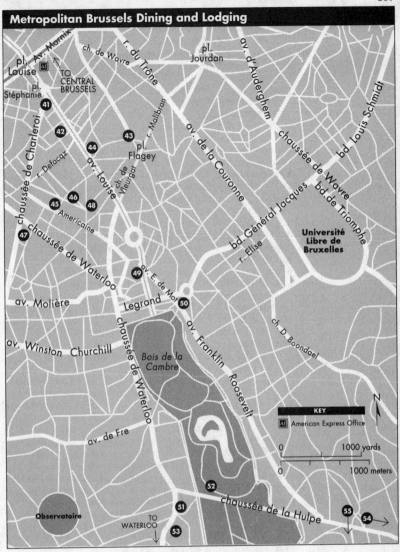

Forum, **47**
Gerfaut, **26**
Hilton, **36**
Holiday Inn, **30**
Ibis, **24**
La Truite d'Argent, **3**
Manos Stephanie, **41**
Metropole, **8**
Novotel, **25**
Orion, **1**
Royal Windsor, **27**

Sabina, **28**
SAS Royal, **10**
Sofitel, **37**
Stanhope, **34**
Sun, **40**

for a round table if you require privacy. *Place du Chatelain 40, tel. 02/640–5388. Reservations advised. Jacket and tie advised. AE, DC, MC, V. Closed Sat. lunch and Sun.*

★ **La Porte des Indes.** The last days of the Raj are recreated in the city's foremost Indian restaurant—the creation of Karl Steppe, a Belgian antiques dealer turned restaurateur. The gracious staff wear traditional Indian attire. The plant-filled lobby, wood carvings, and a soothing blue-and-white decor provide a restful backdrop. The cuisine ranges from a mild pilaf to a spicy *vindaloo* (very hot curry). The "brass tray" offers an assortment of specialties. A vegetarian menu is also available. *Avenue Louise 455, tel. 02/647–8651. Reservations advised. Dress: Casual but neat. AE, DC, MC, V. Closed Sun.*

L'Eléphant Bleu. This is the first of a chain of "Blue Elephant" Thai restaurants that now are to be found also in London, Paris, and Copenhagen. Another brainchild of Karl Steppe, it has led an Oriental food renaissance in Brussels. Thai statuettes and objects d'art fill the gardenlike dining room, and the staff wear beautiful silk costumes. The young, well-to-do clientele comes here for refined exotic flavors, at the same time sweet and spicy. Try the lemon-scented shrimp soup, stuffed chicken wings, or *kaotang natang* (seafood salad with rice cakes). *Chaussée de Waterloo 1120, tel. 02/374–4962. Reservations advised. Dress: casual. AE, DC, MC, V. Closed Sat. lunch.*

Les Capucines. Here's a new restaurant that shows great promise and stands out amid the mediocrity of most Rue Jourdan eateries. The dining room is invitingly green, with huge flower arrangements. Chef Pierre Burtonboy prepares dishes such as grilled fillet of sea bream on a bed of shredded leek dressed with nut oil; lamb interleaved with goose liver, rolled and encased in pastry, with rosemary and thinly sliced potatoes; bitter chocolate mousse with *crème anglaise;* and iced peach soup with mint. *Rue Jourdan 22, tel. 02/538–6924. Reservations suggested. Dress: casual but neat. AE, DC, MC, V. Closed Sun., Mon. dinner, two weeks in Sept.*

Michel Meyers. Only seafood is served in this tiny restaurant just off the Fish Market, which has been enlarged to serve all of 18 diners. The eponymous owner/chef is alone in the kitchen and goes to the nearby market twice daily for the freshest products of the sea. Don't hesitate to take the menu he proposes. It might consist of smoked salmon pâté, lobster with five spices, medallion of monkfish with fresh garlic, and a dessert prepared by Madame la Patronne. *Place du Samedi 18, tel. 02/ 219–2616. Reservations advised. Dress: casual. AE, V. Closed Sun. and mid-July–mid Aug.*

Ogenblik. This small, split-level restaurant in a side gallery off the Galeries St-Hubert has all the appurtenances of an old-time bistro: green-shaded lamps over marble-topped tables, sawdust on the floor, and laid-back waiters. There's nothing casual about the cuisine, however: boned chicken with sweetbreads and goose liver, *mille-feuille* (thin layers of puff pastry separated by filling) of lobster and salmon, saddle of lamb with spring vegetables. The selection of Beaujolais is particularly good. *Galerie des Princes 1, tel. 02/511–6151. No reservations after 8PM. Dress: casual. AE, DC, MC, V. Closed Sun.*

Moderate **Aux Armes de Bruxelles.** Hidden among the tourist traps in the Ilôt Sacré, this restaurant attracts a largely local clientele with its slightly tarnished middle-class elegance and its Belgian classics: turbot *waterzooi* (a creamy stew of potatoes, vegetable, and fish), a variety of steaks, mussels prepared every which way, and french fries, which the Belgians, with some justification, believe they prepare better than anyone else. The place is cheerful and light, and service is friendly if frequently overstretched. *Rue des Bouchers 13, tel. 02/511-2118. Reservations advised. AE, DC, MC, V. Closed Mon. and June.*

In 't Spinnekopke. This is where true Brussels cooking has survived and continues to flourish. It was a coaching inn in the 18th century, and low ceilings and benches around the walls have remained. You can choose among a hundred artisanal beers, and many of the dishes are made with beer, including *carbonnade* (a beef stew with lambic beer). *Place du Jardin aux Fleurs 1, tel. 02/513-2497. Reservations advised. AE, DC, MC, V. Closed Sat. lunch and Sun.*

★ **La Manufacture.** Housed in a former workshop where expensive Delvaux handbags were made, La Manufacture has been cleverly transformed into a contemporary-looking restaurant, with tables of polished stone, brick walls, and friendly servers wearing long leather aprons. The cooking is stylish and modern as well: goat-cheese raviolis with radish butter, Dublin Bay prawns steeped in ginger and accompanied by great crusty bread. *Rue Notre-Dame du Someil 12, tel. 02/502-2525. Reservations advised. AE, DC, MC, V. Closed Sat. lunch and Sun.*

★ **La Quincaillerie.** This means "The Hardware Store," and that's precisely what it used to be. A gleaming zinc counter downstairs accommodates oyster lovers, and tables are perched on the mezzanine. The staff is young, quick, and pleasant. The cuisine is inventive, with especially high marks for the game dishes. There's also a low-calorie menu. *Rue du Page 45, tel. 02/538-2553. Reservations recommended. AE, DC, MC, V.*

La Roue d'Or. The murals in the Roue d'Or pay extravagant homage to Magritte, the great surrealist. Bowler-hatted gentlemen ascend serenely to the ceiling, a blue sky inhabited by birds of paradise. The good cuisine includes traditional Belgian fare as well as such staples of the French brasserie repertoire as lamb's tongue vinaigrette with shallots, pig's feet salad, or veal kidneys with watercress cream. *Rue des Chapeliers 26, tel. 02/514-2554. Reservations advised. AE, DC, MC, V. Closed weekends and mid-July-mid-Aug.*

Le Nouveau Chez Nous. This bustling, value-for-money place, in a small house in quiet Boitsfort, offers a four-course menu with a wide choice of dishes and two kinds of regional wine. Typical dishes include salad of prawns with raspberry vinegar and entrecote with broccoli. *Rue de Middelbourg 28, tel. 02/673-5393. Reservations suggested. AE, DC, MC, V. Closed Sun. dinner, Mon., and last 3 weeks of Aug.*

Les Petits Oignons. This airy 17th-century restaurant in the heart of the Marolles has been furnished with plants and bright modern paintings. It places no demands on your palate, but the ambience makes you feel good and well looked after. Pâté of goose liver with champagne *ratafia* (liqueur) and leg of lamb with potatoes au gratin are among the choices. *Rue Notre-Seigneur 13, tel. 02/512-4130. Reservations suggested. AE, DC, MC, V. Closed Sun. and Aug.*

Le Wine Bar. As the name implies, this is a place for some serious wine tasting, but there's much more to it. The setting is a series of 17th-century vaulted cellars, which you enter from an alley off Rue des Minimes. You can have just a light dish to go with the wine—oxtail salad or a salad with roast quail with cinnamon—or choose the more substantial plat du jour, often a *pot-au-feu* (hot pot). *Rue des Pigeons 9, tel. 02/511–4493. Reservations advised. Dress: casual. AE, DC, MC, V. Closed Sat. lunch, Sun., and July 15–Aug. 15.*

Vincent. In a town where most of the more fashionable places now concentrate on seafood, Vincent remains unapologetically a red-meat stronghold. Sides of beef and big slabs of butter in the window announce what awaits you. You pass through the kitchen on your way to the dining room, which is decorated with naive hand-painted tiles. *Rue des Dominicains 8, tel. 08/511–2303. Reservations advised. AE, DC, MC, V. Closed Aug.*

Inexpensive   **Adrienne.** It's the huge cold buffet that packs them in year after year at this upstairs restaurant just around the corner from Avenue Toison d'Or. The look is rustic, with red-and-white-check tablecloths, and you can eat on the terrace in summer. The location is great for uptown shopping and movies, and it's also fun for kids. *Rue Capitaine Crespel 1A, tel. 02/511–9339. Reservations recommended for lunch. AE, DC, MC, V.*

Boccaccio. The Moroccan husband and Swedish wife who own the restaurant serve generous portions of Italian-inspired food in this super-friendly hole-in-the-wall shaped like a diner with a tiny kitchen at one end. It's popular with airline crews—not a bad recommendation. *Rue du Marché-aux-Fromages 14, tel. 02/512–2929. AE, DC, MC, V.*

★ **Le Cambodge.** The tables and walls are white in this corner restaurant, tastefully decorated with Cambodian statuary. It's packed for lunch and dinner seven days a week with a youngish, mostly professional crowd. Try the *banh-xeo* (rice pancakes with pork and shrimps). *Rue Washington 77, tel. 02/537–7098. Reservations advised. AE, DC, MC, V.*

Chez Jean. Jean Cambien runs a reliable restaurant, unchanged since 1931, with oak benches against the walls backed by mirrors on which the dishes of the day are written up in whitewash. Waitresses in black and white serve poached cod, mussels cooked in white wine, chicken waterzooi, and other Belgian dishes. *Rue des Chapeliers 6, tel. 02/511–9815. Reservations advised. No credit cards. Closed Sun.–Mon.*

★ **Chez Leon.** This started as a tiny restaurant almost 90 years ago and has expanded to occupy eight old houses in the middle of the Ilôt Sacré, and it now serves a ton of mussels a day. It does serve other Belgian specialties, such as eels in green sauce, but potfuls of steaming mussels, served with frites and beer, are the trademark. *Rue des Bouchers 18, tel. 02/511–1415. No reservations. No credit cards.*

Falstaff. This huge tavern with a pure Art Nouveau interior fills up for lunch and keeps going until 5 AM with an ever-changing crowd. The only contemporary touch to the traditional Belgian food is provided by the cordless electronic order pads wielded by the cheerful waitresses. Make sure you go to the original Falstaff at No. 19, not its next-door neighbor. *Rue Henri Maus 19, tel. 02/511–8789. No reservations. AE, DC, MC, V.*

Le Faste Fou. Well situated in the Place Louise area Faste Fou is crowded with office workers at lunch. There is counter service downstairs and table service upstairs in a bare and noisy dining room devoid of decor; friendly servers and good food make up for it. The menu offers substantial salads and complete meals. *Rue du Grand-Cerf 21, tel. 02/511–3832. No reservations. Dress: casual. AE, DC, MC, V. Closed Sun.*

Le Paradoxe. This natural-food restaurant serves seafood and vegetarian dishes in a greenhouselike setting. Samosas with rice, scampi with kiwi, and vegetable plates are on the menu, as well as dishes like tofu schnitzels. There's live music (folk, jazz, or classical) Friday and Saturday nights. *Chaussée d'Ixelles 329, tel. 02/649–8981. Reservations required Fri.– Sat. AE, DC, MC, V. Closed Sun. and second half of July.*

Lodging

Brussels has seen a boom in hotel-building over the past few years in response to the increase in business and diplomatic travel; three out of four visitors come here on business. Most business travel takes place in winter, so a number of hotels offer reduced rates on weekends and in July and August. Most hotels in the Moderate and Inexpensive categories tend to be more functional than welcoming. However, they are almost without exception clean, comfortable, and well located.

Tourist Information Brussels (TIB) publishes an annual hotel guide listing prices and facilities. You can obtain a copy by writing to TIB (Hôtel de Ville, 1000 Brussels). It contains a reservation form, to be sent to Belgium Tourist Reservations (Box 41, 1000 Brussels 23, tel. 02/230–5029). If you arrive in Brussels without reservations, check the **Reception Office** (tel. 02/722–3000) at the airport. The **TIB** at Grand'Place (tel. 02/513–8940) will also arrange reservations locally. The youth organization **Acotra** (Rue de la Madeleine 53, tel. 02/514–4690) has a room-finding service for youth hostels. These services are free, but you will be asked for a deposit, which is then deducted from your hotel bill.

Quoted hotel rates always include 6% value added tax, 9% city tax and 16% service charge, so there are no surprises when you get your bill. All rooms have bath or shower, color TV, and direct-dial telephone unless otherwise indicated. The prices below are for two people in a double room and include Continental breakfast unless otherwise stated. Highly recommended hotels are indicated by a star ★.

Category	Brussels
Very Expensive	over BF8,000
Expensive	BF5,500–BF8,000
Moderate	BF3,500–BF5,500
Inexpensive	under BF3,500

Very Expensive **Carrefour de l'Europe.** Opened in 1992, this hotel is meant to appeal to travelers to whom personalized service is more important than price. The standard rooms, with salmon-pink carpeting and green-and-russet bedspreads, are not as large as you might expect. The glass-and-marble lobby isn't very big, either, but the adjoining tavern cum brasserie is, and it has a separate entrance. The basement haute-cuisine restaurant, Charlemagne, specializes in seafood. *Rue du Marché-aux-Herbes 110, tel. 02/504–9400, fax 02/504–9500. 63 rooms. Facilities: 2 restaurants, bar, business center, conference rooms, garage. AE, DC, MC, V.*

★ **Hilton.** One of the first high rises in Brussels back in the 1960s, it outclasses most other Hiltons in Europe and is continuously being refurbished floor by floor. The corner rooms are the most desirable. The location near the Porte Louise is great for high-class shopping. There is a fine panoramic view from the 27th-floor restaurant, the En Plein Ciel (buffet lunch only). The second-floor restaurant, the Maison du Boeuf, nouvelle cuisine based on local products, much appreciated by guests from the nearby Ministry of Foreign Affairs. *Boulevard de Waterloo 38, tel. 02/504–1111, fax 02/504–2111. 370 rooms. Facilities: 3 restaurants, 2 bars, health club, garage, conference center; breakfast not included. AE, DC, MC, V.*

Holiday Inn. Only the logo and the shoeboxlike structure remain of the traditional Holiday Inn. Built in 1971 but completely refurbished in 1989, this attractive hotel has a spacious, marble-floored lobby and an airy lounge bar. The rooms remain rather dark, for the original architect did not seem to believe in large windows. Here is where you find the widest range of exercise facilities in town, and jogging tracks start at the front door. *Holidaystraat 7, Diegem, tel. 02/720–5865, fax 02/720–4145. 310 rooms. Facilities: restaurant, bar, health club, tennis courts, pool, airport courtesy bus, conference rooms. AE, DC, MC, V.*

Royal Windsor. The Royal Windsor, opened in 1974 close to the Grand'Place, has been refurbished, and all rooms are decorated with blond-wood paneling and marble bathrooms. They are, however, on the small side, and the low ceiling in the lobby gives a somewhat cramped feeling. The dining room, Les Quatre Saisons, serves light, imaginative, and expensive French cuisine. There's a disco in the basement, the Crocodile Club. *Rue Duquesnoy 5, tel. 02/511–4215, fax 02/511–6004. 280 rooms. Facilities: restaurant, bar, disco, garage, conference facilities. AE, DC, MC, V.*

★ **SAS Royal.** Located next to the Opera, near the northern end of the Galeries St-Hubert, this hotel opened in 1990 and was an instant success. The floors are decorated in a variety of styles—Oriental (wicker furniture and Asian art), Italian (art deco fixtures and furnishings) and Scandinavian (light-wood furniture and parquet flooring). The greenery-filled atrium incorporates a 10-foot-high section of the 12th-century city wall. The Sea Grill is first-rate. *Rue du Fosse-aux-Loups 47, tel. 02/219–2828, fax 02/219–6262. 281 rooms. Facilities: 3 restaurants, 2 bars, garage, health club, sauna, airline check-in, business center, conference rooms. AE, DC, MC, V.*

Stanhope. This small hotel is the most expensive in Brussels and operates on the principle that if you have to ask the price, you can't afford it. It was created out of three adjoining town houses; all the high-ceilinged, luxuriously furnished rooms and suites are different and have marble bathrooms. Each room has its own name. The Linley features furniture handmade by Viscount Linley, nephew of the queen of England. You can have English afternoon tea in the ground-floor salon, and the downstairs bar serves caviar. *Rue du Commerce 9, tel. 02/506–9111, fax 02/512–1708. 25 rooms and 25 suites. Facilities: restaurant, tearoom, bar, health club, sauna, boardrooms, garden, garage. AE, MC, V.*

Expensive **Amigo.** Just a block from the Grand'Place and decorated in ★ Spanish Renaissance with touches of Louis XV, the Amigo looks more turn-of-the-century than its actual age of 30-odd years. The lobby has been given a face-lift recently, and the hotel is now a member of the prestigious Relais & Châteaux group. Rooms vary in furnishings, size, and price; bathrooms are on the small side. The higher floors have views over the surrounding rooftops. Amigo is popular with those who like their luxury understated, and the service is excellent. *Rue d'Amigo 1–3, tel. 02/511–5910, fax 02/513–5277. 183 rooms. Facilities: restaurant, bar, garage, conference rooms. AE, DC, MC, V.*

Château du Lac. Half an hour from the city center, this mock-Florentine castle is a former Schweppes bottling plant. The large rooms are light beige and well furnished, and the decor in the public rooms is contemporary, mostly white with details picked out in red. The splendid restaurant, Le Trèfle à Quatre, where Michel Haquin is chef, is itself worth the journey for his superb cuisine focusing on fish and game and for the views over the lake. *Avenue du Lac 87, Genval, tel. 02/654–1122, fax 02/653–6200. 38 rooms. Facilities: restaurant, bar, sauna, outdoor swimming pool, conference center. AE, DC, MC, V.*

Clubhouse. On a quiet side street off the chic Avenue Louise, the former Alfa Louise has had a major face-lift that, alas, has also lifted it to a higher price category. The rooms have been redone with pastel walls, salmon-pink carpeting, flower-patterned Laura Ashley–style bedspreads and curtains, and sofa, easy chair and desk. The large, blue-carpeted lobby, opening on a small garden, has a fire in the open hearth on chilly days. *Rue Blanche 4, tel. 02/537–9210, fax 02/537–0018. 81 rooms. Facilities: bar, conference room, garage. AE, DC, MC, V.*

★ **Metropole.** Stepping into the Metropole, you would think you had never left the Orient Express: The hotel has been restored to the palace it was during the Belle Epoque. The lobby, with its enormously high coffered ceiling, chandeliers, marble, and Oriental carpets sets the tone. It is carried through in the bar with potted palms, deep leather sofas, and Corinthian columns; and in the Alban Chambon restaurant (named for the architect). The rooms are discreetly modern in varying shades of pastel (some with trompe l'oeil murals), with large desks and furniture upholstered with the same material as the bedspreads. *Place de Brouckere 31, tel. 02/217–2300, fax 02/218–0220. 410 rooms. Facilities: restaurant, bar, café, conference rooms, airport courtesy bus. AE, DC, MC, V.*

Sofitel. Opened in 1989, the six-floor Sofitel has a great location opposite the Hilton. There's a chic shopping arcade on the ground floor, and you reach the lobby on an escalator. Public rooms and bedrooms are decorated in warm brown and beige tones. The restaurant, back of the lobby, is good and getting better. *Avenue de la Toison d'Or 40, tel. 02/514–2200, fax 02/514–5744. 171 rooms. Facilities: restaurant, bar, conference rooms; breakfast not included. AE, DC, MC, V.*

Moderate **Arenberg.** This hotel near the Cathédrale St-Michel was recently renovated. It is well run and perhaps a bit impersonal. The rooms are decorated in shades of blue and gray; those numbered 17 or 18 on each floor are larger than the rest and have small balconies, though not much of a view. *Rue d'Assaut 15, tel. 02/511–0770, fax 02/514–1976. 155 rooms. Facilities: restaurant, bar, garage. AE, DC, MC, V.*

★ **Cadettt.** The concept of the Cadettt (part of the Swiss Mövenpick Group) is to offer superior rooms with limited services at a moderate price. The Brussels Cadettt, completed in 1991, has large rooms, each with blond-wood furniture, a reclining chair, and good work space. The beige-and-green atrium bar and restaurant serves copious Swiss breakfasts and a limited selection of specialties for lunch and dinner. *Rue Paul*

Spaak 15, tel. 02/645–6111, fax 02/646–6311. 128 rooms. Facilities: restaurant, 2 bars, garage, health club, sauna, seminar facilities; breakfast not included. AE, DC, MC, V.

Forum. If the management would only complete the refurbishing started a few years ago, they would have a great little hotel. As it is, ask for a room on one of the two renovated floors, preferably at the back overlooking the garden. These are done in a light and airy art deco. *Avenue du Haut-Pont 2, tel. 02/343–0100, fax 02/347–0054. 77 rooms. Facilities: bar, garage, conference rooms. AE, DC, MC, V.*

Ibis. The big French hotel chains mass-produce functional hotels that cannot quite shake their motel origins; the rooms and the food are the same from Martinique to New Caledonia. The Brussels Ibis is the least expensive of the newly built old-look, gabled buildings that front on the Place d'Espagne. The no-frills rooms, in blue and gray, are equipped with essentials only: bed, chair, desk, and wardrobe. In the public rooms the house color is a dusky pink. *Rue du Marché-aux-Herbes 100, tel. 02/514–4040, fax 02/514–5067. 170 rooms. Facilities: restaurant, bar, conference rooms, garage. AE, DC, MC, V.*

★ **Manos Stephanie.** The Louis XV furniture, marble lobby, and antiques set a standard of elegance seldom encountered in a hotel in this price category. The rooms have rust-colored carpets, green bedspreads, and good-sized sitting areas. The hotel, opened in 1992, occupies a grand old town house, so the rooms are not rigidly standardized; the split-level No. 103 is especially appealing. The atrium restaurant is enlivened by gaily striped chair coverings. *Chaussée de Charleroi 28, tel. 02/539–0250, fax 02/537–5729. 55 rooms. Facilities: restaurant, bar, conference room, garage. AE, DC, MC, V.*

Novotel. The mock-Renaissance brick Novotel was completed in 1989, a stone's throw from the Grand'Place. The rooms have white walls and russet carpets; all come with a sofa that can sleep an extra person, some with an additional rollaway bed. There's no extra charge for children under 16. One floor is reserved for nonsmokers. The Grill serves French hotel-chain cuisine; it's acceptable but far from exciting. *Rue du Marché-aux-Herbes 120, tel. 02/514–3333, fax 02/511–7723. 136 rooms. Facilities: restaurant, bar, conference rooms, garage. AE, DC, MC, V.*

Inexpensive **Albert Premier.** This hotel has been around since the 1920s, but it was totally renovated in 1988 and done up in blue and gunmetal art-deco style. Among the somewhat somber rooms, the quietest are those facing the courtyard. Quite a few tour groups use the hotel. *Place Rogier 20, tel. 02/217–2125, fax 02/217–9331. 285 rooms. Facilities: bar, conference rooms. AE, DC, MC, V.*

Arcade Ste-Catherine. This big, modern hotel owned by the French Arcade chain overlooks the church of Ste-Catherine and the rather desolate ruins of the Tour Noire (Black Tower). Most rooms can accommodate families with two children on fold-out bunk beds. The decor leans towards the motelish. *Rue Joseph Plateau 2, tel. 02/513–7620, fax 02/514–2214. 235 rooms. Facilities: bar, conference rooms. AE, MC, V.*

Arlequin. The hotel, smack in the middle of the Ilôt Sacré, is reached by an arcade from the very busy pedestrian Petite Rue des Bouchers, or from the slightly seedy Rue de la Fourche. The rooms are furnished with essentials only and may be a bit scuffed, but they are light and airy in shades of gray. Try for one of the corner rooms (those ending with 02). *Rue de la Fourche 17–19, tel. 02/514–1615, fax 02/514–2202. 60 rooms. Facilities: bar, breakfast room. AE, DC, MC, V.*

Gerfaut. In this cheerful hotel opened in 1991, the rooms—in light beige with colorful bedspreads—are of reasonable size. Three- and four-bed rooms are available at modest supplements. Breakfast is served in the bright and friendly Winter Garden room. The location near the Gare du Midi (South Station), though not choice, is convenient. *Chaussée de Mons 115–117, tel. 02/522–1922, fax 02/523–8991. 48 rooms. Facilities: bar. AE, DC, MC, V.*

★ **La Truite d'Argent Welcome.** The smallest hotel in Brussels, owned and operated by a dynamic young couple and giving great value for money, is in a quiet street leading from the Fish Market. The building is an unprepossessing cube, but the rooms are modern, with king- or queen-size beds. Downstairs is a small bistro, named Les Caprices de Sophie for one of the owners. Around the corner is the seafood restaurant that gave the hotel its name. *Rue du Peuplier 5, tel. 02/219–9546, fax 02/217–1887. 6 rooms. Facilities: 2 restaurants, bar, garage, seminar rooms. AE, DC, MC, V.*

★ **Orion.** Here's a really neat idea: a residential hotel where rooms and apartments can be rented by the night. Walls are whitewashed, with details picked out in bright red. All rooms have well-equipped kitchenettes. The reception desk is always manned, but you do your own bed and tidying. Linen is changed weekly. The rates go up 15% in peak seasons, but there are special weekly and monthly rates. Rooms on the courtyard are the quietest. *Quai au Bois-à-Bruler 51, tel. 02/221–1411, fax 02/221–1599. 169 rooms. Breakfast not included. AE, DC, MC, V.*

Sabina. The wallpaper and carpets of this small and old-fashioned hotel may at first make a fusty impression, but the rooms are in fact rather cozy. It's located just off the elegantly neoclassical Place des Barricades and attracts cost-conscious visitors to the European Commission. *Rue du Nord 78, tel. 02/218–2637, fax 02/219–3239. 23 rooms. Facilities: breakfast room. MC, V.*

Sun. The Sun was renovated in 1988 and makes a smart impression. The rooms are on the small side, in cool pastel green, with Lattoflex beds and safes, and the bathrooms are cramped. The attractive breakfast room has a striking glass mural; snacks are served there during the day. The hotel is located on a quiet but slightly dilapidated side street off the busy Chaussée d'Ixelles. *Rue du Berger 38, tel. 02/511–2119, fax 02/512–3271. 22 rooms with bath or shower. Facilities: parking. AE, DC, MC, V.*

The Arts and Nightlife

The Arts A glance at the "What's On" supplement of the indispensable weekly English-language newsmagazine *The Bulletin* reveals the breadth of the offerings in all categories of cultural life.

Theater Nearly all the city's 30-odd theaters stage French-language plays; only a few present plays in Dutch. Avant-garde performances are the most rewarding. Check what's on at **Théâtre Varia** (Rue du Sceptre 78, tel. 02/640–8258), **Théâtre 140** (Avenue Plasky 140, tel. 02/733–9708), and **Théâtre de Poche** (Bois de la Cambre, tel. 02/649–1727).

Music The principal venue for classical music concerts is the **Palais des Beaux-Arts** (Rue Ravenstein 23, tel. 02/507–8200). A smaller and more attractive hall is the **Conservatoire Royale** (Rue de la Régence 30, tel. 02/511–0427). There are also many concerts in various churches, especially the **Eglise des Minimes** (Rue des Minimes 62).

If you're going to be in Brussels in the spring, try to take in some of the concerts that are part of the **Queen Elisabeth Music Competition** (tel. 02/513–0099), for pianists, violinists, singers, and composers in successive years.

The principal venue for rock concerts is the **Forest National** (Avenue du Globe 36, tel. 02/347–0355). For more rock/pop as well as French *chanson,* check also the **Cirque Royal** (Rue de l'Enseignement 81, tel. 02/218–2015) and **Ancienne Belgique** (Boulevard Anspach 114, tel. 02/512–5813).

Opera and Dance   The national opera house is **Théâtre Royal de la Monnaie** (Place de la Monnaie, tel. 02/218–1202). Visiting opera and dance companies often perform at the **Cirque Royal** (Rue de l'Enseignement 81, tel. 02/218–2015).

Art Galleries   Many of the two dozen galleries in Brussels are in the Avenue Louise and Grand Sablon areas. See *The Bulletin* for listings.

Film   First-run English-language and French movies predominate. The most convenient complex of movie theaters is **Acropole** (Galeries and Avenue de la Toison d'Or, tel. 02/511–4238). The biggest—26 theaters—is the futuristic **Kinepolis** (Avenue du Centenaire 1, Heysel, tel. 02/479–5252). The **Musée du Cinéma** (Cinema Museum, Rue Baron Horta 9, tel. 02/507–8370) shows classic and silent movies; reserve the day of the performance. The **Brussels Film Festival** (Palais des Congres, Coudenberg 3, tel. 02/502–2840) is in January.

Nightlife   By 11 PM most Bruxellois have packed up and gone home. But around midnight bars and cafés fill up again as the night people take over. Nightclubs and cabarets are by and large pale imitations of those in Paris. Locals provide their own entertainment.

Bars and Lounges   There's one or more cafés on virtually every street corner, and they are all taprooms in disguise. The Belgians consume vast quantities of beer, some of it with a 10% alcohol content. **La Mort Subite** (Rue de Montagne-aux-Herbes Potagères 7, near the northern end of the Galeries St-Hubert) is renowned as a genuine and unchanged beer hall. **Chez Moeder Lambic** (Rue de Savoie 68 in St-Gilles) claims to stock 600 Belgian beers and a few hundred more foreign ones; **Fluer en Papier Doré** (Rue des Alexiens 53) is quietly surrealistic; Ultieme Hallucinate (Rue Royale 316) is Art Nouveau. People meet for a drink at all hours in the **Falstaff** (Rue Henri Maus 19), **Chez Richard** (Rue des Minimes 2), or 't Kelderke (Grand'Place 15). If you like Gypsy music, try **Le Huchier** (Grand Sablon 42) or the **Ateliers de la Grande Ile** (Rue de la Grande Ile 33).

Brussels's sizable black population, hailing mostly from Zaire, has its own hangouts. One such is **Kwasa Quouca** (Rue de Boetendael 113, tel. 02/344–9836); another is the disco **L'Ecume des Nuits** (Galerie Louise 122A, Place Stephanie entrance; tel. 02/513–5321; from 11 PM Thurs.–Sun.).

Anglo-Saxons flock to **Rick's Café Americain** (Avenue Louise 344). The **James Joyce** (Rue Archimède 34, tel. 02/230–9894) and the **Kitty O'Shea** (Boulevard de Charlemagne 42, tel. 02/230–7875) are as Irish as they come. Among the best hotel bars are those in the **Hilton,** the **Sheraton,** and the **Royal Windsor** (*see* Lodging, *above*), and there's a new karaoke bar in—where else?—the Japanese **Hotel Tagawa** (Avenue Louise 321).

Gay bars include **Tels Quels** (Rue du Marché au Charbon 81, tel. 02/512–4587), **Tek-Tiz** (Place Vielle Halle-au-Blé 46, tel. 02/513–5681), and **Le Duquesnoy** (Rue Duquesnoy 12, tel. 02/502–3883).

Cabarets   **Show Point** (Place Stephanie 14, tel. 02/511–5364) offers striptease, **Chez Flo** (Rue au Beurre 25, tel. 02/513–3152) has transvestite shows, and **Do Brasil** (Rue de la Canserne 88, tel. 02/513–5028) features Latin American entertainment.

Discos   The disco scene warms up around midnight. Most are only open weekends and cater to the under-30 crowd. The most snobbish, where they let you in if they like the look of you, are **Jeux d'Hiver** (Bois de la Cambre, tel. 02/649–0864) and **Mirano** (Chaussée de Louvain 38, tel. 02/218–5772). Others include **Take Off** (Rue Vilain XIIII 55, tel. 640–3870), **Le Vaudeville** (Rue de la Montagne 14, tel. 02/512–4997), and **Crocodile Club** in the Hotel Royal Windsor (Rue Duquesnoy 7, tel. 02/511–4215).

Jazz   There are two contemporary Belgian jazz greats: Toots Thielemans (on harmonica) and the guitarist Philip Catherine. You stand a good chance of catching Catherine at **Travers** (Rue Traversière 11, tel. 02/218–4086). Other places to check out are **Kaai** (Quai aux Pierre de Taille 39, no tel.), **Ecu d'Or** (Place de Brouckere 14, tel. 02/217–4922), **Preservation Hall** (Rue de Londres 3 bis, tel. 02/511–0304), and **Bierodrome** (Place Fernand Cocq 21, tel. 02/512–0456).

Excursions from Brussels

Mechelen

Tourist Information   City tourist office: **Dienst voor Toerisme** (Stadhuis, Grote Markt, tel. 015/29–76–55). **Provincial tourist office: Toeristische Federatie Provincie Antwerpen** (Karel Oomsstraat 11, Antwerp, tel. 03/216–2810).

Getting There   Mechelen is 28 kilometers (17 miles) north of Brussels on the A1/E19 expressway, and just about the same distance from Antwerp (avoid the exit for the almost identically named Machelen, a Brussels suburb). The train trip takes 15 minutes.

Guided Tours   The **tourist office** organizes walks to explore historic Mechelen at 2 PM on weekends from Easter to September, and daily in July and August.

Exploring Mechelen   **Mechelen** (known to French speakers as Malines) is the traditional residence of the Roman Catholic primate of Belgium and has preserved the traditional Belgian specialties of lace making and tapestry weaving. There are also furniture factories producing the heavy oak pieces favored by many Flemish families. Mechelen, finally, is also the center of vegetable production, especially asparagus and *witloof*, the Belgian delicacy known elsewhere as chicory or endive.

Mechelen's brief period of grandeur coincided with the reign (1507–1530) of Margaret of Austria, who established her devout and cultured court in this city while she served as regent for her nephew, later to become Charles V. The philosophers

Erasmus and Thomas More visited her court, as did the painters Albrecht Dürer and Van Orley (whose portrait of Margaret hangs in the Musée d'Art Ancien in Brussels), and Josquin des Prés, the master of polyphony.

For the modern visitor, Mechelen's chief glory is the **St. Romboutskathedraal** on the Grote Markt and more especially the admirably proportioned tower, with its powerful but light vertical lines. It had been planned to reach a height of 167 meters (547 feet), which would have made it the tallest spire in the world, but construction came to an end in the 1520s when it was only 97 meters (318 feet) high. Even so, the tower represents a magnificent achievement by three generations of the Keldermans family of architects. Inside are two remarkable 40-ton carillons of 49 bells each. The interior of the cathedral is spacious and lofty, particularly the white sandstone nave dating from the 13th century. There are numerous paintings, notably Van Dyck's *Crucifixion* in the south transept. *Grote Markt. Open Mon.–Sat. 9:30–4 (until 7 in summer), Sun. 1–5. Check tourist office for tower tours. Carillon concerts Sat. 11:30 AM, Sun. 3 PM, Mon. 8:30 PM.*

Time Out Relax in the 't Voske on the Grote Markt with a local specialty such as *witloofsoep* (cream of endive soup), or *boerenbrood hesp* (open sandwich with ham and salad).

The **Stadhuis** (Town Hall), opposite the cathedral, consists of two contrasting parts. On the left is the palace commissioned by Charles V to accommodate the Grote Raad, the supreme court of the Burgundian Netherlands established by Charles the Bold. Work was abandoned after 20 years, in 1547, but completed in the 20th century in accordance with Rombout Keldermans's original plans. On the right is the sombers, turreted, 14th-century Lakenhalle (Cloth Hall). *Grote Markt. Guided tours of the Stadhuis start at 2 at the Tourist Office.*

Frederik de Merodestraat leads from the square to **Hof van Busleyden,** which houses the Municipal Museum. It, too, was built by the Keldermanses, for Hieronymus van Busleyden, the lawyer and humanist to whom Thomas More dedicated his *Utopia.* The dining room has survived almost intact, and the collection of paintings provides insights into the city's history. *Frederik de Merodestraat 65, tel. 015/20-20-04. Admission: BF75. Open Easter–Sept., Wed.–Mon. 10–noon and 2–5.*

Back toward the town center is **Sint-Janskerk,** which contains a Rubens triptych, the *Adoration of the Magi.* The painter's wife posed as the Virgin. To the right off Klapgat is Schoutetstraat, with the Refuge van Tongerlo and the tapestry workshops of **Gaspard De Wit—Koninklyke Manufactur/Manufacture Royale** (Royal Tapestery Manufacturer), the only place where the ancient and glorious Belgian art of tapestry weaving is still practiced. *Schoutetstraat 7, tel. 015/20-29-05. Guided tours of workshops and collection of antique and contemporary tapestries mid-Aug.–mid-July Sat. 10:30; admission BF150.*

East of the center, near the railway station, you'll find **Spelgoedmuseum Mechelen** (Mechelen's Toy Museum), which houses a vast collection of toys and games, including more than 8,000 tin soldiers ready to do battle on a model of Waterloo. There's also a play area for young and old. *Nekkerspoel 21, tel. 015/20-03-86. Admission: BF60. Open Tues.–Sun. 2–5.*

Dining
By Nancy Coons

Mechelen offers a rewarding variety of restaurants where good eating takes center stage.

★ **D'Hoogh.** In a grand graystone mansion on the Grote Markt, its first-floor (second to Americans) dining room looking over the square, this glamorous landmark presents top-quality *cuisine du marché* (menus based on whatever is freshest in the local market): smoked eel terrine with pistachios, poached goose liver in port jelly with caramelized apples, turbot and zucchini spaghetti in vinaigrette and olive oil. *Grote Markt 19, tel. 015/21–75–53. Reservations required. Jacket and tie advised. AE, DC, MC, V. Closed Sun. dinner, Mon. Expensive.*

Groene Lantaarn. Facing the cathedral, this tidy, pleasant little restaurant has plenty of Flemish charm—a green-tiled stove, crisp linens, and a menu of classics: eel in green sauce, sole, and all sorts of mussels. *Steenweg 2, tel. 015/20–20–27. Reservations suggested. Dress: casual. AE, DC, MC, V. Inexpensive–Moderate.*

't Korenveld. This tiny, old-fashioned bistro has been primly restored and decked with pretty floral wallpaper and tiled table tops. Its cuisine is equally unpretentious, featuring simple fish and steaks at low prices. It adjoins the Alfa Hotel, and has some tables in their bar. *Korenmarkt 20 tel. 015/42–14–69. Reservations suggested. Dress: casual. AE, DC, MC, V. Closed Mon. Inexpensive.*

Leuven

Tourist Information

City tourist office: Town Hall (Naamsestraat 1a, tel. 016/21–15–39). **Provincial tourist office: Toeristisch Federatie Brabant** (Rue du Marché-aux-Herbes 61, Brussels, tel. 02/504–0461).

Getting There

Leuven is 26 kilometers (16 miles) east of Brussels on A3/E40 toward Liège and Germany, or 20 minutes by train.

Guided Tours

There are no regularly organized guided tours of Leuven, but you can arrange with the tourist office for an English-speaking personal guide (BF1,000 for two hours).

Exploring Leuven

Leuven (Louvain to French speakers) is best known for its Catholic university, founded in 1425. One of its rectors was elected Pope Hadrian VI; Erasmus taught here in the 16th century, as did the cartographer Mercator and, in the following century, Cornelius Jansen, whose teachings inspired the anti-Jesuit Jansenist movement. The city was pillaged and burned by the Germans in 1914, when 1,800 buildings, including the university library, were destroyed. In the 1970s, after severe intercultural tensions, the old bilingual university split into a French-language university, which moved south of the linguistic border to Louvain-la-Neuve, and a Dutch-speaking one, which remained in Leuven. Present-day **Katholieke Universiteit Leuven** has a student body of more than 23,000.

The **Stadhuis** (Town Hall) escaped the 1914 fire due to its occupation by German staff. It is the work of Leuven's own architectural master of Flamboyant Gothic, Mathieu de Layens, who finished it in 1469 after 21 years' work. In photographs it looks more like a finely chiseled reliquary than a building; it is necessary to stand back from it to fully appreciate the vertical lines in the mass of turrets, pinnacles, pendants, and niches, each with its statue. The interior contains some fine 16th-century sculpted ceilings. *Grote Markt. Guided tours start from the tourist office weekdays at 11 and 3, weekends (Mar.–Oct.) at 3.*

Time Out   Under the Town Hall, and adjoining a small beer museum, is the **Raadskelder** café, strategically located for the revival of tired city officials and tourists.

Across the square stands the collegiate church, **St. Pieterskerk.** Mathieu de Layens had a hand in this, too, as did Mechelen's Jan Keldermans and Diest's Sulpice van der Vorst. A shifting foundation led to the shortening of the tower in the 17th century and to the replacement of the spire with a cupola in the 18th. The interior is remarkable for the purity of the Gothic nave; the ambulatory and choir have been arranged as a museum of religious art. Its principal treasure is *The Last Supper* by Dirk Bouts, one of the great Flemish primitives of the 15th century and Leuven's official artist. *Admission: BF50. Open Mon.– Sat. 10–noon and 2–5, Sun. 2–5.*

Additional art treasures fill the **Stedelijk Museum,** (Municipal Museum), just off the Grote Markt. They include works by Albrecht Bouts (died 1549), son of Dirk, and Quentin Metsys (1466–1530), a remarkable portraitist, as well as Brabantine sculptures from the 15th and 16th centuries. *Savoyestraat 6. Admission: BF50 (includes access to other museums). Open Tues.–Sat. 10–noon and 2–5, Sun. 2–5.*

A kilometer (½ mile) south down Naamsestraat, past several university colleges, lies the **Groot Begijnhof,** a city within the city where the *beguines* (lay women members of an old religious order) once resided in their tiny individual houses. There are more than 70 of them, carefully restored and now used by the university, as well as an attractive church.

A number of university institutes are located in less congested surroundings in the splendid park of **Arenberg Castle** (tel. 016/ 284010) in **Heverlee,** 6 kilometers (4 miles) south of the city. At Heverlee, too, is the **Norbertine Abbey of Park** (visits Sun. 4 PM; for information call the tourist office), founded in 1128, with its 18th-century water mill, granary, abbey farm, and church.

Dining   **Belle Epoque.** This grand urban town house, by the station, of-
by Nancy Coons   fers the most lavish dining in Leuven, served with considerable pomp. Try the smoked salmon filled with eel mousse and hope for wild hare, in season. *Bondgenotenlaan 94, tel. 016/22–33– 89. Reservations required. Jacket and tie advised. AE, DC, MC, V. Closed Sun.–Mon. Expensive.*

De 4 Seizoenen. On a stark, urban street next to the Binnenhof hotel, this is a simple, attractive restaurant offering several classic dishes, elegantly served: eel in green sauce, grilled sole, rabbit in abbey beer, quail in *jenever* (Dutch gin). There's a reasonable lunch menu. *Maria-Theresiastraat 73, tel. 016/22–89– 89. Reservations suggested. Jacket suggested. AE, DC, MC, V. Closed Sat. lunch, Sun. Moderate.*

Domus. Tucked into a back street off the Grote Markt, this café adjoins the tiny Domus brewery, famous for its honey beer. The ambience is young and casual, the decor authentically rustic: craggy old beams, a brick fireplace, a labyrinth of separate rooms, bric-a-brac, and paisley table throws. The menu offers well prepared omelettes, chicken à la king, and a cream gratin of endive, ham, and cheese, as well as several salads and cold

You've Let Your Imagination Go, Now Get Up And Follow Your Dreams.

For The Vacation You're Dreaming Of, Call American Express® Travel Agency At 1-800-YES-AMEX.*

American Express will send more than your imagination soaring. We'll fly you, sail you, drive you to any Fodor's destination and beyond. Because American Express believes the best vacations happen from Europe to the Orient, Walt Disney® World to Hawaii and everywhere in between.

For dependable service, expert advice, and value wherever your dreams take you, call on American Express. After all, the best traveling companion is a trustworthy friend.

It's easy to recognize a good place when you see one.

American Express Cardmembers have been doing it for years.

The secret? Instead of just relying on what they see in the window, they look at the door. If there's an American Express Blue Box on it, they know they've found an establishment that cares about high standards.

Whether it's a place to eat, to sleep, to shop, or simply meet, they know they will be warmly welcomed.

So much so, they're rarely taken in by anything else.

Always a good sign.

plates. *Tienestraat 8, tel. 016/20–14–49. Dress: casual. No credit cards. Inexpensive.*

Excursion to Hainaut

All the highways leading south from Brussels end up in France, which may serve to remind you that you are in a proud old country that was the nursery of French kings, the rich dowry of dynastic marriages, and for many years the buffer between expansionist France and quarrelsome Flanders. You go through landscape scarred by the industrial revolution and past ancient, fortified farms turned into centers of highly productive agriculture. You'll see the ravages of war and some cathedrals that were spared, and wander through parks and châteaus that are a reminder of the feudal world that was.

Important Addresses and Numbers

Tourist Information Wallonie: tourist office (Rue du Marché-aux-Herbes 61, Brussels, tel. 02/504–0390). **Province of Hainaut:** tourist office (Rue des Clercs 31, Mons, tel. 065/36–04–64). **City tourist offices: Tournai** (Vieux Marché-aux-Poteries 14, tel. 069/22–20–45); **Mons** (Grand'Place 22, tel. 065/33–55–80); and **Binche** (Rue St-Paul 14, tel. 064/33–37–21).

Emergencies **Police:** tel. 101. **Ambulance:** tel. 100. The name of the nearest on-duty **pharmacy** is posted in all pharmacy windows.

Getting There

By Train There is frequent train service from Brussels to Tournai (on the route to Lille) and to Mons (on the route to Paris). Each trip takes about an hour.

By Car Roads leading south from Brussels pass through Flemish-speaking Brabant; thus roads are signposted to Bergen (Mons), Doornik (Tournai), and Rijsel (Lille).

Guided Tours

City tours are organized on request by the **tourist offices** in Tournai, Mons, and Binche. For tours of the southern part of the province, contact the tourist office in **Beaumont** (tel. 071/58–81–91).

Exploring Hainaut

Numbers in the margin correspond with places of interest on the Excursion to Hainaut map.

① Driving south on E19, you're in **Beersel** almost before leaving Brussels. It is the site of a stark 13th-century fort, the **Kastel van Beersel,** surrounded by a moat. One of the rooms is a well-equipped torture chamber. *Lotstraat, tel. 02/504–0461. Admission: BF50. Open Mar.–mid-Nov., Tues.–Sun. 10–noon and 2–6; mid-Nov.–Jan., weekends 10:30–5.*

② From Beersel you can proceed west past St.-Pieters-Leeuw and follow the signs to **Gaasbeek.** The area is called Pajottenland, and you may be familiar with the landscape from Bruegel's works, many of which were painted here. **Gaasbeek**

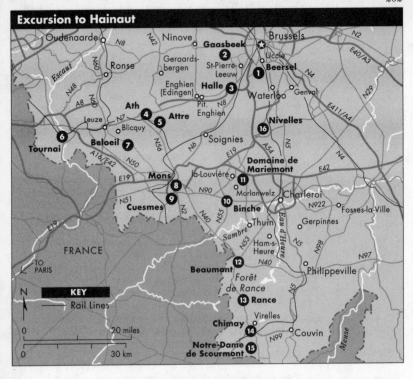

Excursion to Hainaut

Château was restored in the 19th century; it contains outstanding 15th- and 16th-century tapestries. Rubens's will is among the documents in the castle archives. The surrounding park is popular with picnickers. *Groenstraat, tel. 02/532–4372. Admission free. Open Apr.–Oct., Tues.–Thurs. and weekends 10–5.*

3 South of Gaasbeek, **Halle** is worth a stop for its **basiliek** (basilica), which dates from the 14th century. The south portal is decorated with a sculpture of the Virgin and Child surrounded by angels playing musical instruments. Inside, the main religious treasure is the allegedly miraculous Black Virgin; artistically, the focus is on 15th-century sculptures of the apostles from the school of Claus Sluter.

South of Halle on A8 motorway, at the linguistic frontier at Enghien/Edingen, signs begin to refer to Tournai rather than **4** Doornik. From here N7 leads to **Ath,** where amid great jubilation, giants run wild on the fourth Sunday of August during the celebration of the **ducasse,** an event of unknown origin that goes back at least to the 15th century. The principal figures, 4½ meters (15 feet) high, represent Monsieur and Madame Gouyasse (Goliath), the four sons of Aymon on their steed Bayard, Samson, Ambiorix (who faught against the Romans), and Mam'zelle Victoire, representing the town of Ath.

5 In nearby **Attre** stands the splendid **Château d'Attre,** built in 1752 and preserved intact. Among its treasures are paintings by Franz Snyders and Bartolomé Murillo. *Admission: BF120.*

Open mid-Mar.–Oct., weekends 10–noon and 2–6; July–Aug., Thurs.–Tues. 10–noon and 2–6.

⑥ **Tournai** shares with Tongeren the distinction of being the oldest cities in Belgium. It was important in the time of the Romans, and later it was the home of France's Merovingian kings; Clovis was born here in 465. At various times, Tournai has been English, French, and Austrian. Through these vicissitudes the city remained a flourishing center of art. The German bombardment in May 1940 destroyed virtually all the priceless old buildings, with the exception of the **Cathédrale Notre-Dame,** whose five towers, all different, dominate the city today. Begun in 1110 and completed in 60 years, it is the most original work of religious architecture in Belgium and the progenitor of a distinctive style that spread from Tournai down the River Escaut (Scheldt).

You get the best general view of the cathedral from Place Paul-Emile Janson, and you need to walk around it to get the full effect of its vast proportions and the massive silhouettes of the five towers. Inside is an overpowering Renaissance screen in polychrome marble. The transept, almost a cathedral within the cathedral, contains the remains of 12th-century frescoes and well-restored 14th-century windows. In the chapels are paintings by Rubens, Pourbus the Elder, and Martin de Vos. Foremost among the objects in the treasury are reliquaries in gilded copper and silver by two of the great 13th-century silversmiths, Nicholas de Verdun and Hugo d'Oignies. *Place Paul-Emile Janson. Open Easter–Sept., daily 8:30–6; Oct.–Easter, daily 8:30–4:30. Treasury open Easter–Sept., daily 10–noon and 1–6; Oct.–Easter, daily 10–noon and 1–4:30.*

Time Out A l'Bancloque (rue des Chapeliers 46, tel. 069/22–21–49) is a classic Belgian drinking room with high, cottered ceilings and an old stone fireplace.

To see Tournai from the river, take a one-hour trip by sightseeing boat from the landing stage below the Pont des Trous. *Fare: BF80. Hours: May–Aug., Tues.–Sun. at 11, 2:30, and 4:15.*

Tapestry-making has a long tradition in Tournai, and you can see an outstanding selection of tapestries from the Middle Ages to the present day in the new **Musée de la Tapisserie.** One can also see tapestry weaving and restoration in studios in the museum. *Place Reine Astrid, tel. 069/23–42–85. Admission free. Open Wed.–Mon. 10–noon and 2–5:30.*

⑦ From Tournai, head east on A16 in the direction of Mons, keeping an eye peeled for signs to **Beloeil,** home of the princes de Ligne since the 14th century. The 17th-century château is partially a reconstruction from the original plans, following a fire in 1900. It contains fine furniture and tapestries, and the heirlooms include gifts from Marie Antoinette and Catherine the Great, friends of the Maréchal de Ligne; his grandson was offered, but refused, the Belgian crown. The elegant park is patterned on Versailles. Contemporary attractions include a small train that takes you from the château through the vast grounds to Minibel, a reconstruction in miniature of some of the country's finest sites. *Tel. 069/68–94–26. Admission: BF390 for park and château. Open Apr.–Oct., daily 10–6.*

8 A16 takes you quickly on to **Mons,** in the heart of the Borinage mining district, administrative center of the province of Hainaut. Its hilly streets, lined with elegant if grimy 17th- and 18th-century brick houses, have considerable charm. Orlandus Lassus, the 16th-century composer, was a native of Mons. It was at Mons that the British Expeditionary Force first joined battle with the Germans in August 1914. In September 1944, further destruction was wrought by a running battle between advancing American troops and the retreating Germans.

At the highest point stands a remarkable **belfry,** known locally as *le château*, for it is next to the site of the castle of the counts of Hainaut. The 87-meter (285-foot) -high Baroque tower, crowned by an onion dome, was built in the 17th century. Restoration is in progress, and the tower cannot be visited.

Rue des Clercs takes you to the **Eglise de Ste-Waudru** (St. Waudru's Church), named for the wife of a Merovingian dignitary who, legend has it, founded a monastery in the 7th century around which the city developed. The church was begun in 1450 by the ladies of St. Waudru's noble chapter of secular canonesses. The Car d'Or (Golden Coach) carries the reliquary of St. Waudru on Trinity Sunday (first Sunday after Pentecost). *Treasury admission: BF40. Open May–Sept., daily 10–12:30 and 2–6; Oct.–Apr., Tues.–Sun. 10–12:30 and 2–6.*

Time Out You can grab a bite or eat more ambitiously at **Le St-Germain-Saey** (Grand'Place 12), which is also a patisserie.

The whole province, especially south of Charleroi, is dotted with villages celebrating a saint, a battle, a giant, or a medieval marriage—often intertwined traditions—with a procession or *marche militaire*. The origins of the military overtone go back to the era of the Reformation and the Counter-Reformation, when religious processions were guarded by a rural militia. Among the 40-odd military processions, the most notable are those in **Ham-sur-Heure, Gerpinnes,** and **Jumet.**

The area around Mons is dotted with conical slag heaps, grim reminders of its mining past. **Vincent van Gogh** came here as a preacher in 1878, and stayed with a family of miners, the **9** Decrucqs, in **Cuesmes,** just south of the city. It was here that he began drawing the landscape and scenes of the miners' lives. The **house,** in which his room has been reconstituted, still stands. *Rue du Pavillon 3, tel. 065/35–56–11. Open Tues.–Sun. 10–5.*

10 From Mons the Charleroi road, N90, leads to **Binche,** whose center is still intact behind its 25 towers and 1½ miles of ramparts. Binche is the only remaining walled city in Belgium, but it is for its **carnival** that the city is famed. The carnival begins the Sunday before Ash Wednesday, when, first, hundreds of transvestite Mam'zelles dance in the streets to the music of fiddles, barrel organs, and drums, and, later, 1,500 Binche dancers make a procession. Shrove Tuesday is the big day. The Gilles (dancers whose role originated in the 16th century when lords dressed as Incas or Indians, representing recently discovered America, performed to entertain Charles V; the role evolved into an incarnation of the rites of nature) start assembling at dawn, wearing their fantastic costumes of red and yellow. Their magnificent hats are crowned with huge plumes of ostrich feathers, and their white masks are painted with green spectacles and mustaches. To the rhythm of drums, the Gilles move through the streets in a slow, shuffling dance. The day ends with fireworks, but the Gilles continue dancing through the night. Traditionally, they drink nothing but champagne.

The **Musée International du Carnaval et du Masque** contains an extraordinary collection of masks and costumes from all over the world, and there's an audiovisual presentation of the local carnival, in case you're in Binche at the wrong time for the real thing. *Rue du St-Moustier 14, tel. 064/33–57–41. Admission free. Open mid-Jan.–mid-Nov., Mon.–Thurs. 10–noon and 2–5, weekends 10–noon and 2–6.*

From Binche, N563 goes north to the expressway to Brussels. ⑪ On the left at the turn at Morlanwelz is the **Domaine de Mariemont.** There's nothing left of the chateaus that have successively stood here, but the 45-hectare (110-acre) English park is one of the most attractive in Belgium, decorated with sculptures by a number of artists, including Auguste Rodin and Constantin Meunier. The well-laid-out museum contains excellent collections of Chinese art, archaeological finds, and Tournai porcelain. *Chaussée de Mariemont, tel. 064/21–21–93. Admission free. Open Tues.–Sun. 10–6.*

N55 south from Binche leads to the country *Entre Sambre-et-Meuse* (between the area's two principal rivers). Turn left on ⑫ N40 and you're soon in **Beaumont** with its **Tour Salamandre,** all that remains of a major fortified castle built in the 11th century. The tower has been restored and houses a museum of local and regional history. *Tel. 071/58–81–91. Admission: BF40. Open May–Sept., 9–noon and 2–7.*

⑬ To the south on N53 is **Rance,** known for its quarries, which furnished the red marble for St. Peter's in Rome. The excellent **Musée National du Marbre** (National Marble Museum), is here. *Admission: BF100. Open Mon.–Sat. 9:30–6, Sun. 2–6 (until 5 in winter).*

Continuing through the Forêt de Rance, one eventually reaches ⑭ **Chimay,** the home of Froissart, the great 14th-century historian whose chronicles furnished the background information for some of Shakespeare's plays.

The town has more vivid memories of Madame Tallien, a great beauty who was known to revolutionary France as Notre Dame de Thermidor. She narrowly escaped the guillotine, married her protector, Citizen Tallien, and persuaded him to instigate the overthrow of Robespierre. Eventually she was again married, to Francois-Joseph Caraman, prince de Chimay, and ended her days in peace and dignity as mistress of the **Château de Chimay.** The warrant for her arrest, signed by Robespierre, is preserved at the château along with other memorabilia, such as the baptismal robe worn by Napoleon's son, the king of Rome. *Grand'Place, tel. 060/21–18–46. Admission: BF120. Guided tours daily 10–noon and 2–6.*

At **Virelles,** just north of Chimay, you'll find the **Etang de Virelles** (tel. 071/38–17–61), the largest lake in Belgium, at 101 hectares (250 acres). You can rent a rowboat or pedal boat to explore the lake, which is surrounded by woods, and there's a playground on the shore.

Time Out At Virelles, you'll find a moderately priced and hugely popular restaurant called **Edgard et Madeleine** (Rue du Lac 35, tel. 060/ 21–10–71; reservations are essential; closed Tues.).

⑮ South of Chimay is the Trappist monastery of **Notre-Dame de Scourmont.** The abbey cannot be visited, but you can buy the excellent cheese and stout beer produced by the fathers.

On the way back to Brussels, just after A54 rejoins E19, make a final stop at the **Eau-d'Heure Lakes,** a wild and wooded 1,822-hectare (4,500-acre) parkland with grassy valleys and lakes. At La Plate Taille information center, the history of the area is presented in a giant audiovisual show. There are aquariums, models, a panoramic tower, water sports, and marked trails. *N40 between Beaumont and Philippeville, tel. 071/63–35–34. Admission: BF180. Open daily Easter–Sept. 9–6.*

⑯ **Nivelles.** This is one more old town that suffered terribly from bombardment in May 1940, when more than 500 buildings were destroyed. Again, it is the church that survived. The **Collégiale Ste-Gertrude** (St. Gertrude's Collegiate Church) bears the name of the daughter of Pepin the Old, who founded a convent here around AD 650. It is an impressive Romanesque building, with two transepts and choirs at opposite ends. The crypt contains the burial vaults of St. Gertrude and her parents, and vestiges of the five churches that preceded the present one on the same spot. *1-hour tours of the church at 10, 11, 2, 3 and 4. Admission: BF50. Closed Sun. AM.*

Time Out The local Nivelles specialty is *tarte al djote*, a succulent cheese and vegetable pie, served hot. One of the best places to enjoy it is the **Taverne Les Arcade** (Grand'Place).

What to See and Do with Children

There's a full-scale **old steam train** providing service between Charleroi and Mariembourg to the south. *Round-trip fare: BF200. Easter–June and Sept., weekends; July–Aug., Sat.–Tues. and Thurs.*

For the **Centre de Loisirs de l'Orient**, take E42 toward Tournai to Exit 32. The large center has boats, games, barbecues, and a café. *Chemin de Mons 8. Open Apr.–Sept., daily 10–10.*

At Blicquy-Aubechies, near Beloeil, the **Archeosite** is a collection of prehistoric and Gallo-Roman houses, with mud walls, thatched roofs, and authentic interiors, that have been reconstructed according to plans found during their excavation. *Tel. 069/66–29–38. Admission: BF70. Open Nov.–Easter, weekdays 9–5; Easter–Oct., weekdays 9–5, weekends 2–6.*

Off the Beaten Track

Between Mons and the French border is an extraordinary early 19th-century industrial complex, the **Grand-Hornu,** begun in 1810, when coal mining in this area was at its height. The buildings were designed by Bruno Renard, a Tournai architect who worked in the Napoleonic style. Le Grand Hornu includes not only workshops but also, remarkable for the time, lodgings, a school, an arts center, a library and a hospital. *E19, exit 25, tel.*

*065/77–07–12. Admission: BF100. Open Mar.–Sept., Tues.–
Sun. 10–noon and 2–6.*

Villers-la-Ville, 36 kilometers (22 miles) southeast of Brussels,
can be reached through Waterloo and Genappe or east on N237
from Nivelles. At the crossroad north of the village are the remarkable **Villers-la-Ville Abbey Ruins.** St. Bernard himself laid
the foundation stone in 1147, and the robust elegance of the
cloister, dormitories, refectory, and chapter hall, all in true
Cistercian style, are still impressive. *Tel. 071/87–98–98. Admission: BF50. Open mid-Mar.–Oct., daily 10–6.*

Shopping

Mons The smart shops are found in the pedestrian rue de la Chaussée
and around the city's Grand'Place. On Sunday mornings there
is a flea market on the Place Simonet.

Tournai There's a lively pedestrian area, known simply as **Le
Pietonnier,** near the post office. Other shopping streets are Rue
Royale and the streets branching off from the Grand Place.
Lively Saturday morning **markets** take place on the Grand
Place, Place St-Pierre, and Place Paul-Emile Janson, as well as
along the Quai du Marché aux Poissons. Sunday-morning flea
markets are held on Place St-Pierre and in the shopping gallery
off Rue du Cygne. There are many **antiques** dealers in the area
around the Eglise St-Jacques (St. James's Church).

Sports and Outdoor Activities

Archery You can practice crossbow shooting at the **Arbaletriers
Beaumontois** (Parc de Paridaens, **Beaumont,** tel. 071/58–86–
09), or archery in the same town at the **Club Saint-Sebastien**
(Rue de Mons 3, Beaumont, tel. 060/51–23–07).

Golf North of **Tournai** is **Golf Le Chateau** (Chaussée de Courtrai 12,
Ramegnies-Chin, tel. 069/22–61–54). There's a public, 18-hole
golf course west of **Mons, Golf Public** (Rue du Mont Garni 3,
Baudour, tel. 065/62–27–19).

Horseback Riding Horseback riding is popular in many parts of the province, particularly in the less densely populated south. You can arrange
treks with the **Centre Equestre des Fagnes** (Rue de la Fagne 20,
Chimay, tel. 060/41–11–69).

Tennis Try the **Waux-Hall** (Av. Reine Astrid 22, **Mons,** tel. 065/33–90–
89); **Sequoia Tennis Club** (Rue du Sequoia 33, **Ath,** tel. 068/28–
52–64); or **Plaine de Jeux Bozière** (Av. Bozière 1B, **Tournai,** tel.
069/22–35–86).

Dining and Lodging

By Nancy Coons From the ancient Frankish capital of Tournai to the greenery
surrounding Chimay, there's no shortage here of memorable
old inns and atmospheric restaurants.

Chimay **Auberge de Poteaupré.** This casual road stop, built in the 1970s,
Dining and Lodging lies among green, rolling fields and offers plenty of windows to
take in the view; in summer, the back porch opens onto the
grounds. Chimay specialties—rabbit in beer, croquettes of
Chimay cheese, eel *escabèche* (spicy cold marinade of cooked
fish)—are served at long ranks of plain tables that neighbors

share. Rooms upstairs are '70s-minimal, but the views are fine. *Rue Poteaupré 5, B-6480, tel. 060/21–14–33. 11 rooms. Facilities: restaurant (closed Mon.), café. MC, V. Inexpensive.*

★ **Les Virelles.** Just north of Chimay, in the open greenery around the Etang de Virelles, this charming old country inn offers simple, middle-class regional cooking in a pretty, well-weathered beam-and-copper setting. You can have trout or escabèches, or a more ambitious, multicourse menu based on regional plenty (freshwater fish and game). Rooms, named after field flowers, are simple and cozy, some with four-poster beds. *Rue du Lac 28, B-6431 Virelles-Chimay, tel. 060/21–28–03. 8 rooms. Facilities: restaurant (closed Tues.–Wed. dinner), café. AE, DC, MC, V. Inexpensive.*

Tournai
Dining
★ **Le Pressoir.** Tucked down at the end of the Marché aux Poteries, between the cathedral and the Beffroi, this chic, unpretentious restaurant combines historical atmosphere (exposed brick, illuminated oil paintings) with surprising urbanity: The bar draws BCBG (*bon chic–bon genre*) clientele, and the restaurant hosts visiting VIPs. Try saffron-perfumed bouillabaise of *rouget* (red mullet) or confit of farm pigeon with young turnips. *Marché aux Poteries 2, tel. 069/22–35–13. Reservations advised. Jacket and tie suggested. DC, MC, V. Closed weekday dinner. Moderate–Expensive.*

L'Ecu de France. This is popular more for moderate standards (mussels, simple menus) and festive drinks than for its somewhat pretentious à la carte offerings. The setting is warm and welcoming, with polished woodwork: It's designed as an atrium, so diners upstairs can look over the railing at the action in the bar below. *Grand Place 55, tel. 069/22–58–16. Reservations suggested. Dress: casual. AE, DC, MC, V. Moderate.*

Bistro de la Cathédrale. This modernized, brightly lighted storefront restaurant offers a few very reasonable menus and large portions of good, simple, well-prepared food: sparkling-fresh oysters, salads of *crevettes grise* (shrimp), sole meunière, rabbit with prunes. The ambience is casual, the staff friendly. *Vieux Marché aux Poteries 15, tel. 069/21–03–79. Dress: casual. AE, DC, MC, V. Inexpensive.*

Lodging **Cathédrale** (formerly Condor). This is a fully modernized chain-style business hotel, at the foot of the cathedral in the center. The rooms are laminate-spare, and some look onto the small square. *Place St-Pierre, B-7500, tel. 069/21–50–77. 45 rooms. Facilities: restaurant, café. AE, DC, MC, V. Moderate.*

L'Europe. Well placed on the Grand'Place, with rooms looking out toward the Beffroi and historic architecture, this is a comfortable hotel in an old step-gabled house. The rooms have been cheaply redecorated with a lavish touch; most have toilets down the hall. The restaurant/tavern downstairs draws crowds of locals for stone-grilled meats. *Grand'Place 36, B-7500, tel. 069/22–40–67. 8 rooms. Facilities: restaurant, tavern. AE, DC, MC, V. Inexpensive.*

La Tour Saint-Georges. Tucked into a back street behind the Grand'Place, this is a spare, somewhat institutional hotel, with linoleum and terrazzo floors, mixed brocante furnishings, and toilets down the hall. The eager manager will serve evening meals as well as breakfast. *Place de Nédonchel, B-7500, tel. 069/22–53–00. 10 rooms. Facilities: half-board dining, breakfast only. No credit cards. Inexpensive.*

The Arts and Nightlife

The Arts   There are several noteworthy museums in the region: In Tournai the **Musée des Beaux-Arts** (Enclos St. Martin, tel. 069/22–20–43; open Wed.–Mon. 10–noon and 2–5:30) has good collections of Flemish primitives and Impressionists; in Charleroi the **Musée de la Photographie** (av Paul Pastur 11, tel. 071/43–58–10; admission: BF40; open Tues.–Sun. 10–5) features historical photographic exhibits as well as contemporary work; and in Mons the **Musée des Beaux-Arts** (rue Neuve, tel. 065/34–95–55; open Tues.–Sun. 10–6) has interesting temporary exhibitions. In Charleroi the **Palais des Beaux-Arts** (place du Manege 7, tel. 071/31–12–12) is a multicultural center for opera, theater, dance, and popular music.

Nightlife   There's hardly a village anymore that doesn't have its own disco. In **Charleroi** try **La Reserve** at the Palais des Beaux-Arts. **Parisiana** (rue du Commerce 3) has a floor show, and **Le Carré Blanc** (rue Leopold 18) is for the younger set. In **Mons,** the **Voum-Voum** (rue de la Coupe 44) is for dancing and the **New Blue Note** (av Roi Albert 667) is for devotees of jazz.

Ghent, Brugge, and the Coast

Brugge and Ghent are the art cities of Flanders that represent the flowering of the late Middle Ages. The North Sea Coast provided irresistible sandy shores on which the Vikings beached their longboats, and it was to fend off these marauders that Baldwin of the Iron Arm, first count of Flanders, built the original fortifications at both Brugge and Ghent. The cities came to prominence as centers of the cloth trade. Flemish weavers had been renowned since the days of the Romans, but it was in the Middle Ages that they began to use the finest wool from England, Scotland, and Ireland, and their products became truly superior. Thus the English acquired an interest in keeping Flanders from the French. This early form of industrialization also prepared the ground for communal strife, pitting common weavers against patrician merchants.

The destinies of the two cities diverged in the 19th century; Brugge settled into a graceful decline from which it has only roused itself in the last few decades. Ghent, however, embraced the industrial revolution, becoming an important textile center once more. The cities of Kortrijk and Ieper to the south recall the long history of battles fought in the region since the time of Julius Caesar. The North Sea Coast continues to be irresistible to invaders, but now they are sun seekers and beach lovers.

Important Addresses and Numbers

Tourist Information   The **Tourist Office for Flanders** in Brussels is at Rue du Marché-aux-Herbes 61 (tel. 02/504–0390). Information on the area as a whole can be obtained from **Westtoerisme** (Kasteel Tillegem, Brugge, tel. 050/38–02–96). Local tourist offices are located as follows: **Blankenberge:** Leopold III plein (tel. 050/41–22–27); **Brugge** (Dienst voor Toerisme): Burg 11 (tel. 050/44–86–86); **Ghent** (Dienst voor Toerisme): Predikherenlei 2 (tel. 091/25–36–41) and Town Hall (Botermarkt, tel. 091/24–15–55); **De**

Haan: Leopoldlaan 24 (tel. 059/23–57–23); **Ieper:** Stadhuis, Grote Markt (tel. 057/20–07–24); **Knokke-Heist:** Zeedijk 660 (tel. 050/60–16–16); **Kortrijk:** Schouwburgplein (tel. 056/23–93–71); **Nieuwpoort:** Marktplein 7 (tel. 058/23–55–94); **Oostende:** Wapenplein 3 (tel. 059/70–11–99); **De Panne:** Zeelaan 21 (tel. 058/41–13–02).

Emergencies **Police:** tel. 101. **Ambulance:** tel. 100. **Hospital emergency room, Ghent:** tel. 091/40–27–42. The name of the on-duty **late-night pharmacy** is posted in all pharmacy windows.

Arriving and Departing

By Car The six-lane A10/E40 from Brussels passes both Ghent and Brugge en route to Oostende. Traffic is sometimes bumper-to-bumper on summer weekends, making it a better alternative to take N9 from Ghent via Brugge; for Knokke, you branch off on N49. A back road to the resorts southwest of Oostende is N43 from Ghent to Deinze and then N35 to the coast. E17 links Kortrijk with Ghent. A19 links Kortrijk with Ieper and will eventually continue to the coast.

By Train Brugge is a major stop on the important London–Brussels–Cologne railway line. There is half-hourly service from Brussels (50 minutes) and Oostende (15 minutes). All Brussels–Oostende trains (one hour and 10 minutes) also stop at **Ghent.** For train information in Ghent, call 091/21–44–44; in Brugge, call 050/38–23–82; and in Oostende, call 059/70–15–17. There's also train service to Blankenberge and Knokke-Heist.

By Ship **P&O** (in England, tel. 081/575–8555) car ferry has up to eight sailings a day from Dover to Oostende (four hours) and two sailings a day from Felixstowe to Zeebrugge (5½ hours). **North Sea Ferries** (in England, tel. 0482/77–177) offers overnight sailings from Hull to Zeebrugge (14 hours). Foot passengers only are carried by Jetfoil from Dover to Oostende (one hour and 40 minutes, up to five daily crossings).

By Bus **Hoverspeed British Ferries** (in England, tel. 081/554–7061) operates a daily coach service from London to Brugge utilizing Hovercraft for the Dover–Calais crossing.

Getting Around

Brugge The center of Brugge is best seen on foot. The winding streets may confuse your sense of direction, but if you look up, there's always the Belfry to guide you back to the Markt. Sturdy footwear is recommended.

Access for cars and coaches into the old city is restricted. There are only five routes into the city. Most of the cobbled streets have been turned into one-way routes, and the Markt is closed to through traffic. A new computer-controlled traffic light system is being installed on the ring road around Brugge.

By Bus The **De Lijn** bus company (tel. 050/35–54–51; fare BF37, eight-trip tickets BF175) runs most buses every 20 minutes, including Sundays. New minibuses, designed to penetrate the narrow streets, are on order.

By Taxi There are big taxi stands (tel. 050/33–44–44) at the station and at the Markt.

By Bicycle As traffic is of necessity slow-moving, this is a good way to get around Brugge and environs. Bikes can be rented at the **railway station** (BF120 per day with a valid train ticket), at **Eric Popelier** (Hallestraat 14, around the corner from the Belfry, tel. 050/34–32–62; BF150 for four hours, BF250 for the day), or at **Koffiebontje** (Hallestraat 4, tel. 050/33–80–27; same rates).

Ghent Most of the sights in the center of town are within a radius of a kilometer (½ mile) of the Stadhuis (Town Hall), and the preferred way of seeing them is on foot.

By Bus and Tram If you arrive by train, take tram No. 1, 11, or 12 (fare; BF37) for the city center. Tickets can be used on both buses and trams; an eight-trip card costs BF175 at the railway station.

By Taxi There are taxi stands (tel. 091/25–25–25) at the railway station and at major squares.

By Bicycle You can rent a bike at the **train station** (BF120 a day with valid rail ticket). Note: Traffic is quite a bit heavier than in Brugge.

The Coast There's tram service—a happily preserved relic of another
By Tram era—all the way from Knokke to De Panne. The trams are modern, and it's a pleasant ride, but don't expect uninterrupted views of the sea; the tram tracks are on the leeward side of the dike. Tickets cost about BF50 depending on distance. A one-day ticket comes to BF210; a five-day ticket is BF840. For information, call 078/11–36–63.

By Car The coastal road, N34, is very busy in summer. Allow ample time for driving between resorts.

Guided Tours

Brugge Bicycle tours (De Reyghere Bookshop, Markt 12; or Bart
By Bicycle Germonprez, tel. 050/33–12–36, 8–9AM or 9–10PM; cost: BF350) of the city begin at 10 AM every day on the Markt. They last just under two hours.

The **Back Road Bike Co.** (tel. 050/34–68–28) organizes **bicycle** tours covering six villages near Brugge. Mountain bikes are supplied, and the guided four-hour rides take only back roads.

By Boat Independent motor launches depart from five jetties along the Dijver and Katelijnestraat as soon as they are reasonably full (every 15 minutes or so). The trips take just over half an hour. *Fare: BF130 adults, BF65 children. Operated Mar.–Nov.; Dec. and Feb., weekends only.*

By Horse-Drawn You may have to wait for more than an hour for a short ride with
Carriage inadequate commentary and then be asked for "something for the horse." Kids love it, however. Carriages wait in the Burg (cost: BF700; Wed. AM at the Belfry).

By Minibus The 50-minute **Sightseeing Line** tour gives a good if impersonal overview of Brugge's attractions. No visits are included, and the commentary is taped. *The Markt, tel. 050/31–13–55. Fare: BF275 adults, BF180 children. Hourly July–Aug., 10–7; tapering off to Jan.–Feb., 11–1.*

Quasimodo Tours (tel. 050/37–04–70; fare: BF840) operates a "Fields of Flanders" full-day bus tour on Monday and Saturday, March 15 through October 31.

Personal Guides You can book an English-speaking guide through the **tourist office** (tel. 050/44–86–86). Guides charge a minimum of BF1,000 for two hours, BF500 per extra hour. In July and August, groups are consolidated at the tourist office every day at 3 PM; cost per person is BF100 (children free).

Ghent
By Boat

Benelux-Gent Watertoerist sightseeing boats depart from the old landing stages at Graslei and Korenlei for 35-minute trips on the Ghent waterways. *Tel. 091/82–94–18. Fare: BF120 adults, BF70 children. Operated Easter–Oct.*

A full-day **Museum Line** excursion on the River Leie, leaving Ghent at 9 AM and returning at 8 PM, is operated on Thursdays from May to September. *Benelux Co., Recollettenlei 10, Ghent, tel. 091/25–15–05. Bookings required.*

By Horse-Drawn Carriage

Carriages wait in the Sint-Baafsplein to take you on a half-hour trip that gives a general idea of the city center. *Cost: BF600 for up to 4 persons. Operated Easter–Oct.*

By Minibus

Fifty-minute **Sightseeing Line** tours with taped commentary in seven languages give you a quick overview of Ghent's principal sights. *Stadhuis. Tel. 050/31–13–55. Fare: BF275 adults, BF180 children. Mid-Mar.–mid Nov., daily 10, 11, and noon; mid-Nov.–mid-Mar., weekends 10, 11, and noon.*

Personal Guides

In addition to a standard tour, you can ask for accompanied visits to other sights and museums. Guides charge BF1,000 for the first two hours and BF500 per additional hour. For bookings, call **Gidsenbond van Gent** (Association of Ghent Guides, tel. 091/33–07–72, fax 091/33–08–65).

The Coast

Quasimodo (tel. 050/37–04–70; price: BF850) has all-day minibus tours from Brugge on Wednesday and Friday in season. The English-language tour includes a drive along the coast.

Exploring Ghent, Brugge, and the Coast

The wealth of the Flemish cities was created by the weaving trade. The sumptuous clothing so lovingly depicted in numerous paintings was all locally produced. The merchants built their magnificent houses in Flemish style, and they engaged Flemish artists to paint their portraits. Flemish architects designed the churches and town halls. All of this combined to create a remarkable homogeneity, and in that sense Brugge and Ghent are indeed twin towns, and Kortrijk, Ieper, and the others are the closest of kin. It also helped shape the Flemish identity, and even today many a Fleming would, if left to his own devices, build himself a home that would not look out of place in medieval Brugge or Ghent.

Tour 1: Ghent

Numbers in the margin correspond with places of interest on the Ghent, Brugge, and the Coast map.

The Flemish call it Gent; the French, Gand. The English variant, **Ghent,** exists only to prevent a mispronunciation. Long ago, however, the English called it Gaunt, as in John of Gaunt; English links with the city go back to the 14th century.

The city grew up around two 7th-century abbeys, Sint-Pieter (St. Peter) and Sint-Baafs (St. Bavo), and the 9th-century castle of 's-Gravensteen, which dominates the River Leie. The canal joining Ghent and Brugge's port at Damme was dug in the

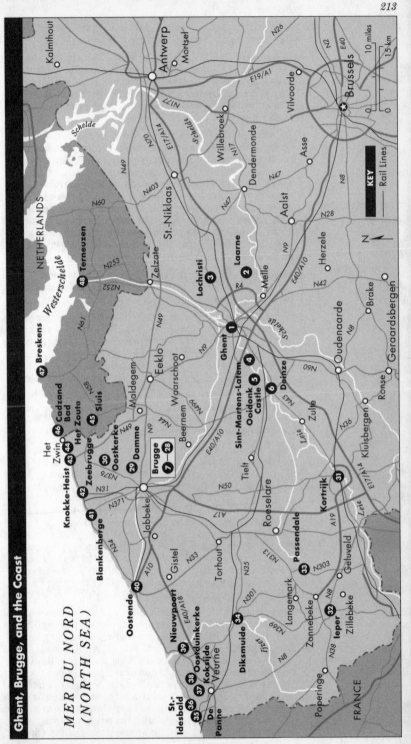

Ghent, Brugge, and the Coast

MER DU NORD
(NORTH SEA)

NETHERLANDS

FRANCE

13th century, and a hundred years later more than 5,000 men were working at the weaver's trade in Ghent.

In the early Middle Ages, the wealthy burghers were loyal to the counts of Flanders, who owed allegiance to the kings of France. But the weavers were dependent for their livelihood on wool shipments from England. Patrician families built fortified houses to make themselves secure in their own town; a few of them still stand.

In 1448, the people of Ghent refused to pay a salt tax imposed by Philip the Good, duke of Burgundy. For five years their militia stood firm against Philip's troops, and when they were finally overwhelmed, 16,000 townspeople perished. Ghent continued to rebel, again and again, against perceived injustices. The emperor himself, Charles V, who was born in Ghent, was not immune to their wrath. He responded by razing the St. Bavo Abbey and suppressing city rights. Religious fervor was added to this volatile mixture when the Calvinist iconoclasts proclaimed a republic in 1577, only to be overthrown by Spanish forces seven years later.

In the 18th century French armies marched on Ghent on four different occasions. This did little to dampen the conflict between French and Flemish speakers in the city.

Ghent was rescued from economic oblivion by a daring young man named Lieven Bauwens, who in 1800 smuggled a spinning jenny out of Britain in a neat reversal of what had happened hundreds of years earlier, when Flemish weavers emigrated to England. Bauwens's exploit provided the foundation for a textile industry that employed 160,000 workers a century later.

To facilitate textile exports, a new canal was built to link Ghent's inland port with the North Sea. It remains the foundation for modern industrial development, drawing a Volvo assembly plant and huge car carriers filled with Hondas.

The best spot to start a walk around Ghent is on **Sint-Michielsbrug** (St. Michael's Bridge), with its view of the glory of Ghent, the three great medieval steeples. Closest by is the tower of the **Sint-Niklaaskerk** (St. Nicholas's Church), the parish church of Ghent's merchants. Its sober, early Gothic style is sometimes called Scheldt Gothic, for it traveled down the River Scheldt from Tournai, where it originated. Next comes the **Belfort** (Belfry), begun in 1314 and not really completed until 1913, when the spire with its gilded details was added, based on the original 14th-century elevation. In the background stands the honey-colored sandstone tower of the Sint-Baafskathedraal (St. Bavo's Cathedral), begun in the 13th century but finished in the 16th in the ornate Brabant Gothic style.

Across the bridge, turn right and walk down the steps to Korenlei. Here is another magnificent view: the **Graslei** on the other side of the River Leie. The row of buildings along this old quay was restored for the World's Fair of 1913. The guild house of the **Vrije Schippers** (Free Boatmen) at No. 14 is a late-Gothic building from 1531; the guild dominated inland shipping. No. 11 is the **Korenmetershuis** (Grain Measurers' House), a late-Baroque building from 1698. Next to it is the narrow Renaissance **Tolhuis** (Toll House), where taxes were levied on grain shipments. It stands side by side with the brooding Romanesque **Koornstapelhuis** (Granary), nicknamed the *Spijker* (Spike), which was built in the 12th century and served its original purpose for 600 years; this was where the grain that the tax men had claimed was stored. The guild house of the **Metselaars** (Stone Masons), finally, is a copy of a house from 1527 constructed on this site in 1913. The original, which stands near the transept of St. Nicholas's Church, has also recently been restored. Every night in season (Fri.–Sat. nights Nov.–Apr.), the Graslei and all other historic monuments are illuminated from sunset to midnight.

From the Grasbrug at the end of Korenlei you have a fine view of the old **Groot Vleeshuis** (Great Meat Hall), an early 15th-century sandstone building on the bank of the Leie, almost at its confluence with the Lieve Canal. Turning back from the bridge and continuing north on Jan Breydelstraat you come to the **Museum voor Sierkunst** (Museum of Decorative Arts), with splendid 18th-century salons and a new contemporary design section. *Jan Breydelstraat 5. Admission: BF80. Open Tues.– Sun. 9–12:30 and 1:30–5:30.*

| Time Out | If you're wandering around after 7 PM, stop in at **Tap en Tepel** (Gewad 7, tel. 091/23–90–00), a wine and cheese house filled with flickering candles and lined with shelves of wine bottles. |

Turn toward the canal on Burgstraat, and as you cross the Hoofdbrug, **'s-Gravensteen**, the castle of the counts of Flanders, looks rather like an enormous old battleship, improbably steaming down the Lieve Canal. Even today, there's a splendid view over the rooftops of old Ghent from its windswept battlements. Rebuilt a number of times—most recently in the 19th century to reflect what the Victorians thought a medieval castle should look like—it has little in common with the original fortress conceived by Count Baldwin (of the Iron Arm) to discourage marauding Norsemen.

Its purpose, too, from protection to oppression as the conflict deepened between feudal lords and unruly townspeople. One of the rooms contains an exhibition of instruments of torture, and there is an *oubliette* (secret dungeon), deep below the floor of another room. It was here that Lieven Bauwens's purloined spinning mule was installed, the first on the Continent; soon the castle's chambers were invaded by clattering looms and flying shuttles, and Ghent became a textile center to rival Manchester.

Many of the workers lived in the **Patershol** area. You reach it by crossing Sint-Veerleplein, taking the Kraanlei, and turning left into one of the narrow lanes. Once a badly neglected slum, this has lately become a desirable address for young and well-to-do families who have converted many of the small houses for their use, interspersed with smart cafés and restaurants.

Back on Kraanlei is the **Museum voor Volkskunde** (Folk Museum), in a 16th-century almshouse. The many small rooms have been reconstructed to convey an idea of life in Ghent a hundred years ago: One room is a grocer's shop, another a tavern, a third a weaver's workshop, and there are several bourgeois rooms. *Kraanlei 65, tel. 091/23–13–36. Admission: BF50. Open Mar.– Nov., daily 9–12:30 and 1:30–5:30; Nov.–Mar., Tues.–Sun. 10–noon and 1:30–5.*

Time Out The popular **Caffe Wolff,** in a Renaissance building at Kraanlei 27, an excellent stop for coffee and cake, a beer, or an aperitif.

Two Baroque houses along Kraanlei have elaborately decorated facades. The panels of No. 79 represent the five senses, crowned by a figure of a flute player, while those of No. 77 illustrate six acts of mercy. The house used to be an inn, and taking in travelers was considered the seventh act.

Across the river stands a small 15th-century cannon on the right, known as Dulle Griet. Up Meersenierstraat is the **Vrijdagmarkt,** a square that becomes particularly lively during the weekly Friday market. It was here that Jacob Van Artevelde urged the people to take up arms against the French in the Hundred Years' War and here that mass meetings of socialists were held to rouse the workers earlier in this century.

Straight ahead, the second street on the right, Belfortstraat, takes you down toward the Town Hall. At the junction of Hoogport is **Sint-Jorishof** (Botermarkt 2), one of the oldest hotels in the world, in business since 1228. The present step-gabled building was constructed in the 1470s.

In the 13th century, when Ghent's population topped 60,000, there were more than a hundred private homes equipped with towers, from which merchant princes could survey the traffic on the Rivers Leie and Scheldt, and the Lieve Canal. One such family was the Van der Sickelens, and their name lives on in the **Kleine Sikkel** from the 14th century on the corner of Biezekapelstraat, a Romanesque town house of unhewn stone; in the **Grote Sikkel** across the street, a less austere building from the 15th century; and in the **Achtersikkel** behind it, the most attractive of the three, with Gothic buildings grouped around a white Renaissance tower. Nowadays, this is the home of the Ghent Conservatory. None of these three buildings is open to visitors.

The **Town Hall** is built in two very different architectural styles. Antwerp's Domien de Waghemakere and Mechelen's Rombout Keldermans were called in to build it in 1516, and they designed a town hall that would put all others to shame. Among its features are the tower on the corner of Hoogpoort and Botermarkt, the balcony expressly built for the announcement of proclamations, the projecting choir of the Magistrates' Chapel, and, above all, the lacelike tracery that embellishes its facade. Before the building could be completed, the taxes imposed by Charles V had drained the city's resources. When work resumed in 1580, during the short-lived Protestant Republic, the Gothic style had fallen from favor and been replaced by that of the Renaissance. *Botermarkt, tel. 091/24–00–24. Admission: BF60. Guided visits only. Mon.–Fri. 4 PM.*

Just across the Gouden Leeuwplein, named for the Golden Lion of Flanders, stands the proud **Belfort** (Belfry), 91 meters (300 feet) high, which symbolizes the power of the guilds in the 14th century. The Belfry contained the documents listing the privileges of the city, protected behind double doors with triple locks, and bells that were rung in moments of danger until Charles V ordered them removed. Now a 52-bell carillon hangs on the fifth floor, and one of the damaged old bells rests at the foot of the tower. *Sint-Baafsplein, tel. 091/23–99–77. Admis-*

sion: BF100. Open daily 10–12:30, with guided visits 10 minutes after each hour.

The Belfry is adjoined by the **Lakenhalle,** (Cloth Hall). Its vaulted basement was used as a prison for 150 years and is now a restaurant.

Across the square on the other side of the Belfry is **St. Bavo's Cathedral,** which contains one of the greatest treasures in Christendom. Originally dedicated to St. John, it became the site for the veneration of Ghent's own saint after Charles V had the old Abbey of St. Bavo razed. The Order of the Golden Fleece—instituted in Brugge by Philip the Good in 1430 and presided over today by King Juan Carlos of Spain as grand master—was convened here in 1559 by Philip II of Spain, and the coats of arms of the 51 knights who attended still hang in the south transept. The remarkably ornate pulpit is carved in white Italian marble and black Danish oak. In one of the radiating chapels hangs a Rubens masterpiece, *Saint Bavo's Entrance into the Monastery.*

It is, however, for the Adoration of the Mystic Lamb, now in the De Villa chapel to the left of the entrance, that crowds throng the cathedral. This stupendous polyptych by Hubert and Jan van Eyck was completed in 1432, and it has had a history as tumultuous as that of Ghent itself. When the iconoclasts smashed St. Bavo's stained-glass windows and other treasures, the painting was hidden in the tower. Napoleon had it carried off to Paris. The panels of Adam and Eve (which Joseph II, a Holy Roman emperor, had found prurient) disappeared and remained lost for a hundred years. The other side panels were sold and hung in a Berlin museum. In 1920 the masterpiece was again complete, but 14 years later a thief removed the panels on the lower left side. He returned St. John the Baptist but apparently died while waiting for a ransom for the panel of the Just Judges. Most people believe the panel is still hidden somewhere in Ghent, possibly even in the cathedral. The whole altarpiece was removed to France for safekeeping during World War II, but the Germans found it and had it taken away. American troops eventually found it in an abandoned salt mine in Austria.

The central panel is based on the Book of Revelations: "And I looked, and, lo, a Lamb stood on the mount Sion, and with him an hundred forty and four thousand, having his Father's name written in their foreheads." There are not quite that many people in the painting, but it does depict 248 figures and 42 different types of flowers, each botanically correct. But statistics do not even suggest its grandeur. It uses a miniaturist technique to express the universal; realism, to portray spirituality. To the medieval viewer it was an artistic *Summa Theologica,* a summation of all things revealed about the relationship between God and the world.

An old tradition identifies the horseman in the foreground of the panel to the immediate left as Hubert van Eyck, while the fourth figure from the left is believed to be his brother Jan. No other work by Hubert van Eyck has survived, and it is thought that he died in about 1426 after working on the altarpiece for four years. Jan was brought from Brugge to continue the work, using brushes so delicate that the finest consisted of a single boar's bristle. It was completed on May 6, 1432.

In the Vicinity **Laarne Castle** lies 13 kilometers (8 miles) east of Ghent, and you
reach it on R4, in the direction of Melle, and then on secondary
② roads to **Laarne.** Built in the 14th century to protect the city's
eastern approaches, it was converted to peaceful use in the
17th; it is one of the best-preserved medieval strongholds in
Belgium. Inside are fine examples of Brussels tapestry weaving and an outstanding collection of silver from the 15th to the
18th century. *Rte R4, Exit 5, Heusden–Laarne, tel. 091/30-
91–55. Admission: BF120. Open July–Aug., daily 10–noon
and 2–6; Sept.–Dec. and Feb.–June, Tues.–Sun. 10–noon and
2–6.*

Return to Ghent on N449 north, turning west on N70 to
③ **Lochristi.** It is the center of the Ghent flower-growing region,
and in season the city and its gardens are a riot of begonias and
azaleas.

The shores of the River Leie have attracted many painters.
Take N43 in the direction of Deinze, and turn off to
④ **Sint-Martens-Latem** with its 15th-century wooden windmill.
Gustave van de Woestyne and his friends worked here in the
early years of this century and were followed by Constant
Permeke and the Expressionists after World War I. In the
neighboring village of **Deurle,** the house and studio of the
Ghent painter Gust De Smet has been turned into the **Museum
Dhondt-Dhaenens.** It contains a major collection of expression-
ist paintings, including works by Permeke, Van den Berghe and
Albert Servaes. *Admission: house and studio, each BF20.
Both open Mar.–Nov., Wed.–Sat. 2–5, Sun. 10–noon and 2–5.*

⑤ On a bend of the river stands **Ooidonk Castle,** a magnificent and
largely untouched palatial abode in Hispano-Flemish style,
still inhabited. It was the property of Count Hoorn, the Flemish patriot executed in 1568 by the Spanish. *Tel. 091/82–61–23.
Admission: BF120. Open Easter–mid-Sept., Sun. 2–5:30;
July–Aug., also Sat. same hours. Park open daily.*

⑥ In **Deinze,** finally, is an attractive Gothic church next to the river, and beside it the **Museum van Deinze en Leiestreek,** with
works by the impressionist Emile Claus as well as by the Latem
group of painters. *Lucien Matthyslaan 3, tel. 091/86–00–11.
Admission: BF40. Open Mon and Wed.–Fri. 2–5, weekends
10–noon and 2–5.*

Tour 2: Brugge

The city may be better known by its French name, Bruges, but
you'll score points with the locals by using the correct Flemish
form. After all, you wouldn't call Liège by the Flemish Luik.

Linked with the estuary of the Zwin on the North Sea by a nav-
igable waterway, the city became one of the most active members of the Hanseatic League in the 13th century, exporting
Flemish cloth and importing fish from Scandinavia, furs from
Russia, wine from Gascony, and silk from Venice. Italian merchants from Lombardy, Tuscany, and Venice set themselves up
in Brugge, and the town established Europe's first stock exchange.

In 1301, the French Queen Jeanne of Navarre was annoyed by
the finery flaunted by the women of Brugge. "I thought I alone
was queen," she said, "and here I am surrounded by hundreds
more." The men of Brugge, in return, were annoyed at being

requested to pay for the French royal couple's lavish reception. One fine morning in May 1302, they fell upon and massacred the French garrison and then went on with the men of Ghent and Ieper to defeat the French cavaliers in the Battle of the Golden Spurs—commemorated to this day as the epitome of Flemish nationalism.

Brugge is where Flemish painting began. In fact, painting with oil was invented by Hubert and Jan van Eyck in the 1420s and spread to Italy at a later date. The art of the so-called Flemish primitives represented a revolution in realism, portraiture, and perspective; it brings their era alive in astonishing detail. Jan van Eyck was named court painter to Philip the Good, duke of Burgundy, who married Isabella of Portugal in a ceremony of ostentatious luxury in Brugge's Prinsenhof in 1429.

The last Burgundian feast in Brugge was the wedding of Duke Charles the Bold to Margaret of York, sister of England's Edward IV, in 1468. In August every five years (next in 1996) it is reenacted in a splendid pageant called the Feast of the Golden Tree, with tableaux of Flemish legend and history as magistrates and guilds welcome the sovereign couple to the city.

At the end of the century adversity struck. Flemish weavers had emigrated across the Channel and taught their trade to the English, who became formidable competitors. Even worse, the Zwin had begun to silt up, and the people of Brugge did not have the nerve or the funds to build the canal that might have saved them. Instead, trade and fortune switched to Antwerp.

In the 19th century, it was British travelers on their way to view the battlefield of Waterloo who rediscovered Brugge and spread its fame as a perfectly preserved medieval town. A novel by Georges Rodenbach, *Bruges-la-Morte* (Bruges, the Dead), brought more visitors but created an image that has been difficult to throw off. The principal industry in Brugge today is, inevitably, tourism. It is also the administrative center of West Flanders and incorporates within its city limits the new port of Zeebrugge as well as some sophisticated industries and two fiercely competitive soccer teams.

The Historic Heart   *Numbers in the margin correspond with places of interest on the Brugge map.*

❼ A good place to start exploring Brugge is the **Markt,** through the centuries the center of the city's commercial life. In the middle stands the statue of the city's medieval heroes, Jan Breydel and Pieter de Coninck, who led the commoners of Flanders to their short-lived victory over the aristocrats of France. On the south side of the Markt stands the 13th-century **Halle** (Cloth Hall). In its heyday it was occupied by stalls where lengths of brightly colored cloth were piled high. The **Belfort** (Belfry) towers above it, rising to a height of 82 meters (270 feet). It commands the city and the surrounding countryside with more puissance than grace. The octagonal lantern that crowns the tower, added in the 15th century, contains the 47 bells of the remarkable Brugge carillon. *Admission: BF80. Open Apr.–Sept., daily 9:30–5; Oct.–Mar., daily 9:30–12:30 and 1:30–5. Carillon concerts Sept.–June, noon Wed. and Sat.–Sun. noon; July–Aug., Mon., Wed. and Sat.–Sun. noon.*

The west and north sides of the market square are lined with old guild houses. Most of them shelter restaurants of unre-

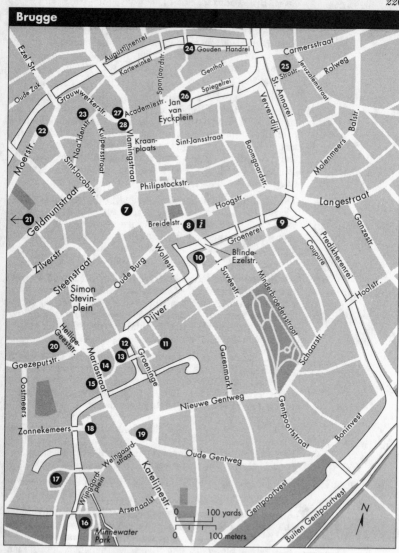

Brugge

Begijnhof, **17**

Brangwyn Museum, **12**

Burg, **8**

Godshuis Onze-Lieve-Vrouw der Zeven Weeen, **19**

Godshuizen De Pelikaan, **9**

Gouden Handrei, **24**

Groeninge Museum, **11**

Gruuthuse Museum, **13**

Hof van Bladelin, **23**

Huidenvettersplein, **10**

Huize ter Buerze, **27**

Markt, **7**

Memling Museum, **15**

Minnewater, **16**

Onze-Lieve Vrouwekerk, **14**

Saaihalle, **28**

Sint-Jakobskerk, **22**

Sint-Salvators-kathedraal, **20**

Speelmanskapel, **21**

Tolhuis, **26**

Vlissinghe, **25**

Walplein, **18**

markable quality that spill out over the sidewalk. On the east stand the provincial government house and the post office, an excellent pastiche of Burgundian Gothic.

8 Breidelstraat, on the left of the Belfry, leads directly to the **Burg.** It is an enchanted square, never more so than when discreetly floodlighted after dark. The Burg derives its name from the fortress built by Baldwin of the Iron Arm, which is long since gone. So is, alas, the Carolingian cathedral of St. Donaas, built around 900 and wantonly destroyed by French Republicans in 1799; the cathedral's site is now a small park.

Opposite, in the corner of the square, stands the small **Heilig Bloed Basiliek** (Basilica of the Holy Blood). The Lower Chapel has kept its austere 12th-century Romanesque character, with massive pillars supporting a low, vaulted roof. The baptismal scene carved on the tympanum is original.

A beautiful Gothic stairway leads to the Upper Chapel, which was twice destroyed—by Protestant iconoclasts in the 16th century and by French Republicans in the 18th—but both times rebuilt. There is a small museum next to the basilica containing the reliquary used to carry a phial thought to contain some drops of the blood of Christ during the annual procession and two outstanding *volets* (shutters) painted by Pieter Pourbus. *Admission: BF20. Open Apr.–Sept., Thurs.–Tues. 9:30–noon and 2–6, Wed. 9:30–noon; Oct.–Mar., daily 10–4.*

Next to the basilica, the gleaming white sandstone **Stadhuis** (Town Hall), built at the end of the 14th century in Flamboyant Gothic, served with its strong vertical lines as the model for town halls in other Flemish cities such as Brussels and Leuven. The figures that originally adorned the facade were smashed by the French Republicans and have been replaced by modern replicas. Inside, a staircase mounts to the Gothic Hall, which has a marvelous double-vaulted timber roof ornamented with 19th-century romantic frescoes. *Admission:* BF40. Open Apr.–Sept., daily 9:30–5; Oct.–March 9:30–12:30 and 2–5.

The Town Hall is linked with the graceful **Oude Griffie** (Office of Records) by a bridge arching over the narrow Blinde Ezelstraat (BlindAss Street). Two centuries younger than its neighbor, it is a mixture of Gothic and Flemish Renaissance elements. The building is topped by an effigy of Justice, flanked by Moses and Aaron. It is now occupied by departments of the city administration.

Squeezed into the corner beside the Office of Records is the tiny **Museum van het Brugse Vrije** (Museum of the Brugge County Council), a remnant of the 15th-century county hall. Its principal treasure is the courtroom with its huge oak and black-marble chimneypiece. A large bas-relief, carved in dark oak by Guyot de Beaugrant depicts a robust, nearly life-size Charles V. *Admission: BF20. Open Feb.–Dec., Tues.–Sun. 10–noon and 1:30–5.*

Where the rest of the county hall once stood is the **Gerechtshof** (Court of Justice), a Baroque palace that now houses the tourist office and other city offices.

Time Out **Opus** 4 is reached through the shopping gallery Ten Steeghere, which starts next to the basilica. It's a good place for a quiet beer, snack, or cake overlooking a pleasant stretch of canal.

Blinde Ezelstraat leads from the Burg across the canal. To the left is Steenhouwersdijk, which overlooks the brick rear gables that were part of the original county hall. The Meebrug (Mee Bridge) offers an especially good view. Farther along the

9 Groenerei stand the **Godshuizen De Pelikaan.** These alms-houses were built in the early 18th century, but others in Brug-ge were built as long ago as the 14th century and as recently as the beginning of the 20th.

Return to the Blinde Ezelstraat bridge and the **Vis Markt** (Fish Market), where fresh seafood from Zeebrugge is sold every day

10 except Sunday and Monday. Just beyond is **Huidenvettersplein** (Tanners' Square), with its 17th-century guild house.

Follow Rozenhoedkaai and its continuation, the Dijver, to the

11 **Groeninge Museum,** set back from the street behind a medieval gate. Although it is small, this is one of the world's essential museums and merits a half-day visit. In the very first room hangs Jan van Eyck's wonderfully realistic *Madonna with Canon Van der Paele.* Van Eyck achieved texture and depth through multiple layers of oil and varnish, and his technique has withstood the ravages of more than five centuries. All the Flemish primitives and their successors—Petrus Christus, Hugo Van der Goes, Hans Memling, Gerard David, Pieter Bruegel (both Elder and Younger), Pieter Pourbus—are repre-sented at this feast. The survey of Belgian art continues through the romantics and realists to surrealists and contem-porary art. *Dijver 12, tel. 050/33–99–11. Admission: BF100. For BF250 you can buy a combination ticket also including the Gruuthuse, Memling, and Brangwyn museums. Open Apr.–Sept., daily 9:30–5; Oct.–Mar., Wed.–Mon. 9:30–12:30 and 2–5.*

Time Out The attractive **Taverne Groeninge** (Dijver 13) is decorated with works by Frank Brangwyn.

12 The **Brangwyn Museum** is in fact next door. The 18th-century house contains hundreds of drawings and paintings by Frank Brangwyn (1867–1956). His father, an architect, had, like a number of other British romantics, settled in Brugge, and the son stayed on to paint many an homage to his adopted city. *Dijver 16, tel. 050/33–99–11. Admission: BF60. Open Apr.–Sept., daily 9:30–5; Oct.–Dec. and Feb.–Mar., Wed.–Mon. 9:30–12:30 and 2–5.*

13 Next on museum row is the **Gruuthuse Museum,** once the home of Lodewijk Van Gruuthuse, a prominent and powerful noble-man of the Netherlands in Burgundian times who financed Edward IV's campaign to regain the throne of England. Room 6, however, is an attractive Gothic interior with a 15th-century mantelpiece and stained-glass windows. *Dijver 17, tel. 050/33–99–11. Admission: BF100. Open Apr.–Sept., daily 9:30–5; Oct.–Mar., Wed.–Mon. 9:30–12:30 and 2–5.*

14 **Onze-Lieve-Vrouwekerk** (Church of Our Lady), a block away, was begun in the 13th century, and the west front with its two round towers is typical of the early Gothic style. The church's most precious treasure is the small *Virgin and Child* by Michelangelo, carved in white marble, which sits in a black marble niche in an altar at the end of the south aisle. The choir contains two mausoleums: that of Mary of Burgundy, who died in 1482 at the age of 25 after a fall from her horse; and that of her father, Charles the Bold, killed in 1477 while laying siege to Nancy in France. *Gruuthusestraat. Open Apr.–Sept., daily 10–11:30 and 2:30–5; Oct.–Mar., 10–11:30 and 3–4:30. Closed Sun. AM except to worshipers.*

⑮ The **Memling Museum** is right across Mariastraat, inside the medieval **Sint-Janshospitaal** (St. John's Hospice). It contains just six works, but they are paintings of breathtaking quality. Hans Memling was born in Germany about 1435 but spent the greater part of his life in Brugge, possibly attracted by the Burgundian court. In the *Altarpiece of St. John the Baptist and St. John the Evangelist,* two leading personages of the court are believed to be portrayed, Mary of Burgundy (buried in the church across the street) as St. Catherine and Margaret of York as St. Barbara.

The Sint-Janshospitaal was founded in the 12th century and remained in use until the early 20th. The middle ward, the oldest of three, was built in the 13th century in Romanesque style. There is a fascinating painting from the 18th century that shows patients arriving by sedan chair and being fed and ministered to by sisters and clerics. *Mariastraat 38, tel. 050/33–25–62. Admission: BF100. Open Apr.–Sept., daily 9:30–5; Oct.–Mar., Thurs.–Tues. 9:30–noon and 2–5.*

To return to the Markt, turn left on Mariastraat, walk up to Simon Stevinplein, and then turn right on Steenstraat.

City of Merchants The **Minnewater** (inner harbor), at the south end of the city cen-
⑯ ter, was created in the 13th century to expand the city's capacity as a trading center. The swans of Minnewater evoke an etymological legend or perhaps a historical truth: In 1488 the people of Brugge imprisoned Maximilian of Austria and decapitated his adviser, Pieter Lanchals. Now, *Lanchals* is very close to the Dutch for "long neck," so when Maximilian was liberated, he ordered Brugge to expiate its crime by keeping swans in the canals of the city in perpetuity.

⑰ The **Begijnhof** is just off Wijngaardplein at the northern end of the Minnewater. This serene close of small whitewashed houses surrounding a pleasant green is at its best in spring when daffodils bloom. If you hear the convent bell, don't hesitate to enter the Renaissance church. The Begijnhof (Beguinage in French) was founded in 1245 by Margaret of Constantinople, primarily as a refuge for widows of Crusaders who had fallen in foreign lands, and the congregation flourished for 600 years. The Beguines have been replaced by Benedictine sisters. Most of the present-day houses are from the 16th or 17th century but have maintained the architectural style of the houses that preceded them. Silence is requested. *Monasterium de Wijngaard, Oud Begijnhof, tel. 050/33–00–11. Admission free; BF45 for a house visit. Open Apr.–Sept., Mon.–Thurs. and Sat. 9:30–noon and 1:45–5:30, Fri. 1:45–5:30, Sun. 10:45–noon and 1:45–6; Oct.–Nov. and Mar., Sun. 10:30–5; Dec.–Feb., Wed.–Thurs. and weekends 10:30–5.*

⑱ To the left from the Begijnhof on Wijngaardstraat and almost immediately left again is **Walplein,** one of Brugge's many delightful squares.

Time Out Here you can choose between **Nieuw 't Walnutje,** for a snack or coffee, and **Straffe Hendrik,** part of the Henri Maes brewery.

From Walstraat, you can walk around Oude Gentweg to look at the attractive **Godshuis Onze-Lieve-Vrouw der Zeven Weeen** (Almshouse of Our Lady of the Seven Sorrows) in Drie Kroezenstraat, and additional almshouses of the 17th century in Nieuwe Gentweg.

Turn right up Mariastraat and branch left into Heilige-Geeststraat, which leads to **Sint-Salvatorskathedraal** (St. Savior's Cathedral), an impressive Gothic brick building with a cluster of chapels radiating from the choir. The upper part of the tower was damaged by fire in 1853 and rebuilt. Inside, the coats of arms of knights of the Order of the Golden Fleece hang above the choir stalls; a chapter was held here in 1478. The finest works of art can be seen in the adjoining cathedral museum and chapter house. They include the *Martyrdom of St. Hippolytus* by Dirk Bouts, and works by Lancelot Blondeel and Pieter Pourbus. *Steenstraat, tel. 050/33–00–44. Admission: BF30. Open Apr.–June and Sept., daily 2–5; July–Aug., daily 10–noon and 2–5; Oct.–Mar., Mon.–Tues. and Thurs.–Sat. 2–5.*

Across Zuidzandstraat and through Zilverpand, a modern shopping mall, Noordzandstraat leads left to the large 't Zand square, where, on the right at the end of Speelmansrei, along the canal, stands a charming chapel. The **Speelmanskapel** was founded in 1421 by the guild of minstrels, who enjoyed exclusive rights to provide the music for public functions. Farther along, on Moerstraat, is **Sint-Jakobskerk** (St. Jacob's Church). As the parish church of the mercantile community, it accumulated so much wealth that it is now almost overencumbered with works of art. Chief among them is the *Legend of St. Lucy* triptych, painted by an unknown master of the 15th century.

To the right on Sint-Jakobsstraat and left on Boterhuis, to Naaldenstraat, is the **Hof van Bladelin,** built in 1451 for Pieter Bladelin, councillor to Philip the Good and one of the richest men in the Burgundian Netherlands. In the courtyard is an arcade with carved stone consoles from Bladelin's time. Under the arcade on the street side, one of the consoles is decorated with three feathers passing through a ring. This was the emblem of Lorenzo the Magnificent; the Medicis bought the Bladelin house in 1466 to serve as both bank and residence. *Naaldenstraat 16. Admission free. Open Apr.–Sept., Mon.–Sat. 9–noon and 2–6, Sun. 10–noon and 2–6; Oct.–Mar., Mon.–Sat. 9–noon and 2–4, Sun. 10–noon and 2–4.*

Across Grauwwerkerstraat and through Pieter Pourbusstraat, Vlamingstraat leads left over the bridge to Augustijnenrei, one of the loveliest of quays. Directly ahead are the three arches of the Augustijnenbrug. Dating from 1391, it's the oldest bridge in Brugge. Crossing it and turning left on the cobbled **Gouden Handrei,** you arrive at the broad main canal, which once flowed all the way to the Markt.

Time Out Across the main canal is the **Vlissinghe** (Blekersstraat 2A). This is the oldest pub in Brugge; people have been enjoying their beer here since 1552.

Follow the branch of the canal that curves right toward Jan van Eyckplein. Ahead is the **Poortersloge,** a late-Gothic building with a slender spire, once a meeting place for the burghers of Brugge. The rampant bear that occupies one niche here shares Brugge's coat of arms with the lion of Flanders.

The present-day canal ends at **Jan van Eyckplein,** which features a statue of the painter. On the right is the old **Tolhuis** (Toll House), built in 1477. The lucrative right to collect tolls on goods to be shipped inland from Brugge was held at the time by Pieter of Luxemburg, whose coat of arms adorns the facade. Next door is a very narrow 15th-century building that was owned by the guild of porters. **Spanjaardstraat,** on the right, leads up to the quay where goods from Spain were unloaded. The house at No. 9 was owned by one Gonzalez d'Aguilera; this is where St. Ignatius of Loyola stayed when he came to Flanders on holidays from his studies at the Sorbonne in Paris.

From Jan van Eyckplein, Academiestraat leads to Vlamingstraat. This intersection was the original Beursplein (not to be confused with the present Beursplein, back of 't Zand). On it is the **Huize ter Buerze** (House of Purses), built in 1453 and recently carefully restored. As early as the 13th century, an inn stood here with a sign of three purses. "Purse" is *bursa* in Latin. It gave its name to the trading that went on here.

The houses of the Venetian and Florentine merchants have disappeared, but the **Saaihalle** (Serge Hall), formerly the Genoese trading house, still stands, just across the narrow Grauwwerkerstraat from the House of Purses. Originally the top floor had a similar crenellated curtain wall, but it has been replaced by a bell-shaped gable. The house (now occupied by the offices of a bank) is entered through an ornate Gothic doorway with a relief of St. George, patron saint of Genoa. On the other side of Vlamingstraat lies **Kraanplaats** (Crane Place). Vlamingstraat leads back to the Markt, then as now at the center of Brugge.

In the Vicinity   *Numbers in the margin correspond with places of interest on the Ghent, Brugge, and the Coast map.*

The road to the small town of **Damme,** just 7 kilometers (4½ miles) north of Brugge, follows a canal lined with tall and slender poplars, all slightly bent by the prevailing breeze. You can ride a bike along the top of the levee, and if the return trip seems too daunting, you can take the bike aboard a miniature paddle steamer, the *Lamme Goedzak*.

In 1134 a tidal wave opened up an inlet of the sea from the Zwin to the neighborhood of Brugge, whose people were quick to build a canal to link up with it. Damme started life as a fishing village at the junction. It became an important port that held exclusive rights to import such varied commodities as wine from Bordeaux and herring from Sweden, and the "Maritime Law of Damme" became the standard for Hanseatic merchants.

It was in Damme's **Onze-Lieve-Vrouwekerk** (Church of Our Lady) that Charles the Bold and Margaret of York were married, and on the facade of the **Stadhuis** (Town Hall) you can see their effigies, the noble duke presenting the wedding ring to his fiancée. Damme was the home of the legendary Tijl Uilenspiegel, whose merry pranks, detailed in Charles de Coster's novel, *La Légende et les aventures héroïques . . . d'Ulenspiegel . . .* (1866), were often directed at the Spanish occupying force.

30 Another mile along the tree-planted canal is its confluence with the Leopold Canal; just past here is the village of **Oostkerke.** Less visited by tourists, it is more in keeping with the peaceful polder landscape.

Time Out For a genuine gourmet meal before returning to Brugge, you can visit **De Waterput** (Rondsaartstraat 1, Oostkerke, tel. 050/ 59–92–56), where you eat what the excellent chef suggests, there being no menu.

Tour 3: Battlefields

The highways south from Brugge and Ghent point in the direction of Flanders Fields, where decisive battles have been waged since the time of Julius Caesar. Here longbowmen fought cavalry in heraldic colors, and here the horrors of World War I were played out.

31 **Kortrijk** (Courtrai to unreconstructed French speakers) is about 50 kilometers (31 miles) south of Brugge and Ghent. The Battle of the Golden Spurs (which the French prefer to call the Battle of Courtrai) was fought immediately outside the city walls, close to the present Groeningelaan. On that fateful July 11, 1302, the poorly armed weavers and other craftsmen from Brugge, Ghent, and Ieper took on the flower of French nobility. The battle had actually been going well for the French infantrymen, but they were brushed aside by the mounted knights, who were spoiling for a fight. A hidden canal, the Groeninge, was the Flemings' greatest ally; many of the knights plunged into it, to be speared by the Flemish pikemen. After the battle, 700 pairs of golden spurs were removed from the bodies and triumphantly hung in the Church of Our Lady in Kortrijk as a votive offering.

A 14-meter-high (45-foot-high) neo-Gothic monument has been erected on the spot where the battle was fought, and it is commemorated on the weekend closest to July 13 with a parade or a tournament (for information, tel. 056/21–78–63). At the **Stedelijk Museum** you can inspect a large-scale model of the city as it was in the Middle Ages, showing the battle site. There is also a copy of the Oxford Chest (of unknown provenance), which is decorated with a series of scenes of the battle. *Broelkaai 6, tel. 056/21–19–92. Open Tues.–Sun. 10–noon and 2–5.*

Like almost every self-respecting Flemish town, Kortrijk can boast a stadhuis, a begijnhof, and an Onze-Lieve-Vrouwekerk. In this case, the Beguinage, with its cobbled streets and whitewashed houses, is an oasis of calm in the busy city, and the church contains a beautiful alabaster figure of St. Catherine from 1380, standing in the Chapel of the Counts of Flanders.

The River Leie passes through Kortrijk on its way to Ghent. In the Middle Ages it was known as the Golden River because of the fields of flax on its banks. The story of this industry is told in a series of tableaux in the **Nationaal Vlasmuseum** (National Flax Museum), installed in an old farmhouse. *Etienne Sabbelaan 4, tel. 056/21–01–38. Admission: BF50. Open Mar.– Nov., Tues.–Fri. 9:30–12:30 and 1:30–6, Mon. 1:30–6.*

Time Out The best dining in town, with prices to match, is at **Restaurant Filip Bogaert** (Minister Tacklaan 5, tel. 056/20–30–34). The chef is famous for his medallion of lobster.

③② Ieper—better known outside Flanders as Ypres, the "Wipers" of World War I—lies 32 kilometers (20 miles) due west of Kortrijk. This city was literally wiped off the face of the earth during the war of 1914–1918. Today's city is a painstaking reconstruction, which was not completed until after World War II. One tradition lives on, the **Kattenwoensdag** (Cat Wednesday) on the second Sunday of May, when cats (stuffed animals these days) are flung from the belfry by the town jester. The tradition goes back to the 10th century, and was part of a renunciation of the devil and his works. Now it is linked to a great parade of cats and floats.

The magnificent **Lakenhalle** (Cloth Hall) is a copy of a building that had stood here since 1304. It houses on the first floor the **Herinnerungsmuseum** (Museum of Remembrance). The bayonets and guns, uniforms and helmets, and medals and shells are all here, as well as useful maps of the battlefields and cemeteries. *Grote Markt, tel. 057/20–07–24. Admission: BF30. Open Easter–mid-Nov., daily 9:30–noon and 1:30–5:30.*

From the Cloth Hall, walking around the cathedral, you can reach **St. George's**, a small British church with an abundance of war memories and the adjoining **Pilgrims' Hall,** built for those who visit Ieper looking for a relative's grave. *Elverdingsestraat 1, tel. 057/21–62–12.*

One of the most moving of war memorials is the **Menin Gate,** five minutes' walk from the Grote Markt on Meensestraat. After World War I, the British built a vast arch in memory of the 300,000 soldiers who had perished nearby. Every night at 8, traffic is stopped at the gate as buglers sound the Last Post. The practice was interrupted during World War II and resumed the night the Germans left, September 6, 1944.

Some 44 million shells were fired over this stretch of the Western Front in the two wars, and a fair number failed to explode. Flemish farmers still turn up about 200 every month, and the bomb disposal experts have to be called in. The poison-gas canisters cause special concern.

There are more than 170 military cemeteries in the area. From Ieper, on N332 toward Zonnebeke, you can stop at **Potijze** to pay homage to the 3,748 whose resting place is the French cemetery. Just beyond **Geluveld,** halfway to Menen, on the site of the Kasteelhof 't Hooghe is one of the few places where bomb craters can still be seen. Follow the signs via Canadalaan and Sanctuary Wood to the **Museum of the Trenches**, which is highly interesting but in a state of some neglect. In addition to photographs, weapons, and assorted objects salvaged from the field of battle, the owner has preserved some of the original trenches and tunnels on his land. You'll need to wear boots to inspect them. *Canadalaan, Zillebeke, tel. 057/46–63–73. Admission: BF95. Open Apr.–Sept., daily 10–8; Oct.–Mar., daily 10–6.*

③③ North of Geluveld is **Passendale,** which gave its name to one of the most murderous battles in history. It is perhaps a hopeful irony that today the name is better known in Belgium as that of the buttery cheese this area produces. Near here is **Tyne Cot,** a

British cemetery with 12,000 graves. A few miles to the west is the German cemetery of **Langemark,** with 44,000 dead.

34 From Langemark, you can take N301 to **Diksmuide,** about 16 kilometers (10 miles) to the northwest. Like Ieper, this town has been completely rebuilt in its original style. A network of trenches west of the town, the Dodengang, can be visited; here Belgian troops faced their German adversaries for four years. In town, an 84-meter (275-foot) tower, the **IJzertoren,** has been erected in honor of the defenders.

Veurne, 14 kilometers (9 miles) west on N35, was the Belgian Army headquarters during World War I. For a town of just over 10,000, Veurne has an amazingly large and sumptuous **Grote Markt,** surrounded by buildings from the 16th and 17th centuries. On the last Sunday of July, a Procession of Penitents is organized in Veurne. On the Saturday preceding August 15, there's a festive late-night market in the Grote Markt.

Tour 4: The North Sea Coast

From De Panne in the southwest to Knokke in the northeast is only 65 kilometers (40 miles), but it's a considerable distance in terms of taste, from middle class to snob appeal. There's a total of 20 resorts, but sometimes it's difficult to know where one ends and the next begins. You can walk for miles along the dike, flanked by modern apartment houses where flats are let by the week or month; for many Belgians, an apartment by the sea is the equivalent of a summer house. All along the coast, parents help their kids fly kites, youngsters ride pedal cars, horseback riders thunder by next to the water's edge, lovers walk arm in arm, dogs chase sticks, children dig in the sand, and sun worshipers laze in deck chairs protected from the North Sea breezes by canvas windbreaks.

Belgians flock to the shore over the weekend all year round. Quite a few profess to like it best in the real off-season, when you can walk along the beach in the pale winter sun, filling your lungs with bracing sea air, and then warm up in a cozy tavern with a plate of steaming mussels.

35 It was at **De Panne,** almost at the French border, that Queen Elisabeth took up residence while King Albert I directed his country's forces from Veurne during World War I. Now it is primarily a family resort, with more than 50 hotels and pensions and an amusement park. The area west of the resort is a national park, **Westhoek** (Dynastielaan, tel. 058/41–13–02), where guided walks are organized in season.

36 **Sint-Idesbald** is also family oriented. For art lovers, the **Paul Delvaux Museum** is dedicated to the surrealist painter. You can follow his development from postimpressionism through expressionism to his very personal style. *Kabouterweg 42, tel. 058/52–12–29. Admission: BF125. Open July–Aug., daily 10:30–6:30; Apr.–June and Sept., Tues.–Sun. 10:30–6:30; Oct.–Dec., weekends and bank holidays 10:30–4:30.*

37 **Koksijde** offers more than beach life. The Hoge Blekker is at 33 meters (108 feet) the highest dune on the coast. Nearby are the ruins of the Cistercian **Duinenabdij** (Abbey of the Dunes) with an archaeological museum. *Koninklijke Prinslaan, tel. 058/51–63–41. Admission: BF75. Open July–Sept., daily 10–6; Oct.–Dec. and Feb.–June, daily 10–noon and 2–6.*

To the north of the abbey stands a new church, **Onze-Lieve-Vrouw ter Duinenkerk** (Our Lady of Sorrows of the Dunes Church), of striking modern design that suggests both the dunes and the sea.

Time Out **Verdonck,** next to the traffic lights on the Koninklijke baan (where the coastal tram runs), has outstanding ice cream and chocolates.

③⑧ At **Oostduinkerke** there are still some horseback shrimp fishers. At low tide, the sturdy horses, half immersed, trawl heavy nets along the shoreline.

③⑨ **Nieuwpoort,** at the estuary of the River IJzer, is where the sluices were opened in October 1914, inundating the polder and permanently halting the German advance. The estuary makes an excellent yachting port, and some 3,000 leisure craft are moored here. Nieuwpoort is also the home of a sizable fishing fleet and a lively fish market.

④⓪ **Oostende** (Ostende in French; Ostend in English) is the largest town and the oldest settlement on the coast, with a history going back to the 10th century. It was a pirate hideout for centuries, and from here Crusaders set sail for the Holy Land. In the early 17th century, Oostende withstood a Spanish siege for three years. One of continental Europe's first railways was built between Oostende and Mechelen in 1838, and regular mail packet services to Dover began in 1846. Modern Oostende leads a double life, as communications center and fishing port on the one hand, and as a fashionable resort on the other.

The painter James Ensor, who was born and spent most of his life in Oostende, has only lately been recognized as one of the great artists of the late 19th century. Using violent colors to express his frequently macabre or satirical themes, he depicted a fantastic carnival world peopled by masks and skeletons. His home, converted into a museum, **James Ensorhuis,** includes his studio. *Vlaanderenstraat 27. Admission: BF50. Open June–Sept., Wed.–Mon. 10–noon and 2–5.*

Paintings by Ensor and his contemporaries can be seen in the **Museum voor Schone Kunsten** (Fine Arts Museum). *Wapenplein, tel. 059/80–53–35. Admission: BF50. Open Nov.–Sept., Wed.–Mon. 10–noon and 2–5.*

Oostende also has a good modern art museum, the **Provinciaal Museum voor Moderne Kunst** (PMMK), where contemporary artists are well represented with works by Pierre Alechinsky, Roger Raveel, Pol Mara, and others. *Romestraat 11, tel. 059/508118. Admission: BF100. Open Wed.–Mon. 10–6.*

Time Out Among the pleasant brasseries and cafés around the Wapenplein in the center of the old town, **Falstaff** has a permanent exhibition of photographs of Oostende in the 1920s.

Along the **Visserskaai** (Fishermen's Wharf), next to the ferry port, fishwives hawk seafood in all its forms from stalls opposite an almost uninterrupted row of fish restaurants.

④① **Blankenberge,** once a small fishing port, has grown into a large resort with more than a hundred hotels and boarding houses. It has the only British-style amusement pier on the Belgian coast, with a modern aquarium and model ships. Blankenberge also has a Kursaal (Casino) and an attractive yachting harbor.

42 **Zeebrugge,** or Brugge-on-the-Sea, is the same size as the parent city, which is 14 kilometers (8 miles) inland. In addition to a sandy beach and a busy fishing port, Zeebrugge's chief distinction is its commercial port. You can tour the harbor and its installations by Euro Line sightseeing boat. *Cost: BF220. 1½-hour sailings June 15–Sept. daily at 11 and 2:30.*

43 **Knokke-Heist,** finally, is where Belgium's BCBG *(bon chic, bon genre)* come to play. It is, in fact, one resort made up of five areas, growing progressively more fashionable as you go north from Heist and Duinbergen on Albert-Strand to Knokke and
44 the splendid villas of **Het Zoute.** Along the Kustlaan, on the leeward side of the dike, you'll find virtually every fashionable shop in Brussels represented by a boutique, and all are open on Sunday. The people strolling along the Zeedijk tend to be bronzed and well dressed. The **Kursaal** (Casino) boasts an enormous chandelier of Venetian crystal, and some of the world's top entertainers come there to perform.

Time Out   The Van Bunnenplein is widely known as the Place M'as-tu-vu (Did-you-see-me Square); it's a gathering place for the chic. The **Belle Epoque** is a good spot to have a drink and people-watch.

The coast has one more treat in store for you, **Het Zwin** on the Dutch border, where Brugge once had its outlet to the sea. Now it's a 152-hectare (375-acre) nature reserve where at certain times salt water washes into the soil, and the flora and fauna are unusual. The best times to visit are in spring for the bird migrations and from mid-July to mid-August for the flowers. Next to the aviary, a former royal villa, the Pavillon du Zoute, serves as an attractive restaurant, and from the top of the dike there's a splendid view of the dunes and inlets. *Ooievaarslaan 8, tel. 050/60–70–86. Admission: BF130 adults, BF70 children. Open daily 9–7.*

Het Zwin continues on the Dutch side of the border. The Dutch province of **Zeeuwsch-Vlaanderen** stretches 60-odd kilometers (about 40 miles) to the mouth of the Scheldt, north of Antwerp. When Belgium declared its independence in 1830, this province stayed Dutch, mostly for religious reasons.

45 The best-known town is **Sluis,** reached from Knokke on N376, (N58 in the Netherlands). This small town shared the wealth of Brugge, for it was on the waterway that linked Brugge with the sea. Today it is home to many shops and restaurants.

46
47 The beach proper begins with **Cadzand Bad,** which has several good hotels, and continues to **Breskens** (where you can take a car ferry to Vlissingen on Walcheren). Zeeuwsch-Vlaanderen is well suited for a holiday with children precisely because the resorts are uncrowded, with wide and quiet beaches.

48 N252 south from the port city of **Terneuzen** links up with R4 to Ghent. There's a second car-ferry service east of Terneuzen, from Kloosterzande on N60 to Kruiningen on Walcheren. Going south on N60 you link up with N49 in Belgium, 26 kilometers (16 miles) from Antwerp.

What to See and Do with Children

Brugge The **Boudewijn Park and Dolphinarium** is near the motorway just over a mile south of the city. There are several daily shows, an educational exhibition, and other attractions. *A. De Baeckestraat 12, St-Michiels, tel. 050/38-38-38. Admission: BF320 adults, BF280 children for all attractions; BF180 adults, BF160 children for Dolphinarium only. Park open Easter–May, daily noon–6; May–Sept., daily 10–6; Sept., Wed. and weekends noon–6. Dolphinarium open daily, shows at 11AM and 4PM, more during peak season.*

The Coast The **Meli Park** at Adinkerke (close to De Panne) has all kinds of fun rides, animals, activities, and even a magic show. *De Pannelaan 68, tel. 058/42-02-02. Admission: BF450 adults, BF420 children. Open Apr.–mid-Sept., daily 10–6.*

In Oostende, youngsters like to visit the windjammer ***Mercator,*** which is moored in the yacht harbor. *Vindictivelaan, tel. 059/70-56-54. Admission: adults BF75, children BF40. Open May, June, Sept. daily 9–noon and 1–6; July, Aug. daily 9–7; Oct., Mar., Apr. weekends 10–noon and 1–5; Nov.–Feb. Sun. 10–noon and 1–4; closed Christmas and New Year.*

Ghent The unusual **School Museum Michel Thiery** highlights geography, fossils, shells, and so on, but the biggest attraction is a sound-and-light show featuring a large scale model of Ghent as it was 400 years ago. *Sint-Pietersplein 14, tel. 091/22-80-50. Admission: BF80 adults, children free. Open Mon.–Thurs. and Sat. 9–12:15 and 1:30–5:15, Fri. 9–12:15.*

Off the Beaten Track

Brugge The **Museum van Volkskunde** (Folklore Museum) is housed in a row of whitewashed almshouses originally built for retired shoemakers and contains various reconstructed interiors: grocery shop, living room, tavern. *Rolweg 40, tel. 050/33-00-44. Admission: BF60. Open Apr.–Sept., daily 9:30–5; Oct.–Dec. and Feb.–Mar., Wed.–Mon. 9:30–12:30 and 2–5.*

Down Balstraat is the privately owned **Jeruzalemkerk,** built by the Adornes brothers in 1428 and still the property of their descendants. Among several family tombs, the black marble mausoleum of Anselm Adornes and his wife is the most striking. *Peperstraat 3. Admission: see below. Open weekdays 10–noon and 2–6, Sat. 10–noon and 2–5.*

The **Kantcentrum** (Lace Center) is at the same address. It is a foundation that aims to maintain the quality and authenticity of this ancient craft. The center includes a lace museum, located in the Jerusalem almshouses in Balstraat, and a lace school where youngsters are taught the intricate art of the bobbins. *Peperstraat 3, tel. 050/33-00-72. Admission: BF40 for all 3. Open weekdays 2–6, Sat. 2–5.*

Ghent The **Sint-Baafsabdij** (St. Bavo's Abbey) east of the center goes back to the 7th century. England's Edward II stayed here with his Queen Philippa, and here it was that she gave birth to John of Gaunt (or Ghent), the future regent. The abbey was already very old when Charles V, another native son, ordered it demolished in 1540. The remnants of the abbey buildings have been left as they were, mostly romantic ruins. The oldest surviving part is an octagonal building from 1171. *Gandastraat 7, tel. 091/*

25–15–85. Admission: BF80 adults, BF20 children. Open Tues.–Sun. 9:30–5.

The **Klein Begijnhof** (Lange Violettenstraat 71) southeast of the center is the best preserved of Ghent's three beguinages. Founded in 1234 by Countess Joanna of Constantinople, it is protected by its wall and portal. The small houses, each identified by a statue of a saint, surround a spacious green and are still occupied by a small number of Beguines, leading the life stipulated by their founder 750 years ago. You may walk through the Klein Begijnhof (quietly, please), but the houses cannot be visited.

South of the city center, in Citadel Park, stands the **Museum voor Schone Kunsten** (Museum of Fine Arts), whose collections include two outstanding paintings by Hieronymus Bosch, *Saint Jerome* and *The Bearing of the Cross;* in the latter Christ is shown surrounded by grotesque faces of unmitigated cruelty. *Nicolaas de Liemaeckereplein 3, tel. 091/22–17–03. Admission: BF80. Open Tues.–Sun. 9–12:30 and 1:30–5:30.*

The lively **Museum van Hedendaagse Kunst** (Museum of Contemporary Art) is located in Sint-Pieters Abdij (St. Peter's Abbey). In addition to hyperrealism, pop art, and the rest, the collection includes works of great vitality by artists of the CO-BRA Group from Copenhagen, Brussels, and Amsterdam. *Sint-Pietersplein 9, tel. 091/22–17–03. Admission: BF80. Open Tues.–Sun. 9:30–5.*

Shopping

Brugge   Brugge has many trendy boutiques and shops, especially along **Steenstraat** and **Vlamingstraat,** both of which branch off from the Markt. **Ter Steeghere** mall, which links the Burg with Wollestraat, deftly integrates a modern development into the historic center. The largest and most pleasant mall is the **Zilverpand** off Zilverstraat, where 50-odd shops cluster in Flemish gable houses around a courtyard with sidewalk cafés.

Street Markets   The Burg is the setting for the **Wednesday Market** (weekly except July–Aug.) with flowers, vegetables, and fruit. The biggest is the **Saturday Market** on 't Zand. The **Fish Market** is held, appropriately, on the Vismarkt, daily except Sunday and Monday. All three are morning events, from 8 to approximately 12:30. On Saturday and Sunday afternoons (Mar.–Oct.) there's a **Flea Market** along the Dijver.

Specialty Stores   Some of the best known of Brugge's many **art and antiques** dealers are 't **Leerhuis** (Groeninge 35, tel. 050/33–03–02), which specializes in contemporary art; **Guyart** (Fort Lapin 37, tel. 050/33–21–59), which is both an art gallery and a tavern (open Thurs.–Tues. 3–10 PM); **Papyrus** (Walplein 41, tel. 050/33–66–87), specializing in silverware; **Classics Kunstatelier** (Oude Burgstraat 32–24), which has the best selection of Flemish hangings.

Brugge has been a center for **lace making** since the 15th century, and such intricate variations on the art as the rose pattern and the fairy stitch, which requires over 300 bobbins, were developed here. Most tourists buy lace as a souvenir costing a few hundred francs, and you can find it in a great many souvenir shops. Handmade lace in intricate patterns, however, takes a very long time to produce, and this is reflected in the price; for

519 M.P.H.

190 M.P.H.

75 M.P.H.

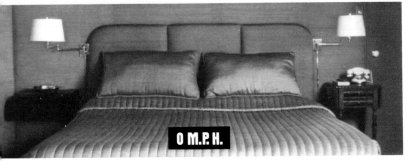

0 M.P.H.

WE LET YOU SEE EUROPE AT YOUR OWN PACE.

Regardless of your personal speed limits, Rail Europe offers everything to get you over, around and through anywhere you want in Europe. For more information, call our travel agent or **1-800-4-EURAIL.**

Rail Europe

work of this type you should be prepared to part with BF10,000 or more. The best shop for the serious lace lover is 't Apostelientje (Balstraat 11, tel. 050/33–78–60), across the street from the Lace Museum (*see* Off the Beaten Track, Brugge, *above*).

Ghent **Veldstraat** and the **Lange Munt** are major shopping streets. There are also several exclusive shopping galleries where boutiques are interspersed with cafés and restaurants, such as the **Bourdon Arcade** (Gouden Leeuwplein) and **Braempoort** (between Brabantdam and Vlaanderenstraat).

Kortrijk Kortrijk was a pioneer in establishing pedestrian shopping streets. Two of the best known are **Steenstraat** and **Wijngaardstraat,** both lined with fashionable and expensive boutiques.

Sports and Fitness

Spectator Sports In Brugge, the main sport is **soccer.** Home games are played at
Brugge the Olympiaparc (Koning Leopold III-Laan 50, St-Andries, tel. 050/38–94–62).

The Coast The Wellington Hippodrome in Oostende is a top track for **flat racing** (tel. 059/80–60–55; open July–Aug., Mon., Thurs., weekends, and bank holidays), and it also holds **trotting races** (tel. 059/80–36–36; open May–Sept., Fri. 6:45 PM).

Participant Sports Information is available from the city's **Sports Service**
Brugge (Walweinstraat 20, tel. 050/44–83–24). The green city wall is ideal for **jogging.** For a more extensive workout, try the Tillegembos provincial domain in St-Michiels.

For **swimming** try the Olympic-size pool at the new Provinciaal Olympisch Zwembad (Olympia Park, Doornstraat, St-Andries, tel. 050/39–02–00). There's also a sauna and solarium.

Tennis clubs include Azalea (Sint-Pieters-Groenestraat 135), 't Vrije (Zuidervaartje 3), and Witte Beer (Damsevaart Zuid 75). Indoor courts are at Bryghia (Boogschutterslaan 37, St-Kruis).

The Coast For information about sports facilities in the area, contact **BLOSO** (Flemish Sports Association, Rue des Colonies 31, 1000 Brussels, tel. 02/510–3411). More detailed local information can be obtained for Knokke (tel. 050/60–43–17); for Oostende (tel. 059/50–05–29); and for De Panne (tel. 058/41–29–71). For information on water sports, contact Vlaamse Vereniging voor Watersport (Beatrijslaan 25, 2050 Antwerp, tel. 03/219–6967).

There are 18-hole **golf** courses at De Haan (tel. 059/23–57–23) and Het Zoute (tel. 050/60–16–16) and practice courses at other locations.

The coast, with its prevailing breeze, offers splendid **sailing** opportunities. Good yacht harbors include Blankenberge, Knokke, Nieuwpoort, Oostende (tel. 059/70–62–94), and Zeebrugge (tel. 052/33–37–62).

At De Panne and Oostduinkerke, where the beach is up to 250 meters (820 feet) wide, the facilities for **sand yachting** are excellent.

Currents can be tricky, and you should **swim** only at beaches supervised by lifeguards. A green flag means bathing is safe;

yellow, bathing is risky but guards are on duty; red, bathing is prohibited. Do not ignore warnings. Many resorts also offer good public open-air pools.

Tennis tournaments are held during the season at Oostende and Het Zoute. There are hundreds of courts along the coast; check with your concierge or the local tourist office.

Windsurfing is extremely popular and special areas have been set aside for it along many beaches. In Oostende, the Flemish Sports Association has set up a water-sports center on the Spuikom waterway (also used for oyster beds).

Ghent Ghent possesses an extensive sports and recreation center only minutes away from the city, the 101-hectare (250-acre) **Blaarmeersen** (Zuiderlaan 5, tel. 091/21–82–66). It is equipped with outdoor and indoor tennis courts, squash courts, roller-skating track, jogging and cycling tracks, and facilities for windsurfing, sailing, canoeing, and camping.

Dining and Lodging

By Nancy Coons Between historic Ghent, romantic Brugge, and the highly developed coastline, Belgium concentrates its greatest variety of hotels and restaurants in this, its most tourist-accommodating region.

Dining Naturally, this is seafood country: Brugge ships in fresh fish daily from Zeebrugge, its waterfront counterpart, and the coast towns serve North Sea delicacies from the source at terrace restaurants whipped by sand and salt air. Even in landlocked Ghent, some 50 kilometers (31 miles) from the coast, locals snack on whelks and winkles (sea snails) as if they were popcorn. You'll inevitably find sole and turbot poached, *barbue* (brill) grilled or broiled, and a limited choice of classic sauces: grilled fish with rich béarnaise or *dijonnaise* sauces and poached fish with only slightly lighter sauce mousseline.

When the Flemish aren't eating their fish straight or in a blanket of golden sauce, they consume it in the region's most famous dish: *waterzooi*, a cream-based white stew flavored with celery, sage, and leeks, with chunks of fish and, occasionally, eel floating in it. Only the citizens of Ghent, deprived of a coastline, prepare their local version with chicken.

If fish is the staple of bourgeois Flemish cuisine, the working man's essentials are *moules* (mussels) and *palings* (eels), the latter as common a source of protein here as chicken or beef is elsewhere in the West. Their flesh is firm, fatty, and sweet, served in long cross-sections that contain an easy-to-remove backbone. The most prevalent preparation by far is "in green," stewed in a heady mix of sorrel, tarragon, sage, mint, and parsley. The side dish? Frites, of course.

For two vegetable delicacies of Flanders, it's worth arranging your visit in springtime: Asparagus, white and tender, is served either in sauce mousseline or with the traditional Flemish garnish of chopped hard-boiled egg and melted butter; and the rarer hops sprouts, sweet, delicate shoots of the hops vine, abundant in March and April in beer-making country.

Lodging Unlike Antwerp and Brussels, Brugge is not a conference town but its opposite: This is where city folk get away for a romantic weekend, and they expect atmosphere in their second-honey-moon suite. Brugge is happy to provide it. Many hotels work hard to supply appropriately Old Flemish decor in the public areas and, when possible, in the rooms. Recent changes in fire codes left Brugge struggling between the obligation to install fire escapes and the desire to preserve its historic landmarks intact: The results are discreet but comforting in this city that often glows with a thousand wood-burning hearths. Ghent, like Brugge, aims at weekend visitors but hasn't developed an industry of romantic hotels; lodgings, with few exceptions, are modern. **Note:** Check with the tourist offices of Brugge and Ghent for package arrangements, in which rooms are reserved and some restaurant meals included, all for a reasonable fixed price. Coast hotels aim for longer visits and often offer half-board plans; in summer, be sure to book well in advance.

Brugge **De Karmeliet.** In a lovely 18th-century house with a graceful
Dining English garden, this culinary landmark offers Bresse pigeon in
★ truffle juice, ravioli of *foie d'oie* (goose liver), and crisp potato nests with *langoustine* (lobster). The wine cave lives up to the kitchen's standard, which is stratospheric; the ambience is genteel, the service flexible and pleasant. *Langestraat 19, tel. 050/33–82–59. Reservations required. Dress: Jacket and tie advised. AE, DC, MC, V. Closed Sun. dinner, Mon. Very Expensive.*

★ **Den Gouden Harynk.** Few of his colleagues can claim the natural flair of chef Philippe Serruys. Holding forth in a small, unpretentious, antiques-filled dining room just south of the Dijver, he serves international cuisine with an artist's gift, not only for presentation but also for planning, pacing, and inspired combination. The menu dégustation offers langoustines brushed with a light curry blend or foie d'oie on a bed of rhubarb with pink peppercorns. *Groeninge, tel. 050/33–76–37. Reservations advised. Dress: Jacket and tie advised. AE, DC, MC, V. Closed Sun.–Mon. Very Expensive.*

De Witte Poorte. Under low brick vaults and stone arches, with rear windows looking onto a lush little garden, this very formal restaurant offers rich, contemporary French cooking, with an emphasis on seafood. Specialties include *ris de veau* (sweetbreads) in tarragon cream sauce, sole with Zeeland oysters, and a superb dessert cart. *Jan Van Eyckplein 6, tel. 050/33–08–83. Reservations advised. Dress: Jacket and tie suggested. Closed Sun.–Mon. AE, DC, MC, V. Very Expensive.*

't Bourgoensche Cruyce. In one of the most medieval-*looking* buildings in Brugge (though its weathered timbers and sharp-raked roofs were heavily rebuilt at the turn of the century), this restaurant claims one of the most romantic canalside settings as well: Dining-room windows shed warm light over the water, the reflections tinted by the salmon-and-copper decor. The cuisine is equally romantic, including delicate smoked halibut, tender scallops, wild mushrooms, or saddle of hare. *Wollestraat 41, tel. 050/33–79–26. Reservations advised. Dress: Jacket and tie suggested. AE, MC, V. Expensive.*

Breydel–De Coninck. Directly en route between the Markt and Burg, this no-frills luncheonette looks more like a tourist trap than a place for locals to flock to their winter *moules* (mussels)—but they do. Austere pink plastic tablecloths and vinyl banquettes leave the focus on the basics, and while there are token offerings of eel and steak, nothing could be more basic than a crock the size of a chamber pot heaped high with shiny blue-black shells. *Breidelstraat 24, tel. 050/33-97-46. Dress: casual. AE, MC, V. Closed Tues. lunch, Wed. Moderate.*

't Paardje. Off the beaten tourist track, this familial little restaurant concentrates all efforts on a few specialties: Mussels are prepared in six variations, eel in eight, and steak in 11 versions. Its terra-cotta and lace decor is cozy, clean, and unpretentious, and its cooking dependably good. *Langestraat 20, tel. 050/33-40-09. Dress: casual. Closed Mon.-Tues. nights. MC, V. Moderate.*

★ **De Zinc.** Here's a bistro with a history: Master chef Patrick Provoost, once one of the most respected chefs in Flanders, had a car accident and went into a coma. Recovery followed, and with it epiphany: *Simplify!* Nowadays his once-somber dining room is full of smoke, Beaujolais, and children, and Provoost turns his expert attention to simple home cooking, exquisitely prepared: pheasant in cabbage, grilled *chèvre* (goat cheese) on raisin toast, entrecote in peppercorn sauce. *Achiel Van Ackerplein 2, tel. 050/33-64-65. Reservations suggested. Dress: casual. AE, MC, V. Closed Wed. Moderate.*

★ **Sint Joris.** Among the dozen or so competitive brasseries crowded along the Markt, this low-key spot maintains a more civilized profile than its neighbors'. Flowers, linens, candles, a roaring fire, and a comfortable clutter of ceramics and copper warm the dining room, and you'll find a choice of either sheltered or open terrace. The cooking is a cut above average as well, and regional dishes are exceptionally well prepared: Fish-based *waterzooi*, eel in green sauce, and mussels. *Markt 29, tel. 050/33-30-62. Dress: casual. AE, DC, MC, V. Inexpensive/Moderate.*

De Tassche. Though you may feel far removed from the romance of old Brugge, you'll be compensated by the attention, commitment to detail, and overall sincerity of this husband-and-wife-run restaurant. A wide range of simple dishes, from cheap steak and frites to grilled sole, are served in a setting of pink damask and copper, and the cooking comes from the heart: Even the frites are hand-cut, and the chef cruises the dining room like a true gastronome. *Oude Burg 11, tel. 050/33-03-19. Dress: casual. DC, MC, V. Inexpensive/Moderate.*

★ **Staminee De Garre.** Tucked in an alley off the well-worn Breidelstraat, this tiny two-tiered coffeehouse is a brick-and-beam oasis, offering Mozart and magazines along with plunger coffee and 136 beers—four of them variations on the house brew. There are simple cold platters and grilled sandwiches, attractively served, and traditional nibbles of cheese with the heartier beers. *Off Breidelstraat, tel. 050/34-10-29. Dress: casual. No credit cards. Inexpensive.*

Taverna Curiosa. Don't be put off by the aggressive posters, menus, and broadcast music that spill onto the street: Downstairs, this cross-vaulted crypt makes a comfortable, atmospheric hideaway from tourist traffic and an ideal place for conversation, a light meal, and one of myriad beers, many of them local. Snacks include omelettes, sandwiches, and *visschotel* (smoked fish plates), as well as pancakes and ice cream. *Vlamingstraat 22, tel. 050/34-23-34. Dress: casual. Closed Mon. AE, MC, V. Inexpensive.*

Tom Pouce. Despite its somewhat geriatric air—heavy velour drapes, splashy carpet, cracked crockery, noisy open service bar—this stuffy old urban tearoom dominates the Burg every afternoon as tourists, shoppers, and loyal retirees dig into warm apple strudel, airy waffles, and their tour de force: hot *pannekoeken,* light, eggy, and vanilla-perfumed, with a pat of butter and a sprinkle of dark brown sugar. There are lunch plates as well. *Burg 16–17, tel. 050/33–03–36. Dress: casual. AE, DC, MC, V. Closed Mon. Inexpensive.*

Lodging

★ **De Tuilerieen.** This stately 15th-century mansion was converted to a sumptuous hotel in 1988 and furnished with genuinely patrician taste: discreet antique reproductions, weathered marble, and warm mixed-print fabrics in shades of celadon, slate, and cream. The firelighted bar is filled with cozy tartan wingbacks, and the breakfast room has a massive mantel and a coffered ceiling. Despite its aristocratic air, this is a welcoming stop. Caveat: Canal views entail traffic noise; courtyard rooms are quieter. *Dyver 7, B-8000, tel. 50/34–36–91. 26 rooms. Facilities: breakfast rooms, bar, indoor pool, whirlpool, sauna, solarium. AE, DC, MC, V. Very Expensive.*

Die Swaene. Lavishly decorated in every period excess, this hotel tries harder. Its situation—fronting on one of the prettier canals in the heart of the tourist center—makes it particularly appropriate for splurging honeymooners, who will be rewarded with swagged tulle, crystal, and any number of marble nymphs. (Its most popular room is a relatively subdued converted Flemish kitchen with stone fireplace and carved four-poster.) There's an upscale French restaurant. *Steenhouwersdijk, B-8000, tel. 50/34–27–98. 24 rooms. Facilities: restaurant, bar. AE, DC, MC, V. Expensive/Very Expensive.*

Bryghia. Restored in 1965 and renovated in 1989, this 15th-century landmark (once a German/Austrian trade center) now sports seamless modern room decors with beechwood cabinetry and soft pastel florals. The management works hard on details of comfort, offering in-room teakettles, flowers, valet parking, and mosquito repellent when the canal waters run slow. *Oosterlingenplein 4, B-8000, tel. 50/33–80–59. 18 rooms. Facilities: breakfast room. AE, DC, MC, V. Expensive.*

Duc de Bourgogne. This could be the closest you'll come to Old Flanders, surrounded by the plush, stuffy luxury of tapestry, fresco, stone, leather, fringe, and gilt that fill this dark and atmospheric restaurant/hotel. Its greatest draw is its dining room, which angles out over a canal and serves rich, if dated, French cuisine. Rooms are freshly decorated with rich prints and tile baths; canal views cost slightly more, but second-floor dormers (view included) are budget-rate. *Huidenvettersplein 12, B-8000, tel. 50/33–20–38. 10 rooms. Facilities: restaurant, bar. AE, DC, MC, V. Expensive.*

★ **Oud Huis Amsterdam.** Freshly renovated and packaged like a fine gift, this snug, central retreat combines the grace of the two noble 17th-century houses it occupies with the polish and luxury of a new first-class property. Antique details—tooled Cordoba wallpaper here, rough-hewn rafters and Delft tiles there—have been preserved, and slick services—international newspapers, umbrellas—superimposed. Owner Philip Traen has even mounted ancestral artworks in an old master vein. Rooms with canal views also overlook a busy street; roofline views in back are calmer. *Spiegelrei 3, B-8000, tel. 50/34–18–10. 18 rooms. Facilities: garden, bar. AE, DC, MC, V. Expensive.*

Pandhotel. Its faded gentility dating not only from the 1830s, when it was built as a private mansion, but also from 1979, when it was renovated as a hotel, this member of the Romantik chain mixes a jewel-box neoclassical decor with modern touches—dark ceramic baths, a skylit breakfast room. Services are business-oriented, and the location is central to tourism. *Pandreitje 16, B-8000, tel. 50/34-06-66. 24 rooms. Facilities: breakfast room, bar. AE, DC, MC, V. Expensive.*

★ **Ter Brughe.** A 1989 renovation of this 15th-century step-gabled house created a slick, modern, efficient hotel in which the decor might seem generic (beige and bamboo) but for those heavy beams, tempera murals, and leaded-glass windows. There are exposed brick barrel vaults in the bar, and you can throw bread to the ducks from the breakfast room, which opens directly onto the canal. *Oost-Gistelhof 2, B-8000, tel. 50/34-03-24. 24 rooms. Facilities: bar. AE, DC, MC, V. Moderate.*

★ **Egmond.** Gracefully placed along the lush Minnewater park, this manorlike inn offers garden views from every room, as well as the odd skylight, parquet floor, fireplace, or dormer-sloped ceiling. Breakfast is served in an oak-beamed hall with a Delft-tiled fireplace. With the park in front and the quiet Beguinage behind, you may feel pleasantly isolated from the touristic bustle of the center, though it's only 10 minutes' walk. *Minnewater 15, B-8000, tel. 50/34-14-45. 9 rooms. Facilities: breakfast room. AE, DC, MC, V. Moderate.*

Europ. Newly acquired by an enthusiastic young management, this mid-price hotel focuses less on historic atmosphere than on basic comforts: Good big beds with Swiss-flex construction are placed in every room, and the breakfast buffet is generous. The hotel was first built in a 1789 house, with a modern wing added in 1970—but the current decor is spare and contemporary in both parts. *Augustijnenrei 18, B-8000, tel. 50/33-79-75. 28 rooms. Facilities: bar. AE, DC, MC, V. Moderate.*

★ **De Pauw.** Homey, familial, and warmly furnished, from the fresh flowers and doilies to the bronzed baby booties in the breakfast parlor, this is a welcoming little inn passed on from mother to daughter. Every room has a name instead of a number, needlepoint cushions, and old framed prints, as well as tiled bath and hair dryer. (Two rooms with shower down the hall are super values.) Breakfast, which includes six kinds of bread and a soft-boiled egg, is served on pretty china. *Sint-Gilliskerkhof 8, B-8000, tel. 50/33-71-18. 8 rooms. Facilities: breakfast room. AE, DC, MC, V. Inexpensive.*

Fevery. The living quarters of the family seem to spill over into the lounge area of this friendly, comfortable hotel; the magazines and knickknacks make you feel like personal guests. There's even a baby monitor so parents can curl up with a drink downstairs after putting a child to bed. The room decor has been recently upgraded (new carpet, fresh chenille), and all rooms have bathrooms. *Collaert Mansionstraat 3, B-8000, tel. 50/33-12-69. 11 rooms. Facilities: bar. AE, DC, MC, V. Inexpensive.*

Jacobs. With all its plush and crystal in the public rooms, this spot may look posh, but the staff are young and friendly, and the breakfast tables are garnished with plastic waste buckets. There are cheap no-bath rooms as well as full-facility doubles, with homey, plain decors. *Baliestraat 1, B-8000, tel. 50/33-98-31. 26 rooms. Facilities: bar. AE, MC, V. Inexpensive.*

Damme/Oostkerke
Dining

't Hemeltje. Despite (or perhaps because of) its lack of period romance, this very simple tavern draws locals for cards, talk, and good, plain food: eel in vegetable broth or fried in butter; grilled ribs or horse meat; cold smoked fish. It's just across from the church, beautifully illuminated at night, where Margaret of York married Charles the Bold. *Kerkstraat 46, Damme, tel. 050/36–07–07. Dress: casual. No credit cards. Closed Tues. dinner, Wed. Inexpensive.*

★ **Siphon.** This sprawling white-brick landmark, along two tree-lined canals, has great casement windows taking in green farmlands. It is often mobbed by fur-coated urbanites on outings in the country. Yet the restaurant is anything but upscale: It's delightfully down-to-earth, with brusque white-uniformed waiters busing eel and wood-grilled lamb chops at checkered-cloth tables, and as many people drink beer as delve into the stellar wine list. *Damse Vaart Oost 1, Damme, tel. 050/62–02–02. Reservations advised. Dress: casual. No credit cards. Closed Thurs. Inexpensive/Moderate.*

Dining and Lodging **De Gulden Kogge.** Along the tree-lined canal that leads straight into Brugge, across from a windmill and farmlands, this tiny inn stresses elegant traditional cooking first (rabbit in cider, poached sea bass with parsley flan) and lodging as an afterthought. While the restaurant is a welcoming mix of oak, brass, and beams, the handful of rooms upstairs are haphazardly furnished and minimally maintained. Two young (and possibly inexperienced) sisters have owned the business since 1990; cuisine is their forte. *Damse Vaart-Zuid 12, B-8340, Damme, tel. 050/35–42–17. 8 rooms. Facilities: restaurant (Expensive). AE, DC, MC, V. Restaurant closed off-season, Wed. dinner and Thurs. Inexpensive.*

Ghent **Guido Meersschaut.** With a direct connection to the nearby fish
Dining market, where Meersschaut has shipped in the freshest catch from the Channel and the North Sea, this small, stylish restaurant offers an extensive menu of seafood. Fresh cold shrimp and snails, their shells still damp with brine, are offered with the aperitif, and the menu includes a courteous four-tongue translation of the encyclopedic list of available fish. Aim for the lightly broiled or poached: The flavors are too fresh to be drowned in that ubiquitous Belgian butter. *Kleine Vismarkt 3, tel. 91/23–53–49. Reservations advised. Dress: Jacket suggested. AE, DC, MC, V. Closed Sun. dinner, Mon. Expensive.*

★ **Het Cooremetershuys.** In a tiny room one flight up from the waterfront on the Graslei, this venturesome little restaurant offers contemporary spins on Belgian classics (wild rabbit with ginger, smoked entrecote) as well as simple standards (lamb shoulder with lentils, fish of the day). The setting combines the best of gallery-chic simplicity and old Flemish atmosphere: wood, brick, and a massive hearth. *Graslei 12, tel. 91/23–49–71. Reservations advised. Jacket suggested. AE, DC, MC, V. Closed Wed. and Sun. Expensive.*

Jan Breydel. This cozy corner restaurant, warmed with exposed brick, oak, and a stone fireplace, offers sophisticated, nouvelle-inspired cooking: beef sautéed with goose liver in acacia honey and raspberry vinegar; turbot stuffed with oysters; strawberry gratin with lime and almonds. Cunning presentation occasionally overshadows substance, but the genial ambience and low-key intimacy compensate for any culinary pretensions. *Jan Breydelstraat 10, tel. 91/25–62–87. Reservations advised. Jacket and tie suggested. AE, DC, MC, V. Closed Mon. lunch and Sun. Expensive.*

Graaf Van Egmond. This 17th-century step-gabled mansion serves unexceptional Frenchified food in a lavish setting with views over the illuminated towers of Ghent. While no expense has been spared in the decor—the walls are papered in rich tapestry fabric; the original oak paneling, ceiling, and fireplace restored to a burnished sheen—costs have been cut in the kitchen, so those peas in the waterzooi may be canned. *Sint-Michielsbrug, tel. 91/25–07–27. Reservations suggested. Jacket suggested. AE, DC, MC, V. Closed Sat. dinner and Sun. Moderate.*

★ **Pakhuis.** A gesture toward see-and-be-seen urban chic, this cavernous bi-level brasserie has been built in a theatrical, retro high-tech style, with copper patina, terrazzo, and Statue of Liberty *torchières.* Daily *plats à l'ancienne* include *choucroute* (sauerkraut), waterzooi, and cassoulet, but the menu's real focus is on trendy upgrades: The house salad combines carpaccio, *saumon mariné minute* (marinated raw salmon), smoked salmon, and foie gras. Pakhuis (which means "warehouse") is a theme restaurant under the same management as La Quincaillerie in Brussels. *Schuurkenstraat 4, B-9000, tel. 91/23–55–55. Reservations optional. Dress: casual. AE, DC, MC, V. Closed Sun. lunch. Moderate.*

Du Progres. This unassuming brasserie—relatively cheap and always full—is typical of its genre in Flanders: Under game trophies and beer posters, heavy meat-based menus are consumed in an atmosphere of thick smoke, clattering service, and incongruous classical music. Fats are impossible to avoid, from the fried cheese croquettes to the inch-thick steaks to the crisp, glistening frites. Toilets—again typically—are hidden in an open courtyard out back. *Korenmarkt 10, tel. 91/25–17–16. Dress: casual. V. Closed Wed. Moderate.*

't Hietekoekske. Its name is Ghent dialect for "pancakes," but the menu offers a few chic, simple daily plates as well as its warm, tender namesakes. The setting is upscale and up-to-date—hanging halogen, framed contemporary art—but the ambience is casual and comfortable, ideal for a break from shopping in this neighborhood of trendy boutiques and department stores. It's open for lunch and afternoon snacks only. *Bennesteeg 1, tel. 091/23–75–66. Dress: casual. No credit cards. Closed Sun. and dinner. Inexpensive.*

Taverne Keizershof. Considerably slicker than its peers and offering large portions of good, solid food, this restaurant is popular with locals. Besides all-day snacks (toasted sandwiches, spaghetti), there are cheap *dagschotel* (daily plates), cold meat or fish plates, mountainous steaks, and *gentse stoverij,* the local beer-marinated stew. The dining room in back has a low vaulted ceiling, crypt-style. *Vrijdagmarkt 47, tel. 91/23–44–46. Dress: casual. MC, V. Closed Sun. Inexpensive.*

De Witte Leeuw. Though there's little more to eat here than omelettes and meaty spareribs, this historic 17th-century building on the waterfront offers warm, dark atmosphere—wooden booths, heavy timbers—and an exceptional list of Belgian beers, including several on draft. It's open until 1AM. *Graslei 6, tel. 091/33–37–33. Dress: casual. No credit cards.*

Lodging **Gravensteen.** If you prefer historic atmosphere over airtight modern convenience, you'll overlook the creaks and austerity within this once-glamorous 1865 structure, its exterior and public spaces restored to the heights of neoclassical excess. Rooms, in contrast, are almost painfully spare (though squeaky-clean) and surprisingly small. The location—by the Gravensteen (Counts' Castle)—is very good, in the midst of the picturesque waterfront. *Jan Breydelstraat 35, B-9000, tel. 091/*

25–11–50. 17 rooms. Facilities: lounge, breakfast room. AE, DC, MC, V. Expensive.

Novotel. Though part of a cookie-cutter look-alike hotel chain, this modern lodging merits mention not only because of its location, in the center of the tourist and shopping area, but also because it manages to compress a sprawl of business-class luxuries—lounges, garden, swimming pool—into what seems to be a small urban space. Some windows open onto the inner courtyard, with its pool and greenery, and some take in the city monuments; decor is slick and standardized. In a city lacking in luxury accommodation, this is the closest thing. *Goudenleeuwplein 5, B-9000, tel. 091/24–22–30. 117 rooms. Facilities: restaurant, bar, swimming pool. AE, DC, MC, V. Expensive.*

Sint Jorishof/Cour St-Georges. Billing itself as the oldest hotel in Europe, this noble old step-gabled inn has housed and feted guests since 1228, from Mary of Burgundy (1477) to Napoleon (1805). Despite generations of renovation, much of its Gothic spirit has been preserved, from the burnished wood restaurant to the stone fireplace in the reception. Rooms, both upstairs and in the annex across the street, are considerably less atmospheric, though new and attractive, with peach-tinted wood and fabrics in Florentine prints. The restaurant serves rich French classics and a few regional specialties. *Botermarkt 2, B-9000, tel. 091/24–24–24. 36 beds. Facilities: restaurant (Moderate/Expensive). AE, DC, MC, V. Expensive.*

Ibis. Its location—at the hub of the old town, on Sint-Baafsplein—compensates heavily for its chain-style decor (bright laminates, a motel-style coffee shop) and service (full business facilities, international reservation service). The early tolling of those massive medieval bells across the street won't let you forget where you are. Back rooms are quieter and have rooftop views. *Limburgstraat 2, B-9000, tel. 091/33–00–00. 120 rooms. Facilities: coffee shop, bar. AE, DC, MC, V. Moderate.*

★ **Erasmus.** From the flagstoned and wood-beamed library/lounge in the basement to the stone mantels in the bedrooms upstairs, every cubic centimeter of this noble 15th-century home has been scrubbed, polished, and decked with a period knickknack, an antique clock, a circle of local lace; Even the tiny garden out back has been manicured like a miniature Versailles. The delightful couple in charge answer the bell pull at night and serve guests their soft-cooked eggs in the parlor in the morning. *Poel 25, B-9000, tel. 091/24–21–95. 11 rooms. Facilities: lounge, breakfast room. AE, DC, MC, V. Moderate.*

Astoria. A small, manorlike brick house on a pollard-lined residential street tucked behind the train station, this simple, family-run hotel mixes '60s simplicity (spare marble, wrought iron) with baroque tastes (Louis XV/XVI, moiré, heavy plush, and music that can be piped into your room). There's a covered terrace and a garden, and a cool, quiet atmosphere quite in contrast to the city center's dark, old-urban style. *Musschestraat 39, B-9000, tel. 091/22–84–13. 15 rooms. Facilities: breakfast room, garden. AE, DC, MC, V. Inexpensive/Moderate.*

Ieper
Lodging
★ **Regina.** Directly on the Grote Markt, in a sturdy neo-Gothic brick building, this is a fresh, comfortable hotel, its generous spaces full of light, its rooms up-to-date. Everything has been upgraded except the windows; traffic noise is the only drawback. *Grote Markt 45, B-8900, tel. 057/21–90–06. 17 rooms. Facilities: restaurant, bar. AE, DC, MC, V. Moderate.*

Knokke-Heist/Het **Aquilon.** Looking like it's the subject of a society house tour in a
Zoute 1953 *Holiday* magazine, this glamorous little Empire-style
Dining mansion from Knokke's nouveau-riche golden age has been
converted into a sumptuous restaurant, where diners sit at
lace-covered tables and look onto a miniature landscaped garden and pond. The food, prepared by chef Marguerite De Spae,
is just as opulent: oysters gratin with almond butter; whole
bass, its juices captured in a solid crust of rock salt; and several
lobster dishes. *Bayauxlaan 70, tel. 050/60–12–74. Reservations required. Jacket and tie advised. AE, DC, MC, V. Closed
high season, Tues. dinner and Wed.; off-season, Mon.–Wed.
Very Expensive.*

Breughel. At the base of an all-new postmodern apartment
building on a quiet cul-de-sac off the beach, this young, chic little urban restaurant offers trendy graphics and high-design
decor to match its cuisine: sole in kiwi with curry sauce; scallops and lobster tails in paprika cream; rabbit with fruit; and
pistachios in Belgian beer. *De Wielingen 5, tel. 050/62–01–00.
Reservations advised. Jacket suggested. AE, DC, MC, V.
Closed Wed. Expensive.*

★ **New Alpina.** Despite token efforts at pink linens and multiple
stemware, this is a seafood diner at heart, where a friendly,
house-proud husband and wife team have served North Sea
classics since 1970. Fresh *raie* (skate), turbot, sole, and shrimp
are served with simple sauces; the multicourse *"menu gourmet"* is a seafood feast. It's just off the beach, by the tourist office. *Lichttorenplein 12, tel. 050/60–89–85. Reservations
suggested. Dress: casual. MC, V. Closed Tues. Moderate.*

Lodging **La Réserve.** This vast country club of a hotel, complete with a
saltwater treatment center and a man-made lake, was built as a
private fantasy-mansion in 1964 and expanded, under various
managements, into the enormous complex it is today. Flowers
and antique-look details do little to warm the airport-style public spaces, but rooms are bright and lovely, in soothing sponge-
painted pastels. You can buy in as far as you like, from a simple
bed-and-breakfast arrangement to a full-out Thalassa-treat-
ment package. It's across from the Casino, three minutes from
the beach. *Elizabetlaan 158–160, B-8300 Albertstrand, tel.
050/61–06–06. 110 rooms. Facilities: restaurant, bar, treatment center, seawater pool, hair salon, sauna, 4 tennis courts,
windsurfing school. AE, DC, MC, V. Very Expensive.*

★ **Katelijne.** A bit out of place in the bustle of high-style boutiques
and traffic snaking along the beachfront, this charming old
whitewashed brick auberge, built in the 1930s in traditional
Flemish style, offers an atmospheric retreat, with fireplace,
Oriental runners, fringed plush, and darkened timbers. The
rooms are equally cozy and dated, though the marble/traver-
tine baths are deluxe. There's a garden and terrace, and a welcoming copper-decked restaurant featuring fish. *Kustlaan
166, B-8300 Knokke-Zout, tel. 050/60–12–16. 15 rooms. Facilities: restaurant, bar, garden. AE, MC, V. Expensive.*

Kortrijk **Damier.** This is a grand little hotel, impeccably renovated and
Lodging superbly appointed, right on the Grote Markt. From its lavish
★ café, with florid plasterwork and chandeliers, to its Laura Ashley rooms, to its beeswaxed oak wainscoting and Persian carpets, it exudes grace and seamless style; there are no musty
corners or creaky halls hiding behind the decor. Despite its rococo facade, the hotel dates from the French Revolution, but
comforts are thoroughly modern. *Grote Markt 41, B-8500, tel.*

056/22–15–47. 49 rooms. Facilities: restaurant, café, terrace café, sauna. AE, DC, MC, V. Very Expensive.

Belfort. Also on the Grote Markt and as attractive as the Damier in its own, less glamorous way, this is a pretty, all-new hotel combining two old properties. The rooms have blond wood, pastels, and tile baths. *Grote Markt 52/53, B-8500, tel. 056/22–22–20. 45 rooms. Facilities: restaurant, café, terrace café. AE, MC, V. Moderate.*

De Panne
Dining

De Braise. Run by the parents of Le Fox's chef, who ran Le Fox (*see below*) when it was a simple tavern, this is the Buyens family's return to their roots: an old-fashioned regional restaurant, offering updated, upgraded local cooking in a homey, bourgeois setting. Though the menu reads like a thousand others in the region—eels in green, turbot poached or grilled, sauce hollandaise/dijonnaise, sole meunière—the portions are generous and the preparation is soigné, and the service is equally sophisticated. *Bortierplein 1, tel. 058/41–59–99. Reservations advised. Dress: casual/jacket suggested. AE, DC, MC, V. Closed Sun. dinner and Mon. Moderate/Expensive.*

Dining and Lodging
★

Le Fox. Chef Stéphane Buyens, like a proper son, has made good, taking over his parents' tavern and creating a prestigious, welcoming gastronomic retreat. Developing dishes such as roast *langoustine* (lobster) tails in sea urchin butter, and turbot in an aromatic mix of 10 oils, herbs, and beet juice, he has drawn a loyal following. They stay in graciously furnished rooms that have windows angled toward the waterfront, and work as many meals into the weekend as they can. The dining room is auberge-cozy and the ambience unstuffy. *Walckiersstraat 2, B-8660, tel. 058/41–28–55. 14 rooms. Facilities: restaurant (Very Expensive), bar. AE, DC, MC, V. Closed all year, Tues.; off-season, Mon. Moderate.*

Soll Cress. In Koksijde-Bad, just east of De Panne, this ungainly, motellike roadhouse offers very good, straightforward North Sea seafood: pan-fried barbue with sauce dijonnaise, rich seafood gratins, mild fish soups. The service is homey and house-proud, and rooms upstairs are well appointed, with up-to-date fixtures and—across the highway, past the high rises—a patch of ocean view. *Koninklijke Baan 225, B-8670 Koksijde, tel. 058/51–23–32. 25 rooms. Facilities: restaurant (Moderate), bar. MC, V. Closed off-season, Tues. Inexpensive.*

Lodging

Sparrenhof. This is a self-contained oasis, cut off from the beachfront scene but only 150 meters (500 feet) from the water. Its pretty pool is cloistered in a garden haven, with many rooms facing onto the greenery. The original building dates from the '50s, and there are still seven comfortable rooms within; the new wing sports flashy bird's-eye veneer and modern furnishings. The restaurant is welcoming year-round, with a wood-burning fireplace and poolside tables. *Koninginnelaan 26, B-8660, tel. 058/41–13–28. 25 rooms. Facilities: restaurant, bar, poolside terrace, pool. AE, DC, MC, V. Moderate.*

Veurne
Dining
★

Driekoningen. Tucked in off the back streets of Beauvoorde, a tiny brick village outside Veurne, this combination coffeehouse and restaurant has elaborate menus and overly complex dishes—salmon filled with endive and foie gras and then topped with caviar—but the simple, well-prepared stuff: sole with hops sprouts is all the fuss you need. The restaurant side, with Villeroy and Boch, flowers, and crystal, is separated from the casual café by a thin screen. *Wulveringemstraat 40, tel. 058/29–*

90–12. Reservations suggested. Dress: casual/jacket suggested. MC, V. Closed off-season, Tues. dinner and Wed. Moderate.

The Arts and Nightlife

The Arts The monthly *Agenda Brugge* (at the tourist office) gives details
Brugge of all events in the city. Check also listings in *The Bulletin*.

The **Festival of Flanders** is the umbrella organization for music festivals in all major Flemish cities. In Brugge it is celebrated the last week of July and the first week of August, and concentrates on early music, including the great Flemish polyphonists. For program information, contact Festival van Vlaanderen (Place Flagey 18, Brussels 1050, tel. 02/648–1484).

There are dramatic and musical performances at the **Stadsshouwburg** (City Theater) in Vlamingstraat (tel. 050/33–81–67).

Ghent Cultural life in Ghent is lively and varied, and it's worthwhile checking *The Bulletin*'s "What's On" section under the heading "Other Towns." Many events take place in the **Kunstencentrum Vooruit** (Vooruit Arts Center, Sint-Pietersnieuwstraat 23, tel. 091/23–82–01), which includes two concert halls, a ballroom, a theater, 10 smaller halls, and an art gallery.

The Festival of Flanders office in Ghent is at Veldstraat 82 (for tickets, tel. 091/25–77–80; for program information, tel. 02/640–1525).

Nightlife Among the nicest hotel bars are **The Meeting** at the Oud Huis
Brugge Amsterdam (Spiegelrei 3, tel. 050/34–18–10), **De Medici** (Potterierei 15, tel. 050/33–98–33), and **Académie** (Wijngaardstraat 7–9, tel. 050/33–22–66).

Discos, mostly catering to a clientele not much older than 20, are clustered around Eiermarkt, back of the Markt: **Coolcat** (Eiermarkt 11, tel. 050/34–05–27), **Ambiorix** (Eiermarkt 11 bis, tel. 050/33–74–00), **The Pick** (Eiermarkt 12, tel. 050/33–76–38); and at 't Zand: **Ma Rica Rokk** ('t Zand 8, tel. 050/33–83–58) and **Graffiti** ('t Zand 9, tel. 050/33–69–09). **Villa Romana** (Kraanplein 1, tel. 050/34–34–53) attracts an older crowd.

Ghent As in most Belgian towns, nightlife in Ghent is a laid-back affair. A few cabarets exist, but the Gentenaars much prefer their pubs and cafés. **Backstage** (Sint-Pietersnieuwstraat 128, tel. 091/33–35–35), a café-restaurant across from the Vooruit center, presents occasional classical and jazz concerts. **Cirque Central** (Hoogpoort 32, tel. 091/25–14–16) is both a café and a disco with an under-25 crowd. The **Brasserie Aba-jour** (Oudburg 20, tel. 091/23–42–08), more relaxed with its cool jazz and art deco ambience, overlooks the Leie.

The Coast The closure rate among seasonal night spots is high; make sure the place you've chosen is still in business. The best bet for quality and consistency in any town is the Kursaal, where casino takings help underwrite the nightclub.

Knokke-Heist is the leader on the coast for nocturnal entertainment. The **Kursaal** (Zeedijk 507, tel. 050/60–60–10) offers dinner-dancing with two orchestras, gala nights with international stars, theater, movies, ballet, and exhibitions. **Patrick's Club** (same address, tel. 050/60–94–17) is in the casino building. Other favorites are the **Gallery Club** (Canada Square 22, tel. 050/60–81–33), **MD's** (Kalvekeetdijk 262, tel. 050/60–72–75), and **Number One** (Zeedijk 509, tel. 050/60–55–04). In **Blankenberge** the popular discos are **The Beatles** (Casinoplein 6, tel. 050/41–16–53), **Old Corner** (Casinoplein 10, tel. 050/41–44–19), **Pebbles** (Zeedijk 104, tel. 050/41–65–36), and **Wit Paard** (Langestraat 40, tel. 050/41–11–00). In **Oostende,** your best bet is the **Sporting Club** (Oosthelling, tel. 059/70–51–11), which is run by the casino. There's a wide choice of night clubs, girlie shows, and discos along Van Iseghemlaan and Langestraat.

Antwerp

The true Flemish name of Belgium's second city is Antwerpen. English speakers use an abbreviated form, and French speakers call it Anvers. Some think the name refers to the way that merchant brigantines sailed up to the central town, which was located *aan het werp* (on the wharf). A more fanciful but much-favored legend tells the story of a Roman soldier, Silvius Brabo, and a giant, Druon Antigon. The giant exacted a toll from boatmen on the river and cut off the hands of those who refused, until Silvius confronted him, cut off the giant's own hand, and flung it—*handwerpen* (hand throwing)—into the River Scheldt. Believe it if you will, but it explains the presence of severed hands on Antwerp's coat of arms.

Great prosperity came to Antwerp during the reign of Emperor Charles V. Born in Ghent and raised in Mechelen, he made Antwerp the principal port of his vast domains, and it became the most important commercial center in the 16th-century world, as well as a center of the new craft of printing. The golden age came to an end with the abdication of Charles V in 1555. He was succeeded by Philip II, whose ardent Catholicism brought him into immediate conflict with the Protestants of the Netherlands. In 1566, when Calvinist iconoclasts destroyed paintings and sculptures in churches and monasteries, Philip responded by sending in Spanish troops. In what became known as the Spanish Fury, they sacked the town and killed thousands of citizens.

The decline of Antwerp had already begun when its most illustrious painters, Rubens, Jordaens, and Van Dyck, reached the peak of their fame. The Treaty of Munster in 1648, which concluded the Thirty Years' War, also sealed Antwerp's fate, for the River Scheldt was closed to shipping—not to be opened again until 1863, when a treaty obliged the Dutch, who controlled the estuary, to reopen it.

The huge and splendid railway station, built at the turn of the century, remains a fitting monument to Antwerp's second age of prosperity; the city hosted universal expositions in both 1885 and 1894. In World War I, Antwerp held off the German invaders long enough for the Belgian army to regroup south of the IJzer. In World War II, the Germans trained many V-1 flying bombs and V-2 rockets on the city, where Allied troops were debarking for the final push.

Antwerp today is Europe's second-largest port. Although ships go in and out in a single day, and sailors on leave are a rare sight on the city streets, Antwerp has retained much of the zest often associated with a port. Some of the old ambiguity also remains. Antwerp has traditionally taken pride in being open to influences from abroad and in welcoming newcomers to the city. Yet in the most recent elections, over a quarter of the votes were cast for a party of the extreme right; it's as if some of the 16th-century iconoclasts had sprung to life again.

Important Addresses and Numbers

Tourist Information The **Toerisme Stad Antwerpen** (Antwerp City Tourist Office) (Grote Markt 15, tel. 03/232–0103, fax 03/231–1937; open Mon.–Sat. 9–6, Sun. 9–5) is located in the heart of the old city. It will assist with hotel reservations. The coordinating office for the Cultural Capital events, **Antwerpen 93** (*see* Highlights '93, *above*) (Grote Market 29, tel. 03/234–1188, fax 03/226–1555), is almost next door. The **Toeristische Federatije Provincie Antwerpen** (Antwerp Provincial Tourist Office) (Karel Oomsstraat 11, tel. 03/216–2810) will help plan trips to see the rest of the province.

Emergencies **Police**, tel. 101. **Ambulance**, tel. 100. **Emergency Rooms:** Middelheim (Lindendreef 1, tel. 03/280–3111); Stuivenberg (Lange Beeldekensstraat 267, tel. 03/217–7111).

Late-night Pharmacies The name of the pharmacy on duty is displayed in all pharmacy windows.

Where to Change Money As well as at banks, money can be changed at **American Express** (Frankrijklei 21), and at **Thomas Cook** (Koningin Astridplein 33). The Exchange Office in the Central Station and **Inter-Change** (Suikerrui 36) stay open late and on weekends.

Travel Agencies **American Express** (Frankrijklei 21, tel. 03/232–5920); **VTB** (Sint-Jacobsmarkt 45, tel. 03/220–3232); **Huybrechts** (Carnotstraat 41, tel. 03/231–9900).

Arriving and Departing by Plane **Deurne Airport** (tel. 03/218–1211), 5½ kilometers (3½ miles) from the city center, is served by several flights a day to London. **Brussels National Airport** (Zaventem) is linked with Antwerp by frequent bus service (hourly 7 AM–11 PM). The trip takes 50 minutes and costs BF220.

Arriving and Departing by Car, Train, and Bus

By Car Antwerp is 48 kilometers (30 miles) north of Brussels. The city is surrounded by a ring road from which expressways shoot off like spokes in a wheel: **A1/E19** south to Brussels and Paris, north to Rotterdam and Amsterdam; **A14/E17** southwest to Ghent and Lille; **A13** southeast to Hasselt and Liège; **A21/E34** northeast to Eindhoven and the Ruhr. For car rentals there are **Avis** (Plantin en Moretuslei 62, tel. 03/218–9496), **Budget** (Frankrijklei 70, tel. 03/232–3500), and **Hertz** (Mechelsesteenweg 43, tel. 03/233–2992).

By Train There are four to five trains an hour from Brussels, and the trip takes about 45 minutes. The train ride north to Rotterdam takes an hour. International Inter-City trains between Paris and Amsterdam stop at Berchem Station south of the city center rather than entering the downtown Central Station (Koningin Astridplein, tel. 03/233–3915).

Getting Around Antwerp

By Tram and Subway You can travel by tram all over central Antwerp. Some operate underground as the pre-Metro system. The most useful subway line for visitors links the Central Station (Metro stop *Diamant*) with the left bank via the Groenplats (for the cathedral and Grote Markt). Your BF37 ticket is good for one hour on all forms of public transport; BF180 will buy you unlimited travel for a 24-hour period. Tickets are available at **De Lijn** offices (tel. 03/218–1411) at the Diamant, Opera/Frankrijklei, and Groenplats Metro stops, and at the tourist office.

By Bus Municipal bus lines (tel. 03/218–1411) mostly begin outside the Central Station in the Koningin Astridplein. Longer distance buses start from the Franklin Rooseveltplaats.

By Taxi There are taxi stands in front of the Central Station and at other principal points. It is often easier to call for one: **Antwerp Taxi** (tel. 03/238–3838), **ATM** (tel. 03/216–0160), or **Metropole Taxi** (tel. 03/231–3131).

Guided Tours

By Minibus **Sightseeing Line** (based in Brugge, tel. 050/31–13–55) operates 50-minute orientation tours with cassette commentary. Tickets (BF330 adults, BF200 children) are sold on the bus, which departs Grote Markt daily at 2, 3, and 4 from mid-March to mid-November. It runs weekends, mid-November to mid-March.

By Boat **Flandria** (tel. 03/231–3100) operates 50-minute boat trips on the River Scheldt, departing from the Steenplein pontoon (next to the Steen) daily every hour on the hour from 10 to 4 from Easter to September (fare: BF220 adults, BF120 children), as well as boat tours of the port (2½ hours), which leave from Quay 13 near Londonstraat (May–Aug., daily 10:30 and 2:30; Easter–Apr. and Sept., Sun. and bank holidays only; fare: BF350 adults, BF200 children).

Personal Guides Qualified guides can be engaged through the City Tourist Office, which requires a couple of days' notice. The price for two hours is BF1,000, and BF500 for each additional hour.

Highlights for First-Time Visitors

Bourla Theater (Tour 2: Rubens and Diamonds)
Grote Markt (Tour 1: The Old City)
Museum Mayer van den Bergh (Tour 2: Rubens and Diamonds)
Onze-Lieve-Vrouwekathedraal (Tour 1: The Old City)
Plantin-Moretus Museum (Tour 1: The Old City)
Rubenshuis (Tour 2: Rubens and Diamonds)
St. Carolus Borromeuskerk (Tour 1: The Old City)
Provincial Diamantmuseum (Tour 2: Rubens and Diamonds)
Steen (Tour 1: The Old City)
Zoo (Tour 2: Rubens and Diamonds)

Exploring Antwerp

Numbers in the margin correspond with places of interest on the Antwerp map.

Tour 1: The Old City The triangular **Grote Markt**, the heart of the Old City, is lined on two sides by guild houses and on the third by the Renais-

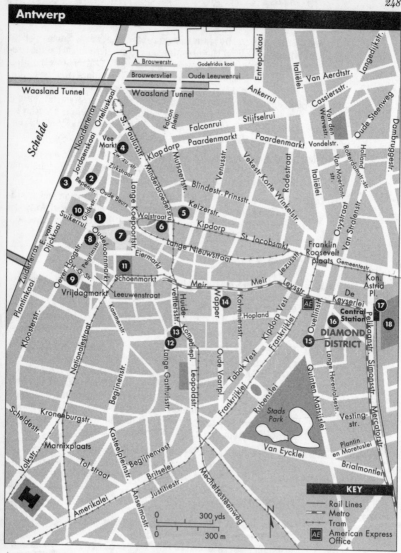

Waasland Tunnel

Waasland Tunnel

Schelde

A. Brouwerstr.

Brouwersvliet

Godefridus kaai

Oude Leeuwenrui

Entrepotkaai

Italiëlei

Van Aerdtstr.

Langedijkstr.

Cassiersstr.

Oude Steenweg

Dambruggestr.

Ankerrui

Stijfselrui

Van den Wervestr.

Vondelstr.

Falcon plein

Falconrui

Paardenmarkt

Paardenmarkt

Noorderterras

Orteliuskaai

St. Paulusstr.

Klapdorp

Mutsaertstr.

Venusstr.

Vekestr. Korte Winkelstr.

Rodestraat

Rotterdamstr.

Van Moerlant str.

Italiëlei

Holland str.

Vee Markt

Zw. zu-str.

Zirkstraat

Blindestr. Prinsstr.

Jordaenskaai

Rapenstr.

Oude Beurs

Lange Koepoortstr.

Minderbroedersrui

Wolstraat

Keizerstr.

Oststraat

Van Stralenstr.

Suikerrui

Gildk.str.

Oudekoornmarkt

H.G. str.

Pelgrimsstr.

Eiermarkt

Kipdorp

St. Jacobsmkt.

Jezusstr.

Franklin Roosevelt plaats

Van Schoonhovestr.

Gemeentestr.

Kon. Astrid Pl.

Zuiderterras E. van Dijckkaai

Oever Hoogstr.

Lange Nieuwstraat

Leysstr.

De Keyserlei

Plantinkaai

Schoenmarkt

Leeuwenstraat

Meir

Meir

Wapper

Central Station

Pelikaanstr.

Vrijdagmarkt

Huidevetterstr.

Komediepl.

Kolveniersstr.

Hopland

Kipdorp Vest

Frankrijkei

Hessenbrug

Quellinstr.

DIAMOND DISTRICT

Lange Herentalsestr.

Simonsstr.

Mercatorstr.

Kloosterstr.

Nationalestraat

Begijnenstr.

Lange Gasthuisstr.

Leopoldstr.

Oude Vaartpl.

Tabak Vest

Frankrijkei

Quinten Matsijslei

Vestingstr.

Kronenburgstr.

Kasteelpleinstr.

Begijnenvest

Frankrijkei

Rubenslei

Stads Park

Plantin en Moretuslei

Brialmontlei

Scheldestr.

Marnixplaats

Tol straat

Britselei

Van Eycklei

Volkstr.

Amerikalei

Anselmostr.

Justitiestr.

Mechelsesteenweg

N

KEY
— Rail Lines
Metro
Tram
Æ American Express Office

0   300 yds
0   300 m

① sance **Stadhuis** (Town Hall). Antwerp's Town Hall was built in the 1560s during the city's golden age, when Paris and Antwerp were the only European cities with more than 100,000 inhabitants. In the facade, the fanciful fretwork of the late-Gothic style has given way to the discipline and order of the Renaissance; the public rooms are suitably impressive, though the heavy hand of 19th-century restoration work is much in evidence. *Admission: BF30, Open Mon. 9–noon, Tues.–Fri. 9–3, and Sat. noon–4. No access during official receptions.*

The huge fountain splashing water over much of the square is crowned by the figure of the legendary Silvius Brabo. He has been about to fling the hand of the giant into the River Scheldt for the past hundred years. Cafés line the square, most with terraces where it is especially pleasant to linger on a Monday night in summer, listening to the cathedral carillon.

Another famous monster slayer, St. George, is perched on top of the 16th-century guild house at Grote Markt 5, while the dragon appears to be falling off the pediment. Walk around the Stadhuis and along Gildekamersstraat; as you emerge on the north side of the square, take the second street left, Wisselstraat.

Time Out Among the many Italian restaurants around the Grote Markt, **La Terrazza** (Wisselstraat 2), run by brothers Saverio and Arturo, features reasonable prices and authentic cuisine.

Turn left again on Oude Beurs and you come immediately upon little Spanjepandsteeg and the house called **De Spieghel** (The Mirror). Originally built for the archers' guild, it was bought in 1506 by Pieter Gillis, a leading humanist. At the beginning of his most famous work, Sir Thomas More describes how, on a visit to Antwerp, he is walking back from Mass in the cathedral with Gillis when they encounter a traveler who tells them of his adventures on an island named Utopia. Erasmus, another friend of Gillis's, had the first edition of *Utopia* printed in Leuven.

② You can't miss the step-gabled **Vleeshuis** (Butchers' Hall), just a block away, for it remains one of the tallest buildings in the Old City, although it was completed for the Butchers' Guild in 1503. The designer was Herman de Waghemakere, member of a family of architects who did much to embellish their native city. The walls were built of alternating bands of brick and sandstone, creating an oddly pleasing layered effect. In the old days, the ground floor was used as a meat market, while the upper floors were occupied by a banquet hall and council chambers. Most of the space is crammed with miscellaneous antiquities of local origin. The collection of musical instruments on the top floor is particularly interesting for its harpsichords dating from the time when Ruckers of Antwerp meant to the music world what Steinway means today. *Vleeshonweistraat 38–40, tel. 03/233–6404. Admission: BF75; ticket good also for the Brouwershuis (see Off the Beaten Track, below). Open Tues.–Sun. 10–5.*

③ The block-long Repenstraat leads to the quay and the **Steen**. The 9th-century fortress was built to protect the western frontier of the Holy Roman Empire against the counts of Flanders. Charles V had the Steen partially rebuilt, and one can distinguish the darker, medieval masonry extending midway up the walls from the lighter, 16th-century upper level. The Steen was used as a prison for centuries. It now houses the **National Scheepvaartmuseum** (National Maritime Museum), where a large collection of models, figureheads, instruments, and charts is on display. *Steenplein, tel. 03/232–0850. Admission: BF75. Open Tues.–Sun. 10–5.*

The Steen is the only survivor of the original waterfront. Many houses were torn down in the 19th century to make room for the wide, straight quays that nowadays are practically deserted, the port having moved north of the city proper. The promenade starting at the Steen, **Noorderterras**, remains a very popular place for a Sunday stroll along the Scheldt, 500 meters (550 yards) wide here. "God gave us the river," say the Antwerpers, "and the river gave us all the rest."

4 At the end of the promenade, descend the steps, veer right across the quay, and head for the newly renovated **Sint-Pauluskerk** (St. Paul's Church), whose Baroque steeple can be seen over the rooftops. The church itself is late Gothic, built for the Dominicans by Domien de Waghemakere, but the interior was subsequently embellished—crammed, some would say—with a wealth of Baroque statuary, furnishings, and paintings, including the *Scourging of Christ* by Rubens. You have to walk around the church to find the entrance. *St. Paulusstraat 20–22, tel. 03/232–3267. Admission: BF30. Open daily May–Sept. 2–5; Oct.–Apr. 9–noon.*

From the Veemarkt in front of St. Paul's, you can zigzag through the old streets and alleys—first along Zwartzusters-straat, then right on Stoelstraat (at No. 11 stands the last remaining, but restored, wooden house in Gothic style), left on Zirkstraat, and right on Lange Koepoortstraat to the second street on the left, **Wolstraat.** This is the street where many English wool merchants settled in the 16th century, and the houses are distinguished by their Baroque portals, especially those at Nos. 7 and 30. You can enter through the gate of No. 37 to discover a well-preserved inner courtyard surrounded by 15th-century almshouses.

5 Turning left on Minderbroedersrui and right almost immediately on Keizerstraat, you arrive at the **Rockoxhuis**, the splendid Renaissance home of Nicolaas Rockox, first burgomaster (mayor) of Antwerp, who moved here in 1603. Rockox, a humanist and art collector, was a friend and patron of Rubens, and two of the painter's works hang here. One is *Madonna and Child*, in fact a delicate portrait of his first wife, Isabella, and their son Nicolaas; the other is a sketch for the *Crucifixion*. The collection also includes works by Van Dyck, Frans Snijders, Joachim Patinier, Jordaens, and David Teniers the Younger. The setting is important; rather than being displayed on museum walls, the paintings are shown in the context of a patrician Baroque home, furnished in the style of the period. *Keizerstraat 10, tel. 03/231–47–10. Admission free. Open Tues.–Sun. 10–5.*

6 The Jesuit church of **St. Carolus Borromeus** is just off Wolstraat. The front and tower are generally attributed to Rubens, and his hand can certainly be seen in the clustered cherubim above the entrance. The facade suggests a richly decorated high altar, inviting the spectator to enter the church. The interior also bears the imprint of Rubens and his group. *Hendrik Conscienceplein 12, tel. 03/33–8433. Admission: BF20. Open Mon. and Wed.–Fri. 7:30–1, Sat. 7:30–noon and 3–6:15.*

The square is one of the most attractive in Antwerp, flanked by the harmonious Renaissance buildings of the Jesuit convent, now occupied by the City Library. Wijngaardstraat, with its restaurants and art galleries, leads toward the Grote Markt.

Time Out **Het Elfde Gebod** (The Eleventh Commandment, Torfbrug 10) nestles under the cathedral. One of the most original of Antwerp's many cafés, it is crammed with plaster saints and angels salvaged from old churches. The beer is good, and you can have a pleasant meal of bread and cheese.

7 Continue to the cathedral entrance on Handschoenmarkt (Glove Market). **Onze-Lieve-Vrouwekathedraal** (Our Lady of Sorrows Cathedral) is the city's Gothic masterpiece, recently restored. It is the largest church in the Low Countries. Work started in 1352 and continued in fits and starts until 1584, but even so the whole is a totally homogeneous monument of stone and light thanks to a succession of remarkable architects, including Peter Appelmans, Herman and Domien de Waghemakere, and Rombout Keldermans the Younger. The 123-meter (404-foot)-high north spire is a miracle of lightness. The tower contains a 47-bell carillon (played Fri. 11:30–12:30 and Mon. in summer 8PM–9PM).

The cathedral's art treasures were twice vandalized, first by Protestant iconoclasts in 1566, and again by the French at the end of the 18th century. The latter carried off masterpieces of art as though they were their rightful booty; some but by no means all have subsequently been returned. Other works have been donated or purchased to make up an outstanding collection of 17th-century religious art, including three Rubens altarpieces. Among them, his *Assumption of the Virgin Mary*, painted for the high altar, is a characteristic swirling apotheosis in which the Virgin is carried upward by massed ranks of *putti* (cherubs) and *amoretti* (cupids) toward the angel waiting to crown her. The Assumption has been cunningly hung so that the rays of the sun illuminate it exactly at noon. *Groenplaats 21, tel. 03/231–3033. Admission: BF30. Open weekdays 10–5, Sat. 10–3, and Sun. 1–4.*

8 A few steps to the left from the front of the cathedral is Oude Koornmarkt, with many old step-gable houses. At No. 16 begins the **Vlaaikensgang**, a quiet cobblestone lane that preserves the mood and style of the 16th century. The alley ends in Pelgrimsstraat, where there is a great view of the cathedral spire. Turning your back to it, you quickly reach Reyndersstraat, where the **house of** the painter **Jacob Jordaens** stands at No. 6. This gem of Baroque art, with its very attractive courtyard, rivals the Rubenshuis (*see* Tour 2, *below*). *Reyndersstraat 6, tel. 03/233–3033. Admission: BF75. Open Tues.–Fri. 10–5.*

Time Out There's another secret courtyard near the Jordaens house. It's at Leeuwenstraat 18 and features a good café, **De Groote Witte Arend,** an old convent where the music tends to be by Vivaldi or Telemann. The menu lists 34 different types of beer.

Just to the left is Leeuwenstraat, which leads to Vrijdagmarkt.
9 On the south side of this square stands the **Plantin-Moretus Museum,** named for Christophe Plantin, who established the Plantin Press here in 1576. Philip II of Spain appointed Plantin exclusive printer of liturgical books, and thousands were exported every year to Spain and its possessions. His greatest achievement was the *Biblia Regia* (in Room 16): eight large volumes containing the Bible in Latin, Greek, Hebrew, Syriac, and Aramaic, complete with notes, glossaries, and grammars.

The first three rooms were the family quarters; they contain several portraits by Rubens. Others remain as they were when occupied by accountants, editors, and proofreaders. The printing workshop, finally, contains Plantin's 16 printing presses. Two typefaces designed here, Plantin and Garamond, are still in use. The presses are still in working order, and one can, in fact, purchase a copy of Plantin's sonnet "Le bonheur de ce monde," an ode to contentment, in any of seven European languages and printed on an original press. *Vrijdagmarkt 22, tel. 03/233–0294. Admission: BF75. Open Tues.–Sun. 10–5.*

Down the lane on the left of the museum, it's worth stopping at the **Huis Draecke** (Heilige-Geeststraat 9), a well-preserved patrician dwelling. The courtyard can be entered. The small chapel on the left is from the 15th century, while the rest is late Gothic. Turn right into Hoogstraat, now a pedestrian precinct.

Time Out | On the waterfront is the striking new **Zuiderterras Café,** a nautically inspired five-story complex of stainless steel, copper, glass, and concrete that also includes an art gallery.

On the way back to the Grote Markt, you can cross the
10 Suikerrui to the **Etnografisch Museum** (Ethnographic Museum). This new museum—opened in 1988—contains excellently displayed collections illustrating art, religion, and daily life in Africa, the Americas, Asia, and the South Seas. *Suikerrui 19, tel. 03/220–8211. Admission: BF75. Open Tues.–Sun. 10–5.*

Tour 2: Rubens and | The bustling **Groenplaats,** just south of the cathedral, is
Diamonds | adorned with a statue of Pieter Paul Rubens himself. He wears
11 a sword as a badge of his rank, for he was truly a Renaissance man who in addition to his prodigious artistic output found time to undertake a number of diplomatic missions, culminating in the negotiation of a peace treaty between Spain and England and knighthoods from both Charles II and Philip IV.

From the southeast corner of the square, Schoenmarkt leads up toward Meir, Antwerp's most elegant shopping street, punctuated at this end by the **Torengebouw,** built around 1930, which Antwerpers proudly proclaim as Europe's first skyscraper.

Huidevettersstraat, to the right, leads to Lange Gasthuis-
12 straat and the outstanding **Museum Mayer van den Bergh,** a private art collection amassed in the 19th century by a passionate connoisseur, Fritz Mayer van den Bergh. The collection includes treasures such as a life-size polychrome statue from about 1300 of St. John resting his head on Christ's bosom. It is, however, the two Bruegel paintings that make this small museum a must. One is his witty, miniature illustrations of *Twelve Proverbs* based on popular Flemish sayings. The other is *Dulle Griet,* often referred to in English as Mad Meg. It shows an

irate woman wearing helmet and breastplate—a sword in one hand, and food and cooking utensils in the other—striding across a field strewn with the ravages and insanity of war. Nothing could be farther from the Bruegelian villages than this nightmare world, whose hallucinations are akin to those of Hieronymus Bosch's fevered imagination. On an emotional level, it is among the most powerful antiwar statements ever made. A footnote: Mayer van den Bergh bought *Dulle Griet* for BF488 in 1894; today it is priceless. *Lange Gasthuisstraat 19, tel. 03/ 232-4237. Admission: BF75. Open Tues.–Sun. 10–5.*

⑬ In Komedieplaats (by way of Huidevettersstraat), on the right, is the neoclassical **Bourla Theater,** a well-preserved playhouse from the 1830s, which has been completely restored, complete with Viennese café in the rotunda.

Time Out In Arme Duivelstraat (Poor Devil Street), just off the square in Antwerp's Quartier Latin, is an attractive bistro called **De Varkenspot.** The menu has Flemish specialties.

⑭ On Wapper, one block away, stands **Rubenshuis,** the carefully reconstructed home of the painter as patrician. Only the elaborate portico and temple, designed by Rubens in Italian Baroque style, were still standing earlier in this century. They figure in several of his own paintings as well as in works by Van Dyck and Jordaens. Drawings by Rubens and his pupils and old prints were used to recreate the brick and sandstone house— kitchen, dining room, bedrooms—and the huge studio. Some Rubens paintings hang in the house (an early *Adam and Eve,* an *Annunciation,* a self-portrait), but nothing like the 300-odd pieces that his widow promptly sold off after his death in 1640. *Wapper 9, tel. 03/232-4751. Admission: BF75. Open Tues.– Sun. 10–5.*

From Wapper you can turn right on Meir, and right again onto Kolveniersstraat. At No. 16 stands **Kolveniershof,** the Renaissance guild house of the harquebusiers, who sported the long-barreled firearms also called hackbuts.

On the opposite side of Meir is the elegant 18th-century **Osterriethhuis,** now occupied by a bank. The continuation of Meir, Leysstraat, crosses the broad Frankrijklei and becomes De Keyserlei. On your right is the **Diamond District,** a few nondescript city blocks bordering on the Central Station to the east. Shop signs in Hebrew and the characteristic Hasidic clothing and ringlets worn by many men are the only clues that this area is any different from the rest of Antwerp. Below the elevated railway tracks a long row of stalls and shops gleams with jewelry and gems, a bit like New York's West 47th Street.

Diamond cutting began in Brugge but moved to Antwerp in the 16th century along with most other wealth-creating activities. Given Antwerp's twin preoccupations with beauty and money, craft and trade both flourished. Twenty-five million carats are cut and traded in Antwerp every year, more than anywhere else, and the industry employs some 18,000 people, divided among 6,000 independent firms. In addition to cutters, grinders, and polishers, there are about 3,000 traders, of whom two-thirds are Jewish and 20% Indian, with a heavy sprinkling of Lebanese and Armenians. Nearly all come from old diamond families. Some of Antwerp's Jews managed to flee Belgium during the war, but many more perished in the camps.

15 Turning right off Meir into Appelmansstraat you come quickly to Lange Herentalsestraat and the **Provinciaal Diamant-museum** (Provincial Diamond Museum). Maps, models and videos tell the story of the diamond trade, and exceptional jewelry is displayed in the treasure room. *Lange Herentalsestraat 31–33, tel. 03/231–8645. Admission free. Open daily 10–5; demonstrations Sat. PM.*

In this business, security is of the essence, and traditionally visitors have not been able to see much of the bustling activity.
16 To remedy this situation, the industry has created **Diamondland.** The spectacular showrooms have three floors of slide shows and films, showcases of rough and polished diamonds, and several diamond cutters at work. *Appelmansstraat 33A, tel. 03/243–3612. Open Mon.–Sat. 9–6.*

Time Out **Panache** (Statiestraat 17), north of De Keyserlei, is an Antwerp institution. It's the best sandwich bar in town and also serves a limited selection of hot dishes.

17 The Neo-Baroque **Centraalstation** (Central Station) at the end of De Keyserlei was built between 1895 and 1905 during the reign of Leopold II, a monarch not given to understatement. Architect Louis Delacenserie's magnificent exterior and splendid, vaulted ticket-office hall and staircases call out for hissing steam engines, peremptory conductors, scurrying porters, and languid ladies wrapped in boas. Alas, most departures and arrivals are humble commuter trains. The square in front of the station, Koningin Astridplein, does little to honor that glamorous and tragic queen; it is depressingly seedy, and the blocks north of it are best avoided.

18 East of the station the **Antwerp Zoo** offers a refreshing change from most city center zoos. A Moorish villa is home to the rhinoceroses, an Egyptian temple is the elephant house, and the thriving okapi family graze around an Indian temple. There's also a dolphinarium, an aquarium, and a house for nocturnal animals. The Antwerp Zoo celebrates its 150th anniversary in 1993. *Koningin Astridplein 26, tel. 03/231–1640. Admission: BF305 adults, BF190 children. Open daily 8:30–6:30; winter, daily 8:45–5:45.*

Excursion from Antwerp

Lier The small town of **Lier** lies 17 kilometers (10½ miles) southeast of Antwerp on N10. It may seem a sleepy riverside town, but it has long attracted poets and painters and has even known its moment of glory. It was here in 1496 that Philip of Burgundy married Joan of Aragon and Castile (known as Philippe le Beau—Philip the Handsome—and Juana la Loca—Joans the Mad). From that union sprang Emperor Charles V.

The **Sint-Gummaruskerk,** where they were wed, is yet another product of the De Waghemakere–Keldermans partnership. It is well endowed with stained-glass windows from the 15th and 16th centuries. Those in the choir were the gift of Maximilian of Austria, who visited in 1516, and he can be seen in one of them with his wife, Mary of Burgundy.

Along the riverside, willows bend over the water, and in summer, boats can be hired for 40-minute sightseeing rides. *Netelaan, weekends 2–8.* The Kleine Nete flows straight through the heart of the town; the Grote Nete and a canal also encircle the center.

Across the river is the **Zimmertoren,** a 14th-century tower renamed for Louis Zimmer, who designed its astronomical clock with 11 faces in 1930. His studio, where 57 dials show the movements of the moon, the tides, the zodiac, and other cosmic phenomena, is inside the tower. *Zimmerplein 18, tel. 03/489-1111. Admission: BF40. Open daily 9-noon and 1-7; winter, 9-noon and 1-5.*

Time Out   If you want sustenance, don't pass up the delicious syrup-filled biscuits, Lierse Vlaaikens, which are the local specialty.

Nearby is the **Begijnhof,** which differs from most other beguinages in that its small houses line narrow streets rather than being grouped around a common. A Renaissance portico stands at the entrance, and on it a statue of St. Begge, who gave his name to this congregation and who probably derived his own from the fact that he was *un begue* (a stammerer).

What to See and Do with Children

The **Antwerp Zoo** is perhaps the greatest attraction for the younger generation in Antwerp (*see* Exploring Antwerp, Tour 2, *above*). **Planckendael,** the breeding station for the zoo, is a huge park where more than a thousand animals live in a state of almost total freedom. *Southeast of Mechelen, 25 km (15 mi) from Antwerp: Leuvensesteenweg 582, Muizen, tel. 015/41-49-21. Admission: BF280 adults, BF180 children. Open Apr.-Sept., daily 8:30-6:30; Oct.-Mar. daily 10-5.*

Kids can see the entire city in miniature at **Mini-Antwerpen** in a transformed quayside warehouse. *Hangar 15, Scheldekai, tel. 03/237-0329. Admission: BF130 adults, BF100 children. Open daily noon-6.*

The region's chief amusement park is **Bobbejaanland,** which has 45 rides, plus slides, swings, and shows. *43 km (27 mi) from Antwerp on E313, exit Herentals West, direction Kasterlee; Steenweg op Olen, Lichtaart, tel. 014/55-78-11. Admission: BF510. Open Apr.-June and Sept., daily 10-6; July-Aug. 10-7.*

Off the Beaten Track

North of the Old City, close to where the port begins, stands the **Brouwershuis** (Brewers' House), which dates from 1553. This is part of the Nieuwstad, or New Town, planned by Gilbert van Schoonbeke, who designed a system to siphon off water from the Herentals Canal; the horse-powered treadmill can be seen on the ground floor. It worked so well that it remained in operation until 1930. The house was also used by the Brewers' Guild, and their meeting room on the first floor, hung with gilt leather, is one of the handsomest rooms in Antwerp. *Adriaan Brouwerstraat 20, tel. 03/232-6511. Admission: BF75 (included in the price of a visit to Vleeshuis; see Exploring Antwerp, Tour 1, above). Open Tues.-Sun. 10-5.*

Berchem is a bit farther out in the same direction, the first train station on the line to Brussels. The 19th-century entrepreneur Baron Edouard Osy and his sister Josephine Cogels, bought up an old castle, demolished it, and built some refreshingly eccentric houses reflecting the confident and eclectic tastes of that era. There are houses in renaissance, Greek classical, and Venetian styles, but most of all there are a number of beautiful Art Nouveau buildings, especially at the southern end of Cogels Osylei and Waterloostraat.

South of the Old City, in Leopold de Waelplaats, is the **Koninklijk Museum voor Schone Kunsten** (Royal Museum of Fine Arts). The permanent collection is long on monumental Rubens works and short on more intimate paintings; the prosaic explanation is that the latter were more easily taken away from Antwerp. Rubens's friends and followers are also well represented. The collection of Flemish primitives is perhaps even more rewarding; it includes works by van Eyck, Memling, Roger van der Weyden, Joachim Patinier, and Quinten Metsys. On the ground floor there's a representative survey of Belgian art of the past 150 years—Emile Claus, Rik Wouters, Permeke, Magritte, Delvaux, and especially James Ensor. *Leopold de Wadplaats 1–9, tel. 03/238–7809. Admission free. Open Tues.– Sun. 10–5.*

South of the beltway—above the tunnel for the expressway to Brussels—is the 12-hectare (30-acre) **Middelheim Park** with its **Openluchtmuseum** (Open Air Sculpture Museum). There are close to 500 sculptures in this very attractive setting, providing an excellent survey of three-dimensional art from Rodin to the present. There is also a new pavilion that houses smaller or more fragile sculptures. *Tel. 03/828–1350. Admission free, except during Biennial exhibitions. Open Tues.–Sun. 10–dusk, (i.e., 5 PM in midwinter; June–July, 9 PM).*

Shopping

Antwerp takes pride in being young, with-it, and trendy, and this is reflected in the city's shops and boutiques, which are as smart as they come.

Shopping Streets The elegant **Meir,** together with its extension to the east, **De Keyserlei,** and at the opposite end, **Huidevettersstraat,** is where the smart and long-established shops are. Shopping galleries branch off from all three—**Century Center** and **Antwerp Tower** from De Keyserlei, **Patio** from Meir, and **Nieuwe Gaanderei** from Huidevettersstraat.

The boutiques along pedestrian malls often cater to more avant-garde tastes. The best-known area is **De Wilde Zee,** consisting of Groendalstraat, Wiegstraat, and Korte Gasthuisstraat. Another pedestrian area is **Hoogstraat,** between Groto Markt and Sint-Jansvliet, with its appendix **Grote Pieter Potstraat.** Here you find good second-hand bookshops and all kinds of bric-a-brac.

Street Markets Public auction sales of furniture and other second-hand goods are held on **Vrijdagmarkt** (Wed. and Fri. 9–noon) from 9 to 5. There's an antique market on **Lijnwaadmarkt** (Easter–Oct., Sat. 9–5), just north of the cathedral. Oudevaartplaats (a block south from Rubenshuis on Wapper) is home to the most popular and animated of Antwerp's markets, the **Vogelmarkt** (bird market, Sun. 9–1). It includes flowers and plants, fruit and vegetables, and lots of pets.

The **Rubensmarkt** (Rubens Market, Aug. 15 annually) is held on the Grote Markt, with vendors in 17th-century costumes hawking everything under the sun.

Specialty Stores

Clothing A group of fashion designers collectively known as the Antwerp Six has been making waves internationally. Two of them, Ann Demeulemeester and Dirk Bikkenbergs, are represented at **Louis** (Lombardenstraat 2, tel. 03/232–9872). Other leading fashion boutiques are **Modepaleis** (Nationalestraat 16, tel. 03/233–9437) and **Closing Date** (Korte Gasthuisstraat 15, tel. 03/232–8722).

Gifts **Calico House** (Zand 1, tel. 03/233–6023) specializes in quilts and patchwork. **Extra Large** (Oude Beurs 30, tel. 03/232–9841) is a place for outsize, fun gifts.

Diamonds Diamonds are an excellent investment for individual customers, as well as for the many dealers who come to Antwerp for them; they can be bought tax-free. (Note: tax-free does not mean duty-free when you return home.) If you are not an expert, you can rely on the advice given by the staff at **Diamondland** (Appelmansstraat 33A, tel. 03/243–3612). The quality of the stones is guaranteed by a Diamond High Council certificate.

Sports and Fitness

Golf The **Royal Antwerp Golf Club** (George Gapiaulei 2, Kapelle-op-den-Bos, tel. 03/666–8456), 22 kilometers (14 miles) from the city, is the oldest. **Ternesse** Golf Club (Uilenbaan 15, Wommelgem, tel. 03/353–0326) is the closest to town, 9 kilometers (5½ miles) away.

Skating Two popular skating rinks are **Antarctica** (Moerelei 119, Wilrijk, tel. 03/828–9928) and **Zondal** (Ruggeveldlaan 488B, Deurne, tel. 03/325–0374).

Tennis Courts at **Het Rooi** (Berchemstadionstraat 73, tel. 03/239–6610) rent for BF200–BF300 per hour. Tariffs at **Beerschot** (Stadionstraat, tel. 03/220–8687) are a bit lower, at BF150 an hour. Try to book courts for as early in the day as you can.

Spectator Sports

Most indoor sports events are staged in the **Sportpaleis** (Schijnpoortweg 113, tel. 03/326–1010) just outside the ring road northeast of the city center, including cycling and tennis championships.

Dining

By Nancy Coons Belgium's second city—its Flemish capital and one of the most active ports in the world—offers an impressive variety of restaurants and even some ethnic options, though not on the level of its once-more-colonially inclined Dutch neighbors. In fact, despite a certain amount of exotic influence, Antwerp remains remarkably conservative in its culinary tastes, focusing with understandable devotion on fish—fish presented with few frills in even the finest restaurants, often poached or steamed, and accessibly priced. From the chilled welks and winkles (sea snails) picked out of their shells with pins, to piles of tender little *crevettes grises* (gray shrimp), to the mammoth turbot heavy with steamy white flesh, the odor of salt air and fresh brine is never far from your table. The ubiquitous *moules* (mussels) and eels, showcased in middle-class restaurants throughout the city center, provide a heavier, heartier version of fish cuisine; they are bought alive from wholesalers, and are thus irreproachably fresh.

Very Expensive **La Preuse.** This retired pleasure cruiser is far from a tourist
★ trap. In fact, it's one of Flanders's finer dining spots, on land or water. Serving fresh and straightforward seafood in an unpretentious atmosphere, the restaurant offers views across the tidal river Scheldt and just enough bobbing on the waves to remind the diner of how local the fish is. Whole turbot is presented in its kitchen steamer before being filleted and served with fennel, carrots, and cream-thickened stock; bass is cooked in salt-crust and served with saffron butter. There's plenty of meat as well: beef in Pomerol with marrow, lamb in orange rind and basil. The ambience is relaxed, almost casual. *Ponton Steen, tel. 03/231–31–51. Reservations required. Jacket and tie suggested. AE, DC, MC, V. Closed Sun.–Mon.*

★ **Sir Anthony Van Dijck.** Hidden down an ancient, twisting brick alley in the old town, this group of 16th- and 17th-century houses has been transformed into a spectacular, atmospheric restaurant. Diners sit under high, massive beams and stone pillars, surrounded by fresh flowers and heavy carved wood, and eat light, if conservative, *cuisine du marché* (food of the market): plump poached oysters in cream sauce with minced leeks and zucchini and a parade of artfully prepared fish. The ambience is hushed and formal, the service discreet. *Oude Koornmarkt 16, tel. 03/231–61–70. Reservations required. Jacket and tie advised. AE, DC, MC, V. Closed weekends.*

Expensive **In de Schaduw van de Kathedraal.** Cozier and more traditional than the wave of contemporary restaurants dominating the scene, this comfortable little dining room faces the cathedral square and, in warm weather, sets up terrace tables in its namesake's shadow. Try the nutmeg-perfumed gratin of endive and crevettes grises or steamed sole with scampi in fresh basil. *Handschoenmarkt 17, tel. 03/232–40–14. Reservations suggested. Jacket suggested. AE, DC, MC, V. Closed June–Sept., Tues.; Oct.–May, Mon.–Tues.*

★ **Neuze Neuze.** Its chichi name ("nose-nose," referring to what children call an Eskimo kiss) sets the tone: This is a young, fashionable dining spot with a downtown air, an arty mix of intimate, old-beamed rooms with halogen and waitresses in matching stretch velour. But the cooking is strictly uptown— terrine of goose liver and pear, sautéed scallops with leeks, monkfish rolls with caviar—and the service is smooth. The wine list is exceptionally deep. *Wijngaardstraat 19, tel. 03/232–57–83. Reservations advised. Jacket suggested. AE, DC, MC, V. Closed Sun.*

★ **Preud'homme.** Don't be put off by the eclectic pomp: turgid Verdi and Puccini tapes, unfocused interior design (modern glass and stone with a 400-year-old painted wood ceiling), signed pewter platters under the china. Despite these excesses, the cooking is confident and superb, from delicate timbales to feather-light vinaigrettes, from expertly poached fish to meats artfully served. Showy service reflects the decor, but not the food—which is right on track. *Suikerrui 28, tel. 03/233-42-00. Reservations advised. Jacket and tie suggested. AE, DC, MC, V. Closed Oct.–May, Tues.*

't Silveren Claverblat. Neither as chic nor as suave as its trendier competitors in this category, with problems in pacing and lacking in visual flair, this popular young-professional rendezvous has trouble getting past the prestige dishes (foie gras, truffles)—but when it does, it serves good, light, contemporary French cuisine (marinated raw salmon, home-smoked salmon with its roe, lobster in creamy-sweet sauterne sauce) in generous portion. *Grote Pieter Potstraat 16, tel. 03/231-33-88. Reservations advised. Jacket and tie suggested. AE, DC, MC, V. Closed Sat. lunch and Tues.*

Moderate **Het Nieuwe Palinghuis.** This is a good, Old Antwerp landmark, with dark wood, pottery, and a comfortable bourgeois air, and its seafood specialties—above all, its *paling* (eel)—are well prepared and reasonably priced. There's eel in green sauce, grilled turbot, grilled scallops, and sole in lobster sauce. *Sint-Jansvliet 14, tel. 03/231-74-45. Reservations suggested. Jacket suggested. AE, DC, MC, V. Closed Mon.–Tues.*

★ **De Grootte Ganz.** Oozing Old Town atmosphere, this romantic, candlelit café/restaurant stretches along an underground, vaulted stone crypt. Unpretentious food—endive-and-beer soup, *stoofpotje* (stew of fish and seafood), sole with mussels, rabbit, and steaks—is served at narrow wooden tables with benches, while a house magician wanders from table to table. *Pelgrimstraat 15, tel. 03/234-08-09. Reservations suggested. Dress: casual. AE, DC, MC, V. Closed Mon.–Tues.*

De Peerdestal. For chalkboard specials (mixed grill, scallops *maison*) and café standards (mussels, fish, steaks), this beam-and-brick stable is an appealing place for a casual meal. It has been renovated in a two-story atrium design, with checkered-cloth tables scattered around the open loft and stools around the pine-topped bar below. *Wijngaardstraat 8, tel. 03/231-95-03. Dress: casual. AE, DC, MC, V. Closed Sun.*

★ **Rooden Hoed.** Though it was founded by an Alsatian family in the 1930s, this atmospheric restaurant/tavern is pure Old Antwerp (the building itself dates from 1467), with high, dark wainscoting topped with pottery and knickknacks. Classic *cuisine bourgeoise* and Antwerp specialties are combined here— eel, oysters, sole, and mussels dominate. However, some more ambitious (read: pretentious) dishes—Chateaubriand, turbot *Noilly Prat*—try to lift the restaurant into an altogether uncalled-for higher class. *Oude Koornmarkt 25, tel. 03/233-28-44. Reservations suggested. Dress: casual. AE, V. Closed Wed.–Thur.*

Inexpensive **'t Brantyser.** This old café, with dark rafters, brick, and stucco in two open levels, offers more than just drinks and the usual snacks: There are imaginative salads (endive with bacon and Roquefort), fish and meat dishes, and affordable specials. *Hendrik Conscienceplein 7, tel. 03/233-18-33. Reservations suggested at lunch. Dress: casual. No credit cards. Closed Mon.*

Kiekekot. Antwerp students satisfy their craving for spit-roasted chicken and frites at this no-frills "chicken coop," which offers a juicy, golden half chicken for little more than its retail price. *Grote Markt 35, tel. 03/232–15–02. No reservations. Dress: casual. No credit cards.*

Overzetboot. This is the best of the mussel joints that vie for tourists between the Steen and the cathedral. Mussels come in the usual variety, and the rest of the menu is a simple mix-and-match: Eel, sole, turbot, steaks, and chicken are offered in a choice of sauces (béarnaise, *archiduc, poivre crème,* mousseline), all of them prepared in advance, and most of them rich. The setting is pleasantly casual, with beer and paper mats. *Suikerrui 8, tel. 03/226–02–64. Reservations suggested. Dress: casual. AE, DC, MC, V. Closed Tues.*

Viskeuken. Translated simply as "Fish Kitchen," this restaurant is as honest as its name. The fish and oysters displayed in its windows are cooked and served in as straightforward a manner as a landlubber could wish, and at reasonable prices. There are paper placemats over the linens, and there's enough ceramic tile, stucco, and beams to give the steamy setting a modicum of charm. *Korte Koepoortstraat 10, tel. 03/233–08–66. Reservations suggested. Dress: casual. AE, DC, MC, V.*

Lodging

By Nancy Coons Antwerp hotels are in the throes of complying with a new fire code, and many inexpensive and family-scale lodgings have not been able to fulfill the new requirements, which include moving elevators and adding new fire escapes. Thus, at least in the early '90s, there are very few inexpensive hotels in town. One option for flexible travelers: Several small houses run on an hourly rate, serving the universal need for illicit rendezvous. They are not for prostitutes, and many tourists find them perfectly functional. They average BF1,500 for an overnight stay (doubles, of course). Ask at the tourist office for the nicer of the lot. **Note:** The tourist office can reserve hotel rooms for you up to a week in advance for reduced prices. You pay a deposit of BF200, which is deducted from the price of the room. Write for a reservation form and return it, specifying your needs. Also, if you land in Antwerp on a weekend, you'll benefit from tremendous reductions on hotel rooms, as most are filled with expense-account businesspeople during the working week. The hotels below are categorized by their weekday price; some fall easily into a lower range on weekends.

Very Expensive **Alfa DeKeyser.** This is one of the more deluxe versions of a business hotel, with music piped into the muffled anonymity of the corridors. Newly refurbished "executive" doubles sport postmodern pear-wood cabinetry and granite-look laminate. Standard doubles, though not as up-to-date, are fresh nonetheless. Ask for a room in the back, overlooking an Astroturfed "court." It's just next door to the train station and zoo. *De Keyserlei 66–70, B-2018, tel. 03/234–01–35. 117 rooms. Facilities: restaurant, bar, indoor pool, whirlpool, sauna, solarium, fitness center, non-smoking rooms. AE, DC, MC, V.*

Alfa Theater. This is a more modest member of the Alfa group but just as convenient to the station, with less decorative flash than the DeKeyser and none of the sports facilities, but most of its other comforts. Surprisingly, the windows have been left single-glazed, so it's important to aim for higher floors or back rooms. *Arenbergstraat 30, B-2000, tel. 03/231–17–20. 85 rooms. Facilities: restaurant, bar. AE, DC, MC, V.*

Carlton. With a number of its rooms overlooking the greenery of the Stads park, this is an unusually comfortable version of the generic modern business hotel. Built new in 1988, with air-conditioning in every room, it offers the current vogue in decor (burled-look laminate, marble-look tile) and all amenities (hair dryers, trouser presses). The back rooms are quieter but lack the park views. *Quinten Matsijslei 25, B-2018, tel. 03/231–15–15. 127 rooms. Facilities: restaurant, bar. AE, DC, MC, V.*

★ **De Rosier.** Leaving would-be competitors in the deluxe market behind by several laps, this is the only choice in town—if not in the country—for luxury on an intimate scale. Literally clois-tered behind discreet double doors (it functioned as a cloister from 1932 to 1972), this lovely hotel is nearly invisible from the narrow back street it faces, focusing inward instead on the aris-tocratic garden court and its sumptuously furnished interiors. Downstairs, guests move freely from Louis Quinze to Empire to Victorian chinoiserie; rooms upstairs vary from skylighted, modernized garrets to the beamed-and-leaded-glass suite in pure Old Antwerp style. The mansion dates from 1627. *Rosier 21–23, B-2000, tel. 03/225–01–40. 12 rooms. Facilities: break-fast room, garden terrace, indoor pool. AE, DC, MC, V.*

Expensive **Antigone.** Directly across the street from the sheltered wharf on the River Scheldt, this group of town houses was rescued from a tradition of *bordellerie* and was converted, in 1988, into a legitimate hotel. Now its interiors are slick and contempo-rary, with a neo–art deco air and pale, rosy pastels. Despite double windows over the street and river, you'll sleep better in the back. *Jordaenskaai 11–12, B-2000, tel. 03/231–66–77. 17 rooms. Facilities: breakfast room, bar. AE, DC, MC, V.*

★ **Firean.** This Art Deco gem, built in 1929 and restored in 1986 not only to its architectural style but also to the welcoming grace of its era, offers sweet relief to travelers benumbed by the uniformity of chain hotels. Its location—a residential neighborhood south of the center but on the way into town from the Brussels expressway—reinforces the tranquillity inside, expressed in fresh flowers, rich fabrics, and a tasteful mix of antiques and reproductions. Breakfast eggs come in floral-print cozies, and jazz piano is discreetly piped into public areas but doesn't leak into the rooms—which are sanctuaries. *Karel Oomsstraat 6, B-2018, tel. 03/237–02–60. 12 rooms. Facilities: breakfast only. AE, DC, MC, V.*

Villa Mozart. Mozart didn't stay here, though he did spend time in Antwerp on his travels with his father, but this small, modern hotel is devoted to him, every room named after a char-acter in his operas. Decor is appropriately fussy, with floral-print Austrian blinds, but the emphasis is on business-class comforts: air-conditioning, electronic security. The rooms are slightly cramped—due, in part, to the generous beds—but many look out toward the cathedral. It's in a pedestrian area, and thus quiet. *Handschoenmarkt 3–7, B-2000, tel. 03/231–30–31. 25 rooms. Facilities: restaurant, bar. AE, DC, MC, V.*

Moderate **Cammerpoorte.** All modern but comfortably nestled in the Old Town, this simple hotel was opened in 1990 and recently added seven new rooms. The structure is solid, the rooms are slick, with all-weather carpet and graphite-look laminate. The breakfast buffet is served in a conference-room atmosphere. *Nationalestraat 38–40, B-2000, tel. 03/231–97–36. 46 rooms. Facilities: breakfast only. AE, DC, MC, V.*

Columbus. This old, central building has been nicely recast as a chic, modern retro hotel, with Art Nouveau references and fresh room decor. Renovated in 1991 and expanded in 1992, with new windows and all-white tile baths, it offers business-class comforts on a comfortable, personal scale. *Frankrijklei 4, B-2000, tel. 03/233–03–90. 24 rooms. Facilities: bar, breakfast only. AE, DC, MC, V.*

★ **Prinse.** Set back from the Old Town streets in an enclosed courtyard, this 400-year-old landmark is a solid new member of the Relais du Silence (quiet inns) group. It was opened in 1990, with a neutral, modern look—black leather, soft blues, all-tile baths—and offers peace and quiet with its business amenities. *Keizerstraat 63, B-2000, tel. 03/226–40–50. 30 rooms. Facilities: breakfast only. AE, DC, MC, V.*

Inexpensive **Antverpja.** Owned by the managers of the Cammerpoorte and
★ just up the street, this small, familial pension has been scrubbed and decorated with the enthusiasm of a home owner by its proud proprietor. Breakfast is served in the tidy brick-and-lace café downstairs, while rooms—on landings up the narrow staircase—are full of bright pastels and sad-clown art. *Steenhouwersvest 55, B-2000, tel. 03/231–28–36. 9 rooms with toilet and shower. Facilities: breakfast only. AE, DC, MC, V.*

Florida. Considerably less attractive but as close to the train station as you can get without sleeping on a bench, this big, weary railroad hotel has single-glazed French windows that open over the noisy street. Decor is tired—pink chenille, scarlet carpet, creaky armoires—but the breakfast room was fixed up in recent decades, and prices justify all. Some rooms have full bath facilities. *De Keyserlei 59, B-2018, tel. 03/232–14–43. 51 rooms. Facilities: breakfast only. V.*

Rubenshof. This glorious mid-Victorian mansion has been left alone in its public spaces, decaying in its own grand excess, with rococo plasterwork, torn silk wallpaper, and an Art Nouveau breakfast nook. Upstairs, unfortunately, rooms have been tacked together and cut out of walls meant to last a millennium. The decor is seedy, but functional. Single windows let in lots of boulevard noise. Yet prices, with or without bath, are the lowest around, and the glimpse of the past that they purchase may justify the discomfort for some. *Amerikalei 115–117, B-2000, tel. 03/237–07–89. 20 rooms. Facilities: breakfast only. MC, V.*

The Arts and Nightlife

The Arts Check *The Bulletin* for details on arts events in Antwerp.

Antwerp has acquired a reputation for innovative and exciting ballet, and its school is internationally renowned. The principal company is the **Koninklijk Ballet van Vlaanderen** (Royal Flanders Ballet, Britselei 80, tel. 03/234–3438). The opera is nearby: **Koninklijke Vlaamse Opera** (Royal Flanders Opera, Frankrijklei 3, tel. 03/233–6685).

The **Koninklijke Philharmonisch Orchester van Vlaanderen** (Royal Flanders Philharmonic) can most frequently be heard at **De Singel** (Desguinlei 25, tel. 03/248–3800), where modern and contemporary music is often performed. Another venue for classical music is the **Koningin Elisabethzaal** (Koningin Astridplein 23, tel. 03/233–8444), where there are also rock concerts. Visiting rock musicians can also be heard at the **Sportpaleis** (Schijnpoortweg 113, tel. 03/326–1010).

The flagship of the over two dozen theaters in Antwerp is the **Koninklijke National Schouwburg** (KNS, Theaterplein 1, tel. 03/231–0750). Two independent theaters of special interest are **Vrije Val** (Namenstraat 7), and **Monty** (Montignystraat 3–5). The **Poppenschouwburg Van Campen** (Van Campen Puppet Theater, Lange Nieuwstraat 3, tel. 03/237–3716), puts on traditional puppet performances in Flemish dialect.

Nightlife There are 2,500 taverns in Antwerp—one per 200 inhabitants.

Bars The most famous is probably the **Bierhuis Kulminator** (Vleminckveld 32–34, tel. 03/232–4538), which stocks, cools and pours 550 different kinds of beer, including EKU-28, the strongest beer on earth. Other bars in the Old Town include **Pelgrom** (Pelgrimsstraat 15, tel. 03/234–0809), a 16th-century tavern; **De Engel** (Grote Markt 3, tel. 03/233–1252), an ordinary café but the most popular in town; **Blauwe Steen** (Ernest van Dijckkaai 34, tel. 03/231–6710), with buskers performing Antwerp music; and **Beveren** (Vlasmarkt 2, tel. 03/231–2225), an old-fashioned café. **Il Mondo** (Grote Pieter Pot 6, no tel.) is small and caters to the fashionable fringe, while next door **De Spiegelbeeld** (tel. 03/225–3010) is large and unpretentious.

Discos The best-known upscale disco remains **Jimmy's** (Van Ertbornstraat 12, tel. 03/233–3515), but it is challenged in popularity by a new place in the red-light district, **Café d'Anvers** (Verversrui 15, tel. 03/226–3870), where the music is as mixed as the clientele. Other discos of note are **Prestige** (Anneessenstraat 18, tel. 03/225–1717) and **New Casino** (Kloosterstraat 70, tel. 03/237–8846). Check opening hours.

Gay Bars These include **Oscar Wilde** (Van Schoonhovestraat 84, tel. 03/226–1118) and **Marcus Antonius** (Van Schoonhovestraat 82, tel. 03/231–4384) for gay men; for gay women, there are **Shakespeare** (Oude Koornmarkt 24, tel. 03/231–5058) and **Lady's Pub** (Waalsekaai 56, tel. 03/238–5490).

Jazz Clubs There isn't live music every night in these clubs, so check beforehand. Try **Swingcafé** (Suikerrui 13, tel. 03/233–1478), **De Muze** (Melkmarkt 15, tel. 03/226–0126), or **De Hopper** (Leopold De Waelstraat 2, tel. 03/248–4933).

Excursion to Limburg

Limburg is the easternmost Flemish-speaking province, stretching from the sandy moorlands of the Kempen area in the north to the fertile plains of the Hesbaye, which the Flemings call Haspengouw, with its prosperous-looking farms, orchards, and undulating fields. On the east it borders on the narrow Dutch corridor stretching south to Maastricht. Its history and spiritual affinity are closest to Antwerp's.

Two great physical features have shaped much of Limburg's recent economic history. One is the coalfields, formerly very extensive but now concentrated in the area between Houthalen and Beverlo, north of Hasselt. The other is the Albert Canal, which leaves the Meuse just north of Liège to follow a course parallel to the river and then veers off across the country to carry the heavy Liège traffic to Antwerp. Thanks to the canal, Genk is a center for the auto and petrochemical industries.

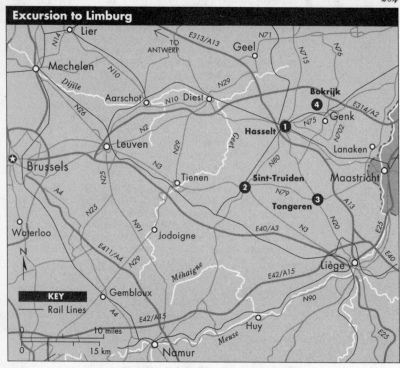

Excursion to Limburg

Important Addresses and Numbers

Tourist Information   The Provincial Tourist Office for Limburg is at Thonissenlaan 27 (tel. 011/22–29–58). City Tourist Offices are located at Lombaardstraat 3, **Hasselt** (tel. 011/22–22–35); Grote Markt 68, **Sint-Truiden** (tel. 011/68–68–72); and Stadhuisplein 9, **Tongeren** (tel. 012/23–29–61).

Emergencies   **Police:** tel. 101. **Ambulance:** tel. 100. The address of the on-duty **late-night pharmacy** is posted in all pharmacy windows.

Getting There

By Car   Hasselt is 77 kilometers (48 miles) from Antwerp on A13/E313, almost as the crow flies.

By Train   You can get to Hasselt by train from Antwerp, Brussels, and Liège, but there are quite a few stops en route.

Exploring Limburg

Numbers in the margin correspond with places of interest on the Excursion to Limburg map.

Limburg has the youngest population in Belgium, and it is the province where the rate of development is fastest. This is particularly noticeable in **Hasselt,** a town with busy shopping streets, innovative museums, and lively music life.

Hasselt enjoys the slightly raffish distinction of having had gin distilling as its major industry, and one of the country's oldest surviving distilleries, from 1803, has become the **Nationaal Jenevermuseum**, *jenever* meaning "gin" in Dutch. A tour of the installations ends in the paneled tasting room, which features a menu of gin of various ages, flavors, and proofs from two dozen Belgian distilleries. *Witte Nonnenstraat 19, tel. 011/24–11–44. Admission: BF60. Open Tues.–Sun. 10–5, weekends 2–6.*

Stadsmuseum Stellingwerf-Waerdenhof (Stellingwerf-Waerdenhof Municipal Museum) consists of two impressive mansions whose interiors have been turned into a strikingly modern space with white walls, red balconies, and large mirrors in which the collection of decorative arts has been dramatically arranged. *Maastrichterstraat 85, tel. 011/24–10–70. Admission: BF60. Open Tues.–Sun. 10–5, weekends 2–6.*

The third among Hasselt's unusual museums is the **Modemuseum** (Fashion Museum), installed in a 17th-century hospital, which illustrates the development of fashion trends over the past two centuries. *Thonissenlaan 73, tel. 011/22–60–08. Admission: BF60. Open Tues.–Sun. 10–5, weekends 2–6.*

Time Out   **La Galette** (Fruitmarkt 26) is an ice cream parlor whose product is 100% homemade, free of all additives, and very good.

In the **Sint-Quintinus Kathedraal** you'll find the **Stedelijk Beiaardmuseum** (Carillon Museum) at the top of several flights of wooden steps. The 47-bell carillon is one of the best in the country. *Vismarkt, tel. 011/24–10–70. Admission: BF60. Open June and Sept., weekends 2–6; July–Aug., Tues.–Fri. 2–5, weekends 2–6 concert July, Aug., Sun. 3.*

② **Sint-Truiden** is 19 kilometers (12 miles) southwest of Hasselt on N80. This is the center of the fruit-growing district; in spring thousands upon thousands of trees are in bloom. The town developed around the abbey founded by St. Trudon in the 7th century. The **Begijnhof** (Beguinage), dating from 1258, has a well-restored church, from the end of the 13th century. It is now the **Provinciaal Museum voor Religieuze Kunst** (Provincial Museum of Religious Art) and is known for its 38 frescoes, executed over four centuries. *Begijnhof, off Speelhoflaan; tel. 011/68–85–79. Admission: BF100. Open Apr.–Oct., Tues.–Fri. 10–noon and 1:30–5, weekends 1:30–5.*

At the **Festraets Studio** you can see the astronomical compensation clock, constructed by Camille Festraets out of 20,000 mechanical parts. It is more than 6 feet tall and weighs more than 4 tons. *Begijnhof 24, tel. 011/68–87–52. Admission: BF60. Visits Easter–June and Sept.–Oct., weekends 1:45, 2:45, 3:45, and 4:45; July–Aug., Tues.–Fri. 9:45, 10:45, 1:45, 2:45, and 3:45, and weekends 1:45, 2:45, 3:45, and 4:45.*

Lace making has been revived in Sint-Truiden over the past few decades with a great deal of originality. The results can be seen at the **Museum van Hedendaagse Kantwerken** (Contemporary Lace Museum) in the school of the Ursuline sisters. *Naamse Straat 5, tel. 011/68–23–56. Admission: BF25. Open Sun. and bank holidays 10–noon and 2–6.*

The **Sint-Gangulfskerk** is worth the small detour to Diester-straat. It is a Romanesque basilica from the 11th century and has recently been carefully restored.

In **Zoutleeuw,** a couple of miles west of Sint-Truiden, is the **Sint-Leonarduskerk** (St. Leonard's Church), which dates from the 13th century and is quite out of proportion to the town's present population. The great treasure is one of the finest brassware pieces in Belgium, a tall paschal candlestick incorporating a Crucifixion scene, made by Renier van Thienen in 1453. *Open Mon.–Sat. 9:30–noon and 1:30–6, Sun. 1:30–5 (winter, Sun. 1:30–4).*

❸ **Tongeren,** 20 kilometers (12½ miles) east of Sint-Truiden on N79, is one of the two oldest cities in Belgium (the other being Tournai). It started life as a Roman army encampment. Here Ambiorix scored a famous but short-lived victory over the Roman legions in 54 BC. The Roman city was considerably larger than the present one; over the centuries following its foundation, it was repeatedly sacked and burned. By the end of the 13th century, the city had retreated within its present limits and enjoyed the occasionally burdensome protection of the prince bishops of Liège. The Moerenpoort gate and sections of the ramparts remain from that period.

Tongeren's outstanding sight is the 12th-century Romanesque cloister in the **Onze-Lieve-Vrouwebasiliek** (Basilica of Our Lady). The Chapter House contains the Treasury, also known as the **Basilica Museum Tongeren.** This is the richest collection of religious art in the country, including a 6th-century ivory diptych of St. Paul, a Merovingian gold buckle from the same century, and a head of Christ sculpted in wood in the 11th century. *Grote Markt, tel. 012/23–57–19. Admission: BF20. Open May–Sept., daily 9–noon and 2–5; Oct.–Apr., by appointment, tel. 012/23–14–17.*

The basilica is a very handsome Gothic church, dating in part (the central nave up to the pulpit, the choir, and the south transept) from 1240. The candlesticks and lectern from 1372 are the work of Jehan de Dinant, one of the outstanding artists of metal working who flourished in the cities of the Meuse Valley. The basilica has excellent acoustics and is used for symphony concerts on Saturdays during the Festival of Flanders.

❹ Exit 30 from A13/E313 takes you via Genk to **Bokrijk,** the largest (550 hectares/1,360 acres) open-air museum in Europe. The nature reserve shows the unspoilt Kempen country of heather and pine, sand and broom, with marshes and ponds frequented by waterfowl. There's also a big playground with pony rides and other attractions, and a sports center with tennis courts, minigolf, and even a soccer field.

Time Out | **In den Dolphin** is an old Flemish inn where you can enjoy traditional fare such as spicy sausages, smoked ham, rich cheeses, and red Rodenbach beer.

Most of Bokrijk's charm derives from the carefully restored farm buildings, which have been transplanted from Limburg and other Flemish provinces. Each building has its own custodian, many of whom are mines of local folklore. The interiors are filled with old peasant furniture and ancient utensils. *Bokrijk Domein, Genk, tel. 011/22–45–75. Admission: BF180 adults, BF60 children, under 7 free. Open Apr.–Oct., daily 10–6.*

What to See and Do with Children

Bokrijk (*see* Exploring Limburg, *above*) is certainly the leading contender for family fun in the province.

At **Lanaken,** near the Dutch border northeast of Tongeren, you can rent a horse and wagon through the local tourist office and set off for a one-day excursion along a route mapped out for you. *Tel. 011/72–24–67. Open May–Oct.*

Sports and Fitness

For general information on sports facilities and opportunities, contact the **Sportdienst** (Diestersestraat 46, Sint-Truiden, tel. 011/68–11–90).

The local tourist offices can supply maps and information on attractive **bicycle** trails. Two of the most popular are the **Trudofietsroute,** 54 kilometers (33½ miles) long, based on the travels of St. Trudon, and Tongeren's **Tongria** route, 45 kilometers (28 miles) long.

Golf aficionados will find excellent facilities in Hasselt (Vlaams-Japanese Golf & Business Club, Vissenbroekstraat 15, tel. 011/22–37–93). The 18-hole course is for members only, while the nine-hole training course is open to the public.

Dining and Lodging

By Nancy Coons

With its combination of historic towns and idyllic country, this region offers an attractive mix of bucolic inns and burnished urban cafés.

Hasselt
Dining
★

De Egge. This charming little one-horse restaurant offers the best efforts of a young couple who believe in their excellent taste: The decor is pretty and discreet, with whitewashed brick and café curtains, and the cooking is imaginative and beautifully executed. Try monkfish on a bed of leeks, or goat cheese brushed with honey and fresh thyme and served hot on a bed of julienned apple, endive, and *mâche* (lamb's lettuce). *Walputstraat 23, tel. 011/22–49–51. Reservations suggested. Jacket suggested. AE, DC, MC, V. Closed Thurs. Moderate.*

Majestic. This big, leaded-glass, high-ceilinged tavern on the Grote Markt has a grand, historic feel, and it draws locals for drinks, cards, snacks, and light meals: sandwiches, trout, steak, and a cheap daily menu. *Grote Markt, tel. 011/22–33–30. Dress: casual. AE, DC, MC, V. Inexpensive.*

Dining and Lodging

Hostellerie Roerdomp. Just south of Hasselt, on the flat suburban stretch outside Diepenbeek, this all-modern reproduction of traditional step-gabled architecture sits on its own green grounds, surrounded by enormous lawn sculptures of creatures (a bat, a fly). Quarters are quiet, tidy, and up-to-date nonetheless, and it's an easy drive into town. There's a good, Moderate restaurant that tests the skills of students from Hasselt's. *Nieuwstraat 62, B3590 Diepenbeek, tel. 011/32–26–60. 17 rooms. Facilities: restaurant. AE, DC, MC, V. Moderate.*

Century. Despite its placement at a major intersection of the busy inner ring, this modest urban hotel has handy access to the pedestrian street that cuts through the center of the old town. Rooms are spare but freshly painted, with old linoleum and dated fixtures. Nonetheless, the restaurant downstairs is popular and appealing, serving good middle-class brasserie fare. *Leopoldplein 1, B-3500, tel. 011/22–47–99. 16 rooms. Facilities: restaurant, bar. AE, DC, MC, V. Inexpensive.*

Lier
Dining
't Suyckeren Schip. Just across from the church, this restaurant offers *cuisine bourgeoise:* steaks with a variety of sauces, and five different preparations of sole. The setting has an informal, comfortable, brick-and-beams look. Sunday crowds come after church. *Rechtestraat 49, tel. 03/489–01–40. Reservations suggested. Jacket suggested. AE, DC, MC, V. Moderate.*

Sint-Truiden
Dining
De Fakkels. In an extravagantly decorated 19th-century town house, with tapestries, carved wood, leaded glass, and terrazzo floors, this ambitious restaurant offers well-executed French cooking: *pot-au-feu de St-Pierre aux raviolis de langoustines* (John Dory stew with lobster ravioli), sweetbreads on a bed of zucchini and mushrooms. *Stationstraat 33, tel. 011/68–76–34. Reservations advised. Jacket and tie advised. AE, DC, MC, V. Closed Sun. dinner, Mon. Expensive.*

Century. A classic old tavern/restaurant on the Grote Markt, with oak, green-plush banquettes, and great windows framing the market scene, this simple spot is as comfortable for a drink as for a meal. Typical "snacks" include half a roasted chicken with frites and salad, omelettes, steaks, sole, and sandwiches. *Grote Markt 5, tel. 011/68–83–41. Dress: casual. AE, DC, MC, V. Closed Tues. dinner. Inexpensive.*

Lodging
★
Regency. Recently expanded and renovated from its origins as an early 19th-century town house, this city hotel offers two styles: Graceful old rooms with high, molded ceilings, or those in the new wing, all modern and freshly installed. It's on a quiet street but close to the city center. *Schepen Dejongstraat 43, B-3800, tel. 011/68–48–81. 30 rooms. Facilities: restaurant, bar. AE, DC, MC, V. Moderate.*

Tongeren
Dining
★
Clos St. Denis. This enormous 17th-century farmhouse with attached barns has been completely restored as a fresh, elegant country inn, where chef Christian Denis serves extravagant fare: grilled turbot in Chablis butter; gratin of oysters in champagne and caviar; raviolis of *foie d'oie* (goose liver) in truffle cream. There's *choucroute* (sauerkraut) with suckling pig and mustard as well. Four dining rooms outdo each other for period luxury—burnished parquet, Persian runners, chinoiserie. *Grimmertingenstraat 24, Vliermall-Kortessem, tel. 012/23–60–96. Reservations required. Jacket and tie advised. AE, DC, MC, V. Closed Mon.–Tues. Very Expensive.*

Dining and Lodging
Lido. Rich in its own atmosphere, this old hotel/restaurant faces the historic square. Inside, you'll find a kind of faded, Vermeer-like grace: leaded glass, heavy dark oak, and "Persian" rugs thrown over the café tables. Rooms upstairs are considerably less memorable, their tumbledown pomp mixed with cheap modern materials. The menu features steak, trout, and sole, but also quail and *pintadeau* (guinea fowl) in whiskey. *Grote Markt 19, B-3700, tel. 012/23–19–48. 5 rooms. Facilities: restaurant (Moderate), tavern. DC. Restaurant closed Fri. Inexpensive.*

The Meuse and the Ardennes

Wallonie is everything that Flanders is not. The northern half of the country is flat, the *"platte land"* of Jacques Brel's songs. The south is hilly, even mountainous. You visit Flanders primarily for its historic towns; Wallonie attracts people who enjoy its rapid streams, deep forests, and hamlets. The northerners are all Dutch speakers; the southerners speak French, but one in three also understands Walloon, a dialect descended from demotic Latin; the linguistic frontier corresponds roughly to the northern boundary of the Roman empire. Flanders has a sense of regional identity going back a thousand years; Wallonie consists of several smaller regions joined together not much more than 150 years ago.

The Meuse Valley The Meuse River rises in France and reaches the sea in Holland under a different name, the Maas. It is in Belgium that it reveals real character, at first foaming along narrow ravines. In Dinant it is joined by the Lesse and flows, serene and beautiful, toward Namur, overlooked by ancient citadels. At Namur comes the confluence with the Sambre, tainted from its exposure to the industries of Charleroi. The river becomes broad and powerful, and gradually the pleasure craft are replaced by an endless procession of tugboats and barges.

From the name of the river is derived the adjective "Mosan," used to describe an indigenous style of metalworking of extraordinary plasticity. It reached its finest flowering in the 12th and 13th centuries with masters such as Renier de Huy, Nicolas de Verdun, and Hugo d'Oignies. They worked with brass, copper, and silver to achieve artistic levels equal to those of the Flemish painters a couple of centuries later.

Roman legions commanded by Julius Caesar marched up the Meuse valley 2,000 years ago and made it one of the principal routes to Cologne. Later, it served a similar purpose for Charlemagne, linking his Frankish and German lands. The French came through here under Louis XIV and again under Napoleon; a century later it was the turn of the Germans pushing west and south in World Wars I and II. They were seen off here, too.

The Ardennes The Ardennes are an ancient mountain range worn down to wooded hills, largely bypassed by modern development, where villages and isolated farmhouses all have slate walls and slate roofs, and where you can walk alone for hours. German is spoken in cafés and restaurants in the easternmost reaches of the country, and shop and road signs are in that language. German is in fact spoken by less than 1% of the Belgian population but is one of the three official languages. These cantons were part of the Duchy of Limburg for centuries. They were awarded to Prussia after the Napoleonic wars and reverted to Belgium a century later.

Liège Many Belgians feel that visiting Liège, gateway to the Ardennes, is almost like going abroad. The Liègeois, for their part, see little reason for going to Brussels; if they hanker for bright lights, they head for Paris. They are the most Francophile among the Francophones, and it was no accident that

Georges Simenon could so easily transplant the cafés and streets of the Liège of his boyhood to Maigret's Paris.

The history of Liège does differ fundamentally from that of the rest of the country. For eight of its 10 centuries it was an independent principality of the Holy Roman Empire, from the time Bishop Notger transformed his bishopric into a temporal domain at the end of the 10th century. His successors had to devote quite as much time to the defense of the realm—much larger than the present province—as to pastoral concerns. The power of the autocratic prince bishops was also hotly contested by the increasingly independent-minded cities. The end was brought about by the French Revolution, which many Liègeois joined with enthusiasm. The ancient cathedral of St. Lambert was razed, and the principality became a French *département*.

The 19th century, after Belgian independence in 1830, saw an upsurge in industrial activity. The first European locomotive was built in Liège, and the Bessemer steel production method developed; it is to the burning furnaces that Liège owes its nickname *la cité ardente* (the Fiery City). Drawing on a centuries-old tradition of weapons manufacturing, the Fabrique Nationale started to build precision firearms, and Val-St-Lambert began to produce glassware that has gained wide renown.

Belgian Luxembourg The Belgian province of Luxembourg is almost twice as large as the independent Grand Duchy of Luxembourg. Luxembourg made common cause with Belgium against the Dutch in 1830, but while Belgium gained its freedom, the Grand Duchy remained under Dutch domination for another 50-odd years; meanwhile Leopold I of Belgium had claimed the western half. This is the largest and, with just a couple of hundred thousand inhabitants, by far the most sparsely populated province of Belgium. Here you can rough it in great comfort and fill your lungs with fresh mountain air. It's a land of forests and dairy farms, slate gray houses and fortresses perched on high rocks, swift streams, and flowering meadows.

Important Addresses and Numbers

Tourist Information The tourist office for **Wallonie** as a whole, Office de Promotion du Tourisme, is at Rue du Marché-aux-Herbes 61 in Brussels (tel. 02/504–4390). The provincial tourist office for the **Meuse Valley** is at Rue Notre-Dame 3, **Namur** (tel. 081/22–29–98). City tourist offices: **Dinant** (Rue Grande 37, tel. 082/22–28–70) and **Namur** (Square de l'Europe Unie, tel. 081/22–28–59).

The provincial tourist office for **Liège** is at Boulevard de la Sauvenière 77 (tel. 041/22–42–10). The **Liège** city tourist office is at En Féronstrée 92 (tel. 041/22–24–56) and is open weekdays 9–6, Saturday 10–4, and Sunday 10–2. Other city tourist offices in the region are at Marktplatz 7, **Eupen** (tel. 087/55–34–50); Hospice d'Oultremont, Quai de Namur 4, **Huy,** (tel. 085/21–29–15); Place de Rome 4, **Malmédy** (tel. 080/33–02–50); Rue Royale 41, **Spa** (tel. 087/77–25–19); and Ancienne Abbaye, **Stavelot** (tel. 080/88–23–30).

The provincial tourist office for **Belgian Luxembourg** is at Quai de l'Ourthe 9, La Roche-en-Ardennes (tel. 084/41–10–11). City tourist offices are located at Place MacAuliffe 24, **Bastogne** (tel. 061/21–27–11); Bureau du Château-Fort, **Bouillon** (tel. 061/46–62–57), and (during the high season) at Porte de

France, also in Bouillon (tel. 061/46–62–89); Hôtel de Ville, Place du Marché, **La Roche-en-Ardenne** (tel. 084/41–13–42); and Place de l'Abbaye, **St-Hubert** (tel. 061/61–12–99).

Emergencies **Police,** tel. 101; **ambulance,** tel. 100.

Late-Night Addresses of all-night pharmacies are posted in all pharmacy
Pharmacies windows.

Arriving and Departing

Meuse There are two to three trains an hour from Brussels to Namur.
By Train The trip takes an hour from Brussels's Gare du Midi; 10 minutes less from Brussels's Gare du Nord. For train information in Namur, call 081/22–37–01.

By Car Namur is 64 kilometers (40 miles) from Brussels on the A4/ E411 motorway, which continues to Luxembourg and on to eastern France, Germany, and Switzerland. It is 61 kilometers (38 miles) from Liège on A15/E42, which continues to Charleroi and links up with E19 to Paris.

Liège There are 20 trains a day from Brussels. The trip takes an hour
By Train from Brussels Nord, 10 minutes more from Brussels Midi. All express trains from Oostende to Cologne stop at Liège. So do international trains from Scandinavia and Hamburg to Paris. Liège's station is the Gare des Guillemins (tel. 041/52–01–30).

By Car Liège is 97 kilometers (60 miles) east of Brussels on A3/E40, which continues 122 kilometers (76 miles) to Aachen and Cologne. The distance from Antwerp is 119 kilometers (74 miles) via A13/E313. Paris is 360 kilometers (224 miles) from Liège on A15/E42, which links up with A7/E19 near Mons.

Belgian Thus there are half a dozen daily connections from Brussels to
Luxembourg Bastogne, but you have to change at Libramont, and the trip
By Train takes 2½ hours. Secondary lines run into the region from Liège and Namur, but services are neither frequent nor fast. For information call the railway station in Bastogne (tel. 062/21–11–08.)

By Car The main artery through the region is the A4/E411 highway from Brussels.

Getting around Meuse and the Ardennes

The Meuse Valley There's hourly train service between Namur and Dinant. The
By Train trip takes about 20 minutes. From April to August, excursion steam trains are operated from Dinant to Givet, across the French border, and east–west from Treignes to Momignies. Each takes about two hours round-trip. For reservations, call 081/22–11–99 or 060/31–24–40.

By Car The main route from Brussels is the A4/E411 motorway. Elsewhere in the region, you travel chiefly on two-lane roads.

Liège Taxis are plentiful and can be picked up at cabstands in the
By Taxi principal squares. Call a cab at 041/67–66–00.

By Bus A single trip on a bus in the inner city costs BF32, and eight-trip cards sell for BF162.

The Ardennes Having your own wheels is almost indispensable in exploring
By Car the Ardennes. The northeast is traversed by two motorways, A3/E40 from Brussels via Liège to Aachen, Cologne, and

points east, and the nearly completed A27, which runs south from E40 via Verviers to St. Vith and stops at the German border.

Belgian Luxembourg *By Car*

The road network seems to have been designed to get cars through Luxembourg as fast as possible rather than to serve its towns. Thus St-Hubert and Bouillon are on either side and about 25 kilometers (16 miles) from A4/E411, and La Roche-en-Ardennes is about 15 kilometers (9 miles) away on E5 from Liège and on the old N4 from Namur. Some secondary roads are four-lane highways, but most are two-lane.

Guided Tours

The Meuse Valley

Boat tours ranging from short excursions to full-day trips are available in both Dinant and Namur; for details, contact **Compagnie des Bateaux** (Rue Daoust 64, 5500 Dinant, tel. 082/22–23–15). For trips from Dinant, contact also **Bateau Bayard** (Rue Caussin 13, 5500 Dinant, tel. 082/22–60–16).

With some advance planning, you could probably arrange to sail the entire length of the Meuse from France to Holland by sightseeing boats. In Huy, river trips are organized on the *Bateau Val Mosan* (Quai de Namur 1, tel. 025/21–29–15).

In Liège, excursions are arranged onboard *Le Pays de Liège* (Port des Yachts, tel. 041/87–43–33) from Liège (departure 8:30 AM from the right bank next to the Passerelle bridge) to Maastricht and return, with a three-hour stop in the Dutch city, arriving in Liège at 6:45 PM.

Liège

Your best bet is to hire an English-speaking guide from the city **tourist office** (En Féronstrée 92; BF1000 for two hours, BF500 per additional hour).

If you understand French, you're welcome to join a guided walking tour starting from the tourist office. *En Féronstrée 92. Cost: about BF100. Apr.–June and Sept.–Oct., weekends 2 PM; July–Aug., daily 2 PM.*

Exploring the Meuse and the Ardennes

Numbers in the margin correspond with places of interest on the Meuse and the Ardennes map.

This region is crowded with Belgian vacationers and weekend visitors, especially in July and August.

Tour 1: The Meuse Valley

1 At **Han-sur-Lesse**, 60 kilometers (37 miles) south of Namur on A4/E411, at Exit 23, are the magnificent **Grottes de Han** (Han Caves), which have been visited by tourists since the 1850s. Before that, they had provided refuge for threatened tribes since Neolithic times. Tickets are sold in the center of the small town, where you board an ancient tram that carries you to the mouth of the cave. Multilingual guides take groups through 3 kilometers (2 miles) of dimly lit chambers, with occasional glimpses of the underground River Lesse, past giant stalagmites, into the vast cavern called the Dome, 145 meters (475 feet) high. The final part of the journey is by boat. The trip takes about 90 minutes. *Rue J. Lamotte 2, tel. 084/37–72–13.*

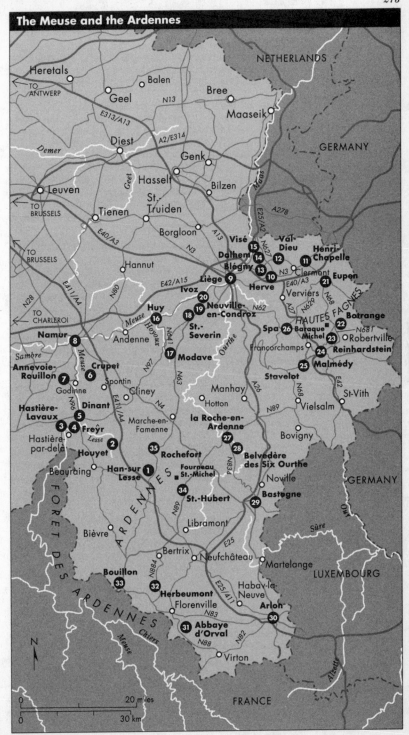

The Meuse and the Ardennes

NETHERLANDS

GERMANY

Heretals
TO ANTWERP
Geel
Balen
Bree
Maaseik
N13

E313/A13

Diest
A2/E314

Genk

Leuven
TO BRUSSELS
Hasselt
Bilzen
Demer
Geet
Tienen
St.-Truiden
TO BRUSSELS
E40/A3
Borgloon
A13
N3
Visé
Val-Dieu
Henri-Chapelle
Hannut
Dalhem
15
14
12
11
Clermont
Eupen
N28
E411/A4
N80
Blégny
13
10
N3
E40/A3
Verviers
21
TO CHARLEROI
E42/A15
Liège
9
Herve
N62
Ivoz
20
Neuville-en-Condroz
N68
HAUTES FAGNES
N629
Huy
16
19
18
St.-Severin
A27
Botrange
22
Namur
8
Andenne
Hoyoux
17
Modave
Spa
26
Baraque Michel
23
Robertville
N681
Sambre
Meuse
Crupet
6
N97
Ourthe
Francorchamps
Reinhardstein
24
Annevoie-Rouillon
7
Godinne
Spontin
N641
N63
Manhay
A26
Stavelot
25
Malmédy
Hastière-Lavaux
5
Dinant
Cliney
N4
Hotton
N89
N68
Vielsalm
St.-Vith
3
4
Freÿr
Marche-en-Famenne
la Roche-en-Ardenne
Bovigny
E42
Hastière-par-delà
Lesse
2
35
Rochefort
27
Beauraing
Houyet
1
Han-sur-Lesse
Fourneau St.-Michel
28
Belvédère des Six Ourthe
Noville
GERMANY
A
R
D
E
N
N
E
S
34
St.-Hubert
29
Bastogne
Our
Bièvre
N89
Libramont
Sûre
F
O
R
E
T
Bertrix
N884
Neufchâteau
E25
Martelange
LUXEMBOURG
D
E
S
Bouillon
33
32
Herbeumont
Florenville
N83
Habay-la-Neuve
E25/A11
Arlon
30
A
R
D
E
N
N
E
S
31
Abbaye d'Orval
N88
N82
Virton
Alzette
Meuse
Chiers

N

0   20 miles
0   30 km

FRANCE

Admission: BF265 adults, BF185 children. Open Apr.–June and Sept.–Nov., daily 10–4; July–Aug., daily 10–6.

Time Out At the **Taverne Ardennaise** (Rue des Grottes 2), you can enjoy regional specialties such as *civet de marcassin* (jugged wild boar) washed down by a locally brewed Trappist beer.

The Lesse is one of the liveliest tributaries of the Meuse, and shooting the rapids in a kayak has great appeal to the adventure-minded. The starting point for organized river trips is **2** **Houyet,** near Exit 22 on the motorway. The 21-kilometer (13-mile) ride takes you through two rapids and past the eagle's-nest Walzin castle to Anseremme on the Meuse, just south of Dinant. Train service back to the starting point is available, and reservations are recommended. *Lesse-Kayaks, Place de l'Eglise 2, Anseremme, tel. 082/22–43–97. Price: BF250–BF600. Open Apr.–Oct., daily embarkation at Houyet 9:30–11.*

The Meuse is at its most attractive upstream from Dinant, and it's worth crossing the river and driving along it at least as far **3** as **Hastière-Lavaux.** Its charmingly named twin town, **Hastière-par-Delà**—on the other side of the river—has an 11th-century church, well worth seeing, in Romanesque Mosan style. The drive back toward Dinant offers many vistas over the river to the towering rock formations on the opposite shore.

4 **Freÿr,** on the left, is considered the best rock-climbing center in Wallonie. The **Château de Freÿr** is an impressive Renaissance building with beautiful interiors decorated with 17th-century woodwork and furniture. Louis XIV visited here during the siege of Dinant in 1675. The park has been laid out in accordance with the design principles of Le Nôtre, the French landscape architect. *Domaine de Freÿr, Waulsort, tel. 082/22–22–00. Admission: BF160. Guided visits July–Aug., weekends 2–6.*

Just before Dinant, the needle-shaped **Rocher Bayard** looms on the right bank. Legend has it that Bayard, the steed of the four Aymon brothers who were the implacable foes of Charlemagne, split the rock with his hoof. The passage was widened by the troops of Louis XIV as they advanced on the city.

5 **Dinant** has a most scenic location; unfortunately, its strategic importance led to its involvement in an interminable series of wars. The French word *dinanderie*, meaning the art of brass- and copper-working, is derived from Dinant, where it was developed in the 12th century and spread downstream to Namur and Huy. The copperware sold today in Dinant's souvenir shops is not, alas, of the same quality.

Dinant was the birthplace of the 17th-century painter Joachim Patenier, who worked in Antwerp; his biblical scenes are set in landscapes recognizably inspired by the Meuse Valley. Another native son was Adolphe Sax, inventor of the saxophone.

The 13th-century collegiate church of **Notre-Dame** huddles under the citadel. The bulbous blue bell tower is a 17th-century addition. Back of the church is the starting point for cable cars to the **Citadel,** which is not as ancient as you might think, for the ancient fortifications were razed in 1818 by the Dutch, who replaced it with a new fort just before they were evicted. The view is splendid, and there is an arms museum. *Le Prieuré 25, tel. 082/22–21–19. Admission plus cable car: BF160 adults, BF120 children. Open Mar.–Oct., daily 10–4, until 6 in summer; Nov.–Feb., Sat.–Thurs. 10–4.*

On the left bank about 450 meters (1,500 feet) from the bridge on the road toward Philippeville you'll come to the entrance to the cave called **La Merveilleuse,** whose many stalactites are remarkably white. A visit takes about 50 minutes. *Route de Philippeville 142, tel. 082/22–22–10. Admission: BF140. Open Apr.–June and Sept., daily 11–4; July–Aug., daily 10–6.*

Time Out   Dinant has two specialties: *flamiches* (cheese, egg, and butter tarts), to be eaten piping hot; and the hard, spicy *couques,* made with carved molds in many fanciful shapes from pastry and honey. The streets are lined with cafés. The **Patisserie Solbrun** offers the advantage of a great view over the river.

From N96 toward Namur, cross the river just after Anhee for a 23-kilometer (14-mile) detour. From Yvoir, take the steeply rising N937 to **Spontin.** The moated **Château de Spontin** is an excellent example of medieval architecture, with a Renaissance brick superstructure. The drawbridge can still be operated, and there are secret staircases and lookouts. The castle is still inhabited, and the interior presents the same contrast between austerity and elegance as does the exterior. *Chaussée de Dinant 8, tel. 083/69–90–55. Admission: BF100. Open for guided visits (approx. 45 min.) July–Aug., daily 10–5; by appointment, Sept.–June.*

6   In nearby **Crupet** stands a massive, river-encircled square dungeon from the 12th century; it was the stronghold of the powerful French Carondelet family for centuries.

You return to the Meuse at Godinne, and at the other end of the
7   bridge is **Annevoie-Rouillon.** A greater contrast to medieval keeps cannot be imagined than the **Château et Jardins d'Annevoie** (Chateau and Gardens of Annevoie). The 12-hectare (30-acre) park is a happy blend of 18th-century French landscaping and romantic Italian garden design, remarkable for its use of natural waterfalls, fountains, and ponds to animate the gardens with their flower beds, lawns, statues, and grottoes. The château blends perfectly with the gardens; the furniture, paneling, and family portraits all contribute to an ambience of elegant refinement. *Route des Jardins, tel. 082/61–15–55. Admission: BF200 adults, BF100 children. Gardens open Apr.–Oct., daily 9–7; chateau open 9:30–1 and 1:30–6:30 daily July–Aug., weekends May–June, Sun. Apr. and Sept.*

8   You enter **Namur** under the shadow of the Citadel, perched on a cliff on the promontory overlooking the confluence of the Meuse and the Sambre. The city is the seat of the body governing the affairs of the semiautonomous French-speaking community, chosen as a compromise acceptable to Charleroi and Liège, both of which are twice as large. Much of the center of Namur is a pedestrian zone, with cafés, art galleries, and boutiques. The appealing streets are lined with pink-brick 17th-century houses, and here and there is a rich Baroque church. Namur is a university town, and the student population helps liven up what passes for nightlife around the Rue St-Loup. Right in the center is the quiet Place du Marché-aux-Légumes, with the **Eglise de Saint-Jean Baptiste** (St. John the Baptist's Church).

Time Out On this square you'll find a new café in an old building, **Le XVIIIe,** so named for its stuccoed 18th-century ceiling. The specialty is pancakes with generous fillings.

The **Institut des Soeurs de Notre-Dame** (Institute of the Sisters of Our Lady) is the home of the **Trésor Hugo d'Oignies.** The crosses, reliquaries, and other religious artifacts, made by Brother Hugo for the priory in nearby Oignies in the beginning of the 13th century, were rescued during the bombardments of 1914. The finesse with which he worked the silver and enamel inlays, often with miniature hunting scenes, was remarkable, and Hugo d'Oignies has been recognized as one of the masters of Art Mosan. *Rue Billiart 17, tel. 081/23–04–49. Admission: BF20. Open Wed.–Sat. and Mon. 10–noon and 2–5, Sun. 2–5. Closed bank holidays.*

The **Musée Archéologique** (Archaeological Museum) is installed in the handsome 16th-century Butchers' Hall on the waterfront. It contains Roman and Merovingian antiquities from the Namur area, and the collection of jewelry from the 1st century to the 7th century includes some magnificent specimens. *Rue du Pont, tel. 081/23–16–31. Admission: BF40. Open Mon. and Wed.–Fri. 10–5, weekends 10:30–5.*

A special museum, dedicated to the work of Namur's leading 19th-century artist, is the **Musée Felicien Rops.** Rops was a friend of Baudelaire and illustrated his and many other books. A surrealist before his time, Rops created works by turns satirical and erotic. *Rue Fumal 12, tel. 081/23–03–21, ext. 520. Admission: BF100. Open July–Aug., daily 10–5; Sept.–June, Wed.–Mon. 10–5.*

You can reach the **Citadelle** (Citadel) by car up the hairpin curves of a mile-long road called La Route Merveilleuse, or you can ride up by cable car. From the plateau at the top you have great views in all directions. The 15th-century bastions were further fortified by the Spanish. The Dutch also constructed fortifications here, called the Fort d'Orange. *Route Merveilleuse 3, tel. 081/22–68–29. Admission: BF180 adults, BF120 children. Open daily June–Sept., daily 11–7, May and Oct., weekends 11–7. Cable car: BF100.*

There are several museums on the site, including the **Musée Provincial de la Forêt** (Provincial Forestry Museum), contained in an old hunting lodge, which gives an overview of the region's fauna and flora. *Route Merveilleuse 9, tel. 081/74–38–94. Admission: BF50. Open Easter–Oct., Tues.–Sat. 10–noon and 2:30–6; Sun. 2:30–6; Nov.–Easter, Tues.–Sun. 2:30–6.*

Tour 2: Liège

❾ The bustling city of **Liège**—Luik to the Flemish and Dutch, Lüttich to the Germans—is in many ways quietly romantic. Surrounded by hills, it sits deep in the Meuse Valley at the confluence with the Ourthe. Here the river is slate-gray, and pleasure craft play second fiddle to coal barges and tankers. Liège is a city riddled with secret courtyards, narrow medieval lanes, and steeply stepped streets. Above all, it is a city of joie de vivre, where you easily get into conversation with strangers. The institution that best expresses the Liège spirit is the *café chantant,* where everyone is welcome to burst into song and frequently does.

The **Place de la Cathédrale** is a pleasant square with flower beds in the center, lined with sidewalk cafés on two sides, and flanked by the north wall of the Gothic **Cathédrale St-Paul** (St. Paul's Cathedral). Inside, you'll see some handsome statues, including one of St. Paul by Jean Delcour. Other graceful works by this 18th-century sculptor dot the old city. The cathedral's most highly prized possessions are found in the **Treasury**, especially the *Reliquaire de Charles le Téméraire* with gold and enamel figures of St. George and the bold duke himself on his knees; curiously, their faces are identical. This reliquary was presented to Liège by Charles the Bold in 1471 in expiation for having had the city razed three years earlier. *Admission: BF40. Open Apr.–Sept., daily 7:30–12:30 and 2–6; Oct.–Mar., daily 7:30–12:30 and 2–5.*

From the Place de la Cathédrale, turn left on Pont d'Avroy. Despite the name, there's no bridge in sight. Many street names here reflect a maritime past, when the arc of the Boulevard de la Sauvenière, which surrounds the district, was a branch of the river. Pont d'Avroy is crammed with shops and cafés, giving a taste of what the neighborhood is like. Everyone in Liège knows it by its informal name of **Le Carré.**

Time Out   **Le Panier Fleuri** (20 Pont d'Avroy) is a period piece from the Belle Epoque. This combination tavern and brasserie serves Belgian beer, 200 brands of spirits, and 80 different permutations of ham and cheese on toast.

Three blocks from the Pont d'Avroy is Place Xavier Neujean and the **Eglise St-Jean** (St. John's Church), an octagonal church founded by Prince Bishop Notger in the 10th century and heavily restored. Here you can see the *Sedes Sapientiae* (Seat of Wisdom), a magnificent wood carving of the Virgin and Child from 1220—one of the finest sculptural examples of Art Mosan. *Place Xavier Neujean, tel. 041/23–70–42. Open Mon.–Sat. 3–5:45, Sun. 10:30–1 and (in summer) 7:30–9.*

Time Out   On the Rue St-Adalbert in a single block there are more than half a dozen antiques dealers, as well as a traditional Liègeois café, **Le Seigneur,** and two student hangouts, **Le Saloon** and **Les Trois Frères.**

Bearing left, you come to the charming and animated triangular square called **Vinâve-d'Ile,** where a fountain is ornamented by a Virgin and Child by Delcour.

Liège's most prestigious shopping addresses are along the covered Passage Lemonnier, which stretches from here to the Rue de l'Université. On the left you come to the Place de la République Française. Turn right into the narrow medieval lane called Rue de la Wache to the **Eglise St-Denis** (Church of St. Denis), also founded by Bishop Notger, with a handsome reredos portraying the Suffering of Christ. *Place St-Denis, tel. 041/23–57–56. Open Mon.–Sat. 9–6, Sun. 9–11:30.*

Turning left from Place St-Denis, you shortly arrive at a true eyesore, the Place St-Lambert. What should be the city's most prestigious square has in fact been a hole in the ground for more than 20 years. It's as though the destruction of the cathedral has cast a spell on the site. The word is that a solution has been agreed upon and work is about to start, but the Liègeois aren't holding their breath.

On the other side stands the enormous **Palais des Princes-Evèques** (Palace of the Prince Bishops), rebuilt at different stages since Notger's days. The present facade dates from after the fire of 1734. It's worth picking your way across the square to have a peek inside the colonnaded 16th-century courtyard, which has remained unchanged. Each column is decorated with different stone carvings of staggering variety. The palace is now used by local government offices and law courts, which explains the presence of police and metal detectors.

Just to the left as you leave the palace is the **Place du Marché** (Market Square), as old as the city itself. For centuries, this was where the city's commercial and political life was concentrated. A number of the old buildings surrounding it were among the 23,000 houses destroyed by German "flying bombs" toward the end of World War II. In the center stands the **Perron,** a large fountain sculpted by Jean Delcour, a symbol of municipal liberty.

Time Out The **Café à Pilori** (Place du Marché 5) is another essentially Liègeois tavern, with a large fireplace and beamed ceiling. It sells good pub-style food and its own homemade brew called La Rousse, a mellow brown beer.

Turning down En Neuvice toward the Meuse, you can take the first passage to the left, a 1-meter-wide (3-foot-wide) alley called Rue du Carré. The second right is Rue de la Goffe, which takes you past several attractive houses on the right and, on the left, the **Halle aux Viandes** (Butchers' Hall), from the 16th century, a handsome building that served its original purpose until rather recently. Thus one arrives at the riverside.

On Sundays from 9 AM to 2 PM, this is the site of the mile-long street market known as **La Batte,** ranging from bric-a-brac and foodstuffs to songbirds and pets to clothing, books, records, and toys. Visitors from neighboring Holland and Germany descend regularly on Liège to join the locals at the Sunday market, but it's not so much the merchandise that makes it attractive as the good-natured ambience.

A couple of blocks downstream you come upon Rue St-Georges, which takes you into the **Ilôt St-Georges,** an interesting example of urban archaeology. Twelve dilapidated buildings were taken apart, brick by brick, and put together again to form an attractive architectural whole. Here, too, is the new **Musée de l'Art Wallon,** containing works by Walloon artists from the 17th century to the present day, including Magritte and Delvaux. *Féronstrée 86, tel. 041/22–08–00. Admission: BF50. Open Tues.–Sat. 1–6, Sun. 11–4:30.*

Farther down the quay stands the handsome neoclassical **Musée d'Armes** (Armaments Museum). Napoleon slept here, and there's a portrait of him as first consul by Ingres. Liège was famed for its arms manufacturing from the Middle Ages on, and the collection includes many rare and beautifully executed pieces. *Quai de Maestricht 8, tel. 041/23–31–78. Admission: BF50. Open Mon., Thurs., and Sat. 10–1; Wed. and Fri. 2–5; guided visits 1st and 3rd Sun. of month, 10 and 11:30.*

Next door is the **Musée Curtius.** This patrician mansion was built in the style typical of Mosan Renaissance for the arms manufacturer Jean Curtius in the 16th century. Among its archaeological and decorative art treasures are three outstanding pieces: a 12th-century tympanum, representing the Apollonian Mystery; the Virgin of Dom Rupert, from the same century; and, above all, Bishop Notger's Evangelistery, an exquisite 10th-century manuscript of the gospels. *Quai de Maestricht 13, tel. 041/23-20-68. Admission: BF50. Open Mon., Thurs., and Sat. 2–5; Wed. and Fri. 10–1; guided visits 2nd and 4th Sun. of month, 10 and 11:30.*

Time Out   A la Bonne Franquette (En Féronstrée 152) is a no-frills neighborhood eatery where you can enjoy a meal or snack.

Liège's greatest treasure awaits you in the **Eglise St-Barthélemy** (St. Bartholomew's Church). Follow Rue du Mont-de-Piété to an archway (an *arvô* in the local patois), turn left, and then turn right. The entrance to this Romanesque church retains its original aspect of sober austerity. The nave has been touched up in baroque fashion, and the choir is under restoration. In this church stands the brass masterpiece of Art Mosan, the Baptismal Font of Renier de Huy, which dates from the period between 1107 and 1118. The high relief figures of the five Biblical baptismal scenes are of an extraordinary suppleness, and there is also great variety among the 10 oxen on which the font rests. *Place St-Barthélemy, tel. 041/23-49-98. Admission: BF50. Open Tues.–Sat. 10–1 and 2–5, Sun. 2–5.*

Leaving the square in front of the church by the Rue des Brasseurs and bearing right at the first opportunity, you reach the **Cour St-Antoine,** a hidden square combining postmodern architecture with Mosan Renaissance buildings and a daring use of color. In the old days, prominent citizens in the service of the prince bishops lived along En Hors-Château. Their servants were tucked away in tiny houses up narrow mews, or *impasses.* As late as the 1970s it was believed that the best approach to urban redevelopment was to tear them down. Luckily, common sense prevailed, and many small houses have been restored to mint condition. The **Impasse de l'Ange** and its neighbor **Impasse de la Couronne** are fine examples. Here, as in many other places around Liège, you find a number of *potales* (wall chapels), devoted mostly to the Virgin or Saint Roch, the latter venerated as the protector against epidemic diseases.

As you return toward the center on Hors-Château, the **Montagne de Bueren** ascends as a broad flight of 373 steps toward the Citadel. The stairway is not much more than a hundred years old, but it evokes the memory of Vincent van Bueren, a leader of the resistance against Charles the Bold. In 1468 he climbed the hill with 600 men, intending to fall upon the duke and kill him. Betrayed by their Liègeois accents, they lost their lives instead, and the city was pillaged and burned. Charles was loved in Burgundy, but he never had much press in Liège.

At the foot of the stairs, you can turn left through the cobbled **Impasse des Ursulines,** which mounts to the small and peaceful Beguinage. Next to it stand old buildings rescued from demolition elsewhere in Liège. Continuing uphill, you come to a gate in the wall on the left. Push through it, and you're in a large and verdant hillside park. From Rue du Pery, you can return down the Montagne de Bueren.

Back on Hors-Château, you come to the last two museums of note, past another Delcour fountain. The **Musée d'Art Religieux et d'Art Mosan** (MARAM) has inherited the treasures of the old diocesan museum. They include an 11th-century *Seat of Wisdom*, two centuries older than its namesake in St. John's. This is a stiff and stern-faced Virgin, reflecting a more austere age. *Rue Mère Dieu 11, tel. 041/23–18–93. Admission: BF50. Open Tues.–Sat. 1–6, Sun. 11–4.*

Across the courtyard, in the old Franciscan convent, is the **Musée de la Vie Wallonne** (Museum of Walloon Life), where carefully reconstituted interiors give a vivid and varied idea of life in old Wallonie, from coal mines to farm kitchens to the workshops of many different crafts, as well as a court of law complete with a guillotine. One gallery is populated by the irreverent marionettes—Tchantchès and his band—who have always represented the Liège spirit. *Cour des Mineurs, tel. 041/23–60–94. Admission: BF50. Open Tues.–Sat. 10–5, Sun. 10–4.*

You can follow Rue des Mineurs back to the Place du Marché.

In the Vicinity
Herve Region

The gently rolling **Herve region,** northeast of Liège, is a land of orchards and fields, hedgerows and copses. Herve has given its name to a particularly pungent cheese, which connoisseurs rank with Switzerland's Vacherin and Britain's Stilton.

⑩ You get to the village of **Herve** most easily by taking E40 toward Aachen and following N3 northeast from Exit 37. Nearby is the **Fort de Battice,** which held out against the Germans for 12 days in May 1940 while the German tanks rolled on into France. *Route d'Aubel, tel. 087/31–13–50. Admission: BF100. Open last Sat. of Mar.–Nov., at 1:30.*

⑪ Farther along N3 you'll come to the Cimetière de **Henri-Chapelle,** an American military cemetery that is the resting place of 7,989 GIs who fell in the Battle of the Bulge during the last winter of World War II. The crosses and steles are ranged in arcs converging on the central monument, which also contains a small museum. From here, there is a great view over the plateau of Herve. *Route de Henri-Chapelle, Hombourg, tel. 087/68–17–73. Open Apr.–Sept., daily 8–noon and 1–6, Oct.–Mar., daily 8–noon and 1–5.*

⑫ In the opposite direction, you pass through attractive villages such as **Clermont,** where you can take N650 to **Val-Dieu.** The ancient but much rebuilt abbey here is open for visits and sells lo-
⑬ cal produce. N642 will take you on to **Blegny,** where it is possible to visit the old colliery. The wealth of Liège was based on coal, which was mined from the Middle Ages until 1980. An audiovisual presentation illustrates this history, and former miners lead tours of the facility. A complete visit takes 3½ hours. *Complexe Touristique de Blegny, Rue Lambert Marlet 23, tel. 041/87–43–33. Admission: BF370 adults, BF245 children. Open Apr.–June and Sept.–mid-Oct. daily, 9:30–3:30; July–Aug., daily 9:30–5.*

⑭ To the north is **Dalhem,** formerly a walled town, with castle ruins and an old keep.

At **Mortroux**, the **Musée de la Vie Régionale de Mortroux** (museum of the life of the region) has been installed in an old farm where syrup, cider, butter, and cheese are still produced in the old, artisanal way. There's also a rustic self-service restaurant, where you can try local beers and the celebrated Herve cheese. *Chemin de Trembleur, tel. 041/76-62-97. Admission: BF50 adults, BF30 children. Open Apr.-mid-Sept., daily 10:30-7 PM.*

15 **Visé** on the Meuse was sacked and burned early in World War I and abandoned when the survivors fled to Holland. It is an old town, proud of its ancient guilds of crossbowmen and harquebusiers, each of which maintains a small museum. The reliquary of Saint Hadelin, in the collegiate church, is decorated with scenes of his life, presumed to have been done by Renier de Huy, the master of the baptismal font in Liège. Water sports are available off the Ile Robinson.

Huy and the Condroz
16 The small and charming town of **Huy** (pronounced "we") on the River Meuse is 33 kilometers (20 miles) southwest of Liège off A15/E42. It is an ancient place; its city privileges of 1066 are the oldest that have been preserved in Europe. The Gothic **Eglise Collégiale de Notre-Dame** (Collegiate Church of Our Lady) has a rose window, the so-called Rondia, with a diameter of 9 meters (30 feet), and its treasury contains several magnificent reliquaries, two of them attributed to Godefroy de Huy, who followed in the footsteps of Renier. *Admission: BF40. Open daily 9:15-noon and 2-5:30.*

On the Grand' Place is the **Hôtel de Ville** (Town Hall), in Louis-XV style, and in the center stands a remarkable copper fountain, the Bassinia; the bronze cistern decorated with saints dates from 1406, and in the 18th century the Austrians topped it all with their double eagle. From the square one can wander through winding alleys to the old Franciscan monastery, which is now the **Musée Communal**, a mine of local folklore and history, with an exceptional Art Mosan oak carving of Christ. *Rue Van Keerberghen, tel. 085/21-29-15. Admission BF30. Open Apr.-Oct., Mon.-Sat. 2-6, Sun. 10-noon and 2-6.*

An easy way to get a great view of town and country is to take a mile-long ride on the cable car from the left bank of the Meuse, across the river and to the cliff-top fort. This **Citadelle** was part of the defenses built by the Dutch in the early 19th century. During World War II it served as a prison for resisters and hostages. *Chaussée Napoleon, tel. 085/21-53-34. Admission: BF100. Open Apr.-Sept., daily 9:30-6.*

17 It's in Huy that the Meuse is joined by the Hoyoux, clearest and coldest of the rivers of the Ardennes. Following its valley south on N641, you come to **Modave** with its 17th-century **Château des Comtes de Marchin**, on a cliff overlooking the river. Its elegant rooms feature stuccoed polychrome ceilings. The hydraulic machinery that brought water from the river to the cliff top was copied in France to bring water from the Seine to the Palace of Versailles. *Tel. 085/41-13-69. Admission: BF125 adults, BF75 children. Open Apr.-mid-Nov., daily 9-6.*

18 You are now in the heart of the **Condroz**, a fertile plateau of the lower Ardennes remarkable for the opulence of its farms and manors. Traveling toward Liège on N63, you reach **St-Severin** on the left, with the beautiful and harmonious Romanesque **Eglise de Sts Pierre et Paul** (Church of Sts. Peter and Paul) from the 12th century, one of the best preserved in Belgium. The architecture is based on that of the Abbey of Cluny in Burgundy, of which this was once a priory. *Tel. 041/71–40–34. Open daily 10–6. In case of temporary closure, ring the bell at No. 17 in the churchyard.*

⑲ Where N63 forks, take the road to the left, N677. You arrive in **Neuville-en-Condroz,** the site of the **Cimitière Americian des Ardennes,** final resting place for 5,327 soldiers of the U.S. First Army who fell in the Ardennes, at the Siegfried Line, and around Aachen. The memorial, decorated with an immense American eagle, contains a nondenominational chapel. *Route du Condroz, tel. 041/71–42–87. Admission free. Open Apr.–Sept., weekdays 9–6; Oct.–Mar., weekdays 9–5.*

⑳ At **Ivoz**-Ramet on the Meuse, turn right on N90 and you arrive at the **Cristalleries du Val-St-Lambert.** You can see glassblowers and engravers at work, walk through well-restored factory buildings from the 19th century, see an exhibition of museum and contemporary glassware, and visit the shop. *Admission: BF100 adults, BF50 children. Open Apr.–Dec., Tues.–Sun. 10–5; Jan.–Mar., weekends and bank holidays 10–5.*

Tour 3: Eupen to Spa

㉑ **Eupen,** 40 kilometers (25 miles) east of Liège, is a newcomer as Belgian towns go, dating from the 18th century. The church, with its bulbous towers and extravagant altars, is typical of the period. Following N68 in the direction of Malmédy, you are soon in dense woods, which then open up into the **Hautes Fagnes** (High Fens). This is now a national park of almost 4,300 hectares (10,500 acres). Here the vistas open over vast tracts of moor, with bushes and copses, harboring rich and varied vegetation and bird life. The marshland is waterlogged, and wooden walks have been laid out across the area. You're well advised not to stray from them and to be exceedingly careful with fire in dry periods. Starting points are clearly marked.

㉒ Just past the Baraque Michel (Michael's Shack, named for a former innkeeper), take N676 toward Robertville and you'll reach the Centre Nature à **Botrange,** where you can get a professional introduction to the flora and fauna of the High Fens. Parts of the area can only be visited with a guide, especially the peat bogs and the feeding areas of the *capercaillies* (grouse). You can book an individual guide in advance, and you can also rent boots and bikes. *Robertville, tel. 080/44–57–81. Admission: BF60. Open Dec.–Oct., daily 10–6; walks, Sun. 1.*

㉓ Schloss **Reinhardstein,** the loftiest and possibly the best-preserved medieval fortress in the country, is reached by a kilometer-long walk. It sits on a spur of rock overlooking the River Warche and has been in the hands of such illustrious families as the Metternichs, who spawned the prince who masterminded the Congress of Vienna in 1815. The castle has been well restored; the Hall of Knights and the Chapel are gems. *Robertville, tel. 080/44–68–68. Admission: BF150 adults, BF60 children. Tours mid-June–mid-Sept., Sun. 2:15, 3:15, 4:15, and 5:15; July–Aug., also Tues., Thur., and Sat. 3:30.*

The High Fens act as a huge sponge; dams have been built on some of the rivers that drain them, and water sports are available on the artificial lake at **Robertville** and neighboring **Bütgenbach.**

㉔ Malmédy and its neighbor Stavelot formed a separate, peaceful principality, ruled by abbots, for 11 centuries before the French Revolution. The center of Malmédy was destroyed during an air raid in December 1944. Most years there's at least a short skiing season. The carnival, beginning on the Saturday before Lent, is among the merriest in Belgium. To learn more about it, you might want to visit the **Musée du Carnaval**. *Place de Rome 11 (3rd floor; no elevator), tel. 080/33–70–58. Admission: BF50 adults, children free. Open July–Aug., daily 3–6; Sept.–June, weekends 2:30–5:30. Closed carnival and Lent.*

Time Out **Le Floreal** (Place Albert I) serves breakfast, lunch, dinner, and snacks such as *jambon d'Ardennes.*

㉕ Stavelot is only 15 kilometers (9¼ miles) from Malmédy, but its traditions differ. Here carnival is celebrated on the fourth Sunday in Lent and is animated by a couple of thousand Blancs-Moussis, dressed in white with long capes and bright red long noses, who swoop and rush through the streets. Stavelot, too, was badly damaged in the Battle of the Bulge, but some picturesque old streets survived, particularly Rue Haute (off Place St-Remacle). Remacle founded the abbey in 647, and his reliquary, now in the **Eglise Saint-Sébastien** (St. Sebastian's Church), is one of the wonders of Art Mosan. Dating from the 13th century, it is 2 meters (6½ feet) long and is decorated on the sides with statuettes of the apostles and, on the ends, of Christ and the Virgin. *Place du Vinâve, tel. 080/86–44–37. Admission: BF40. Open daily (except during services) 10–noon and 2–5.*

Only a Romanesque tower remains of the **Ancienne Abbaye** (Old Abbey). The present buildings date from the 18th century, and the refectory has become a concert hall. The old stable has been converted into a **Musée d'Art Religieux Régional** (Regional Museum of Religious Art), and the vaulted cellars of the abbey have been put to somewhat anachronistic use in housing the **Musée du Circuit de Spa-Francorchamps** (Museum of the Spa-Francorchamp Racecourse), which displays Formula I racing cars, sports cars, and motorcycles illustrating the history of motor racing since 1907. *Tel. 080/86–27–06. Admission: BF100 adults, BF40 children; valid also for Museum of Religious Art. Open daily 10–12:30 and 2:30–5:30 (winter to 4:30).*

㉖ The road from Stavelot north to **Spa** runs through very attractive landscape. Spa is indeed the original spa. The Romans came here to take the waters, and they were followed over the centuries by crowned heads such as Marguerite de Valois, Christina of Sweden, and Peter the Great. Less welcome was Kaiser Wilhelm II, who established his general headquarters in Spa in 1918. By then Spa was already past its prime. During the 18th and 19th centuries, Spa had been the watering place of international high society, and many gracious houses remain from that period. The pleasures of the cure and the surroundings were supplemented in those days by high-stakes gambling, playing *pharaon* or *biribi* for rubles, ducats, piastres, or francs. Today's casino is more sedate.

The two best-known sources in the center of town—locally known as *pouhons*—are the **Pouhon Pierre-le-Grand** and the

Pouhon Prince-de-Condé, which can be visited by tourists as well as *curistes* (people taking the cure). The price for a glass straight from the source is a modest BF7. *Open Easter–Oct., daily 10–noon and 2–5:30; Nov.–Easter, weekdays 2–5, weekends 10–noon and 2–5.*

Tour 4: Belgian Luxembourg

㉗ **La Roche-en-Ardenne** is 77 kilometers (48 miles) from Liège, 127 kilometers (79 miles) from Brussels, and 66 kilometers (41 miles) from Namur. It's a small town, beautifully situated, and is packed with tourists and trippers in the summer season, when it's wise to avoid it on weekends. However, the main attraction is a trip out of town to admire the view, and the principal part is played by the River Ourthe, a torrent that splashes through a landscape of great beauty. Follow N834 south and turn left on N843 to Nisramont, which has an excellent view. Cross the river and go left on N860 to Nadrin, and left again on

㉘ N869 to the **Belvedère des Six Ourthes.** A 120-step climb to the top of the observation tower will reward you with a magnificent view of the quintessence of the Ardennes: wooded hills and meandering river valleys. You can return on the pretty N860, following the banks of the Ourthe toward La Roche.

㉙ You reach **Bastogne** by going southwest on N89 and then southeast on N4. La Roche and a number of other Ardennes towns were also destroyed during the Battle of the Bulge, but Bastogne was the epicenter. The town was surrounded but held by the American 101st Airborne Division. The weather was miserable. On December 22 Brigadier General MacAuliffe was invited to surrender. His four-letter-word reply, "Nuts!" is one of the famous quotes from World War II. On December 26, the skies cleared and supplies could be flown in, but it took another month before the last German salient had been wiped out.

Colline du Mardasson (Mardasson Hill), just east of the town, is the site of a memorial to the Americans lost in the battle. Mosaics by Fernand Léger decorate the crypt with its three chapels, Protestant, Catholic, and Jewish. The **Bastogne Historical Center,** next to the memorial monument and built in the shape of a five-pointed star, illustrates the ebb and flow of the battle with photos, films (including footage shot during the battle), uniforms, and arms. *Tel. 061/21–14–13. Admission: BF195. Open Mar.–Apr. and Oct.–mid-Nov., daily 10–4; May–June and Sept., daily 9:30–5; July–Aug., daily 9–6.*

The **Victory Memorial Museum** expands on the same theme. The museum traces the progress of World War II from Africa to Berlin with the help of realistic reconstructions, using 200 vehicles, arms, uniforms, materiel, and a film compiled from contemporary sources. There's also a souvenir shop and a specialized book shop. *Messancy (40 km/25 mi south of Bastogne on E25), tel. 063/21–99–88. Admission: BF295 adults, BF175 children. Open Feb.–Dec., daily 9–5; summer, daily 9–6.*

㉚ In **Arlon,** the **Musée Luxembourgeois** contains a number of Roman tombstones from the first three centuries AD, sculpted with reliefs of mythical or allegorical figures as well as scenes from daily life. There is also a section featuring Merovingian tombstones and jewelry. *Rue des Martyrs 13, tel. 063/22–12–*

36. Admission: BF50. Open mid-June–mid-Sept., Mon.–Sat. 9–noon and 2–5, Sun. 9–noon and 2–4:30.

You are now in the southernmost part of Belgian Luxembourg, La Gaume, which is part of Lorraine rather than the Ardennes. N83 leads west to Florenville, where you can turn south on N88 to reach the **Abbaye d'Orval** in the middle of the woods, almost on the French border. This abbey, founded by Italian Benedictines in 1070, gradually became one of Europe's richest and most famous. Destroyed twice by French troops in the 17th and 18th centuries, the monastery was finally re-consecrated as a Trappist abbey in 1948. The medieval and 18th-century ruins are remarkable. The tomb of Wenceslas, first duke of Luxembourg, is in the choir of the abbey church, and outside it is the spring where Mathilde, duchess of Lorraine, once dropped her wedding band, only to have it miraculously returned by a trout. The monks are known not only for their spirituality, but also for the excellence of their bread, cheese, and potent Trappist beer. *Villers-devant-Orval, tel. 061/31–10–60. Admission: BF60. Open daily (except Mon. AM in winter) 10–noon and 2–5.*

The focus of this region is the Semois River, flowing west to join the Meuse. A few miles west of Florenville you can head north on N884 to **Herbeumont,** a thousand-year-old village with a hilltop castle ruin, which offers a splendid view of the river valley. Just to the north, N865 west follows the river from Mortehan/Cugnon to Dohan (both possible starting points for kayak trips to Bouillon), Noirefontaine, and Bouillon.

The small town of **Bouillon** was capital of a duchy almost equally small, which managed to remain independent for 800 years. Its most famous native son, Godefroy de Bouillon, sold it to the bishop of Liège in 1096 in order to improve his cash flow before departing on the first crusade. Bouillon owed its independence to the **Château Fort,** an impressive example of medieval military architecture. Successive modifications have done little to alter the personality of this feudal stronghold with its towers, drawbridge, guardroom, torture chamber, dungeons, and enormous walls. *Rue du Château, tel. 061/46–62–57. Admission: BF140 adults, BF70 children. Open Mar.–June and Sept.–Nov., daily 10–5; July–Aug., daily 10–7; Dec., Wed.–Sun. 10–5; Jan. and Feb., weekends 10–5.*

St-Hubert is 56 kilometers (35 miles) northeast of Bouillon on N89. Its name recalls the patron saint of hunters. According to legend Hubert, hunting in these woods on Good Friday in 683, saw his quarry, a stag, turn its head toward him, and its antlers held a crucifix. Hubert lowered his bow, and later went on to become a bishop and a saint. On the first Sunday in September, Mass in the old basilica is played with hunting horns, followed by a historical procession, and on November 3, St. Hubert's feast day, animals are blessed.

North of the town is, appropriately enough, the **Parc à Gibier de St-Hubert,** where one can observe the animal life of the Ardennes—deer, mountain sheep, and wild boars. *Rue St-Michel, tel. 061/61–17–15. Admission: BF60 adults, BF40 children. Open daily 9–6.*

To the north past Han-sur-Lesse (*see* Tour 1, *above*) is **Rochefort,** where the caves excavated by the River Lomme are even wilder and colder than those at Han-sur-Lesse. *Drève de Lorette, tel. 084/21–20–80. Admission: BF150 adults, BF105* *children. May–Aug., visits every 45 min. 9:45–5:15; April and Sept.–mid-Nov., 10, 11:30, 1:30, 3, and 4:30.*

You are now only 13 km (8 mi) from A4/E411 and the network of motorways.

What to See and Do with Children

The Meuse Valley The **Réserve d'Animaux Sauvage** (Wildlife Reserve) in Han-sur-Lesse, which covers more than 240 hectares (600 acres), provides an opportunity to see the wildlife, past and present, of the Ardennes, including stags and wild boars, lynx and bears, bisons and wild oxen. *Rue J. Lamotte 2, tel. 084/37–72–13. Admission: BF170 adults, BF120 children. Open May–Aug., daily 10–5; Mar.–Apr. and Sept.–Nov., daily 10–4.*

Mont-Fat in Dinant, 122 meters (400 feet) above the city, offers the combination of a guided tour of prehistoric caves and a chairlift ride to an amusement area. *Rue en Rhée 15, tel. 082/22–27–83. Admission: BF200 adults, BF150 children. Open Easter–Sept., daily 10:30–7.*

The **Reine Fabiola** center in the Citadel grounds at Namur includes a large playground with miniature golf, go-carts, boat rides, and electric cars. *Route Merveilleuse, tel. 081/22–68–29. Admission and hours as for the Citadel (see Tour 1, above).*

Liège The **Wegimont Domaine** is just a few minutes south of E42 at Exit 37. An area of 20 hectares (50 acres) around the château offers sporting facilities, fishing, rowing, swimming in a heated outdoor pool, minigolf, and signposted walks. *Soumagne, tel. 041/77–10–20. Admission: BF90 adults, BF55 children. Open May–Aug., daily 9–8.*

Eupen to Spa At **Telecoo**, chairlifts take you up from Coo to a plateau where there's a splendid view of the Ambleve River valley and an extensive amusement park. *Stavelot, tel. 080/68–42–65. Admission: BF480. Open Mar.–mid-Nov., daily 10–7; mid-Nov.–Feb., weekends 10–7.*

You get to the **Monde Sauvage Safari** (Savage World Safari) at Deigné near Aywaille on E25 south from Liège, Exit 46. The safari park, home to a number of different species of African animals, is visited by car or tourist train. This is followed by a visit on foot to a zoo with lions, tigers, polar bears, and others. *Fange de Deigné 3, tel. 041/60–90–70. Admission: BF200 adults, BF140 children. Open mid-Mar.–mid-Nov., daily 10–7.*

Belgian Luxembourg On a very different note, you'll find a **Musée du Jouet** (Toy Museum) in Ferrières (motorway A26, Exit 48). Its collection consists of more than a thousand early 20th-century toys. *Route du Lognoûle 6, tel. 086/40–01–98. Admission: BF50 adults, BF20 children. Open July–Aug., weekends 2:30–5:30.*

Off the Beaten Track

Liège To the northwest of central Liège, the **Fort de Loncin** has remained as it was at 5:15 PM on August 16, 1914, when a German shell scored a direct hit, killing most of the garrison. *Route de Bruxelles, tel. 041/26–24–34. Admission: BF60. Open Wed.–Sun. 9–6; winter, Wed.–Sun. 9–5.*

The right bank of the river, **Outremeuse** (On the Other Side of the Meuse), is a sort of Alternative Liège. It was the home of two personages, Georges Simenon and Tchantchès. Simenon left Liège as early as he could, and only one of his more than 400 books, *Le pendu de Saint-Pholien*, is set in the city; nevertheless the tourist office arranges occasional Simenon walks for his fans. Tchantchès is strictly a local character, a marionette that impersonates the "true Liègeois"—caustic, irreverent, and funny. His home is the **Musée Tchantchès.** *Rue Surlet 56, tel. 041/42–75–75. Admission: BF20. Open Tues. and Thur. 2–4.*

The **Aquarium** and **Musée Zoologique,** on the waterfront, owned by the University of Liège, presents 300 different species in 30 carefully created biotopes, while the museum collection of 18,000 pieces illustrates the process of evolution. *Quai Van Beneden 22, tel. 041/43–49–18. Admission: BF100. Open daily 10:30–12:30 and 2–6.*

The **Maison de la Métallurgie** (House of Metallurgy) is south of Outremeuse. Huge 19th-century steel mills have been converted into a museum of industrial archaeology, including a 17th-century Walloon forge. *Boulevard Raymond Poincaré 17, tel. 041/42–65–43. Admission: BF50. Open weekdays 9–5.*

On the attractive new University of Liège campus at **Sart Tilman,** a wooded plateau south of the city, is the **Musée en Plein Air** (Open-Air Museum) conceived by architect Claude Strebelle. It contains many contemporary sculptures and some murals, all integrated with the striking modern architecture. *Domaine Universitaire Sart Tilman, tel. 041/56–22–20. Admission free. Accessible at all times.*

The **Eglise St-Jacques** (St. James's Church) is a few blocks south of Liège's center. The grimy exterior belies a wonderful interior in which marble, stained glass, and polished wood combine to create an outstanding visual harmony. The glory of the church is the Gothic vaults, decorated in intricate patterns of vivid blue and gold and containing myriad sculpted figures. *Place St-Jacques, tel. 041/22–14–41. Open Mon.–Sat. 8–noon.*

Shopping

Huy   The artisans of modern Huy produce pewter plates that make attractive souvenirs; one of the best shops is **Les Potstainiers Hutois** (Avenue des Fosses 34).

Liège   Department store chains in Liège include **C&A** (Feronstree 84), **Sarma** (Place St-Lambert), **Inno-BM** (Place du Maréchal Foch 1), and **FNAC** (same address). The La Batte **street market** is in full swing every Sunday between 9 AM and 2 PM.

The **Carré** is almost exclusively a pedestrian area, with boutiques and shops. The most important shopping arcades are the **Passage Lemonnier** (between Vinâve d'Ile and rue de l'Univérsité), **Galérie en Ile** (between Vinâve d'Ile and rue du Pot d'Or), **Galérie du Pont d'Avroy** (off the street of the same name) and **Galérie Nagelmackers** (between Place de la Cathédrale and rue Tournant St-Paul).

Glassware from Val St-Lambert can be found in a number of shops and most advantageously at the glassworks in Seraing (*see Tour 2, above*). **Firearms,** an age-old Liège specialty, are still handmade to order by some gun shops, notably Lebeau-Courally (Rue St-Gilles 386, tel. 041/52–48–43).

Sports and Fitness

The Meuse Valley
Biking
You can rent mountain bikes at **Meuse et Lesse** in Dinant. *(Rue Caussin 13, Dinant, tel. 082/22–61–86).*

Boating
Rowing is popular, and boats can be hired under the auspices of the **Clubs Nautiques** at Namur and Dinant. If you find riding a kayak down the Lesse a bit too tricky, canoeing on the Meuse may be more to your liking. Contact **Meuse et Lesse** (*see* Biking, *above*).

Climbing
The sheer cliffs along the Meuse lend themselves extremely well to rock climbing, and many hopeful mountaineers learn the skills here for more dramatic exploits. Contact **Club Alpin Belge** (Belgian Alpine Club), Boulevard de la Meuse 109, Jambes, tel. 081/30–31–19).

Fishing
Fishing is permitted on several stretches of the Meuse, where it is mostly of the sitting-on-the-bank kind, and on some livelier tributaries. Licenses can be purchased at local post offices (Dinant: Rue St-Martin).

Horseback Riding
The Provincial Tourist Office can supply a list of more than 20 stables, and the region is great for horseback riding. Horses can be hired for about BF500 per hour, and several stables organize treks of several days with overnight accommodations.

Sailing
Sailing is extremely popular, with yacht harbors at Namur, Profondeville, Dinant, and Waulsort. Contact **Royal Nautique Club de Sambre et Meuse,** (Chemin des Pruniers 11, Wepion, tel. 081/46–11–30).

Liège
Participant Sports
Boating. There's a yacht harbor along the Boulevard Frère Orban, and water sports are popular upstream from the Pont Albert I. Another water-sports center is the Ile Robinson at Visé.

Golf. The **Royal Golf Club du Sart Tilman** (Route du Condroz 2, Ougrée, tel. 041/36–20–21) has 18 holes. Another 18-hole course is at **International Gomzé Golf Club** (Gomzé-Andoumont, tel. 041/60–92–07).

Swimming and Skating. The **Palais des Sports de Coronmeuse** (Quai de Wallonie 7, tel. 041/27–13–24) provides facilities for swimming in a heated outdoor pool in summer and skating in winter.

Spectator Sports
Motor racing. Motor sport fans know **Francorchamps** (near Spa) as one of Europe's top racing circuits. The Formula I Grand Prix de Belgique race is run in August, and there are several other motorcycle and automobile races throughout the year. Contact Intercommunale du Circuit de Spa-Francorchamps (Route de l'Eau Rouge 280, Francorchamps, tel. 087/27–51–38) for information.

Eupen to Spa
Golf
There's a lovely 18-hole golf course at **Balmoral** (tel. 087/77–16–13), just outside Spa.

Horseback Riding
The **Worricken Sports Center** (rue Worricken 9, Bütgenbach, tel. 080/44–69–61) offers horseback riding.

Skiing
Venues for downhill and cross-country skiing are dotted around the region. Equipment is generally available locally. Snow con-

ditions vary wildly, however; check before setting out by calling Belsud (tel. 02/504–0280) in Brussels.

Tennis The **Worricken Sports Center** (*see* Horseback Riding, *above*) has tennis facilities.

Water Sports Water sports can be enjoyed at Robertville and Bütgenbach (*see* Horseback Riding, *above*).

Virtually all the rivers of the Ardennes are great for canoeing, and the meandering Amblêve is one of the best. Single or double kayaks can be rented at **Cookayak** (Stavelot, tel. 080/68–42–45) for a 9-kilometer (5½-mile) ride from Coo to Cheneux (about 1½ hours) or a 23-kilometer (14-mile) ride to Lorcé (about 3½ hours). Bus service back to the starting point is provided.

Belgian Biking in these parts is for those with sturdy legs. Mountain
Luxembourg bikes can be rented from **Ardenne Adventures** (*see* Canoeing, be-
Biking *low*), **Ferme de Palogne** (*see* Canoeing, *below*), and **Moulin de la Falize** (Bouillon, tel. 061/46–72–75). The last is a multisport facility with a swimming pool, bowling alleys, a sauna, and a fitness room.

Canoeing The rapid rivers are ideal for canoeing in this part of the Ardennes. Kayaks can be rented by day or by distance, generally with return transportation to the point of departure. For the River Ourthe, contact **Ardenne Adventures** (La Roche-en-Ardennes, tel. 084/41–13–47; kayaks Apr.–Oct., rafting Nov.–Mar.); **Ourthe Detente Kayak** (Bomal, tel. 086/21–26–71; Apr.–Oct.); or **Ferme de Palogne** (Vieuxville, tel. 086/21–24–12). For the Semois River, contact **Les Rapides du Saty** (Bouillon, tel. 061/42–62–00; Mar.–Oct.) or **Les Tritons-Semois** (Bouillon, tel. 061/46–63–91; Easter–Sept.).

Cross-country It is possible to ski cross-country for a few precious winter
Skiing weeks at the **Centre de Tourisme Équestre** (*see* Horseback Riding, *below*) and at **Moulin de la Falize** (*see* Biking, *above*).

Horseback Riding Contact the **Centre de Tourisme Équestre** (Grand-Halleux, tel. 080/21–64–43), which offers both instruction and treks.

Dining and Lodging

By Nancy Coons Eating in the Ardennes is one of the most straightforward pleasures Belgium has to offer. The territory is chockablock with atmospheric gray-stone inns. The cuisine is, redolent of forest and farm, with ham, sausage, trout, and game in the forefront. The region's *charcuterie* (cured meats and sausages) is some of the best in central Europe. Ardennes sausage, neat and plump, is made with a blend of veal and pork, smoked over smoldering oak; its flavor is a wholesome compromise between simple American summer sausage and the milder Italian salamis. The real charcuterie star, is *jambon d'Ardennes*, ham that is salt-cured raw and delicately smoked so its meat—surely the most supple among its Parma and Westphalian competitors—slices up thin, moist, and tender, more like a superior roast beef than ham. Restaurateurs offer generous platters of it, garnished with crisp little gherkins and pickled onions or, if you're lucky, a savory onion marmalade.

Though game figures prominently throughout Belgian cuisine, nowhere is it more at home, and rarely do you find it fresher, than in these deep, forested hills. Cooks pride themselves on buying their game *à poil*—that is, fresh and furry—from the back of the hunter's station wagon. *Lièvre*, a specialty, is true hare, an enormous rabbit with sail-sized ears and haunches thick with dark flesh. Its most delicate meat lies along the backbone (saddle or *râble*) and can be roasted and served in tenderloin-like slices. The rest of the hare is often, well, gamier (that is, stronger flavored), which prompted the invention of another Ardennes treat: *civet de lièvre*, a rich, aromatic, marinated stew often thickened with blood. A second popular Ardennes stew is *civet de marcassin*, made from the meat of young wild boar, closer to veal than to pork, but considerably more pungently flavored. Ardennes game is usually served with poached fruit and *airelles*, cranberrylike red berries; it also is cooked so often with *genièvre* (juniper berries) that the French call this seasoning *à l'ardennaise*.

Trout offers diners a slightly lighter meal, though once poached in a pool of butter and heaped with toasted almonds it may be as rich as red-meat alternatives. One pleasant relief, though not always available, is *truite au bleu:* Plunged freshly killed into a boiling vinegar stock, the trout turns steely blue and retains its delicate flavor.

Hotel rooms in this region tend to be low-priced, even if there's an outstanding restaurant downstairs. They tend to fill up on weekends and during summer high season (June–Aug.). If you prefer to eat somewhere other than in the hotel you've booked, clear it with the management: You're often expected (and sometimes obligated) to eat in their restaurant. Many hotels offer *demi-pension* (half-board) arrangements, as well as "gastronomic weekends," which include two or three lavish meals with two nights' lodging.

Bastogne
Dining

Au Luxembourg. Among the many brasserie/cafés that line the Place McAuliffe, this lace-cloth restaurant offers more than waffles and beer: There are inexpensive plate lunches, game specialties, and good freshwater fish. *Pl. McAuliffe 25, tel. 061/21–12–26. Dress: casual. AE, DC, MC, V. Inexpensive.*

Wagon-Restaurant Léo. Originally a tiny chrome railroad diner, this local institution has spilled over across the street into the new, chicly refurbished Bistro Léo. In the restaurant, huge platters of plain Belgian standards—mussels, trout in riesling, steak Americain (tartare), frites—are served up; in the bistro, only cold ham plates, quiche, and homemade lasagne are the fare. *Rue du Vivier 8, tel. 061/21–65–10. Dress: casual. MC, V. Inexpensive.*

Lodging

Du Sud. Airy and solid in its new, post-war form, this straightforward little hotel kept its local atmosphere—oak details, game trophies, tile floors—and offers simple comforts. Back rooms are quietest. *Rue de Marche 39, B-6600, tel. 061/21–11–14. 13 rooms. Facilities: café, breakfast only. MC, V. Inexpensive.*

Le Brun. Despite the pride and care lavished on public areas—burnished oak, beveled glass, tile mosaic—this town landmark has only superficially updated its rooms upstairs, with old plumbing fixtures, armoires, and wiring. New paint and wallpaper do give it a fresh look, and renovation work should be finished before 1994. *Rue de Marche 8, B-6600, tel. 061/21–54–21. 20 rooms. Breakfast only. AE, DC, MC, V. Inexpensive.*

Dining and Lodging
★

La Ferme au Pont. Located on a country road between Bastogne and La Roche, this idyllic little farmhouse inn has forests surrounding it and the Ourthe rushing just behind. Dating from 1747, with whitewashed brick, flower boxes on every sill, and a dining room taking in views of the landscaped greenery behind, the inn offers good, simple cooking—grilled ham, smoked trout—and comfortable rooms decked with ivy-print fabrics. *16 kilometers from Bastogne on N-34, near Ortho. B-6983, tel. 084/43–31–61. 7 rooms. AE, DC, MC, V. Inexpensive.*

Bouillon
Dining and Lodging
★

Au Gastronome. This swank Paliseul auberge, once a roadside café, explores the usual stellar routes of haute gastronomy but specializes in a local delicacy: suckling pig, roasted in its crisp skin, its juices blending with those of its stuffing of green pepper and lime. The setting is unpretentious, if a little stuffy, but rooms upstairs are pleasantly old-fashioned, in shades of pink and cream, with floral prints. *Rue Bouillon 2, B-6850 Paliseul (northwest of Bouillon), tel. 061/53–30–64. 10 rooms. Facilities: restaurant (Very Expensive; reservations required; jacket and tie suggested; closed Sun dinner, Mon.). AE, DC, MC, V. Moderate.*

★

Auberge d'Alsace. In the center of Bouillon, with the River Semois across the street and the château towering behind, is this ambitious little hotel/restaurant. Having had the interior rebuilt from the ground up, the proprietress has lavished the rooms with flashy fabrics, brass, lacquer, lace, and the occasional baldachin. Striking a similar tenuous balance between store-bought chic and Old Ardennes, the restaurant downstairs offers good cooking nonetheless: monkfish with kiwi, curried shrimp, but also home-smoked trout and homemade *civet de marcassin* (stew of preserved young boar). *Faubourg de France 3, B-6830, tel. 061/46–65–88. 18 rooms. Facilities: restaurant (Moderate; closed off-season, Mon. dinner, and Tues.), café, terrace café. AE, MC, V. Inexpensive.*

De la Poste. This is the most historic and atmospheric hotel in town, but not consistently the most comfortable. Since Napoleon III, Emile Zola, and Victor Hugo stayed at this 1730 stagecoach stop, its original rooms have been left virtually unchanged, balancing burnished oak and antiques with aged fixtures and afterthought baths. The all-new annex, built in 1990, offers airtight comfort. Downstairs, the grandeur remains intact, with a charming mix of Victorian antiques and rustic brocante. The restaurant stretches along the riverfront; the menu features French classics. *Place St-Arnould 1, B-6830, tel. 061/46–65–06. 80 rooms. Facilities: Restaurant (Moderate), bar, terrace café. AE, DC, MC, V. Inexpensive.*

Gai Repos. Perched on a narrow terraced bluff high above town, looking across the Semois Valley toward the château, this tiny renovated hotel/restaurant offers views from most rooms, including the dining room. Though floors are still creaky and plumbing exposed, the decor is fresh and simple. Dining is relaxed, with straightforward, generous dinners cooked to order by the owner—lamb chops with mustard sauce, veal in cognac, trout. *Rue au Dessus de la Ville 4, B-6830, tel. 061/46–82–62. 6 rooms. Facilities: restaurant (moderate; closed off-season, Tues.), bar. AE, MC, V. Inexpensive.*

Dinant and Environs
Dining

Le Vivier d'Oies. This country inn lies northeast of Dinant, about 3 kilometers (2 miles) east of Yvoir, in a lovely stone farmhouse with a modern stone-and-glass wing. The ambience is strictly urbane, and the cuisine is above reproach: goose liver sautéed with caramelized pears, farm duck with honey and cinnamon, trout with caviar. *Rue Etat 7, Dorinne, tel. 083/69–95–71. Reservations advised. Jacket and tie suggested. AE, DC, MC, V. Closed Tues. dinner, Wed. Expensive.*

Le Jardin de Fiorine. Newly opened in May 1991 and a great success already, this young, ambitious restaurant holds forth in a restored gray-stone mansion with a pretty garden behind. Specialties include a fine lobster and sweetbread salad, satiny lobster flan with Chablis, veal in tarragon and pears, and roast pigeon with corn cakes. *Rue Georges Cousot 3, Dinant, tel. 082/22–74–74. Reservations advised. Jacket suggested. AE, DC, MC, V. Closed Wed. Moderate/Expensive.*

Thermidor. All the elements are here for a mediocre meal—stodgy bourgeois decor with game trophies, an excess of wine glasses, the combination of the words *"touristique"* and *"gastronomique"* on the same menu—yet the cooking here is all it should be: old-time French cuisine, sauces made fresh on the spot, a few experiments in new combinations. Try the grilled salmon steak with fresh-whisked mustard sauce, or chicken breast with a drizzle of vanilla butter. *Rue Station 3, Dinant, tel. 082/22–31–35. Reservations suggested. Jacket suggested. AE, MC, V. Closed Mon. dinner, Tues. Moderate.*

Dining and Lodging
★

Auberge de Bouvignes. This 1830 roadhouse just north of Dinant combines beautifully restored architecture—beams, stonework, whitewashed brick—with a chic decor and superb cooking. Its wine caves are blasted into the solid stone bluff behind, and its rustic bedrooms overlook the Meuse. Lobsters of all kinds are a specialty as in a ragout with asparagus, morels, and fresh pasta; or there may be Bresse pigeon with braised endive and truffles. *Rue Fétis 112, B-5500 Bouvignes-sur-Meuse, tel. 082/61–16–00. 6 rooms. Facilities: restaurant (Very Expensive; reservations required; jacket and tie advised; closed Sun. dinner, Mon.) AE, DC, MC, V. Inexpensive.*

★

Le Mosan. In Anseremme, just downstream from Dinant, this welcoming old roadside hotel sits right on the riverbank. It's very well kept, with fresh, light decor in pretty pastels—worth the mild discomfort of bathrooms down the hall. Downstairs, the traditional restaurant offers trout specialties, kidneys, and steaks, either on the glass porch or in the charming dining room. *Rue Dufrenne 2, B-5500 Anseremme-Dinant, tel. 082/22–24–50. 8 rooms, 0 with bath. Facilities: restaurant (closed off-season, Mon.; Moderate). AE, DC, MC, V. Inexpensive.*

Durbuy
Dining and Lodging

Le Sanglier des Ardennes. Dominating the center of town, with back windows overlooking the river, it has a stone fireplace, beams, and public spaces punctuated by glass cases hawking perfume, leather, and French scarves. The restaurant offers grand French cooking with some regional touches. Rooms are classic pastel-modern, with a businessy look. *Rue Comte d'Ursel 99, B-5480, tel. 086/21–32–62. 45 rooms. Facilities: restaurant (closed off-season, Thurs.), bar, garden, terrace café. AE, DC, MC, V. Expensive.*

★

Du Prévôt. Tucked back on cobblestone streets in the old section of town, this is a cozy, familial old haven, with its main building dating from the 17th century and its additions loyal to the style. Rooms are big and up-to-date, with plush appointments. The restaurant features an open grill, so you can make your choice: sizzling lamb chops, salmon steaks, or trout. *Récollectines 71, B-6940, tel. 086/21–28–68. 10 rooms. Facilities: restaurant (closed Wed.), bar, courtyard café. AE, DC, MC, V. Moderate.*

Lodging **Vieux Durbuy.** This affiliate of the Sanglier sits off the main
★ route, on a tiny old-town back street. A former residence dating from the 17th century, it's an atmospheric stage setting of tapestry, polished wood, and weathered stone: The fireplace in the breakfast room has graceful caryatids. Rooms are full of antiques, with baths in Delft-like tile. *Rue Jean de Bohême 80, B-6940, tel. 086/21–32–62. 12 rooms. Facilities: garden, breakfast only. AE, DC, MC, V. Moderate.*

Han-sur-Lesse **Des Ardennes.** Run casually and not very well maintained, this
Dining and Lodging is a good roadhouse stopover for families visiting the caves. Rooms are musty, with spongy beds and old bath fixtures; those overlooking the garden are more pleasant. Guests are required to eat in the hotel, which is no great punishment: There's good regional cooking with some French fuss, friendly and competent service, and an unusually well-chosen wine list. *Rue des Grottes 2, B-5580, tel. 084/37–72–20. 26 rooms. Facilities: Restaurant (closed off-season, Wed.; Moderate), bar, terrace café. AE, DC, MC, V. Inexpensive.*

Henri IV. In a much quieter setting, back from the highway outside town with forest behind and fields in front, this is more like a country inn than its competitors. It was built in 1948 for the new wave of tourism, and rooms have been kept up to date with a bit of handiwork and fresh decor. The restaurant features *la poule au pot d'autre fois* (old-fashioned stewed chicken, made with ham, turnips, and cabbage) and its own trout. *Rue des Chasseurs Ardennais 59, B-5580, tel. 084/37–72–21. 8 rooms. Facilities: restaurant (closed off-season, Thurs.; Moderate), bar, terrace café. AE, MC, V. Inexpensive.*

Huy **Du Fort.** Tucked under the Citadel, across from the arching
Dining and Lodging bridge over the Meuse, this is the simplest of roadhouses, but
★ its rooms have been carefully decorated and maintained at a solid middle-class level, and its owners pamper you in the unpretentious tavern downstairs. There's a brief, standard menu with trout, sole, or chicken, each with frites and salad, at reasonable prices. *Chaussée Napoléon 6, B-4500, tel. 085/21–24–03. 34 rooms, some with sink only. Facilities: restaurant, bar. AE, DC, MC, V. Inexpensive.*

Liège **Vieux Liège.** The money you spend here on classic, old-school
Dining French cuisine—foie gras, lobster, beef in three-pepper sauce—functions less as a cost of fine dining than as a museum entry fee into one of Belgium's extraordinary buildings, a sprawling, appealingly ramshackle cross-timbered beauty dating from the 16th century. Interiors, all creaking parquet and glossy wood beams, have been furnished in Old-Master luxury—Delft tiles, brass, pewter, Oriental runners. *Quai de la Goffee 41, tel. 041/23–77–48. Reservations suggested. Jacket and tie suggested. AE, DC, MC, V. Closed Sun., Wed. night. Very Expensive.*

★ **Ma Maison.** This sleek, intimate little restaurant chose to showcase its timbers and casement windows in cool, modern decor, focusing its energies instead on varied, imaginative cooking, chic presentation, and discreet service. Daily specialties may include skate in a cool aspic of bouillabaisse, tiny beignets (fritters) of ham in mustard sauce, airy potato pancakes with minced smoked salmon, and a smörgåsbord of cunning sweets. *Rue Hors-Château 46, tel. 041/23–30–91. Reservations advised. Jacket suggested. AE, DC, MC, V. Closed Sun., Mon. Expensive.*

Lodging **Cygne d'Argent/Petit Cygne.** This modest hotel and its nearby annex offer a backstreet retreat from the noisy Boulevard d'Avroy. Room decor is dated but well maintained, with baths in good order. In the 18th-century Petit Cygne down the block, with its great hallway and tall windows, rooms have only been superficially modernized; breakfast can be delivered from the main hotel. *Rue Beeckman 49, B-4000, tel. 041/23–70–01. 29 rooms. Facilities: Breakfast only. AE, DC, MC, V. Moderate.*

Metropôle. Upstairs in this very basic station hotel, the rooms have been left to sag a bit—stuffy old furniture, orange chenille. Windows are double-glazed, however, and back rooms are downright quiet. Some cheaper rooms have no bathroom. *Rue des Guillemins 141, B-4000. Tel. 041/52–42–93. 28 rooms, some without bath. Facilities: Breakfast only. AE, DC, MC, V. Inexpensive.*

★ **de l'Univers.** A cut above most train station hotels, this landmark has been kept up to date with double windows, sharp room decor (business-class beige and burgundy), and a modernized brasserie/bar downstairs. *Rue des Guillemins 116, B-4000. Tel. 041/52–28–04. 49 rooms. Facilities: Restaurant, bar. AE, DC, MC, V. Inexpensive.*

Malmédy **Au St-Esprit.** In the very center of this now-thriving town (well
Dining and Lodging recovered and even friendly to Americans despite being acci-
★ dentally bombed three times in December 1944), this solid, comfortable hotel combines fresh decor (pretty floral prints, fresh linens in the rooms) with regional charm (fireplace and beams downstairs). The restaurant features Ardennes specialties, of course—ham, trout, game—on a number of moderately priced menus. *Place de Rome, B-4960, tel. 080/33–03–14. 9 rooms, 3 with sink only. Facilities: restaurant. AE, DC, MC, V. Inexpensive.*

Namur **Le Temps des Cerises.** On a narrow old-town street chockablock
Dining with little restaurants, this retro café serves rich, hearty
★ fare—fish soup with *rouille* (garlic and red-pepper sauce), homemade sausages, kidneys in garlic-juniper sauce—in artful but generous portions. The setting is charmingly Old Belgium, with lace café curtains, vintage postcards, knickknacks, and furniture and paneling painted a glossy cherry red. *Rue des Brasseurs 22, tel. 081/22–53–26. Reservations suggested. Dress: casual. V. Moderate.*

Dining and Lodging **Château de Namur.** Situated at the top of the Citadel's bluff above the city, in a grand old mansion built in 1930, this is a hotel school first and foremost, with much of its former grandeur subjugated to its current role as a teaching vehicle. Public spaces are spare and underfurnished, but rooms are comfortable and fresh and the views above reproach. Ask for a corner, with double views. In the dining room, students practice the art of serving rough-edged but ambitious French cooking. *Avenue Ermitage 1, B-5000 tel. 081/74–26–30. 29 rooms. Facilities: restaurant, bar. AE, DC, MC, V. Expensive.*

★ **Saint-Loup.** Making a real break away from posh old city hotels and jazzy new chains, this central lodging is urban to the core, converting an 18th-century town house to an avant-garde downtown delight. Rooms have been designed in super-mod angles and candy-bright colors, some with marble baths; downstairs, lovely old spaces (including a quiet, green garden court) have been slicked up with halogen and high-tech furniture. *Rue St-Loup 4, B-5000, tel. 081/23-04-05. 10 rooms. Facilities: restaurant (Moderate/Expensive), bar, garden court. AE, DC, MC, V. Expensive.*

★ **Ferme du Quartier.** Just outside Namur, near the Bouge exit from the highway, this delightfully restored old stone farmhouse stands in a silent country oasis. Interiors are modern, in natural materials, with some brick-vaulted ceilings and beams. The locals dine in its simple, traditional restaurant on varieties of steak, rabbit in mustard sauce, grilled salmon, or *pintadeau* (guinea fowl) in beer. Rooms in the converted barn are smaller but even quieter than those in the main house. *B-5004 Bouge-Namur, tel. 081/21-11-05. 14 rooms. Facilities: restaurant, bar. AE, DC, MC, V. Inexpensive.*

Lodging **Beauregard.** Newly built into a wing of the Casino, this is a polished, fashionable business hotel, with vivid color schemes (lime, salmon, teal) and sleek room decor. Rooms with wide views of the river cost slightly more (as of April 1993). Breakfast buffet is served in a vast, windowed hall with more river views. *Avenue Baron de Moreau 1, B-5000, tel. 081/23-00-28. 51 rooms. Facilities: access to Casino Club (restaurant/bar) and Casino. AE, DC, MC, V. Moderate.*

La Roche-en-Ardenne **La Huchette.** Though a bit out of place in this hardy forest resort, this middle-class restaurant serves good, classic French *Dining* cooking—delicate quenelles of pike in lobster *coulis* (broth), salmon tournedos in tarragon, pigeon with red cabbage—in a decidedly unrustic setting of pink, brass, and terra-cotta. *Rue de l'Eglise 6, tel. 084/41-13-33. Reservations suggested. Jacket suggested. AE, MC, V. Closed Tues. dinner, Wed. Moderate/Expensive.*

★ **Du Midi.** This tiny old cliffside hotel is worth a visit for the food, which is the Real Thing: straightforward regional specialties, simply and stylishly served. Game in season is superbly cooked (tenderloin of young boar in old port) and served with *gratin Dauphinois* (scalloped potatoes) and poached pear; air-dried Ardennes ham comes with candied onions. The setting is local—oak, green plush, brass lamps, spinning-wheel chandeliers—though not old. *Rue Beausaint 6, tel. 084/41-11-38. Reservations suggested. Dress: casual. AE, DC, MC, V. Moderate.*

Dining and Lodging **La Claire Fontaine.** On the forest highway leading from E40 to ★ La Roche, this grand old whitewashed-brick lodge sits comfortably on wooded grounds, its windows taking in green views on all sides. The Son-Renard family have left the crooked old woodwork intact and filled the lounges with overstuffed furniture, antiques, and Oriental rugs. Upstairs, rooms are less picturesque, though some on the second floor have been slicked up with bright colors and modern fixtures. The son is the chef de cuisine; he buys his game "in the fur" and offers weekend gastronomic specials. *Route de Hotton 64, B-6980, tel. 084/41-12-96. 26 rooms. Facilities: restaurant, bar. AE, MC, V. Moderate.*

★ **Les Genets.** Even the rooms are pretty in this romantic old sprawl of a mountain inn, with its stenciled wallpaper and homey-chic mixes of plaid, paisley, and chintz. Picture windows take in valley views on two sides. The restaurant offers gastronomic menus (grilled and smoked trout salad with hazelnut vinaigrette, pigeon in juniper). They prefer guests to take demipension. *Corniche de Deister 2, B-6980, tel. 084/41–18–77. 8 rooms. Facilities: restaurant (closed off-season, Wed.–Thurs.; Moderate), bar. AE, DC, MC, V. Inexpensive.*

Rochefort
Dining and Lodging

Les Falizes. On the edge of town, on the way to Han-sur-Lesse, this is yet another comfortable, up-market country inn. It is cozily furnished with old oak, leaded glass, a working fireplace, and overstuffed furniture; sizable rooms upstairs are furnished with a palatable mix of Victorian plush and florals. The focus is food, however: *chartreuse* (layered mold) of sole and beets; pigeon roasted in truffle juice; duck-liver *pot au feu* (hot pot). *Rue de France 90, B-5580, tel. 084/21–12–82. 6 rooms. Facilities: restaurant (closed off-season, Mon. dinner and Tues.; summer, Tues.; Expensive), bar. AE, DC, MC, V. Inexpensive.*

★ **La Malle Poste.** Despite its location on the main road through town, this former *relais de poste* (coach stop), dating from the late 18th century, affects a grand, manicured garden. Its architecture merits the fuss, as the stonework, moldings, and burnished oak of the main house evoke a lavish past. The new wing, built into a neighboring building, is more rustic, with exposed timbers and heavy stone. The restaurant specializes in luxuries—foie gras, lobster, and pigeon—though they do a mean truite au bleu as well. *Rue de Behogne 46, B-5580, tel. 084/22–11–13. 11 rooms. Facilities: restaurant (closed off-season, Mon. and Thurs.; Moderate/Expensive) bar, garden, terrace. AE, DC, MC, V. Inexpensive.*

★ **Trou Maulin.** Just past the center, at the edge of green fields and forest, this is a lovely little country inn. The husband cooks, the wife serves, and both keep up the pretty garden and the creaky-cozy lodgings upstairs, with quirkily shaped rooms squeezed in and furnished in a homey mix. While there are well-executed regional specialties—game, trout—chef Boubet shows even greater skills with *abats* (organ meats): sweetbreads, kidneys, and calf brains. *Route de Marche 19, B-5430, tel. 084/21–32–40. 7 rooms. Facilities: restaurant (closed off-season, Tues. dinner and Wed.; Moderate), bar, terrace café, garden. AE, MC, V. Inexpensive.*

Lodging
★

Le Vieux Logis. This is a delightful small hotel *sans restaurant* in a 300-year-old home that housed the abundance of "chateau cousins" who lived below the castle. From the date, 1696, visible on the fireback behind a log fire in the lounge to the ancient plank floors, the setting transports guests to the past—despite the traffic whizzing by out front. Rooms have been decorated by the owner with pretty Delft-look wallpaper and real antiques. *Rue Jacquet 71, B-5580, tel. 084/21–10–24. 11 rooms. Facilities: garden, breakfast only. MC, V. Inexpensive.*

Spa
Dining
★

La Brasserie du Grand Maur. This graceful 200-year-old city mansion now houses a lovely, traditional restaurant, where visitors sample menus of good regional specialties, somewhat Frenchified: *sole aux crevettes grises* (sole with tiny gray shrimp), trout, and game. The setting, all polished wood, linens, and antiques, makes the meal. *Rue Xhrouet 41, tel. 087/77–36–16. Reservations suggested. Jacket suggested. AE, DC, MC, V. Closed Mon.–Tues. Moderate.*

Old Inn. A simple, slightly touristy little lunch stop on the main

American Express offers Travelers Cheques built for two.

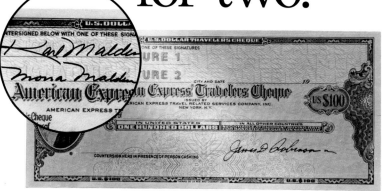

American Express® Travelers Cheques *for Two*. The first Travelers Cheques that allow either of you to use them because both of you have signed them. And only one of you needs to be present to purchase them.

Cheques *for Two* are accepted anywhere regular American Express Travelers Cheques are, which is just about everywhere. So stop by before your next trip and ask for Cheques *for Two*.

Travelers Cheques

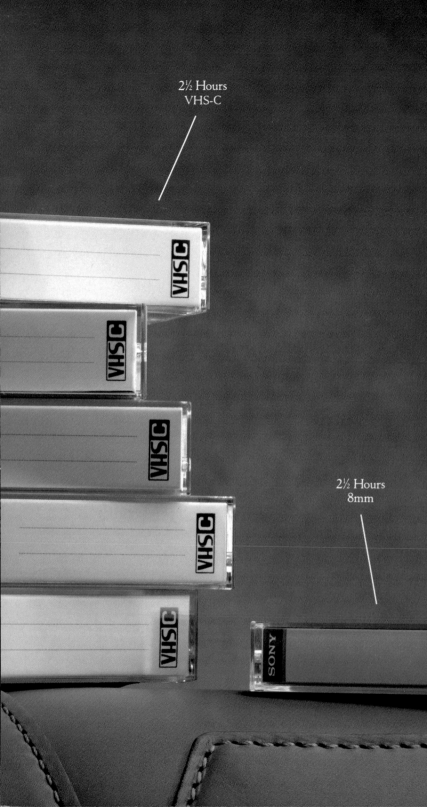

2½ Hours
VHS-C

2½ Hours
8mm

SONY

PACK WISELY.

Given a choice, the seasoned traveler always carries less.

Case in point: Sony Handycam® camcorders, America's most

popular. They record up to 2½ hours on a single tape.

VHS-C tapes record only 30 minutes.* And why carry five tapes

when you can record everything on one? Which brings us

to the first rule of traveling: pack a Sony Handycam camcorder.

street, across from the baths, this beamed and wainscoted restaurant serves inexpensive regional menus (ham, game) as well as mussels and crêpes. It's one step up from a tavern, with pink linens covered by paper mats with ads for local businesses. *Rue Royale 17, tel. 087/77–39–43. Dress: casual. AE, DC, MC, V. Closed off-season, Wed. Inexpensive/Moderate.*

Lodging
★ **Cardinal.** Offering a real taste of old Spa, this grand urban resort hotel opened in 1924—but, the host asserts, it was completely renovated in 1948. Its period decor and interior architecture is completely intact and fresh as new. Have tea in the muraled salon, hot chocolate in the beautiful all-oak café, or dinner in the swanky chandeliered dining hall. Most rooms are 1948-modern (smooth gold oak paneling). *Place Royale 21–27, B-4880, tel. 087/77–10–64. 30 rooms. Facilities: restaurant, bar, tearoom. AE, DC, MC, V. Expensive.*

The Arts and Nightlife

Liège
Check times at **Infor-Spectacles** (En Féronstrée 92, tel. 041/22–11–11). You can also buy tickets there. For all sorts of events in Liège, look under "Other Towns" in *The Bulletin.*

The Arts
Liège has its own opera company, the **Opéra Royal de Wallonie,** (Théâtre Royal, Rue des Dominicains, tel. 041/23–59–10).

The city also has its own symphony orchestra, **l'Orchestre Philharmonique de Liège.** The Wallonie Chamber Orchestra and other ensembles participate in the annual Festival de la Wallonie, with concerts also in Spa and Stavelot.

The most interesting **theater** performances in French or Walloon are generally at the **Théâtre de la Place** (Place de l'Yser, tel. 041/42–81–18). It's also worth checking out what's on offer at **Les Chiroux** (Place des Carmes, tel. 041/23–19–60) or at the **Foyer Culturel du Sart Tilman** (*Domaine Universitaire, tel. 041/56–32–99*). You can see **puppet theater** performances featuring the irrepressible Tchantchès at the grandly named **Théâtre Royal Ex-Impérial de Roture** (Rue Surlet 56, tel. 041/42–75–75; Wed. 2:30 PM and Sun. 10:30 AM), at the theater of the **Musée de la Vie Wallonne** (Cour des Mineurs; tel. 041/23–60–94 same hours), and at the **Théâtre Al Botroule** (Rue Hocheporte 3, tel. 041/23–05–76; Sat. 8:30 PM for adults, Wed. 3 PM for children).

Nightlife
The Liègeois have an amazing ability to stay up until all hours, and nightlife is booming on both sides of the Meuse. The Carré quarter, on the left bank, is favored by students and those who go to a show first and decide to go out afterwards. Two *cafés chantant* (singing cafés), than which nothing is more typical of this city, should be tried: **Les Olivettes** (Rue Pied-du-Pont des Arches, tel. 041/22–07–08) and **Les Caves de Porto** (Féronstrée 144, tel. 041/23–23–25), which also welcomes jazz. Other cafés with lots of traditional ambience include **Le Seigneur d'Amay** (Rue d'Amay, tel. 041/22–00–44) and **La Taverne St-Paul** (Rue St-Paul, tel. 041/23–72–17) near the Cathedral. Rue Tête-de-Boeuf contains some fashionable clubs and discos such as **Estoril** (tel. 041/21–09–37).

You go to the Roture quarter in Outremeuse more specifically for a night's entertainment. There's hardly a house without a café, club, or jazz hangout. Here's where the best jazz clubs are, including **Le Lion s'envoile** (En Roture 11, tel. 041/42–93–

17) and **Le Cirque Divers** (En Roture 13, tel. 041/41–02–44). Both branch out from time to time into literary and other kinds of happenings. Or you may choose to finish the evening more quietly in an ambience of Liège folklore at the **Café Tchantchès** (Rue Grande-Beche, tel. 041/43–39–31).

Stavelot The **Stavelot Chamber Music Festival** (tel. 080/86–27–34) is held
The Arts every August.

5 Luxembourg

By Nancy Coons

Entering the eponymous capital of tiny Luxembourg across the Grande-Duchesse Charlotte Bridge, first-time visitors are greeted by an awe-inspiring view: Up and down the length of the Alzette River stretches a panorama of medieval stonework—jutting fortification walls, slit-windowed towers, ancient church spires, massive gates—as detailed and complete as a 17th-century engraving come to life. Then the visitors turn left—and enter the 20th century. The Boulevard Royal, little more than five blocks long, glitters with glass-and-concrete office buildings, each one containing a world-class bank and untold, anonymous, well-sheltered fortunes. There's plenty of time to gawk, because traffic, thick with Jaguars, Mercedes, BMWs, crawls through town, dodging extravagant new roadworks and construction projects. Luxembourg, once sovereign to lands that stretched from the Meuse to the Rhine, reduced over the centuries to a powerless pawn and lobbed from conqueror to conqueror like a tennis ball, until recently little more than a cluster of meager farms and failing mines, flaunts new wealth, new political muscle, and the fourth-highest standard of living in the world.

The Grand Duchy of Luxembourg, one of the smallest countries in the United Nations, measures only 2,597 square kilometers (999 square miles), less than the size of Rhode Island. It is dwarfed by its neighbors—Germany, Belgium, and France—yet from its history of invasion, occupation, and siege, you might think those square miles built over bedrock of solid gold. In fact, it was Luxembourg's very defenses against centuries of attack that rendered it all the more desirable: From AD 963, when Charlemagne's descendant Sigefroid founded a castle on the high promontory of the Bock, the duchy encased itself in layer upon layer of fortifications until by the mid-19th century its very invulnerability was considered a threat to those *not* commanding its thick stone walls. The more impregnable it became, the more desirable it became; the more its enemies tried to grasp it, the greater its holder's efforts to thicken the shell.

It all started when Sigefroid, a beneficiary of the disintegration of central Europe that followed Charlemagne's death, chose a small gooseneck carved by the Alzette to develop as a fortress and the capital of his considerable domains. Thanks to his aggressions and the ambitions of his heirs, Luxembourg grew continuously until, by the 14th century, its count, Henry IV, was powerful and important enough to serve as Henry VII, king of the German nations and Holy Roman emperor. In fact, in that epoch, Luxembourg contributed no less than five kings and emperors to the empire, including Henry VII's son, the flamboyant John the Blind (Jean l'Aveugle), who, despite leading his armies, to slaughter in the Battle of Crécy (1346), remains a national hero.

After his death, Luxembourg commanded the greatest territory it would ever rule—from the Meuse to Metz and the Moselle—and its rulers Charles IV, Wenceslas I and II, and Sigismund carried the name of the House of Luxembourg to pan-European renown. If Luxembourg had a golden age, this was it, and it was short-lived. Plague, the decay of feudalism, marital and financial intrigues among leaders who rarely if ever set toe in Luxembourg—all these factors finally left the duchy vulnerable, and Philip the Good, duke of Burgundy, took it by storm in 1443.

From that point on, Luxembourg lost its significance as a geographical mass and took on importance as a fortress. It was controlled from 1443 to 1506 by Burgundy, from 1506 to 1714 by Spain (with a brief period—1684 to 1697—under Louis XIV of France), and from 1714 to 1795 by Austria; Napoleon took it from the Habsburgs in 1795. Each, in taking the fortress, had to penetrate miles of outworks whose battlements, pointed like the arms of stars, were thrust into the threatening countryside. And having penetrated the outer defenses, the aggressor faced a citadel perched on sheer stone cliffs with weapons bristling from every pore, its soldiers outnumbering its citizens. To take it by frontal attack was out of the question; the solution, usually, was siege and starvation.

Having been torn and ravaged for 400 years by conquerors' games of tug-of-war, Luxembourg continued to provoke squabbles into the 19th century, when Prussia's leader, Bismarck, Solomon-like, decided that no one should have it at all. Named a grand duchy in 1815 and granted independence in 1839, Luxembourg was declared an independent and neutral state in 1867 by the Treaty of London, and its battlements were dismantled, stone by stone. What remains of its walls, while impressive, is only a reminder of what was one of the strongholds of Europe—the "Gibraltar of the North."

Today Luxembourg is besieged again, this time by bankers and Eurocrats. Its more than 120 banks rival Switzerland's, and just outside the old city a new colony has been seeded, a self-contained ecosystem of *fonctionnaires* for the European Community, the heir to the Common Market. Fiercely protecting its share of the expanding bureaucracy from Strasbourg and Brussels, which, with Luxembourg, form the triumvirate of capitals that head the EC, the duchy digs its heels in once again, this time fighting not only for independence but also for its new-found prosperity and clout. Thus the national motto takes on new meaning: *Mir wölle bleiwe wat mir sin* (We want to stay what we are)—nowadays, a powerful, viable grand duchy in the heart of modern Europe.

And yet, really, all this new wealth and power has very little to do with the average Luxembourger, beyond increasing exponentially the value of his cabbage patch. This was, and remains, an agricultural country, a close-knit, self-contained community of small farmers who, until the 19th century, suffered a plague of natural and political disasters and produced little more than enough to support themselves. In 1878 breakthroughs in both farming and mining technology turned the country around (ironically, it was discovered that a new, efficient technique for purifying iron ore created an indispensible by-product: fertilizer) and started a boom that ended up putting Luxembourg on 20th-century maps.

Luxembourgers have remained proud farmers at heart, trading their Bruno Magli shoes for garden clogs every weekend and digging row upon row of brussels sprouts and cabbage; until the mid-'60s, foreign residents were hard put to find greengrocers, as the natives grew their own fruits and vegetables. Often wealthy enough to mortgage Grandpapa's now astonishingly valuable farmlands and buy each of their children suburban bungalows as wedding gifts, many Luxembourgers nonetheless scrub their sidewalks weekly, keep their manure pile in front of the adjoining barn (in old times this was a meas-

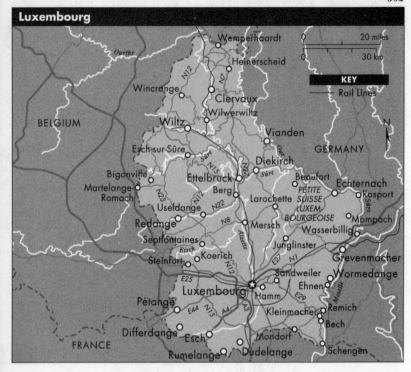

urable status symbol), play in the community band, spend Sunday afternoon at the local *jeu de quilles* (bowling) café, and walk to the cathedral every year to thank the Virgin for sparing their forefathers from the plague.

Threatened and encroached upon for a thousand years, isolated by Luxembourgish, their only recently codified Frankish dialect, and now smothered under a new eruption of foreign laborers and Eurocrats, the Luxembourgers are a far from effervescent lot; the public face is dour, sober, hardened against foreign approach. Nor are they socially promiscuous among themselves, entering each other's homes only on formal invitation. The family is sacred, and though children are expected to go to university in Brussels, Strasbourg, or Cologne (there is no university here), they also are expected to come home, where they will often live and lunch until marriage—and sometimes after. While their education prepares them to deal with the world in French, German, and English, they are only truly at home in their mother tongue—and few in the world besides Mother speak it.

Observing the Luxembourgers out on a Sunday afternoon in their loden-green overcoats as they walk their long-haired dachshunds down their tidy streets, past their shutterless, unsentimental modernizations of ancient buildings; speak their guttural dialect, with its scraps of Alttrier-Moselle German and flinty, scolding tone; and treat themselves to their afternoon coffee and cake, a visitor might conclude that Luxembourg is a Germanic culture at heart. Hitler tried to convince them of it: Suppressing Luxembourgish, converting French names, he launched a campaign to convince Luxembourgers to come *Heim ins Reich*—to come home to the fatherland as ethnic Germans. Yet a visit to any war museum will show that the Luxembourgers weren't having any of it, and that the majority have yet to forget that the German invasions left Luxembourg hideously scarred, that thousands of its men were conscripted during the German occupation and sent as so much cannon fodder to the Russian front. There are Luxembourgers today who refuse to drive German cars and who will welcome American veterans come back to trace the *Route de la Liberation*.

Yet that era is passing, too, and the Germans, like the Spanish, the French, and the Dutch who conquered before, have been for the most part forgiven—and even accepted as frequent tourists. Today Luxembourg welcomes all nationalities as visitors; they swarm through its ruins, churches, museums, forests, and vineyards every summer. And whatever their origin, Luxembourg greets them, quite often, in a common tongue. Centuries of occupation have prepared the inhabitants well for such grudging hospitality. But despite—or perhaps because of—the onslaught, Luxembourg remains intact, autonomous, independent: *Mir wölle bleiwe wat mir sin.*

Before You Go

Government Tourist Offices

In North America 801 2nd Avenue, New York, NY 10017, tel. 212/370–9850.

In the U.K. 36–37, Piccadilly, London W1V 9PA, tel. 071/434–2800.

Tour Groups

General-Interest Tours Listed below is a sample of the tours and packages that concentrate on Luxembourg. *See* Tour Groups in Chapter 1, *above*, for tours that cover more than one country in the region. Most tour operators request that bookings be made through a travel agent—there is no additional charge for doing so. For additional resources, contact your travel agent or the tourist office of Luxembourg.

From the U.S. **Olson Travelworld** (Box 10066, Manhattan Beach, CA 90226, tel. 310/546–8400 or 800/421–2255) tailors excursions in Luxembourg for individuals or groups.

From the U.K. **Time Off Ltd.** (Chester Close, Chester St., London SW1X 7BQ, tel. 071/235–8070) has packages from two to seven nights to Luxembourg.

Package Deals for Independent Travelers

Extra Value Travel (683 S. Collier Blvd., Marco Island, FL 33937, tel. 813/398–4848 or 800/255–2847) offers self-drive tours of Luxembourg that include hotel choices and car rental. **Jet Vacations** (1775 Broadway, New York, NY 10019, tel. 212/474–8700 or 800/538–0999) offers Flexiplan Europe, a choice of hotels, car rentals, airport transfers, and sightseeing options for Luxembourg. **Travel Bound** (599 Broadway, Penthouse,

New York, NY 10012, tel. 212/334–1350 or 800/456–8656) offers packages to Luxembourg for a minimum of three to six nights.

When to Go

Luxembourg is a northern country—parallel in latitude to Newfoundland in Canada—and experiences extreme changes in day- and night-length from season to season. Thus late spring, summer, and early fall allow you long days that stay light up to 10 o'clock; in winter, however, be prepared for dusk closing in before 4 PM. There's rarely a long spell of heavy snow, but winters tend to be dank and rainy. Many attractions, especially outside the city, maintain shortened visiting hours (or close altogether) from late fall to Pentecost (late spring), except for a brief time around Easter. Summer is tourist time, when Luxembourg polishes up its sightseeing train, and restaurants set out terrace tables under the sycamores; gardens are in full bloom and weather can be comfortably hot. Spring is attractive as well, but it is riddled with church holidays and inconvenient closings.

Climate The following are average daily maximum and minimum temperatures for Luxembourg.

Luxembourg								
Jan.	38F	3C	**May**	65F	18C	**Sept.**	67F	19C
	31	– 1		47	8		50	10
Feb.	40F	4C	**June**	70F	21C	**Oct.**	56	13C
	31	– 1		52	11		43	6
Mar.	50F	10C	**July**	74F	23C	**Nov.**	45F	7C
	34	1		56	13		38	3
Apr.	58F	14C	**Aug.**	72F	22C	**Dec.**	40F	4C
	40	4		54	13		32	0

Festivals and Seasonal Events

Apr. 12. At the **E'maischen** fair on Easter Monday, ceramic bird-flutes (*Peckvillchen*) are sold to usher in spring.

May 16. During **Octave** (beginning the fifth Sunday after Easter) since the 17th century when the Holy Mother spared the devout from a raging plague, grateful villagers have walked from their local church to the cathedral in Luxembourg City, accompanied by chants, incense, and often the community band. During Octave, a fair holds forth in the Place Guillaume, offering arcade games, crafts, and food stands selling fried sausages, fried potato patties, fried crepes, fried waffles, and the traditional batter-fried *merlan* (whiting).

May 30. During Echternach's **Spring Sprangprocession** (Dance-Procession) (Whitsun Tuesday), the most famous spring pageant, the townspeople dance through the streets, hopping from one foot to the other, chanting prayers to St. Willibrord.

June 23. Luxembourg's National Day honors its beloved duke with parades and ceremonies; the night before, there's a spectacular fireworks show launched from the Pont Adolphe.

Aug. 15–31. The **Schobermesse** (trade fair begun in 1340) dominates the Parking Glacis (near the Grande-Duchesse Charlotte bridge), with rides and games as well as the usual abundance of greasy treats.

What to Pack

Clothing Bring a wool sweater, even in summer; if you hit a rainy spell, a raincoat and umbrella may prove indispensable, as rain often takes hold for weeks at a time. Practical walking shoes are important, whether for rough cobblestones or forest trails. Women here wear skirts more frequently than do women in America, especially those over 35: If you would rather fit in with the natives than with fellow tourists, a casual skirt is appropriate for day wear. Men would be wise to include a jacket and tie, especially if you're planning to visit one of the upper-echelon restaurants.

Miscellaneous Americans will need an electrical adapter for hair dryers and small appliances. Voltage is 220, with 50 cycles, so you may want to invest in portable appliances with changeable voltage and cycles. You will need to adapt the plug to fit Luxembourg outlets; Luxembourg plugs have two round prongs, the thicker of two standard options.

Taking Money Abroad

Luxembourg, as an international banking capital, makes it easy for travelers to pay with credit cards or to withdraw cash advances. Make sure the bank (or shop, restaurant, or hotel) has a sticker in the window for the credit card you wish to use. There is no limit to the amount of cash you can bring into Luxembourg.

Luxembourg Currency

The Luxembourg franc (abbreviated Flux), equivalent to the Belgian franc and used interchangeably with it within Luxembourg, comes in notes in denominations of 100 and 1,000 francs; Belgium issues 500- and 5,000-franc notes as well. Coins are issued in denominations of 1, 5, 20, and 50 francs; you will rarely be required to use the 50-centime piece. If you're traveling in France as well, be careful not to mix up French 10-franc pieces with Belgian and Luxembourgian 20-franc coins; the French coin is three times as valuable. At press time, rates of exchange average Flux 35 to the U.S. dollar, Flux 60 to the pound sterling, and Flux 23 to the Canadian dollar. Rates fluctuate daily, so be sure to check at the time you leave.

What It Will Cost

As Luxembourg continues to prosper, the cost of living skyrockets annually, pumping up real estate costs and thus prices everywhere. Yet hotel and restaurant prices tend to be up no more than 5% over last year's. Because of Luxembourg's tax privileges, gasoline, cigarettes, and liquor continue to be notably cheaper here than in neighboring countries; you'll find combination gas station/liquor stores clustered at every border crossing. High-octane, lead-free gas costs about 21 Flux a liter; in Belgium, you'll pay 29 Flux or more.

Taxes A visitor's tax of 5% for overnight stays is included in your hotel bill. Value-added taxes (TVA) are in upheaval now as the European Community makes gradual adjustments toward equality; in 1992, they range from 3% to 15%, depending on the type of purchase. Purchases of goods for export only to non-EC countries may qualify for a refund; ask the shop to fill out a refund form. You must then have the form stamped by customs officers on leaving either Luxembourg, Belgium, or Holland. A minimum purchase of Flux 3,000 is required before you're eligible for a refund.

Sample Costs Cup of coffee, Flux 50; glass of beer, Flux 40; movie ticket, Flux 170–200; 3-mile taxi ride, Flux 500 (10% higher nights, 25% higher Sundays).

Passports and Visas

U.S. If your passport has been lost or stolen, report the loss/theft to the main police station (rue Glesener, near the train station). Stop by a photo booth and have three 2x2-inch photos taken (light background), and then bring them to the U.S. Embassy, along with the police report. They will ask you for proof of citizenship; if you have no other proof, they can trace your social security number through a Washington, D.C., computer to find your latest passport registration. If all goes smoothly, they can offer you a new, fully valid passport within minutes of confirmation. The lost passport fee for adults is $65; for children under 18, $40.

British Follow the same procedure as Americans, bringing standard European-scale portrait photos along. Depending on your remaining documents and their ability to trace your passport records, you should be able to have at least a temporary passport that day.

Customs and Duties

On Arrival **Americans and other non-EC members** are allowed to bring in no more than 200 cigarettes, 50 cigars, one liter of spirits or sparkling wine, two liters of wine, 50 grams of perfume, and .25 liters of toilet water. **EC members** may bring in 300 cigarettes (200 if bought in a duty-free shop), 75 cigars, 1.5 liters of spirits or sparkling wine, five liters of wine, 75 grams of perfume, and .375 liters of toilet water.

On Departure **U.S. citizens** may bring home $400 worth of foreign merchandise as gifts or for personal use without having to pay duty, provided they have been out of the country for more than 48 hours and provided they have not claimed a similar exemption within the previous 30 days. Every member of a family is entitled to the same exemption, regardless of age, and the exemptions can be pooled. For the next $1,000 worth of goods, inspectors will assess a flat 10% duty, based on the price actually paid, so it is a good idea to keep your receipts. Included in the $400 allowance for travelers over the age of 21 are one liter of alcohol, 100 cigars, and 200 cigarettes. Any amount in excess of those limits will be taxed at the port of entry, and it may be additionally taxed in the traveler's home state. You may not bring home meats, fruits, plants, soil, or other agricultural items.

British citizens may bring home the same quantity of goods they were allowed to carry into Luxembourg (listed above). Because of strict rabies control, no pets or animals may be brought into the United Kingdom.

Canadian citizens may bring home 50 cigars, 200 cigarettes, and 40 ounces of liquor. Be sure to carry receipts for your purchases abroad, as any totaling more than $300 will be taxed.

Language

Luxembourg is a linguistic melting pot, with its citizens speaking an essentially oral tongue called Lëtzeburgesch (Luxembourgish) descended from an ancient dialect of the Moselle Franks. Luxembourgers themselves are educated in German while learning French, eventually completing higher studies in French; the current generation also learns English and is, for the most part, easily conversant. The language used for government documents is French, but many are translated into German as well; a simple church service will often include German, French, Luxembourgish and a soupçon of Latin. Within the tourist industry, most Luxembourgers you'll meet will speak some English with you, better French, and even better German; but they'll talk *about* you in Luxembourgish.

Staying Healthy

Whatever their linguistic leanings, Luxembourgers cleave to their Germanic roots when it comes to cleanliness, scouring their sidewalks and airing their linens. Its tap water is as safe to drink as that of any other urban source, though widespread manure fertilization and heavily salted streets in winter may make you think twice; most locals drink bottled water. Otherwise, the greatest health threat to be found here is to your waistline.

Car Rentals

Luxembourg is one of the cheapest sources in Europe for rental cars, with easy pickup at the airport and at the train station in Luxembourg City (*see* Chapter 1, *above*). A valid driver's license from your own country is required, as is proof of insurance.

Traveling with Children

Getting There A car is by far the best way to get around with children in this tiny country, where few rail connections and limited bus excursions make it difficult to sightsee beyond the main attractions.

Rentals The National Tourist Office publishes a free pamphlet listing available holiday flats and houses and all their facilities. There's also a new brochure for "Rural Holidays" listing a number of farms that take in visitors.

Baby-sitting Services **Action Familiale et Populaire** (tel. 2–11–11) offers names of screened baby-sitters in the Luxembourg City area; **Luxembourg Acceuil** (tel. 4–17–17) offers a similar service.

Hints for Disabled Travelers

In Luxembourg, the Ministry of Health handles provisions for disabled people. Most trains and buses have special seats for the handicapped, and handicapped spaces are available in parking lots.

Further Reading

The Grand Duchy of Luxembourg: The Evolution of a Nation-hood by James Newcomer (University Press of America, Lanham, MD, 1984) is an extensive, fairly readable history of the Grand Duchy's early woes. *A Time for Trumpets* by Charles B. MacDonald (William Morrow and Company, New York, 1985) gives a blow-by-blow, 600-page account of the Battle of the Bulge.

Arriving and Departing

From North America by Plane

Airports and Airlines **Icelandair** is the only airline to offer direct flights from the U.S. (New York, Washington, D.C., Orlando), with a stopover in Reykjavik. However, most of the main international airlines—**British Airways, Northwest, KLM, Sabena, Lufthansa**—offer connections (usually with **Luxair**) allowing you to fly to London, Frankfurt, Amsterdam, or Paris, then connect into Luxembourg as a final destination with little or no additional cost. All flights land at **Findel Airport,** 6 kilometers (4 miles) from the city center. Their numbers, locally and in the United States: British Airways, tel. 34–83–47 or 800/247–9297; Icelandair, tel. 40–27–27–27 or 800/223–5500; Luxair, tel. 43–61–61; Sabena, tel. 2–12–12 or 800/632–8050.

Flying Time Brussels–Luxembourg, 45 minutes; New York–Brussels, eight hours; Chicago–Brussels, 11 hours, including connections through JFK. Reykjavik–Luxembourg, three hours, plus New York–Reykjavik, six hours, or Orlando–Reykjavik, 7½ hours.

From the U.K. by Plane, Car, and Train

By Plane
Airlines **Luxair,** the Luxembourg airline that connects to all major airports in Europe, has regular flights to London (reservations, tel. 43–61–61; information and arrivals/departures, tel. 4798–2311), as does **British Airways** (information, tel. 34–83–47).

Flying Time London–Luxembourg, 1 hour and 15 minutes.

By Car and Ferry The entire Benelux region is easily accessible in a day from London and the southeast. Several companies operate sailings direct to the Belgian ports of Oostende and Zeebrugge. Sailings are most frequent from the south coast ports; during the summer months from Dover there are up to six sailings daily to Zeebrugge, and nine to Oostende, by the **P&O European Ferries/RTM** (tel. 0304/20–33–88) consortium. The travel time on these routes is upward of 3½ hours, depending on the crossing you choose. If you take the **Sally Line** (tel. 0843/59–55–22) from Ramsgate, you'll dock in Dunkerque, minutes from the Belgian coast and direct autoroute connections to Luxembourg; the trip is longer, but there are cinemas, a good restaurant, and even a discotheque on board. The quickest (but most expensive) way is from Dover to Calais via the Hovercraft link, operated by **Hoverspeed** (tel. 0304/24–02–41). After a mere 35-minute crossing, you continue south from Calais to Lille and cut across Belgium, via Mons, Charleroi, and Namur, to reach Luxembourg. If weather and short queues permit, you'll make it from the south coast to Luxembourg in five hours. You also can take a standard ferry from Dover to Calais, with P&O alternating departures with **Sealink** (tel. 0233/64–70–33).

Fares vary considerably according to season, journey time, number of passengers, and length of vehicle. However, the approximate cost of crossing the Channel by ferry on one of the short sea routes in high summer, with an average vehicle of 14 feet (4¼ meters) and two adult passengers, works out to about £110 one way. By traveling off-peak, early in the morning or late evening, or in June and September, you can reduce costs.

By Train Take an early morning train from Victoria Station to Dover, ferry by speedy **Jetfoil** to Oostende, train to Brussels, then cross the tracks at the Gare du Midi and continue into Luxembourg, arriving early that evening. It's advisable to reserve seats for the whole trip (including Jetfoil) in advance. The route can also be covered by using the conventional car ferry service from Dover to Oostende, but the extra time taken for the Channel crossing makes for a long day.

Staying in Luxembourg

Getting around Luxembourg

By Train Train travel within the Grand Duchy is very limited; a north–south line connects Luxembourg City with Clervaux in the north and Bettembourg in the south; another line carries you to Grevenmacher and Wasserbillig, along the Moselle. For additional information, write or call the **CFL** (9 place de la Gare, Boite Postale 1803, L-1019 Luxembourg, tel. 49–24–24).

By Bus The Luxembourg bus system carries tourists and citizens to points throughout the Grand Duchy; most buses leave from the train station. You can buy an *horaire* (bus schedule) to plan complex itineraries, or you can ask at the tourist office for suggestions on a logical schedule for getting to, say, Vianden or Echternach from Luxembourg City. The **Oeko-Billjee,** a special day ticket (Flux 120), allows you to travel anywhere in the country by bus or rail from the time you first use it until 8 AM the next day. They're available at the **Centre Aldringen,** the underground bus station in front of the central post office (corner rue Aldringen and av. Monterey; av. Monterey 8A) and at any train station.

By Car The best way to see Luxembourg outside Luxembourg City is by car, as castles and attractive villages are scattered around and connected by pleasant, well-maintained country roads. Observe standard middle-Europe driving laws: *Priorité à droite* (yield to the right) applies here and should be strictly observed; drivers may shoot out from side streets at top speed without glancing to their left. Speed limits are 50 kph (31 mph) in built-up areas, 90 kph (55 mph) on national highways, and 120 kph (75 mph) on expressways.

Telephones

Local Calls Public phones are relatively rare, except at post offices and in cafés, usually near the toilets. A local call costs Flux 5 or 10, depending on the phone booth; pick up the receiver, slip in the coin, listen for the tone, then dial. No area codes are necessary within the Grand Duchy.

International Calls To dial direct internationally, start with the country code (001 for the U.S., 0044 for the U.K.), then dial the local number. A **Telekaart,** available with 50 or 150 time units, works in special-ly equipped booths, usually in post offices, where they are sold. The AT&T U.S.A. Direct number out of Luxembourg is 08000111. Phone cabins for timed long-distance calls are provided inside most post offices; you may be required to make a down payment before the call. Luxembourg's country code is 352. To make an international call without direct access, you must dial 0010.

Operators and Information For international information, dial 016; for local information, dial 017.

Mail

Postal Rates Airmail postcards and letters weighing less than 20 grams cost Flux 22 to the United States. Letters and postcards to the United Kingdom cost Flux 14.

Tipping

In Luxembourg, service charges of 15% are included in your restaurant bill; for a modest meal, most people leave the small change. At a grander restaurant, you will be expected to leave a larger tip—up to 10% extra when a large staff is involved. A tip of Flux 50 per bag is adequate for porters. Cab drivers expect a tip of around 10%.

Opening and Closing Times

Most shops open at 9 and close at noon, reopening at 1:30 or 2 and closing for the night at 6. Many banks now stay open through the lunch hour, opening at 8:30 and closing at 4:30. Nearly all shops and businesses stay closed Monday mornings.

Shopping

As Luxembourg has only partially and recently abandoned its rural roots, its citizens are for the most part unsentimental about the traditional blue-and-gray crockery and burnished pewter that once furnished every home; nowadays, they prefer their indigenous Villeroy & Boch vitro-porcelain in jazzy, modern designs. Nonetheless, all three can be found in most home-furnishings and gift shops. For souvenirs, there are lovely photography books on Luxembourg's historic sites, as well as reproduced engravings of the city in all its fortified glory. *Taaken*, miniature cast-iron firebacks with bas-relief scenes of Luxembourg, are made by the Fonderie de Mersch and are available in gift and souvenir shops.

Sports and Outdoor Activities

Biking The Luxembourg National Tourist Office, as well as those of Luxembourg City, Diekirch, and Mersch, all publish booklets suggesting cycling tours within the grand duchy; good routes include Ettelbruck–Vianden and Luxembourg City–Echternach.

Boating/Watersports The Wiltz and the Clerve rivers offer challenging waters for small craft or canoes, but the Our, with its wooded gorges, is the wildest; the Sûre is most rewarding, for its length and for the thrills it offers. For further information, write to the **Fédération Luxembourgeoise de Canoë et de Kayak** (rue de Pulvermuhle 6, Luxembourg). People windsurf and sail on Lac de la Haute Sûre.

Camping Visitors from all over Europe, but especially the Netherlands, descend on Luxembourg's campgrounds every summer, making them sociable, populous places, often near forests and riverfronts. Write for the pamphlet "Camping/Grand-Duché de Luxembourg," made available through the national tourist office. The **Fédération Luxembourgeoise de Camping et de Caravaning** (route d'Esch 31, L-4450, tel. 59–12–74) also publishes information.

Fishing If you're in search of trout, grayling, perch, and dace—as well as relaxation—apply for a government fishing permit from the **Administration des Eaux et Forêts** (Boite Postale 411, L-2014 Luxembourg, tel. 40–53–10), and a local permit from the owner of the waterfront, which is in many cases your hotel.

Hiking/Walking Luxembourg is full of well-developed forest trails, often on state lands with parking provided. "171 Circuits Auto-pedestres," a book with 171 maps of walking itineraries, is available in bookshops for Flux 895. Trails will be full of strollers late Sunday afternoons, the traditional time for such outings.

Hunting The District Commissioners of the Administration des Eaux et Forêts (*see* Fishing, *above*) also issue one- or five-day hunting permits on request, but the application must be franked by the owner of the hunting rights for the area.

Dining

"French quality, German quantity"—that's an apt and common description of Luxembourg cuisine. A quick study of local posted menus might lead visitors to think the locals eat nothing but *cuisine bourgeoise*—veal with cream and mushrooms, beef entrecôte with peppercorn sauce, veal *cordon bleu* (breaded veal stuffed with ham and cheese)—all served in generous portions, with heaps of *frites* (french fries) on the side. Yet this tiny country has its own earthy cuisine, fresh off the farm: *judd mat gardebohn'en* (smoked pork shoulder with fava beans), *E'slecker* ham or *jambon d'Ardennes* (pearly-pink raw-smoked ham served cold with pickled onions), *choucroûte* (sauerkraut), *treipen* (blood pudding), *kuddelfleck paniert* (plain breaded tripe), *fierkeljelli* (suckling pig in aspic), batter-fried *merlan* (whiting), and spicy *gromperekichelcher* (fried potato patties). A few restaurants still feature them, for sentimental locals as well as for visitors. More upscale additions to the national specialties are *ecrevisses* (crayfish), cooked with local wine, and all manner of trout. In Luxembourg City, though, you're as likely nowadays to find Chinese, Thai, Japanese, Indian, Mexican, and—leading the ethnic selections by several laps—Italian, its hold on the dining scene due in part to the vast immigration of Italian miners who settled and assimilated at the turn of the century. (Pizza, in fact, is Luxembourg's de rigueur fast food.) Of course, Belgium's penchant for *moules* (mussels) has leaked over the border; here, they're savored with the local white wines. And some of Luxembourg's French cuisine isn't so bourgeois: There are more star-studded *gastronomique* restaurants per capita than in any other European country. Many restaurants—including some of these world-class venues—offer an accessibly priced menu at lunch.

Luxembourg takes pride in its Moselle wines, grown on the hills that rear up from the riverside and take maximum advantage of the region's muted sunlight. Their bottles—slim and tapered—and some of their names suggest Alsatian and German wines, and they do share a certain straightforward fruitiness with these fellow white wines. But Luxembourg's versions are sharper and lighter, and when poured from an iced bottle into a green-stemmed glass, they're an ideal counterpoint to a cream-sauced veal dish—or a platter of choucroûte. The best names: a crisp Riesling or Auxerrois, a dry Pinot Gris or a rounder Pinot Blanc, and the rare, rosé-like Pinot Noir. More commonplace varieties, often served in pitchers or by the glass, are Rivaner and Elbling.

Luxembourg's Moselle wines lend themselves well to the French aperitif called *kir*, a glass of white wine tinted pale pink with a touch of *cassis* (black currant liqueur), a version of which is made in the castle village of Beaufort. After a meal, be sure to try the local eaux-de-vie, reducing the fruity essence of *quetsch* (a little blue plum), *mirabelle* (halfway between a plum and a yellow cherry), *kirsch* (cherry), or—for the hard core—*grain*, the latter best mixed in a mug of strong coffee.

Though Luxembourg is a hardworking business town, its workers drop everything at noon and rush home, jamming the streets, to a leisurely hot meal, then rush back, jamming the streets once more, at 2 PM. Many restaurants offer a relatively speedy *plat du jour* (daily one-course special) for those who don't commute twice a day. Evening meals at home tend to be an early cold supper of ham, sausage, dark bread, and cheese; the evening meal out is a celebration and is enjoyed at length, à la Française. The Sunday noon meal is the most important of the week, and the best restaurants are booked up with three-generation families, who plan to spend the afternoon eating and drinking before their late-afternoon stroll, after which the menfolk retire to the local pubs.

Price categories in the Dining sections are based on a three-course meal without beverages or additional tip. Italian restaurants are rated Moderate, but simple pizza or one-course pasta meals would fall well within the Inexpensive range. Service is included.

Very Expensive	over Flux 2,500
Expensive	Flux 1,200–2,500
Moderate	Flux 600–1,200
Inexpensive	under Flux 600

Lodging

Hotels in Luxembourg tend to be tidy and straightforward, with prices considerably higher in the city than in the surrounding countryside; outside town, prices vary remarkably little. Hotels outside the city may well close up during low season—late fall to Easter—so check in advance with the tourist office. Breakfast is usually included in the price; that information, along with prices, should be posted at the door, at the front desk, or in the room itself. A 5% visitors' tax is automatically included in the price. Rooms with bathtub tend to cost slightly more than rooms with showers; specify your preference.

Very Expensive	Flux over 6,000
Expensive	Flux 3,500–6,000
Moderate	Flux 2,500–3,500
Inexpensive	under Flux 2,500

Categories are based on the nightly rate for a standard double room with bathroom and Continental breakfast, though the latter may not always be included in the room price. A 5% visitors tax is included in the price.

Luxembourg City

If you visit one place only in the Grand Duchy of Luxembourg, it will be, of course, Luxembourg-Ville (Luxembourg City), the city of 79,000 people in a nation of 400,000. Here, at leisure, you can explore all the must-sees—the fortifications, the old cobbled streets, the parks, the cathedral, the museum—and, after shopping, relax in a shaded terrace café, listening to street musicians or a brass band. For first-time visitors to Europe with big eyes—those who plan to take in Paris, Florence, Stonehenge, and the Matterhorn in 10 days—it can be "done" in a day; indeed, many train travelers check their bags in a station locker and make a satisfying tour of the town without spending the night. But if you have more time to ration, you may find quiet little Luxembourg a romantic base for excursions and a lovely place at night, with its illuminated monuments and walls and its inviting public squares.

Important Addresses and Numbers

Tourist Information The Luxembourg City tourist office (place d'Armes, tel. 22–28–09) is open mid-September–mid-June, Monday–Saturday 9–1 and 2–6; mid-June–mid-September, weekdays 9–7, Saturday 9–1 and 2–7, Sunday 10–noon and 2–6.

Embassies U.S.: Boulevard Emmanuel Servais 22, tel. 46–01–23.

U.K.: Boulevard Franklin Roosevelt 14, tel. 22–98–64.

Canada (in Brussels): Avenue de Tervuren 2, B-1040 Brussels, tel. 0032/2–735–60–40.

Emergencies **Police, Ambulance, Doctors, Dentists:** Dial the central emergency number, 012, for instructions in English on where to go in case of medical or dental emergencies. Do *not* go to the nearest hospital, as it may not accommodate you—hospitals firmly adhere to a rotation schedule for handling emergencies.

Where to Change Money	Banks throughout Luxembourg display "Change" signs in their windows and doors; there's also a *bureau de change* at the central rail station, open 9–9.
English-language Bookstore	The **Magasin Anglais** (Allée Scheffer 19, tel. 2–49–25) carries some English books among its teas, greeting cards, Weet-a-bix, chutneys, and custard mixes.
Late-night Pharmacies	Check in the windows of pharmacies for a sign listing the *pharmacie de garde* (pharmacy on duty), or call 012.
Travel Agencies	**American Express** is located at rue Origer 6–8, 1-2269 (tel. 48–67–57). **Wagons-Lits Tours** is at rue Aldringen 6 (tel. 46–03–15). **Sotour**, at place du Théâtre 15 (tel. 46–15–14), offers several English-speaking agents.

Arriving and Departing by Plane

Airport and Airlines	Luxembourg's Findel Airport, 6 kilometers (4 miles) from the city center, serves the entire grand duchy, particularly by Icelandair.
Between the Airport and Center *By Bus*	Luxembourg city bus No. 9 leaves the airport at regular intervals for Luxembourg City's main bus depot (place de la Gare), located just beside the train station. Buses Nos. 2, 4, and 11 go to the city center. Individual tickets cost Flux 30. As city buses make stops along the way, you may be willing to pay more for the **Luxair** buses, which leave hourly 6 AM–10 PM, heading non-stop for the train station. Tickets cost Flux 120.
By Taxi	To the center, a taxi ride will cost about Flux 600.

Arriving and Departing by Car, Train, and Bus

By Car	The proper motorway exits for Luxembourg City are poorly indicated for newcomers; if you're arriving from France, watch for "Belgique/Brussels–Liège/Luxembourg aeroport" with "centre-ville" in fine italics; from Belgium, exit for Strassen and turn left on the route d'Arlon. From Germany, the motorway empties directly into the center.
By Train	Luxembourg is served by frequent direct trains from Brussels (under three hours) and Paris (four hours). From Amsterdam, you travel via Brussels (six hours). Most connections from Germany channel through Koblenz.

Getting around Luxembourg

By Bus	Luxembourg City has a highly efficient bus service. The blue-and-yellow buses outside the city train station will take you all around town and also to some of the outlying areas. Get details about services at the information counter in the station arrivals hall. Fares are low, but for an extended stay, the best bet is to buy a 10-ride ticket (Flux 240), available from banks or from the bus station in the Aldringen Center. Other buses, connecting Luxembourg City with towns throughout the country, leave from the train station. For information on bus routes or departures, call the information desk at the train station (tel. 49–24–24) or write to Clemins de Fer Luxemborgeois (9 place de la Gare 1803, L-1018 Luxembourg).
By Taxi	Taxis (tel. 48–22–33 or 40–52–52) are available at stands by the central post office and at the train station.

By Car As traffic is unusually thick for a city this size, and problems are compounded by extravagant roadworks, you will be wise to deposit your car in a central parking area, either Parking Glacis (near the Grande-Duchesse Charlotte bridge), or in Parking Knuedler, under the place Guillaume.

On Foot Luxembourg's diminutive scale allows you the luxury of covering nearly every neighborhood on foot.

Guided Tours

Orientation Sales-Lentz (26 rue de Curé, L-1368, tel. 46–18–18) offers tours of the city 9:30–11:30 every morning during the peak tourist season (Apr.–Oct.) and several days a week in winter. The tours leave from the bus station, next to the railway station, platform 5, or from place de la Constitution, under the Gëlle Fra, and visit the historic sights of the center, the new European area, and some of the villas on the city outskirts, together with the military cemeteries. Tours cost Flux 290. Another tour of the city and countryside takes visitors to the monuments of Luxembourg City, the cemeteries, and on to the village and restored castle at Bourglinster. Tours run 2:30–5:45 every Saturday and Sunday during April, May, and October; from June through September, they run every Tuesday, Thursday, Saturday, and Sunday. Other more complete tours of the sights in the grand duchy are available for groups of 10 or more.

Special-Interest Tours Luxembourg Live! is a guided minitrain tour of the Old Town and Petrusse Valley, with multilingual commentary and dramatic music; tickets are sold at the bus booth on the place de la Constitution, and trains leave every 45 minutes (11:30–5:30, later in midsummer). Tours last 60–90 minutes. Tickets cost Flux 220 for adults, Flux 160 for children 4–15; families with up to two children, Flux 650; additional children, Flux 140.

Walking Tours A self-guided City Tour offers visitors a cassette player and earphones with a choice of commentaries on cassette: either "Discovering Luxembourg" (45 minutes, Flux 170) or "Luxembourg the fortress" (60 minutes, Flux 190). The players and cassettes are available for rental at the bus booth on the Place de la Constitution.

Highlights for First-Time Visitors

Bock/Corniche
Casemates
Cathédrale Notre-Dame
Citadelle St-Esprit
Diekirch (excursion)
Echternach (excursion)
Grand Ducal Palace
Maquette
Moselle wine country (excursion)
Musée National
Vianden Castle (excursion)

Exploring Luxembourg City

Numbers in the margin correspond with points of interest on the Luxembourg City map.

Luxembourg City

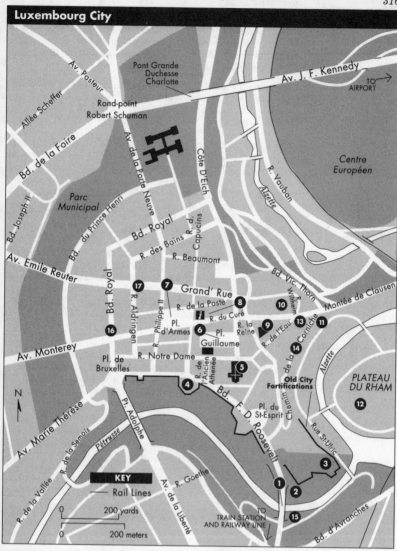

This walk takes you through the maze of ancient military fortifications of Luxembourg City, now transformed into peaceful paths. Begin at the train station, in the southern section of the city. As you head right from the station toward the city center, along avenue de la Gare, you will pass through a bustling shopping district.

❶ Take the **Passerelle** (Viaduct), a 19th-century road bridge that links the station with the valley of the Petrusse. The Petrusse is more of a brook than a river and is now contained by concrete, but the valley has become a singularly beautiful park. From here you'll see the rocky ledges—partly natural, partly man-made—on which the city was founded.

At the cathedral end of the Viaduct, immediately on the right, ❷ take the steps and curving sidewalk up to the **Monument de la Solidarité Nationale** (National Monument to Luxembourg Unity), with its perpetual flame. It was erected in 1971 to commemorate Luxembourg's sacrifices and survival during World War II. The stark walls and enclosed chapel are dedicated *"D'Hémecht hiren Doudegen 1940–1945"* ("From the homeland to their dead"). To the right of the monument, continue up the road along some of the typically wedge-shaped remains of the ❸ old city fortifications, known here as the **Citadelle du St-Esprit** (Citadel of the Holy Spirit). This 17th-century citadel was built by Vauban, the great French military engineer, on the site of a former monastery. From the "prow" you'll see wraparound views: the three spires of the cathedral, the curve of the Alzette, and the incongruous white tower of the European Parliament secretariat.

Retrace your steps along the old city fortifications, cross boulevard F.D. Roosevelt, and continue on to the **place de la Consti-** ❹ **tution,** marked by the war memorial, a striking gilt *Gëlle Fra* (Golden Woman). She was destroyed by the Nazis in 1940 and rebuilt, with original pieces incorporated, in 1984. Here you'll find the entrance to the ancient **Casemates** (military tunnels) carved into the rocky **Petrusse** fortifications. At the height of her power and influence, Luxembourg was protected by three rings of defenses comprising 53 forts and strongholds. During the many phases of the fortress's construction, the rock itself was hollowed out to form a honeycomb of passages running for nearly 24 kilometers (15 miles) below the town. Ten gates controlled admittance through the walls, and the town was, in effect, 178 hectares (440 acres) of solid fort. The Casemates served not only defensive purposes but were also used for storage and as a place of refuge when the city was under attack. Two sections of the passages are open to the public. These sections contain former barracks, cavernous abattoires, bakeries, and a deep well. *Place de la Constitution. Admission: Flux 50 adults, Flux 30 children. Open Easter, July–Sept. daily 10–5.*

Back across boulevard Roosevelt, take rue de l'ancien Athénée past the former Jesuit college, now the National Library. On rue Notre-Dame, to your right, is the main entrance to the late- ❺ Gothic **Cathédrale Notre-Dame.** There's an attractive Baroque organ gallery and a crypt containing the tomb of John the Blind, Luxembourg's beloved 14th-century king of Bohemia and count of Luxembourg. The valley side of the church was rebuilt in 1935; the roof of the main tower was rebuilt after a fire in 1985. *Open daily 7:30–noon and 2–7; crypt open only by request.*

6 Opposite the cathedral lies the **place Guillaume,** known locally as the Knuedler, a name derived from the girdle worn by Franciscan monks who once had a monastery on the site. On market days (Wednesday and Saturday mornings) the square is a mass of retail fruit and vegetable stands, vivid flower vendors, cheese and fish specialists, and a few remaining Luxembourg farmers who bring in their personal crop of potatoes, apples, cabbage, and radishes—as well as homemade jam, sauerkraut, and goat cheese. That's Grand-Duke William II on the bronze horse; he reigned from 1840 to 1849, while Luxembourg was flush with new independence. The Hotel de Ville (Town Hall), its stairs flanked by two stone lions, was inaugurated in 1844.

7 Opposite the Town Hall, leave the place Guillaume through the yellow sandstone arched passageway, then turn left. The **place d'Armes,** lined with symmetrical plane trees and strung with colored lights, was once the innermost heart of the fortified city; today it is the most welcoming corner of town, and in fine weather its cafés and benches are full of locals and tourists. The bandstand shelters visiting bands, who offer concerts every summer evening. Every second and fourth Saturday, a *brocante* (antiques/flea) market fills the square. The tourist office holds forth on the southwest corner, in the **Cercle Municipal,** with its bas-relief of the Countess Ermesinde granting Luxembourg its charter of freedom in 1244.

8 Behind the tourist office, look for the doorway marked Forteresse de Luxembourg: **Maquette.** Inside, there's a relief model of the fortress at various stages of its construction. *Rue du Curé, tel. 4796–2496. Admission: Flux 40 adults, Flux 20 children. Open Sept.–June, Sat. 10–1 and 2–6; July–Aug., Wed.–Sun. 10–12:30 and 2–5:30.*

9 Continue two blocks down rue du Curé and turn right; on the left you'll see the city's finest building, the **Grand Ducal Palace.** (It's currently under a clever—and extravagant—trompe l'oeil scaffolding screen, being restored in anticipation of Luxembourg's turn as Cultural Capital of Europe in 1995.) Portions of the building were constructed in the late-16th century as part of the town hall commissioned by Peter Ernst, the count of Mansfeld and then governor; the elaborate ornamentation bears the stamp of the Spanish Renaissance. (You can see the cross of Burgundy on one of the consoles supporting the balcony.) While the royal families used to reside here, they now use the palace for business and entertaining—though, during the restoration, the duke works in temporary offices in the Villa Vauban, in the municipal park.

To the right of the palace, turn left and continue up rue de l'Eau into the city's most ancient quarter. Here, rue de l'Eau turns into a tiny cobbled street and leads downhill to the right; some say this portion is the oldest street in town. It empties into a large, open crossroads, called the **place Marché aux Poissons;** this is the site of the old fish market and originally the crossing point of two Roman roads. Look to your right: Just up and behind the Pizzeria Um Bock, you'll see an oriel (bay-window tower) inscribed with the national motto.

10 To your left stands the **Musée National** (National Museum), set in an attractive row of 16th-century houses. The Gallo-Roman collection, on the ground floor, features a fascinating assortment of small, local treasures—toga buckles, miniature dei-ties—unearthed along the ancient routes that crisscrossed Luxembourg in the first centuries AD. This is the home of the 8th-century altar stone that guarded the tomb of St. Willibrord in Echternach; it's the oldest known of its kind. There's a series of rooms reproducing middle-class home life in 17th- to 19th-century Luxembourg, more models of the city's fortifications, and a collection of art ranging from old masters to local heroes, including the notable works of Luxembourg's own Joseph Kutter (1894–1941) and Sosthène Weiss (1872–1941). *Marché-aux-Poissons, tel. 47–93–30. Admission free. Open Tues.–Fri. 10–4:45, Sat. 2–5:45, Sun. 10–11:45 and 2–5:45.*

Time Out Down rue Wiltheim, which runs alongside the museum, you'll find the tavern **Welle Mann** (rue Wiltheim 12, tel. 47–17–83), the quintessentially Luxembourgish museum café. Sit on the tiny terrace and enjoy the magnificent view along the Alzette Valley, or admire the oak, the tile, and the old-city photos and posters inside. As there's no kitchen, only snacks are available—croques monsieurs, pizza baguettes, hot dogs—but the ambience makes it worth the stop.

At the bottom of rue Wiltheim stands the gate of the **Trois Tours** (Three Towers), the oldest of which was built around 1030. During the French Revolution, a guillotine was set up in these towers. To your right, up boulevard Victor Thorn, you ⑪ can clearly see Luxembourg's raison d'être: the **Bock** (from the Celtic "büück," meaning the promontory supporting a castle). Jutting dramatically out over the valley, this tongue of cliff served as the principal approach to the town from Celtic and Roman times until later bridges were constructed. Over its farthest point looms the ruined tower of the castle of Sigefroid himself. He founded the fortress Lucilinburhuc in 963; it was expanded, over the centuries, from this dominant point. In the surrounding ruins, you can walk over stone foundations, tour yet another set of **casemates,** or hang over the wall and take in vertiginous views of the valley, just as Sigefroid did: You'll see ⑫ the **Plateau du Rham** across the way, on the right, and before it, the massive towers of the Wenceslas fortifications, which in 1390 extended the protected area; the blocklike *casernes* (barracks) were built in the 17th century by the French and function today as a hospice for the elderly. Below them, at the bottom of the valley, is the 17th-century **monastery,** which from 1869 to 1984 served as the prison. Looking down the length of the Grund (meaning "valley"), it's easy to imagine the ground covered with thousands of banner-topped tents and campfires waiting out a siege. *Casemates admission: Flux 50 adults, Flux 30 children. Open Mar.–Oct., daily 10–5.*

⑬ Just uphill from the Bock, the prominent church of **St-Michel** looks over the valley, its bulbous steeple visible in all directions. Its congregation dates back to the 10th century, and there are visible signs of the original Romanesque structure to the left of the entrance. Most of the current structure mixes late Romanesque, Gothic, and Baroque, all heavily restored.

⑭ From the Bock, you can continue right along the **Corniche,** scenic ramparts overlooking the Grund, to the newly cobbled Plateau St-Esprit and take the elevator down to the Grund itself; or double back from the Bock to the place Marché aux Poissons and cut left down a steep cobbled street (rue Large) to reach the same point.

Time Out On the Corniche, stop at the shady outdoor tables of **Restaurant Breedewé** (rue Large 9, tel. 2–26–96; you can cut through from rue Large as well) for a drink or a light, French-accented plat du jour. Or at the bottom of the valley, have a pint of bitter or Anglo-American cuisine at the English gathering point, **Scott's Pub** (Bisserwé 4, tel. 47–53–52), where outdoor tables line the picturesque Alzette.

Once considered dank and squalid, twice buried under the flooding Alzette, the Grund is suddenly recherché, and you'll find chic restaurants, exclusive clubs, and skylighted renovated town houses among the tumbledown laborers' homes. Continue down rue St-Ulric and cut left into the **Vallée de la Petrusse,** a broad canyon-park full of willows, cherry trees, and illuminated bluffs. Before you pass under the high Passerelle ⑮ viaduct, you'll see the **Chapelle de St-Quirin** (St. Quirin's Chapel) built into the rocks on your left. The cave it surrounded is said to have been carved by the Celts; it is known to have housed a chapel since at least the 4th century. The relics of St. Quirin, transferred in 1050 from Avignon to Deutz-on-Rhine, spent a night in the chapel. The current structure was first built in 1355 by Teutonic Knights, though it has been repeatedly restored.

Continue through the park, with the cathedral and the Golden Woman looming above you, and cut right, uphill, under the Pont Adolphe. Narrow switchbacks will carry you back up to ⑯ the **boulevard Royal** and the beginning of banking territory. For shopping, cross the boulevard and turn right on rue Notre-Dame, walk two more blocks, then cut left on rue Philippe II. ⑰ This busy shopping street empties onto the **Grand'rue,** Luxembourg's pedestrian-only shopping street, where pastry shops and high-priced clothing boutiques vie for your tourist dollars. From here, it's half a block down rue des Capucins to the place d'Armes.

What to See and Do with Children

Luxembourg City itself is small and congested and, as such, not entirely user-friendly for children. Older kids may enjoy the loud music, dramatic stories, and novelty ride on the **Petrusse Express** (*see* Luxembourg Live! in Special-Interest Tours, *above*). Children often fill the central square of the place d'Armes during the summer **band concerts;** it's easy to have an ice cream at one of the surrounding café tables and dance when the spirit moves. The best **playground** by far is in Merl Park, in a residential neighborhood west of the center; it offers plenty of high-adventure equipment for all ages.

Off the Beaten Track

Walk up boulevard Royal to Rond-point Robert Schuman, named for one of the fathers of the European Common Market, and cross the Grande-Duchesse Charlotte bridge to **Plateau Kirchberg,** a moonscape of modern architecture housing the European Court of Justice and various branches of the **European Community.** Its most prominent structure—at 23 stories, Luxembourg's only skyscraper and, some complain, a bit of an eyesore looming over the old city's graceful stonework—houses the secretariat of the European Parliament.

Shopping

Luxembourg City has a reputation for being expensive, as it shelters a population of bankers and well-paid Eurocrats as well as Luxembourg's own newly wealthy. Thus the city supports a disproportionate share of luxury and designer shops, and its few remaining middle-class shops tend to mark up their goods for a captive audience. Service is usually European-style, meaning the client often isn't allowed to browse alone, but is expected to be shown goods by a clerk. Be warned: The clerks in Luxembourg City and its suburbs have a well-earned reputation for rudeness, as years of struggling with foreigners have hardened them against the onslaught of tourists and *étrangers.* Don't take it personally if they don't return your most ingratiating smile.

Shopping Districts   The **Grand'rue** and radiating streets concentrate the best of high-end shopping; shops along the **avenue de la Gare** and **avenue de la Liberté,** both forking north from the train station, offer more affordable goods.

Department Stores   **Rosenstiel** (4–6 rue Philippe II) recently transformed itself into a glamorous little mini–Trump Tower, with atrium escalators, fountains, marble, brass, and a mix of its own departments with independent boutiques. **Monopol** (branches at Grand'rue 33, avenue de la Gare 42, and avenue de la Liberté 53) has more middle-brow goods, à la Kmart; the English **C&A** chain (place Guillaume 2, and avenue de la Gare 15) sells moderate dry goods.

Street Markets   The main **farmers' market** holds forth in the place Guillaume every Wednesday and Saturday morning. An **antiques fair** takes over the place d'Armes every second and fourth Saturday. The annual **Braderie,** a massive, citywide sidewalk sale, slashes prices on the last weekend in August or the first weekend in September.

Specialty Stores
China   **Villeroy and Boch** porcelain has been manufactured in Luxembourg since 1748. If you have a favorite pattern, this is the place to invest in it: The seconds-quality factory outlet, on the edge of town, offers good reductions on virtually flawless goods and rock-bottom bargains on pieces with slightly visible flaws. The factory (rue Rollingergrund 330) lies on the northwest edge of town. Take bus No. 2 from Aldringen Center, by the post office. The outlet will not ship, so weigh your purchases carefully. The glossy main shop (rue du Fossé 2, between the Grand'rue and the place Guillaume) shows first-quality goods at full price.

Prints   **Correspondances** (rue de la Boucherie 16) carries lovely antique engravings and maps of Luxembourg, along with a serious assortment of antique books. **Galerie Kutter** (rue des Bains 17) offers good framed prints and stationery taken from the works of Luxembourg watercolorist Sosthène Weiss, who painted Cezanne-like scenes of Luxembourg's old town. **Librairie Bruck** (Grand'rue 22) sells maps and engravings in its showroom downstairs.

Sports and Fitness

Biking In Luxembourg City, you can rent bicycles for forays throughout the grand duchy from **Velo en Ville** (rue Bisserné 8, tel. 47/96–23–83), in the Grund.

Golf The golf course at Senningerberg (tel. 3–40–90), about 7 kilometers (4¼ miles) outside the city, has narrow fairways surrounded by dense woods; it is open only to members of other private clubs.

Dining

Luxembourg City has a wide variety of restaurants, offering everything from top French cuisine to simple local specialties; you'll also find an assortment of international choices and a plethora of pizzerias. It's easy to find a fixed-price menu or plat du jour by wandering from restaurant to restaurant, but beware: The best places are often booked up at weekday lunchtime; if you know where you want to eat, phone ahead. Dress is casual unless indicated.

Very Expensive **St-Michel.** Located in a 16th-century building behind the ducal
★ palace, warmly lighted, intimate, and filled with antiques, this is one of the finest restaurants in the region and is rich in historical atmosphere. A five-course *menu dégustation* and a three-course *menu découverte* (discovery) showcase Breton-born chef Pierrick Guillou's extraordinary skills. Specialties include *cotriade croisicaise* (traditional Breton fish stew), *trio d'agneau de Pauillac à la persillade* (prize Pauillac lamb in parsley and garlic), and an exhaustive wine list. The staff is young, skilled, and unstuffy, and the ambience is genuinely welcoming. *Rue de l'Eau 32, tel. 22–32–15. Reservations required. AE, DC, MC, V. Closed weekends.*

Clairefontaine. Airy, bright, and chic, and set on the newly renovated place de Clairefontaine near the Foreign Ministry, this fine gastronomic restaurant offers foie gras specialties, innovative fish dishes such as *vinaigrette tiède de grenouilles et homard* (warm vinagrette of frogs' legs and lobster), and seasonal game (wild duck with truffles). There's a business lunch, a three-course fixed price menu, and a lavish *dégustation*. The wine cellar met with the approval of both French President Mitterrand and the pope. *Rue de Clairefontaine 9, tel. 46–22–11. Reservations required. AE, DC, MC, V. Closed Sat. dinner, Sun.*

Expensive **La Lorraine.** Strategically set on the place d'Armes, with terrace tables under its awnings, this seafood specialist caters to tourists passing by but also serves serious meals upstairs in its dignified dining room. The retail shop around the corner shows off the quality of the restaurant's wares: heaps of briny oysters, glistening turbot and sole, wriggling crabs. Once prepared, they live up to their promise: Baked skate in hazelnut butter with capers and grilled salmon in white wine sauce are good bets. *Place d'Armes 7, tel. 47–46–20. Reservations advised. Jacket advised indoors. AE, DC, MC, V. Closed Sat. lunch, Sun.*

Speltz. In a chic, restored 17th-century house in the middle of the pedestrian shopping area, this stylish, relatively new restaurant caters to a young business crowd by serving a reasonable fixed-price lunch menu that may include lobster in local

Dining
Ancre d'Or, **11**
Bacchus, **12**
Casa d'Italia, **17**
Clairefontaine, **14**
Ems, **28**
Kamakura, **16**
La Lorraine, **7**
La Trattoria dei
Quattro, **23**
Mousel's Cantine, **15**
Osteria del Téatro, **1**
Speltz, **8**
St-Michel, **13**
Taverne Bit, **2**
Um Dierfchen, **9**

Lodging
Alfa, **26**
Arcotel, **21**
Auberge du Coin, **18**
Bristol, **25**
Carlton, **24**
Dauphin, **20**
Empire, **29**
Grand Cravat, **10**
Hostellerie du
Grunewald, **3**
InterContinental, **4**
International, **27**
Italia, **19**
Le Royal, **6**
Nobilis, **22**
Pullman, **5**

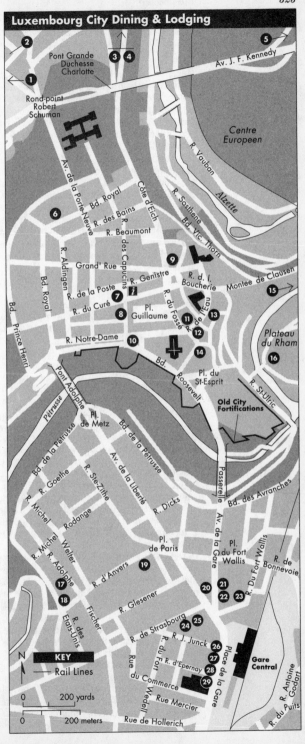

Luxembourg City Dining & Lodging

Riesling sauce with fricasee of mushrooms, or veal kidneys roasted in balsamic vinegar and mustard. *Rue Chimay 8, tel. 47-49-50. Reservations advised. Jacket and tie suggested. AE, DC, MC, V. Closed weekends.*

Moderate **Bacchus.** This relatively new Italian pizzeria attracts an up-scale, downtown set, as much for its location in the historic center and for its slick peach-and-brass decor as for its food, which is straightforward and reasonably priced. Wood-oven pizza and classic pastas are dependable choices. Reserve for a seat in the tranquil courtyard. *Rue Marché-aux-Herbes 32, tel. 47-13-97. Reservations advised. AE, DC, MC, V.*

Um Dierfchen. While you'll find *steak de cheval* (horsemeat) a standard in pubs throughout the region, this simple downtown establishment used to raise its own stock on farms near the French border. Still in the same family but without the farm source, it continues to specialize in entrecote and *tournedos de poulain*—the horsey equivalent of veal. Both colt- and horsemeat come sauced, either with a mild paprika or rich mushroom blend. Other specialties include lentil soup with smoked pork, and steaks of the more customary bovine sort. Portions are astounding, so you'd be wise to skip the first course. *Côte d'Eich 6, tel. 2-61-41. Reservations suggested at lunch. V.*

Kamakura. If heavy Western cuisine palls, take the elevator down from St-Esprit to the up-and-coming Grund and try this chic Japanese restaurant. A number of fixed-price menus offer a variety of delicate, nouvelle-accented dishes, artfully presented and graciously served. À la carte specialties, considerably more expensive, include impeccably fresh sashimi (raw fish) and light tempura vegetables. *Rue Munster 2-4, tel. 47-06-04. AE, DC, MC, V. Closed Sun.*

★ **Mousel's Cantine.** The great Mousel brewery dominates the valley of Clausen (just across the bridge from the Bock), the waters of the Alzette reflecting its old walls. Directly adjoining its works—there are windows that open into the plant and beer taps that feed from tanks within—this fresh, comfortable café serves up heaping platters of local specialties to be washed down with crockery steins of creamy *Gezwickelte Béier* (unfiltered beer). There's braised and grilled ham, sausage, and smoked suckling pig (order in advance, minimum five diners), as well as the usual smorgasbord of *choucroûte* (sauerkraut), *gardebohn'en* (fava beans), and fried potatoes. *Montée de Clausen 46, tel. 47-01-98. Reservations suggested. MC, V. Closed Sun.*

Osteria del Teatro. Across the Parking Glacis from the Municipal Theater, this popular restaurant offers a wide variety of pizzas, *gnocchi* (dumplings), and risottos as well as grilled meats and fish in a lavish decor of scarlet brocade and *faux* Renaissance art. *Allée Scheffer 21-25, tel. 2-88-11. Reservations suggested. AE, DC, MC, V. Closed Thurs.*

★ **La Trattoria dei Quattro.** Despite an undesirable location—on one of the sleazier back streets around the train station—and despite an overabundance of pizzerias in town, this merits a trip off the beaten track. It's set in a 150-year-old town house with an impressive carved wood ceiling and fireplace, and the Sardinian-accented cooking is a cut above the usual. Pastas are all homemade and are rarely run of the mill: Try *maccheroni alla Sarda* (sauced with tomato, onion, tuna, and fennel seeds) or *bucatini alla melanzani e funghi* (with eggplant and mushrooms). There are several good risottos, a mixed fish grill, and *filetto al gorgonzola* (steak with blue-cheese sauce). *Rue Fort-Neipperg 64, tel. 49–00–39. AE, DC, MC, V. Closed weekends.*

Inexpensive **Ancre d'Or.** This tidy, friendly brasserie, just off the place Guillaume, serves a wide variety of old-time Luxembourgish specialties as well as good bourgeois cuisine. Try their *judd mat gardebohn'en* (smoked pork shoulder with fava beans), *kuddelfleck* (breaded tripe), or *treipen*, a pair of rich blood sausages served with red cabbage and apple sauce. Other country classics include a fine version of *tête de veau* (stewed calf's head and tongue with onion vinaigrette) and *choucroûte*. Their veal in cream-and-mushroom sauce is prototypical, and the delicious apple tart (Luxembourgish style, with custard base) is homemade. Try to book ahead; it's usually full on market days. *Rue du Fossé 23, tel. 47–29–73. Reservations strongly advised. MC, V. Closed Sun.*

Casa d'Italia. Though the cooking isn't anything to write home about, you can get a substantial two-course hot meal at absurdly low prices in this comfortable, clublike meeting place crowded with loyal, local Italian immigrants. Order and pay at the cash register when you enter, choosing between a big slab of lasagne followed by roast veal, or pasta in Bolognese sauce followed by plain, fresh mozzarella. *Centro di ristoro Italiano, rue Adolphe Fischer 56, tel. 48–35–68. No credit cards.*

Ems. Directly across the street from the train station, this lively diner equivalent (vinyl booths, posted specials) draws a loyal clientele for its vast portions of *moules* (mussels) in a rich wine-and-garlic broth, accompanied by frites and (unlike in Belgium, where they drink beer) a bottle of sharp, cold Moselle wine. There also are local meat and fish specialties—*tomates aux crevettes* (tomatoes stuffed with mayonnaise-coated tiny shrimp), herring, Thuringer sausages—and substantial ice cream specialties. Food is served until 1 AM. *Place de la Gare 30, 48–77–99. DC, MC, V.*

Taverne Bit. With sanded tabletops and dark-wood banquettes, this is a cozy and very local pub, where you can drink a *clensch* (stein) of draft Bitburger beer (from just across the German border) and have a plate of sausage with good potato salad, a plate of cold ham, or *kachkäse*, the pungent local cheese spread, served with baked potatoes. *Allée Scheffer 43, tel. 46–07–51. No credit cards. Closed Sat. dinner, Sun.*

Lodging

It's more expensive to stay in Luxembourg than in hotels outside the city, but worth it for the convenience of having an interesting home base. Hotels tend to be modern here; more options are clustered around the train station, which is a trek (or a bus ride) from the old town.

Very Expensive **InterContinental.** Rising above the outskirts of Luxembourg like a 20th-century château-fort, this all-modern 19-story deluxe hotel opened in 1985 and competes directly with Le Royal downtown, offering a big indoor pool, good fitness facilities, and gracious rooms with good, broad beds. The restaurant Les Continents attracts locals for its upscale French cooking. *Rue Jean Engling, L-1466, tel. 4–37–81. 344 rooms. Facilities: restaurant, café, bar, terrace, indoor pool, sauna, fitness room. AE, DC, MC, V.*

★ **Le Royal.** Located in the city center, on the Wall Street of Luxembourg and within steps of parks, shopping, and the old town, this is the best choice for luxury. It's solid, modern (opened 1984), and sleek, with a great deal of lacquer, marble, and glass, and all facilities stress business: There are six phone booths in the lobby and a separate counter for faxes and telexes. Rooms are air-tight and climatized, though those facing boulevard Royal have traffic noise leaking through the double-glazed windows. Opt for a back room toward the park if possible. The piano bar is popular, as is the Le Jardin brasserie, especially when the fountain terrace is open. *bd Royal 12, L–2449, tel. 4–16–16. 180 rooms. Facilities: 2 restaurants, piano bar, exercise equipment, pool, hairdresser; sauna (fee), tennis (fee). AE, DC, MC, V.*

Pullman. On the moonscape of the Kirchberg Plateau, surrounded by the architectural experiments of various branches of the European Community, this former Holiday Inn was completely renovated in 1990. It maintains an all-American look (big beds, generic decor) and a friendly attitude. *Centre Europeén, L–2015. Tel. 43–77–61. 260 rooms. Facilities: restaurant, bar, café, garden. AE, DC, MC, V.*

Expensive **Arcotel.** Opened in 1985 on the busy shopping street between the old town and the train station, this airtight, modernized hotel provides a quiet getaway from the city outside. Decorated in warm shades of beige and rose, with polished wood and brass, it offers solid baths and extra comforts—hair dryers in the bathroom, drinks in the Boukara-lined lounge—to make up for the typically small rooms. *Avenue de la Gare 43, L–1611, tel. 49–40–01. 30 rooms with bath. Facilities: breakfast room. AE, DC, V.*

★ **Grand Cravat.** While Luxembourg is quickly bulldozing away its bourgeois past and tacking up the glitziest *nouveau* international styles, this relic—moderately grand, modestly glamorous—continues to hold forth at the best location in town: the edge of the old town, along the Petrusse Valley. Built in several phases since the turn of the century, it features a mix of solid old architectural details—an Art Deco brass elevator, caryatids framing the lounge fireplace—and though corridors have a dated, institutional air, the rooms are fresh and welcoming in a variety of tastefully retro styles. Bathrobes and hair dryers add a bit of luxury. The bar is comfortably swank, though you may want to drink in the adjoining Art Deco coffee shop, another period piece that still draws fur-hatted ladies of a certain age to tea. General Bradley stayed here during World War II. *Boulevard F.-D. Roosevelt 29, L–2011, tel. 22–19–75. 60 rooms. Facilities: restaurant, coffee shop, bar. AE, DC, MC, V.*

★ **Hostellerie du Grunewald.** Just outside the city center, near the InterContinental, this former roadside auberge offers the antithesis of anonymous business travel: a quiet, illuminated garden out back; cozy, old-fashioned lounges crammed with mixed wingbacks, knickknacks, and old master prints; and plush rooms full of Persian rugs, rich fabrics, and cream-patina Louis XV furniture. Serene garden-side rooms are worth booking ahead, though street-side windows are triple glazed. The current owner took over in 1963, upgrading rooms to full comfort and creating the detail-rich decor that merits their membership in the Romantik hotel group. The cozy restaurant, more like an upscale country inn than a city hotel dining room, features classic, luxurious French cuisine, catering to a business crowd with different *menus d'affaires* at lunch and dinner. *Route d'Echternach 10–14, L–1453, Dommeldange, tel. 43–18–82. 28 rooms. Facilities: restaurant (Very Expensive; tel. 42–03–14; closed Sat. lunch, Sun.), garden terrace. AE, DC, MC, V.*

International. In the midst of a gradual upgrade, this large postwar station-area hotel offers a mixed bag of comforts and decors without making a price distinction. Be sure to ask for one of the newly done rooms, with fresh Eurostyle baths and built-in cabinetry; otherwise you may end up with chipped laminate, chenille, and elderly toilets. Despite double-glazed windows on the street side, back rooms are much more desirable. *Place de la Gare 20–22, L–1016, tel. 48–59–11. 60 rooms. Facilities: restaurant. AE, DC, MC, V.*

Moderate **Alfa.** Only hard-core history buffs will want to breach the gloomy corridors of this station-area 1932 landmark, where Generals Patton and Bradley had Christmas dinner in 1944 as the Battle of the Bulge finally swung in favor of the Allies. Indeed, they'll find Patton's big bay-windowed suite virtually unchanged but for the addition of a few cheap pieces of '60s furniture. (Unlike the florid VIP suites many hotels flaunt, Patton's quarters were appropriately spare and grim.) Decor, once simple, is shabby now: Casement windows remain single glazed, and only half the rooms have toilets—yet the architecture maintains some of its Fascist-era grandeur. *Place de la Gare, L–1020, tel. 49–00–09. 100 rooms. Facilities: restaurant, bar. AE, DC, MC, V.*

★ **Auberge du Coin.** At the edge of a quiet, dignified residential area but within easy reach of the station and the old town, this pleasant hotel was completely renovated in 1989 in pure "new Luxembourg" style—that is, stone and terra-cotta floors, wood-framed double windows, polished oak, Persian rugs, and tropical plants. Rooms are freshly furnished in bright knotty pine with new tile baths and oil paintings of the old town. There's a lovely French restaurant and a comfortable oak-and-stone bar as well. Prices are at the high end of this category; the nine-room matching annex down the street has no elevator and costs slightly less. *8 bd de la Pétrusse 2, L–2320, tel. 40–21–01. 23 rooms. Facilities: restaurant, bar. AE, DC, MC, V.*

Empire. Slick, freshly decorated, simple, and aimed at single business travelers (there are only three double rooms), this station hotel offers all comforts and a few bargain no-bath rooms (though all have toilets). A pizzeria and a French restaurant adjoin. *Place de la Gare 34, tel. 48–52–52. 27 rooms. Facilities: restaurant, pizzeria, bar. AE, DC, MC, V.*

★ **Italia.** This is a valuable and remarkably inexpensive find in the train-station area: a former private apartment converted into hotel rooms, some with plaster details and cabinetry left behind. Rooms are solid and freshly furbished, all with private tiled bathrooms. The restaurant downstairs is one of the city's best Italian venues, and prices are considerably higher than those in neighboring pizzerias. In summer, try to dine in the quiet back garden. *Rue d'Anvers 15–17, L–1130, tel. 48–66–26. 20 rooms. Facilities: restaurant, bar, garden. AE, DC, MC, V.*

Nobilis. Built new in 1980 on the busy avenue de la Gare, and decorated in heavy wood and earth tones, this is a welcoming, relatively quiet property with business-class comforts. Despite double-glazing in front, back rooms (over the parking) are considerably quieter and cost only Flux 100 more. Enter through a minimall set in from the street. *Avenue de la Gare 47, L–1611, tel. 49–49–71. 44 rooms. Facilities: restaurant, coffee shop, bar. AE, DC, MC, V.*

Inexpensive **Bristol.** Though rue de Strasbourg is part of the network of questionable streets that lead off the place de la Gare, and thus is lined with strip joints and flophouses as well as legitimate shops and restaurants, this modest hotel offers comfortable, secure lodging and a fresh decor. The lobby/bar is warm and cozy, the breakfast room is lined with game trophies won by the owner's family, and baths are newly refurbished. A few bathless rooms on the first and fourth floors go for bargain rates. *Rue de Strasbourg 11, L–2561, tel. 48–58–30. 30 rooms, 22 with shower/toilet. Facilities: bar for guests only. AE, DC, MC, V.*

★ **Carlton.** In this vast 1918 hotel, buffered from the rue de Strasbourg scene by a rank of stores and opening onto a quiet inner court, tight-budget travelers will find roomy, quiet quarters. Nothing has been renovated, which means the beveled glass, oak parquet, and terrazzo floors are original, but so are the toilets, all located down the hall. The lounge, reception, and breakfast room are vast and lavishly furnished. Upstairs is only a little bleaker: Each room has antique beds, floral-print comforters, and a sink; wood floors, despite creaks, are white-glove clean; and while there's blistered plaster in the shower, the heat works. The maid even leaves an apple when she makes your bed in the morning. *Rue de Strasbourg 9, L–2561, tel. 48–48–02. 50 rooms without toilet. Facilities: breakfast room, bar. No credit cards.*

Dauphin. Another budget option, this modern hotel offers plain, clean rooms with splashy '60s decor—daisy prints, linoleum—and all-private baths. Back rooms avoid heavy street noise. *Avenue de la Gare 42, L–1610, tel. 48–82–82. 36 rooms. Facilities: breakfast room. AE, DC, MC, V.*

The Arts and Nightlife

The Arts Luxembourg City hosts a disproportionate number of arts events for its size, and while many of them are sold out on a season-ticket basis, there are often seats available at the last minute, and there are also independent concerts with tickets sold immediately before. Watch for posters on kiosks, and check at the tourist office on the place d'Armes, where tickets to many events are sold. Tickets to events at the Municipal Theater (Rond-point Robert Schuman, tel. 47–08–95) may be sold at its box office. The *Luxembourg News Digest*, an English-language weekly translating local news from the city dailies, offers up-to-date events listings; it is sold at bookstores and magazine stands. *Weekend* and *Rendez-vous Lëtzbuerg*, both available at the tourist office, also offer listings.

Theater Good traveling plays in French and German pass through the Municipal Theater; there also are English-language amateur productions from time to time. Watch kiosks or check at the tourist office on the place d'Armes.

Music Luxembourg is home to the **Radio-Télé-Luxembourg** (RTL) **Orchestra**, which performs a series of weekly concert pairs, usually on Thursday nights in the Municipal Theater and Friday nights at the Conservatoire de Musique (rue Charles Martel 33, tel. 4796–2950). Watch for posters announcing "Concerts du Midi": They may feature the RTL Orchestra, its members as soloists, or other professional chamber groups, and they are free of charge. They take place at the RTL Villa Louvigny, in the central municipal park. Though Luxembourg supports no opera company of its own, several German companies pass through on tour every season.

Film Luxembourg films are usually shown in their original language, with subtitles in a variety of tongues. If you want to see something other than an English-language film, check the posters to see what language subtitles will be in. The best films in any language usually come to **Cine Utopia** (avenue de la Faiencerie 16, 47–21–09), where reservations are accepted by phone.

Nightlife **Lentzen Eck** (rue de la Boucherie 2, tel. 2–24–77) offers a very
Bars and Cafés traditional old-Luxembourg setting, plus a good list of local eaux-de-vie. The **Cockpit Inn** (boulevard General Patton 43, tel. 48–86–35) pulls together the Icelandair and American residents for mixed drinks and an aviation theme. **Scott's Pub** (Bisserwé 4, tel. 47–53–52) in the Grund makes Brits feel at home; across the way, **Am Häffchen** (Bisserwé 9, tel. 46–16–17) serves cocktails and cocoa in an intimate, retro setting, complete with bookshelves. **Interview** (rue Aldringen 21, tel. 47–36–65) draws a very young, chic crowd (mostly students from the European School) to a setting of Warholesque urban decay. **Taverne Bit** (allée Scheffer 43, tel. 46–07–51) serves draft Bitburger Pils in a cozy German-pub setting. The **George and Dragon** (rue Unden 217, tel. 47–41–86) has an open fire, fish and chips, and Guinness stout on tap. The **piano bar** at the hotel Le Royal (boulevard Royal 12, tel. 4–16–16) has live music and cocktails in a swank setting. **Yucatan** (rue Notre-Dame 13, tel. 2–68–71) draws a stand-up local crowd for mixed margaritas and, as an afterthought, a reasonable approximation of Mexican food.

Discos The enormous **Metropolis** (rue du Fort Neipperg 56–58, tel. 48–22–11) has occasional live music. **Le Biblos** (avenue Monterey 10, tel. 2–32–29) stays open until 3 AM. **Casa Blanca** (boulevard d'Avranches 36, tel. 49–69–40) is the current weekend hot spot, while **Bugatti** (rue des Bains 19, tel. 2–70–66) draws an upscale, flashy crowd. Upstairs at **Jamaïque** (rue Aldringen 23, 47–08–22), there's a mix of soul and country music.

Jazz Clubs **Melusina** (rue de la Tour Jacob 145, tel. 43–59–22) draws top local musicians and touring guests for jazz, rock, and folk.

Excursion to the Luxembourg Ardennes

Vast, rolling green hills and dense fir forests alternate in Luxembourg's northern highlands, the southeast corner of the rocky, wooded Ardennes plateau. Higher, harsher than the duchy's southern *Bon Pays* (Good Country), with bitter winters and unwilling soil, it has remained isolated and inaccessible; indeed, even in the 1940s, no one expected the Germans to attempt attacking across such rough and uneven terrain. They did, of course—twice. The second led to one of the most vicious conflicts in World War II, the Battle of the Ardennes, or the Bulge (*see* Chapter 2, Portraits, *above*). It has been the hunting grounds of kings and emperors, Celts, Romans, and Gauls; shaggy deer and great, bristling wild boar still occasionally charge across a forest road. Castles punctuate its hills and valleys, and rocky rivers and streams pour off its slopes, making this an attractive vacation area for Europeans—especially from the flat Netherlands—to experience wilderness and medieval history. Clervaux, the northernmost point of our tour, lies some 60 kilometers (37 miles) north of Luxembourg City; thus it, and any points below it, lie within reach for a day trip. To follow the complete tour as described below, give yourself at least an overnight stop; though distances are small, roads do tend to wind a bit, so plan on a leisurely drive. If you're interested in tracing the ravages of World War II, allow plenty of browsing time, for there are three museums devoted to the subject in this hardest-hit area. And if you want to hike, you may want to settle in for a wilderness sojourn of two or three days—or more.

Important Addresses and Numbers

Tourist Information **Clervaux:** Syndicat d'Initiative, L-9700, tel. 9–20–72. **Diekirch:** Syndicat d'Initiative, place Guillaume, Boite Postale 29, L-9201, tel. 80–30–23. **Esch-sur-Sûre:** Syndicat d'Initiative, rue de l'Eglise 6, L-9650, tel. 8–93–67. **Vianden:** Syndicat d'Initiative, rue de la Gare 37, L-9420, tel. 8–42–67.

Emergencies *Police* **Clervaux:** tel. 9–28–11; **Diekirch:** tel. 80–31–85; **Esch-sur-Sûre** (Heiderscheid): tel. 8–90–05; **Vianden:** tel. 8–48–41.

Ambulance (throughout Luxembourg) 012

Hospital Emergency Room **Clervaux:** Clinique St-François, tel. 9–10–37; **Diekirch:** Hôpital Sacre Coeur, 80–33–55.

Late-night Pharmacies Inquire at 012 for number and address of the local *pharmacie de garde* (emergency pharmacy).

Getting There

By Car From Luxembourg City, follow signs for Ettelbruck (via route E 420). Driving is by far the most efficient and satisfying way of exploring this region, and roads are well-kept though slow and winding.

By Train Small rail lines out of Luxembourg City can carry you to Ettelbruck, Bourscheid, Clervaux, and Wiltz, but other sites on this tour remain out of reach by train.

By Bus Luxembourg buses connect throughout the grand duchy, both from Luxembourg City and from exterior towns. If you're staying outside the city, invest in the thick *horaire*, which has complete listings of connections.

Guided Tours

Sales-Lentz (*see* Luxembourg City Guided Tours, *above*) offers coach tours to groups of 10 or more.

Exploring the Luxembourg Ardennes

Numbers in the margin correspond with points of interest on the Luxembourg map.

Leave **Luxembourg**'s center via the Côte d'Eich, passing the red Grand-Duchesse Charlotte bridge, and follow signs toward Ettelbruck/Diekirch (RN 7). About 25 kilometers (15 miles) up **❶** the road, past Mersch, you'll reach **Colmar-Berg** and the **Grand Ducal Castle**, where the royal family has maintained their castle quarters for centuries; it is visible from the road (to the left), but well protected from close-up public viewing. Colmar-Berg is also home to a large branch of America's Goodyear tire company.

Another 2 kilometers (1¼ miles) takes you to the outskirts of **Ettelbruck**, an important crossroads; just short of town, take a **❷** right toward **Diekirch.** This small, easygoing city, with a pleasant pedestrian shopping area, offers several points of interest. **Eglise St-Laurent** (St. Lawrence's Church), a lovely, ancient little Romanesque church, has portions dating from as far back as the 5th century. Its earliest incarnation was constructed on the foundations of a Roman temple, the older parts functioning as a cemetery; in 1961, that lower section was uncovered, and with it 30-some Merovingian sarcophagi, many of them containing intact skeletons. Since 1978, the cemetery has been restored and open to the public. Some of the ancient underbelly of the church can be seen through a grate in the nave; you may enter the crypt by an exterior door on the right of the building. At the **Musée Municipal** (Municipal Museum), in the basement of the primary school, there are two more sarcophagi and remains found under the church, along with well-preserved Roman mosaics from the 4th century, found a couple of blocks away; Diekirch is riddled with remains of Roman culture, though most of its treasures were carried away by invading Franks. *Place Guillaume. Admission: Flux 20. Open mid-Mar.–Oct., Fri.–Tues. 10–noon and 2–6.*

In the **Musee de la Bataille des Ardennes** (Museum of the Battle of the Bulge), 10 lifesize, authentically equipped dioramas depict personal aspects of the hardships of the battle. Unlike the museum at Bastogne, this thoughtful, neutral effort sidesteps discussions of strategies and fronts; it brings out individual details instead, from yellowed letters and K rations to propaganda flyers—both German and American—scattered to demoralize already homesick soldiers at Christmastime. All paraphernalia are authentic period pieces. The staff often welcomes veterans personally. *Bamertal 10, tel. 80–89–08. Admission: Flux 120 adults, Flux 80 students under 18. Open 2 weeks at Easter and May–Oct., daily 10–noon and 2–6.*

Diekirch is also the home of the brewery of a beer bearing its name; it is one of the most popular beers in Luxembourg. And you may want to head briefly out of town, following the route to Larochette; as you climb the switchbacks above town, park across from the sign for the **Diewelselter,** an impressive dolmen (stone altar) attributed to the Celts, then walk up the trail marked "D" into the forest (about 15 minutes). No one is sure who piled the great stones that form this ancient arch—or how they did it.

❸ From Diekirch, follow route 17 east and north to **Vianden,** where coming around the last bend, you'll suddenly see a full-length view of its spectacular **castle** rearing up on a hill over the village, replete with conical spires, crenellation, step gables, and massive bulwarks. Its dramatic position enhances the tiny village's medieval air, with its steep, narrow main street and

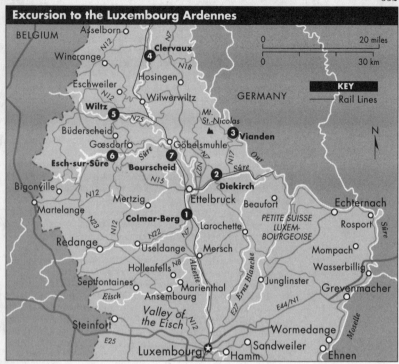

shuttered houses crouched at the feet of the feudal lord. The castle was built on Roman foundations in the 9th century, but its most spectacular portions date from the 11th, 12th, and 15th centuries. It has been completely and, to some eyes, ruthlessly restored, with all-new plaster-, stone-, and woodwork, and track lighting—yet fans of romantic ruins haven't grounds for complaint: It is a fully functional royal castle, still the rightful property of the blue-blooded heirs to the counts of Vianden and the House of Orange-Nassau, so why shouldn't it be up-to-date? *Tel. 8–41–08. Admission: Flux 110 adults, Flux 30 children. Open Mar. and Oct., daily 10–5; Apr.–June and Sept., daily 10–6; July–Aug., daily 9–7; Nov.–Feb., daily 10–4.*

In the village below, the 13th-century **Gothic church** once functioned as a Trinitarian monastery; its ancient cloisters, too, have been restored to sparkling modernity. Down the hill, by the banks of the River Our, the **Musée Victor Hugo** displays letters and memorabilia from the famous French author's sojourn here in 1871. *Tel. 8–42–57. Admission: Flux 25 adults, Flux 15 children. Open Apr.–Oct., daily 9:30–noon and 2–6; Dec.–Mar., Thurs.–Tues. 9:30–noon and 2–6.*

The **Hotel Heintz,** on the main street, billeted American intelligence and reconnaissance (I&R) men in the chilly last days of 1944; one of the bits of intelligence they picked up was the story of Elise Delé, a Luxembourgish farm woman from Bivels, just up the road. On route to her evacuated house to pick up warm clothing, she had been picked up by German soldiers and carried across the Our, all the way to Bitburg. Along the way she witnessed a beehive of activity—soldiers, trucks, artillery, SS troops, and river-crossing pontoons—heading west. With help from the Luxembourg underground, she escaped and described what she had seen to the I&R Americans at the Hotel Heintz. On December 14 her story had made it as far as the First Army headquarters in Spa, but it hadn't crossed the desks of Eisenhower or Montgomery. At 5:30 AM on December 16, the Germans attacked and continued to attack, with a passion and brutality born of desperation, until well after Christmas—and well into Belgium.

From Vianden, wend your way back toward Diekirch, but cut north (right) on a smaller scenic road over Mont St-Nicholas (with widespread views of the Our Valley from its summit) and on to **4 Clervaux.** This forest village, surrounded by deep-cleft hills, draws vacationers to hike, hunt, and visit its sprawling **castle,** founded by the de Lannoi family. It was from this castle that Philip de Lannoi, an ancestor of Franklin *Delano* Roosevelt, left in 1621 to make his fortune in America. The castle was virtually reduced to rubble in the Battle of the Bulge but has been completely restored; there's a small museum inside, with a movingly personal hodgepodge of local photos and memorabilia from the war. You also can visit a collection of models of Luxembourg castles and the recently restored and now permanent exhibition of photo portraits of *The Family of Man,* taken by Luxembourg native Edward Steichen. *Admission: Flux 40 per exhibit. Open July–mid-Sept., daily 10–5; mid-Sept.–June, Sun. 1–5.*

Clervaux is also home to the striking **Benedictine Abbey of Saints Maurice and Maur,** built in 1910 in the style of the Abbey of Cluny and perched high above town. In the pedestrian center, there is a new memorial/appreciation to the Americans who fought in Clervaux in 1944.

From Clervaux, double back to route 7 and head south, then (in about 7 kilometers/4¼ miles) cut west (right) on winding route **5** 25 toward **Wiltz.** This unusual town is divided into two separate levels, with its Oberwiltz (upper town) dominated by the fully restored **castle.** Built in the 12th century, it was completely remodeled in 1631; it now houses a small **Musée de la Battaille des Ardennes** (Museum of the Battle of the Bulge), with documents and photographs from the war. *Tel. 95–74–44. Admission: Flux 50 adults, Flux 25 children. Open June–mid-Sept., daily 10–noon and 1–5.*

Also in town is a **Musée arts et métiers** (Museum of Arts and Trades), which displays tools and objects from old local bakers, tanners, and distilleries. *Tel. 95–74–44. Admission: Flux 50 adults, Flux 25 children. Open June–mid-Sept., daily 10–noon and 1:30–5:30.*

The amphitheater behind the museum hosts the Wiltz Festival of classical music; the rest of the château serves as a retirement home and cannot be visited.

Leaving Wiltz, head south on route 12 to Büderscheid, then continue south briefly on N15. Turn right, cutting through a tunnel in the rock cliff, and in 2 kilometers (1¼ miles) you'll enter **6** pretty little **Esch-sur-Sûre.** Completely circled by densely forested hills, this miniature gooseneck on the River Sûre was once a stronghold, and its ruined **fortress-castle** still towers over the town. (Unrestored, it is open to the public.) Legend has it that an Esch Crusader brought home a Turk's head and hung it outside the castle gate, and that it reappears to this day to warn of disaster; some claim to have seen it before the German invasion in 1940. Nowadays Esch is the gateway to a water recreation area, on the shores of the **Lac de la Haute Sûre,** created by a dam just upstream from town.

Head south again on route 15, then immediately cut left toward Goebelsmühle, following the green Sûre Valley along a wild and isolated winding road. Continue along the river, following signs for Bourscheid Moulin-Plage, where you'll see the roman-tic ruins of **Bourscheid** Castle looming 500 feet above the Sûre, commanding three valleys. Recent restorations have made this rambling hodgepodge of towers and walls more accessible; the views are magnificent, and there's a new snack bar built in. *Tel. 9–05–70. Admission: Flux 80 adults, Flux 50 children. Open Mar.–Sept., daily 10–7.*

From Bourscheid, follow signs to Lipperscheid, from where N7 leads back to Luxembourg City.

What to See and Do with Children

Kids who finally tire of pouring imaginary boiling oil and shoot-ing flaming arrows from Ardennes castles, and who balk at an-other uphill forest hike, will enjoy a trip to swim or windsurf on the waterfront of the **Lac de la Haute Sûre,** accessible on the south shore at Insenborn and on the north shore below Liefrange. There's also a **Musée de la poupée et du jouet** (Muse-um of Dolls and Toys) in Vianden, with antiques dating back to the 16th century. *Grand'rue 96, tel. 8–45–91. Admission: Flux 80 adults, Flux 60 children. Open Easter–Oct., Tues.–Sun. 10–noon and 2–6.*

Off the Beaten Track

For more castles, make an extra circle tour west of **Mersch** (with its own three towers) and visit the **Valley of the Seven Châteaux,** cutting west to Reckange, south to **Hollenfels, Marienthal,** and **Ansembourg** (which has an old castle in the heights and a new one in the valley below), then working west to **Septfontaines** and south to **Koerich.** The castles, in various stages of repair and representing a broad historical spectrum, have not been developed for visitors, but they loom above for-ests and over valleys much as they did in Luxembourg's grand-er days. Follow the road signs marked "Vallée des Sept Châteaux": This rather obscure and never-direct itinerary takes you through pretty farmlands, woods, and—just outside Koerich, at **Goeblange**—to the foundations of two 4th-century **Roman villas,** their underground heating and plumbing sys-tems exposed; the rough cobbles leading into the woods are original, too.

Shopping

There's good, moderate shopping for clothes and kitchen wares in the downtown sections of **Diekirch** and **Ettelbruck.** A few souvenir shops in **Clervaux** and **Vianden** offer rustic goods and (grimly enough) World War II–model war toys for children in-spired by the horrors of Battle of the Bulge museums.

Sports and Outdoor Activities

Biking Bicycles can be rented in Diekirch at **Camping de la Sûre** (tel. 80–94–25) and at **Outdoor Centre** (tel. 80–97–92).

Golf Clervaux (tel. 92–93–95) has an 18-hole course.

Dining and Lodging

Clervaux
Dining and Lodging

Koener/International. These two hotels, owned by brothers and adjoining a shared indoor pool, offer sleek new mall-look decors and modern details; rooms on the International side are somewhat more attractive (and more expensive), with dark-green and brass decors. Neither half, aside from some rooms with forest views, has much Ardennes atmosphere, but both offer full comfort. *Grand'rue 10–14, L-9701, tel. 9–10–67. 50/42 rooms. Facilities: Restaurant (Moderate), café, terrace, piano bar, indoor pool, sauna, solarium. AE, DC, MC, V. Koener: Inexpensive. International: Moderate.*

Du Commerce. Directly below the castle and slightly apart from the hotel-packed center, this spacious, freshly renewed hotel has been in the family for two generations, and shows their pride: It combines slick, spare modernity—tile, stucco, polished oak—with homey old details (fringed lamps, heavy upholstery), and there's an open fireplace in the restaurant. Some rooms have balconies over the river and hills. *Rue de Marnach 2, L-9709, tel. 91032. 54 rooms. Facilities: restaurant (Moderate), bar, garden, terrace café. MC, V. Inexpensive.*

Diekirch
Dining and Lodging
★

Hiertz. This small hotel/restaurant looks stark and unwelcoming from the outside, but inside, its tiny dining rooms are homey little parlors, with heavy carpet, flocked wallpaper, and ornate silver appointments. Sit in the pretty terraced garden on the hill behind for summer aperitifs and after-dinner coffee; for the meal in between, try *rouget* (red mullet) in rosemary cream sauce or roast Vosges quail with juniper berries. The hotel plays second fiddle to the food, but rooms are comfortable, their decor in the same stuffy-lavish vein (green satin, mixed floral stencils) as downstairs; ask for one of the three back rooms facing the garden. *Rue Clairefontaine 1, L-9220, tel. 80–35–62. 8 rooms. Facilities: restaurant (Expensive; closed Mon. dinner, Tues.), garden bar. AE, DC, MC, V. Moderate.*

Esch-sur-Sûre
Dining and Lodging

Beau-Site. At the edge of a village and overlooking the river, this comfortable landmark hotel/restaurant has been updated with new woodwork and fresh tile. The rooms are modern, some with flower boxes and river views. The restaurant offers grilled meats and cream-sauced standards at prices slightly higher than average—but the portions are staggering, and the kitchen cuts no corners. *Rue de Kaundorf 2, L-9650, tel. 8–91–34. 21 rooms. Facilities: restaurant, terrace café. No credit cards. Restaurant closed Wed. Moderate.*

Lipperscheid
Dining and Lodging

Leweck. Just off the main north–south route between Diekirch and Clervaux, this big, comfortable hotel/restaurant has evolved over the years into a fairly luxurious lodging, with an indoor pool, green grounds, and an upscale restaurant. The rooms are modern and airtight; the back rooms (higher priced) take in valley views toward Bourscheid. The restaurant walks a delicate line between deluxe and bourgeois, with rustic pine, copper decor, and highbrow service hovering over the steaks and lamb chops. You can have simpler fare—local ham with frites and salad—in the adjoining casual café. *Route de Diekirch, L-9378, tel. 9–00–22. 25 rooms. Facilities: restaurant, café, garden terrace, indoor pool, tennis court, whirlpool, sauna, solarium, game room. MC, V. Moderate.*

Vianden
Dining and Lodging

Oranienburg. In the same family since 1880, this once-traditional lodging has gone deluxe, decorating its rooms and restaurant in lush, new fabrics and modern, built-in fixtures. Only the café and stairwell retain the old-Vianden atmosphere, with game trophies and burnished oak. The restaurant, Le Chatelain, now contemporary and posh as well, attracts nonguests for its ambitious French cooking and its views toward the village and castle. *Grand'rue 126, L-9411, tel. 8–41–53. 36 rooms. Facilities: restaurant (Expensive), café, terrace, private garden terrace. AE, DC, MC, V. Moderate.*

★ **Heintz.** Expanded from its origins as a Trinitarian monastery, this atmospheric hotel has been in the family for four generations. Its most famous incarnation: American intelligence officers were billeted here during the war, and late owner Grandma Hansen stayed on, working with the Resistance, hiding hams, cash, and Luxembourgers with equal aplomb. The public spaces are rich with history, from the cross-vaulted oak café to the hallways filled with local antiques; rooms are simple and up-to-date. The oldest rooms, on the first floor, have antique oak furniture and original doors, but baths are down the hall; the best rooms are upstairs, with balconies over the garden and fountain. The restaurant offers French classics—grilled beef with béarnaise sauce, salmon in chives, and pure-German apple strudel with vanilla sauce. *Grand'rue 55, L-9410, tel. 8–41–55. 30 rooms. Facilities: restaurant (Moderate), café, garden terrace. AE, DC, MC, V. Inexpensive.*

Aal Veinen. Dark, cozy, and casual, this 1683 *auberge* (inn) serves a menu of simple standards—*bouchée à la reine* (chicken à la king) with frites, omelettes, cold sausage plates—and a wide selection of grilled meats, cooked in full view of the dining area over a sizzling wood fire. (If you've given up on pork chops, this is the place to get reacquainted.) Rooms upstairs are tidy and sparely furnished, with some beams, stucco, and oak armoires. *Grand'rue 114, L-9411, tel. 8–43–68. 8 rooms. Facilities: restaurant, bar. MC, V. Restaurant closed Tues. except Aug. Inexpensive.*

The Arts and Nightlife

The Arts

Wiltz sponsors a popular classical music festival, with concerts in the church and outdoor amphitheater (for ticket and schedule information, call 95–74–44 or write to the Syndicat d'Initiative, L-9516 Wiltz).

Nightlife

For dancing and late-night action, head back to Luxembourg City.

Excursion to Petite Suisse and the Moselle

Important Addresses and Numbers

Tourist Information **Echternach:** Syndicat d'Initiative, Boite Postale 30, L-6401, tel. 7–22–30. **Remich:** Syndicat d'Initiative, Gare Routière, L-5553, tel. 69–84–88.

Emergencies **Echternach:** Police, tel. 72–99–95. Doctor/Dentist/Hospital, tel. 012. **Remich:** Police, tel. 69–86–87. Doctor/Dentist/Hospital, tel. 012.

Getting There

By Car Everything on this excursion can easily be reached by car within 40 minutes of Luxembourg City; there is no rail service connecting these sights.

By Bus *See* Getting Around Luxembourg, *above.*

Guided Tours

Sales-Lentz (*see* Luxembourg City Guided Tours, *above*) offers tours into the Moselle area to groups of 10 or more. To view the Moselle by cruise boat, contact **Navigation Touristique** and its M.S. *Princess Marie-Astrid* (route de Thionville 32, L-6791 Grevenmacher, tel. 75–82–75); this graceful little ship stops at Wasserbillig, Grevenmacher, Wormeldange, Stadtbredimus, Remich, Bech-Kleinmacher, and Schengen; it runs, on average, twice a day between 11 AM and 6 PM; a comfortable itinerary for sightseers would be to leave Remich at 2:30, arrive at Schengen at 3:10, then double back to Remich by 4. Another company offers entertainment on board: **Navitours** (rue de Luxembourg 1, L-6750 Grevenmacher, tel. 75–84–89).

Most of the wine houses along the Moselle offer guided tours and tastings. Contact **Bernard-Massard** (rue du Pont 8, L-6773 Grevenmacher, tel. 7–55–45), **St-Martin** (L-5570 Remich, tel. 69–90–91), and **St-Remy** (L-5501 Remich, tel. 6–90–84).

Exploring Echternach and the Moselle

Leave Luxembourg City via the Côte d'Eich, following signs for **Echternach.** You'll pass through some lovely forests—and some devastated wastelands, where the windstorms of 1990 cut tornadolike swaths through ancient beech timber; the damage is still evident throughout the grand duchy. The next town of consequence is the now bedroom community of Junglinster, where you'll see three transmitter towers and buildings of **RTL** (Radio-Télé-Luxembourg), made famous during World War II and still one of the most powerful radio stations in Europe. Just past town, turn left toward those towers, following signs to **Larochette.** This forest resort, on the western edge of the region known as **Müllerthal** (or, because of its high bluffs, woodlands, and rushing streams, as La Petite Suisse), hosts a striking step-gabled castle that looks down on the town. The castle is privately owned and occupied, but adjoining ruins from an earlier incarnation (with evocative views over the small houses below) may be visited. *Admission: Flux 50.*

From the center of Larochette, cut east, following signs to **Beaufort.** Here yet another splendid ruin, only partially restored to its 15th-century form, rises over green grounds full of sheep and forests full of walking trails. This one is well worth crawling around in: You can step into guard towers with archers' slits, look down wells, visit the kitchen fireplace, cross a drawbridge, and ogle very serious-looking torture equipment in a dungeon, including a rack. At the ticket counter, you can buy (or drink) samples of the local kirsch (cherry eau-de-vie) and cassis (black currant liqueur). *Tel. 8–60–02. Admission: Flux 50 adults, Flux 20 children. Open Apr.–Oct., daily 9–6.*

From Beaufort, head northeast for N10, and follow the River Sûre south to **Echternach,** a flourishing tourist center all but adopted by the Germans across the Sûre, who fill its hotels, restaurants, and monuments every weekend. Their influence is strongly felt, in the all-German-language labels on artifacts and attractions, and in the spic-and-span, better-than-ever restorations—as well as in the shrapnel scars that pock the stonework still, 45 years after the Battle of the Bulge. This ancient town was founded in 698 by Saint Willibrord, who came from Northumberland in England to establish a Benedictine abbey, which thrived until 1795. In the Middle Ages, the Echternach Abbey was known throughout the Western world for its fine school of illuminations (miniature paintings that illustrated holy, hand-copied texts). The magnificent quadrant of abbey buildings dates from the 18th century (though damaged and restored after the war); nowhere else in Luxembourg can you wander among buildings of such noble line and classical scale. Examples of the artwork produced in the abbey can be viewed in the **Musée de l'Abbaye** (Abbey Museum) in the abbey basement, but be aware: They're lavishly colored all-modern reproductions, including the jewel-studded book covers; in fact, virtually everything in the museum is a slick, new reproduction, framed and well-lighted like treasures of antiquity. The originals are not accessible for public viewing. *Admission: Flux 40 adults, Flux 20 children 6–16. Variable hours: usually Pentecost–Oct., daily 10–noon and 2–5; July–Aug., 10–noon and 2–6.*

The once-early-Romanesque **basilica,** built originally in the 11th to 13th centuries but destroyed in World War II and reconstructed in 1952, combines a very spare, squeaky-clean modernism with the few Romanesque details that remain; note the alternating square and round pillars. It was first built to house the remains of St. Willibrord; they were rediscovered after World War I behind an 8th-century altar (on display in the National Museum in Luxembourg City) and are enshrined in the **crypt** in a neoclassical marble sarcophagus. Inside, behind the elaborate carvings, you can just get a glimpse of the simple tooled-stone sarcophagus cut in the 7th century. In the crypt, a few token traces of the original 7th-century chapel, founded by the saint himself, have been left exposed under heavy, modern cosmetic repairs. On a hill just behind the basilica, the **Eglise SS. Pierre et Paul** (Saints Peter and Paul's Church) stands on remains of a Roman castellum and shows, in its spare architecture, signs of Merovingian, Romanesque, and Gothic influence. Every spring, the two churches host one of Luxembourg's most important arts events: the Echternach Festival of Classical Music.

Time Out   Just below Saints Peter and Paul's, have coffee and a sizable fresh pastry at the **Café-Tea Room Zimmer,** and pick up something for later in the adjoining bakeshop/confiserie.

Echternach's cobbled **place du Marché,** in the old town center, offers a charming mix of Gothic arcades and restored medieval town houses, festooned with wrought-iron signs and sculpted drainspouts; the arched and turreted 13th-century **Hôtel de Ville** (Town Hall) is its centerpiece.

On Whittuesday (the eighth Tuesday after Easter), Echternach is transported to the Middle Ages: Pilgrims from throughout the region come to town to join in—and tourists come to watch—the famous Springprozession, a dancing parade down the streets of the town, the marchers bouncing from one foot to the other, all the way to the basilica. Their chanted prayer: "Holy Willibrord, founder of churches, light of the blind, destroyer of idols, pray for us."

Leaving Echternach, follow signs for Wasserbillig/Trier and head south on N10 along the Sûre and the German border, passing **Rosport,** the source of the ubiquitous green-bottled mineral water you will be served wherever you go. You'll also pass several small artisinale schnapps or eaux-de-vie distilleries, making the most of nearby orchards. At Wasserbillig cut through town toward Grevenmacher; at the other end, you will greet the **Moselle,** whose waters nourish Luxembourg's famous vineyards, cultivated since Roman times. The vines cover every exposed slope in sight, and the farther south you drive, the more romantic the scenery becomes. About 6 kilometers (4 miles) down, you'll find **Grevenmacher,** a principal wine center and home of Bernard-Massard (who make a widely exported champagne substitute). Ten kilometers (6 miles) south lies graceful little **Wormeldange,** another key wine center; cut inland and follow signs up into Wormeldange-Haute (Upper Wormeldange) for sweeping views over the Moselle.

Time Out   Stop at Wormeldange's enormous pink-stuccoed **Caves Cooperatives** to sample the local product, as its tidy adjoining pub offers a *dégustation:* a wrought-iron, vine-shaped rack suspending five sample glasses to contrast and compare. There's local grape juice, too, for the designated driver.

Return to the main Moselle highway. **Ehnen,** just down the road from Wormeldange, is worth a stop and a stroll as well, as its narrow old streets, carved-wood doors, and circular church (a 15th-century design reconstructed in 1826) seem frozen in time. It's home to a **musée du vin** (wine museum), set in a typical group of Luxembourgish farm buildings, with pink stucco and cobbled courts. Its rooms are full of tools, equipment, and photographs of the wine-making industry, and there's a demonstration vineyard planted with samples of each of the local varietals. There are labels in English. *Tel. 7–60–26. Admission: Flux 60 adults, Flux 30 children. Open Feb.–Nov., Tues.–Sun. 9:30–11:30 and 2–5.*

Twelve kilometers (7 miles) farther down the highway, **Remich** is a popular waterfront town, where cruise boats roll past a pleasant riverside promenade, and sizable wineries can be visited. You can take a leisurely round-trip boat ride from here to **Schengen,** at the southeast tip of Luxembourg, which intersects with both Germany and France (*see* Guided Tours, *above*).

Just south of Remich, in a small wine village named **Bech-Kleinmacher,** stop at **A Possen,** a 17th-century stone wine maker's house restored and furnished. Its extraordinarily atmospheric displays include a "black kitchen," with a ham-smoking chimney, and a cozy bedroom with a four-poster and homespun linens; there are museum displays on the wine industry, and a toy collection as well. *Rue Sandt 16, tel. 69–82–33. Admission: Flux 100 adults, Flux 40 children 6–12. Open mid-Mar.–Oct., Fri.–Sun. 10–11:30 and 2–7.*

Time Out After viewing the displays, you can stop in the **Waistuff** (wine *stube* or café) to taste the local wine and sample dark bread smeared with *kochkäse,* Luxembourg's favorite cheese spread.

Double back to Remich, then take E27/N2 toward Luxembourg. Just before reaching the city, stop between Sandweiler and Hamm to visit the **American Military Cemetery,** where General George Patton chose to be buried with his men. More than 5,000 soldiers of the Third Army were buried here, having died on Luxembourg soil; there are also 117 graves of unknown soldiers. Each grave is marked with either a Star of David or a simple cross, but they are not separated by race, rank, religion, or origin—except for the 22 pairs of brothers, who lie side by side. Only Patton's cross, identical to the others, stands by itself.

From the parking lot, a small road leads a kilometer toward Sandweiler, and across an intersection to the **German Military Cemetery,** which shelters more than twice as many war dead. During the Ardennes conflict, the U.S. Army Burial Service recovered the bodies from both sides and buried them in two temporary cemeteries, the Americans near Hamm, the Germans near Sandweiler. For the Germans, 300 graves served 5,000 soldiers. Yet another 5,000 had been buried on battle sites throughout the country, with little or no identification, mostly in mass graves. In 1952, those bodies were transferred here. Blunt stone crosses identify multiple burial sites, some marked with names and serial numbers, other marked simply "Ein Deutscher Soldat" (a German soldier). At the top of the lot, a tall stone cross heads the mass grave, where the other 5,000 are, for the most part, identified by a bronze plaque. This is the only German cemetery on once-enemy soil.

What to See and Do with Children

The **Jardin des Papillons** (Butterfly Garden) in Grevenmacher seethes with fluttering wildlife, from butterflies to birds to tropical insects, all enclosed in an attractive greenhouse. *Route du Vin, tel. 75–85–39. Open Apr. 1–mid-Oct., daily 9:30–5:30. Admission: Flux 150 adults, Flux 80 children.*

Off the Beaten Track

If you've seen enough castles and want to wander through dense fir and beech forests, with high limestone bluffs and twisting brooks, drive through the **Müllerthal,** also known as

La Petite Suisse. The forests are rich, and there are *auberges* (inns) sprinkled along the roadside, with terrace tables and welcoming cafés. Starting at Junglinster, follow signs for Larochette, then toward Consdorf and Berdorf, where hotels and restaurants are concentrated.

Shopping

The best souvenirs of this region are meant to be drunk: Moselle wines, both sparkling and regular, can be tasted and purchased in gift packs from most of the caves cooperatives. Artisanale distilleries sell their eaux-de-vie along the Moselle highway, too. And at Beaufort, you can pick up a bottle of their house-label kirsch or cassis.

Sports and Outdoor Activities

Bicycling   In Echternach, contact **Cycles Schmitt** (rue Ermesinde 27, tel. 7–21–48).

Dining and Lodging

Echternach   **La Bergerie.** One of the best restaurants in the region, this
Dining   19th-century farmhouse nestles in an idyllic setting of forest
★   and fields, with windows and a garden-terrace making the most of the expanse of greenery. The graceful, unfussy dining room features the cooking of owner/chef Claude Phal, whose specialties include classics (simple foie gras; turbot in champagne sauce) and sophisticated experiments (smoked sole; young pigeon in pastry, its own juice caramelized). The strawberry gratin in orange butter uses fruit from their own garden; all baked goods are made in their full-scale pastry kitchen. It's a family effort, with wife, son, and daughter-in-law running the restaurant and their off-shoot hotel in Echternach, 7 kilometers (4¼ miles) away (there's a free shuttle between). *Geyershaff, tel. 7–94–64. Reservations required. Jacket and tie advised. AE, DC, MC, V. Closed Sun. dinner, Mon. Very Expensive.*

Dining and Lodging   **Du Commerce.** Tucked back from the place du Marché, with quiet bordering streets and an idyllic garden behind, this simple hotel has been kept in top running order, with efforts at upgrades in every corner. Rooms have fixtures of varying vintage but all-fresh decors, and there's an enormous fitness center free to guests. The restaurant and café are atmospheric, with oak wainscoting, beams, and pink linens; standards (trout, *bouchée à la reine*) are moderately priced and well prepared. *Place du Marché 16, L-6460, tel. 7–23–01. 48 rooms. Facilities: restaurant (Moderate), café, terrace café, garden, fitness room, sauna, solarium. AE, MC, V. Inexpensive.*

Lodging   **La Bergerie.** Managed by the owners of the partner restaurant
★   outside town (*see Dining, above*), this recent (1988) addition to the downtown hotel scene is one of a kind: a small mansion, enclosed in a shady garden, completely converted to creamy, modern luxury, with glistening tile baths, opulent fabrics and cabinetry, and all comforts—except a restaurant, which requires a pleasant shuttle ride into the countryside. Breakfast is served in the big bay window overlooking the garden and fountain, or on the terrace in good weather; croissants come from the restaurant's pastry kitchen. *Rue de Luxembourg 47, L-*

6450, tel. 72–85–04. 15 rooms. Facilities: breakfast only, sauna, solarium, fitness equipment. AE, DC, MC, V. Expensive.

Ehnen
Dining and Lodging
★

Bamberg. Looking for all the world as if a world war had never passed through, this comfortable, friendly old hotel/restaurant, across from the Moselle and flanked by vineyards, maintains a reassuring retro formality: oak wainscoting, leaded glass, ceramics, pewter coasters under cut-glass crystal goblets. The cuisine is equally old school, and just as appealing: plump vineyard snails swimming in butter; boned quail stuffed with grapes and wrapped in pastry; sweetbreads and morels in rich cream sauce. Wines, of course, are local and modestly priced. The breakfast room is a cozy parlor, complete with antiques and a porcelain collection, and some of the stuffy/comfy (chenille, sculptured carpet) rooms upstairs offer balconies toward the Moselle. *Route du Vin 131, L-5416. 14 rooms. Facilities: restaurant, (closed Tues; Moderate/Expensive). AE, MC, V. Inexpensive.*

★ **Simmer.** This Moselle institution, built in 1863 and maintained in a welcoming Victorian-rustic style, is the preferred riverfront retreat of the royal family and political luminaries, though its ambience remains comfortable and homey. Incorporating portions of a 1610 house and the founder's butcher shop, it was taken over by the current family in 1955 and built into an elegant hotel/restaurant. The details they added—a 17th-century fireplace in the dining room, carved oak grotesques paneling the salon—complete the effect of elegant warmth. Rooms are roomy and solid, decked with dated glamour (brocade, gilt, crystal) and some antiques; in front, there are balconies, in back, small suites. Restaurant specialties include braised *brochet* (pike) in cream and *sandre* (pike perch) in local Auxerrois; in summer, you can dine on the full-length, open front porch. It's next door to the wine museum. *Route du Vin 117, L-5416. 17 rooms. Facilities: restaurant (Expensive; closed Tues.), terrace, bar. AE, MC, V. Inexpensive.*

Frisange
Dining
★

Lea Linster. As the first woman to win France's culinary Oscar, the Paul Bocuse d'Or, Ms. Linster has earned international attention and keeps her modest farmhouse—once her mother's rustic café, with *jeu de quilles* (bowling)—full of prominent guests. Have a glass of champagne in the shady garden out back (cows may wander nearby), then relax in the elegant dining room over her prize-winning dishes: lobster with truffled fettuccine and lamb in crisp potato crust. The wine list is weighted toward the high end, as are prices. It's on the southern border, 4 kilometers (2½ miles) east of the Bettembourg exit off the motorway (E25). *Route de Luxembourg 17, tel. 6-84-11. Reservations required. Jacket and tie advised. AE, DC, MC, V. Closed Mon.–Tues. Very Expensive.*

★ **Lëtzebuerger Kaschthaus.** Secure in her success in haute gastronomie, Lea Linster hasn't forgotten her roots; now she's opened a simple farmhouse restaurant to cook nothing but Luxembourg specialties, superbly prepared and served without frills in a comfortably retro setting. Pretty print linens, stenciled wallpaper, and original ceramic flooring make everyone feel at home, from hip young nationalists to fur-hatted ladies of a certain age. Try the green-bean soup, rich bouchée à la reine with sweetbreads, savory lentils with sausage, and mouth-watering fruit tarts. Immediately off the motorway (E25) between Bettembourg and Frisange, it's an easy drive from Luxembourg City. *Route de Bettembourg 4, Hellange, tel. 51–*

65–73. Reservations advised. Dress: casual. AE, DC, MC, V. Closed Tues. Inexpensive/Moderate.

Godbrange
Dining

Dahm. In a cozy farmhouse decorated with game trophies, you can experience the classic Luxembourg meal: *Judd mat gardeboh'nen* (smoked pork with fava beans), *choucroûte* (sauerkraut), and lard-fried potatoes. The choice is limited to this standard menu, or an alternative of cold *jambon d'Ardennes* (Ardennes ham) with frites and salad. Service is notoriously chilly, but the food is good and portions are unlimited. *Rue du Village 22, tel. 7–81–97. Reservations suggested. Dress: casual. AE, DC, MC, V. Inexpensive.*

Remich
Dining

Caves St-Martin. This long, open oak-and-tile sprawl of a restaurant/café offers comfortable old-style dining—fried fish, veal in cream sauce—to be washed down with a bottle of the house specialty, which you can sample on a tour of the winery. *Route du Vin 21, tel. 6–91–02. Reservations suggested. Dress: casual. MC, V. Moderate.*

Lodging
★

Saint-Nicolas. Named for the patron saint of fishermen, whose small shrine adjoins the building, this hotel got its start in 1885 as a *relais* (relay station) for changing teams of horses that hauled barges up the Moselle. Now, under the same family management and fully rebuilt after the war, it offers guests modern facilities but the same roomy scale and grace of its earlier days. There's a long glassed-in front porch with a restaurant, and an open terrace just above, both taking in full-length views of the Moselle, as well as an enclosed garden court for summer breakfasts. Rooms have bright, new fabrics, and some have double casement windows over the river (and highway). *Esplanade 31, L-5533, tel. 69–83–33. 43 rooms. Facilities: restaurant, bar, terrace, sauna, solarium, fitness equipment. AE, DC, MC, V. Moderate.*

Esplanade. This big, postwar waterfront hotel offers much of the same comfort as the Saint-Nicolas but none of the historic tradition. There's a big porch and a terrace café, and plenty of rooms overlooking the waterfront, some with sheltered balconies. *Esplanade 5, L-5533, tel. 6–91–71. 20 rooms. Facilities: restaurant, bar, terrace café. V. Inexpensive.*

Wormeldange-Haut
Dining
★

Schmit-Hengel. Perched high over the Moselle valley, with some windows taking in the view, this is a family restaurant specializing in *cuisine bourgeoise* standards: aspargus in fresh-whisked *sauce mousseline* (sauce with whipped cream), *escalope de veau crème champignons* (veal in mushroom cream sauce), rumpsteak, and *friture de la Moselle* (fried freshwater fish). It's packed with three-generation groups for Sunday dinner. *Berreggaass 9, tel. 7–60–46. Reservations suggested. Dress: casual. AE, MC, V. Closed Tues. Moderate.*

The Arts and Nightlife

The Arts

The **Echternach Festival** of classical music is one of the most important arts events in Luxembourg, bringing in world-class artists and ensembles and showcasing them in the basilica and the smaller Saints Peter and Paul's Church. It takes place in late spring, and tickets sell out quickly; if you're interested, write ahead to Lux-Festival (Boite Postale 30, L-6401 Echternach). Tickets, if available, can be bought in person at the Echternach Syndicat d'Initiative and at the Luxembourg Syndicat on the place d'Armes.

Nightlife For all its touristic charms, if you're interested in late nights and bright lights, this is not the region to linger in—head back for Luxembourg-Ville. The one exception: the small treatment spa Mondorf-les-Bains, on the French border southeast of Luxembourg City, offers **Casino 2000** (rue Flamang, tel. 66–10–10–1), with full gaming facilities.

Vocabulary

Dutch Vocabulary

	English	Dutch	Pronunciation
Basics	Yes/no	Ja,nee	yah,nay
	Please	Alstublieft	**ahls**-too-bleeft
	Thank you	Dank u	**dahnk** oo
	You're welcome	Niets te danken	neets teh **dahn**-ken
	Excuse me, sorry	Pardon	pahr-**don**
	Good morning	Goede morgen	**hoh**-deh **mor**-ghen
	Good evening	Goede avond	**hoh**-deh **ahv**-unt
	Goodbye	Dag!	dah
Numbers	one	een	ehn
	two	twee	tveh
	three	drie	dree
	four	vier	veer
	five	vijf	vehf
	six	zes	zehss
	seven	zeven	**zeh**-vehn
	eight	acht	ahkht
	nine	negen	**neh**-ghen
	ten	tien	teen
Days of the Week	Sunday	zondag	**zohn**-dagh
	Monday	maandag	**mahn**-dagh
	Tuesday	dinsdag	**dinns**-dagh
	Wednesday	woensdag	**voons**-dagh
	Thursday	donderdag	**don**-der-dagh
	Friday	vrijdag	**vreh**-dagh
	Saturday	zaterdag	**zah**-ter-dagh
Useful Phrases	Do you speak English?	Spreekt U Engels?	sprehkt oo **ehn**-gls
	I don't speak Dutch	Ik spreek geen Nederlands	ihk sprehk **ghen** Ned-er-lahnds
	I don't understand	Ik begrijp het niet	ihk be-**ghrehp** het neet
	I don't know	Ik weet niet	ihk **veht** ut neet
	I'm American/English	Ik ben Amerikaans/Engels	ihk ben Am-er-ee-**kahns**/Ehn-gls
	Where is . . .	Waar is _____?	vahr iss
	the train station?	het station	heht stah-**syohn**
	the post office?	het postkantoor	het **pohst**-kahn-tohr
	the hospital?	het ziekenhuis	het **zeek**-uhn-haus
	Where are the restrooms?	waar is de WC	**vahr** iss de **veh**-seh

Left/right	links/rechts	leenks/rehts
How much is this?	Hoeveel kost dit?	hoo-**vehl** kohst deet
It's expensive/cheap	Het is te duur/goedkoop	het ees teh **dour**/**hood**-kohp
I am ill/sick	Ik ben ziek	ihk behn zeek
I want to call a doctor	Ik wil een docter bellen	ihk veel ehn **dohk**-ter **behl**-len
Help!	Help!	help
Stop!	Stoppen	**stop**-pen

Dining Out

Bill/check	de rekening	de **rehk**-en-eeng
Bread	brood	brohd
Butter	boter	**boh**-ter
Fork	vork	fork
I'd like to order	Ik wil graag bestellen	Ihk veel khrah behs-**tell**-en
Knife	een mes	ehn mehs
Menu	menu/kaart	men-**oo**/kahrt
Napkin	en servet	ehn ser-**veht**
Pepper	peper	**peh**-per
Please give me . . .	mag ik [een] . . .	mahkh ihk [ehn] . . .
Salt	zout	zoot
Spoon	een lepel	ehn **leh**-pehl
Sugar	suiker	**sigh**-kur

French Vocabulary

English	French	Pronunciation
Basics Yes/no	Oui/non	wee/no
Please	S'il vous plaît	seel voo play
Thank you	Merci	mare-**see**
You're welcome	De rien	deh ree-**en**
Excuse me, sorry	Pardon	pahr-**doan**
Good morning/afternoon	Bonjour	bone-**joor**
Good evening	Bonsoir	bone-**swar**
Goodbye	Au revoir	o ruh-**vwar**

Numbers one	un	un
two	deux	dew
three	trois	twa
four	quatre	**cat**-ruh
five	cinq	sank
six	six	seess
seven	sept	set
eight	huit	wheat
nine	neuf	nuf
ten	dix	deess

Days of the Week	Sunday	dimanche	dee-**mahnsh**
	Monday	lundi	lewn-**dee**
	Tuesday	mardi	mar-**dee**
	Wednesday	mercredi	mare-kruh-**dee**
	Thursday	jeudi	juh-**dee**
	Friday	vendredi	van-dra-**dee**
	Saturday	samedi	sam-**dee**
Useful Phrases	Do you speak English?	Parlez-vous anglais?	par-lay vooz ahng-**glay**
	I don't speak French	Je ne parle pas français	jeh nuh parl pah fraun-**say**
	I don't understand	Je ne comprends pas	jeh nuh kohm-prahn **pah**
	I don't know	Je ne sais pas	jeh nuh say **pah**
	I'm American/British	Je suis américain/anglais	jeh sweez a-may-ree-**can**/ahng-**glay**
	Where is . . .	Où est . . .	oo ay
	the train station? the post office? the hospital	la gare? la poste? l'hôpital?	la gar la post low-pee-**tahl**
	Where are the restrooms?	Où sont les toilettes?	oo son lay twah-**let**
	Left/right	A gauche/à droite	a goash/a drwat
	How much is it?	C'est combien?	say comb-bee-**en**
	It's expensive/cheap	C'est cher/pas cher	say sher/pa sher
	I am ill/sick	Je suis malade	jeh swee ma-**lahd**
	Call a doctor	Appelez un docteur	a-pe-lay un dohk-**tore**
	Help!	Au secours!	o say-**koor**
	Stop!	Arrêtez!	a-ruh-**tay**
Dining Out	Bill/check	l'addition	la-dee-see-**own**
	Bread	du pain	due pan
	Butter	du beurre	due bur
	Fork	une fourchette	ewn four-**shet**
	I'd like . . .	Je voudrais . . .	jeh voo-**dray**
	Knife	un couteau	un koo-**toe**
	Menu	la carte	la cart
	Napkin	une serviette	ewn sair-vee-**et**
	Pepper	du poivre	due **pwah**-vruh
	Salt	du sel	dew sell
	Spoon	une cuillère	ewn kwee-**air**
	Sugar	du sucre	due **sook**-ruh

Index

Fodor's Travel Guides

U.S. Guides

Alaska

Arizona

Boston

California

Cape Cod, Martha's
Vineyard, Nantucket

The Carolinas & the
Georgia Coast

Chicago

Disney World & the
Orlando Area

Florida

Hawaii

Las Vegas, Reno,
Tahoe

Los Angeles

Maine, Vermont,
New Hampshire

Maui

Miami & the Keys

New England

New Orleans

New York City

Pacific North Coast

Philadelphia & the
Pennsylvania Dutch
Country

San Diego

San Francisco

Santa Fe, Taos,
Albuquerque

Seattle & Vancouver

The South

The U.S. & British
Virgin Islands

The Upper Great
Lakes Region

USA

Vacations in New York
State

Vacations on the
Jersey Shore

Virginia & Maryland

Waikiki

Washington, D.C.

Foreign Guides

Acapulco, Ixtapa,
Zihuatanejo

Australia & New
Zealand

Austria

The Bahamas

Baja & Mexico's
Pacific Coast Resorts

Barbados

Berlin

Bermuda

Brazil

Budapest

Budget Europe

Canada

Cancun, Cozumel,
Yucatan Peninsula

Caribbean

Central America

China

Costa Rica, Belize,
Guatemala

Czechoslovakia

Eastern Europe

Egypt

Euro Disney

Europe

Europe's Great Cities

France

Germany

Great Britain

Greece

The Himalayan
Countries

Hong Kong

India

Ireland

Israel

Italy

Italy's Great Cities

Japan

Kenya & Tanzania

Korea

London

Madrid & Barcelona

Mexico

Montreal &
Quebec City

Morocco

The Netherlands
Belgium &
Luxembourg

New Zealand

Norway

Nova Scotia, Prince
Edward Island &
New Brunswick

Paris

Portugal

Rome

Russia & the Baltic
Countries

Scandinavia

Scotland

Singapore

South America

Southeast Asia

South Pacific

Spain

Sweden

Switzerland

Thailand

Tokyo

Toronto

Turkey

Vienna & the Danube
Valley

Yugoslavia

WHEREVER YOU TRAVEL, *H*ELP IS NEVER FAR AWAY.

From planning your trip to providing travel assistance along the way, American Express® Travel Service Offices* are always there to help.

THE NETHERLANDS

Damrak 66
Amsterdam
31-20-520-7777

92 Meent
Rotterdam
31-10-433-0300

Van Baerlestraat 38
Amsterdam
31-20-673-8550

Venestraat 20
The Hague
31-70-346-9515

BELGIUM

Frankrijklei 21
Antwerp
32-3-232-5920

2, Place Louise
Brussels
32-2-512-1740

LUXEMBOURG

34 Avenue de la Porte Neuve
Luxembourg
352-228-555